Tell It to the Stones

Encounters with the Films of Danièle Huillet and Jean-Marie Straub

Edited by
Annett Busch and Tobias Hering

Sternberg Press

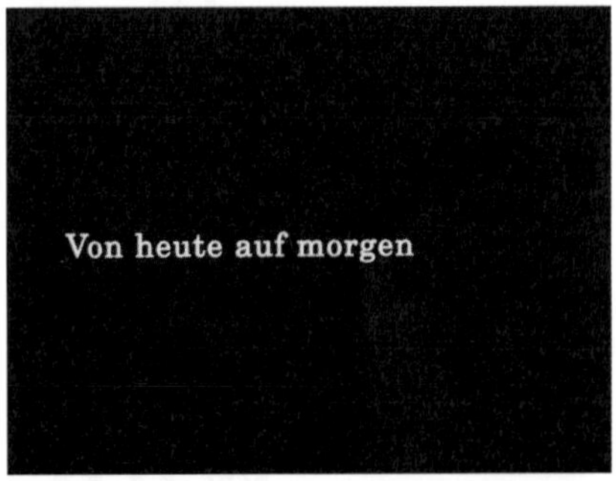

en rachâchant

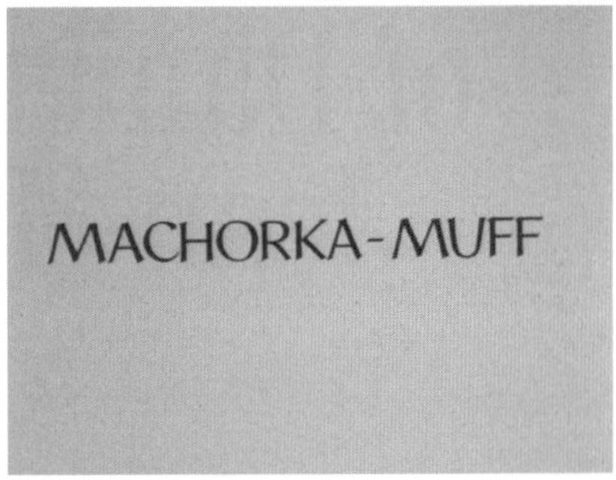

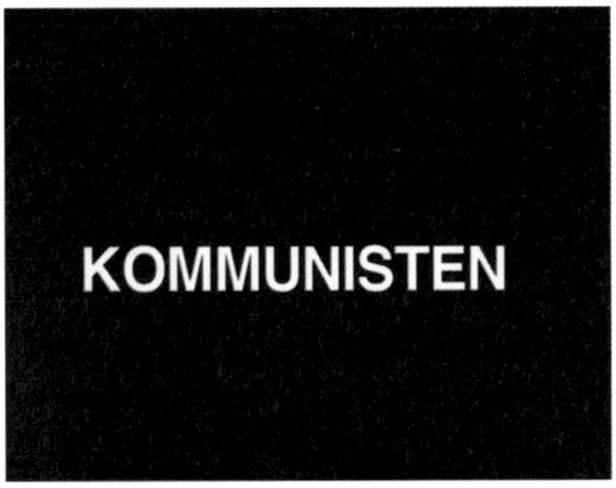

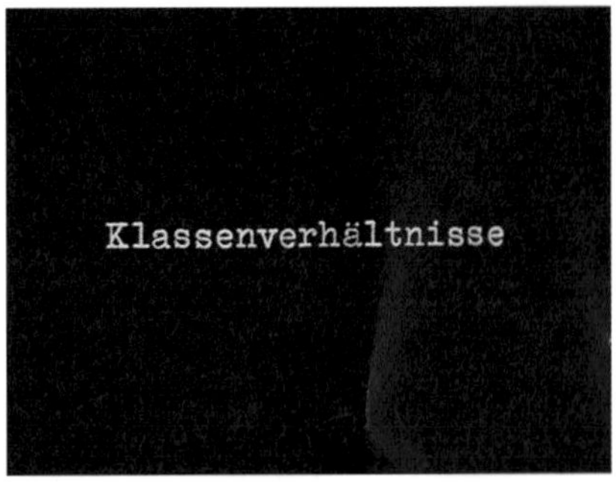

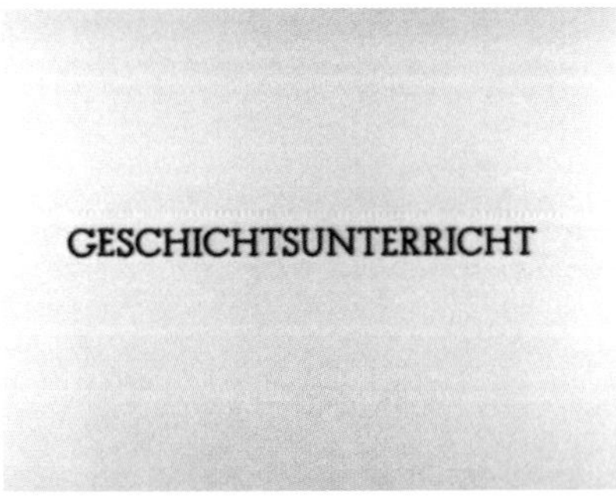

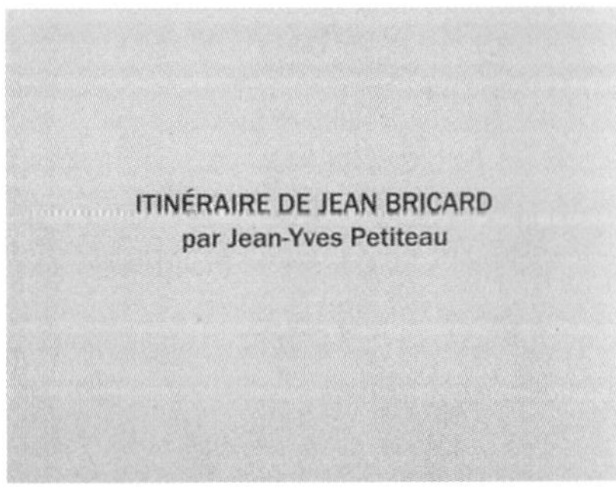

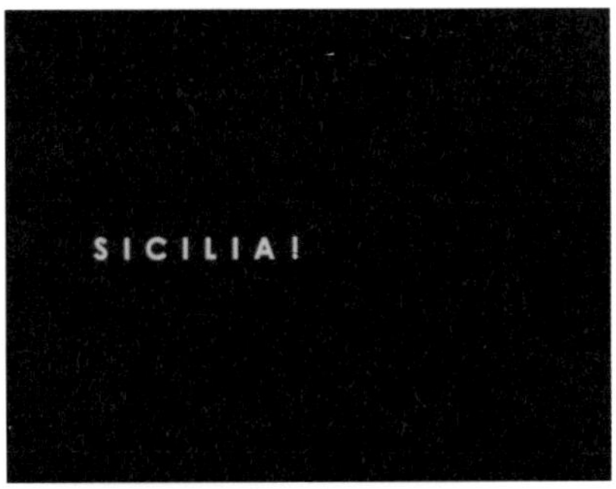

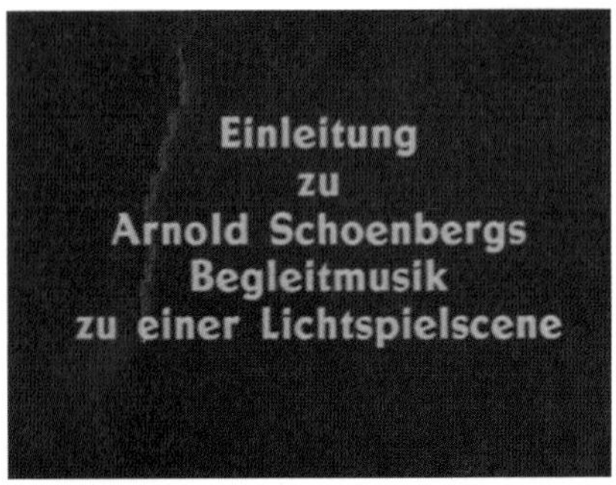

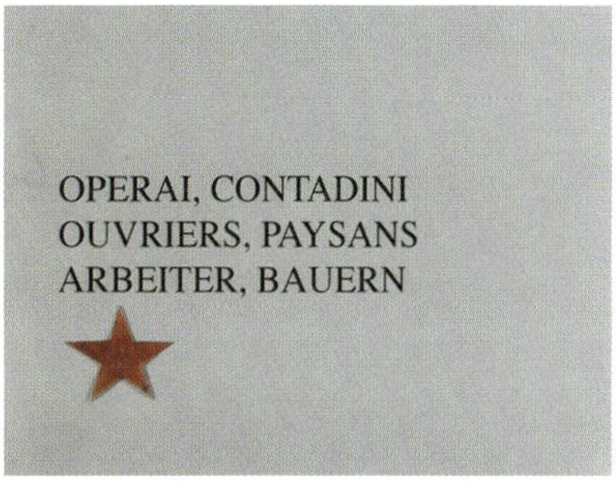
OPERAI, CONTADINI
OUVRIERS, PAYSANS
ARBEITER, BAUERN

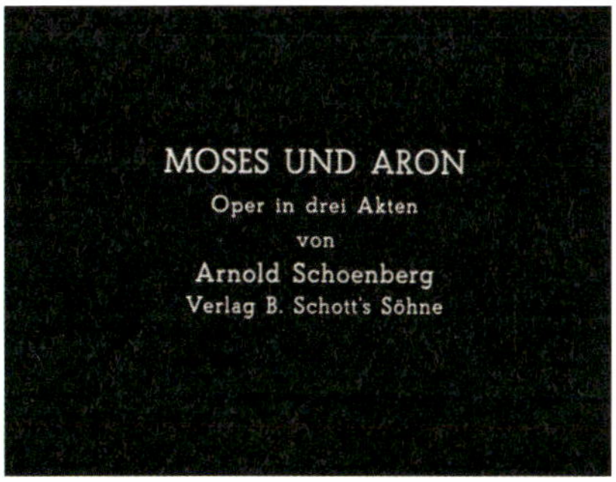
MOSES UND ARON
Oper in drei Akten
von
Arnold Schoenberg
Verlag B. Schott's Söhne

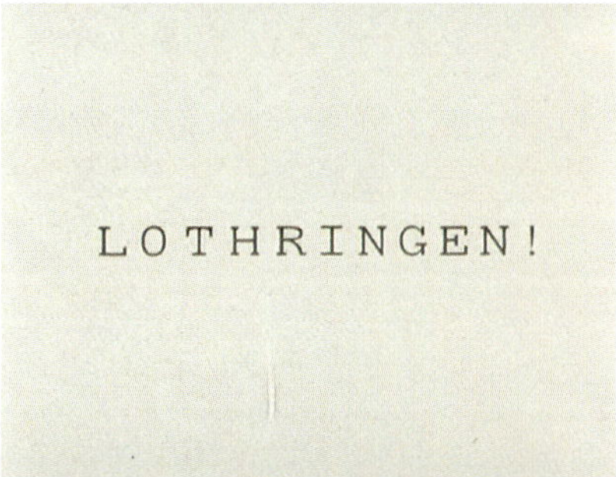
LOTHRINGEN!

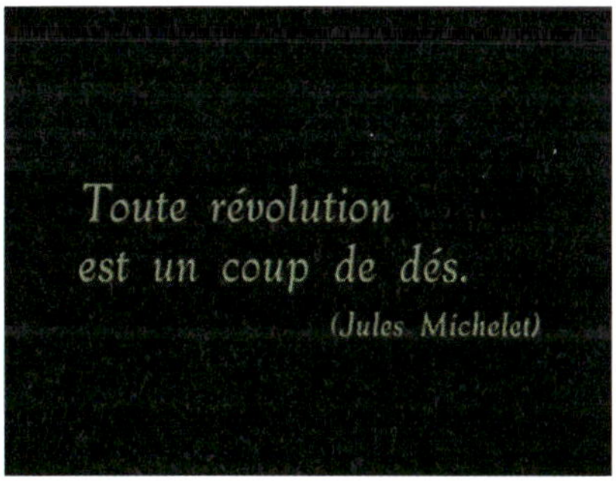
Toute révolution
est un coup de dés.
(Jules Michelet)

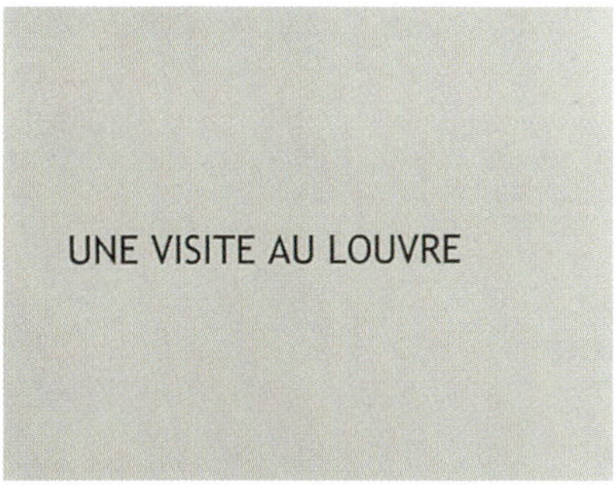
UNE VISITE AU LOUVRE

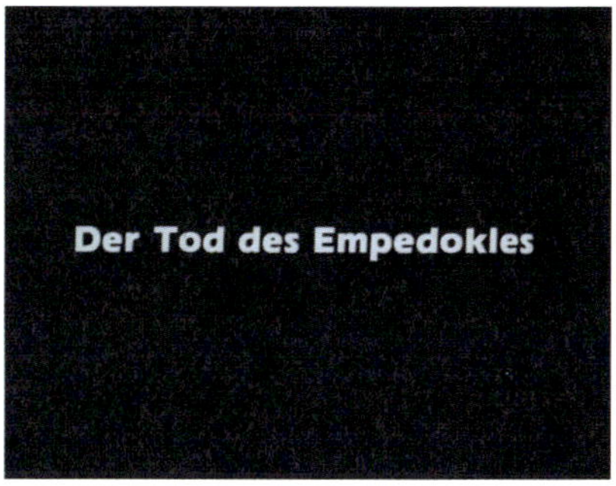
Der Tod des Empedokles

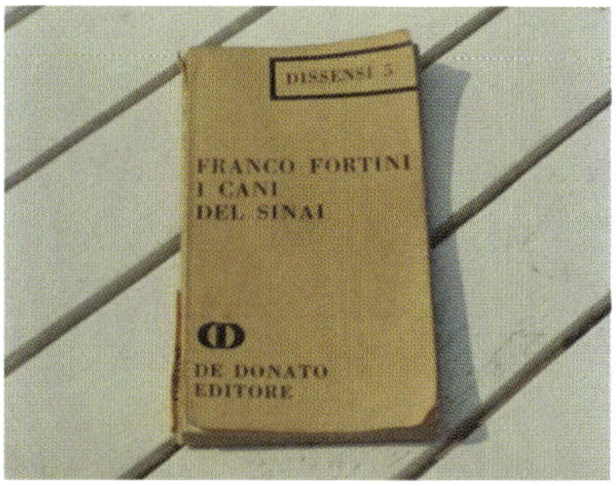
DISSENSI 5
FRANCO FORTINI
I CANI
DEL SINAI
DE DONATO
EDITORE

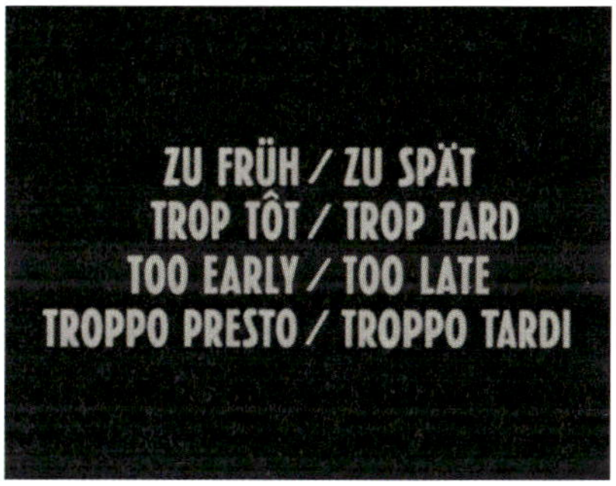
ZU FRÜH / ZU SPÄT
TROP TÔT / TROP TARD
TOO EARLY / TOO LATE
TROPPO PRESTO / TROPPO TARDI

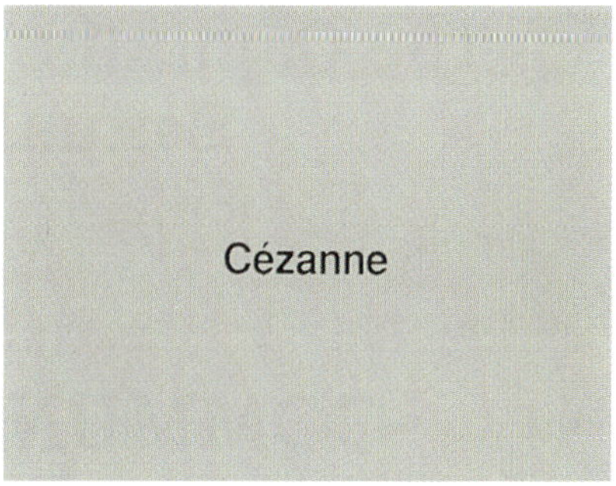
Cézanne

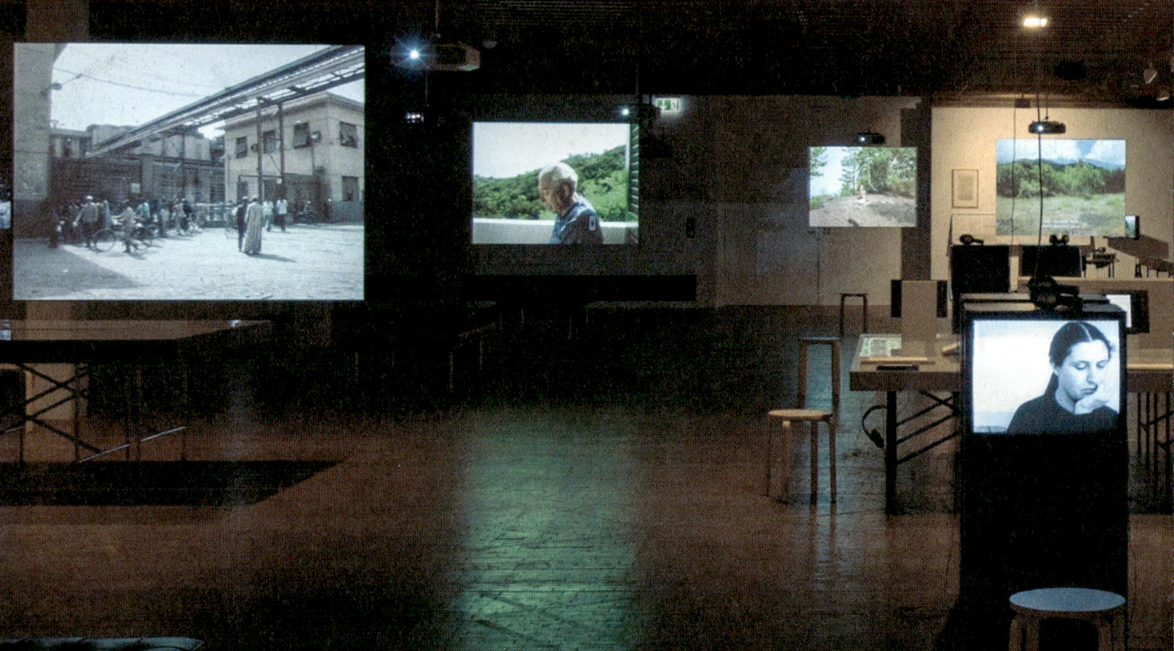

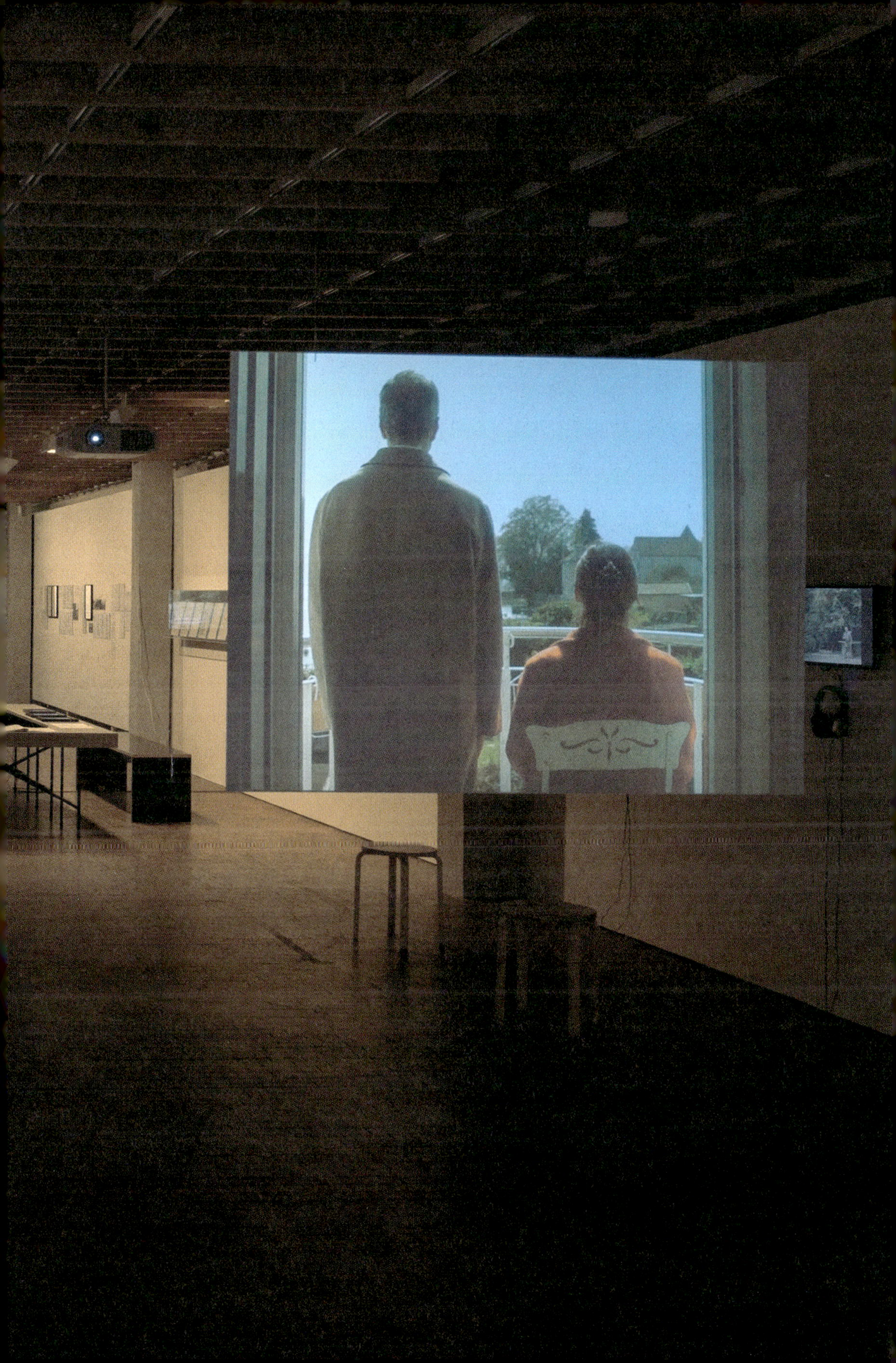

Annett Busch, Tobias Hering

Opening

As a leitmotif for arranging the various elements of the exhibition “Tell it to the Stones,”[1] we adopted the compositional method Jean-Marie Straub applied for *Kommunisten* (2014), “this dream of a thing.”[2] Blocks of previous films, edited into new sequences, combined with one newly shot to recirculate and build new relations among each other in response to a new title. We extended these circles and invited artists to respond to the importance of the two filmmakers with their own way of thinking and working. It was an approach that we carried into the compilation of the book contributions to initiate new unfinished conversations. An invitation for chance encounters, to encourage the joy of not having a navigation system at hand, and to start from the middle of things, remembering “everything is the main thing.”[3]

1

“We met at an early age,” is the beginning of Peter Nestler’s homage “For Danièle and Jean-Marie,” and it also opens this compilation. I never met Danièle Huillet, and I met Jean-Marie Straub quite late, at the opening of the retrospective at Centre Georges Pompidou in Paris in May 2016. We didn’t talk much then, and we didn’t on any of the three further occasions on which we met. I was reminded several times that I came late to the work of Huillet and Straub, but hoped that being relatively “unmarked” by their work could eventually turn out to be beneficial for my contribution to this project.

When is a good time? Is this a good time to discover or rediscover the work of Danièle Huillet and Jean-Marie Straub?[4] A common expression of alienation with regard to their films has been to call their characters, costumes, ways of speaking “outdated.” Who would do such things now? But if not now, when? The timeliness of things said and done is often discussed by Huillet and Straub. In a way each of their films demands contemporaneity with untimely things—texts, dialects, thoughts, dedications, acts. Their untimeliness stirs discomfort with what is timely and prevalent. In their films, what is there is haunted by what is not there (not anymore, not yet).

> [W]hoever watches the film has the possibility to ask how that came about; whether it *must* be or whether

1 “Tell it to the Stones: The Work of Danièle Huillet and Jean-Marie Straub,” curated by Annett Busch and Tobias Hering, was an Akademie der Künste, Berlin project in collaboration with BELVA Film, Zeughauskino, Kino in der Brotfabrik and fsk Kino. Exhibition guide and program of the cycle of events, including Rencontres, Schoenberg Week, and a complete retrospective: huilletstraub-berlin.net. As for the title’s meaning see: Patrick Primavesi, “Violence and the Stones,” in the present volume, 478–491.

2 See Ted Fendt, “The Dream of a Thing: Straub’s *Kommunisten*,” Notebook Feature, 17 March 2015, mubi.com

3 Karlheinz Stockhausen in reference to Anton Webern and the principles of twelve-tone technique in, “Letter to Jean-Marie Straub.” First published in *Film*, no. 2, 1963.

4 It was high time, we argued, for a thorough presentation around Danièle Huillet and Jean-Marie Straub’s films in Berlin, where their last retrospective had been in 1990. Huillet and Straub were elected members of the Akademie der Künste in 1998. The protocols of the inaugural meetings of the Academy’s section for film and media art even suggest that they had been shortlisted

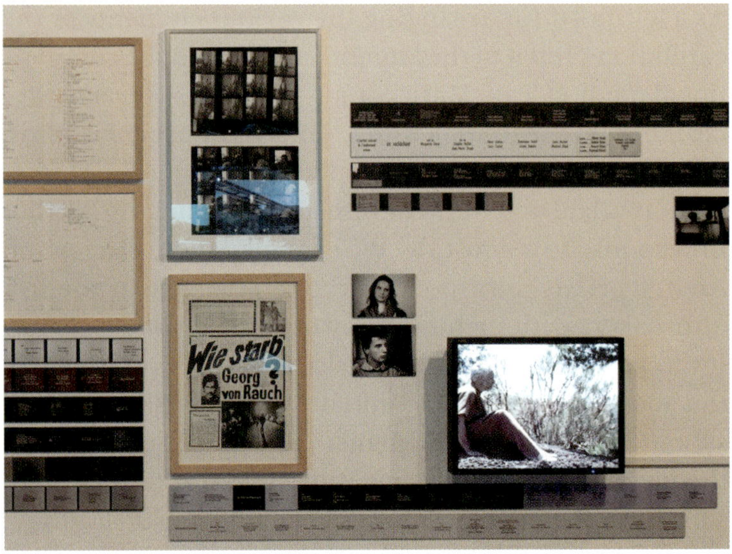

> it ought to be. Brecht never spoke of *Distanzierung* [distantiation]; the Americans and the English misinterpreted it. He spoke of *Verfremdung* [estrangement], to show things in such a light that they become strange.[5]

Rather than filling their frames with what "ought not be," Huillet and Straub have opted to make seen and heard what is worth fighting for. While many of their films are dedicated to an endangered social or natural environment, none of them shows what could be immediately identified as an image of destruction.[6] Some of their films were ten years in the making and then appeared, like *Chronicle of Anna Magdalena Bach*, just in time to be dedicated to an ongoing struggle. They lend themselves to be re-dedicated again and again, and that is what "Tell It to the Stones" is about.

2

"Tell it to the Stones" ran parallel to a comprehensive Harun Farocki festival—over two months in autumn 2017 in Berlin. The timing seemed adverse, but once the date was set and planning had begun, the events developed their own momentum. The friendly competition became a powerful statement in itself, indicated by the sheer number of events, and the many interrelations that were made visible. During the juxtaposed presence of these very divergent forms of radical filmmaking, among overlapping

for membership as early as October 1984, but were not elected. In December 1999, the Akademie der Künste dedicated a two-night program to films by Huillet and Straub with them present. Audio recordings from the Academy's archives of Q&As after these screenings were part of the exhibition in 2017.

5
"A Thousand Cliffs," Jean-Marie Straub in conversation with Elke Marhöfer and Mikhail Lylov, trans. John Barrett, originally published in *Der Standpunkt der Aufnahme – Point of View*, ed. Tobias Hering (Berlin: Archive Books, 2014). Republished in the present volume, 364–391.

6
The only exception seems to be the sequence of archival images in *Introduction to Arnold Schoenberg's "Accompaniment to a cinematographic scene"* (1972) showing footage of U.S. Air Force bomb missions in Vietnam and a photograph of the dead communards of Paris. The implications of danger, fear, violence, and their representation in this film are discussed in Ming Tsao's contribution to the present volume, 102–123.

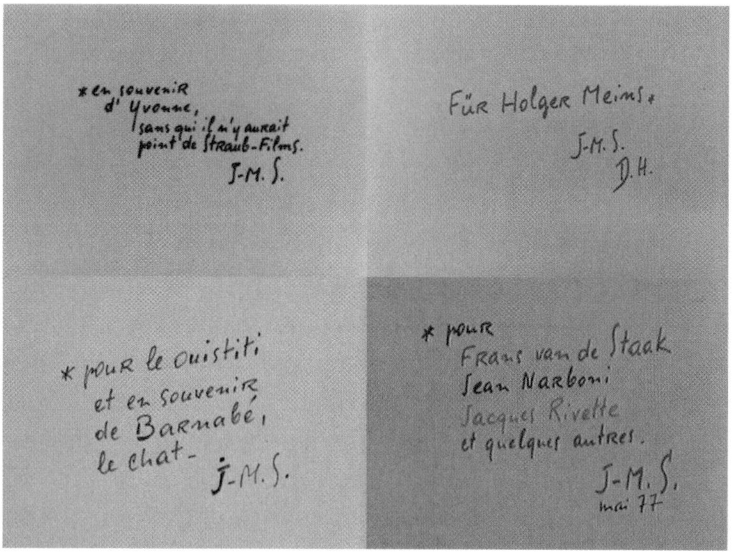

audiences commuting between Kino Arsenal, Akademie der Künste, and the cinemas Brotfabrik, Zeughauskino, fsk, in conversations informed by chance encounters and double features, something became tangible yet difficult to grasp, which could be described as a desire to participate in something that is bigger than just a film screening. A feeling, maybe, of being part of something that is timely, which seems easier to create with Farocki's films than with those by Huillet and Straub.[7]

Forty years earlier, in a letter to the "straubs," written on a typewriter but signed by hand with "Harun," Farocki describes that after having finished the shooting of "Verbindungsrohr,"[8] which later became known as *Between Two Wars,* he invited all who had participated in its making to a sample screening and afterwards "we showed cani."[9]

> your film felt very lonely, what we shot seemed to me to be popular like an operetta. [...] I didn't think at all, didn't talk about it and in the end I had understood everything. with this film we have made something, I am sure and not arrogant, that exceeds our own importance by far.[10]

The lines of the somewhat enigmatic letter may be striking simply for their directness, in the relation Farocki attributes to the "straubs" the dichotomy between loneliness and the popular. What could it mean that a film feels lonely? However, the idea of having possibly realized something popular does not give Farocki much confidence. A

7
What resonates here is the concept of "a people who are missing" as formulated by Gilles Deleuze. See "What is the Creative Act?," in Gilles Deleuze, *Two Regimes of Madness. Texts and Interviews 1975–1995* (New York: Semiotext(e), 2007), 329. Picked up in a conversation with Antonio Negri, "Le devenir révolutionnaire et les créations politiques," published in *Futur Antérieur* 1: Printemps 1990. "Of a people who are missing: on films by Danièle Huillet and Jean-Marie Straub" was also the title of an exhibition and ciné-club I co-curated with Florian Schneider at Extra City, Antwerp, 2009. The "people are missing" often accompanies the filmic oeuvre of Straub Huillet as a mockery regarding the number of spectators, who at times are few. The more interesting aspect would be that a people is not just a quantity, but has to be created and re-created. And what does it tell us, that the people are not missing? Could we imagine the films of Huillet and Straub being popular?

few lines further he states, "we are much less consolidated, [...] we are like children, drawn to evil and wickedness."

The letter is dated 6 October 1977, a month after Hanns-Martin Schleyer was kidnapped and two weeks before the so-called "Stammheim Death Night." A political radicalization had developed its own dynamics in confrontation with the state power, leading to isolation—and something of a gloomy confusion permeates Farocki's letter, without even a mention of any political event. Another two years earlier, Straub and Huillet had dedicated *Moses and Aaron* to Holger Meins, who had died in prison during a hunger strike in 1975. In "My Key Dates," published in *Libération* in 2003, Straub gives an idea of the weight and significance of a dedication, an unexpectedly explicit reference that can make us see a political link not evident in the film itself. It's the year 1968.

> *Chronicle* exists at last! During its screening in Munich, I dedicated the film to the peasants of the Bavarian Forest and to the Vietcong (B52s were bombing Hanoi every day). A young student from the Berlin film school, Holger Meins, who has just seen the film in Frankfurt, declares it the most important film in the history of cinema.

And a few lines further Straub recalls: "We dedicate *Moses and Aaron* to him. Twenty-four frames in the opening credits that attract the censorship of the directors of the third German television channel, the film's co-producer."[11]

Beyond the chance intersection of different timelines, the coincidence of Holger Meins' death and finishing the edit of *Moses and Aaron*—Straub draws another connection: "Didn't Moses [...] begin his 'career' [as a prophet] as a terrorist by killing a tax collector? He took refuge in the desert."[12] Holger Meins was in the same first year of the newly founded film school, DFFB, 1966, in Berlin as Harun Farocki, they knew each other well. "We never discussed the 'question of armed struggle' as it used to be known. We only ate together when we were working or traveling together, we only drank beer together when we met by chance at a screening or a political gathering."[13] Many years later, in 2012, Farocki wrote in an email to Ute Holl that he "was recently in Regenbogenkino to 'introduce' two films by the Straubs (can't understand them otherwise). No

8
Asked by *Frankfurter Rundschau* in 1976, "What cultural-political activities of others could convince or stimulate you?" Straub answered "Das große Verbindungsrohr" (the large connecting tube), referring to Farocki's "compilation text" published in *Die Republik*. See "Drei Fragen zur 'Kulturdebatte,'" in *Danièle Huillet, Jean-Marie Straub: Schriften*, ed. Tobias Hering, Volko Kamensky, Markus Nechleba, Antonia Weiße (Berlin: Vorwerk 8), 200. Farocki once mentioned, referring to *Between Two Wars*: "Maybe I made the film only to be recognized by Straub." In Tilman Baumgärtel, *Harun Farocki – Vom Guerrillakino zum Essayfilm* (Berlin: b-books, 2002), 147. Quoted from Ilse Müller, *Film als Zitat*, Universität Osnabrück (unpublished thesis, 1981).

9
Refers to *Fortini/Cani*, dir. Jean-Marie Straub, Danièle Huillet, 1976. Based on the book *I cani del Sinai* (*The Dogs of the Sinai*) by Franco Fortini.

10
"Ein Brief an die Straubs (Oktober 1977)," February 2018, on www.harun-farocki-institut.org.

11
Jean-Marie Straub and Danièle Huillet: Writings, ed. Sally Shafto, Katherine Pickard (New York: Sequence Press, 2016), 264.

12
Writings, 264.

one there under 55, unfortunately!" While in Kassel

> about 100 people sat in the theater and watched Straub from 9 in the morning till 3 at night. The copy of *Moses und Aron* was almost entirely red. For some the dedication to Holger Meins was more important than anything else.[14]

3

"It has come too soon for our death—too late for our life," was how Jean-Marie Straub and Danièle Huillet commented on the Special Lion for "invention of cinematic language in the ensemble of their work," which the Venice Film Festival awarded to them in 2006. The remark was the opening statement of a three-part note—later published as "Three Messages to the 63rd Venice International Film Festival"[15]—read on their behalf during a press conference by actress Giovanna Daddi, a long-time collaborator from the Teatro Francesco di Bartolo in Buti and a protagonist in their latest film, *Quei loro incontri* (2005), which screened in the Venice competition that same year. Huillet and Straub did not attend the festival and were hence awarded in absentia. While their communiqué contains a sobering resumé of the scarce recognition given to their films in Venice in the past,[16] it might be more interesting to read it as a triptych on time and timeliness. After all, the opening line contains a reference to their film *Too Early/Too Late* (1980–81), whose title takes up on a remark by Friedrich Engels in a letter to Karl Kautsky discussing political options in post-revolutionary France, the timeliness of "plebeian fraternization" and the use of violence, or terrorism quite literally, by Robespierre and the Commune. "What they [plebeian fraternity] wanted, nobody could tell; until long after the demise of the commune Babeuf put a name to it. While the commune's aspirations for fraternity came too early, Babeuf again came too late."[17] Or, of course: "How many masters' houses need to be set on fire, how many need to be killed in the streets and squares before the world turns just and we can say it's ours?"[18]

If the communiqué stirred some commotion, it was for its final part, in which Straub refuses "to be festive in a festival where there are so many public and private police looking for terrorists—I am the terrorist," he claims and,

13 Harun Farocki, "Staking One's Life: Images of Holger Meins," in *Harun Farocki: Working on the Sight-Lines*, ed. Thomas Elsaesser (Amsterdam: Amsterdam University Press, 2004), 83–91.

14 See Ute Holl, *The Moses Complex – Freud, Schoenberg, Straub/Huillet*, trans. Michael Turnbull (Zurich/Berlin: diaphanes, 2017), 318–319.

15 "Three Messages to the 63rd Venice International Film Festival," in *Writings*, 272–273. Retrospectively, the Venice statement's opening line may also bring to mind the proximity to Danièle Huillet's death, who passed away only four weeks later.

16 The second part of the communiqué consists of a faithful list of the altogether six times Straub attended the Venice film festival, once as a film critic (in 1954), and five times on the occasion of a film by them shown in the festival, including a 1966 screening "paid for by Jean-Luc Godard."

17 "Engels an Kautsky in Wien, 20. Februar 1889" [Engels to Kautsky in Vienna, Feb 20, 1889], in *Karl Marx, Friedrich Engels: Werke*, Vol. 37 (Berlin: Dietz, 1967), 156.

18 One of several quotes from Cesare Pavese's *La luna e i falò* (Turin: Giulio Einaudi, 1950) which amount to about half of the text volume of "Three Messages."

paraphrasing Franco Fortini, “so long as there’s American imperialistic capitalism, there’ll never be enough terrorists in the world.” While those who cared to be offended by this statement hastened to make Straub look irrelevant, it strangely seems to remain one of the most circulated quotes by him. Even in the context of “Tell it to the Stones” in 2017, I was repeatedly asked by journalists to comment on it.

Maybe Straub himself commented on it when, having been invited to contribute to an “homage to Italian art” for the Italian pavilion of the Venice biennial in 2015, he submitted a video copy of the last ten minutes of their film *History Lessons* (1972), taken from a grossly red-tinted 16mm print stored at the Museum of Modern Art in New York, and titled it, *In omaggio all’arte italiana*. In Straub’s own words, *History Lessons* is “a film which relates the primordial relations between business and democracy, capitalism and imperialism.”[19] On a textual level, the ten-minute excerpt that he used for *In omaggio all’arte italiana* relates to the final lesson which the “young man” in the film is made to learn.[20] “En voilà un film obscur,” is how blogger Moizi commented on it on senscritique.com.[21] Probably unencumbered by the film’s presentation in Venice (in a custom-built miniature pavilion with maximum efforts to give back to the “pink film” the gravity of a piece of great art), Moizi makes the best of his/her puzzlement:

> My explanation is that Straub is showing a film, and in order to do that, he films a film reel projected on a screen. We see there all the artefacts due to time, the film starts slipping, the English subtitles disappear and leave us facing a work in German... That’s quite a particular way to break the fourth wall, in order to make the spectator understand that she is watching a film.

Given under the headline “étrange, c’est étrange...” (strange, that’s strange...), Moizi’s notes describe in all clarity what I think is the desired effect of Brecht’s (and Huillet-Straub’s) use of *Verfremdung* (estrangement), *to show things in such a light that they become strange*—and to come to grips with what one is actually looking at, and why things are the way they are and not otherwise.

> I should say that even if I didn’t get the point, I appreciate the questions surrounding the work, one

19 Synopsis of *History Lessons* in German in Straub’s handwriting on a loose sheet of paper kept at the Fondo Straub-Huillet at the Cineteca di Bologna.

20 See also Luisa Greenfield’s essay “History Lessons By Comparison” in the present volume, 268–293.

21 “étrange, c’est étrange...” blog post by “Moizi,” www.senscritique.com, June 6, 2018.

that's at least unique, since besides Godard I don't know many directors who use pieces of their films, who quote themselves etc., in order to make something else.

Straub has put an old and forgotten thing back into place. Has it come too soon, too late?

And I'm not even talking about what is happening in our field, still so young, the famous 'restorations' of films—the refusal of any patina, because of the idiotic and arrogant idea that you can act as if time has not passed.[22]

'Untimely' is a derogative term only for those who believe in the linearity of progress, and who choose to consider the world we presently live in as the best possible. With Danièle Huillet and Jean-Marie Straub, however—their films, their acts, their texts—we are always in for a negotiation of things too early / too late. When, for instance, is the appropriate time for these lines of dialogue from their film *From the Cloud to the Resistance* (1978), written by Cesare Pavese in 1950 and quoted in their 2006 message in response to an invitation to be festive under the eyes of police in Venice?

The other day I passed by La Mora. There's no longer the pine tree at the gate. He had it cut down, the accountant, Nicoletto. The lout. He had it cut down because beggars would stop in its shade and beg. Understand?

4

"During the film, when we tied Aaron, I was thinking of Lumumba." A thought, more than ten years after the murder of Lumumba, not something that occupied the news at the time in the mid-1970s, mentioned by Straub probably only once in a conversation with Pascal Bonitzer, Serge Daney and Jacques Bontemps, printed in *Cahiers du cinéma*[23] in 1975. What was Straub thinking of—Aaron's posture, an image of a defeated body lying on the ground? Aaron's vision of an arrival (after traversing the desert) against that of Moses, who imagined a continuing traversal, "the idea of nomadism, tout simplement," as Straub con-

22 Danièle Huillet, "Quite a lot of pent-up anger," in *Writings*, 231.

23 Jean-Marie Straub and Danièle Huillet, "Conversation avec Jean-Marie Straub et Danièle Huillet. Par Jacques Bontemps, Pascal Bonitzer et Serge Daney," *Cahiers du cinéma*, no. 258/259, (1975): 8. "During the film, when we tied Aaron, I thought of Lumumba. And when Moses said: 'Let him free!' we no longer see Aaron (he is already off-screen), we de-framed him during this last sentence 'Für seine Freiheit, dass es ein Volk werde' [For their liberty, that they become a people], in order to re-frame Moses. And Moses destroys Aaron, but, in doing so—and this seems obvious, at least I hope so—Moses destroys himself, although he is right in sending the people back into the desert, adding: 'In der Wüste seid ihr unüberwindlich und werdet das Ziel erreichen' [In the desert you are invincible and will achieve the goal]."

densed Moses and Aaron's disagreement a few sentences later. Whatever Straub had in mind exactly, to think of someone while filming somebody else and to mention it, opens up a net of invisible but present relations and a different starting point of reflection—a process of indirect understanding. How does a thought materialize and influence the making of an image, and knowing it, how does it change the way we see it? Like a riddle we kept recalling, "I was thinking of Lumumba..." while preparing the "encounters" series during the "Tell it to the Stones" program cycle, not to solve it, but rather as a question of how to create and narrate connections that do not appear obvious at first sight—and also as a calling to leave Europe (in our minds), without arrival.

5

What became an exhibition, then a series of events, including talks, workshops and concerts, a complete retrospective, and now this book, was built on and informed by personal and intellectual encounters between people like Peter Nestler who could say about Huillet and Straub, "We met at an early age," and others who had only begun to relate to their films after Danièle Huillet wasn't there anymore, or who were having their first encounters with them through peer-to-peer platforms online. Some we asked to participate because we saw a peculiar engagement in their work with that of Huillet-Straub. Louis Henderson had explored stratigraphic images in the context of today's media landscapes, strewn with litter of post-colonial violence, and was just starting to conceive of a film around Toussaint Louverture. Ala Younis had come across *Too Early/Too Late* at a time when this film was being rediscovered as an early herald of the Arab Spring—an affirmation which she found riddled with misreading and which she set out to balance with a more careful exploration of the film's actual agency then and now. Oraib Toukan had briefly discussed the same film in a lecture investigating the combination of landscape shots with soundtracks in cinematic representations of Palestine.[24] When we took that as a cue to contact her, she had just come back from a visit to the archaeological site Iraq al Amir in Jordan, conceiving of a film composed of photographs she had taken there and local tales about the site she had recorded.

24 Oraib Toukan's lecture "Gardening a pitiless mountain dreamed of faraway with its owner only a passing shadow," held at Makan art space, Amman, in December 2011, was subsequently published as "A lecture in three parts, in between the odd discussion," in: *Tin Soldiers*, ed. Ala Younis (Amman, 2012).

With some others we only guessed that there was an affinity. When we met Jan Werner we might have imagined *Machorka-Muff* or *Nicht versöhnt* resampled by Mouse on Mars, but he had his mind set on *Antigone* and suggested a concert performance with Astrid Ofner, which became the closing event of the program cycle in 2017. We had always intended the "project" to consist of such unanticipated encounters, to be a work-in-progress and to also include perspectives from artists, writers and researchers for whom Huillet and Straub were a relatively recent influence. Rather than claiming a place for their work in history, we were looking for ways to make watching a film, or reading an interview or a text by Huillet and Straub the beginning of something new, now.

The book became possible because the encounters and experiences of 2017 had created a desire to follow up. A driving force in this process was Ming Tsao who not only felt an urge to write about his own process of composing *Refuse Collection* for the 2017 event, a new composition based on Schoenberg, Huillet-Straub, and J.H. Prynne, but who also wished to see the contributions of others made permanently accessible, and to hear and read more.

6

"I shall not go back to school any more. Because at school they teach me things I don't know"—these two sentences enter the kitchen in singsong, in French. "Child Ernesto" recites, standing straight with his big glasses, between a mother peeling potatoes and a father sitting next to the window, reading the paper and smoking. His refusal to go back to school culminates in a conversation among parents, teacher and child in an empty classroom and Ernesto's answer to the teacher's question: "And how does child Ernesto plan to learn what he doesn't know yet?"—"En rachâchant!"—"What is that?"—"A new method." And also the title of the short film.[25] "This excellent production of seven minutes is the ideal complement to a program. First, because it proves that the Straubs are funny. Second, [...] their strange relation to the idea of education..."[26] Stated in one of the many beautiful texts written by Serge Daney accompanying the filmmaking of Huillet and Straub over more than two decades.

25 *En Rachâchant,* dir. Danièle Huillet, Jean-Marie Straub, 1982, based on the short story, "Ah! Ernesto" by Marguerite Duras.

26 Serge Daney, "Straub rachâche," first published in *Libération,* April 7, 1983. Translated into English by Laurent Kretzschmar and Andy Rector, published March 17, 2019, kinoslang.blogspot.com.

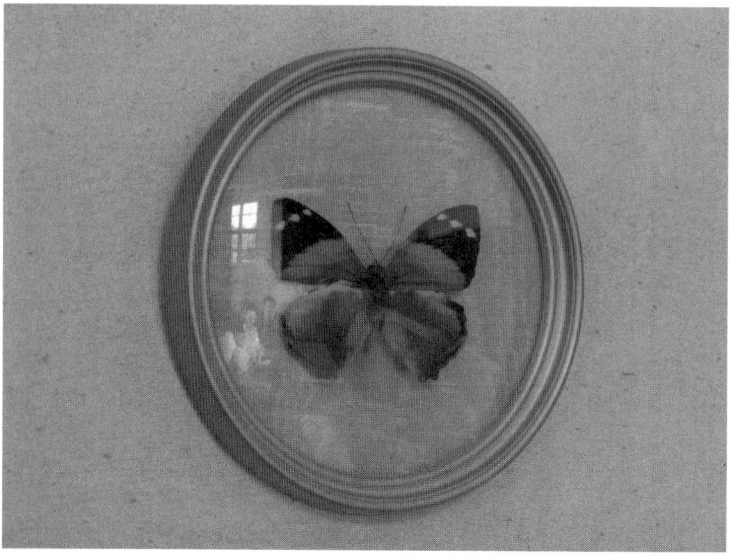

"En rachâchant" is an invented expression. According to the critic Yann Lardeau in *Cahiers du cinéma* at the time, "it onomatopoetically hints at harping on, harking back, buying back, muttering, mumbling, chewing, knowing, fretting, fuming and murder-ing!" By "re-de-de re-see-see re-pee-pee-ting!" as in a translation suggested by Ina C. Jaeger and Ciba Vaughan.[27] Ernesto has left the room. The flabbergasted teacher and parents are left alone to find out what it could mean. An idea of the new method could emerge if we add another short sentence by Serge Daney, taken out of context, noted in "A Tomb for the Eye (Straubian Pedagogy)"—"Everything is in the present."[28]

If we turn Ernesto's refusal into a request: What could it mean that we should learn what we know already? Asked to describe a pinned up butterfly behind glass, framed as a picture, Ernesto answers: "a crime."—"And what is this, a football?" The teacher tries to joke, pointing to the globe on his desk and gets as reply from his pupil: "Un football, une pomme de terre et la terre (a football, a potato and the earth)." Ernesto refuses to acknowledge the general agreement on a name through an ironic linking of words and form. Awareness seems to be situated and created through interrelations between image, designation, and abstraction—and a new meaning, a critical evaluation, by reading and naming what we see as an image. To learn what we already know also means to learn how things matter to us, beginning to realize the history of what we see, which is not evident. That everything in the present has to be

27 *Ah! Ernesto, story by Marguerite Duras, pictures by Bernhard Bonhomme,* trans. Ina C. Jaeger, Ciba Vaughan (Harlin Quist Books, 1972)

28 Originally published as "Un tombeau pour l'oeil (En marge de 'L'Introduction à la musique d'accompagnement pour une scène de film d'Arnold Schoenberg' de J.-M. Straub)" in *Cahiers du cinéma* 258–259 (July–August 1975). English translation by John Barrett in *Der Standpunkt der Aufnahme – Point of View* (359–363); also accessible in a translation by Stoffel Debuysere on www.diagonalthoughts.com, May 25, 2013.

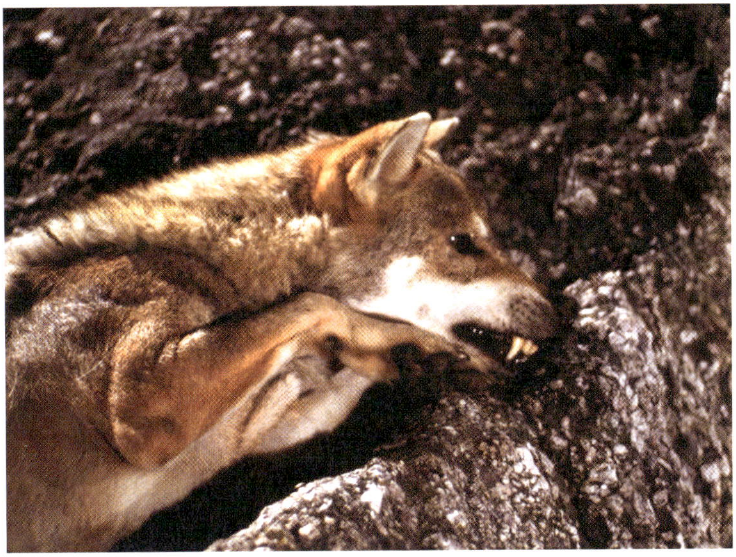

learned while we know it already. By "chewing" (listed as a possible translation of "en rachâchant"), a kind of bodily activity of remembering (das Gelernte durchkauen), we combine and recombine the old and the new, the known and not yet known, the relation between absence and presence, of what is not visible in the picture, but might appear through listening or by giving it a (new) name. Similar to the absent presence of the work of a network which materializes on film—it's there and we know it, but we are trained not to see it and therefore forget about it.

29 *Apparatus*, ed. Theresa Hak Kyung Cha (New York: Tanam Press, 1981), Preface.

7

From the beginning, our idea was to focus attention on the *work* of Danièle Huillet and Jean-Marie Straub. Work, in the sense of labor, not oeuvre, was a key word that opened an area of attention and research, beside and around the actual films. It comprises parallel processes of research, writing, traveling, waiting, and taking care, whose relation to a film are not always evident at first sight or only become relevant much later, in another context, for another film. A great source for these aspects of the work are letters, and it was usually Danièle Huillet who would write them. In 1981 she had a mail correspondence with the artist Theresa Hak Kyung Cha who had apparently asked her and Jean-Marie Straub for a contribution to her book project *Apparatus*—"a collection of Autonomous Works on the apparatus of cinema."[29] In the Theresa Hak Kyung Cha archives at Berkeley Art Museum / Pacific Film Archive (BAMPFA) there are

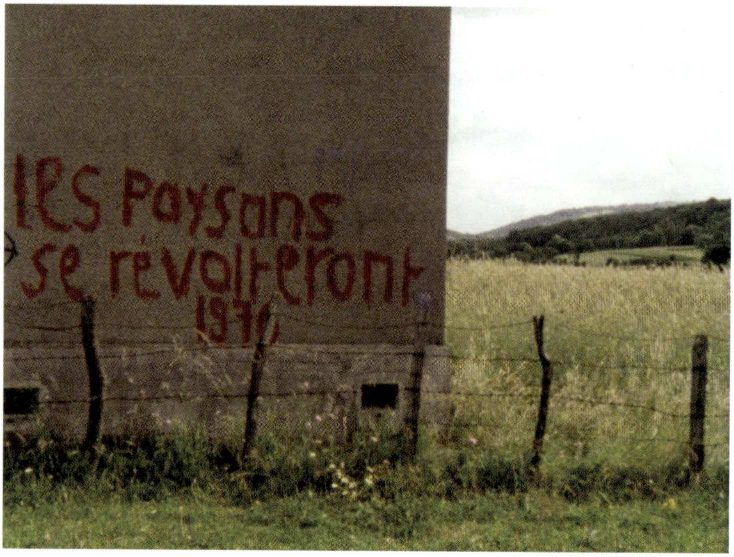

three letters by Danièle Huillet written between January 21, 1981 and April 1, 1981 (or 1982?).[30] They testify to the precision that Danièle Huillet applied at all stages of her work, and they give a glimpse of Huillet-Straub's exceptional generosity, which so many of their collaborators have described. When someone asked them for something, they would usually get it—or something else. The cinema programmer and cinephile Heimo Bachstein, one of the first to regularly screen their films in Germany in a small-town cinema in Marktheidenfeld, was provided with leftover film frames for his collection over many years.[31] When asked during a Q&A about the long tracking shot of a Munich street which they filmed for *The Bridegroom, the Actress and the Pimp* (1968) and which Rainer Werner Fassbinder adopted for his *Liebe ist kälter als der Tod* (1969), Straub said: "We gave it to him, because he had asked for it and we had no reason to refuse."[32]

Apparently, Theresa Hak Kyung Cha had first asked Huillet and Straub to write a text about their work process.[33] In her response, Danièle Huillet mentions time and nerve consuming preparations for "having all our films coming out in Italy" and their effort "to find money and finish a film called TOO EARLY TOO LATE." For these reasons, she writes,

> we have really no time to work out what you want from us for APPARATUS, and no will either at that moment. <u>But</u>: Jean-Marie wants me to tell you that we have said what we have to say and even too

30 For learning about this correspondence, I am indebted to Paolo Caffoni who first spoke to me about *Apparatus*, and to Stephanie Cannizzo at BAMPFA who sent me scans of the letters. The third letter is undated, but "1st April" is mentioned by Huillet as the date of writing. All letters are typewritten and hand signed.

31 See *Kino-Enthusiasmus. Die Schenkung Heimo Bachstein*, ed. Volker Pantenburg, Katrin Richter (Weimar: Lucia, 2016), 98–99.

32 "Leben bedeutet, eine Form zu verteidigen," *Schriften*, 348.

33 Cha's own letters to Huillet do not seem to be part of the BAMPFA archive. Their content can roughly be surmised from Huillet's replies.

> much in a thing called ENTHUSIASM, printed in London from a friend called Andi Engel and which you could have phoning in New York Dan Talbot, New Yorker Films 3621243–3621416 and telling him we told you to ask him to give you this magazine (there is a fountain and a photo with Jean-Marie and me on the front page) (black and white). The best thing in it, says Straub, the one which tells more about how we work, is, from page 32 to 55, A WORK JOURNAL OF THE STRAUB/HUILLET FILM 'MOSES AND AARON' by Gregory Woods *and* [typed in red ink] NOTES ON GREGORY'S WORK JOURNAL by Danièle Huillet. Andi Engel is to be found, if you need any further information, at ARTIFICIAL EYE, 211 Camden High str, London NW17BT.

In her response to this, Theresa Hak Kyung Cha must have asked for work material from the shooting of *Too Early/Too Late* and for a shooting script of *Every Revolution is a Throw of Dice* (1977). Again Danièle Huillet refuses, and then offers. No script of the Mallarmé film ever existed, and as to *Too Early/Too Late*: "We don't like anything published about a film which still doesn't exist (call it superstition...)." However, she offers some photographs of the shooting to be requested from camera assistant Caroline Champetier. In lieu of an actual shooting script of *Every Revolution* she offers a post-shooting script, previously published by an "Italian magazine,"

> which is very precise: I send it to you here, together with the English translation we made together with two english+american friends [Misha Donat and Gregory Woods] before subtitling the film, and some photographs of the shooting (made by Andrea Spingler; but you need no permission, if you want to publish some of them; she is a friend and a nice girl).

What is printed in *Apparatus* is a compilation of this material, which Danièle Huillet suggested not as consolation for what she and Straub did not want to, or could not deliver, but as what they found to be appropriate to tell about their work with and within the cinema apparatus. After receiving the book, Danièle Huillet thanks Theresa Hak Kyung

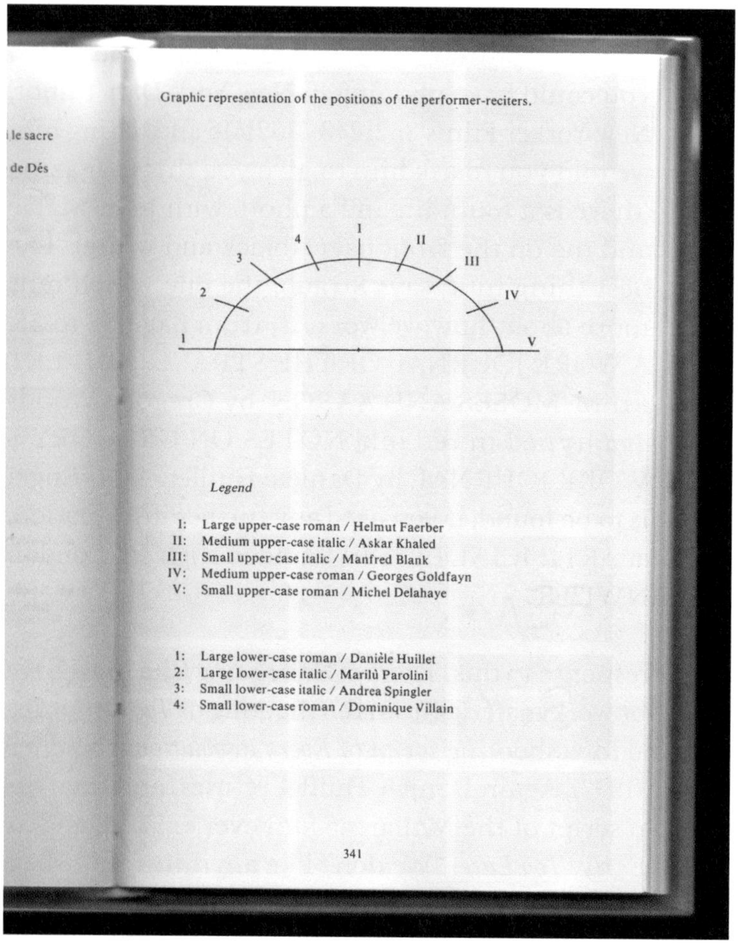

Graphic representation of the positions of the performer-reciters.

Legend

I: Large upper-case roman / Helmut Faerber
II: Medium upper-case italic / Askar Khaled
III: Small upper-case italic / Manfred Blank
IV: Medium upper-case roman / Georges Goldfayn
V: Small upper-case roman / Michel Delahaye

1: Large lower-case roman / Danièle Huillet
2: Large lower-case italic / Marilù Parolini
3: Small lower-case italic / Andrea Spingler
4: Small lower-case roman / Dominique Villain

341

Cha, lists a number of unfortunate mistakes in spelling and layout, and invites her to visit them in Rome, "if we don't see each other in New York."

8

> Before watching their films, it is useful to recall that Straub is a trained grammarian. This is a discipline which presupposes a special, typically French love of language; the audacious idea of fathoming the nature of language in a methodically extra-linguistic manner. All their films may be grasped this way: as stories on a threshold, as undertakings of the in-between.[34]

Frieda Grafe wrote this on the occasion of a Huillet/Straub retrospective at the Munich Film Museum in 1997, as if she were writing about her own undertaking to abstract viewing (and listening) experiences, translating the grammar of image and sound as texts that explore the in-between.

34 Frieda Grafe, "Patrioten im Niemandsland," in *Geraffte Zeit*, Schriften, Vol. 8, ed. Enno Patalas (Berlin: Brinkmann & Bose, 2005), 88.

Both Grafe's writings on film and Huillet and Straub's films require considerable effort to talk about what actually "happened." Spending time with and in a film by Huillet and Straub also means falling out of time and allowing a reboot of our sensorial system. Which can be a refuge, but also inconvenient, sometimes soporific, or exhausting. The difficulty "to make use" of the films is embedded in their aesthetics of resistance—the commitment and care it takes to actually produce and realize (not just state) a politics of polyvocality through images, voices, sound, and tones to become an aesthetic experience. To be taken seriously as spectators can create a feeling of loneliness; we are not told what to think, but we are generously offered an encounter, and as with any encounter, it requires mutual activity to make it an adventure, which is the fundament of a non-representational cinema for a people. An absence of topic-related information requires a different effort to translate the politics of sound, image, and representation back into the realm of political discourse. The call for a multiplicity of translations (from film to text), to enrich the discursive zones, not to reduce film to discourse, is something we try to unfold on the following pages.

35 kinoslang.blogspot.com, March 17, 2019.

In the "editor's note" to *En Rachâchant* on his *Kino Slang* blog, Andy Rector recalls a way of talking that escapes the restrictions and order of communication and language:

> I take pleasure in this adapted translation, as it reminds me of the word mischief that Straub gets up to when contemplating things in public: 'In the beginning the earth was without form and void. Your formless form, your formless formed, informed, invertebrate...' from *Where Does Your Hidden Smile Lie?* (dir. Pedro Costa, 2001); or his occasional use of 'caca-pipi-talism'; or the following while presenting *Othon*: "A muh-muh-muh-modern tragedy. Police pitfall. Political pitfall. A polis-puh-puh-puh-puh.[35]

9

This is what I meant yesterday when I said: we caught a political conscience like one catches the chickenpox. I should have answered that it was not through Karl Marx that we discovered the class struggle, but through the obstacles that we experienced when attempting to make a precise film, which was CHRONICLE OF ANNA MAGDALENA BACH. This lasted from 1958 to 1967, so ten years. This is where we realized what social violence is, the class struggle, etc. Reading Marx after that, we said to ourselves: 'Now here's a perfectly clear, just, and realistic analysis of the state of things.'[36]—Huillet, Strasbourg, 1993.

We cherished Danièle Huillet's revelation that time is a method and a weapon, something she said during a Q&A in Stockholm in 2004 (a recording of which could be seen in the exhibition at Akademie der Künste.) It is a moment when Straub, after having taken the better part of the speaking time as usual, shows signs of exhaustion. A man in the audience has asked them if they are able to say what for them "embodies the integrity of a work of art." Straub is at a loss with the question. Danièle paraphrases it for him: "Whether we are able to describe what for us is the integrity of the material we use in our films." Straub: "You mean if something resists us, and if it is worth the craft work that will eventually result in a film? Is that your question?"—"Which part of the material is one allowed to touch and which not?" explains the person who had asked, and then Danièle replies, "In this respect there's no difference between a text, or any other pre-existing work, and a tree or the earth or the sky, that you want to show, or the people." Then the recording indicates a (presumably short) gap, and when it continues, it is still Danièle who speaks:

> I believe that the only method one can apply—I already said this to someone after yesterday's discussion—is time. Patience and time. And that is true for everything, not only for the texts, but also for a musical score. If you do *From Today Until Tomorrow*,[37] you need to take your time and patience to read the score, in order to discover where there are articulations that allow you to cut.
>
> Straub: One can call it articulations, one could also call it the "veins." The sculptor, when receiving a chunk of marble, he must first sit down and discover the veins. Nothing to do with "time is money."
>
> Huillet: So, the only weapon one has is time. Because people with money never have time. That's

36 kinoslang.blogspot.com, May 1, 2020.

37 Arnold Schoenberg's one-act opera, *Von heute auf morgen* (*From Today Until Tomorrow*) was staged and filmed by Danièle Huillet and Jean-Marie Straub for their 1996 film of the same name. See also Diedrich Diedrichsen's essay "The Revolutionary Dream of Marriage versus the Capitalist Reality of Sexuality" in the present volume, 68–77.

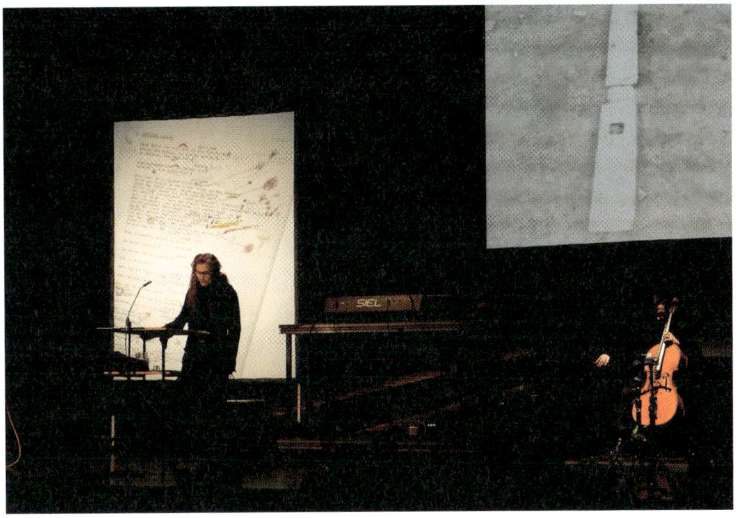

totally clear: money must be reinvested as quickly as possible. No time to lose there. But if you have time, you are still stronger in the long run.
Straub: Yes, even in a world like the one we have come to live in by now.
Huillet: But you pay for this, of course. That's clear. You pay nevertheless.[38]

38
The scene of this dialogue also appears in Peter Nestler's homage to Huillet and Straub, *Verteidigung der Zeit* (*Defense of Time*, 2007). Nestler was in the audience during these conversations in the Filmhuset in Stockholm in 2004. The complete transcript of the two Q&As, serendipitously recorded on video by Mike Jarmon, was first published in Swedish in the magazine *Walden*, no. 7/8, 2017, and recently in German in *Danièle Huillet, Jean-Marie Straub: Schriften*.

10

The films are what they are thanks to the effort that goes into making them. [...] And the greater part of the work during pre-production and when shooting is namely that—to avoid the clichés, and to blow them up, to dynamite them. There's a word that has frayed with usage, that has turned into something of a cliché. It is linked to *dialectic*. Damn! One should never say or show something in which one cannot sense the possibility of its opposite as an intrinsic resistance.[39] —Jean-Marie Straub

39
"A Thousand Cliffs," in the present volume, 388.

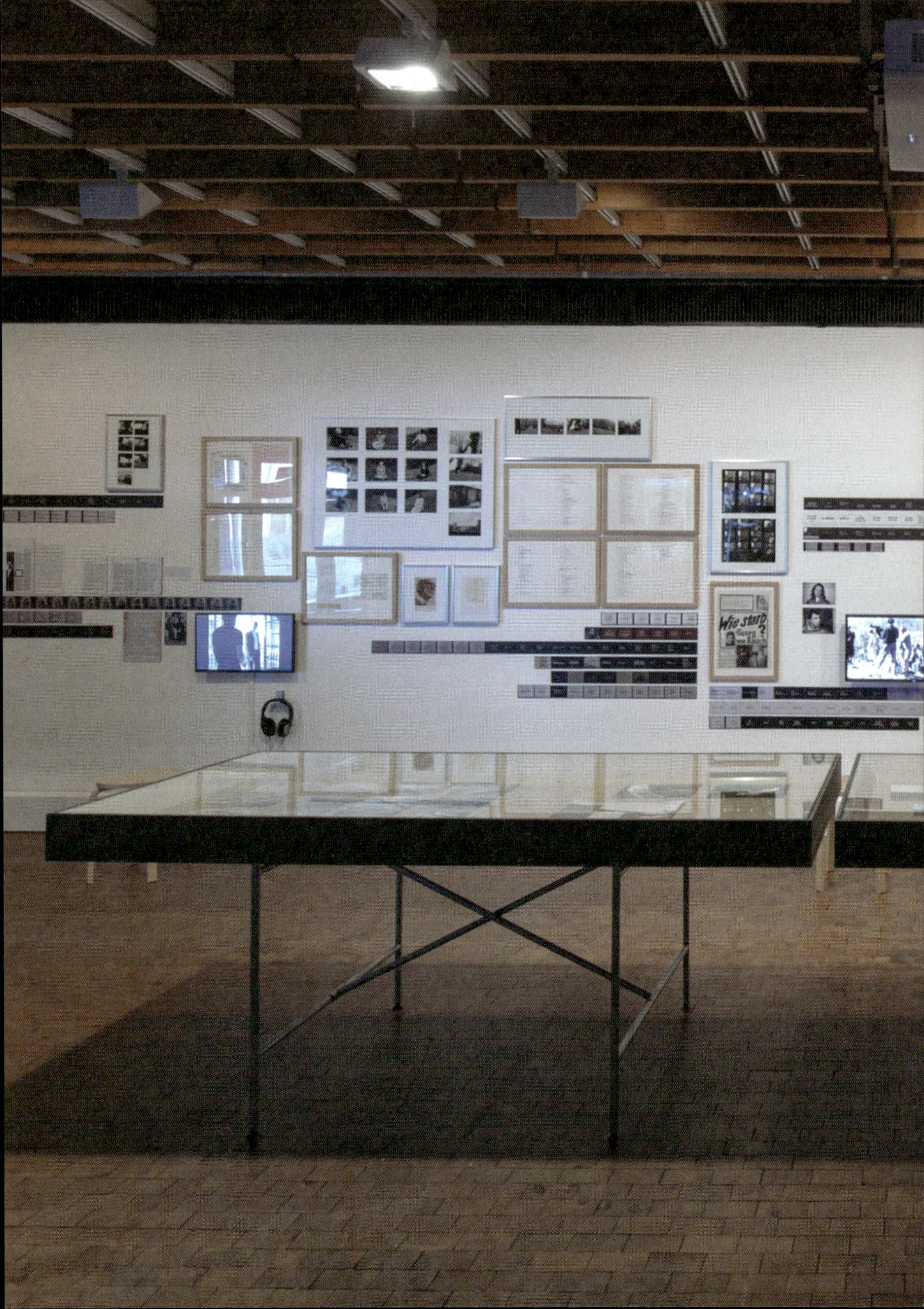
Wie starb
Georg
?

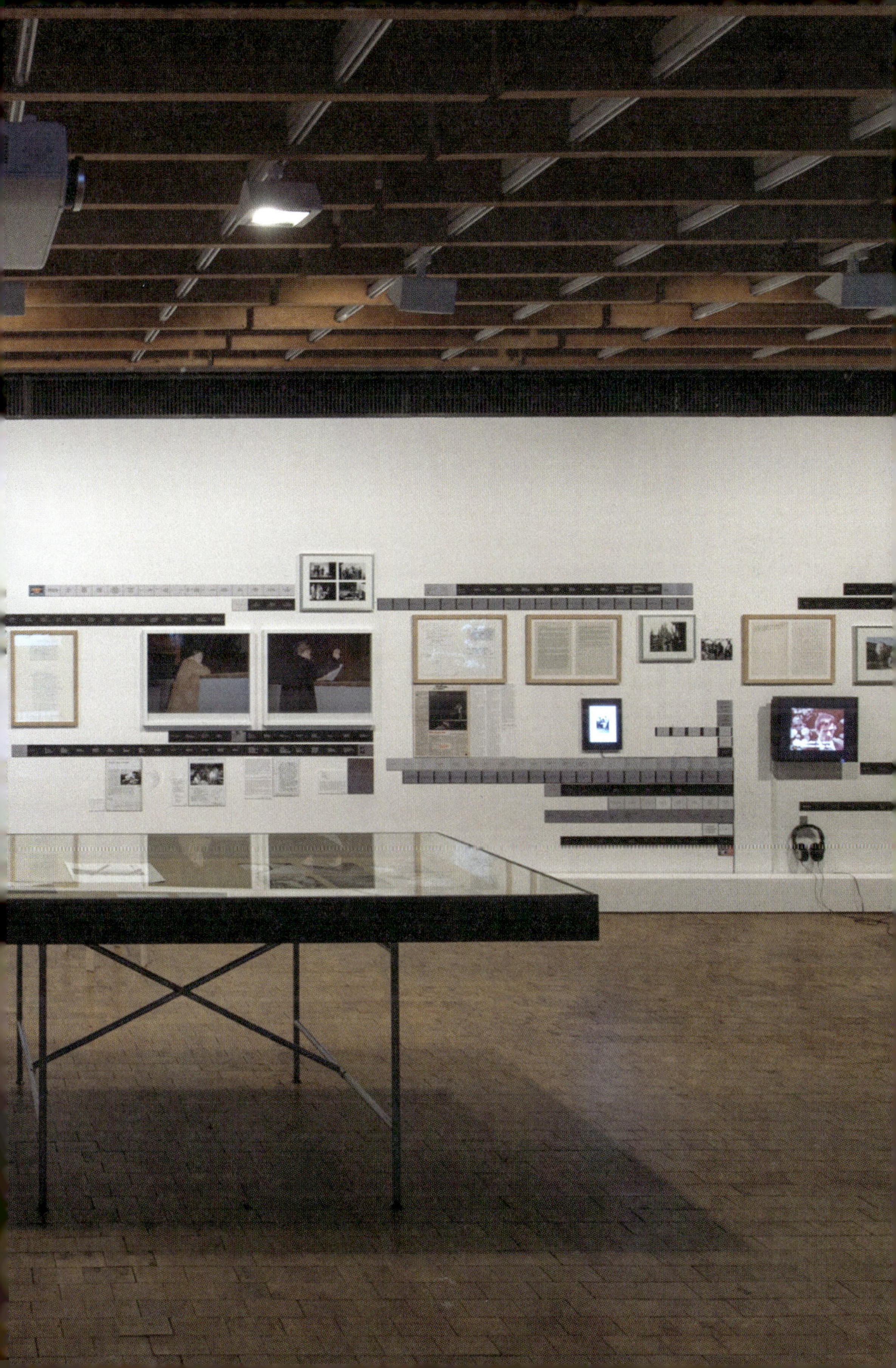

FILMOGRAPHY

[Based on the detailed filmography in *Jean-Marie Straub & Danièle Huillet*, edited by Ted Fendt (Vienna: SYNEMA, 2016), revised by Klaus Volkmer and Antonia Weiße for *Danièle Huillet, Jean-Marie Straub: Schriften* (Berlin: Vorwerk 8, 2020). The dating refers to the year in which a film was finished, as was the habit of Huillet and Straub, and not to the year of a film's first public screening, as is commonly done.]

1962 *Machorka-Muff*, West Germany, 35mm, B&W, 18 min. "Ein bildhaft abstrakter Traum, keine Geschichte. Jean-Marie Straub." ("A metaphorically abstract dream, not a story.") Script based on the story, "Hauptstädtisches Journal," by Heinrich Böll. Production dates and locations: ten days in September 1962, Bonn and Munich.

1964/65 *Nicht versöhnt oder Es hilft nur Gewalt, wo Gewalt herrscht* (*Not Reconciled, or Only Violence Helps Where Violence Rules*), West Germany, 35mm, B&W, 52 min. Text based on the novel *Billard um halbzehn* by Heinrich Böll. Production dates and locations: six weeks in August–September 1964, and two weeks in April 1965 at 45 different locations in and around Cologne, Eifel, and Munich.

1967 *Chronik der Anna Magdalena Bach* (*Chronicle of Anna Magdalena Bach*), West Germany, 35mm, B&W, 93 min. Script based on the *Necrology* by Carl Philipp Emanuel Bach and J. F. Agricola (1754), from texts (letters and memoirs) by Johann Sebastian Bach and other period documents. Main locations: Eutin castle (Prince of Anhalt-Cöthen's castle); Preetz, monastery church (organ loft no. 3, Cöthen Cathedral); Stade, St. Wilhaldi and St. Cosmae churches (organ loft no. 1, St. Thomas Church in Leipzig; organ loft no. 2, at the university); Leipzig, facade of the city hall (Leipzig marketplace); Lüneburg Abbey (St. Thomas School: refectory, Cantor's lodgings); Haseldorf castle (Cantor's lodgings: composition room; superintendent's lodgings); Lübeck, Füchting court (municipal counsel's room, Leipzig Town Hall); Nuremberg, National Germanic Museum (Cantor's lodgings: music room); Freiberg in

Saxony, cathedral (organ loft no. 5, Notre-Dame of Dresden church); Grosshartmannsdorf, church (organ loft no. 4, St. Sophie of Dresden church); East Berlin, Opera House ("Apollo" room). Production dates: August 20–October 14, 1967.

1968 *Der Bräutigam, die Komödiantin und der Zuhälter* (*The Bridegroom, the Actress, and the Pimp*), West Germany, 35mm, B&W, 23 min. Script based on *Krankheit der Jugend (Pains of Youth)* by Ferdinand Bruckner, condensed by Jean-Marie Straub, and three poems by Juan de la Cruz translated into German by Jean-Marie Straub, Danièle Huillet and Helmut Färber. Production dates and locations: half-day in the Action Theater (Munich) on April 1, 1968, and four days in Munich, May 1968.

1969 *Les yeux ne veulent pas en tout temps se fermer–ou Peut-être qu'un jour Rome se permettra de choisir à son tour (Othon)* (*Eyes do not want to close at all times or Perhaps one day Rome will permit herself to choose in her turn [Othon]*), West Germany/Italy, 16mm, color, 88 min. Based on *Othon* by Pierre Corneille. "This film is dedicated to the very great number of those born into the French language who have never had the privilege to get to know the work of Corneille; and to Alberto Moravia and Laura Betti who obtained permission for me to shoot on Palatine Hill and in the gardens of Doria-Pamphilj villa in Rome. J.-M. S." Production dates and location: four weeks in Rome, August–September 1969.

1972 *Geschichtsunterricht* (*History Lessons*), Italy/West Germany, 16 mm, color, 85 min. Adapted from the novel fragment *Die Geschäfte des Herrn Julius Caesar* (*The Business Affairs of Mr. Julius Caesar*) by Bertolt Brecht. Production dates and locations: three weeks in Rome, Frascati, Trentino-Alto Adige and Elba, June–July 1972.

1972 *Einleitung zu Arnold Schoenbergs Begleitmusik zu einer Lichtspielscene* (*Introduction to Arnold Schoenberg's "Accompaniment to a Cinematographic Scene"*), West Germany, 16mm, color/B&W, 15 min. Texts: Arnold

Schoenberg (letters to Wassily Kandinsky, April 20 and May 4, 1923) and Bertolt Brecht (extract from a speech to the International Congress in Defense of Culture, 1935). Production dates and locations: one day in Rome and one in Baden-Baden (TV studios), in June and October 1972.

1974 *Moses und Aron* (*Moses and Aaron*), Austria/Italy/France/West Germany, 35mm (two shots in 16mm), color, 105 min. “For Holger Meins*, J-M.S., D.H.” Script based on, *Moses und Aron. Opera in three acts by Arnold Schoenberg*, (Mainz: B. Schott’s Söhne, 1958). Script dated: Berlin, late 1959–Rome, early 1970. Production dates and locations: two shots in Luxor, Egypt (shots 42 and 43, pans over the Nile Valley), 16mm, May 1973; six weeks recording the orchestra in Vienna; five weeks in the amphitheater in Alba Fucens (Abruzzo, Italy), and Lake Matese (last shot, Act III) in August–September 1974.

1976 *Fortini/Cani*, Italy, 16mm, color, 83 min. The film is known as *Fortini/Cani*, but the title does not appear in the film, which opens with a shot of the cover of Franco Fortini’s book *The Dogs of Sinai* from which the text is drawn. Production dates and locations: three weeks in June 1976 in Cotoncello (Elba), Marzabotto, Sant’Anna di Stazzema, San Terenzo, Vinca, San Leonardo/Frigido, Bergiola (Apuan Alps), Florence, Milan, Rome.

1977 *Toute Révolution est un coup de dés* (*Every Revolution is a Throw of the Dice*), France, 35mm, color, 10 min. “*for Frans van de Staak, Jean Narboni, Jacques Rivette and some others. J.-M.S. May 77.” Based on, *Un coup de dés jamais n’abolira le hasard* by Stéphane Mallarmé (1897). Production dates and locations: May 9–10, 1977 in Père-Lachaise cemetery, Paris.

1978 *Dalla nube alla resistenza* (*From the Cloud to the Resistance*), Italy/West Germany, 35mm, color, 105 min. Based on texts by Cesare Pavese, *Dialoghi con Leucò* (*Dialogues with Leucò*), (Turin: Einaudi, 1947) and *La luna e il falò* (*The Moon and the Bonfires*), (Turin: Einaudi, 1950). “*in memory of Yvonne without whom there would be no Straub-Films J.-M.S." Production dates and locations: five weeks in Maremme, Monte Pisano, Tripalle near Pisa, in the Langhe (Piedmont), June–July 1978.

1980/81 *Too Early/Too Late,* France/Egypt, 16mm, color, 100 min. Texts: a letter from Friedrich Engels to Karl Kautsky (February 20, 1889); an excerpt from "Die Bauernfrage in Frankreich und Deutschland" by Friedrich Engels ("The Peasant Question in France and Germany," *Die Neue Zeit*, 1894–95); statistics in first part excerpted from the *cahiers de doléance*; postface to *La Lutte de classes en Égypte* (*Class Struggles in Egypt from 1945 to 1968* (Paris: F. Maspero, 1969) by Mahmoud Hussein. Production dates and locations: first part–two weeks in France, June 1980; second part–three weeks in Egypt, May 1981.

1982 *En Rachâchant,* France, 35mm, B&W, 7 min. Based on the short story, "*Ah! Ernesto!*" (Boissy-Saint-Léger: Harlin Quist, 1971), by Marguerite Duras. Production dates and locations: August 1982, Straub-Huillet's apartment in Paris and Saint-Ouen (school).

1983 *Klassenverhältnisse* (*Class Relations*), West Germany/France, 35mm, B&W, 130 min. Based on the novel by Franz Kafka, *Der Verschollene* (*Amerika*) (Frankfurt am Main: S. Fischer Verlag). Production dates and locations: July 2–September 20, 1983 (Hamburg and Bremen), September 21–25, 1983 (New York and St. Louis).

1985 *Proposta in quattro parti* (*Proposition in Four Parts*), Italy, video, color and B&W, 41 min. 1. *A Corner in Wheat*, D.W. Griffith, 1909, 14 min. in its entirety, silent. 2. *Moses und Aron*, Arnold Schoenberg, 1932; Straub-Huillet, 1974. 3. *Fortini/Cani*, Franco Fortini, 1967, Straub-Huillet, 1976. 4. *Dalla nube alla resistenza*, Cesare Pavese, 1948–50, Straub-Huillet, 1978. Video montage conceived and edited by Jean-Marie Straub for Enrico Ghezzi's TV program, *La Magnifica ossessione*, broadcast on R.A.I. 3 over forty hours from December 25–26, 1985.

1986 *Der Tod des Empedokles; oder: wenn dann der Erde Grün von neuem euch erglänzt* (*The Death of Empedocles or When the Green of the Earth Will Glisten for You Anew*), France/West Germany, 35mm, color, 132 min. The film is based on the first version (1798) of Hölderlin's unfinished *Der Tod des Empedokles*. Huillet and Straub established the script in collaboration with D.E. Sattler, the editor of Hölderlin's complete works, *Frankfurter Hölderlin-Ausgabe* (Frankfurt am Main: Roter Stern, 1975). Production dates and locations: eight weeks in a park in Dona Fugata (Ragusa, southern Sicily) and on Mount Etna, late May–late July 1986.

1988 *Schwarze Sünde* (*Black Sin*), West Germany, 35mm, color, 42 min. Text: from the third version (1799) of *Der Tod des Empedokles*, established with D.E. Sattler. Production dates and locations: three weeks on Mount Etna (altitude: 1900 m.), late July and August 1988.

1989 *Cézanne. Dialogue avec Joachim Gasquet* (*Les éditions Bernheim-Jeune*) (*Cézanne. Conversation with Joachim Gasquet [Bernheim-Jeune Editions]*), France/West Germany, 35mm, color, 51 min. Text: adapted from "Ce qu'il m'a dit...," by Joachim Gasquet, *Cézanne* (Paris: Éditions Bernheim-Jeune, 1921, republished in 1926). The film includes a full reel of *Madame Bovary* (Jean Renoir, 1934, based on the novel by Gustave Flaubert) about the "comices agricoles" as well as two excerpts from *The Death of Empedocles* and various documents (photos of Cézanne by Maurice Denis, paintings by Cézanne). Production dates and locations: three weeks in Paris, London, Edinburgh, Basel, Ascona and Mount St.-Victoire in September–October 1989. The film also exists in a German version that is twelve minutes longer than the French version.

1991 *die Antigone des Sophokles nach der Hölderlinschen Übertragung für die Bühne bearbeitet von Brecht 1948 (Suhrkamp Verlag).* (*The Antigone of Sophocles after Hölderlin's Translation Adapted for the Stage by Brecht 1948 [Suhrkamp Publishers]*), France/Germany 35mm, color, 100 min. Text: a version reworked for the stage by Brecht in 1948 of Hölderlin's German translation (1800–1803) of Sophocles' tragedy *Antigone* (441 BC) without Brecht's prologue. The play was performed at the Schaubühne in Berlin (premiered May 3, 1991), and had a single performance on August 14 at the Teatro di Segesta. Production dates and location: five weeks at the ancient Teatro di Segesta (Sicily), Summer 1991.

1994 *Lothringen!* Germany/France, 35mm, color, 21 min. Text: adapted from *Colette Baudoche. Histoires d'une jeune fille de Metz* (*Colette Baudoche: Story of a Young Girl from Metz*) (Paris: F. Juven, 1909). Production dates and locations: Metz and surrounding areas, Koblenz, June 1994.

1996 *Von Heute auf Morgen* (*From Today Until Tomorrow*), France/Germany, 35mm, B&W, 62 min. Opera in One Act by Arnold Schoenberg, libretto Max Blonda, 1929. "Dedicated to Helga Gielen, Dieter Reifarth, André and Dominique Warynski." Production location: Hessischer Rundfunk Studio, Frankfurt.

1998 *Sicilia!* France/Italy, 35mm, B&W, 66 min. "*For the Ouistiti and in memory of Barnabé the cat. J.-M.S." Constellations, dialogues from the novel, *Conversazione in Sicilia* by Elio Vittorini 1937–38. Performed at the Teatro Francesco di Bartolo in Buti, Italy, April 1998, prior to shooting. Production locations: Buti, Messina, Syracuse, Grammichele.

2000 *Operai, contadini* (*Workers, Peasants*), Italy/France, 35mm, color, 123 min. Text: almost the entirety of chapters XLIV to XLVII from the novel *Le Donne di Messina*, 1st edition published in 1949, 2nd edition, partially re-written in 1964. Performed at the Teatro Francesco di Bartolo in Buti, June 2000. Production dates and location: Summer 2000, Buti, Italy.

2000 *Il Viandante* (*The Wayfarer*), Italy/France, 35 mm, B&W, 5 min. "*for Danièle!"—*L'arrotino* (*The Knife Sharpener*), Italy/France, 35mm, B&W, 7 min.
Both of these films are re-edited sequences using alternative takes from *Sicilia!*.

2002 *Il Ritorno del Figlio Prodigo* (*The Return of the Prodigal Son*), Italy/France/Germany, 35mm, color, 29 min. Alternative version of shots 40–46 and 63–66 of *Workers, Peasants*, focusing on the character Spine.

2002 *Umiliati: che niente di fatto o toccato da loro, di uscito dalle mani loro, risultasse esente dal diritto di qualche estraneo (Operai, contadini – seguito e fine)* (*Humiliated: that nothing produced or touched by them, coming from their hands, proves free from the claim of some stranger [Workers, Peasants – continuation and end]*), Italy/France/Germany, 35mm, color, 35 min. Premiered together with *Le Retour du fils prodigue—Humiliés.*

2001–2003 *Il Ritorno del Figlio Prodigo–Umiliati* (*The Return of the Prodigal Son–The Humiliated*), Italy/France/Germany, 35mm, color, 64 min. Text: Elio Vittorini, 1948–49 (excerpts from *Women of Messina*). *Umiliati* was performed at the Teatro Francesco di Bartolo in Buti, Italy, May 31, June 1–2, 2002.

2002 *Dolando,* Italy/France/Germany, 35mm, color, 7 min. Film made during the stage production of *Umiliati*. Three shots showing Dolando Bernardini, an actor in the film, singing a few verses a capella of *La Gerusalamme liberata* by Torquato Tasso, which he knew by heart. Followed by an alternative take of the last shot of *Workers, Peasants* (2000).

2003 *Une visite au Louvre* (*A Visit to the Louvre*), France, 35mm, color, 48 min. (1st version), 47 min. (2nd version). Text: “Ce qu’il m’a dit…,” extracts from *Cézanne* by Joachim Gasquet, 1921.

2005 *Quei loro incontri* (*These Encounters of Theirs*), Italy/France, 35mm, color, 68 min. Text: the last five *Dialogues with Leucò* by Cesare Pavese. Performed at the Teatro Francesco di Bartolo in Buti, Italy, May 2005.

2006 *Europa 2005, 27 Octobre (Cinétract)* (*Europe 2005, 27 October*). France, MiniDV, color, 10 min. Shot near the Clichy-sous-Bois power transformer where Zyed Benna and Bouna Traoré died from electrocution on October 27, 2005 while running from the police.

2007 *Le Genou d'Artemide* (*Artemide's Knee*), Italy/France, 35mm, color, 26 min. (1st version, subtitled in French), 27 min. (2nd version, not subtitled). "*for Barbara." Text: "La Belva" ("The Beast") by Cesare Pavese from *Dialoghi con Leucò*. Performed at the Teatro Francesco di Bartolo in Buti, Italy, May 2007. Production dates and location: June 11–18, 2007, Buti, Italy.

2007 *Itinéraire de Jean Bricard* (*Itinerary of Jean Bricard*), France, 35mm, B&W, 40 min. (2 versions). "For Peter Nestler." Script based on "Itinéraire de Jean Bricard" by Jean-Yves Petiteau, *Interlope la curieuse* (Nantes), no. 9/10, June 1994. Filmed in December 2007 on and around Coton Island, on the Loire.

2008 *Le Streghe, femmes entre elles* (*The Witches, Women among Themselves*), France/Italy, 35mm, color, 21 min. After "Le Streghe" ("The Witches") from *Dialogues with Leucò,* written by Cesare Pavese. First performed at the Teatro Francesco di Bartolo in Buti, June 5, 2008. Production dates and location: Buti, Italy, June 16–20, 2008.

2009 *O somma luce* (*Oh Supreme Light*), Italy/France, HD, 16:9, color, 18 min. (2 versions). Based on "Canto XXXIII" of *Paradise* from the *Divine Comedy* by Dante Alighieri. Production dates and location: Buti, Italy, September 7–10, 2009.

2009 *Joachim Gatti*, France, HD, color, 1 min. 30 sec. Text by Jean-Jacques Rousseau, from the preface to the *Discourse on the Origin and Foundations of Inequality Among Men* (1755). Produced for *Outrage et Rebellion*, a collective film conceived by Nicole Brenez and Nathalie Hubert in response to the blinding of filmmaker Joachim Gatti from a flash-ball shot by a police officer during a protest in Montreuil in July 2009. Production dates and location: Buti, Italy, September 2009.

2009 *Corneille – Brecht,* France, MiniDV, color, 26 min. 43 sec. (1st version), 26 min. 27 sec. (2nd version), 26 min. 55 sec. (3rd version). Texts: *Horace* (1640) and *Othon* (1664) by Pierre Corneille; *Das Verhör des Lucullus* (*The Trial of Lucullus*, 1939) by Bertolt Brecht. Production dates and location: Jean-Marie Straub's apartment, Paris, July 2009.

2010 *L'inconsolable* (*The Inconsolable One*), Italy, MiniDV, color, 15 min. (1st version), 15 min. 17 sec. (2nd version). Text: "L'inconsolabile" from *Dialoghi con Leucò* by Cesare Pavese. Production dates and location: September 6–9, 2010, Buti, Italy. Performed at the Teatro Francesco di Bartolo in Buti on September 3, 2010.

2010 *Un héritier* (*An Heir*), France, MiniDV, color, 20 min. 23 sec. (1st Version), 21 min. 5 sec. (2nd Version). Text: Maurice Barrès, *Au service de l'Allemagne* (*In the Service of Germany*, 1905), chapter 8. Production dates and locations: September 14–22, 2010, Ottrott, France.

2011 *Schakale und Araber* (*Jackals and Arabs*), France, MiniDV, color, 10 min. 43 sec. (1st version), 10 min. 35 sec. (2nd version). Text: Franz Kafka, "Schakale und Araber" (Jackals and Arabs, 1917). Production dates and location: April 22–29 and May 1, 2011, Jean-Marie Straub's apartment, Paris.

2011 *La Madre* (*The Mother*), Italy, HD, color, 20 min. 9 sec. (1st version), 20 min. 9 sec. (2nd version), 19 min. 38 sec. (3rd version). Text: "La Madre" from *Dialoghi con Leucò* by Cesare Pavese. Performed at the Teatro Francesco di Bartolo in Buti on September 13, 2011. Production dates and location: September 4–8, 2011, Acciaiolo, Italy.

2012 *Un conte de Michel de Montaigne* (*A Tale by Michel de Montaigne*), France, HD, color, 34 min. Text: Michel de Montaigne, *Essais* (Book II, Chapter 6), "De l'exercitation." Production dates and location: August 6–11, 2012, Paris.

2013 *La Mort de Venise* (*The Death of Venice*) France, HD, color, 2 min. Commissioned by the Venice Film Festival for the omnibus film, *Venezia 70—Future Reloaded.*

2013 *Dialogues d'ombres* (*Dialogue of Shadows*), France, HD, color, 28 min. Text: *Dialogues d'ombres* (*Dialogue of Shadows*, 1928) by Georges Bernanos. Production dates and location: June 15–20, 2013, La Boderie, Athis-de-l'Orne, France.

2013 *À propos de Venise (Geschichtsunterricht)* (*Concerning Venice [History Lessons]*), Switzerland, HD, color, 22 min. 39 sec. Text: "La mort de Venise" in *Amori et dolori sacrum* (1916) by Maurice Barrès. Includes an extract from *Chronicle of Anna Magdalena Bach* (1967). Production dates and location: October 12–14, 2013, Rolle, Switzerland.

2014 *Kommunisten* (*Communists*), Switzerland/France, HD, color, 70 min. "For Jacques-Henri Michot and Giorgio Passerone," two parts based on the novel *Le temps du mépris* by André Malraux, followed by excerpts from: 1. *Operai, contadini* (2000), 2. *Trop tôt, trop tard* (1980/81), 3. *Fortini/Cani* (1976), 4. *Der Tod des Empedokles* (1986), 5. *Schwarze Sünde* (1988). Production dates and location: Summer/Autumn 2014, Rolle, Switzerland.

2014 *La Guerre d'Algérie!* (*The Algerian War!*), France, HD, color, 2 min. Based on a story by Jean Sandretto (inexploré no. 23). Production dates and location: October 3–4, 2014, Jean-Marie Straub's apartment, Paris.

2015 *L'Aquarium et la Nation* (*The Aquarium and the Nation*), France, HD, color, 31 min. 18 sec. Text extract from the novel, *Les noyers de l'Altenburg* (*The Walnut Trees of Altenburg*) by André Malraux. Includes an excerpt from *La Marseillaise* by Jean Renoir. Production dates and locations: February 2015, restaurant Chez Ming, Rue Forest, Paris 18ème, and Société Française de Psychologie Analytique–l'Institut C.G. Jung, Paris.

2015 *Pour Renato* (*For Renato*), Italy/France, HD, color, 8 min. Montage of a scene from *Othon* (1969), and set photos made for Renato Berta's birthday party at Stadtkino Basel on April 1, 2015.

2016 *Où en êtes-vous, Jean-Marie Straub?* (*What are you up to, Jean-Marie Straub?*) Switzerland, HD, color, 9 min. 30 sec. The film was commissioned by Centre Georges Pompidou for the retrospective "Jean-Marie Straub, Danièle Huillet," May 27–July 3 2016.

2018 *Gens du Lac* (*People of the Lake*), Switzerland, HD, color, 19 min. Based on the novel by Janine Massard (Éditions Bernard Campiche, 2013). Production dates and location: end of September 2017, Rolle, Switzerland.

2020 *La France contre les robots* (*France against the robots*), Switzerland, HD, color, 4 min. 48 sec. (1st edit), 4 min. 54 sec. (2nd edit). Based on the essay "La France contre les robots" by George Bernanos. Production date and location: November 30, 2019, Rolle, Switzerland. "For Jean-Luc."

Peter Nestler

FOR DANIÈLE AND JEAN-MARIE

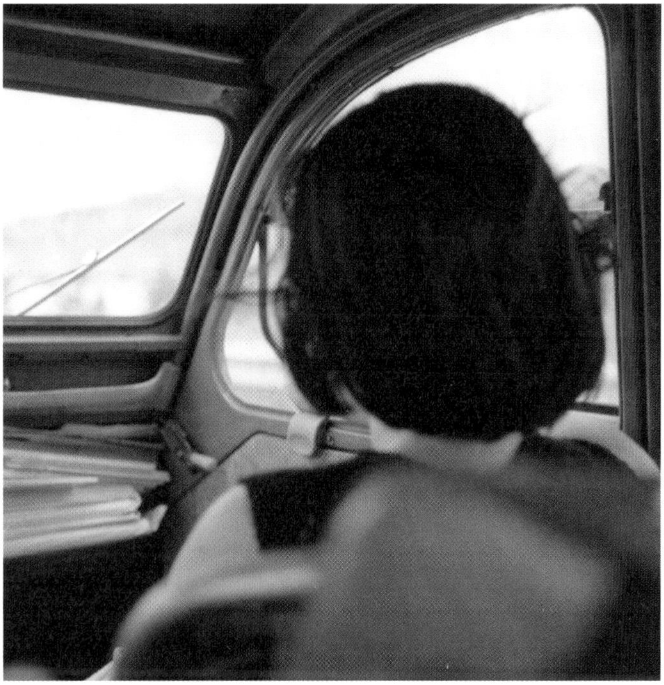

We met at an early age.

In 1958, Jean-Marie and Danièle moved away from Paris, first to Amsterdam and then to Munich. They lived in a small apartment in a high-rise near the Hauptbahnhof on Schwanthaler Straße. They came to Germany partly in order to prepare their first and biggest film project, *Chronicle of Anna Magdalena Bach*, partly because Jean-Marie didn't want to end up in prison because of his refusal to take part in France's war against the Algerians ("my friends," said Jean-Marie). In his home city of Metz, he had already been involved in an action against racism—racism against Algerians—and the French police there mistreated him. In the early 1950s, Jean-Marie studied in Strasbourg, Nancy and in Metz where he founded a film club with a very vibrant program of important films. In 1954, he moved from Eastern France to Paris and he met Danièle there. In the following years, he watched and worked on film shoots for the directors Abel Gance, Jean Renoir, Jacques Rivette, Robert Bresson, and Alexandre Astruc—then the revolution in Algeria began.

At this time, he was already attempting to find a place for his Bach film. He talks about this in Manfred Blank's beautiful, vibrant film portrait, *Die Beharrlichkeit des Blicks*:[1]

1 *Die Beharrlichkeit des Blicks*, dir. Manfred Blank, 1993.

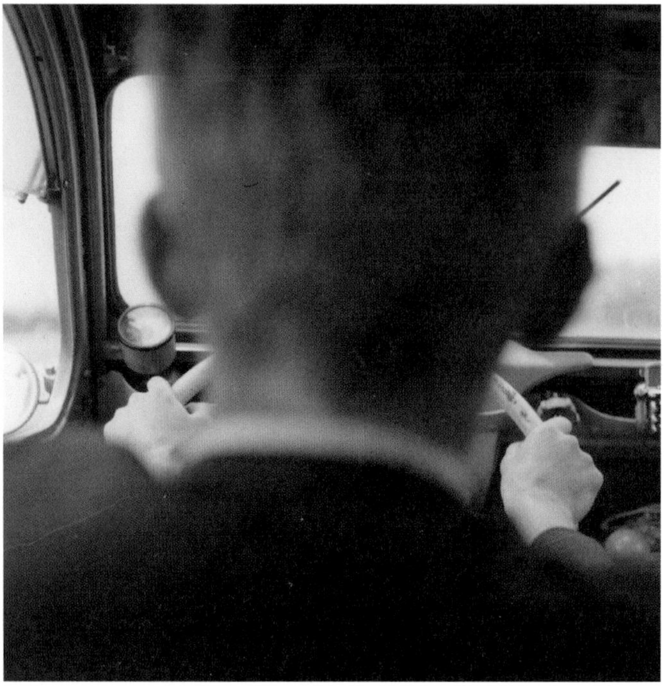

Jean-Marie: I thought of a film about Bach. That was in 1954. And since at the time I wasn't thinking about filmmaking at all, which surprises me... I immediately thought of Bresson for this film. [...] I thought that with this project, he could continue what he had achieved with *Diary of a Country Priest*. I mean, with a literary text there and with a musical text here. As Bazin said: the literary text as *matière esthétique brute* and not filmed or rewritten for the film. Then I thought, maybe someone could try or continue the same thing with a musical fabric. And I, who was only hardly there, had explained this to him, he listened patiently, I also didn't say much—he was a little shy and I was very shy—then he looked at me and said: "Yes, but this is your film, there is only one person who can make this film and that's you." And then I was in a trap. The other trap was Danièle. Because we met in 1954 in a *Gymnasium*, Lycée Voltaire. And when Bresson pushed me into the trap, I asked her—because I was of course immediately in love—I asked her if she wanted to write the script with me and prepare the film. And I can tell you one thing: I would probably never have made a film if I had remained alone. Because I wouldn't have found the courage and I was too

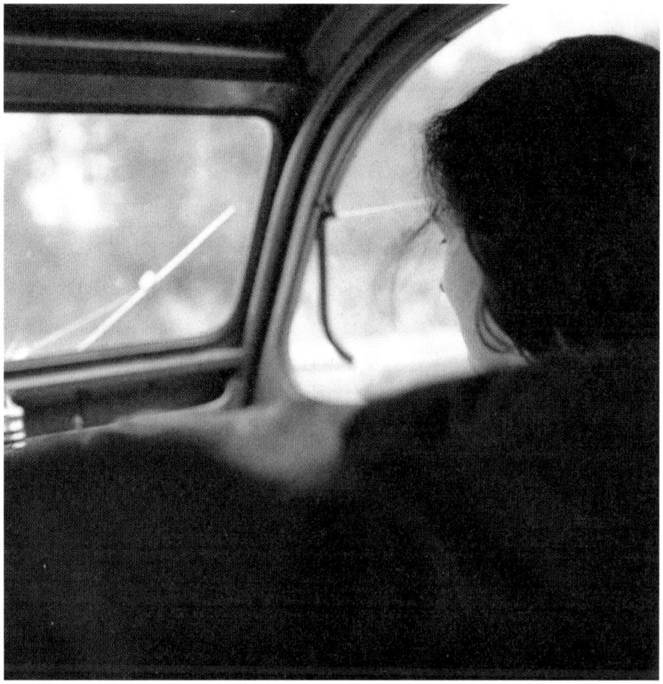

> lazy and still am. And I would probably have failed or given up, or...

When Jean-Marie and Danièle came to Germany, it was not easy to find the financing for the Bach film—this struggle took years. During this time, they both researched possible shooting locations and Bach's manuscripts in West and East Germany. They asked permission to shoot in these locations as well as for the sheets of music written by Bach, for documents and letters from the period. In Amsterdam, they met organist and harpsichordist Gustav Leonhardt, who was professor of harpsichord at the Academy of Music in Amsterdam and Vienna at the time. It took them a while to convince Leonhardt to appear in the film in the role of Johann Sebastian Bach and to be recorded playing Bach's music before the camera. Leonhardt was a bit wary at first and wanted to know exactly what the film was all about. Jean-Marie and Danièle explained. In the end, he said, "I'll do it." In the years of research and looking for money for the big *Chronicle of Anna Magdalena Bach* project, "out of impatience," Jean-Marie and Danièle made a first short film in 1962, *Machorka-Muff*, based on a text by Heinrich Böll, and then in 1964/65 the longer film *Not Reconciled or Only Violence Helps Where Violence Rules*. I first met them in 1964 when they were visiting a potential shooting location in Munich for the planned film *Not Reconciled*: it was the parlor of a big, former upper-class ground floor apartment in the Bogenhausen neighborhood located near the Isar and across from the English Garden. I lived there. I'd rented a small room where the maid would once have lived. The apartment was owned by friends (he was a poet, she was a singing coach). They suggested I be at home during the location scout. It would definitely be interesting for me to meet these French filmmakers and to talk with them since I was also involved in film. On the day when Jean-Marie and Danièle came and also approved this shooting location—a music parlor with a sofa, a baroque religious statue, and a big, black piano in the middle of the room—the three of us sat on the sofa drinking tea and eating cookies, talking about film, what film could be, what film should and should not be. We really agreed: important were attention and preciseness, reverence and caution in relation to what one found or organized in front of the camera. We didn't want to change anything. Jean-Marie and Danièle express this shared attitude in Manfred Blank's film. For me, it is spoken from the soul.

Jean-Marie chooses his words before a background of tall grass and a bit of woods.

JM: And otherwise I simply believe that in general there are—as far as art is concerned—only two families of artists: those who assume the right—sometimes brilliantly, sometimes only arrogantly—to transform the world; and those who try to see the world and to become a mirror that is as clean as possible. It also means for Cocteau: "Les miroirs feraient bien de réfléchir davantage." Mirrors would do well to reflect more. Of course, there is also abstraction in Cézanne's work but it always goes back to so-called nature, meaning to what he was looking at and what made his eyes red and him dizzy. Which is why he said: "Look at this mountain, once it was fire." Because it is not enough to see a mountain and to paint it. One must know what is behind it, thousands of years before and in between and so on, otherwise one does not see the forms. And then one can also not convey them. Anyway, I was wrong, there is a third family of artists. These are the paratroopers.

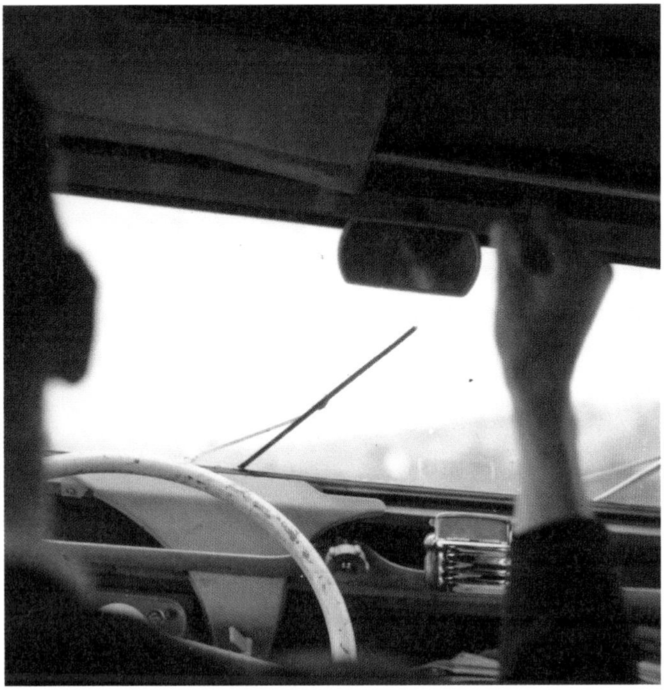

And they represent 99% of cinema today. These are people who simply fall out of the sky somewhere and, “boop,” the camera is already rolling. And they film something that they have never even seen once, not taking the time to look at it. And in order to show something, one has to have seen it; in order to see something, one has to have looked at it for years. And Cézanne did this.

Danièle: The way Cézanne saw the mountain was barely still visible from up there. And we had to wait until the fog had cleared a little so that we could see something. And Jean-Marie waited a little off to the side and suddenly he called me over and said: “Come and take a look at this!” There are sometimes clouds in Cézanne’s work that are green. And of course one always thinks the man was a little crazy; no cloud is green. And suddenly on that day at that time, there were clouds that were green. And he had the patience to see them. And we could have died without ever seeing them if we had not been forced to wait.

JM: But it must be said, film is also not painting. Film works with photography. And that is a blessing.

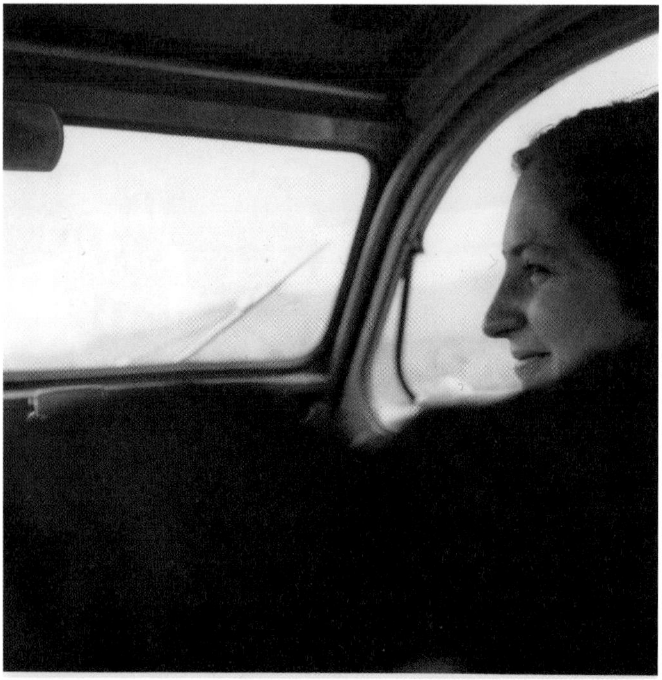

> There is also nothing worse than the many young people today who twice a year send me a script where they write at the beginning: "We drive along here and the light must be like Goya or Vermeer van Delft." That's all nonsense since one must light things as they are and try to understand the space where one is filming one's characters and so on. And that's it.

Jean-Marie and Danièle wanted to see what kind of films I had made so far. So one day in a small studio in Munich I showed them my first three short films: *Am Siel*, *Aufsätze*, and *Mülheim (Ruhr)*. They didn't say anything during the films. When we left the studio, they didn't say anything. After a while, Danièle, almost inaudibly and with a small grin: "*Aufsätze* is very beautiful." We went to the exit in silence, Jean-Marie looking at the floor. "What do you think?" I asked him. "Ohhhh..." he groaned and lightly patted his neck with his palms, "this *Mülheim*..." I later understood that they liked all three films a lot. And my reaction to their first film from 1963, *Machorka-Muff*, was the same. This film was freeing—as if a window had been opened. The esteemed weekly paper *Die Zeit* had written it off with the words: "A lot of noise for nothing...the film laments German rearmament." When Danièle and Jean-Marie were preparing to shoot *Not Reconciled or Only Violence Helps Where Violence Rules*, the Südwestfunk gave me the chance to shoot a film about the village Ödenwaldstetten. I rented a room on the land of an old farmer, spent a few weeks researching in the village and the surrounding area, and would talk with this retired farmer in the evening. I took notes on what appeared important to me. A lot of his comments are re-used in the film and create a kind of framework out of language and history that encompasses all of the sequences. I didn't meet with Jean-Marie and Danièle then, but we corresponded.

A year later, Michel Delahaye came to Munich. He was a film critic for *Cahiers du cinéma* and friends with Jean-Marie and Danièle. Delahaye was investigating German film production of the time. He described his findings in the *Cahiers* under the title "Allemagne – ciné zero." A screening was organized in Munich and Delahaye saw my films and those of other young filmmakers like Rudolf Thome, Max Zihlmann, and Klaus Lemke. Film critics, producers, and distributors were invited. During the screening of my short film *Mülheim (Ruhr)*, a commotion broke out in the theater. There was a shot filmed in the working class neighborhood Styrum in which an old couple walks with a stroller along the gray wall of a house on which someone years before had written "*Hinein in die KPD*" ("Join the German Communist Party"). A distributor in the audience stood up and said out loud, "Now I know who I'm dealing with!" left the theater, and slammed the door. Michel Delahaye had composed himself after a while and during another shot with an old man hiking in a foggy park, he shouted "Bravo!"

Not Reconciled was premiered at the Berlinale, although not in competition. It was shown in a sidebar event. The majority of film critics as well as filmmakers in the country rejected *Not Reconciled*. It was also a generous gift to German cinema in year zero. The transcript of the Q&A makes for appalling but also tiring reading. Delahaye briefly summarized the discussion in *Cahiers du cinéma*:

> Jean-Marie Straub's *Nicht Versöhnt* was screened out of competition [...]. This film is a masterpiece (and also one of the boldest experiments ever attempted in cinema), following the paths already traced by Dreyer, Bresson, Rossellini, Resnais. At the very least: the most important German work since Lang and Murnau. [...] Straub's film breaks many of the

"rules." In Germany (where critics are in any case forced by their vanity to find something to criticize in every film), a work is not defined in light of theories. It is therefore practically condemned to always be something that is too much or not enough in relation to common theory. This is a vicious circle since by definition a masterpiece is always something more than its own rules. You won't escape by saying purely and simply that the film is beautiful. Because the word is already suspicious, almost fascistic, since it is not "objective" and you will only be forgiven if you can explain on the spot the reasons and criteria behind your judgment as well as the theory it is based on, responding in passing to a few trifles like: how can society be changed? Or, what is art? If you don't perform, you are declared bankrupt. One of the rules Straub breaks is language. There is "movie German," the language of the acting school spoken by professional speechifiers during the post-synchronization of German or foreign films—it is the only authorized language. Germans are not allowed to hear their own language in films. *Nicht Versöhnt*, of course, was shot with direct sound and the critics hear, aside from a light Cologne accent, the vibrations and intonations characteristic of any voice "in action." And they immediately started shouting that their ears and language were being massacred. How to explain this? They cannot or do not want to understand how Dreyer, Bresson, Resnais, and Godard (and *Alphaville*?) "massacre" their language. Moreover, Straub moves progressively toward recitation when (one reason out of a thousand) dealing with reading a very literary text by Böll, (and very beautiful) whose literalness and literary-ness he wants to maintain. To try to make himself understood, Straub calls on Brecht. Blasphemy! Because if Germany ended up accepting Brecht, it would only be within the confines of a patented orthodoxy. As for the camera: you aren't allowed (?), one person said, to shoot a film with only one lens (well, it was shot with seven!) and another: you don't have the right (?) not to move the camera (someday someone will have to count the number of pans and tracking shots in N.V.).[2]

2
Michel Delahaye, "Berlin entre deux chaises," *Cahiers du cinéma*, no. 171 (October 1965): 14.

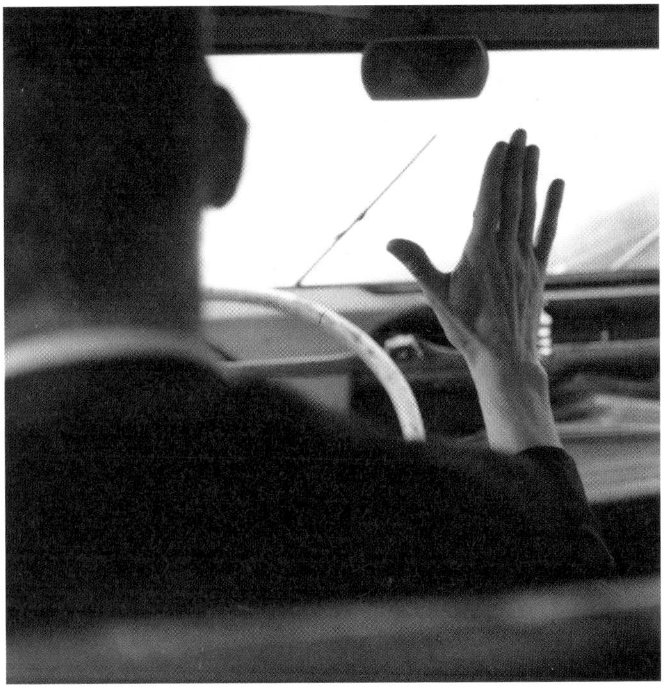

Already in 1980, in the magazine *Filme—Neues und Altes vom Kino*, Jochen Brunow published a conversation that he had with Jean-Marie and Danièle under the title "Der Maschine Widerstand leisten" ("Resisting the Machine") in which, among other things, they talk about what history is in their films.

Brunow: Something however that clearly differentiates your films from Fritz Lang's is how they deal with film time and film space.

Straub: Yes, that may partly come from our small personalities, but it is also a question of generations. What we can manage in this direction was not yet possible in Fritz Lang's time. It also comes from how we are forced into a situation of shooting films outside the industry, which was not the case for Fritz Lang. He was lucky to belong to a generation for whom it was still possible to make products within the industry that one could still be responsible for.

B: Today in *Dalla nube alla resistenza* (*From the Cloud to the Resistance*) I had the feeling during the transition to the last part...

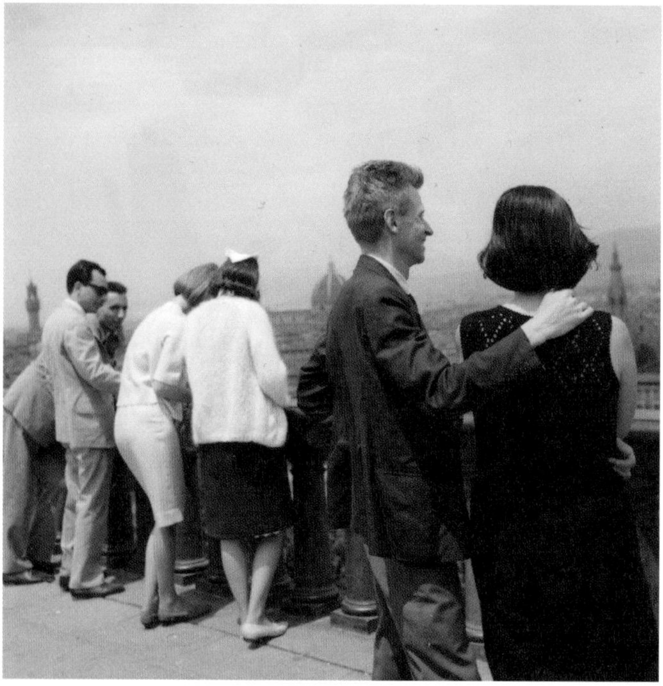

S: ...to the so-called contemporary part, to the post-war part, in which the people are dressed in costumes that look like what we wear today, right?

B: Yes, exactly at this point, I had the idea that the position of film space and film time in your films is occupied by history.

S: You'll have to try explaining that to us. That sounds very flattering, but I'd like to understand better.

B: The codes of narrative cinema treat space and time, so real space and real time, in so far as they try to reconstruct them: the goal is to produce an illusion. In your films, film space and film time are treated so that history is produced. I don't mean the representation of history as a subject, but history as something existing in the film itself.

S: These illusions that you've named... that's right, I think. In these exist partly consciously, partly unconsciously—I think consciously for the most part—our concern: to dynamite them.

B: I can't express this any more precisely. It was an idea I had while watching *Dalla nube*. I had trouble with the subtitles too. Since so much is said, one is really chained to the subtitles and can't really focus on the image.

S: We're back to the point that this kind of film is basically only for Italians and that *Not Reconciled* and *Machorka-Muff* and so on are only for German-speaking countries. There is a limit one must accept. The industry's goal is for something like this to no longer to exist. They want to make more and more international products—and they will manage to do so.[3]

3 Jochen Brunow, "Der Maschine Widerstand leisten," *Filme—Altes und Neues vom Kino*, no. 1 (1980): 29–35.

Bernard Sobel in Manfred Blank's Die *Beharrlichkeit des Blicks*:

> I have to be in shape to watch a film by the Straubs. It's demanding... It's exercise. I don't get comfortable in a chair and "poff." No. They expect me to work, to collaborate. I think that means a film by the Straubs from the viewer's side demands that he is a creator at the same time.

Translated from German by Ted Fendt.

Jan Lemitz

BLOCKBUSTER

BILDER VON KRIEGEN

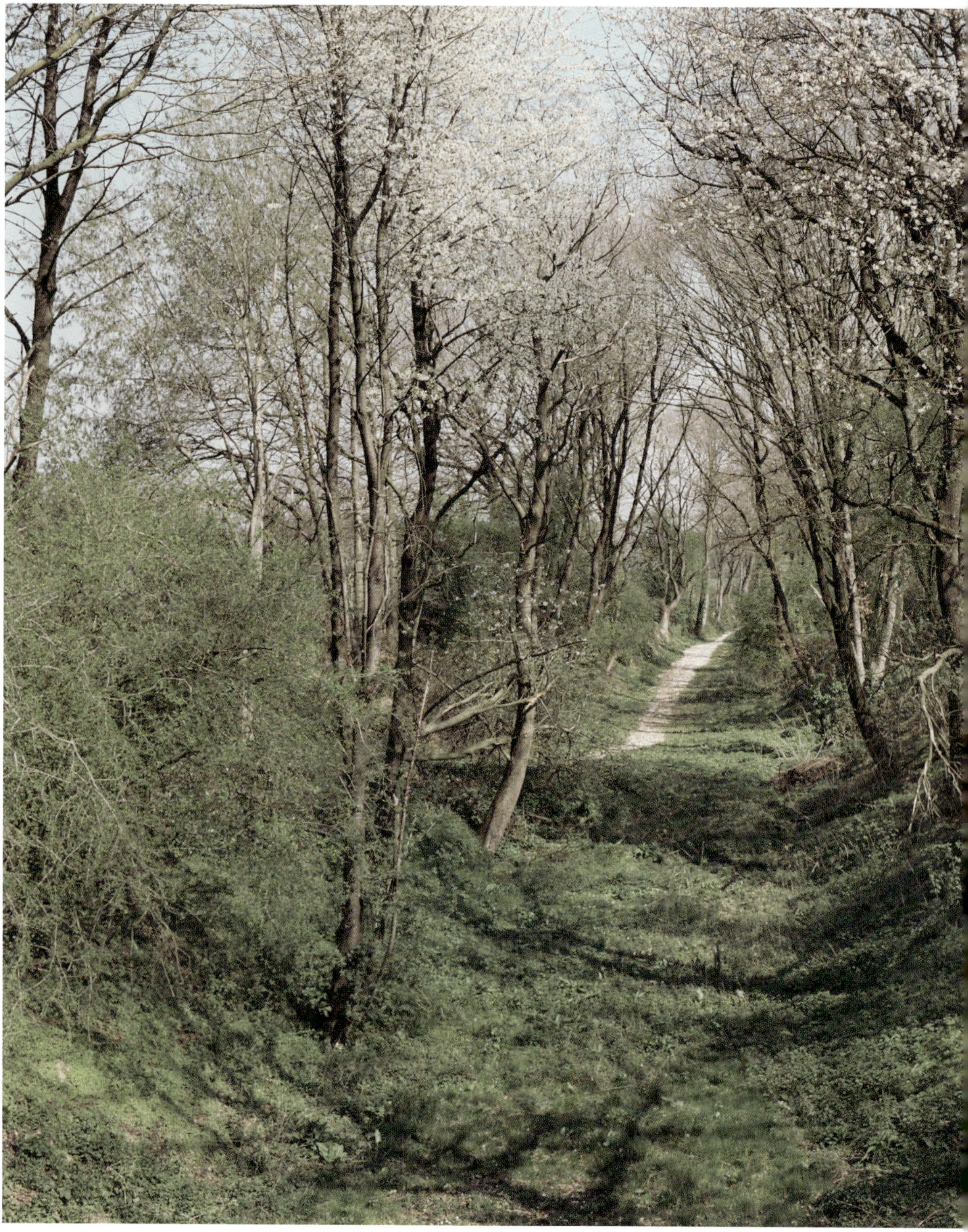

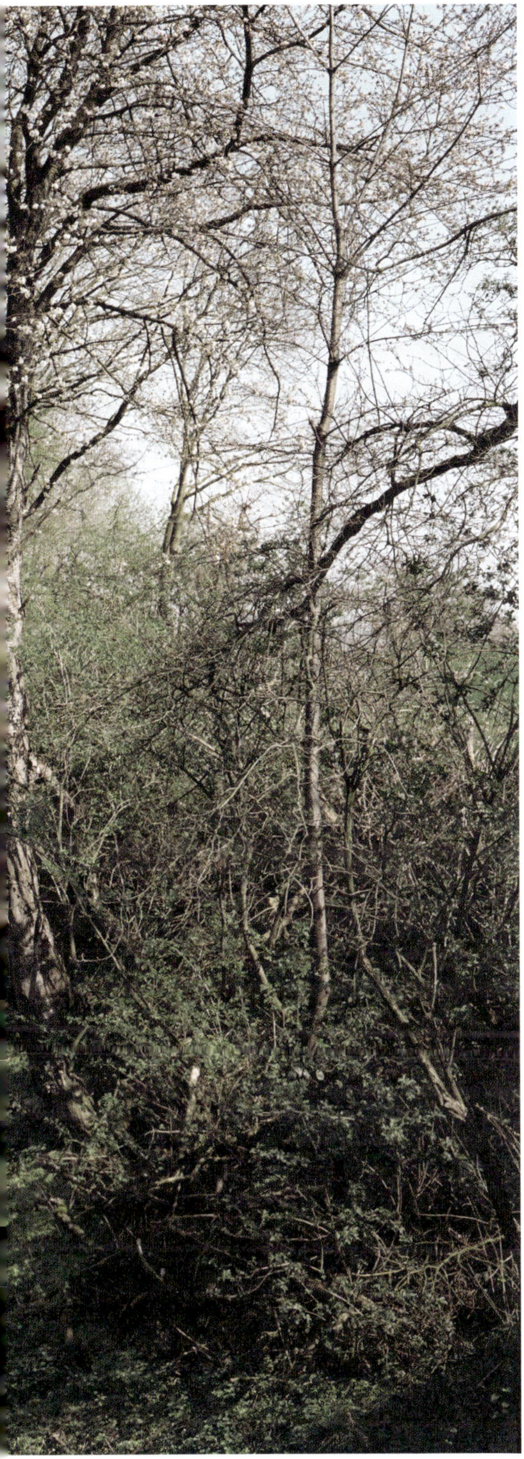

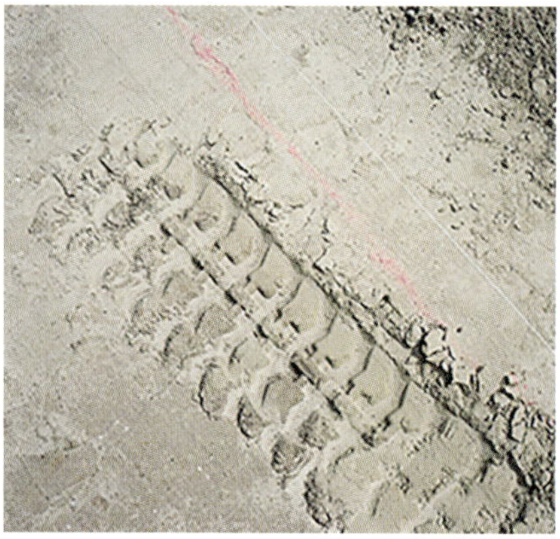

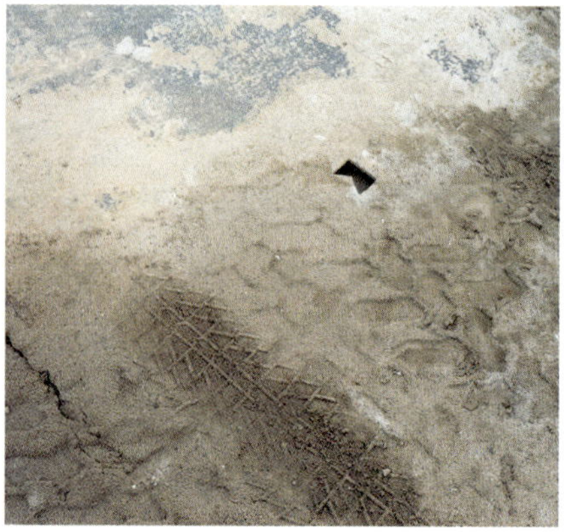

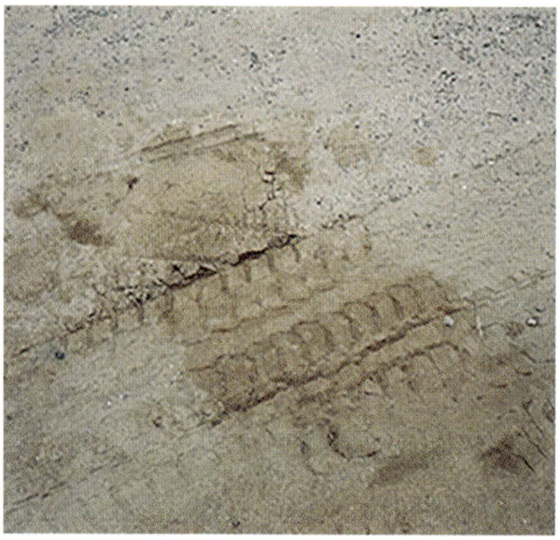

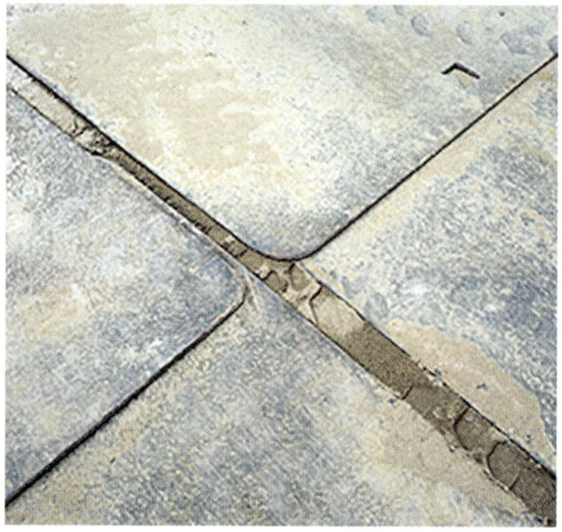

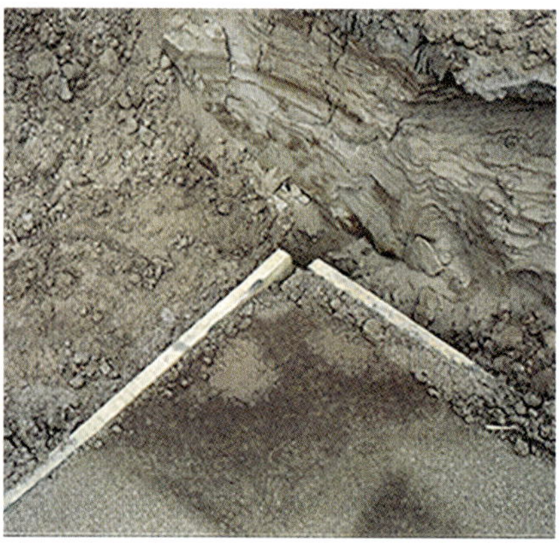

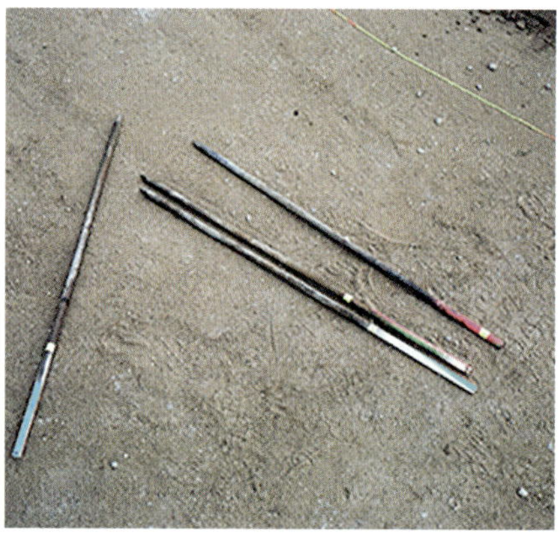

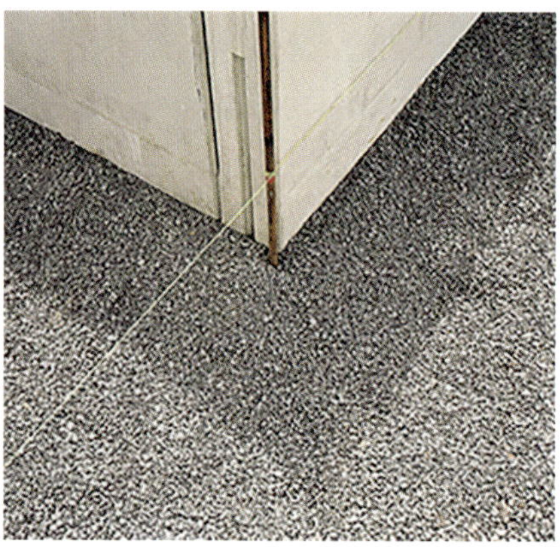

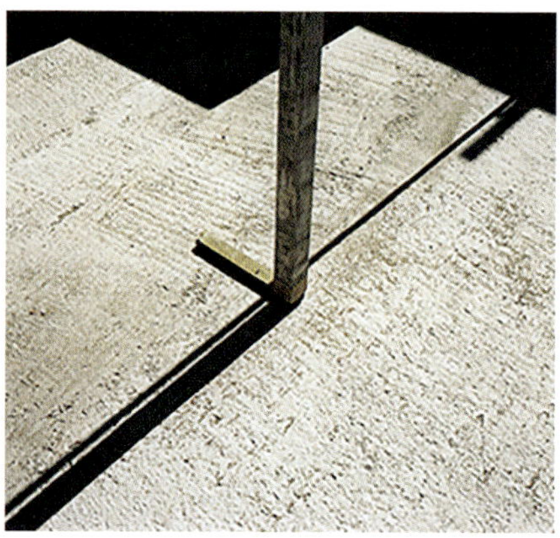

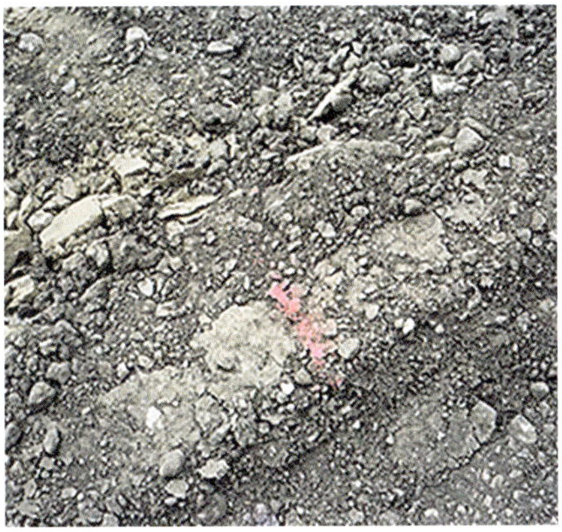
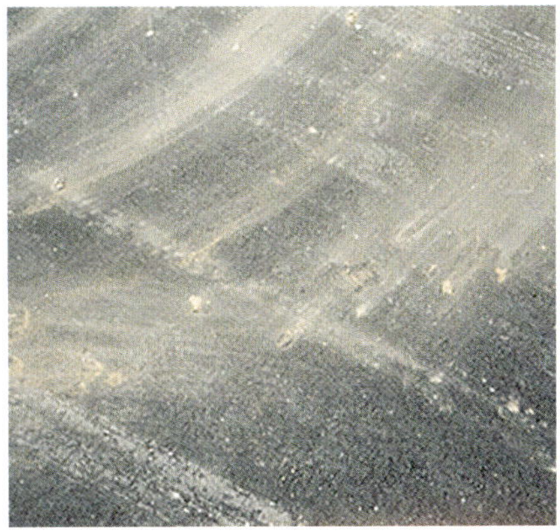
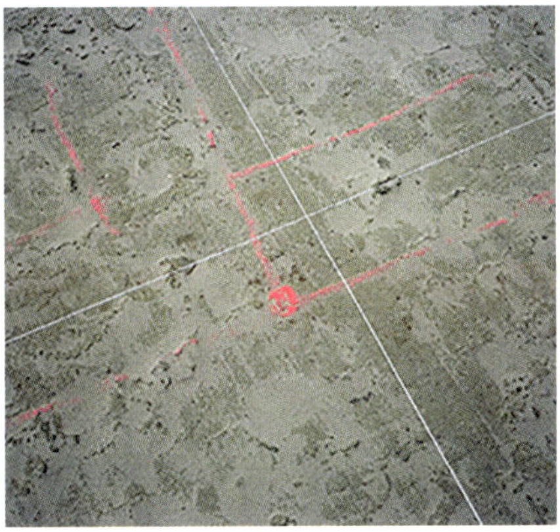
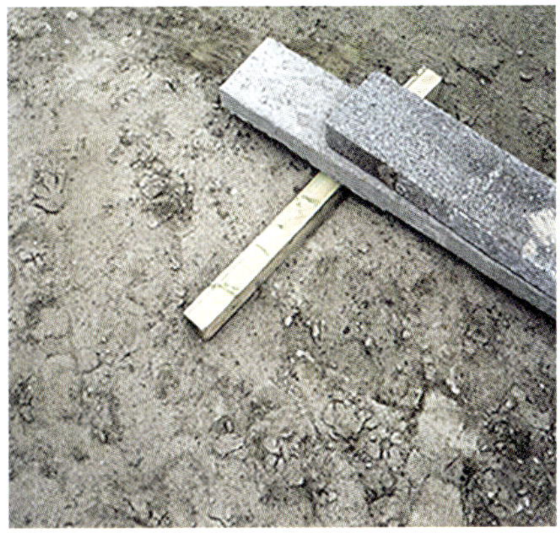
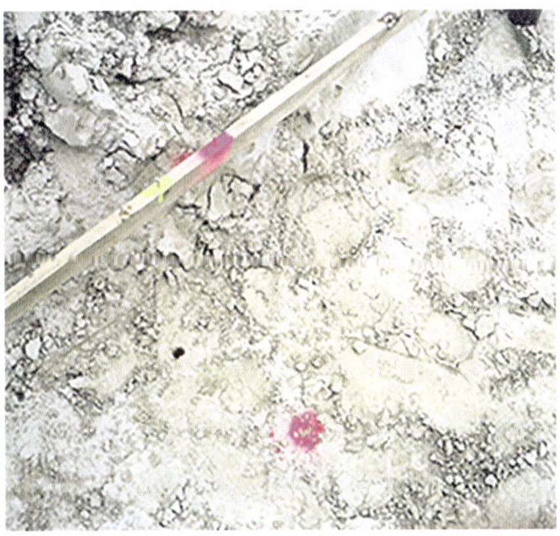
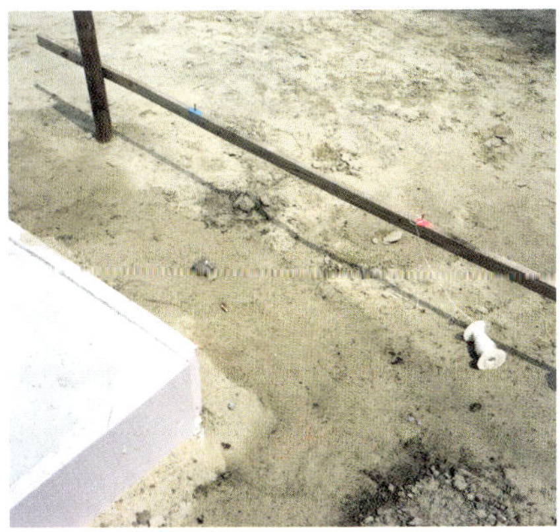
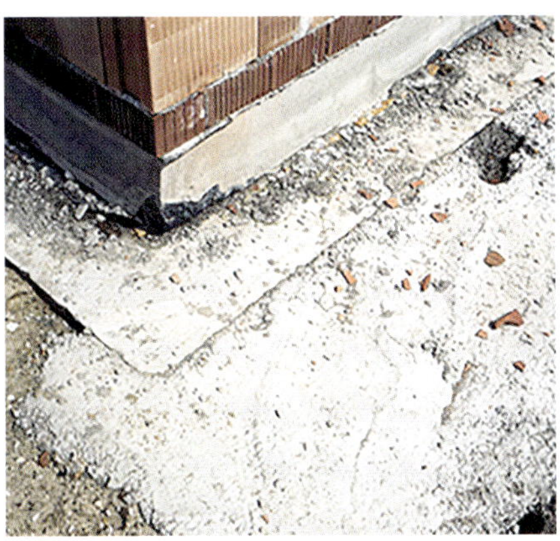
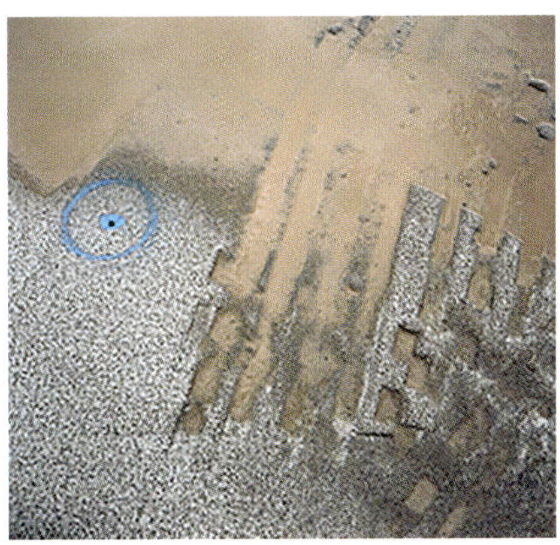

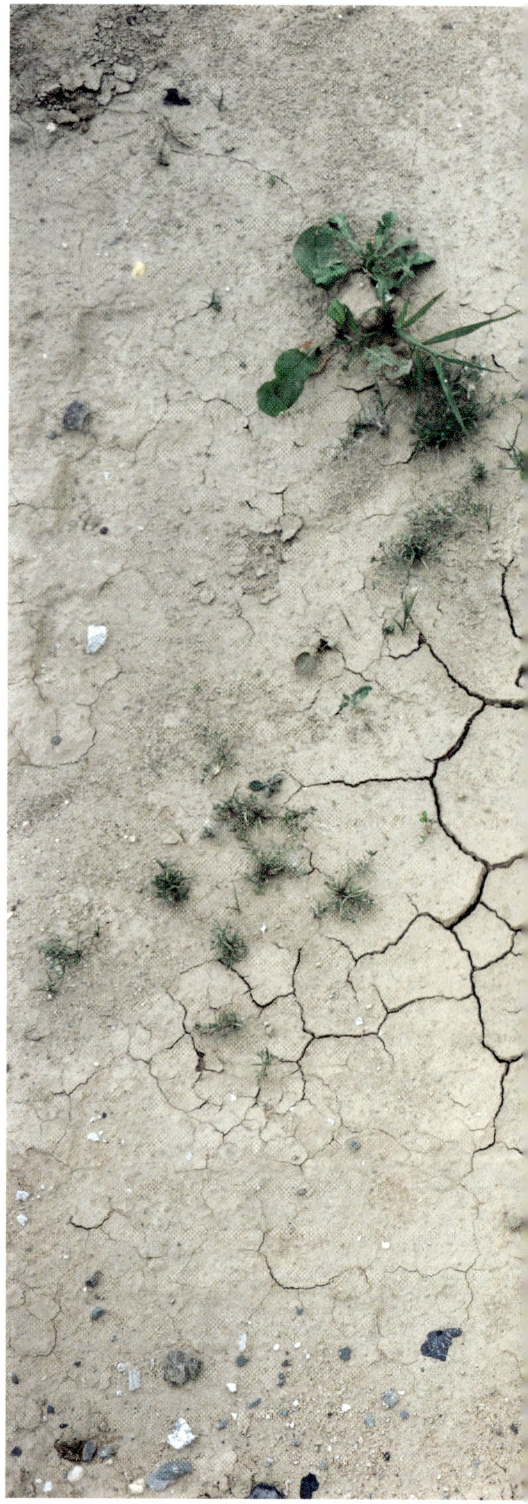

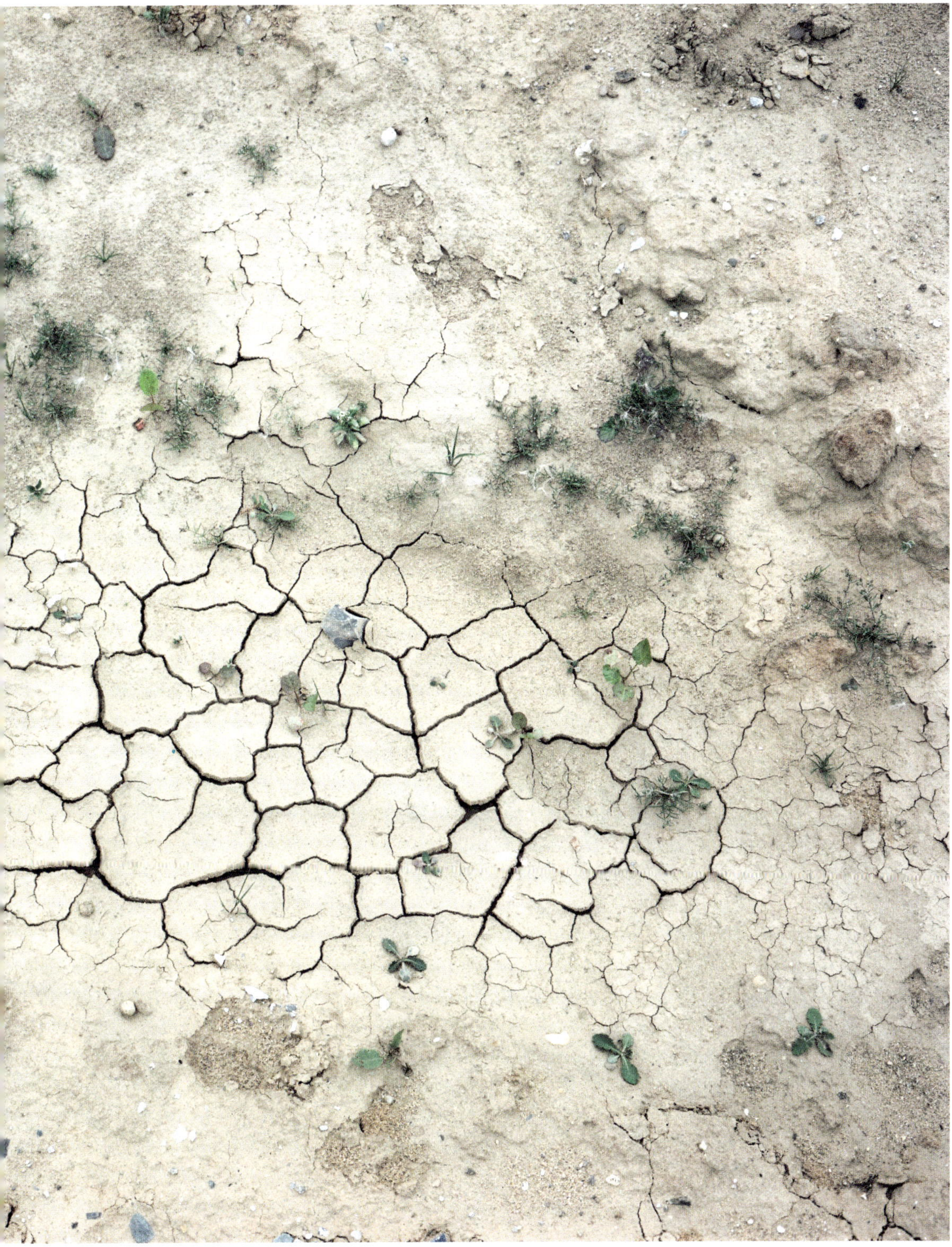

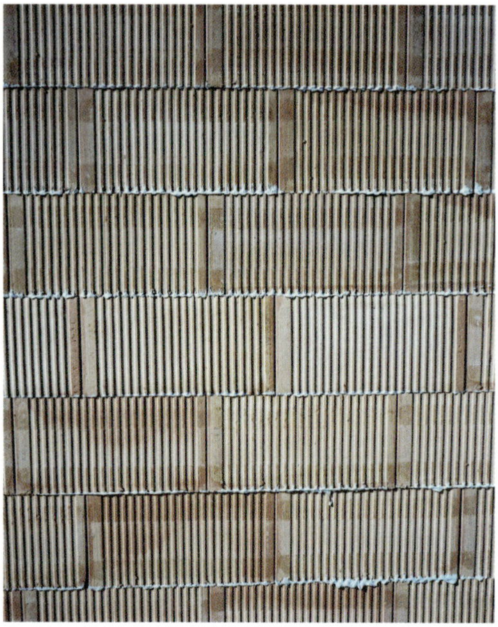

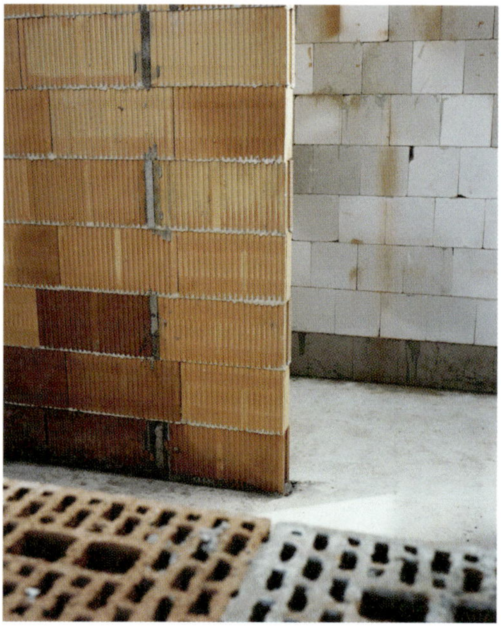

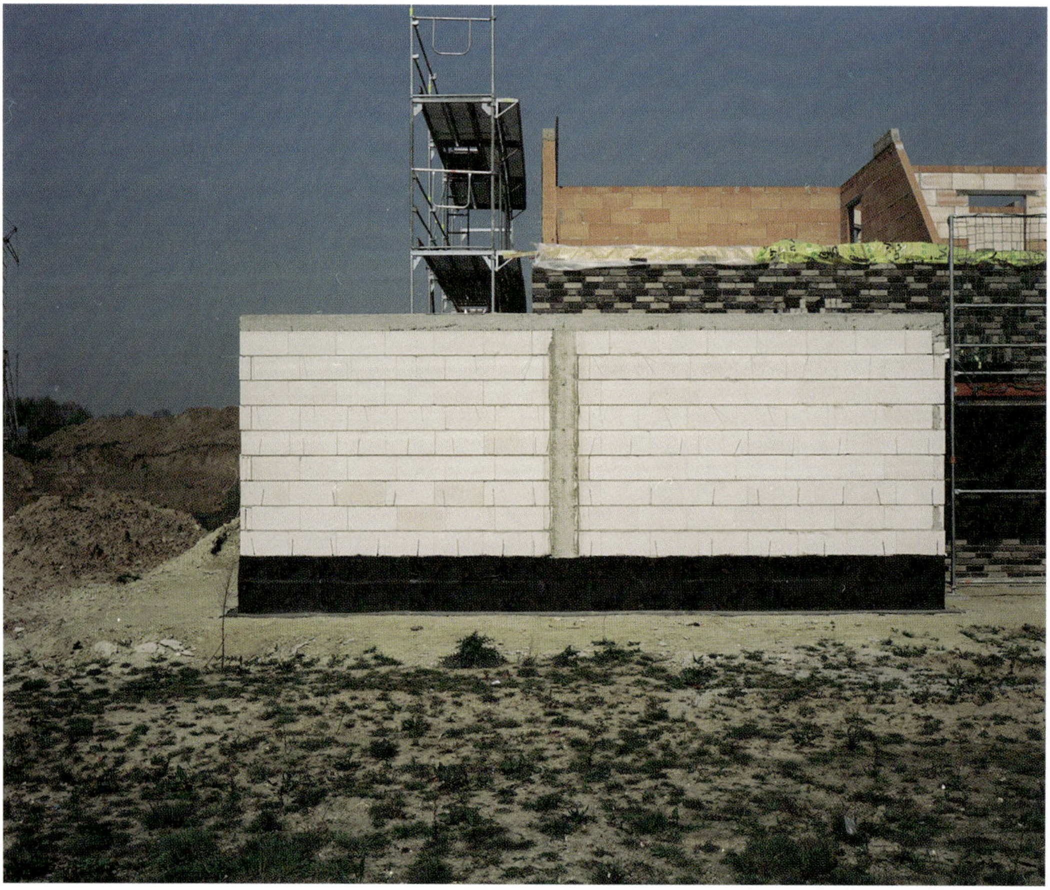

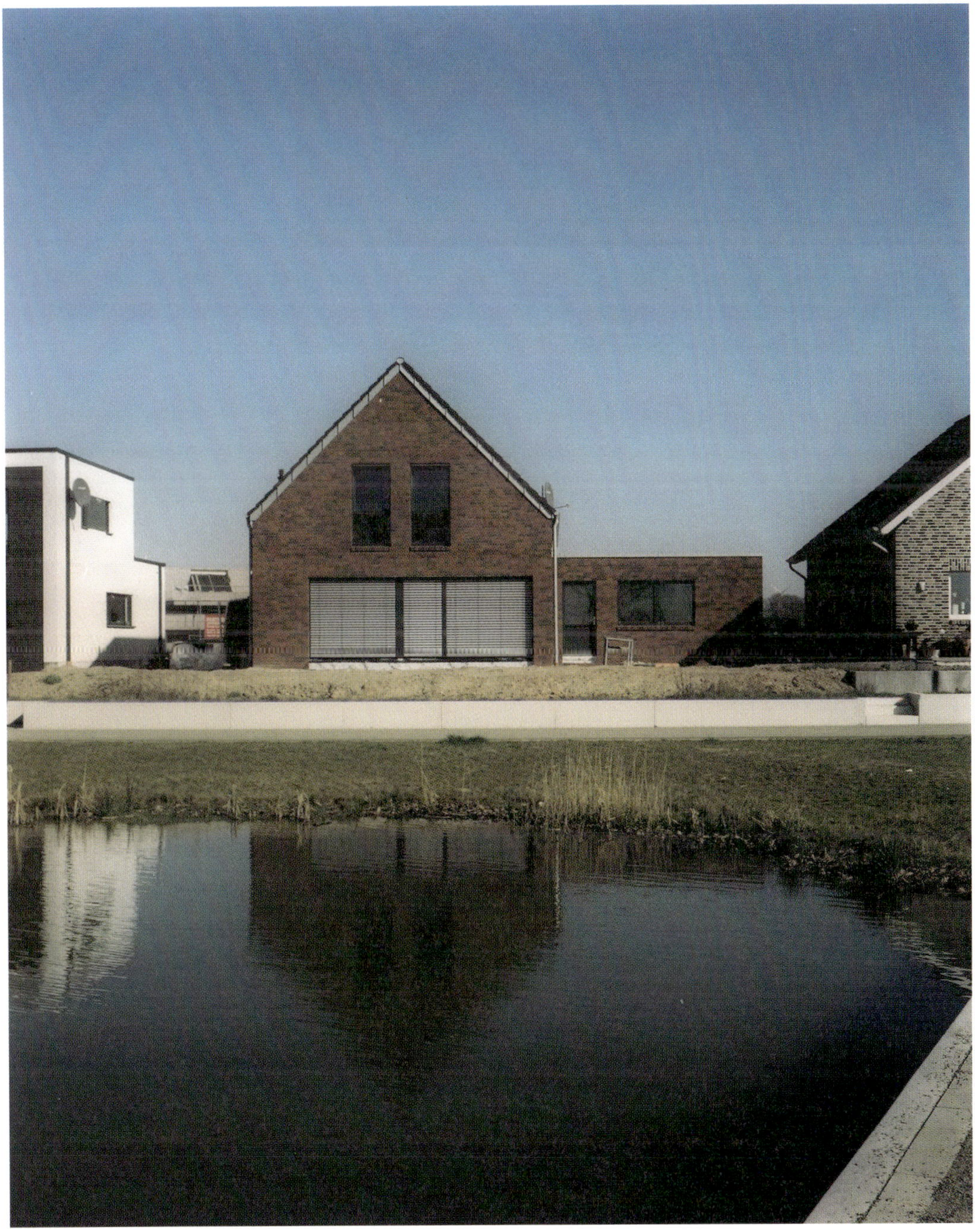

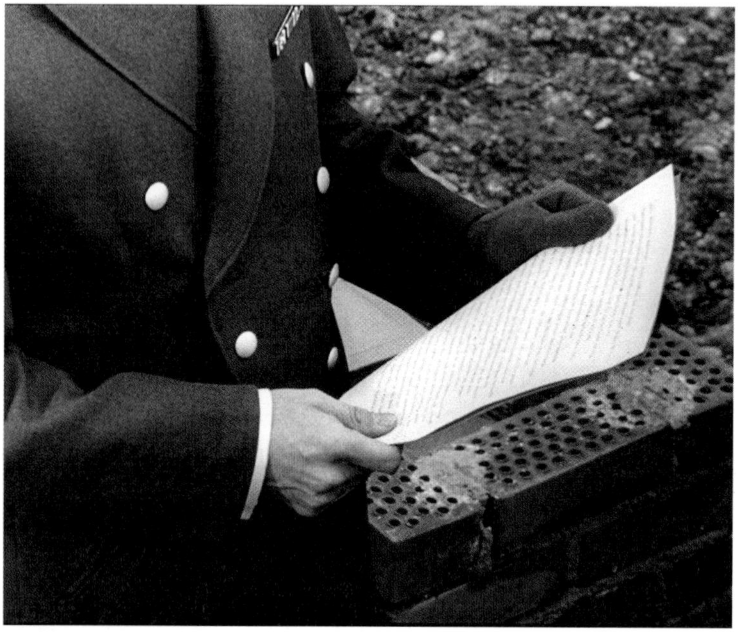

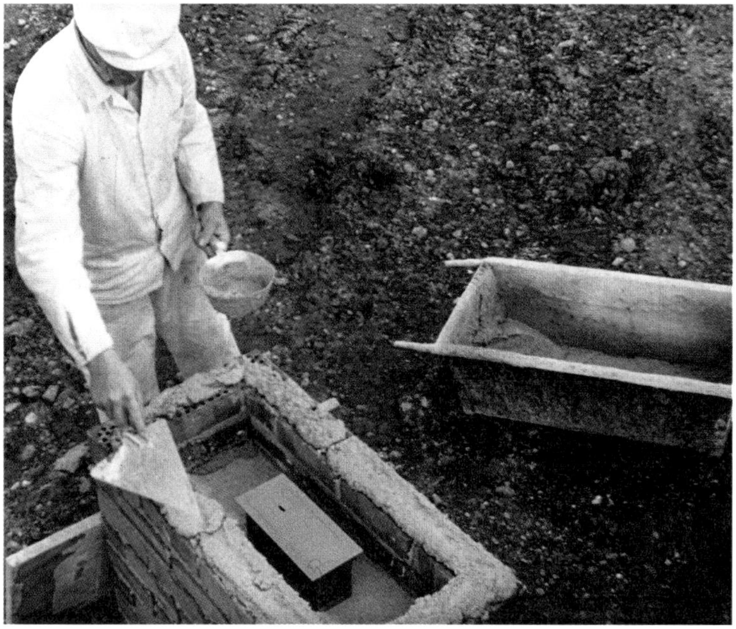

Operation Blockbuster aimed at the military breakthrough of the Allied forces near Uedem on the Lower Rhine in early 1945. With the intent of paving the way for the crossing of the River Rhine, the fighting left the vast majority of towns and villages in the region in complete devastation. Today, the term blockbuster connotes different means of representation of military conflicts, their mediatization as well as their public reception.

The photos were taken during the redevelopment of the former Reichswald barracks in the city of Goch during the last few years. Established in the early 1950's, the facilities were first used by British forces and then, after West German rearmament, handed over to the Bundeswehr in 1962. Since the demolition of the barracks the area is being reintegrated into the city; properties are up for sale in plot sizes—a public park surrounding a lake is being designed.

The photographs depict perspectives onto a landscape continuously exposed to processes of partially violent transformation. Like in Huillet-Straub's debut film *Machorka-Muff*, the images allude to the limitations of visualizing the military complex, its spatial conditions as well as the narratives and scenarios often-times hovering between fiction and references to reality, pointing at the discrepancies between visibility and concealment.

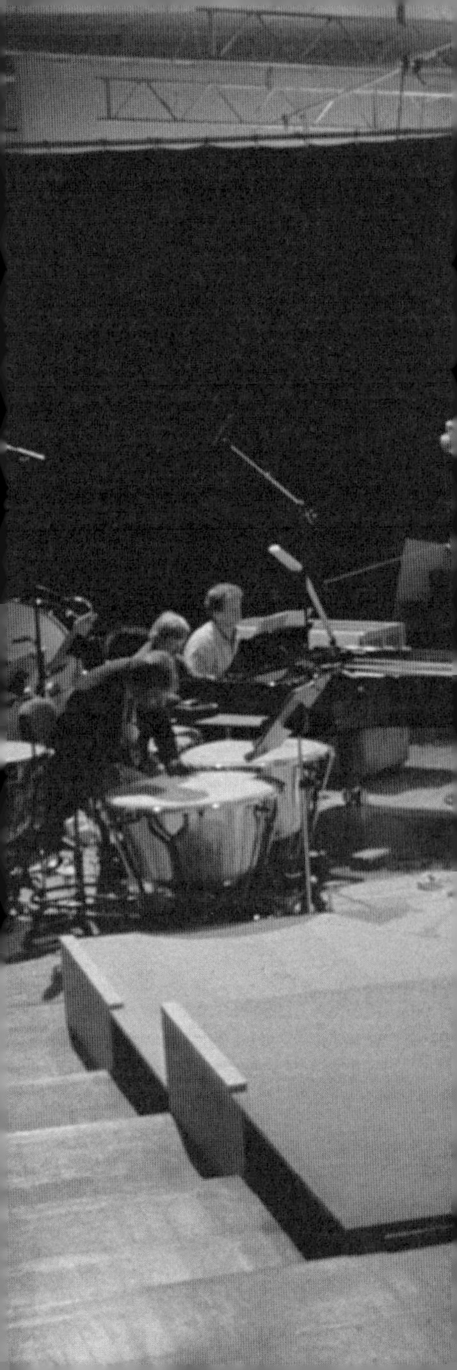

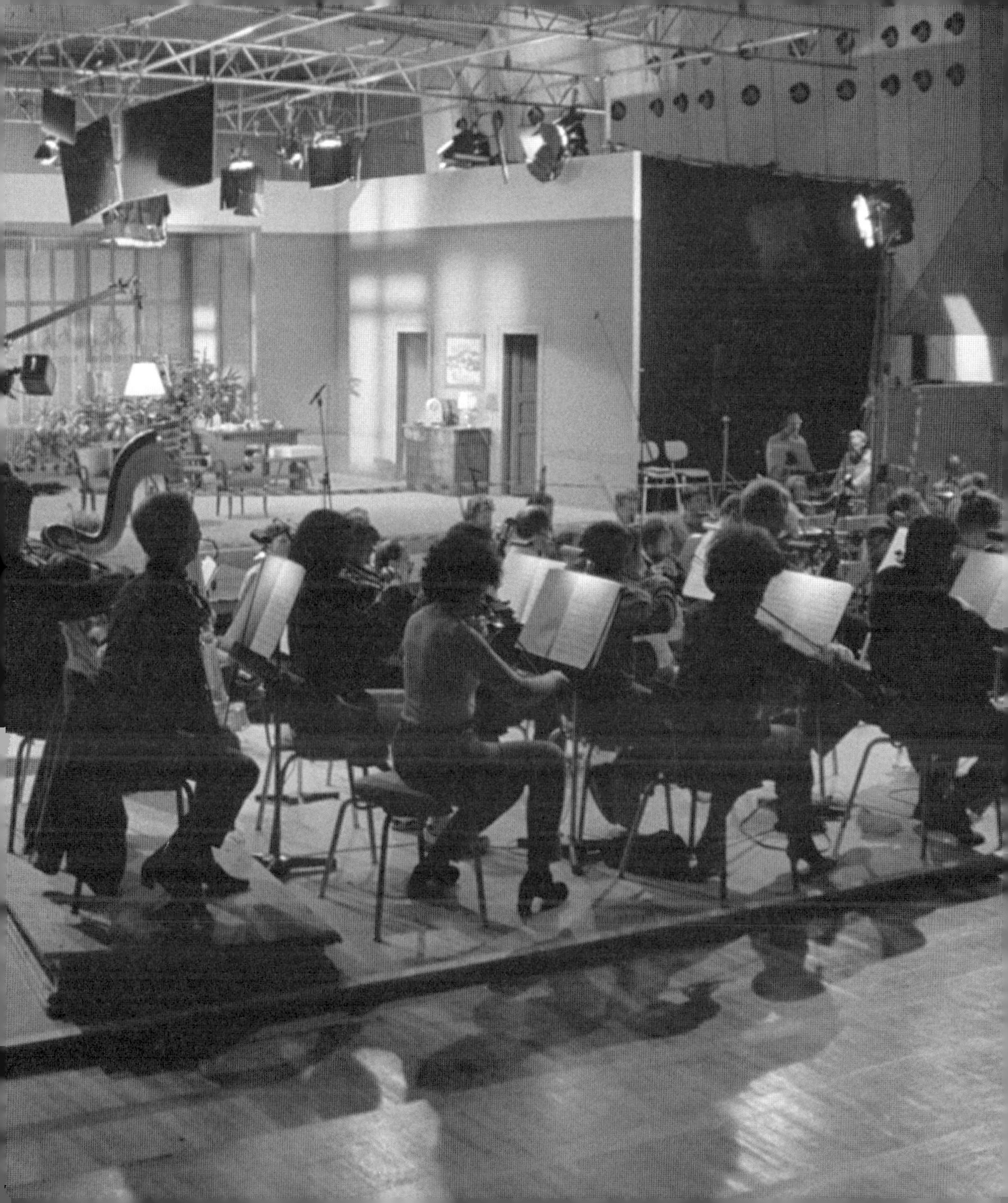

Diedrich Diederichsen

The Revolutionary Dream of Marriage versus the Capitalist Reality of Sexuality

Sometime in March 1971, Georges Perec added the short "Dream No. 69" to his dream journal, *The Dark Room*:

> Jean-Marie Straub's film, *Othon*, inspired by the Corneille play, has a different name. Maybe it's the Corneille play that has a different name? Actually, there's another text too, hidden beneath the first, which I try in vain to decipher.[1]

The film does indeed have a lengthy subtitle, *Die Augen wollen sich nicht zu jeder Zeit schließen oder vielleicht eines Tages wird Rom sich erlauben seinerseits zu wählen* (Eyes do not want to close at all times, or perhaps one day Rome will permit herself to choose in her turn), which is as mysteriously appealing as it is difficult to remember. Moreover, the title explicitly refers to the difficulty of entering the state in which Perec perceives that the title or another piece of text is missing: the curse and blessing of closed eyes.

The period of closed eyes, the night, has its place between today and tomorrow. *Von Heute auf Morgen* (*From Today Until Tomorrow*) is a film title without a subtitle but not without dreamlike qualities, both as a film and in its plot. A married couple comes home in an agitated state; it is already late; they are arguing. They undergo a transformation, becoming strangers to each other, or pretending to do so. Finally, each persuades the other that he or she desires someone else. Somebody rings the doorbell, looking to collect the gas bill in the middle of the night—the kind of thing that only happens in a dream. Finally, the two desired others appear in person. Everyone knows this is also something that can only happen in a dream: the person we momentarily flirted with walks into the house hours later to supply the arguments, the illustrations, and even the occasion—temptation—of a marital spat that, as we know, has actually long been on the horizon. But the temptation is mastered; the marriage survives. The struggle lasts precisely one night, from today to tomorrow. And when the events of a night are condensed into forty-five minutes, and when, in addition, desired others who aren't there are conjured up and made present, it is clear that what we are witnessing is a dream, even if, thanks to its high speed, screwball-like density, and clarity, the participants seem quite awake. But in addition to their very precise hard work in an uncluttered studio of the Hessischer

1 Georges Perec, *La Boutique Obscure: 124 Dreams*, trans. Daniel Levin Becker (Brooklyn, NY: Melville House, 2012).

Rundfunk and the extremely fast pace not just of the finished opera but—as Schoenberg repeatedly indicated—of the composition process itself, there is also a stratum of the work's production that may have something to do with dreaming.

Von Heute auf Morgen is an extremely fast-paced film. This is surely connected with the unique conditions of its production. Every scene was shot using the original sound of the live in-studio orchestra and had to be continued in such a way as not to cause any discrepancies at the interfaces between the scenes. There are more than sixty scenes, and every time the shutter fell, the orchestra had to come in at just the right moment, so that the editing of the images was effectively dictated by the orchestra's precision. Although the meticulous work this demanded informs all of Straub/Huillet's films in other ways as an aesthetic and ethical imperative, not all of them display it so breathlessly. For example, there are very different, almost casual-looking, but equally precise means of directing in a film like *Trop tôt, trop tard* (*Too Early/Too Late*)—here again a title with two temporal indications, in this case, however, not as endpoints but as long since exceeded limits. This is immediately apparent from the films. But even if one isn't familiar with the aesthetic and technical background of the production of *Von Heute auf Morgen*, one can see that the actors are concentrating intensely, that they are having to work at high speed and with great precision. The synchronized cooperation of such disparate ensembles as orchestra, singers, and film crew, however, also affords great pleasure in the empathic identification with the success of these precise operations. To whom? The audience!

It is surprising, however, that what moves at this frenetic pace is a plot that takes aim against a principle, which is itself associated with freneticism and speed in the development of society: fashion. The often staid despisers of fashion with their attachment to ostensibly timeless frameworks for living feel almost threatened by the urban quickness, street-smart elegance, and breathlessness that this opera exudes in its movements. But it is precisely against ironic, freewheeling, street-smart modern urban people that the opera directs its criticism, and it does so in the name of a tradition that, by contrast, has always been combatted by bohemians, nightlife denizens, subculturalists, and artist types: marriage. There are various biographical explanations in the Schoenberg literature for what occasioned this remarkably witty and elegant defense of marriage against the threat posed by elegance and wit. The libretto was in all probability the work of Schoenberg's second wife, Gertrud, who wrote it under the pseudonym Max Blonda—itself a name which might have been that of the founder of a new wave band in 1980. Schoenberg's tragic divorce from his first wife, who died shortly thereafter, is also suggested as a motivating factor.

When the film came out in 1997, the directors were asked about the critique of fashion in a number of different interviews and responded with various readings of it. Speaking to Isabelle Graw in *Texte zur Kunst*,[2] Jean-Marie Straub refers to neoliberal reforms carried out in the name of modernity as a cautionary example of fashion: "Modernizing means privatizing, plundering, and destroying everything with a fixed idea of growth and development in mind." But Danièle Huillet also pointed to fascism as a fashion that Schoenberg and Blonda would have been thinking of: "There is a moment where the wife says, 'when fashion dictates depravity.' When you hear the way she sings that, you realize that depravity can extend to the yellow star for Jews. That's part of it too." And Straub adds: "[Schoenberg] knew that people can be driven to anything by fashion, even the idea of the gas chamber."[3] And in another interview, this one with Artem Demenok: "Schoenberg knew that fashions can be annihilating. Annihilating. That they can become extremely diffuse, like poison gas. That people inhale such fashions and turn into cripples, almost without noticing it. And that the process goes faster and faster."[4] Schoenberg himself writes in a text that was read on the radio when the one-act opera was broadcast on the "Berliner Funkstunde" ("Berlin Radio Hour") on February 27, 1930:

> *Von Heute auf Morgen* is intended as a comic opera: it only shows what takes place between today and tomorrow and doesn't hold true or apply any longer than that. [...] It shows that it would be dangerous to tamper with the fundamental things for the sake of fashion.[5]

2 Isabelle Graw, "Moderne Menschen. Ein Interview mit Danièle Huillet und Jean-Marie Straub von Isabelle Graw," *Texte zur Kunst*, no. 27, 1997.

3 Graw, "Moderne Menschen," 52.

4 Klaus Volkmer, Klaus Kalchschmid, Patrick Primavesi, eds., *Von heute auf morgen. Oper, Musik, Film. Drehbuch und Materialien zum Film von Danièle Huillet & Jean-Marie Straub und zur Oper von Arnold & Gertrud Schoenberg* (Berlin: Vorwerk 8, 1997), 95.

5 Arnold Schoenberg, "Über *Von heute auf morgen* op. 32," in *Stile herrschen – Gedanken siegen: Ausgewählte Schriften*, ed. Anna Maria Morazzoni (Mainz: Schott, 2007), 410.

And speaking of an effect he hoped it would have on its listeners: "It may fortify some who are weak. [...] Perhaps he'll dare to remain decent after all."

Rejecting fashion in this manner also means identifying with the status quo. And this, together with the fact that the fashionable woman in the opera is also the emancipated woman as popularly conceived, and moreover that the opposite of fashion's depredations and the decency that actually deserves our allegiance are represented, of all things, by the old heteronormative model of a division of labor and life possibilities of marriage as shaped by the interests of men, led to some critical questioning on the part of the aforementioned interviewers. First, they suggested that a fashion, which champions new forms of sexual expression and new ways of life against marriage and male dominance, was to be welcomed. And second, it was not to be compared with the coming into fashion of fascism—supposing it was even legitimate to describe the latter's success in these terms. While Straub explains that he does not believe in a "sexual liberation rooted only in fashion," both filmmakers, Straub and Huillet, soon take a different angle on the question. The point is made later in a few different interviews that not only was the text, the libretto, written by a woman; the central and most efficacious character is also the wife, who brings her tipsy, euphoric husband with his dreams of unbridled sexual freedom back to his senses, and does so with a stereotypical feminine wile that comes right out of the arsenal of traditional comedy.

The enemy, as Straub said repeatedly in the three interviews mentioned from the late 1990s, was not so much fashion as such but the bourgeois fantasy of the femme fatale. The femme fatale is introduced as a paradoxical figure of bourgeois ideology. She allows the bourgeois to do what—according to a bon mot that Straub passes off as a quotation from Marx in a conversation with Rainer Bellenbaum[6]—occupies ninety percent of the bourgeoisie's time as a class, that is to say, cheating on each other in love. This is why the femme fatale was invented: she threatens and yet ultimately stabilizes marriage, since she is punished in the end—as happens, for example, to Lulu, a femme fatale who commanded significant attention in Viennese opera

6 Deutsche Welle TV, Kulturmagazin "Kunst & Co.," 1996.

composer circles and was forced to die a horrible death at the hands of Jack the Ripper.

This conflict—the battle against the institution of the femme fatale—together with the essentially emancipatory goal of liberating women from the awful choice of being either the undesired wife or a Lulu-like sexual commodity consumed to death, generates an additional antagonism—toward Alban Berg. Although Berg did not complete his *Lulu* during his lifetime, he began adapting the well-known story more than a year before *Von Heute auf Morgen*. Straub explained that, while he respected Berg and considered him a great composer, he did not *like* him, in human terms, as it were. Schoenberg, he suggested, had much more than mere respect for Berg, and yet his opera and above all the film *Von Heute auf Morgen* were also a protest against *Lulu*. What helps against the femme fatale and her system, fashion? Love. As Straub observed to Robert Bramkamp: "Schoenberg was Jewish. He counters Lulu and the myth of the femme fatale with das *Hohe Lied der Liebe.*[7] Why not?"

7 Translator's note: Literally the *great song of love*, the German name for the Bible's *Song of Songs*.

Why not? Hadn't love long since broken in two in the modern age—into an institution called marriage and a desire that longs for something outside it—in part precisely because the conditions of its captivity had loosened? Yes, but dialectically, both of the pieces thus liberated contain elements of an original utopian love that was both at once, institution and desire, institution *through* desire, since desire always wishes to take permanent possession of its object and permanence leads to institutions. Thus, even after love's disintegration, energies survive that oppose the tendency of the liberated elements to fly off in different directions. But how can those energies triumph? Can they do so in the repetitive processes of the reality of marriage or only in the dreamlike, abbreviated night in which all of the forces are briefly presented as arguments and then love, because it embodies the union of opposites, holds the better cards?

The fear of fashion can also be derived from another constellation. Fashion opposes patriarchal law; but for Straub/Huillet, the latter is still better than the anomie of unfettered capitalist fashion, which they claim leads straight to fascism. As an artist, however, Schoenberg called a law into question more fundamentally than an avant-gardism driven by short-term rebellious impulses ever could. Instead of attacking the principle of law itself, he created a new one: composition using the twelve-tone row. In the opera *Von Heute auf Morgen*, the principles of his compositional method are for the first time realized pervasively and consistently in an opera, hence in a more or less narrative format. The defined row, D–E flat–A–C sharp–B–F–A flat–G–E–C–B flat–F sharp, its retrograde, inversion, and retrograde inversion determine the pitch sequences, and for the first time they are also assigned in a narrative sense to individual characters, who can employ the row's various versions (retrograde and inversion) in their own different states and transformations. Thus, they are able to switch their position from pro- to anti-marital fidelity while still remaining within the established framework of the twelve-tone row. This method of composition scales back the role played by musical convention in musical order, but without calling into question or abandoning the determinacy and order of the musical events as such.

Schoenberg's innovation is thus a fundamental transformation, but one that does not call the centrality of rules or laws into question as the foundation of Western composition. This is something, however, that *was* done at the same time by jazz, which came into fashion at the time when *Von Heute auf Morgen* was written and was also taken as a model and inspiration by opera composers and writers, from René Schickele to Ernst Krenek. Krenek's *Jonny Spielt Auf* (*Johnny Strikes Up*) is regarded as one of the so-called *Zeitoper*, or "operas of the time," which Schoenberg, according to another of his comments that did not explicitly refer to Krenek, ranged among the passing fashions and hymns to the fashionable that deserved to be combatted. But the greatest threat was that the twelve-tone method itself, which exerted a considerable influence on other composers—there were even disputes regarding its paternity—would be seen as a fashion. It was enormously important to Schoenberg that the method followed necessarily from the tonal material according to fundamental laws, that it wasn't arbitrary or mechanical and anti-creative but concerned the material essence of music. Idea takes precedence over style, as his most famous essay argues.

This may explain why the opera fights, as it were, on two fronts at once. It promotes a transformation of the law, but one that operates very close to and in competition with a false novelty, for which the word "fashion" stands here. Since it stands on the side of the law, it stands on the side of marriage; since it stands on the side of transformation, it must touch on fashion and then in the end propose a better marriage, a twelve-tone marriage; this is *marriage with love*. Love is the musical meaning achieved by transformation but transformation *of the law*. Despite this position's dialectical character, it is a difficult fit for the emancipatory Marxist position of Straub/Huillet. In their interview with Isabelle Graw, there are points at which they seem to squirm a bit at finding themselves on the side of the misogynistic and heteronormative prison of marriage. Nevertheless, they evince a clear sympathy for Schoenberg's artistic and ethical position, precisely where the latter marks itself off from Berg and Krenek; that sympathy has to do with Straub/Huillet's artistic program.

That program is less the totally determined and yet completely anti-conventional conception of dramatic speech in their work, which has often, quite plausibly, been compared to musical stipulations (although it is also much more than that), since it does not replace meaning with music but involves a rhythmic, prosodic sharpening of the meaning of dialogues. Rather, the connection with their artistic program lies in the fact that Straub/Huillet were working in a genre or with a medium in which it has long been, and perhaps still is unclear what is a good law and what is a hollow convention. Compared to the culture of the old European bourgeoisie and its operas, film is much more open to the suspicion that it does not become more truly itself through innovation but loses itself again and again to a fashion that selects its models and forms purely in the interest of conformity. Straub/Huillet's position here is not a simple one: their reference points are precisely not the formulations of an alternative cinema or the canon of art house or much less experimental film. On the contrary, in the interviews conducted for the premiere of *Von Heute auf Morgen*, Howard Hawks is repeatedly mentioned—certainly no anti-fashionable ascetic and no supporter of misogynistic theories of marriage but one of Hollywood's first feminist men. Lubitsch is also mentioned twice. What is clear is that, if the struggle against fashion and in favor of the anti-modern posture, as articulated by Straub, includes the closing scene of *Bringing Up Baby*, it has nothing to do with the opposition between bourgeois high art and low mass-cultural fashion but concerns the question of the possibility of protest—or, as Straub rails in the *Texte zur Kunst* interview: "There is such a thing as the idea of resistance—dammit!"

Resistance to the modern world and the construction of the femme fatale is here a resistance distinguished by the fact that it takes beautiful forms, that it seeks to specify with the utmost precision exactly how the eyes should be batted and exists in décors very much like those of fashion, whether of the conformist or nonconformist variety. This resistance simply consists in a higher degree of *justified determinacy*, in knowing better, more often, and more precisely why something should be done one way rather than another. Greater determinacy alone would mean the conversion of the commodity into bureaucracy, of market into state, but justified decisiveness is the subsoil of aesthetic resistance.

There is another director—against whom Jean-Marie Straub railed on a few occasions—who, one year after *Von Heute auf Morgen*, also adapted a Viennese marriage story for the screen: Stanley Kubrick in *Eyes Wide Shut*. Apart from that, of course, he does everything differently—for example, he uses Shostakovich rather than Schoenberg—but the text on which his film is based, Arthur Schnitzler's *Traumnovelle* (*Dream Novella*), nevertheless has a few things in common with Max Blonda's libretto. The fact that everything is decided in a single night, a certain form of precipitation, the fact that the mind of a marriage is shifted into high gear and subjected to a dreamlike acceleration, and the way all this is accomplished are subsumed under the notion of the dream. At the end of Kubrick's film, Nicole Kidman and Tom Cruise walk through a department store, and here too truth seems to come from the mouth of a child. But the married couple also express the only thing that can save their marriage, a return to sexuality—even if this realization occurs in the toy section of a department store in a manner which suggests that the dream is not yet over. In Straub/Huillet's film, there is no such solution—

apart from the child, which they take from Schoenberg/ Blonda. But this is not just a consequence of the fact that the Schoenbergs were a conservative married couple; it also has to do with the fact that, for Straub/Huillet, what matters in this act of resistance to the modern world is not first and foremost complying with the imperative that a viable counterproposal be developed, but the act of resistance itself, its possibilities and artistic consequences—and finally a frenetic pace, a dreamlike frenzy, that does not derive its seductive power from the act of letting go, from the relaxation of constraints—as we might like to think today—but from the justified determinacy of all decisions. The fact that, historically, it is jazz that prevailed, and not just for bad reasons, is another story. The notion that responsibility begins in dreams is an idea (and a short story title, "In Dreams Begin Responsibilities") of the Jewish American writer Delmore Schwartz; it could also stand as the motto for this opera film.

Translated from German by Jim Gussen.

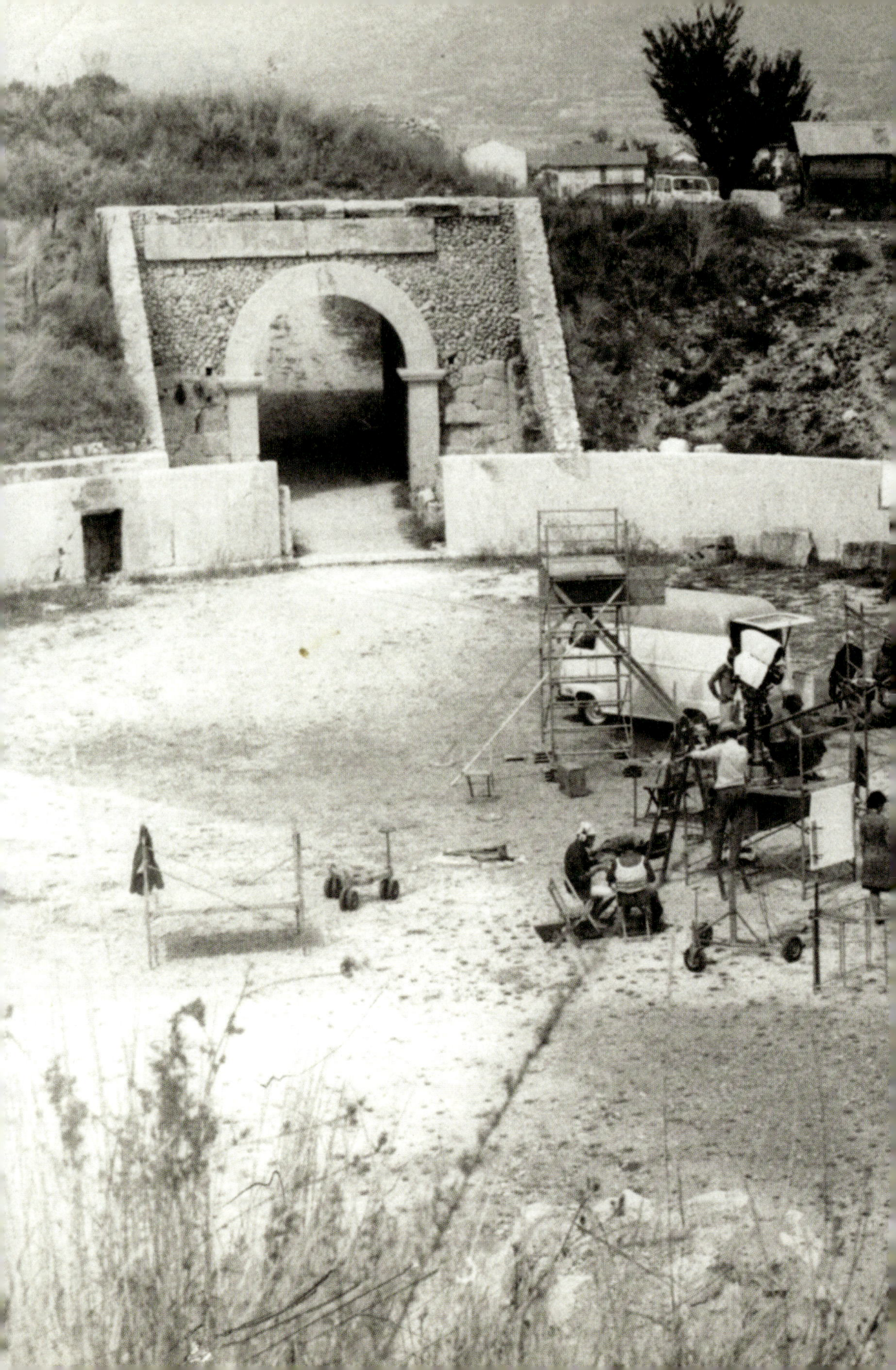

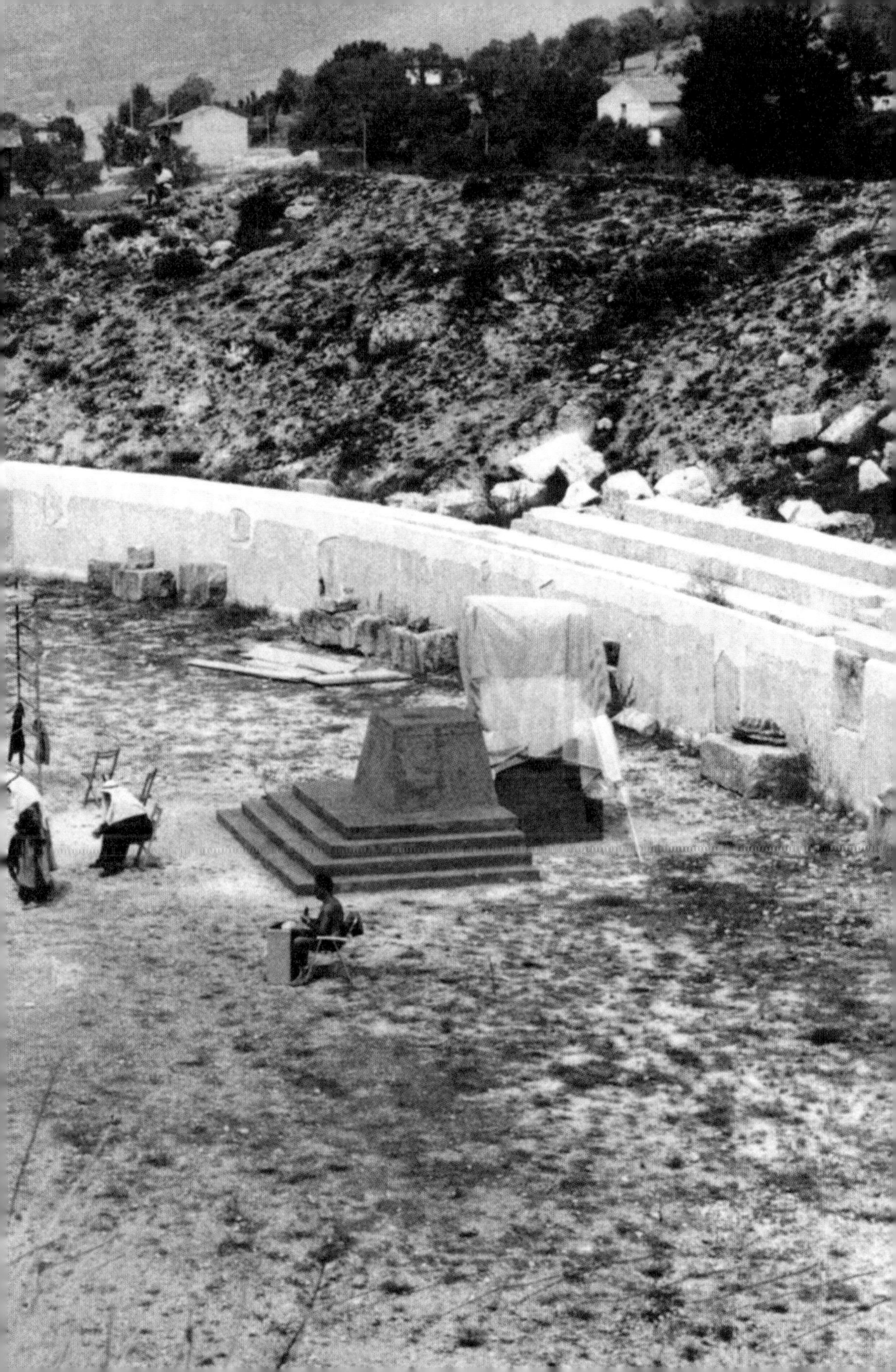

Ute Holl

COMMUNISM AS AESTHETIC PROCEDURE

Ein Busch, irgendein Kiesel, sogar ein Termitenhügel manchmal: dem Wind genügt das. An ihm richten Wächten sich aus und wachsen sich zu Dünen aus; sie bilden Ketten und Wälle, werden ei-, herz-, oder sternförmig.

— Raoul Schrott[1]

Considering the cinema of Danièle Huillet and Jean-Marie Straub as a constant construction site for communism includes, as has often been remarked, a certain ambivalence regarding the issue of the people and the popular. On the one hand, their films deal with historical and political conditions of workers and peasants, focus on suppression and call for revolt. The plea for the empowerment of people may on the other hand be felt as contradictory to their idiosyncratic cinematic forms as well as their choice of texts, a rather classical canon of established literature and high culture—Corneille, Montaigne, Hölderlin, Mallarmé and Kafka for instance, including the communists Pavese, Fortini, Vittorini and Brecht, and, for that matter, Bach and Schoenberg in terms of music. In addition, their strict filmic forms tend to disconcert cinema-goers out for entertainment and have contributed to a certain exclusivity of the typical Straubian audience: instead of enlightening a subaltern public to learn "en rachâchant,"[2] their films have attracted a stern bunch of academic specialists, connoisseurs, mostly male and many bookworms. Then again, published letters and memories document lifelong affectionate friendships with all collaborators, a renowned conductor, as well as a sound assistant, an Egyptian journalist, and a Sicilian bricklayer.[3] Where then does their films' hidden people lie? The way people are staged, framed, and filmed in the cinema of Huillet/Straub directly opposes contemporary images of the people and contemporary iconic representations of communism. In the 1970s and 80s, when their films increasingly focused on the nexus of the people and the law, as in *History Lessons* (1972), *Moses and Aaron* (1974) *Too Early/Too Late* (1980/1981) or *Class Relations* (1983), the popular communist notion was enforced by retro-realist images such as *Il quarto stato*, Guiseppe Pellizza da Volpedo's oil painting, depicting peasant hunger protests of the late 19th century in classical centralized perspective, led by sturdy men and frail women. This iconic signature of the revolutionary people was accordingly adapted in the

1 Raoul Schrott, *Die Wüste Lop Nor: Novelle* (Munich/Vienna: Carl Hanser Verlag, 2000), 79. "A bush, a pebble, sometimes even a termite hill: this will do for the wind. Cornices develop on it and grow onto dunes, develop chains and walls, become egg-, heart- or star-shaped," trans. Ute Holl.

2 *En rachâchant* (France, 1982) is a seven-minute film by Huillet and Straub based on Marguerite Duras' short story "Ah Ernesto!" (1971). Its title, a neologism referring to the sound of the word "researching" in French, *en recherchant*, or, as the schoolboy who is the hero of the film demands: to find out by oneself.

3 Danièle Huillet, "Sickle and Hammer, Cannons, Cannons and Dynamite! Danièle Huillet and Jean-Marie Straub in Conversation with François Albera," in *Jean-Marie Straub & Danièle Huillet*, ed. Ted Fendt (Vienna: SYNEMA, 2006), 123.

arts by Joseph Beuys or Bernardo Bertolucci. The films of Huillet/Straub, however, saturated with a different historical experience and devoid of false utopian spirit, are directed against such sentimentalities. Against all idealization and iconic shorthand, they are concerned with particular people, either historical or those whom they came to know during their filmwork and accordingly felt akin to. In *Workers, Peasants*, shot in 2000, texts of Elio Vittorini's *Le donne di Messina* (*Women of Messina*) are read by workers and peasants, "almost illiterate people,"[4] as Huillet underlines. Accounts and memories of fascism and the *resistenza* are spoken as a fugue of opposing voices and carried by the material voices of those who read or recite the text. "What interests us is how the text is embodied in human beings, dialogues, not the plot."[5] The idea of making a film popular or "a part of the people,"[6] then is not to simplify or adapt it to popular or mass cultures, but to insert bodies of living people as a means of resistance against conventional, bourgeois, specialists' receptions of texts. As in *From the Cloud to the Resistance* (1978) and as in several poems of Friedrich Hölderlin, for that matter, it is not as mortals that people confront the gods, but as the living! People are opposed to the immortals not because they will eventually die but because they have decided to live and be alive.

According to Straub, addressing people in a film is the opposite of aiming at the applause of masses, risking, meanwhile, that their films escape their attention:

> Films that pretend to be made for the masses are really made to keep them in their place, to violate them, or to fascinate them. Consequently, these films are made in such a way that they don't give people the liberty to get up and leave. Our films are made so people can leave if they want.[7]

Theirs is a cinema of disobedience. It seems that, rather than underlining this positive freedom of determining one's own time, the work of Huillet/Straub has often been described in negative terms, as "ascetic, minimalist, avant-garde, anti-illusionist, antinarrative, anticinematic, and static,"[8] according to Barton Byg's overview of critiques. This is also true for Gilles Deleuze's repeated formula, molded on Klee, that in the political cinema of Huillet/Straub the people is missing, even if he gives it a productive twist: according to Deleuze, Huillet/Straub belong to

4 Huillet, "Sickle and Hammer," 123.

5 Straub, "Sickle and Hammer," 120.

6 Huillet, "Sickle and Hammer," 123.

7 Straub quoted according to John Gianvito, "Tough Love," in *Jean-Marie Straub and Danièle Huillet*, 144.

8 Barton Byg, *Landscapes of Resistance: The German Films of Danièle Huillet and Jean-Marie Straub* (Berkeley: University of California Press, 1995), 4.

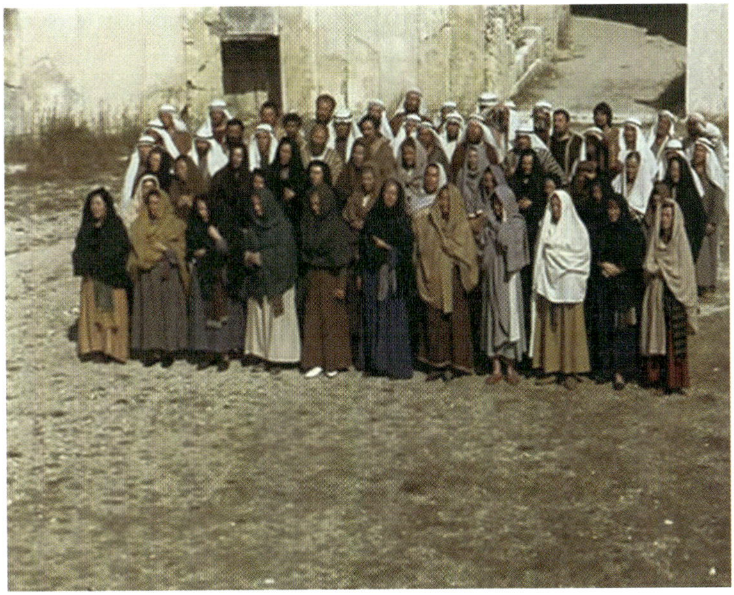

"the greatest political filmmakers in the West, in modern cinema" exactly because "they know how to show how the people are what is missing, what is not there."[9] A closer description of their aesthetic procedures, however, will reveal that Huillet/Straub are less concerned with the absence of a people than with constructing a productive dispositive of communism, from which people might emerge as equals.

In his study *On Populist Reason*, Ernesto Laclau, drawing on structuralist theory, argues that in order to provoke the appearance of the people, three procedures need to be simultaneously introduced: the acknowledgement of a primordial heterogeneity, the implementation of differences and the logics of equivalence. To begin with, an order of heterogeneous, particular differences is organized so as to structure a grid of possible actions or aesthetics. These differences have then to be inscribed within an equivalential chain.[10] In deliberately exposing the particularity of people then, Huillet and Straub do not try to represent a people—or its absence—but rather establish the structures that facilitate the formation of a people or peoples. Communism in their films concerns the set of equal relations allowing for a "construction of the people [which] is the political act par excellence."[11]

The basic procedure of Huillet/Straub's filmwork concerns the focus on the particular and the distribution of particular elements to create fields of equal dispersal. Straub

9 Gilles Deleuze, *Cinema 2. The Time-Image* (Minneapolis: University of Minnesota Press, 1989), 215.

10 Ernesto Laclau, *On Populist Reason* (London: Verso, 2005), 78 and 121.

11 Laclau, *Reason*, 154.

repeatedly describes this in interviews. The first measure taken is to break down all context into the basic elements of its construction. When discussing direct sound, for instance, Straub refers to "waves" as the common denominator of filmic perception, seeing and hearing. Decisions concerning staging, framing, recording and montage have to consider this. The universality of waves accounts for the equal importance of images and the sonic, as light, music, sounds or noises: "The greatest part of the waves that film contains come from the sound..."[12] Secondly, the equal operational availability of visual or sonic elements is the precondition for all forms of filmic movements and emotions: "The waves that a sound transmits are not just sound waves. Waves of ideas, of movements, and of emotions also travel across sound."[13]

Huillet/Straub's meticulous concern with film stock, optics, lighting, as well as recording and mixing devices stems from the idea to work from materialities, so that no industrially preformatted procedures should enter the filmic process.[14] This is true for the organization of direct sound recordings as well as for camera movements. Their specific use of the pan, for instance, flattens out the landscape, produces an equal value of all its elements, and liberates it from perspective and representational rules.[15] Their framing and use of optical measures constructs equivalential relations, including the hors champ as an unseen but not abstract presence in the films. The procedure of producing equals then starts, as opposed to the reception-based theory of Jacques Rancière, with the material and materialistic processes of filmmaking. The working methods of two of the artists that Huillet/Straub have paid particular attention to, Friedrich Hölderlin and Arnold Schoenberg, prove them to be precursors in the field, in that both have also struggled with concepts of equal distribution in inventing forms to resist and radically reconfigure the aesthetics of their times. For both, these aesthetics are related to spatial reconfigurations. Hölderlin as well as Schoenberg related their spatial and relational concerns to the issue of the people.

12 Jean-Marie Straub, Danièle Huillet, "Interview on Direct Sound," in *Jean-Marie Straub and Danièle Huillet: Writings*, ed. Sally Shafto, Katherine Pickard (New York: Sequence Press, 2016), 156.

13 Straub, *Writings*, 156.

14 See Danièle Huillet's considerations on material and procedures in "Notes on Gregory's Work Journal," in *Writings*, 277–331. "We are going to use this new negative [...] testing if there is progress over the preceding one or if, indeed, it serves Kodak mainly as an industrial progress..."

15 See my chapter "Panorama Politics: about the Pan," in Ute Holl, *The Moses Complex. Freud, Schoenberg, Straub/Huillet* (Chicago: University of Chicago Press, 2017), 194–221.

In his revolutionary effort to put a native reversal ("vaterländische Umkehr") into practice, Friedrich Hölderlin, taking the term literally, had turned toward verses as points of inversion and return of realities. While the process of the native reversal was an open one to him, it could have ended in "wilderness or a new form,"[16] just as his poetry was adapted by German national socialists and left-wing revolutionaries alike, the production of a new people was closely linked to radical poetic reconfigurations of language. To transform language into Gesang, song or poetry are procedures of producing an equivalence of elements. Walter Benjamin had thus observed that the people, "the Volk as the symbol of poetry [has] the task of fulfilling Hölderlin's cosmos."[17] In his poetry, Hölderlin had not only used the rhythmic equalizer of antic meters, Alcaeic, as in "Thränen" (Tears) or Asclepiadeic as in "Blödigkeit" (Timidness), or even hexameters as in "Menon's Lament for Diotima." Hölderlin had also used the open space of the white page in order to set his words according to rhythmic patterns, allowing, in early phases of his poems and plays, for large parts of the page to remain empty. He was thus pointing toward the possibility of materially distributing words on a page long before Stéphane Mallarmé (whose poem "Un coup de dés jamais n'abolira le hazard" is central in Huillet/Straub's film *Toute révolution est un coup de dés* of 1977) experimented with the empty spaces between signs. Hölderlin's new way of working with space became very visible in the critical Frankfurt edition of his works, on which Huillet and Straub had in fact based their studies for Hölderlin's *Empedokles*. The editor, D.E. Sattler, returned to early manuscripts to demonstrate that semantics and syntax of the verses are evoked through a rhythmical distribution of words on a page, meticulously reconstructing how, in early versions, spaces were intentionally left blank.[18] In this way, Hölderlin enforced his resistance against all conventions in the use of language and texts, and that includes, inverting ways of speaking German.

The rigor to transform the spoken German, to turn it, so to speak, into broken German, in order to distill different sorts of experiences from it, is a central concern of Danièle Huillet and Jean-Marie Straub. The idiosyncratic emphasis they put on the pronunciation of texts during rehearsals

16 Friedrich Hölderlin, "Notes on the Antigone," in *Essays and Letters*, ed. Jeremy Adler and Charles Louth (London: Penguin Classics, 2009), 331.

17 Walter Benjamin, "Two Poems by Friedrich Hölderlin—'The Poet's Courage' and 'Timidity,'" in *Walter Benjamin: Selected Writings 1: 1913–1926*, ed. Marcus Bullock and Michael W. Jennings (Cambridge, MA and London, UK: Belknap Press of Harvard University Press, 1996), 18–47; "Und so als Symbol des Gesanges hat das Volk den Kosmos Hölderlins zu erfüllen," Walter Benjamin, *Aufsätze, Essays, Vorträge*, ed. R. Tiedemann, H. Schweppenhäuser (Frankfurt/Main: Suhrkamp, 1977), 114.

18 See Friedrich Hölderlin, "Empedokles I," in *Sämtliche Werke. Frankfurter Ausgabe*, ed. D.E. Sattler (Frankfurt/Main, Basel: Stroemfeld/Roter Stern, 1985), Vol. 12, 13.

with actors and actresses, their attention toward the impact of each syllable in a sentence in order to preserve an equal valence and relevance of words against the adaptation of language through accustomed and seemingly natural habits thus retrieves its genealogy in Hölderlin. It is a technique to liberate hidden and historically lost emotions that have survived, petrified like traces of dinosaurs, in the textures of the literatures which Huillet/Straub revive in their films. Apart from this archaeological retrieval of historical senses and emotions, however, Hölderlin's work also turns out to open an understanding of Huillet/Straub's approach to the issue of the people.

Walter Benjamin's essay on two related odes by Hölderlin: "Dichtermut—The Poet's Courage and Blödigkeit—Timidness"[19] written in the first winter of war 1914/15, names two fundamental aspects which also seem crucial for the cinema of Huillet/Straub: firstly, that these poems of Hölderlin's concern the intrinsic relation between the poet and the people, and, for that matter, the issue of the gods and the law. And secondly, in comparing these two related poems as a transformation of a basic set of verses, Benjamin observes that in his odes, Hölderlin works on the reconfiguration of space and an intentional disorganization of spatial laws, consequently attacking hierarchies and social orders. Benjamin discusses the second ode, "Blödigkeit," as a turn toward the oriental as opposed to the Greek based forms of "Dichtermut." The second ode's oriental and mystical poetical principle, which "overcomes limits,"[20] is able to abolish the Greek formative principle of the earlier ode and will eventually form a spiritual cosmos out of "pure relations of intuition, sensual existence,"[21] hence a new form of immediated perception. Benjamin is able to unfold his argument already with respect to the first two lines of the poems which focus firstly on "the living," as a more radical substitute for the people in Hölderlin's poetry, and secondly on a new haptic and flat space as it was also being rediscovered by art historians of Benjamin's time, the early 1900s, to challenge the laws of perspective.[22] According to Benjamin, the people and spatial orders remain connected in Hölderlin's work, the central issue for the artist being the problem of where to belong, whom to relate to, whom to speak for, as in the first verses of "Blödigkeit":

19 Bullock and Jennings, editors of Benjamin's essay, translate "Blödigkeit" as "Timidity." Michael Hamburger translates Hölderlin's poem as "Timidness."

20 Benjamin, "Two Poems," 34.

21 Benjamin, "Two Poems," In German: "Das ist das orientalische, mystische, die Grenzen überwindende Prinzip, das in diesem Gedicht so offenbar immer wieder das griechische Gestaltende Prinzip aufhebt, das einen geistigen Kosmos schaffte aus reinen Beziehungen der Anschauung, des sinnlichen Daseins … ." in Benjamin, "Zwei Gedichte," 124.

22 See Wilhelm Worringer and Alois Riegl, or, in terms of architecture and the ornamental, Siegfried Kracauer.

23 Friedrich Hölderlin, *Selected Poems and Fragments*, ed. Jeremy Adler, trans. Michael Hamburger (London: Penguin Books, 1998), 100–101.

Sind denn Dir nicht bekannt viele Lebendigen?
Geht auf Wahrem Dein Fuß nicht, wie auf Teppichen?
Of the living, are not many well-known to you?
On the truth don't your feet walk as they would on rugs?[23]

The first version of the poem, "Dichtermut," had begun differently. According to Benjamin, this version still "lives in the Greek world"[24] and remains attached to the myth:

Sind denn dir nicht verwandt alle Lebendigen?
Nährt zum Dienste denn nicht selber die Parze Dich?
Is not all that is alive close and akin to you, Does the Fate not herself keep you to serve her ends?[25]

For "Dichtermut," which deals with the death of the poet, Benjamin maintains that the courage of the poet is supplied by a yet unknown force, and is justified from "another and alien order—that of the relationship with the living."[26] Here, Hölderlin's cosmos is not yet fulfilled with song or sound as with people, on the contrary, it is still attached to a higher force: "The deeper right, by which the poet associates himself with and feels himself related to his people, those who are alive, cannot be felt in this poem."[27] Only in the second version of the verses, the earlier image of poets as being "poets of the people"[28] turns into their being the "tongues of the people,"[29] a new relationship that is authorized by the new spatial interlacing of poet and people. It is here that the "oriental" comes in as the concrete experience of the flatwoven fabric, the rug, or the knotted carpet—a very concrete experience, incidentally, for Benjamin, son of an antiques dealer familiar with oriental fabrics and techniques. The people as well as the poet and the gods then are equally inserted into a flat and haptic space, but specifically the poet and the people are enmeshed as in a single texture, as Benjamin puts it, "Now, depersonalized, the people appear (may we compare this with Byzantine mosaics?) as if pressed in the surface, around the great flat figure of its sacred poet."[30] Space here as an "oriental" or ornamental structure has turned into a production device for a set of new differences increasing probabilities for equal relations. The new space constitutes and contains a world of particularities, derived from the specific place it obtains in the neo-oriental space of equal elements as in the patterns of rugs, carpets or mosaics: "Immanent to everything

24 Benjamin, "Two Poems," 23. Benjamin, "Das Gedicht lebt in der griechischen Welt" in "Zwei Gedichte," 110.

25 Hölderlin, *Selected Poems*, 99.

26 Benjamin, "Two Poems," 23. See Benjamin, "Zwei Gedichte," 109: "Noch begründet sich der Mut des Dichters seltsam aus einer andern, fremden Ordnung. [...] Was hat dem dichterischen Mut die Volksverwandtschaft zur bedeuten? Nicht fühlbar wird im Gedicht das tiefere Recht, aus dem der Dichter seinem Volk, den Lebendigen, sich anlehnt und ihnen verwandt fühlt."

27 Benjamin, "Two Poems," 23.

28 Hölderlin, *Selected Poems*, 99.

29 This is metrically deferred in Michael Hamburger's translation, see Hölderlin, *Selected Poems*, 101 and 103.

30 Benjamin, "Two Poems," 28; cf. Benjamin, "Zwei Gedichte," 116: "Nun erscheint—dürfen wir es byzantinischen Mosaiken vergleichen?—entpersönlicht das Volk, wie in der Fläche gedrängt um die flache große Gestalt seines heiligen Dichters."

determinative in space is its own determination. Every situation is determined only in space, and is only determinative in space."[31] The aesthetic procedure has thus created a new sense of beauty, out of which "the people appear."

Finally, as Benjamin points out, Hölderlin turns his poetological resistance against a hierarchical organization of space into a political argument. Referring to the middle verses of "Blödigkeit," Benjamin points toward the equivalential chain of social elements that follows: Gods perform like men, wild animals join heavenly creatures and the cantos of princes as of those of poets is joined with the people:

> For since gods grew like men, lonely as woodland beasts And since, each in his way, song and the princely choir Brought the Heavenly in person back to earth, so we too, the tongues of the people, have liked living men's company.[32]

From this central turning point of the ode, Benjamin concludes, the order of the world tumbles and the once distinguished powers string into a chain or row of equals: "So that here, at the center of the poem, men, heavenly ones, and princes—crashing down from their old orders, as it were—are linked to one another."[33] While it is true here that the figure of a god remains, the god Hölderlin invokes is kinship, a father "who to rich men and poor offers the thinking day,"[34] a god distributing intellectual wealth and force equally, thus enlightening the living "en rachâchant" as a general public. The method of "linking to one another," zu einander reihen, as in a chain or row, is an artist's, but also a divine procedure.

From Walter Benjamin's analysis of Hölderlin's work, Huillet/Straub's transposition of verse into filmic structures, inserting sonic and visual elements on absolutely equal terms, suddenly appears integrated into a longer tradition of poetological procedures. Dissolving the world into particulars, the differential procedures, is a means of disassembling ideas or ideological assumptions, and of analyzing them in relation to cinematic experience. Producing particulars in redetermining the singular place of all things and living beings in space is also to make them precious beyond capitalist or religious value systems. Then, in the editing process, they are reassembled according to the logics of equivalence.

31
Benjamin, "Two Poems," 27; cf. Benjamin, "Zwei Gedichte," 115. "Allem Bestimmenden im Raum ist immanent dessen eigene Bestimmtheit. Jede Lage ist im Raum allein bestimmt und allein in ihm bestimmend."

32
Hölderlin, *Selected Poems*, 103.

33
Benjamin, "Two Poems," 25; cf. Benjamin, "Zwei Gedichte," 112: "So daß hier, um die Mitte des Gedichts, Menschen, Himmlische und Fürsten, gleichsam abstürzend aus ihren alten Ordnungen, zu einander gereiht sind."

34
Cf. Hölderlin, *Selected Poems*, 102: "Unser Vater, des Himmels Gott || Der den denkenden Tag Armen und Reichen gönnt."

In an essay on Hölderlin's late poetry published fifty years after Benjamin, Theodor W. Adorno called this procedure of equal distribution paratactical, stating that Hölderlin "was allergic to the expectable, preset and interchangeable quality of linguistic convenus,"[35] allergic, one might add, to any preformatted exchange value of words. Adorno explains Hölderlin's poetological strategy as one that radically resists subordination. With the same nonchalance Hölderlin had adopted while supporting national revolts, he was also determined to disturb any sort of order of family, kinship, or the state. Aware of traditions of emancipation he focused on his own willful verse-making techniques, obviously unfazed by the incomprehension and contempt often expressed by his contemporaries. His method points toward a general attitude even when it focuses on the transformation of language: "Hölderlin's technique [...] is not lacking in boldly formed hypotactic constructions, still the parataxes are striking-artificial disturbances that evade the logical hierarchy of a subordinating syntax."[36]

In an attempt to rescue Hölderlin from Martin Heidegger's nationalistic appropriation, specifically in terms of "Volk" as a very German concept of people, Adorno refers to the later ode, "Stimme des Volkes" (Voice of the People), to explain the counter-forced tension on the poetic subject which, in the paratactical destruction of linguistic conventions, experiences a painful disconnectedness. "The detached, form-giving subject, absolute in the double sense, becomes aware of itself as negativity," but, exactly through the loss of firm linguistic grounds, it also becomes aware of the presence of a fictional or poetic community: "aware of an isolation that does not abolish / is not abolished by the fiction of a positive community."[37] The community, one might paraphrase Deleuze, is perceptibly missing here, or in the more dialectical terms of Adorno: "Precisely because he revered Rousseau, as a poet Hölderlin no longer abides by the *contrat social*."[38] Following a subtext of Adorno's essay, one might interpret his reading of Hölderlin's poetology as assembling elements of an aesthetics of insubordination. The procedure of equalizing linguistic elements is, for Adorno, a liberating but also a violent act: "Set free, language appears paratactically disordered when judged in terms of subjective intention,"[39] a statement which sounds

35 Theodor W. Adorno, "Parataxis. On Hölderlin's Late Poetry," in: T.W.A., *Notes to Literature, Volume Two*, ed. Rolf Tiedemann, trans. Shierry Weber Nicholsen (New York: Columbia University Press, 1974), 129–130.

36 Adorno, "Parataxis," 131.

37 The German "... einer Vereinzelung, die doch keine Fiktion positiver Gemeinschaft tilgt," dialectically indicates "aware of an isolation that no fiction of a positive community can abolish," as Nicholsen translates; cf. Theodor W. Adorno, "Parataxis. Zur späten Lyrik Hölderlins," in T.W.A., *Noten*.

38 Adorno, "Parataxis," 135–136.

39 Adorno, "Parataxis," 135.

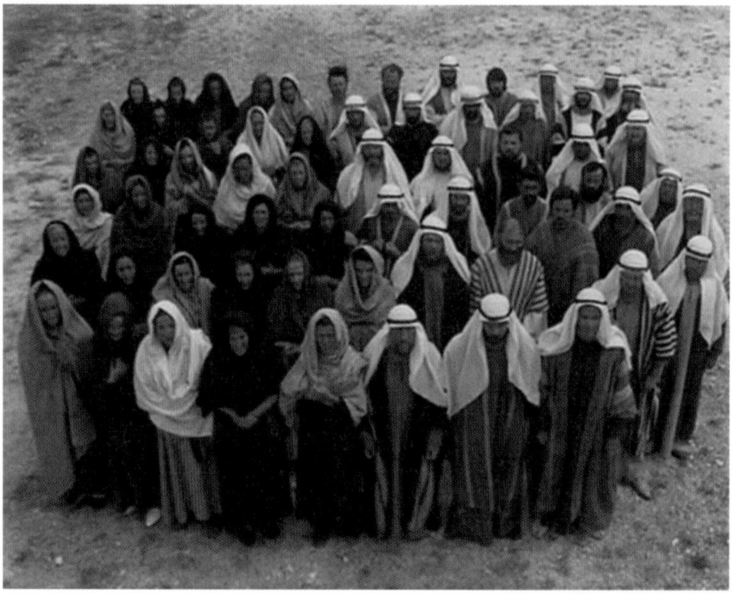

harsher in German where Adorno actually speaks of language as being "paratactically shattered."[40]

Taking the cue from Walter Benjamin who had described Hölderlin's poetic procedure as "linking one to another," working according to chains or rows (Reihen), Adorno continues to describe "the transformation of language into a serial order" which he accordingly qualifies as "music-like."[41] Undoubtedly here Adorno had also thought of Arnold Schoenberg and composition on the basis of rows—which he had studied with Schoenberg's student Alban Berg. Since Huillet and Straub in their extended work on Schoenberg, specifically in their singular transposition of the opera *Moses und Aron* into a film in 1974, had carefully studied his basic procedures of composing, it is worthwhile to recall Schoenberg's ideas on techniques of equal distribution in music, and to relate it to the initial idea of this opera: the issue of the people, the law and the question of insubordination in times of danger and exile.

POETOLOGIES OF THE DESERT

In his considerations of a new technique of composition which he first delivered as a lecture at the University of California in Los Angeles on March 26, 1941, Schoenberg explains that his "Method of Composing with Twelve Tones Which are Related Only with One Another"[42] is a procedure of abstraction, transferring an idea into music, and

40
Cf. Adorno, "Parataxis. Zur späten Lyrik Hölderlins," 475: "Losgelassen, freigesetzt, erscheint [die Sprache] nach dem Maß subjektiver Intention parataktisch zerrüttet."

41
Adorno, "Parataxis," 130–131.

42
Arnold Schoenberg, "Composition With Twelve Tones," in: A.S., *Style and Idea* (New York: Philosophical Library, 1950), 107.

simultaneously an aesthetic procedure, relating a form, as Schoenberg had it, "psychologically speaking, to a feeling of beauty."[43] As a conservative musicologist, Schoenberg relies on the fact that in music history, sound or the organization of tone-color had not, as one might think, been an idea of coloring an otherwise mathematically formed idea, as in the difference of *disegno* and *colore* in painting, but that sound-coloring itself had always been "the radiation of an intrinsic quality of ideas..."[44] Schoenberg, in a Kantian twist, is opting for a close relation between the particular and the idea by very practically increasing the range of differences of sounds. It is here that Huillet/Straub find their model in relying on the basic material elements of cinema in order to communicate abstract historical ideas, such as class relations or lessons in historiography.

Without going into details of composing with twelve-tone sets or rows, suffice it to underline that it follows the basic rule that no tone should be repeated unless all others have sounded. The composer uses a specific series of the chromatic scale, a row, as well as its inversion, retrograde and retrograde inversion to achieve an equivalential chaining. Schoenberg's concept can be summarized as creating absolutely equal relations between all tones, avoiding any impression of emphasis on a singular one, which might then be misunderstood as a central root or a tonic that submits the sound to a central ruling harmony.[45] Even if tones are clustered in groups, "this grouping serves primarily to provide a regularity in the distribution of the tones."[46] Setting out from the classical notational system—for which, incidentally, he devised a mechanical typewriter—Schoenberg not only worked in the horizontal plane of distribution according to the rule of the row, but also in the vertical dimension of simultaneity, in other words, paratactically and syntactically. In terms of an aesthetics of equal relevance, it is intriguing that he should pay specific attention to the spaces in-between, spaces that then transcend the traditional concept of intervals in Pythagorean relations, in that they are no longer subordinated to harmonies.[47]

The logics or the rule of twelve-tone composition and its rapidly changing "idea-emotional structure"[48] of music is hard to perceive, as even Schoenberg admits, however, the impression of the sounds as being equally distributed in a

43 Schoenberg, "Composition With Twelve Tones," 103.

44 Schoenberg, 138.

45 Schoenberg, 116.

46 Schoenberg, 11.

47 Schoenberg, 109.

48 Schoenberg, 138.

planified audible field is the most prominent characteristic of his music. It follows the idea of equal distribution as in the sands of a desert, at the same time autonomically developing structures according to its own inherent rule of the row. As opposed to composing in keys and harmonies, which submit a piece to a certain spirit or temper, the range of colors and expressions in twelve-tone-music establishes a new form of open sonic space. It "corresponds to the principle of *the absolute and unitary perception of musical space.*"[49] At the same time, in superimposing new and unheard of tone-colors, sounds may also meander between music and noise, human and inhuman, instrumental and environmental effects, "overcoming limits," as Benjamin had observed for Hölderlin's poetological procedures, opening new sonic spaces.

The opera *Moses und Aron*, based on a single set, opens in fact with an example of a complex sound between the human and the instrumental. According to the score, a sung "O---" should resound pianissimo from the orchestra pit through the darkness of the auditorium before the curtain rises. Six solo voices intonate it, while sitting next to six solo instruments playing "in unison with them":[50] soprano and flute, mezzo and clarinet, alto with English horn, and, a bar later, tenor, baritone, and bass with bassoon, bass clarinet, and cello. The sound forms an acoustic buzzing, fusion, and confusion of instruments and bodies. Only nine bars later will four more voices be added, the sound crystallized into particular voices and words that turn out to represent "The Voice from the Burning Bush."[51] It is the moment of indistinction, however, that puts the audience into the same awkward situation of Moses grazing his sheep in the desert, irritated by what he cannot distinguish as pure noise or a voice, as mere disturbance or a divine order. And it will be the motive of confusion through a set of increasing differences and equal probabilities that makes the setting of the opera, in the camp in the desert, with the people discussing their fate in face of the mountain of god and the absence of a leader. In this crisis, suspended before the law, Schoenberg, himself persecuted as a Jew and later on his way into exile when he composed—and never finished—the opera, enfolds the confrontations of two positions: Moses, committed to the abstract ideas, the words and the law, and Aron, dedicated to the particular and sensual perception. In this sense, the situation before the law raises a musical,

49 Schoenberg, 115–116. Italics added.

50 Arnold Schoenberg, *Moses und Aron, Oper in drei Akten*, Studien-Partitur (Mainz: Edition Schott), bar 1.

51 Schoenberg, bars 1–14. For the question of whether the initial vocalize belongs to Moses' call or not, see Marc M. Kerling, *"O Wort, du Wort, das mir fehlt:" Die Gottesfrage in Arnold Schoenbergs Oper Moses und Aron. Zur Theologie eines musikalischen Kunst-Werkes des 20. Jahrhunderts* (Mainz: Matthias-Grünewald-Verlag, 2004), 57ff.

an aesthetic and a religious question at the same time.[52] In their adaptation of the opera, Huillet and Straub will add a political, probably an ecological one. Working toward communism, in their films, is not only a matter of cinematically creating a matrix for equal relations, but also of opening up a space of unknown relations including those between men and animals, spaces and climates—including, as Hölderlin saw it, "heavenly ones and princes," that had to "crash down from their old orders."[53] A people appears as a secondary phenomenon of this view of the world, just as the people of the opera becomes an issue after Moses had received the message of its oppression from the sound of the bush. With the help of film technology and filmic procedures, Huillet/Straub's film deploys a dense concept of communism as the force of creating new and equal relationships.

To increase the confusion of the initial sound of the opera, Schoenberg had had the eccentric idea of technically augmenting the alienation, suggesting for a staging that "it might be feasible to separate the voices from each other off stage [although remaining visually in contact] using telephones which will lead through loud-speakers into the hall where the voices will then coalesce."[54] It is from this idea of technically separating and then remixing tone colors and sounds, that Huillet/Straub have taken their unique sonic solution for the cinematic adaptation of the opera which was eventually shot in an amphitheater near Alba Fucens in the Abruzzan mountains. As Straub explained in an interview with the *Cahiers du cinéma*:

> *Moses und Aron* is a technical adventure on the level of sound recording that no one had previously dared [...]. I had dreamed of it from the very beginning, and the sound engineer also thought that it was right ... to record the orchestra alone first and then have the singers sing over it.[55]

The orchestral parts and all off-screen choral sequences were thus pre-produced at the Austrian Broadcasting Corporation (ORF) in Vienna to provide a very dry, reverb-free, four-channel mono version on narrow tape for the shooting of the film.[56] The prerecorded tracks supported the singers during their open-air performances via small speakers installed among the choristers. The soloists sang equipped with small earplugs to be able to follow

52 See Matthias Schmidt, "Vor dem Gesetz. Zur religiösen Dimension eines musikalischen Begriffs bei Schoenberg," in *Arnold Schoenberg und sein Gott: Bericht zum Symposium Juni 26. – 29. Juni 2002*, ed. Christian Meyer (Vienna: Arnold Schoenberg Center, 2003), 299–310.

53 Benjamin, "Two Poems," 25.

54 Schoenberg, *Moses und Aron*, footnote to bar 9.

55 Translated from Jean-Marie Straub and Danièle Huillet, "Conversation avec Jean-Marie Straub et Danièle Huillet (Moïse et Aaron). Par Jacques Bontemps, Pascal Bonitzer et Serge Daney," *Cahiers du cinéma* 258–259 (1975): 23.

56 Michael Gielen, *Unbedingt Musik. Erinnerungen* (Frankfurt: Insel, 2005). My translation, U.H.

the orchestral sounds, which had to be carefully kept out of the sensivity range of the microphones. In the arena of the theater with all its reverberation effects and ambient noises, the voices of chorus and soloists were recorded with several microphones on booms for two of the three Nagra-IV devices present.[57] In order to hear the orchestra parts, Michael Gielen, the conductor, who stood on a mobile pedestal, had to wear "a headphone which covered both his ears, preventing him from hearing what those he was conducting were singing."[58] During the shoot in the amphitheater, sound engineer Louis Hochet added the Vienna studio recordings as a sort of "live" synchronization to those of the singers. After editing, the synchronized material only had to be dynamically mixed.

The micromovement of separating voices, music, and sounds, which Schoenberg had implied both in his composition and in his stage directions was thus established on a large scale in Huillet/Straub's filming. To form a new sonic space, they integrated all sorts of particular effects: Voices in cultural framings of a technical studio were mixed with voices on location, disturbed by the wind or modulated by animal sounds. Reverberations of different historical architectures were mixed—and this was possible only

> because the Straubs and their sound engineer had found out through experiment that the natural reverberation of the studio in Vienna more or less corresponded to that of the arena in Alba Fucens, where the shoot took place.[59]

The circumstances of a theater ruin in mid-1970s Italy, irregularity in the electric frequency, old copper cables, all point to the fragile situation of a synchronization that never submitted to a central metricalization of the music but much rather corresponds to a paratactical shattering of orders. The paratactic acoustic space that Huillet/Straub devised included the disturbances caused by the radical separation of parameters to produce new layers of sound fields—and the linking of elements according to equal relations. After technically isolating the participants—singers, peasants, technicians, musicians, and animals—and then superimposing the particular phenomena in the two stages of mixing to form an absolutely hybrid space, the complete sound of the film-opera, "the absolute and unitary perception of the filmic space,"[60] would be perceived for the first

57
For more details see Danièle Huillet, "Notes" in *Writings*, 277–331; see also: "Propos de JM Straub publiés dans *Le Film Français*" in NEF Diffusion, *Moise et Aaron*, Presse Information. I thank Volko Kamensky for sharing this document from the archives of the Fondo Straub-Huillet, Cineteca di Bologna.

58
Huillet, "Notes," in *Writings*, 293.

59
Translated from Michael Gielen, "'Aus einem Gespräch mit Michael Gielen.' Wolfram Schütte spricht mit Michael Gielen," *Filmkritik* 221/222 (1975): 281.

60
Schoenberg, "Composition," 115–116.

time in the cinematic screening. It is in the mosaic space of the cinema that a new sort of people, technologically evoked and enhanced, makes its appearance.

In her preparations for the film, Danièle Huillet had produced a historical study on the life and customs of Semitic nomads in the Middle East, largely drawing on Adolphe Lods' book *Israël, des origines au milieu du VIIIe siècle avant notre ère*, first published in 1930. In her notes, Huillet underlines that the desert is a hybrid space of different cultures.[61] The film transposes this idea of the desert onto a set of relations, connecting the architecture of the theater and its *arena*—Latin literally for sand—to the single characters, exposed to wind and climate, as well as to peasants acting and to the animals filmed in their movements and sounds. Huillet/Straub's way of filming is distinguished by the complete refusal of a central order or regime: neither the technicians, nor the actors, nor the directors dictate the procedures, but the filming captures and thus documents the intricate interaction of all elements. Here of course they act more radically than Schoenberg had probably envisioned his opera to be realized. However, John Cage had qualified even the music of Schoenberg, a well-known conservative, in this sense: "Schoenberg's method is analogous to a society in which the emphasis is on the group and the integration of the individual in the group."[62] The art of integrating without submitting the particular to a central idea or a totalitarian law is the art in question.

61 Danièle Huillet, "Small Historical Excursus," *Writings*, 161–176.

62 John Cage, "The Future of Music. Credo," *Silence* (Cambridge, 1971), 3–7: 5.

DIFFERENCES AND COMMUNISM: DANIÈLE HUILLET AND JEAN-MARIE STRAUB

The initial shot of the film-opera, corresponding to the sounds of Moses' confusion, begins with a close-up on the back of the prophet's head and then moves in a single take across the arena of the amphitheater up into its ruins, across brush and bushes of abandoned olive orchards and a deserted plain to stop, with the end of the first musical movement in front of a double peaked mountain. This pan exposes the gaze to a once cultivated landscape that is now thoroughly pervaded by cultural techniques of industrialized societies. This is true for the landscape as well as for the camera technology that reveals it. The pan strings the particular elements into a series of equals; it frees and simultaneously alienates the landscape of its perspective order, opening this cinematically estranged new serial space to the gaze of the audience. But the audience still needs to make all necessary distinctions by itself: does it want to see a sublime landscape or rather the wastelands of capitalist economies that exploit peasants and workers? Does it want to see a historical setting or an analysis of the peasants' situation of the seventies? In this sense, the pan is a collective movement that awaits distinction, that demands a series of particular and individual decisions—as opposed to a homogeneous mass reception—to become reality. It is from this beginning that French film critics suggested the people of the film are actually hidden in filmic procedures or cultural techniques, such as, for instance, the pan:

> *Cahiers du cinéma*: The striking thing in *Moses and Aaron* is that the people are conceived like a gaze. It is a gaze that requires us to satisfy it.
>
> Straub: My thought just now was that the people, despite everything, are the gaze. Okay, so what then suddenly causes the gaze to bring about the pan? It isn't Aaron who brings about the pan, and not the connection between Moses and Aaron. For Moses is never linked to the people through a pan (apart from the one that passes him by). Moses is never linked to the people through any kind of camera movement—apart from the pan of his "calling," (Burning bush = people in the *hors-champ*.)[63]

The metonymical relationship of pan, burning bush, small chorus, and people, a bundling of technical, musical, cinematic, and political conceptions, connects the film's diverse levels from the very beginning. For Straub, making people's films then, constructing cinematic communism, is an issue of learning to perceive without a central guiding force on the gaze, as it is iconic for the singular god:

> One must realize that with civilization, the peasants invented gods. One must realize that what the invention of monotheism means, that it is very difficult to do without gods. That it will still take us centuries to get there and that doing without gods like the Voltairian bourgeoisie did is certainly no solution. It's only cynicism.[64]

63 Translated from Straub/Huillet, "Conversation," 13–14.

64 Jean-Marie Straub, "Sickle and Hammer," 119.

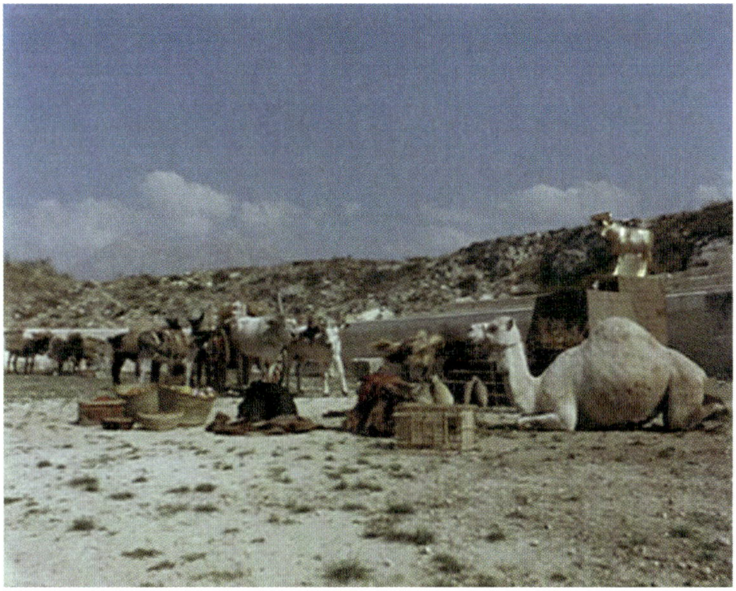

Straub's enterprise of making and seeing films is one of unlearning monotheism. This is true not only in terms of a Kantian responsibility of using one's own understanding without another's guidance, but it practically means a radical analysis of the world, taking it apart with filmic means, so that it resists any conventional category. And this is specifically true for the modern category of the real, "la catégorie du réel," which Roland Barthes, in 1968, had denounced as a mode of creating the effect of realism in modernity, the hidden implicit signifier of realist art.[65] The goal of Huillet/Straub's films is much rather to construct new and equal relationships for a coming society or people. Here, they prove to be precise communists:

> The theoretical conclusions of the Communists are in no way based on ideas or principles that have been invented, or discovered, by this or that would-be universal reformer. They merely express, in general terms, actual relations springing from an existing class struggle, from a historical movement going on under our very eyes.[66]

As opposed to Kant, who in his *Critique of Judgement* had based the art of making distinctions on the sensus communis and aesthetic differences and had defined the beautiful as an end to itself, "without linkage, as it were, to other beautiful things,"[67] the cinema of Huillet and Straub prepares the ground for all sorts of possible linkages, multiplied and made equal, as Straub maintains: "Jeder sei wie

65 Roland Barthes, "L'Effet de Réel," *Communications* 11 (1968): 84–89. Thanks to Peter Ott for hints and critical remarks.

66 Karl Marx, Friedrich Engels, *The Communist Manifesto*. Authorized English Translation, edited and annotated by Frederick Engels, published online by the Socialist Labor Party of America, www.slp.org.

67 Hannah Arendt, *Lectures on Kant's Political Philosophy*, ed. Ronald Beiner (Chicago: University of Chicago Press, 1992), 7. In her lectures, Arendt reads Kant's *Critique of Judgement* and the beautiful as a political program.

alle (Each be as all). It's Empedocles' big speech that I call Hölderlin's communist utopia."[68] This communist construction is based on and enforced by technical measures: the manifold layers of synthesized sounds, the complex construction of cinematic spaces and hence the opening of specific gazes which will then prepare for the formation and appearance of a people. But it is as difficult to get rid of guided and centrally organized forms of perception as it was for the proletarians Marx addresses to lose their chains. However, he writes: "They have a world to win."[69]

Danièle Huillet, in her notes on the shooting of *Moses and Aaron*,[70] carries the argument further. For her it is not just the expulsion of a single God but the introduction of new cinematic differences such as a cinematic time as duration, filmic space as an open field, montage as a way to think about the hitherto unrelated, and the appearance of unforeseen phenomena captured by the cinematic apparatus: movements of light the wind makes in leaves of trees, the marks of the sun on pale Austrian singers' noses, sounds of animal's hooves on dry and sandy ground, climatic elements that rule a space, a culture or a people. For Huillet, the camera is a Vertovian apparatus to reveal the normally unseen, as she maintains, "an apparatus for radiography, a mirror that helps to see and… hear, to discover, under the accumulation of habit and clichés, reality—the truth?"[71] Cinema is the art of establishing links to the unseen, the overlooked, the hitherto unknown things in their own right. But as opposed to a fetishism of the real which Barthes exposes in the arts of the Sixties, an interspersing of elements of the real to stitch the signifier directly to the bare referent, Huillet and Straub show the entire series of linkages that cinema can produce, an intricate network of particular things, senses, sights and sounds.

One set of shots illustrating this is a sequence accompanying the construction of the *Golden Calf*. It begins with the image of a glaring sculpture of a calf, seen behind Aaron, who, while law-maker Moses does not return from the mountain, tries to calm the protesting people in explaining that sensual images and material things are connected by an intrinsic principle. This, says Aaron, is just as reliable as an unchangeable law. Aaron is opting for a sort of materially based set of rules, a sort of flexible economy, a

68
"Questionnaire on May 1968," *Writings*, 267.

69
Marx, Engels, *The Communist Manifesto*, 40.

70
Huillet, "Notes," 277–331.

71
Huillet, "Interview: No appeasement," *Writings*, 252.

gold-standard[72] instead of a pure monotheistic law or else, a radically revolutionary economy:

> This image attests that in everything that is, a God lives! Unchangeable, like a principle, is the material, the gold, which you have given. Seemingly changeable, like everything is, secondary, is the shape which I gave it. Revere yourselves in this symbol![73]

Huillet/Straub cut this propaganda-piece of Aaron's short by immediately adding a wide-angle shot of a group of animals, including donkeys, oxen, and a white camel. Huillet recounts:

> We will shoot three very long takes, for such a shot one must film and allow for life to carry on its own flow. Georges [Vaglio] takes the sound, for we hold out for the breathing and the noises of the harness or of the cart—very beautiful.[74]

Then, through the roofless, clear southern *parodos* of the amphitheater, shepherds wearing theatrical costumes drive more animals, herds of sheep and cows, into the arena, with movements that recall cultural techniques of a few thousand years. These different layers show that the film is not concerned with historicizing but with analyzing historical forms of representation and reality. The shot entangles cultural and natural history in recorded gestures, traces, and voices. Here, Schoenberg's music is again overlaid by many kinds of animal noises, whose tone colors, at the end of a long orchestral section that juxtaposes extreme and eccentric *glissandi* with quasi oriental rhythms, mingle with those of the instruments. String instruments and woodwinds merge with the whistling and shouting of the herdsmen, percussion instruments merge with the clattering of the sheep's hooves, the voices of oxen and contrabassoon merge, in the way that previously the Voice from the Burning Bush was a mix of instruments and voices, breathing and vibrating.

In this scene of driving the herds, filming had to wait, as Huillet writes, for the rhythm of the shot to evolve. But as opposed to the sequence of the Burning Bush,[75] the call synthesized here from animal voices and instruments is no longer a call from a god or a transcendental otherworld,

72
This economic subtext suggests itself, since the post-war Bretton Woods agreements, a set of rules to balance economic powers, failed just as the film was being shot, leaving the field open to venture, and vulture capitalism. Aaron's allusions to gold as a token of social peace might suggest, at least for 1970s audiences, an option for the capitalist utopia of a self-controlling monetary system based on gold reserves (including US American economic supremacy). Moses opposes all of that in his defense of an immaterial universal, or rather "an omnipresent, unperceived and inconceivable" law, as Moses addresses the new god in the beginning of the opera.

73
Schoenberg, Act II, Scene 3, bars 308–319. English translation by Danièle Huillet.

74
Huillet, "Notes," 327.

75
See Huillet, "Notes," 329–330: "We start again a second time: it is better, the rhythm picks up."

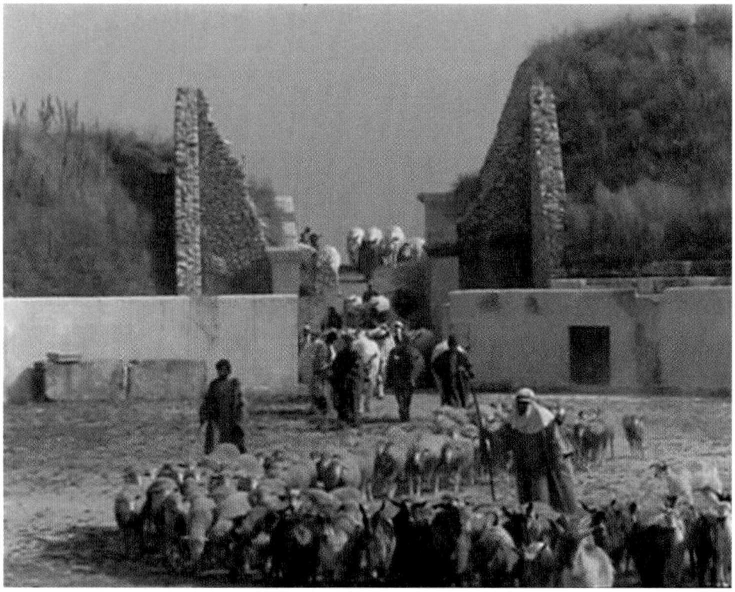

but a call from the living. It is a concrete sonic mixture of beings, things, instruments, and probably recording machines: animal and mechanical. In this shot, every single viewer is challenged to make a distinction: not to think of gods but of living conditions. These also appear during the dance of the butchers that follows: laying on the altar, confronted with other antique fragments of architecture, are chunks of meat as a reminder of a capitalist society separating production and consumption, and the injustice of the distribution following it. The images of living things, objects and people here are not a confrontation of cultural images with pure or real life, on the contrary, they are again a series of images that allow observers to perceive and think in terms of historical constellations and class relations. This however implies to "overcome limits," as Benjamin put it for Hölderlin.[76] Or as Laclau explains, "the emergence of the 'people' as a historical actor is thus always transgressive *vis-à-vis* the situation preceding it."[77]

76 Benjamin, "Two Poems," 34.

77 Laclau, *On Populist Reason*, 228.

The particular beauty of the particular sounds in the sequence of animals, herdsmen and butchers, the breathing of dancers and animals alike, reminds us that we too are living beings, distinguished from immortals or gods, making our own distinctions. The films of Danièle Huillet and Jean-Marie Straub remind us that "it is very difficult to do without gods," but we have a world to win by doing so.

Ming Tsao

Refuse Collection

Schoenberg/Lachenmann – Straub/Huillet – J.H. Prynne

Drohende Gefahr, Angst, Katastrophe (Threatening danger, fear, catastrophe) are the words that preface the score to Schoenberg's *Begleitmusik zu einer Lichtspielscene* (Opus 34, henceforth *Begleitmusik*) from 1930, which was commissioned by the Heinrichshofen Verlag in Germany.[1] The commission was for a film score that Schoenberg ultimately abandoned in favor of the more abstract program of *Drohende Gefahr, Angst, Katastrophe,* perhaps similar to the typical tone poems found by a composer such as Richard Strauss.[2] An accompanimental film would, in Schoenberg's view, subordinate the music to the images presented giving the music a more illustrative account of these sensations. By abandoning the accompanimental film, Schoenberg believed that only music as a non-conceptual medium could convey such sensations directly to a listener.

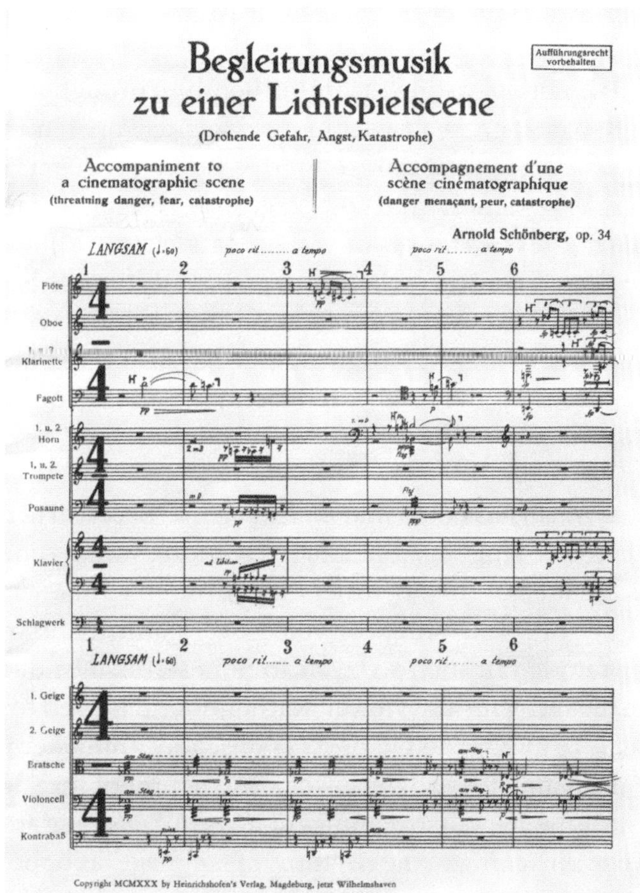

Arnold Schoenberg,
Begleitmusik zu einer Lichtspielscene, 1930

1 Ursula Böser, *The Art of Seeing, The Art of Listening: The Politics of Representation in the Work of Jean-Marie Straub and Danièle Huillet* (Frankfurt am Main: Peter Lang GmbH, Europäischer Verlag der Wissenschaften, 2004), 72.

2 Schoenberg had a very particular program in mind for composing specific images into the music that is similar to a work such as Strauss' *Alpine Symphony* as indicated below.

I. Quiet – short (the calm before the storm)
II. The threatening Danger appears
III. The Threatened becomes anxious
IV. The Danger draws closer
V. The Threatened become aware of the Danger
VI. The Danger grows
VII. The fear grows ever greater
VIII. Catastrophe
IX. Collapse

An alternative version that Schoenberg considered for the final two images was: VIII. The Danger passes, IX. Alleviation of the Tension of the Threatened (salvation, deliverance). See J. Daniel Jenkins, ed., *Schoenberg's Program Notes and Musical Analyses, Schoenberg in Words,* vol. 5, (New York: Oxford University Press, 2016), 329.

Jean-Marie Straub and Danièle Huillet's *Einleitung zu Arnold Schoenbergs Begleitmusik zu einer Lichtspielscene*, 1972 (henceforth *Einleitung*) is a "desynchronized reaction" to Schoenberg's *Begleitmusik* by enlisting a number of representational strategies (such as interviews, photo montages, documentaries, texts, etc.) in the attempt to create an image that captures the sensations of Schoenberg's music. Included in their accompaniment are dialogues through various kinds of montage such as the letters between Schoenberg and Kandinsky, Brecht's 1935 address to the International Congress of Writers for the Defense of Culture as well as the juxtaposing of photos and documentary newsreels that depict the effects of violence from the mass executions by the Versailles forces at the end of the Paris Commune of 1871, the American bombing of Vietnam and the Nazi extermination camps. Situated within these materials is the seeming "biopic" about Schoenberg himself followed by stills of photos and paintings of Schoenberg as well as documentary-like readings of the letters and address by Günter Peter Straschek and Peter Nestler (who are filmed in a broadcasting recording booth). Throughout the film are black spaces that act more as lacunae preventing a seamlessly integrated context for this variety of materials.[3] Such an experience wants to engage us with what becomes visible in these instances of violence and catastrophe, for the viewer to construct their own *counter-shots* to a history that is presented by means of discontinuous montage and not narrative integration, through what film critic Serge Daney notes as "the stubborn rejection of all the forces of homogenization."[4]

Martin Walsh has noted that *Einleitung* is a "deconstruction of cinematic language," particularly in the way it repositions the idea of the documentary through a materialist lens.[5] Sound—including the voice-over commentary—is foregrounded in such a way as to not establish or determine meaning for the viewer. Rather, sound is used to involve us in a more active process of seeing and listening, and ultimately toward our own construction of meaning. The documentary-like readings of texts in *Einleitung* attenuate one's listening to the rhythms of language, as opposed to simply its meaning, and thereby reassert the materiality of the spoken text. Yet the heterogeneity of materials in *Einleitung* is not seamlessly fused together into a linear

3 Böser, *The Art of Seeing*, 83.

4 Serge Daney, "A Tomb for the Eye (Straubian Pedagogy)," in *Der Standpunkt der Aufnahme – Point of View: Perspectives of Political Film and Video Work*, ed. Tobias Hering (Berlin: Archive Books, 2014), 359.

5 Martin Walsh, *The Brechtian Aspect of Radical Cinema* (London: British Film Institute Publishing, 1981), 85.

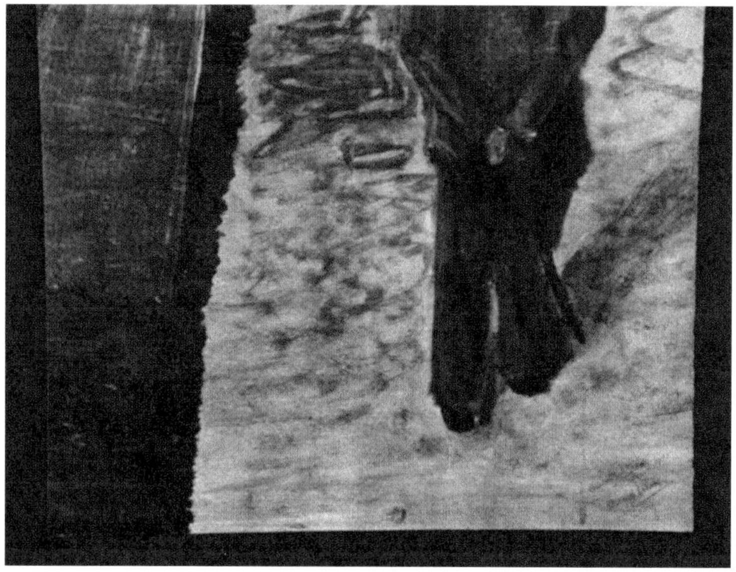

Fragment of Arnold Schoenberg's painting *Gehendes Selbstportrait* from Huillet-Straub's *Einleitung zu Arnold Schoenbergs 'Begleitmusik zu einer Lichtspielscene'* (1972).

narrative or argumentation, but rather organized through the montage of independent tableaux-like moments that refuse commentary or interpretation in order to explicate their meaning. Such a practice of *soft* montage (i.e., montage through an inclusive "and" rather than an exclusive "or" as suggested by the practices of Harun Farocki or late Godard)[6] recalls Ezra Pound's ideogrammic method in poetry where *luminous details* are brought into focus through the raw juxtaposition of concrete facts.[7] According to Benoît Turquety, *Einleitung* functions through the ideogrammic method by juxtaposing a series of concrete events and thus forms "a constellation without any explicit connection" whose coherence is maintained rhythmically and energetically.[8]

With soft montage in film, one can achieve a kind of semantic spark or jump when two things are placed together that are not normally associated with the same field of reference or meaning, particularly when the possible connections between the two things are maximized. Sometimes these sparks can follow in quick succession, producing disturbance patterns of their own, similar to the effect that one finds in the atonal music of Anton Webern. In this music, electricity continuously jumps between juxtaposed musical figures as a way to gain energy in a context where tonal grammar, phrasing and rhythm are severely

6 Harun Farocki, *Weiche Montagen/ Soft Montages*, ed. Yilmaz Dziewior (Bregenz: Kunsthaus Bregenz, 2011), 206.

7 Hugh Kenner, *The Pound Era* (Berkeley: University of California Press, 1971), 152.

8 Benoît Turquety, *Danièle Huillet, Jean-Marie Straub: "Objectivists" in Cinema*, trans. Ted Fendt (Amsterdam: Amsterdam University Press, 2020), 159.

reduced. The Cambridge poet J.H Prynne produces a similar reaction in poetic discourse maintaining cohesion through energetic sparks among, "extended trains of unfamiliar words and phrases which break the rules for local sense" so that "discourse levels and fields of reference are switched abruptly and without sign-posts," and the construction of relationships and pattern-making can occur in new ways.[9] The energy in which the structure of a work unfolds over time constitutes its *rhythm* that then becomes coterminous with its temporal experience. This potential of rhythm to generate energy, force and violence are key characteristics for critiquing a lyric subjectivity intrinsic to an expressionist poetics of music.

Coherence in the films of Straub and Huillet is often supported by techniques such as rhythmic patterning, abrupt juxtapositions, asymmetric relationships, serial variations and repetitions, thus creating temporal structures similar to those in music composition. As Straub has remarked,

> One needs a rhythm even before one starts shooting the film, or works at the cutting table. One needs to know why one chooses particular angles from which to film, how long the individual shots will last, and then choose another standpoint or an identical one, but nearer, or the same, only a little more distant.[10]

In both poetry and music, the tensions between rhythm and meter are ways in which new resistances might be made appreciable, since counting and the use of numbers (syllables and line breaks in poetry or rhythm and meter in music) enables one to apprehend the proportion of one thing to another, including their possible incommensurability. Incommensurability can destroy the integrity of syntax and argument through which the lyrical features of music become prominent, thus challenging a place of stability in which events can be apprehended, related and given meaning through lyrical expression.

The methodology of Straub and Huillet involves precisely constructing the framework for each shot and then allowing contingencies to manifest so that freedom evolves from its opposite: "One should never say or show something in which one cannot sense the possibility of its opposite as an intrinsic resistance."[11] These contingencies are referred to as "unforeseen factors" that arise from within

9 J.H. Prynne, "Difficulties in the Translation of 'Difficult' Poems," *Cambridge Literary Review*, 1/3 (Easter 2010): 157.

10 Elke Marhöfer, Jean-Marie Straub, Mikhail Lylov, "A Thousand Cliffs," in *Der Standpunkt der Aufnahme*, 322. Reprinted in the present volume, 376.

11 Straub, "A Thousand Cliffs," in the present volume, 388.

the work itself and are an integral part of the subject matter that establish the work as a "site of resistance."[12] "If you have a great deal of patience, it is charged with contradictions at the same time. Otherwise it doesn't have the time to be charged. Lasting patience is necessarily charged with tenderness and violence."[13] In a similar vein, as Prynne has remarked in the context of poetic composition, "Nothing taken for granted, nothing merely forced, pressure of the composing will as varied by delicacy, because these energies are dialectical and not extruded from personality or point of view."[14]

What does it mean for a work to become a site of resistance? Cognitive engagement depends less upon perception as on the experience of resistance, which forms the surrounding world of a subject's activity when things present themselves through their inertial force. Instead of intelligibility as a criterion of knowledge, resistance can "make accessible the fact of a thing's existence without impairing its status as a substantial, independent entity,"[15] a way of affirming the world around us without completely jettisoning the role of the subject.[16] It is through resistance that a model of perception is expanded beyond a subject's limit of the perceivable world in an attempt to record the manifold richness of how things are.[17] This projective expansion includes much more than any apparent intention of the subject whereupon *contingency* becomes a necessary part for pushing outward toward reality; a closer engagement with what there is, including a conception of agency and feeling that is not distinctly identified with a personal subject. In this sense, a site of resistance in the films of Straub and Huillet contextualizes what knowledge is valuable and what paths of action are potentially possible.

II

An important aspect of *Einleitung* is its fundamental repositioning of the idea of *accompaniment*. The composer Hanns Eisler suggested that in Schoenberg's music, words are always secondary—or accompanimental—to the music, for example in the opera *Moses und Aron*. As Straub suggests,

> Eisler argues for this divorce between the two parts of the opera, the words and the music. I think

12
"A Thousand Cliffs," 378.

13
Tag Gallagher, "Straub Anti-Straub," *Senses of Cinema,* no. 43 (2007): 2.

14
J.H. Prynne, "Poetic Thought," *Textual Practice,* 24(4) (2010): 597.

15
J.H. Prynne, "Resistance and Difficulty," *Prospect 5* (Winter 1961): 27.

16
Levi Bryant, Nick Srnicek, and Graham Harman, eds., "Towards a Speculative Philosophy," in *The Speculative Turn: Continental Materialism and Realism* (Melbourne, Australia: re.press, 2011), 5.

17
J.H. Prynne, "Mental Ears and Poetic Work," *Chicago Review,* vol. 55., no. 1 (2010): 126.

however that Eisler is wrong, and that the work really is a unity. This is the conclusion that I've come to, more and more surely, as I've studied over the text of the opera and listened to the music accompanying it, to the structure and rhythm of the music."[18]

What Straub proposes is the idea of *polyphony* between music and text where each contribute equally to the aesthetic experience. The idea of accompaniment itself suggests a form of violence through the enforcement of a relationship that Straub and Huillet fundamentally question, a relationship often of subordination and hierarchization. The one place in *Einleitung* where Straub and Huillet do force a relation hangs upon the word "but" (*aber*) that links Brecht's public address, which connects fascism with capitalism, to Schoenberg's letter to Kandinsky in which he states he does not want to be exception to Kandinsky's anti-Semitism, thus implying that it requires an act of violence to reveal the often hidden connections between racism and capitalism.

Grammar, the way in which images, words and sounds are connected (and often forced together) is constantly threatening to fall into subjectivity and violence through the lyrical procedures of desire to establish meaning. *Einleitung* juxtaposes a series of concrete events that form a heterogeneous constellation without any explicit connections, whose coherence is maintained rhythmically and energetically. Schoenberg and Brecht, in their respective work, each created an image of such catastrophe that could only be captured through a refusal of the "homogenized forces of representation," including a refusal of an artistic expression that confines itself to an exiled and protected space in contemporary culture.

Schoenberg's renunciation of a tonal (and hierarchical) structure is not a refusal of musical grammar in itself. He is still invested in grammar as a way to renew musical language to the point where it becomes possible once more to explore the pure elaboration of musical thoughts. For Schoenberg, the whole task of art is to unexpress the expressible, whereas the expressible are those sanctioned meanings made possible and contained by conventions.[19] These conventions are established through the musical grammar and syntax of how connections are made—the

18
Joel Rogers, "*Moses and Aaron* as an object of Marxist reflection: Jean-Marie Straub and Danièle Huillet interviewed," *Jump Cut*, no. 12/13 (1976): 61.

19
Walsh cites Roland Barthes' idea of "expressing the inexpressible" to frame Schoenberg's music. Walsh, *The Brechtian Aspect of Radical Cinema*, 82.

foundation of a musical language—where, as Adorno notes,

> every musical phenomenon points beyond itself, on the strength of what it recalls, from what it distinguishes itself, by what means it awakens expectation. The traditional doctrine of musical forms has its sentence, phrase, period, and punctuation. Questions, exclamations, subordinate clauses are everywhere, voices rise and fall, and, in all of this, the gesture of music is borrowed from the speaking voice.[20]

The term *vocables* comprises chords and their progressions, melodic phrases, gestures and most importantly, cadences; i.e., those expressive aspects of a musical language that are found in tonality but have their origins in the speaking voice.

The composer Helmut Lachenmann has expanded the concept of vocables through the notion of the *Strukturklang* (structure-sound), where expressive aspects of a composition are generally stable rhetorical devices—gestures and cadences grounded in the language of late Romanticism and early Expressionism—against which the materiality of sound production becomes perceptible and creates resistances.[21] A Strukturklang engages the listening not so much through the perception of sound, as through the experience of resistance to the lyrical procedures of an expressive subject. In Lachenmann's music, the materiality of sound production presents itself as *noise* in the music, noise not only in the disruption of expressive intent but also in the physicality of performance. A Strukturklang is a musical process that requires an active listening whereby a sound's internal time or *Eigenzeit* is coterminous with one's experience of it.[22]

In opposition to the Strukturklang is the *Texturklang* (texture-sound) that is experienced as "object-like" (where one appreciates the sound long before it has ended). A Texturklang is a point of orientation for a listener as an extended moment of passive listening that creates a subject-position in the musical experience.[23] In other words, Texturklänge (texture-sounds) are moments of relief that give a listener the impression that a full listening experience is manageable and understandable. Such points privilege a humanist center from which lyrical procedures such

20 Theodor W. Adorno, "Music, Language, and Composition," trans. Susan Gillespie, *The Musical Quarterly,* vol. 77, no. 3 (Autumn 1993): 401, 405.

21 Ming Tsao, "Helmut Lachenmann's 'Sound Types,'" *Perspectives of New Music,* vol. 52, no. 1 (Winter 2014): 217–238.

22 Tsao, "'Sound Types,'" 217.

23 Tsao, "'Sound Types,'" 220.

as gestures and cadences (i.e., Lachenmann's *Kadenzklänge*) make for an authentic language of personal agency. The desiring "I" as the expressive subject is composed into the music through these *Klangtypen* (sound-types) against the material resistances of sound production.

Lachenmann's *Kadenzklänge* (cadence-sounds) derive from the grammar of tonality: phrasing, antecedent/consequent relations, attack/resonance, cadence, period forms and symmetry. These tonal shapes also inform Schoenberg's *musical idea* (musikalischer Gedanke) where notions of motive, gestalt, phrase, theme, rhythm, harmony and form, shape the wholeness of the musical work.[24] These musical shapes generate vocables or gestures in which a speaking subject is inscribed into the music, including Schoenberg's notion of lyricism, where the *musical idea* is made possible by representing a feeling "subject" in the musical discourse.[25] Schoenberg's idea of a musical prose can therefore be seen as a perceptual process of expansion that begins from the outward intention of a subject which takes the limit of the perceivable world as a basis and is elaborated through an encounter with resistance beyond that limit. This is the case for how subjectivity is encoded in Schoenberg's monodrama *Erwartung* and explains why there is so much resonance between music and poetic composition, between Adorno's *musique informelle* and poet Charles Olson's *projective verse*.[26] The language of expanding outwards, disrupting boundaries and increasing the "world's available reality" is abundant in both of these ideas.

Perhaps a more radical idea of the musical gesture and subjectivity in music is the anti-humanist orientation of Ferneyhough's *figure* where gestures arise not from stable rhetorical devices against which the materiality of sound can place pressure, but through *lines of force* as structural categories in which musical processes conflate with musical objects (i.e., processes as "shadows thrown by objects in time").[27] At the center of a musical gesture is no nucleus of tangibility but instead a system of relationships. What matters is what happens between gestures, between sounds where lines of force can arise and generate *figural energies* in the act of moving from one discrete musical gesture to another.[28] Ferneyhough's gestures arise not from an

24 Arnold Schoenberg, *The Musical Idea and the Logic, Technique, and Art of Its Presentation*, ed. Patricia Carpenter and Severine Neff (New York: Columbia University Press, 1995), 102–103.

25 Arnold Schoenberg, "Heart and Brain in Music" in *Style and Idea: Selected Writings*, trans. Leo Black (Berkeley: University of California Press, 1984), 53–76.

26 Theodore W. Adorno, "Vers une musique informelle" in *Quasi una Fantasia* (London: Verso, 1998), 269–322 and Charles Olson, "Projective Verse" in *Collected Prose*, ed. Donald Allen and Benjamin Friedlander (Berkeley: University of California Press, 1997), 239–249.

27 Brian Ferneyhough, "Il Tempo della Figura," in *Collected Writings*, 34–36 and "Adorno Presentation" Goldsmiths College, London, 21 February 1998 (unpublished document).

28 Ferneyhough, *Collected Writings*, 35. Note that Olson mirrors the same idea when he writes, "At root (or stump) what is, is no longer THINGS but what happens BETWEEN things, these are the terms of the reality contemporary to us - and the terms of what we are." Charles Olson, *Collected Prose*, 138.

expressive first person, as with Schoenberg or Lachenmann, but through impersonal forces applied to the language of music where music's rhetorical tropes are twisted and damaged in order to unexpress the expressible. It is through the resistance of these rhetorical materials that the lines of force become apparent and are harnessed for a new kind of lyricism to manifest. Paraphrasing Straub, one must intelligently respect the existing space in order to take in its lines of force against which expressive devices could emerge without being derivative of a represented content.[29]

In comparison to Schoenberg's "idea" or Lachenmann's Strukturklang, Ferneyhough's *figure* maps out a lyrical subjectivity in more radical ways, always denying a stable subject-position of intent and desire by placing expression itself as a matter of transition from one state to another. The dense polyphony and rhythmic complexity of Ferneyhough's music works between multiple networked relationships, shifting from measure to measure in ways that, similar to the poetry of Prynne,

> sustain rapid alignments and realignments and provide both a conceptual topography and a virtual history of association. Accumulated meaning is systematically dismantled as the syntactical structures defeat any attempts to memorize connections and relationships.[30]

This is not a music that leads the listener back to its composer, but to a musical language as a theoretical structure that begins to explore the limits of a humanist mode of expression and attempts to move beyond it.

29 Daniel Fairfax, "Straub/Huillet–Brecht–Benjamin–Adorno," *Quarterly Review of Film and Video*, vol. 29 (2012): 41.

30 Ian Davidson, *Radical Spaces of Poetry* (London: Palgrave Macmillan, 2010), 160.

III

In J.H. Prynne's "Refuse Collection" (2004), the parataxis of a lyrical poetic language, with its documentary quotations from the everyday language of capitalism and media representation, attempts to create an image of another catastrophe, the atrocities of Abu Ghraib in Iraq. Such a poetic language is conveyed through a formal sense of poetic rhythm in a similar vein to Straub and Huillet's formal sense of filmic rhythm. Akin to the tension created about and across the montage between shots in Straub and Huillet's film, Prynne situates the tension about and across line-endings where "there is a kind of dialectical unsettling because line-endings and verse divisions work into and against semantic overload in the poetic work."[31]

As Colin Winborn has suggested "to 're-fuse' is 'to fuse or melt again', and 'refusion' is 'the act of pouring back'. Almost all of Prynne's work is concerned with the 're-fusing' of seemingly incommensurate or incompatible discourses; it turns also on the 'refusion' of self into other" where "military, economic and scientific discourses all collide, sometimes within the crash zone of a single term."[32]

The first stanza of "Refuse Collection":

> To a light led sole in pit of, this by slap-up
> barter of an arm rest cap, on stirrup trade in
> crawled to many bodies, uncounted. Talon up
> crude oil-for-food, incarnadine incarcerate, get
> foremost a track rocket, rapacious in heavy
> investment insert tool this way up. This way
> can it will you they took to fast immediate satis-
> faction or slather, new slave run the chain store
> enlisted, posture writhing what they just want
> we'll box tick that, nim nim. Camshot spoilers
> strap to high stakes head to the ground elated
> detonator like a bear dancing stripped canny
> sex romp, webbing taint. Confess sell out the
> self input, yes rape yes village gunship by
> apache rotor capital genital grant a seed trial
> take a nap a twin.

Prynne's poem "Refuse Collection" fuses a variety of discourses without achieving a harmonious co-existence and union of parts. Indeed as Winborn continues, ""Refuse Collection" is suspicious of the idea that anything is truly 'collectable' as part of a projected 'whole,' particularly in terms of knowledge. It condemns a culture of excess in which human life has come to be seen as 'refuse,' mere matter for the 'spectacle dump'; and yet the poem is itself a waste product, a space in which words and phrases that would be flushed away by other poets come to be deposited. It is in this sense a 'Refuse Collection,' a disorderly gathering of verbal detritus."[33] The text of "Refuse Collection" "brutally assaults the idea of 'autonomous' and 'unique' subjectivity. 'You' merges with 'we' or 'they,' what is 'inside' is also revealed

31 Prynne, "Poetic Thought," 599.

32 Colin Winborn, "'Derangement from deep inside': J.H. Prynne's 'Refuse Collection,'" *PN Review 175*, vol. 33, no. 5, 55.

33 Winborn, "'Derangement from deep inside,'" 56.

as 'outside,' and what is 'over there' blends disconcertingly with what is 'here' and 'at home': we are all complicit and accountable. This is the darker side of Prynne's concern with the 'refusion' of self into other. The whole text urges us to resist being 'collected,' brought on side, by a war-mongering government." Prynne's text critiques the idea of establishing consensus.

"Refuse Collection" is a poem that is absent of clear subject-positions in the context of imperatives for committing unethical acts (such as "Kick them around" and "stamp on non-white body parts"). As Nandini Ramesh Sankar has pointed out, "Refuse Collection" "progressively refines a strategy of combining the problem of guilt and social agency with the formal device of pronominal ambiguity" implying that there is "the abdication of any clear subject-position."[34] The use of the imperative in combination with the act of torture suggests that agency is conflated with complicity, most notably in the confusion of pronouns. For example, the juxtaposition of *you* and *they* creates an unresolved ambiguity regarding agency: "This way/can it will *you they* took to fast immediate satis-/faction or slather." With the ambiguity between pronouns, the individual lyric voice is dislocated and passes through the collective, embedding it into a much larger historical and social context that makes it complicit with acts of collective violence.

34
Nandini Ramesh Sankar, *Poetics of Difficulty in Postmodern Poetry* (PhD diss., Cornell University, 2012), 188.

Such an ambiguity makes the poem critical of a self-righteous anti-war *us* as well as an *us* that is responsible for the atrocities. The poem accepts neither a position of despair or self-righteousness from which one can deny responsibility. It critiques the notion that in a democracy one can find those spaces in which free and rational discourse between equals might exist. Prynne, along with Straub and Huillet, is critical of any form of expression that seeks to encode universal human feelings. Such expression is essentially a Romantic sensibility in that it seeks to locate a unifying personal consciousness at the center of the phenomenal world, almost entirely controlled by the first person pronoun or character point of view, and implies a fixed, stable perspective in an otherwise unstable world. Similarly, music whose vocables are equally controlled by the first person pronoun—gestures and forms of expression that fall into the tropes of Lachenmann's

Kadenzklänge—also become a music of nostalgia, an unconscious desire for a utopian space where new expression is thought to be possible based on earlier experiences of harmony and closure.

Nostalgia is *the* potential problem in the music of Lachenmann where the materiality of sound production—experienced as noise—simply is not enough to destabilize the rhetorical tropes, gestures, Kadenzklänge and the hierarchical structuring of his musical language derived from tonality. The problem of subjectivity in music is entirely tied to the phenomena of Klangtypen, in particular the Kadenzklang whose shape evokes the shadows of the spoken voice and its intentional declarations (rhythm, pacing, emphasis, breath, sound-patterning and rhyme). In this sense, Schoenberg's *Begleitmusik* still is committed to a representational music by composing into the music through expressive vocables, a sense of subjectivity or agency, that feels *Drohende Gefahr, Angst, Katastrophe*. Although the hierarchical tonal structure is abandoned with respect to pitch, the rhetorical tropes—the language-like aspects of music derived from tonality—are maintained (as in Pierre Boulez' critique of Schoenberg's twelve-tone music).[35] Both Schoenberg's and Lachenmann's is a music fully endowed with consciousness: Schoenberg's *musical idea* and Lachenmann's Strukturklang develop from an organicist conception of music whereby notions of subjectivity—such as a relatively stable speaking "I" within an otherwise unstable (or non-hierarchical) musical discourse—are constructed through the lyrical procedures they employ.

Straub once said that language is colonization, referring to the fixing of stable meanings through the solidification of signifier and signified into an identity. Straub and Huillet seek to undo this solidification by focusing on the rhythmic and musical attributes of spoken language, insofar as the sonic materiality of language is reasserted.[36] Language, including filmic language of images and sound, is too often complicit in the acts of violence that *Einleitung* brings together through montage. Indeed, as Prynne states in his note on war and language,

> The idea that there is an innocent or unwounded condition of language in any of its historic or con-

35
Pierre Boulez, "Schoenberg is Dead," in *Stocktakings from an Apprenticeship*, trans. Stephen Walsh (Oxford: Clarendon Press, 1991), 209–214.

36
Walsh, *The Brechtian Aspect of Radical Cinema*, 86.

> ceptual formalizations, from which at some determined point in war-like operations it can passively fall into victim-damage and victim-anguish...is false and dangerous and absurd.[37]

The grammar of language, in particular, can create and manipulate connections between events to participate in "the mounting up of a war program, in advance of the hostilities and to justify their methods."[37] My belief is that music is also complicit in the condition of language, particularly through its speech acts, which inform musical shapes and gestures—the language of music—that have over history become emotional carriers of language's sense.

In "Stars, Tigers and the Shape of Words," Prynne writes that

> if language is a social code of interactions, in which performance is an expressive procedure within a context of sense-bearing acts, then anything that can count towards meaning may do so; intonation, style-level, choice of words and their sounds and echoes.[38]

The lyrical aspects of spoken language, which I believe are at the basis of music composition, do not in themselves create meaning or sense but endorse it through such parameters as rhythm, meter, pacing, sound-patterning and rhyme: all the expressive skills of "word-painting" or imitation found in the history of composed music. This "style of sound," as suggested by the poet Alexander Pope with regard to Prynne's "Stars, Tigers and the Shape of Words," is a "signifying code that is potentially sense-bearing, or at least sense-confirming and sense-enhancing" and "can be managed so as to give innumerable motivated echoes of non-arbitrary confirmation to the sense or idea."[39] It is the "innumerable motivated echoes" that, when detached from the sense or idea (as the "shadows" of speech acts), become the language of music.

I am particularly interested in how noise and interference are coded back into these language-like aspects of music (i.e., the idea of *reverse transcription*) so that moving from the play of sound and gesture—the material of music—to music's materiality (its "grain of voice" so to speak) can become the start of an ecological approach to music composition. This ecology is constituted through a feedback

37 J.H. Prynne, "A Quick Riposte to Handke's Dictum about War and Language," *Quid 6* (2000): 25.

38 J.H. Prynne, *Stars, Tigers and the Shape of Words: The William Matthews Lectures* 1992 (London: Birkbeck College, 1993), 1.

39 J.H. Prynne, *Stars, Tigers and the Shape of Words*, 6.

loop that continually registers between the physical characteristics of sound (its materiality, spectrum and noise), music's language-like aspects (Klangtypen derived from aspects of tonality such as gesture, phrasing and cadence), music's aura (as stratified layers of historical and cultural associations), and music's compositional structuring through various kinds of processes—primarily serial and mathematical—that can work into and against music's language-like aspects. Such an ecological approach can already be gleaned in the manner in which Straub and Huillet methodically work with their actors in the reading and reciting of texts where the "innumerable motivated echoes"—the varied musical aspects of speech-acts including intonation, pacing and emphasis—are worked into and against the meaning of the text thereby producing a rich counterpoint. Indeed, their film scripts are filled with musical indications for the actors such as accelerando, rallentando, pizzicato, forte, pianissimo, etc.

IV

My musical composition for 18 musicians, *Refuse Collection,* is an attempt to bring together Schoenberg's music, Straub-Huillet's film, and Prynne's poem under the rubric of a noise-bearing "speculative music composition" that *reverse* transcribes Schoenberg's Opus 34 through the rhythmic and metric forces of Prynne's poem in such a way that a listener comes to hear a counter-melody against the original music as *Begleitmusik* ("accompanimental music") to the forces of the original work. Under the pressure of Prynne's poem, my musical composition begins to show the scars of Schoenberg's original music by working against it. Indeed, in Schoenberg's theoretical writings, the true nature of *accompaniment* is defined as counterpoint (an inherent *working against)* so that sufficient resistance is encountered in the act of listening to meet the continuing demand for palpable texture in human affairs. My aim, as a composer, is not to entirely dispense with an organicist orientation, but to orient my materials toward virology, as a parasite that disrupts music's communicative and lyrical point of view. In biology, "the virus integrates with the host cell's genome, replicating along with it but remaining dormant until the right sort of conditions emerge for it to reactivate."[40] These reactivations of usage codes from

40 Sam Solnick, *Poetry and the Anthropocene: Ecology, biology and technology in contemporary British and Irish poetry* (London and New York: Routledge, 2017), 172.

Schoenberg's expressionist musical language under certain compositional conditions provide the basis for my *Refuse Collection*.

Below is the syllabic structure of the first stanza of Prynne's poem and the resulting initial metric structure for my *Refuse Collection*, where addition signs indicate small breaks due to punctuation with occasional regroupings in order to generate more manageable metric lengths (such as 8 = 4 + 4). Measures in square brackets are additional measures that lie outside the syllabic count of the poetic line that I added later for temporal reasons. The syllabic count generally informs the numerator of each measure and only occasionally the denominator. The denominator of each measure is generally freely chosen in such a way as to keep a musician counting *only* on each specific measure. Thus, rarely does the continuation of a beat continue across two or more measures such as 4/4 followed by 3/4. In such a context, the denominator will be changed to enact a tempo change, for example, 4/4 followed by 3/5. Furthermore, when the denominator is the same for two or more successive measures, then the numerator is arranged in such a way as to prevent more global groupings. For example, 3/16 followed by 5/16 could easily be regrouped as 8/16 or 4/8. If the denominator is not changed, then another measure will be inserted between them such as 3/16, 4/16, 5/16 thus preventing a more common metrical grouping to emerge. These changes force a musician to continually count and concentrate on the immediate measure at hand in order to generate energy in the performance of the music by preventing more global perspectives on the music's rhythm from materializing, whereby a musician's concentration can relax.

To indicate the formal divisions in the original poem between stanzas, fermatas were placed in the music. For example, after the last 5/16 measure ("take a nap a twin"), a fermata of three seconds is placed to indicate the end of the first stanza in the poem. The formal structure of the poem interrupts the structure of Schoenberg's music in unpredictable ways, thereby preventing clear tension/relaxation relationships that mimic the rhythms and breathing of the speaking voice from manifesting while still demanding an active listening. By applying an

	Resulting Musical Meter	Syllable Count per Line
To a light led sole in pit of, this by slap-up	4/4, 4/10, 4/3	8+4=(4+4)+4
barter of an arm rest cap, on stirrup trade in	7/20, [11/16], 5/10, [5/4]	7+5
crawled to many bodies, uncounted. Talon up	6/5, 3/16, [6/3], 3/5	6+3+3
crude oil-for-food, incarnadine incarcerate, get	4/12, 4/5, 4/4, 1/3	4+8+1=4+(4+4)+1
foremost a track rocket, rapacious in heavy	6/8, 6/8	6+6
investment insert tool this way up. This way	9/20, 2/5, [4/4]	9+2
can it will you they took to fast immediate satis-	7/12	14=7*2
faction or slather, new slave run the chain store	5/3, [5/16], 6/4	5+6
enlisted, posture writhing what they just want	6/5 (doubling 3 and omitting 8)	3+8
we'll box tick that, nim nim. Camshot spoilers	6/5, 4/12	4+2+4=6+4
strap to high stakes head to the ground elated	11/16	11
detonator like a bear dancing stripped canny	3/4	12=3*4
sex romp, webbing taint. Confess sell out the	2/3, 3/7, 5/8	2+3+5
self input, yes rape yes village gunship by	3/12, 4/5	3+8=3+(4*2)
apache rotor capital genital grant a seed trial	4/5	16 = 4*4
take a nap a twin.	5/16	5

additional structure to the original Schoenberg *Begleitmusik*, one can test its solidity through the music's resistance to it, often creating breaks and cracks in Schoenberg's music that work against its narrative so that its materiality becomes palpable.

The presence of the irrational measures (where numbers other than powers of 2 are in the denominator) produces continual, abrupt shifts in tempi and pacing that halts or deflects the forward movement of musical discourse by breaking off this movement before it can complete itself. Such ruptures in the continuity of discourse force upon us an awareness of the musical linguistic medium (gestures, phrasing, relations of antecedent/consequent) by denying a sense of completion and cadence. As in Prynne's "Refuse Collection" where systematic spacing of the verse never coincides with syntactical cuts, the connections between the identifiable parts of musical phrases and gestures become difficult to grasp.

My reverse transcription of Schoenberg's *Begleitmusik* is composed of interlacing quotations and palimpsests from various sources, often working anonymously below the work's surface. This helps to disrupt the lyrical intentions of Schoenberg's original so that no consistent subject-position is ever maintained within the musical discourse thus denying any gestures, phrasing and cadencing that come to represent clear emotional desires or psychological states in the music. My intention is to displace musical expression as something apart from desire and individual subjectivity, an expression that is "beyond memory, appetite, greed, and all the other consolations for predatoriness that make up the spiral curve of bourgeois autobiography."[41]

Part of displacing musical expression in this way is through transcribing the shapes and gestures of music—in this case, primarily from Schoenberg's *Begleitmusik*—onto a rhythmic grid that is unstable with a continually shifting, unpredictable metric ground against which the transcribed materials can never find a central point for intentionally clear expressions and declamations (a stable "I") to manifest, particularly since tempo is never consistent for more than a measure of time. A rhythmic and metric grid that registers a performer's musical actions is similar to the precision with which Straub and Huillet craft the performance of spoken language, where each inflection and stress is rhythmically calibrated and ultimately works against the

41 Keston Sutherland, "Hilarious absolute daybreak [Brass, 1971]" in *Glossator Practice and Theory of the Commentary*, vol. 2 (2010), 131.

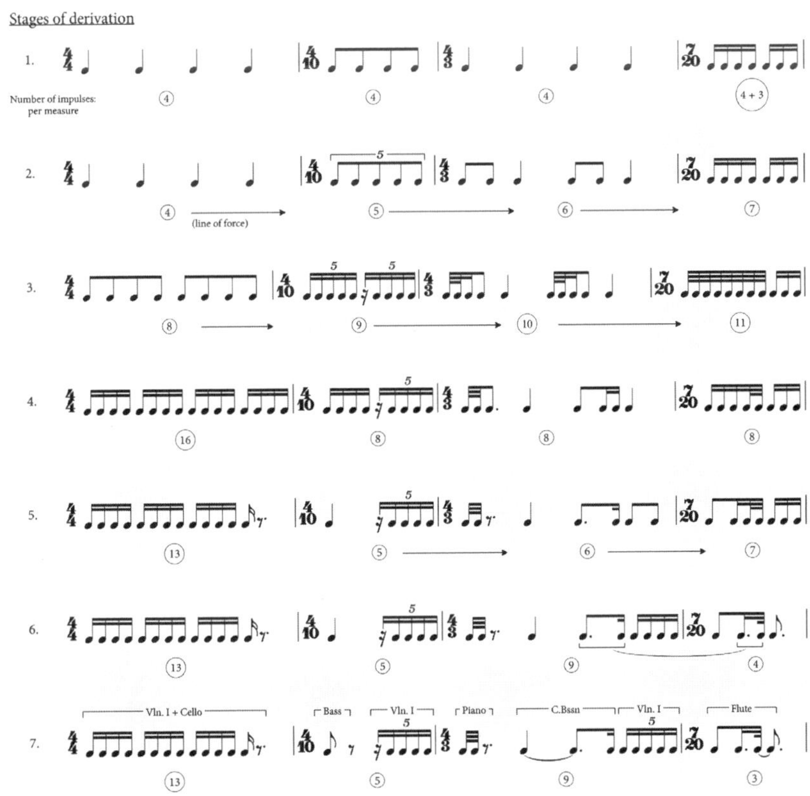

Ming Tsao, *Refuse Collection sketch*, 2017

Refuse Collection

The score is in C

Ming Tsao
2017

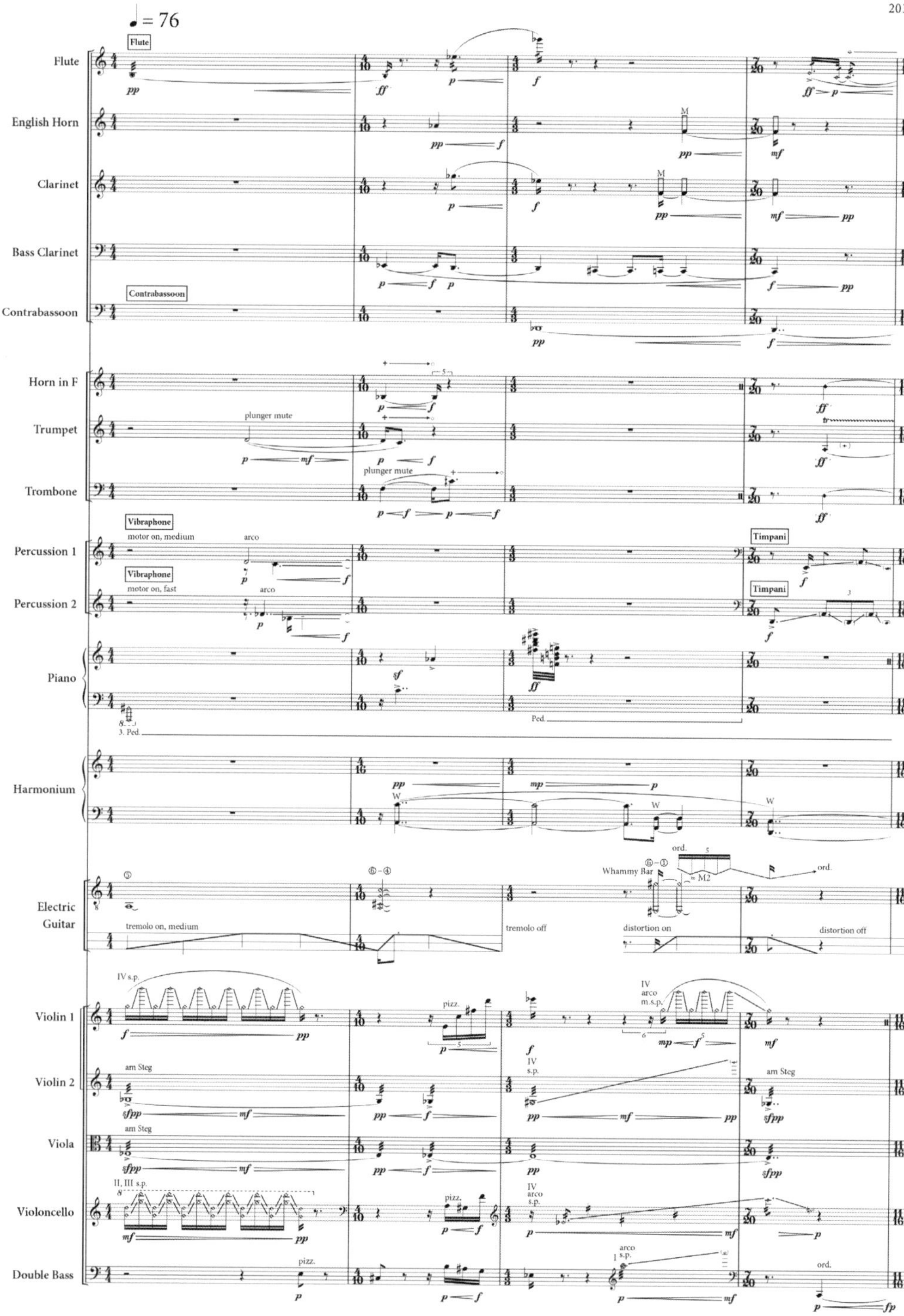

intentionally expressive aspects of the text and its intended meaning. The rhythmic grid for my *Refuse Collection* is constructed from the meter scheme suggested by the poem. The previous image, *Refuse Collection sketch*, shows the composite rhythmic sketch for the opening four measures (based on the first one and a half lines of Prynne's poem "Refuse Collection") in many stages of development.

V

How can musical lyricism, through its gestures, cadences and song, be attained in an era where the effects of human expression have become problematic? Through my composition *Refuse Collection*, scraps and filings from various musical references that lie outside of my immediate musical consciousness and whose language is fundamentally at odds with my own expressive desires, accumulate so that music's materiality exceeds human agency and can dissolve an ego-centered expressiveness in favor of a more encompassing subjectivity. The nature of my *Refuse Collection* suggests the recuperation of discarded materials as *waste* through a discontinuous montage of musical fragments based on Schoenberg's music, but whose *rhythm* is informed by Prynne's poem.

> Waste signifies noise, excess and rubbish, which stands as a rebuke and challenge to instrumental systems because rubbish is what is left when the operation of the forces of homogenization are complete and nothing should be left.[42]

In my reworking of Schoenberg's *Begleitmusik*, rhythm and meter are destabilizing musical forces on instrumental actions in order to foreground the materiality of sound production through a noise-bearing aesthetic. The waste that is a product of music's materiality can tune into the accumulated layers of signification accrued through music's evolution and reactivate past codes as the contamination of damaged forms.

Such a reworking of Schoenberg's Opus 34 attempts to provide another image of *Drohende Gefahr, Angst, Katastrophe* that is defined through the cracks and rough textures of Schoenberg's original music. My *Refuse Collection* is lyrically expressive, which means that subject-positions[43] can exist for a listener to engage with the music as expressive

42 N. H. Reeve and Richard Kerridge, *Nearly Too Much: The Poetry of J. H. Prynne* (Liverpool: Liverpool University Press, 1995), 10. Composer John Cage even uses the term "courageous wastefulness" as an aesthetic for music composition. See James Pritchett, *The Music of John Cage* (Cambridge: Cambridge University Press, 1993), 157.

43 Eric F. Clarke, *Ways of Listening: An Ecological Approach to the Perception of Musical Meaning* (Oxford: Oxford University Press, 2005), 91–92.

gestures and cadences of intention, potentially forming aspects of a compositional language. In my music, these subject-positions are never *stable* points of orientation (as they are with Schoenberg or Lachenmann) and thus my music critiques the idea of any unifying personal "voice" or agency speaking from behind the musical language. Indeed, subjectivity in my music emerges from those areas of contact between the materiality of sound production and a musical expression that is fractured and destabilized throughout. If there is the presence of a lyrical voice, it is then made insecure, with the possibility that it may open up at any moment to other forms of expression with which it must cohabitate and find dialogue. Listeners should listen "beyond anthropocentric terms, including the ways in which the resistance of the world—its conflicting and dynamic materiality—exceeds subjective desire, conceptual thought and technological control."[44] My music is a *materialist* music, akin to Straub's notion of a "materialist image"—a sound world outside of consciousness, rather than a sound world fully endowed with consciousness, where a listener is not directed by my own subjective desire for expression but is required to rethink subjectivity and expression within a larger domain of possible sounds.

What the lyrical domain of music opens to is what John Cage would refer to as "anarchic harmony" where sound is freed from a human intentionality and reaches into the artlessness of nature, not nature as socio-historically mediated nature, but closer to what Quentin Meillassoux calls "the great outdoors."[45] The sudden allusion to musical materials from other time periods impose shifts of scale that immediately disrupt any sense of personal, unmediated perception. They make a subject-position for listeners to orient themselves insecure and incomplete, thus providing a challenge to the humanist paradigm. The sound world that my music evokes manifests from the contingencies that appear when one reverse transcribes many layers of musical sources with sound's materiality into a dense and rhythmically unstable Strukturklang. Through reverse transcriptions, connected roots among sounds begin to develop their own internal agency and activity, and separate themselves from my expressive intentionality as a composer. Noise in my music is then not merely disruption of signal or material resistance toward lyrical intent (as in

44 George Clark and Redmond Entwistle, "We do everything for this art, but this art isn't everything: Notes on Danièle Huillet and Jean-Marie Straub," *Vertigo Magazine*, vol. 3, no. 6 (Summer 2007): 2.

45 "Harmony is freed from structural responsibility," or rather, harmony lies outside thinking. Pritchett, *The Music of John Cage*, 49. "The great outdoors" is that which is "not relative to us, and which was given as indifferent to its own givenness to be what it is, existing in itself regardless of whether we are thinking of it or not; that outside which thought could explore with the legitimate feeling of being on foreign territory—of being entirely elsewhere." Quentin Meillassoux, *After Finitude: An Essay on the Necessity of Contingency*, trans. Ray Brassier (London: Bloomsbury Academic, 2008), 7.

the music of Lachenmann) but quite possibly those interferences that lie outside the reach of humanity because they are the result of material and cultural forces passing through many stratified layers of accumulated earth.

My music engages with a "lyric of the Anthropocene" that sensitizes a listener to become more mindful of our history, environment and the organic connection of music to the world and to nature. As Straub has noted, "We have something concrete beneath our feet, the earth, and we must have the ability to enjoy the earth, so as to be in a position to protect it." And in the same context: A film "has to do with geology. [...] Geology is the study of that which is not visible, or barely so; that which is underneath."[46] Music composition should understand its corruptions as well, not by avoiding expression but by fully understanding music's relation to language, to speech and to song in order to deconstruct the rhetorical tropes that are so prevalent in the culture of today's "new music" that is still dominated by Romantic sensibilities. Music also must become a defense of the earth, as we cannot afford another alternative.

46 "A Thousand Cliffs," 385, 389.

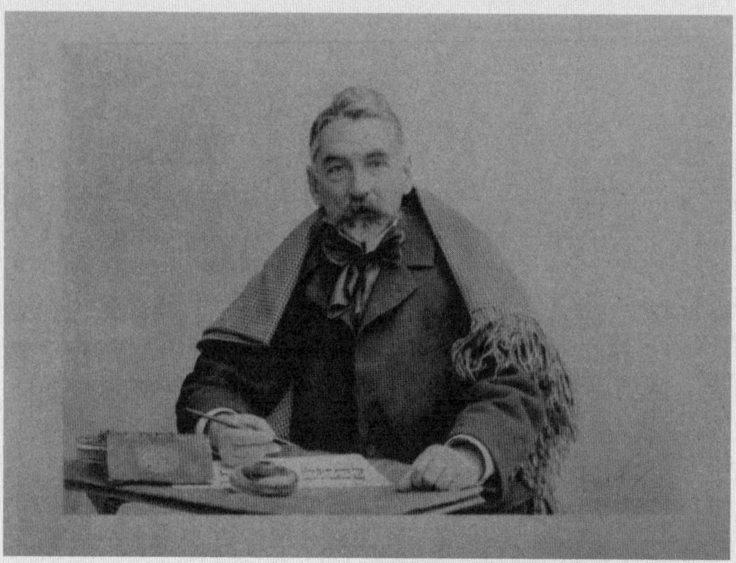

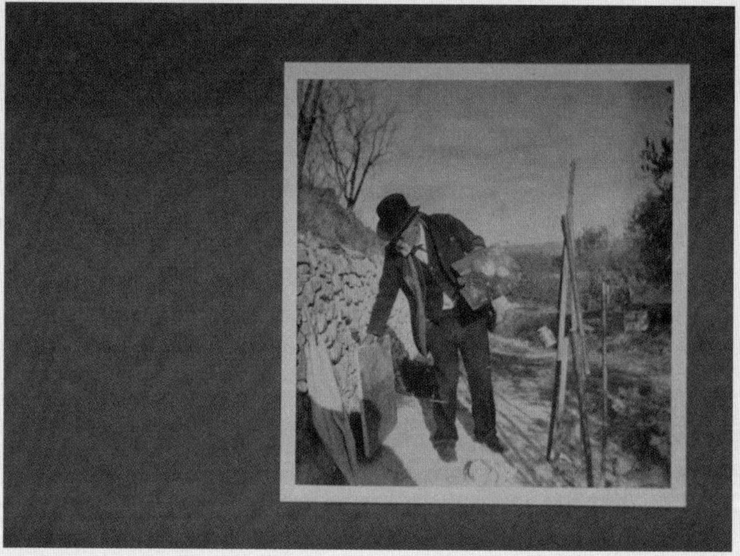

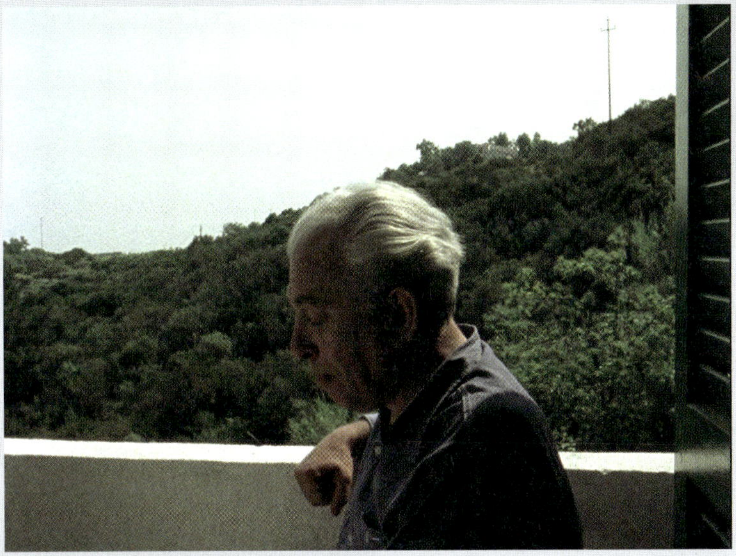

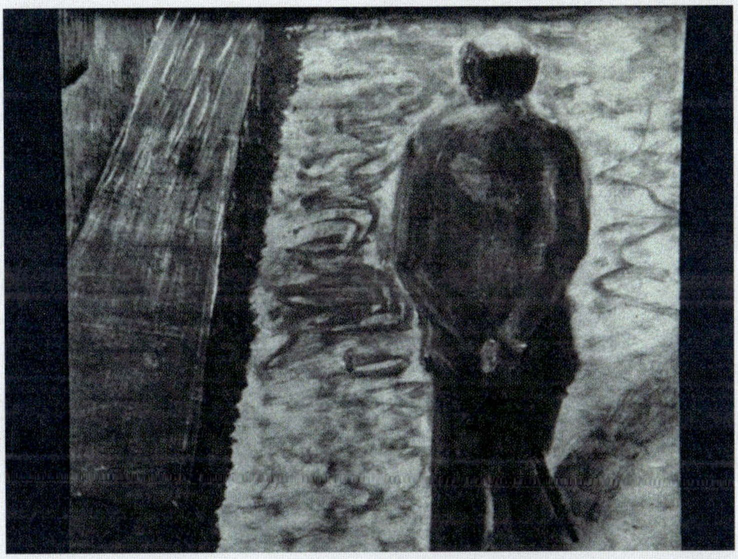

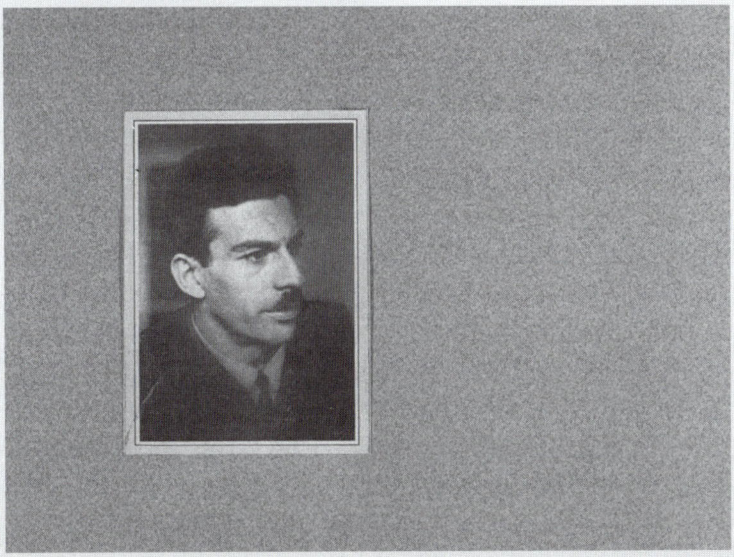

Rembert Hüser, Nikolaus Wegmann

Philologists at Work

And that people discover less and less how traditional our films are, how deeply rooted in a tradition: I just don't understand it.[1]

August 1987.

1987 is the year of Hölderlin; 1984 was the year of Kafka. There was also already a year of Corneille, a year of Brecht, one for Mallarmé; Pavese had one as well. And there will be more such years. The classics have to get moving and stay in motion. They do so by becoming films. In 1987, Jean-Marie Straub and Danièle Huillet's *The Death of Empedocles* was premiered at the Berlin Film Festival; in 1984 it was the film *Class Relations*, based upon Kafka's *Der Verschollene.*[2] Again, a film by Straub/Huillet. But not only Kafka, there were also Corneille, Brecht, Mallarmé, Pavese, Schoenberg, Bach, and several more.

These films set examples; we can learn from them: "Yesterday we watched *L'Enfant sauvage* [by François Truffaut], and because it's a beautiful, good, and clever film, it struck me that many shots could have been slightly more precise. That's what happens watching Straub. [...] When the child runs toward the river, the camera strangely approaches the riverbank. The [camera] movement should have been initiated a little earlier."[3] That a filmmaker (Farocki) observes something in another filmmaker's work (Truffaut) is not remarkable. He obviously has learned to observe as a spectator. Whoever only watches films but has seen Straub/Huillet could advance a similar argument. Straub/Huillet furnish the viewer with criteria for film viewing; they teach film. And nothing less than the basic rules of film. Yet, the two French filmmakers are not making educational films, but full-length features. To be more precise: feature films that are readings. They film the "great texts."

Reading precedes filming. Trivial though this may be, who among the filmmakers adapting literature seems to really know this? Moreover the filmmaker has to read the classics first. Yet, that is the domain of literary studies. Their reading of a text is first and foremost one of interpretation. Ever since the hermeneutics of Romanticism this has meant: reading what is not written. Around 1800, alongside the letter, the spirit was discovered. And ever

1 Jean-Marie Straub, "Gespräch mit Danièle Huillet und Jean-Marie Straub," in *Klassenverhältnisse von Danièle Huillet und Jean-Marie Straub nach dem Amerika-Roman 'Der Verschollene' von Franz Kafka*, ed. Wolfram Schütte (Frankfurt am Main: Fischer, 1984), 49.

2 First published in English as *Amerika*, subsequently republished as *The Man Who Disappeared*, *The Missing Person*, and *Lost in America*.

3 Harun Farocki, "Rückblick (1): Auszüge aus Gesprächen," Hartmut Bitomsky et al., *Filmkritk* no. 313 (January 1983): 21.

since, the spirit has been continuously rediscovered anew, whether as never-ending variations on the text's deeper meaning or as a document of an external reality that precedes the text. On the other hand, for many on the fringes of the discipline, there are new and yet traditional activities that run counter to this culture of interpretation, just as with scholarly editing. Before any interpretation, the question of the text itself arises, about its transmission, and its form. Texts do not exist in a "pure" or authentic form. A text emerges by dint of readings, based upon decisions, conjectures and emendations, even if it is part and parcel of the gesture of philological work to let the lore story decide for itself. Only that which can be proven with the "facts" of the text shall have validity.

But the hoped-for result fails to materialize. In the end of the quest there is not a single "original text," but rather the insight that a classic is at most the result of an alignment. The impression of an immutable dimension vanishes even before any philosophical-literary interpretation occurs. This becomes apparent in the case of the classic author Hölderlin and the Frankfurt Edition of D. E. Sattler. And what are the possibilities if one wants to film a text and finds oneself confronted with decisions that are difficult to verify? When one has a text at hand, but doesn't believe in unity? Without further ado, Straub/Huillet have edited the text themselves. The Frankfurt Edition of the *Empedocles* volume had yet to be published, but the editor made photocopies of the Hölderlin manuscript available to the filmmakers. Half a year later, the result of Danièle Huillet's editorial work was being discussed with Sattler.

To read: but how? In the manner of positivist edition micrology or according to speculative interpretation? Is every reading mired in this scientific-historical polemic? Or, as Nietzsche puts it, "to be able to read off a text as text without interposing an interpretation."[4] Nietzsche was indeed skeptical whether there could be a theory or even an instruction manual for such an "other" philology. But perhaps there are philological works, or readings of the classics that come close to this objective—as is the case with films by Straub/Huillet. Film critics and audiences find them troublesome. Instead of a Hölderlin that educated readers know from their schooldays, they are con-

4 Friedrich Nietzsche, *The Will to Power*, trans. Walter Kaufmann and R.J. Hollingdale (New York: Vintage Books, 1968), 266.

fronted with the classic in a form that exposes the text for what it is: a load of work. Variations, the unresolved, the open-ended—all that which in Beißner's Stuttgart edition is found exiled in the annotation apparatus, that is out of the way of the interpretative reading—are now situated where it makes sense: right in the middle. A classic on the screen that is no longer a result. The irritation is great: "the film doesn't even let me guess what Straub/Huillet had in mind with Hölderlin's fragments [...] the two directors neither offer philosophical discourses nor a drama in which different ideologies are pitted against one another."[5] Here, "with silent anger, Straub/Huillet sacrifice everything we are accustomed to from film aesthetics. With downright manic obsession, any kind of junk images have been ejected from this film. What remains are the orators, Sicily's nature, long, statuesque shots, ritualistic repetitions. Everything that was near and dear has been cut."[6] And yet, their work is not infrequently lauded in the highest terms. Despite all the objections, it seems that everyone agrees that foundation work has been executed here. "The radical boldness of Jean-Marie Straub and his partner in art Danièle Huillet is consistently breathtaking."[7] Nobody insinuates arbitrariness or dilettantism in any form.

As has been said, we can learn from Straub/Huillet. To read, for example. They modestly approach the great texts, the classics. The text is neither the playground for avant-garde film experimentation, nor mere evidence of a general theory that reads it as an expression of other intentions. With Straub-like frankness: "I'm a filmmaker, not a theorist."[8] This modesty (Huillet even sometimes uses the word humility) also means that texts are not used as message-bearers of a truth that should ultimately be evoked or visualized: "We wanted to peruse Kafka's text *Amerika* to simply peruse it."[9] There's no promise of a lofty interpretation; just respect, the feeling that every access to the text must be doubt-ridden, irrespective of how it's justified. "I think we have to strive to remain very humble not alone about what we do, but also in what we say and claim."[10] Or, with the two filmmakers' typical brevity, which risks being misconstrued by all well-read readers: "By the way, I wasn't thinking of anything during the shooting."[11] Straub/Huillet concede—as a methodological

5 Hagmut Brockmann, "Mißverständnis vom Massenmedium Film. Im Wettbewerb Filme aus der Bundesrepublik und Spanien," in *Volksblatt Berlin* (February 27, 1987): 16.

6 Dietrich Kuhlbrodt, in *Konkret*, no. 5, 1987.

7 Ponkie, "Wenn Pausen hörbar werden. Straub/Huillets Hölderlinwerk, Truebas Sexmoral und Schraders Familiendrama," in *AZ*, (February 28, 1987).

8 Barbara Bernauer, Wolfram Schütte and F.W. Vöbel, "Gespräch mit Jean-Marie Straub," in *Filmstudio*, no. 48, (January-March 1966): 6.

9 Schütte, *Klassenverhältnisse*, 45.

10 Manfred Blank, Gerhard Metz, Berthold Schweiz, Susanne and Ulrich Röckel, "Wie will ich lustig lachen, wenn alles durcheinandergeht. Danièle Huillet und Jean-Marie Straub sprechen über ihren Film *Klassenverhältnisse*," in *Filmkritik*, no. 333–4 (September-October 1984): 270.

11 Bernauer et al., "Gespräch," 6.

premise—the superiority of the text. They accept, as the philologist de Man stated with regard to his own work-attitude, an inner authority in the text. It is the working hypothesis of the philologist par excellence, even if de Man knows that it is "merely" a hypothesis, and that he actually knows better...[12] No particular subject, no characteristic interpretation of reality can measure up to what has survived throughout history, what each and every interpretation has resisted: "I think there's more to it than the petty thoughts we might have. Because whenever we come across such material, we have no clarity about it."[13]

All this must be a disappointment for those who read text and film as though they were the work of authorial intention. It is not a sophisticated program or a strictly thought-through aesthetic that is decisive here. Modesty turned into a "method" corresponds rather to the application of philological and cinematic crafts. It is thanks to this that their shooting script is a product of reading the classics. Whoever doesn't want to see "something" in a text right away needs be on their guard, however. It isn't easy to break free from that which schools and universities have taught their students ever since the dawn of the 19th century and continue to teach: to read between the lines instead of reading the lines themselves. "Spirit" instead of "letters," content instead of words and texture. Straub/Huillet have made us aware that we can read differently, that reading doesn't inevitably follow a single pattern across all historical eras. Today's reader is unfamiliar with their attitude to the text: they assume the role of a school student with regard to the text—albeit a student from a class that is no longer the norm. Contrary to that modern reading habit whereby the reader invariably interprets the text on first reading it, Straub and Huillet's initial approach to the text is to simply copy it. "The first thing I do is to start copying down [...]. I buy an exercise book and copy my book like a school student, and once I've copied it, I'm happy."[14] Still, copying does not mean mechanically making a duplicate. Rather, copying here is meant more in the tradition of the ancient didactics of reading; it is "reading with a plume in the hand." By dint of this simple manual operation, the text is not fathomed for a deeper voice: the text itself has no soul.[15] "It's a much more profane matter: it structures itself, it builds up: but

12
Cf. Stefano Rosso, "An Interview with Paul de Man," in Paul de Man, *The Resistance to Theory* (Minneapolis: University of Minnesota Press, 1986), 118.

13
Karsten Witte, "Interview [mit Danièle Huillet und Jean-Marie Straub]," in *Herzog/Kluge/Straub*, ed. Peter W. Jansen and Wolfram Schütte (Munich, Vienna: Hanser, 1976), 211.

14
Schütte, *Klassenverhältnisse*, 46.

15
Harun Farocki, "Einfach mit der Seele, das gibt es nicht. Gespräch mit Jean-Marie Straub," in *Filmkritik*, no. 317 (May 1983): 246.

then I already know where I've got to stop, what weight a block must have in relation to the preceding block and the one that follows."[16] Questions about meaning and content lose their priority. Straub and Huillet's handling of text is characterized by that monumental reading of history that Nietzsche's pupil Foucault has recommended to historians. "[...] history now organizes the document, divides it up, distributes it, orders it, arranges it in levels, establishes series, distinguishes between what is relevant and what is not, discovers elements, defines unities, describes relations."[17]

The reference point for Straub/Huillet isn't theory, however, but film tradition, for example Erich von Stroheim. Unlike any other filmmaker he has shown things, monumentally presented his cinematic objects with a sense of monumentality: "Stroheim was the greatest. Why? Because [in his films] every moment is monumental, every figure, every space."[18]

A text is anything but an accomplice to one's own intentions. According to Straub, one must engage with the text as though it was something strange after all with which we struggle. "And this strange thing must first be assembled on paper."[19] Construction of series, sequences, blocks, paragraphs, chunks—and not content, meaning, symbols, psychology, intentions—this reconstruction work on the textual fabric cannot be replaced by a congenially kindred spirit: "There's no such thing as just simply doing it with the heart and soul."[20]

And even this method, consisting in a reserve with regard to an interpretative access to the text, (interpretation: what is that?) can be double-checked. For one can never be sure not to impose interpretations onto a text, or to read clichés into it. That's why Straub and Huillet work as a team; one controls and corrects the other: "I fight with my wife, in other words, the script emerges by dint of a dialogue with her: alternately, either she or I assume the role of the spectator. For me, to write a shooting script means fighting against myself, against my own stereotyped-ideas. Hence, the ideas I had at the outset are rarely usable, for they are mostly clichés."[21] The yardstick requirement for a successful shooting script is the frame, as Straub calls it,

16 Schütte, *Klassenverhältnisse*, 46.

17 Michel Foucault, *The Archaeology of Knowledge*, trans. A.M. Sheridan Smith (New York: Pantheon Books, 1972), 6.

18 Blank et al., "Wie will ich lustig lachen," 273.

19 Farocki, "Einfach mit der Seele," 243.

20 Farocki, 242.

21 Gino Doni, "Ein Drehbuch ist nichts. Es ist dazu da, um weggeworfen zu werden. Ein Gespräch mit Jean-Marie Straub," *Filmreport*, 19 (1969): 2.

"a structure that is thoroughly empty, so that I'm sure that whenever I shoot I'm absolutely unable to have any more intentions. I constantly strive to eliminate all intentions—expressive intentions."[22]

This demands constant exertion. The usual reading in quest of meaning, which has become the cultural norm in the film or the book medium, can only be eliminated through repeated retractions and deletions: "We kept on deleting until we no longer had any scenes or episodes left—just what Stockhausen referred to as *Points*."[23] Speakers and actors, too, have to pull their weight. The acquired "meaning-laden weighty" speech they have learned in their training should not be expressed as the result of an undesirable interpretation. This is their reason for working with amateurs, often those with German as a second language. They seem to find it easier to achieve the speech level that is characteristic of Straub/Huillet's films. Whatever articulation and accentuation is added to a particular sound, a word, or a sentence—and what mostly serves as a directive for interpretation—comes across as strange in their films. Strange because the usual expressive quality of speaking aloud is absent here. The way they speak, however, doesn't in any way come across as sterile or monotonous. Rather, each speaker is supposed to incorporate their own speech-patterns, rhythm, and modulation ability—and not their own interpretation or a conventionalized psychology of expression—into the shooting script. Just as a musician brings his musicality to a score. "We determine the pauses and stresses with each of them, and then— once we've worked out the score—Danièle re-types the texts [...] on a sheet of paper, and it then visually resembles a poem, with line breaks and so on. This poem is then learned and reeled off by the performers, recited, performed using variations in movements, tone, posture."[24] A goal that not infrequently involves an enormous number of re-runs: "always let things happen slowly."[25]

And what if the spoken score also went through this joint process with the actors, if the narrators' own modulations were written down? In that case, the shooting script has already served its purpose: "It's there to be tossed away [...] It's merely a guideline. I never pick up the shooting script while I'm filming."[26]

22 "Tribüne des Jungen Deutschen Films. III. Jean-Marie Straub," *Filmkritik*, no. 119 (November 1966): 608.

23 Straub, "Tribüne des Jungen Deutschen Films," 607.

24 Schütte, *Klassenverhältnisse*, 55–56.

25 Wilhelm Roth, Günther Pflaum, "Gespräch mit Jean-Marie Straub und Danièle Huillet," *Filmkritik*, no. 194 (February 1973): 71.

26 Straub, "Ein Drehbuch ist nichts," 1.

The second part of the shooting script scarcely differs. In the same way that everything is structured "with a plume in the hand," that the manner of speaking and gestures are initially determined on paper, the camera settings and the respective placements for those in the shot are also determined in advance; "the dramatic space is [also] organized in advance."[27] A sketchbook is used for this purpose; it records the camera trajectories for sequence shots. And here again, this sought-after precision that ought to be a little more systematic without ever becoming in itself a system: "So I tried to invent something systematic, a possible point where the camera remains fixed for the entire sequence. This doesn't mean that it's nailed down to that spot; the camera position can vary slightly from one shot to the next [...] And what I then do is discover series [...] and then I have to vary within these series [...] If you lack imagination, then you'll have nothing on screen."[28]

27
Filmbüro Hamburg, Seminar in the Filmhaus with Jean-Marie Straub and Danièle Huillet, protocol by Rembert Hüser, March 2–22, 1987.

28
Farocki, "Einfach mit der Seele," 243–244.

29
Schütte, *Klassenverhältnisse*, 52.

Notwithstanding this exceptionally precise, disciplined creative process, there is room for coincidence. "Perfection and coincidence are not mutually exclusive. If anything, the power of coincidence only seems to unfold in what is firmly constructed: "If we shoot a shot twenty times [...] and we aim to achieve a steady rhythm both in the text and in the movements and also in the relations between text and movements [...] then coincidence will invariably fall our way."[29] It will fall our way—and not be arbitrarily brought about. Whether it occurs or not seems to be a matter of attitude to the text.

The choice of filming-location is equally determined by diligence and precise craftsmanship. Locations are selected in terms of their coherence. Coherence entails being equally suitable for image and sound. The benchmark of coherence (implicitly) demarcates, differentiates itself from the typical norm of expressive cinema, in which the sound is dubbed and in which only beautiful shots are sought. Once a location has been determined, the circle of specialists expands. Other craftsmen are called upon to assess the project in terms of their individual specialist fields and to put their experience to the cause. Cameramen and sound-engineers are called upon: "Louis had already had time to test the acoustics of the amphitheater a year beforehand, when we had him come from Paris to see and hear our amphitheater—for we were greatly apprehensive. [...] Louis asked if we would envisage filming elsewhere. 'No,' we told him. 'Well then,' he said, 'we'll have to solve the difficulties as they come along."[30] The entire working process of a Straub/Huillet film is organized strictly according to the division of labor, "never undertake a job that others can do better"[31]— work is not simply delegated, however. Whoever collaborates on the film is one of the greats in their field. And yet, their work is rigorously set out: "We usually come up with solutions for the image. In other words, when the camera crew shows up, they don't have much scope for any great ideas. Each individual shot belongs to a whole, something the camera crew often forgets."[32] And yet, notwithstanding this tight framework, the skills of these specialists remain discernable as their own signature.

But how does all this artisanal diligence yield a film? In itself, the reduction and compression work does not create a "whole." What ensures the cohesion of the individual work steps? It cannot be a substantive moment. Those radical political statements that Straub/Huillet make at press conferences at most play a marginal role in their film work. Rather, their political rhetoric is a byword for the pathos of collective work:

> If now and then I feel discouraged, if I'm not quite sure that I'm strong enough and sufficiently smart to hold out till the end, I tell myself that if Mao and his peasants managed to bring about such upheaval in their country, it would be the height of failure if we couldn't succeed in completing a film.[33]

It would never occur to Straub/Huillet to compromise their cinematic work on account of imposing a political intention. "There's not one single situation [...] and not one single relation between people which we hadn't experienced, [...]. But we didn't interfere there. That's the difference between what *we* are doing and what Godard is doing."[34] Still, the work process itself sheds lights on the question of the *oeuvre*: "Using location sound is a method to which we're very attached and which is very decisive for us."[35] For Straub/Huillet, location sound correlates space (visual shot, cf. sketchbook) and dialogue (score, cf. shooting script). Ultimately, it combines text and image, forging unity by dint of a manual process, and not through meaning. One can discern successful takes during the film shoot by ear: "If

30
Danièle Huillet, "Appunti sul giornale di lavorazione di Gregory," *Filmkritik*, no. 225 (September 1975): 402. English translation from: *Danièle Huillet, Jean-Marie Straub: Writings*, ed. Sally Shafto, Katherine Pickard (New York: Sequence Press, 2016), 283.

31
Straub, Filmbüro Hamburg, 1987.

32
Straub, 1987.

33
Huillet, "Appunti," 411.

34
Blank et al., "Wie will ich lustig lachen," 270.

35
Witte, *Herzog/Kluge/Straub*, 213.

we shoot thirty-two times, there might be five [takes] that were complete [...] not only do we listen while shooting, but Danièle also listens. Alone at first, while I'm preparing the upcoming shot, she sits apart with the sound technician. They listen to the last take together. [...] Then it's my turn. If we decide, we'll stop at that point; if we have the two good takes or if we can make another better one [...], then we do it or not. But before we do that, we listen."[36]

Their specific treatment of sound follows in the tradition of the great film realists (Renoir), who attached importance to their own sound direction. With Straub/Huillet/Hochet, Godard's dream of transferring sound-takes without having to resort to mixing has meanwhile practically become a reality: in the Hölderlin film, the direct sound from the individual takes can basically be played in unmodified form. Each sound signal that appears in a recording comes from just one single go. If the voice of the actor playing Empedocles originated off-screen in the long shot of nature, it was recorded simultaneously with the sounds of nature one hears. Off-screen sounds and loops are treated just like synchronous sounds and are not added afterward. The separation which technology facilitates—somewhat similar to seeking out "beautiful (sound) loops" for the "beautiful shots"—has no place here. Straub/Huillet's special editing technique has radicalized this process even further. Sound and image tracks are edited with hard cuts; overlapping and crossfading are ruled out. Straub described the result for ZDF [German public-service broadcaster]: "The text spoken in the film is the complete and original French text by Pierre Corneille. The actors read, memorized, practiced, and rehearsed it for three months and it was then—recited entirely by heart—recorded over four weeks in the same place and time, always simultaneously with the image."[37] Unity no longer guarantees transcendental meaning, but rather a coherence among the techniques used. "If at any moment you keep your eyes and ears open for all of this, you'll find the film even more exciting and notice that everything here is information—even the pure sensual reality of the space that the performers leave vacant at the end of each act."[38]

Through their emphasis on film craft Straub/Huillet have repeatedly spoken out against the cinema of expression

36 Roth, "Gespräch," 75.

37 Jean-Marie Straub, "Einführung zur Fernsehaufführung (*Othon*). Jean-Marie Straubs *Othon*," *Filmkritik*, no. 169 (January 1971): 16.

38 Straub, "Einführung zur Fernsehaufführung," 16.

and content. And yet, there is no film without interpretation. Even Straub/Huillet interpret—intentionally and unintentionally. It begins with the question of the version of the text and continues with the simple fact that as filmmakers they make "images." But what does a film by Straub/Huillet show? It is easier to say what it doesn't: there is no dramaturgy of meaning in their films that wants to enact a reality "pre" text and film. That is exactly why audiences and film critics find them so difficult. "Film is [...] not there in order to show anything [...] in order to express anything, [...] in order to demonstrate something. These are all just pitfalls"[39] which the filmmaker has to shun.

In our eyes, what distinguishes their films is their anachronistic way of looking at the text. There are strong grounds for arguing that the exceptional level of craftsmanship that Straub/Huillet demand in the making of each of their films, and which they uncompromisingly realize, ultimately discovers something which "modern" readers and viewers don't (any longer) perceive: "indifference of the text with regard to its referential meaning."[40] This is an essential quality of a text, in that it explains why a text is constantly being reproduced in new interpretations. That which produces a text and which nevertheless exists regardless of any reference to a reality is its grammar. Even the most non-grammatical text/film is just a divergence from grammar... In order to be able to perceive this general quality, however, a text must first be kept free of any referentiality. We need to differentiate how a text is perceived and how it is interpreted. Everyday experience won't suffice in this regard. It merely camouflages the incompatibility between grammar and meaning.[41] To look at a text not only from the perspective of its meaning, imposes extreme discipline during the film production phase and also demands unusually hard work for audiences. Are the films by Straub/Huillet a school for reading and viewing? At least if you take Straub's statements literally, because had he not become a filmmaker, then, according to his answer to the corresponding question, he would have become a grammar teacher. Grammar teacher.[42] Straub and Huillet's interest in film, in text, and in the pedagogical-didactic commitment happen to coincide. It would be a misunderstanding to deduce their motives from autobiographical "anguish" or related intentions: "to implicate the artist in

39 Straub, "Tribüne des Jungen Deutschen Films," 608.

40 Paul de Man, "Promises (Social Contract)," in *Allegories of Reading. Figural Language in Rousseau, Nietzsche, Rilke, and Proust* (New Haven and London: Yale University Press, 1979), 268.

41 de Man, *Allegories*, 269.

42 Barbara Bronnen, "Gespräch mit Danièle Huillet und Jean-Marie Straub," in *Die Filmemacher. Der neue deutsche Film nach Oberhausen*, ed. Barbara Bronnen and Corinna Brocher (Munich, Gütersloh, Vienna: Bertelsmann, 1973), 41.

the oeuvre belongs to the 19th century; that has nothing to do with me."[43] The "content" that is most important to them is the reality of the text and of the film. And that only reveals itself to those who can read and see. To read correctly, whether a book or a film, does not just mean to read without interpretation. It is these very rules of the text that impose the question of interpretation, of meaning—(at times) against the filmmakers' intentions: "but we don't interpret anything."[44] A reading that is not (also) designed for meaning doesn't seem possible. Without a reference, the text would remain potentially open for meaning, open to every conceivable meaning that only a reader with a thousand eyes could read—concurrently. Limited skills or cultural habits preclude that. Even two images reduced to zero expression, even arbitrarily juxtaposed camera shots, trigger the viewer's association of meanings and, according to Béla Balázs, invariably seem to have to impart something—and not: all sorts of things.[45]

This is also the case for Straub/Huillet when they watch their own films. Meaning is also realized behind the back of the filmmaker: "I believe that all this only came into the film by coincidence, a kind of symbolism that I didn't deploy intentionally."[46] No "content," yet a theme now emerges: "There is no theme, initially. We seek out something and a theme only exists once the film has been shot; we only discover it once the film is finished."[47] Still, there are equally explicit, deliberate gestures of meaning, such as in the Hölderlin film (*The Death of Empedocles*), where to accompany the line, "Is there no avenger?," a knife is pulled out of the earth, or in the Kafka film (*Class Relations*), where a Bach cantata is used to introduce the Nature Theater of Oklahoma. The intended goal of getting by without interpretation can thus only count as a fictitious threshold. Rather, it is a matter of protecting oneself against the excess of meaning (that is presented) "To do something that is contrary to the norm, the opposite of (...) what society does. That means no inflation."[48] And that equally means being able to deal with the interpretations implicitly or explicitly offered by Straub/Huillet.

43 Blank et al., "Wie will ich lustig lachen," 270.

44 Blank et al., 272.

45 Béla Balázs, *Early Film Theory—Visible Man and The Spirit of Film*, trans. Rodney Livingstone, ed. Erica Carter (New York, Oxford: Berghahn Books, 2011), 125.

46 Bernauer et al., "Gespräch," 6.

47 Bernauer et al., 8.

48 Blank et al., "Wie will ich lustig lachen," 273.

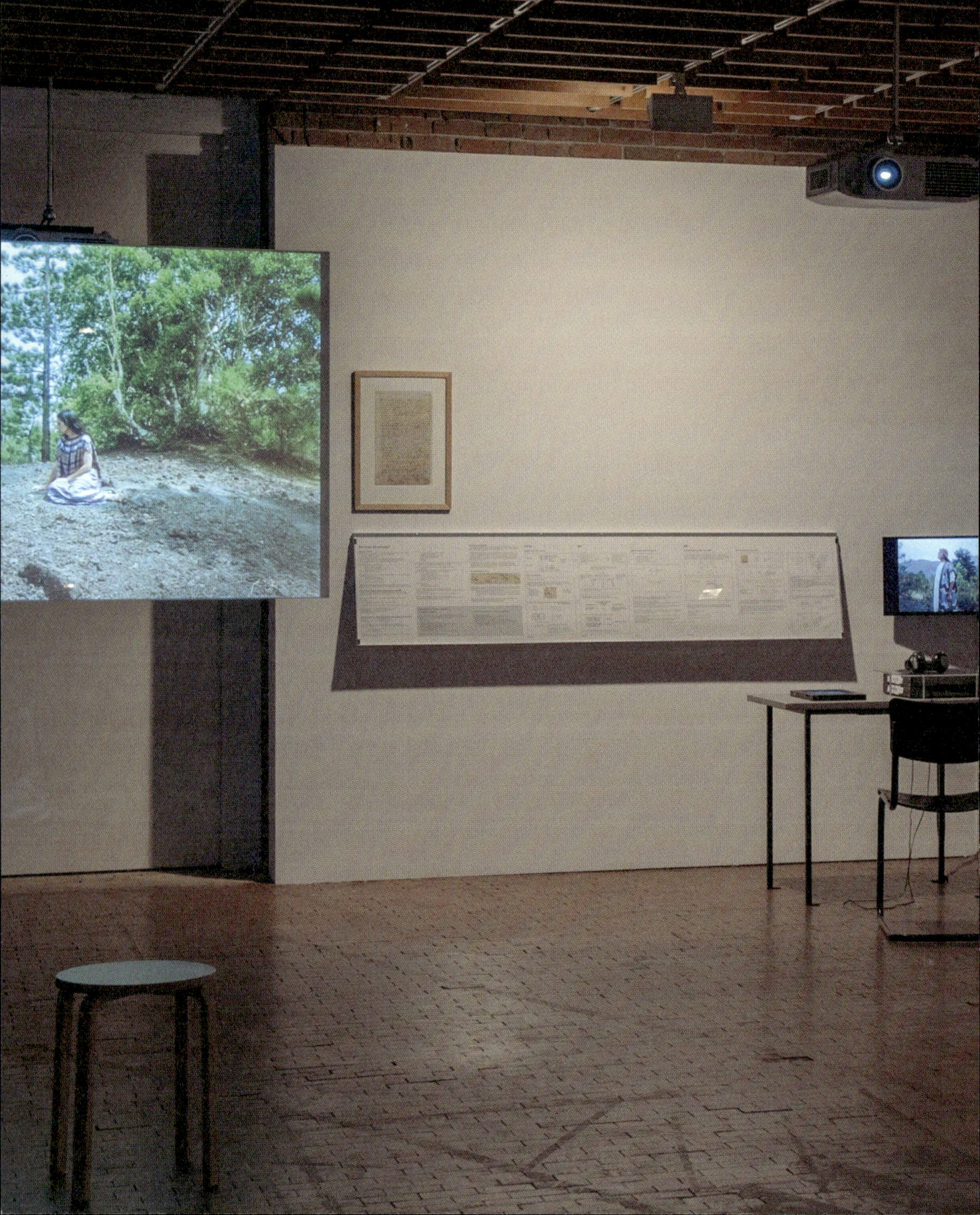

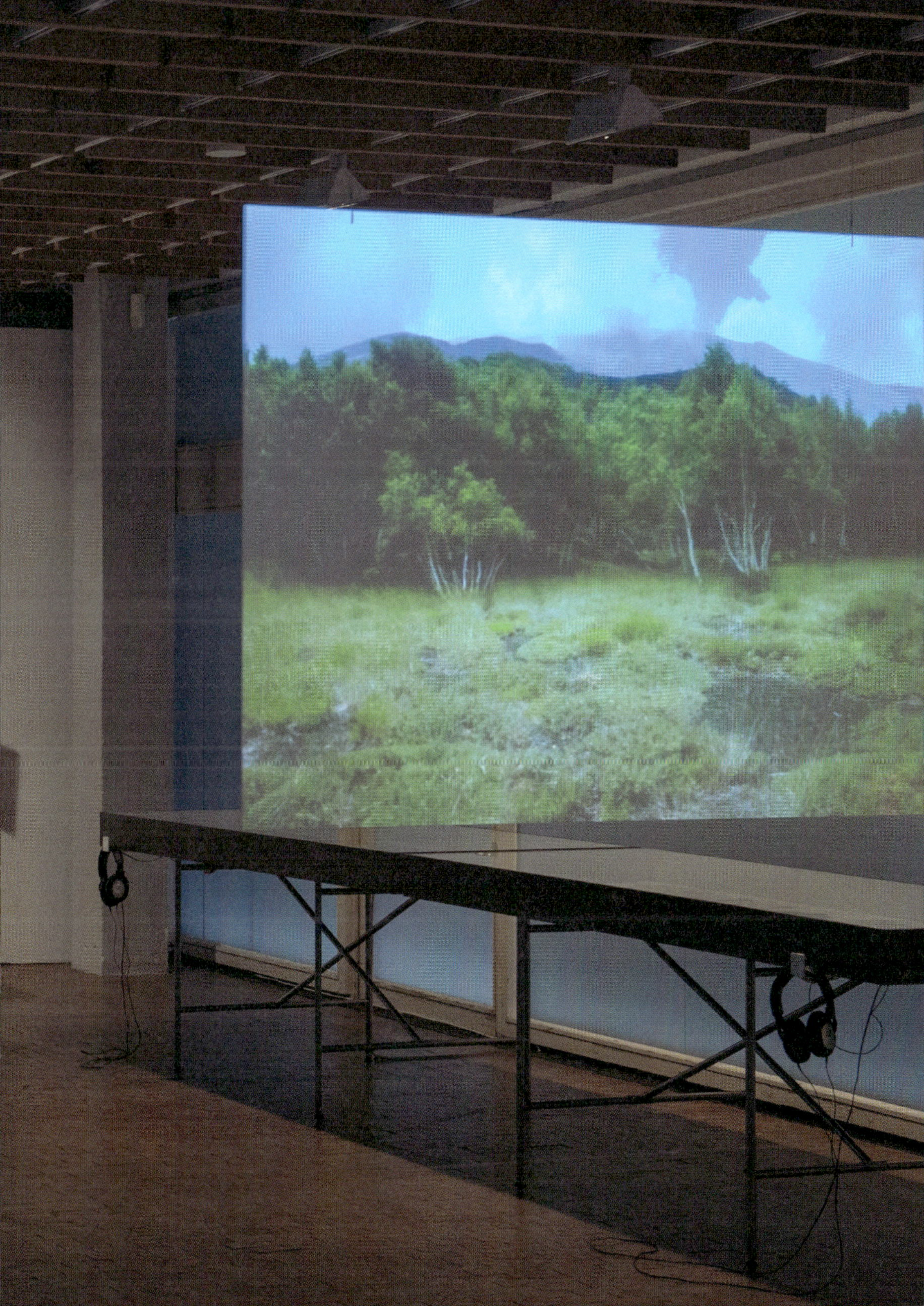

Barbara Ulrich

"HAST DU NICHT ALLES MIR GESAGT?" AND HÖLDERLIN'S *NATIVE REVERSAL* AS RESPONSE

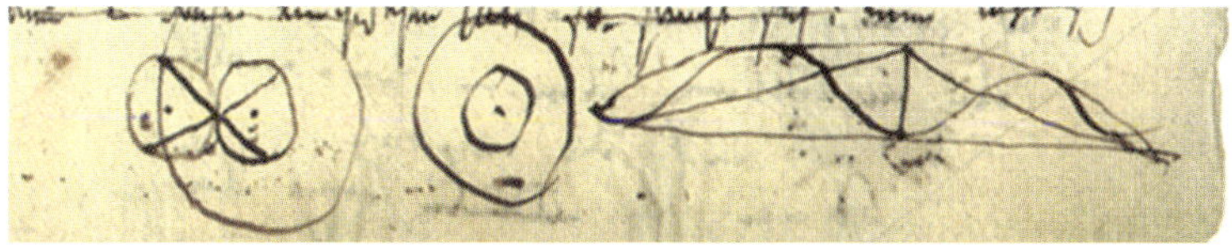

Johann Christian Friedrich Hölderlin was born in Nürtingen, Germany, on the river Neckar on 20 March 1770 and died on 7 June 1843. His contemporaries turned their backs on him, transforming their incomprehension of his work into a diagnosis of the author's madness. But Nietzsche, still a student in 1861, admired him and was among the very first to grasp his magnitude. As for Heidegger, at the end of the 1930s, in *Beiträge*, he writes, "The historical destiny of philosophy culminates in knowledge of the necessity to create a hearing for the words of Hölderlin."[1] Nothing less! In 1990, the Straubs edited and kept secret an unusual object whose discovery in 2017 pushes me, through the question posed in it, to try to understand the major and still under-discussed importance of Hölderlin for comprehending our so-called post-modern world and the healing of its wounds.

Hölderlin wrote poems, some theoretical essays, and an epistolary novel, *Hyperion*, doubtless his best known work besides the verse from the hymn *Patmos,* "Where there is danger, grows / also what saves," which was already rediscovered thirty years ago, I think, for an advertisement for Électricité de France or a toothpaste company. When he completed the writing of *Hyperion* in 1797, in a letter Hölderlin announced his intention of pursuing the composition of a *Trauerspiel*, whose hero would be a Sicilian from the 5th century B.C., the philosopher, and doctor Empedocles. Hölderlin did not wish to write a (Greek) tragedy, but something equivalent to one for his own time, using new forms and new subjects closer to our own modern understanding. Despite three incomplete drafts and a theoretical text, he never managed to finish the work, and its abandonment marks the shift that would distance him from paths he had explored up until then with his friends Hegel and Schelling. One thinks of their years together at the Tübinger Stift in the middle of the French Revolution. The first sketches of German Idealism were born out of their friendship and proximity. They tried to understand the workings of the mechanisms of the world, discovered in the past, observed in the present, and upon which they wanted to

1 Martin Heidegger, *Contributions to Philosophy (Of the Event)*, trans. Richard Rojcewicz and Daniela Vallega-Neu (Bloomington: Indiana University Press, 2012), 334.

act for a better future. While still maintaining this ambition, Hölderlin would definitively move away from their common base. In the theoretical text, "The Basis of Empedocles," written just prior to the third and final draft of the play, he performs, as he would later say in "Remarks on 'Antigone,'" a "reversal of all modes of representation and forms," a form of the *native reversal*[2] or, to put it differently, of the paradigms determining how we perceive the world. This is enormous and, to return to a metaphor of Malraux's, it is as if a fish were suddenly to see its own aquarium. And moreover, as if he were to see other aquariums and other fish.[3]

HOMMAGE À VERNON, "HAVE YOU NOT TOLD ME EVERYTHING?"

For decades, Hölderlin held a central place in the work of Danièle Huillet and Jean-Marie Straub. Their two films, *The Death of Empedocles* and *Black Sin*, based on the first and third versions of the mourning-play[4] (see timeline p. 144), are well-known. It is also well-known that excerpts from both films are "quoted" in later Straub films. Completely unknown, however, was the existence of the film *Hommage à Vernon*, whose unexpected discovery in the spring of 2017 raised exciting questions.[5]

What do we know about this work? An initial viewing revealed that it contains 17 outtakes of the 28th shot from *Black Sin* compiled onto one reel of 35mm positive film without color timing and a reel of unmixed magnetic sound with a total running time of 10'18". It contains the end of the dialogue between Manes (on screen, played by Howard Vernon) and Empedocles (off screen):

> M: How goes it with us? Do you see it so certainly?
> E: You tell me, you who see all!
> M: Let us be still, o son! and always learn.
> E: You used to teach me, learn today from me.
> M: Have you not told me everything?

There is nothing remotely comparable to this in the entire work of Straub and Huillet. Presumably spliced together at the editing table after the completion of the last of the film's four edited versions, the two reels were deposited by Straub and Huillet on 6 November 1990 in the archive of

2
Friedrich Hölderlin, "Remarks on 'Antigone,'" *Friedrich Hölderlin: Essays and Letters on Theory*, trans. Thomas Pfau (Albany: State University of New York Press, 1988), 114. One of Hölderlin's key concepts, the *Vaterländische Umkehr* or native reversal, elsewhere translated as national reversal or patriotic reversal. The latter terms emphasize an exterior entity: a nation or country with which one identifies or that represents an ideal toward which the return should be directed. Prior to any and all abstractions and generalizations, however, *Vaterland*—fatherland or home country—very concretely refers to the time and place within whose spiritual and cultural laws one is born and which determine our interior sensibility, our way of being in the world. Hölderlin is very real and very concrete. The native reversal is a complex and ambiguous concept the poet uses in his late work—for example, at the end of "Remarks on 'Antigone.'" The understanding of this concept has divided and continues to divide the highly divergent estimations of Hölderlin's work. We are attempting an interpretation in relation to the film *Hommage à Vernon*.

3
See Jean-Marie Straub's film *L'Aquarium et la Nation* (2015).

4
Translator's Note: In a footnote to his translation of *The Death of Empedocles*,

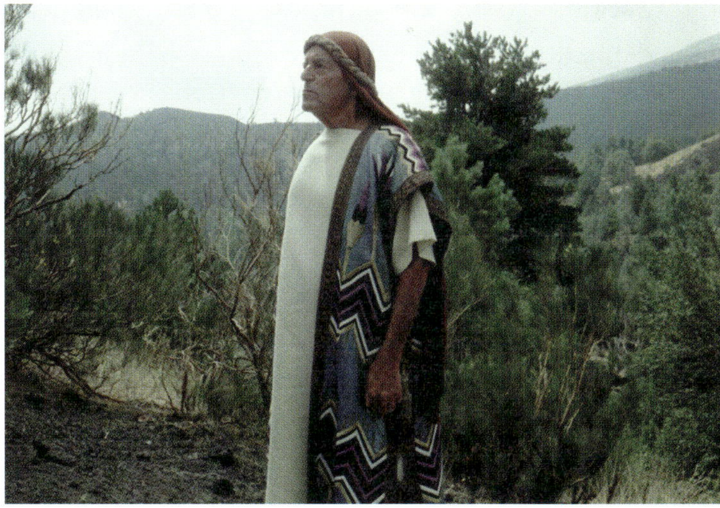

Howard Vernon *in Hommage à Vernon.*

Arsenal cinema in Berlin[6] under the title *Hommage à Vernon* where they, as far as is known, remained untouched until the spring of 2017. Jean-Marie Straub, whom I immediately asked about the film, only said, "Howard was always very kind to us." An unusual answer, why bury an *homage* in an archive? There isn't the slightest trace in Danièle Huillet's notebooks and none of the people I could ask had heard of this work. There must be another reason and the answer must mean something different.

We find a clue in an interview from 1988 in which Jean-Marie Straub says, "Empedocles' charm in the third version is different and I don't know what attracted us to him. Maybe I will know when the editing is finished. Maybe I'll never know."[7] And when the editing was finished... they responded with *Hommage à Vernon*! What does the existence of this film mean? Where is its place?

What was it about Hölderlin that attracted the filmmakers? The first and most well-known answer is that he drafted what Straub calls, following Bertaux, the "communist utopia" that Empedocles sustains in the first film. This is the promise of a possible, coming, peaceful, and joyful coexistence of humans on earth, and even more, the renewed reconciliation of humans with nature in all of its aspects. In my opinion, this is also the deepest concern of all of Straub and Huillet's work. If it is correct to assume that any major work grows out of and is sustained by a single, autonomous, hidden leitmotif that also provides it direction,

David Farrell Krell explains his choice to translate *Trauerspiel* as "mourning-play": "The German word *Trauerspiel* may most often be taken as synonymous with *Tragödie*. Yet because mourning, *die Trauer*, constitutes such an important motif for Hölderlin's work, from his early novel *Hyperion*, through his drama *Der Tod des Empedokles*, to his late hymns, it seems best to use the English word *tragedy* only when its German cognate appears. I accept the risk of offending the English/American ear with the more literal *mourning-play* for *Trauerspiel*." David Farrell Krell, Preface to Friedrich Hölderlin, *The Death of Empedocles* (Albany: State University of New York Press, 2008), vii.

5
The print was noticed during preparations for the exhibition and retrospective "Sagen Sie's den Steinen/Tell it to the Stones" at Akademie der Künste, Berlin. An earlier draft of the present text was prepared for this exhibition.

6
Today known as Arsenal–Institute for Film and Video Art, in 1990 it was operating under the name, Freunde der deutschen Kinemathek (Friends of the German Cinematheque).

7
Quoted in "Le plus et le moins," an article signed by Jean-Marie Straub, in *Pardo News* (Festival Newsletter of the Locarno Film Festival), August 7, 1989.

then we could say the leitmotif of Straub-Huillet's work is the demand that the coexistence of human beings and that which they produce and construct, in the broadest sense: culture, should be an answer corresponding to and worthy of that which precedes us when we come into the world and that surrounds us, meaning: nature—the complex and wonderful micro- and macrocosmic organization from which we originate and of which our earth is one of its most beautiful gems.

In their multifaceted political, psychological, aesthetic, and historical aspects, all of Straub and Huillet's films can be understood as variations of this basic theme and demand. This is an initial response to the question regarding the importance of Hölderlin's work, it offers a site and a home to Straub and Huillet's artistic and personal leitmotif.

TIMELINE:
HÖLDERLIN – STRAUB/HUILLET – EMPEDOCLES

The Hölderlinian "Empedocles"

Hölderlin finishes *Hyperion* and writes a "modern mourning play." The model for the hero is the Greek doctor, seer, and philosopher Empedocles who lived in Sicily in the 4th century B.C. and committed suicide in the flames of Etna. Different stages:

1797	*Empedocles*, Ode
1797	*Frankfurter Plan (Frankfurt plan)*
1797/98	Work on the first version of the mourning play
1799	Abandonment of work on the first version and beginning of the second version
1799	Abandonment of work on the second version
1799	"Basis of Empedocles" and draft of the third version Development of the first act of the third version
1800	Abandonment of the third version This ends with the draft of the final chorus of the first act, "New World."

There is no finalized version of the planned mourning play.

The Hölderlinian "Empedocles" in
the Films of Straub-Huillet

Early reading of *Hyperion*, says Straub.

1987 *The Death of Empedocles*, based on the first version of the mourning play

1989 *Black Sin*, based on the third version

1989 *Hommage à Vernon*, outtakes of shot 28 from *Black Sin*

1999 *Cézanne*, inclusion of shots 34–37, 43 and 127 from *The Death of Empedocles*

2015 Shot 127 from *The Death of Empedocles* becomes the fifth act of *Communists*. The 30th shot from *Black Sin* becomes the sixth and final act of *Communists* with only two words: "New World."

HÖLDERLIN AND EMPEDOCLES

We know that Hölderlin himself worked on the subject of Empedocles for many years. It gave him trouble because, in the chosen subject matter, he first discovered a problem that could perhaps be called his own leitmotif. For years, together in debates with his friends Hegel and Schelling —and Fichte, he had tried to find an answer to the defining questions of his era concerning the relationships of nature and culture, unity and multiplicity, absolutism and contingency, and God and man in extenso, as well as the question of the relativity of perception and the possibility of objective truth. This intellectual exercise, nourished by the soil of the speculative piety of Württemberg, was initiated and challenged by the immediate political reality of the French Revolution and its promises, of the resulting "terreur," and of the massive presence of the hero Napoleon, in whom Hegel saw the personification of the world spirit on horseback whereas Beethoven furiously erased the dedication of "Eroica" after his hero proclaimed himself emperor. The idea of the harmonic coexistence of enlightened minds in a just community—which was utopic (having not yet found its place, its topos) in Hölderlin's time and remains so today—is seeking the laws for its possible realization.

Empedocles is also a hero, a Greek hero, and Hölderlin, who wanted to compose a modern mourning-play, was looking to give him character traits corresponding to his own time. What was paradigmatic in the late 18th century age of Enlightenment and which went unquestioned, since its historical origins were in a powerful connection of Christian dogma with Platonic ideas, was the conviction of the superiority of mind over matter, of the world of ideas over concrete *Dasein*, of the general over the specific, as well as the moral, judgmental, and evaluative interconnection that the mind, generality, nature, and ideas are "good," while material, specificity, culture, and concrete life here in the world are "bad." Equally important is the idea that the progress of reason and science automatically lead to an improvement of human society and its relationships.

Just like the hero Napoleon promised to free France from the shackles of political feudalism and the straitjacket of religion, to lead the *citoyens* into the promised land of liberty, equality, and fraternity, Empedocles announces to his people in Agrigento that it is now time to break out of a limited life of narrow circumstances. Hölderlin (also) means his homeland in Württemberg, he means the shackles of the dusty theology under which he suffered in Tübingen, and he means ossified authorial structures, "This is the time of kings no more," Empedocles states very clearly.

And yet, what took place concretely in the neighboring country? The dream was over and the revolution devoured its children. Was this a historical accident or a structural malfunction, which is to say a fundamental impossibility? What had to be rethought if the failure of the revolution was not a historical—meaning a punctual and therefore avoidable—accident, but that it meant something different and deeper?

Hölderlin left the first version of his dramatic text incomplete and began a second, which, however, he quickly aborted. As if to gain distance, he set himself to writing a theoretical text, "The Basis of Empedocles." In this text, it became clear to Hölderlin that he was dealing not with an avoidable accident, but with a structural impossibility, and it is here that he lays the basis in it for the native reversal, that which saves, because it grows alongside danger. One can wonder why, after this fundamental text, Hölderlin once again began a dramatic version that nevertheless, through its predefined contents—Empedocles and the suicide on Etna—could not integrate what is already acknowledged and formulated theoretically in "The Basis of Empedocles." Near the end of the third version stands the question, "Have you not told me everything?" The answer from Hölderlin/Empedocles is, "O no!"

If the reversal of the highest ideas emerged in concrete terror (exemplary in the French Revolution), not through an accident of history but out of ignorance of fundamental laws of nature, then this must be recognized so that it is not repeated... since it continues to be repeated again and again. There appears to be a kind of "curse" blocking the "good" from establishing itself.

Or, translated into the terminology of the Straub-Huillet leitmotif, mechanisms seem to be at play that apparently impede our human understanding and conduct—culture—from being "good," and "beautiful" and "brilliant" like that which we have been given: a starry night, a flower, or an ant hill, or the migratory patterns of birds.

Why do we destroy so much and why have we made so little progress in the pacification of our relationships since the beginning of the world? Why does the dream escape us and what have we so far not understood?

Let's try to discover what Hölderlin saw and announced between 1798 and 1800, "Have you not told me everything?"

HÖLDERLIN'S ATTEMPTS AT EMPEDOCLES

a) In the first draft, Empedocles is living in the gardens of Agrigento, loved and admired by the people and in intimate communion with nature and the gods. This status intoxicates him and he begins to take himself for a god. As soon as he declares this publicly, the spiritual luster, the halo that made the citizens see him as an exceptional being, disappears. He is no more than a human among humans. He suffers terribly and does not know what to do—live like this from now on? He cannot bear the thought and he has only one desire, which is to return to the earlier, fusional state—proximity and intimacy with the gods. But that is now only possible through death, suicide on Etna. Here is how this situation looks:

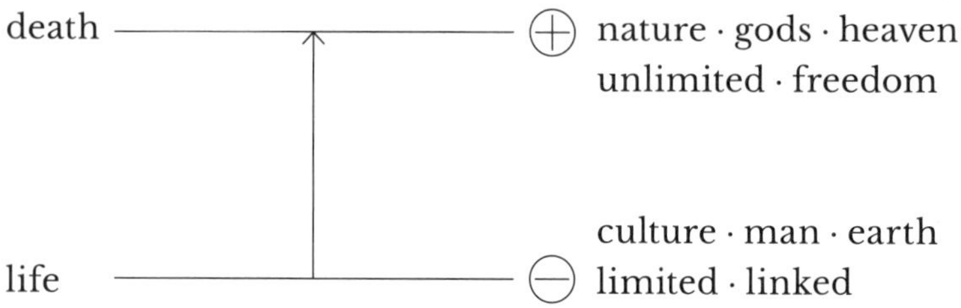

The diagram employs a "less/more" paradigm of bivalence, which was, culturally, very powerful in Hölderlin's time and still is today in our own since it is one of the bases of our perception. In Hölderlin's time, one often looked back to Ancient Greece, in relation to which and to whose unrivaled excellence one felt "less." This is a look backward of "less than what is" toward "the more that was."

8
A book devoted to this fundamental yet under examined question has just been published, Clément Layet, *Hölderlin, la démesure et le vivant* (Paris: Vrin, 2020).

But this paradigm of bivalence also produces the opposite movement of "less than what is" toward "more that should be," providing the basic impulse to all educational movements, systems of philosophic and religious salvation, and therefore to all holy wars.

Although opposites, if one draws these two movements on a temporal axis, the paralyzing "backward" and the militant "forward" are the same in their affirmation of the bivalent dichotomy and desire to leave the inclined plane of less-toward-more, of limited toward unlimited, of subjugation toward freedom. This also means, from culture toward nature. See Empedocles.

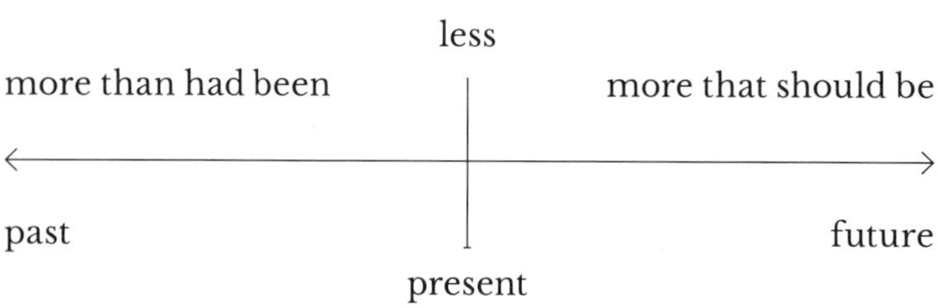

Empedocles is therefore perfectly integrated in his time, but his trajectory does not satisfy his author. We are in 1799.

b) Since "The Basis of Empedocles" is a fundamental, theoretical text seeking to establish the rules behind the world's laws of motion—which, being universally valid, are even meaningful for the construction of a mourning-play—Hölderlin poses the question at the beginning: How does it happen that a unity (or purity: unmixed) can split itself into a multiplicity and in this manner launch a movement?[8] He says that through the initial "excess of intensity,"[9] the "conflict has arisen, that the tragic ode conjures up at the very outset in order to depict what is pure."[10] He then goes on to describe the resulting movement.

It is born from the encounter on a line of two different principles he calls "pure spirit" and "consciousness, reflection, or spiritual sensuality."[11] They meet and then separate but are transformed. A bit later in the essay, these two principles, whose characteristics are strictly opposite, are called "the general" and "the particular" and, later still, "nature" and "culture/art." At this point, Hölderlin describes their movement more precisely: the general in its greater generality contracts in order to arrive at its most concentrated. But when it has reached this extreme particularity, it makes a reverse movement and spreads out in order to find its initial generality again. The particular makes the opposite movement. It tends toward the general and reaches it, but it can no longer consider it, it can only feel it—there is no more differentiation. In order to consider it and therefore differentiate, it must withdraw toward its particularity. Here is the diagram:

a)

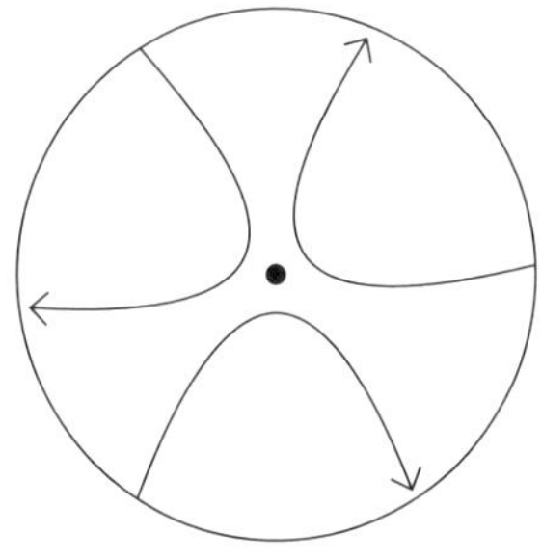

General
Divine · Aorgic
Unconscious · Nature

b)

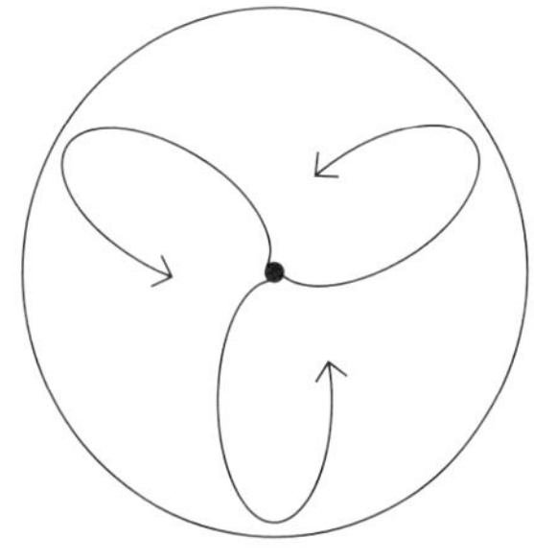

Particular
Human · Organic
Conscious · Culture

9
Translator's note: In his notes on the first version of *The Death of Empedocles*, translator Krell writes, "The word *innig* is most often translated here as 'intense,' yet it also carries the meaning of intimacy. The word has often been translated, especially in the philosophical literature, as 'interior,' in the sense of the interior life of subjectivity. This is in my view quite misleading. Rather, *Innigkeit* suggests the intensity of ecstasy, of standing outside oneself. The confusion may arise from the association of *Innigkeit* with intellectual intuition. Here Max Kommerell's analysis is helpful: 'Tragedy in Hölderlin's sense is the genre that uncovers [*die enthüllende Gattung*]. For according to its very definition it contains an intellectual intuition, i.e., something that cannot be achieved by a concept, something that within poetic forms pertains to the mythic state of life—namely, the perception of the individual within the whole, as of the whole in the individual. Here we also have Hölderlin's concept of *Innigkeit*, which means an amicable dwelling-with-one-another of opposites.' (MK 331). Amicable and intimate, yes—but also intense to the point of ecstasy." In Hölderlin, *The Death of Empedocles*, 226.

10
"The Basis of Empedocles" in Hölderlin, *The Death of Empedocles*, 142.

11
Hölderlin, 142.

And here is the shift that gets Hölderlin on his way, with a magisterial and unexplained gesture, he straightens out the bivalent inclined plane. Nature's "more" and culture's "less" disappear. There is an "equivalence" that one might almost call "naïve" because it makes any judgment impossible. Likewise, how do we separate nature and culture, mind and matter, thought and feeling, human and divine? This is a new view, absolutely contrary to our Western habits of seeing in perspective and making value judgments!

Then Hölderlin returns to Empedocles and he is joined by a partner, Hermocrates. In the first draft of the text, the latter is a calculating, vengeful priest, but now he is Empedocles' equal. Because they are humans belonging to the "particular–organic" sphere, both are inscribed in diagram b) above. We know Empedocles wants to eliminate the tension between the particular (human sphere) and the general (divine sphere), meaning he will immobilize the possible movement through suicide. He takes a one-way path. The new Hermocrates that Hölderlin now brings to life, on the other hand, accepts the opposition between the two spheres and, even more, he "wants to unite extremes to a consciousness," his own in fact, and keep them—and himself—alive in as much tension as possible. He wants to "take upon himself a destiny."

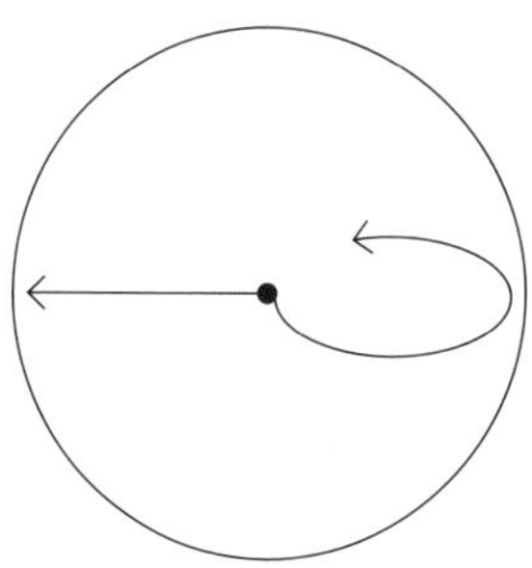

It is a key moment in the argument and with an equal amount of timidity and fervor Hölderlin concludes: When the particular has rediscovered its particularity, it contains henceforth both itself and nature. And this may be among the highest things that man can experience. It is a possible experience of Totality. Hölderlin also calls it *Innigkeit*, "intensity,"[12] and represents it in the drawing in the middle of the banner reproduced at the top of this essay. It is the point surrounded by two circles.

12
See footnote 9.

This is the "Basis of Empedocles" that crosses and breaks the foundations of speculative idealism while simultaneously distancing itself from romanticism. Hölderlin tells us that the highest possible human experience is not ecstatic and eccentric; accomplishment is not elsewhere, but here in the "return to." It is not a matter of "leaving behind" (in a Hegelian *Aufhebung*), but of bringing back into oneself; the man of the future, says Nietzsche, must be heavy, "gravid," and a bearer of fruits: rich, full, round.

Although unapparent and discrete, Hölderlin's gesture is unheard of and spectacular because by straightening the bivalent inclined plane, things that were previously incomparable due to the different values they had been attributed, suddenly become comparable. Indeed, a comparison endangers hegemonic positions. One can now compare other impulses of life—feelings, for example—to reason. We can compare matter to the mind or the flesh to logos. To compare is to balance, to include and not exclude. Hölderlin thus puts himself in total contradiction with the ideology that has established our history and dominates our philosophy and sciences based on the hegemony of reason, the high depository of all knowledge, exclusive and absolute judge of truth.

c) *Schwarze Sünde (Black Sin)*

On these new foundations, Hölderlin undertakes the third and final attempt at writing his mourning play. But having seen the "proper" form of behavior for our times in Hermocrates, we understand that Empedocles, still inclined toward fleeing, is in trouble. Thus, as he prepares to leave, Hölderlin has a second character appear whom he names Manes. Historically, Manes is known as having been a Zoroastrian priest and the founder of Manicheanism. In Hölderlin's play, he becomes Empedocles' former master who asks him if he is sure about having the right to leave like this. Alluding to the planned suicide, he says "Only for one is it right, at this time, / only one is ennobled by your black sin." The allusion to Christ, the half-god founder of our era who left for the divine sphere early, is clear. In a certain way, Empedocles is himself a Christ figure and if Empedocles is a double for Hölderlin, the question is: Can a word redeem the world? Where will that which saves come from?

"Black sin," *Schwarze Sünde*, is also the unusually punchy title of the Straubs' film. Sin? Would the protestant theologian Hölderlin make an allusion to the Christian dogma forbidding suicide? That would be stopping a bit short. Let's instead ask: Why does he use this expression? Etymologically, both in Greek and Hebrew—and Hölderlin spoke both languages—sin means, "to aim to the side" or miss the target, the goal. If we think back to Hölderlin's sketch of intensity, it looks like a target. And if we think about Hermocrates' movement, his center (his consciousness) is like the center of the target that, following a centrifugal movement from consciousness to the general *aorgic*,[13] is touched at each return in the centripetal movement. Whereas Empedocles' one-way movement no longer touches anything but becomes lost.

THE NATIVE REVERSAL AS THE ATTITUDE OF WHAT SAVES

The abandonment of the inclined plane of bi-valency and the establishment of an equi-valency in "The Basis of Empedocles"—and now? The question repeated seventeen times in *Hommage à Vernon* is still ringing in our ears, "Have you not told me everything?"

Indeed, Hölderlin did not say everything in 1800. He would say it piecemeal in hymns he wrote, in letters, in notes on his translations of Sophocles' *Oedipus* and *Antigone*. He would talk about "Greece – Hesperia,"[14] "to seize oneself – to hit a mark,"[15] "that which is foreign – that which is one's own,"[16] "fas – nefas."[17] These are the reference points for the native reversal (along with "unite extremes to a consciousness" and "take upon oneself a destiny," which we know already) that he would henceforth begin to deploy in a "reversal of all modes of representation and forms."

These are enigmatic words. What is this native reversal? We said that Hölderlin was looking for and found a law of motion for the living, whose form with regards to people was the native reversal. Recalling the diagrams above, we can now specify that it is a concretization of the schematically drawn curve of Hermocrates' life in "The Basis of Empedocles" marked by the circumstances and their

13 *Translator's note:* the *aorgic* (das Aorgische) is a term coined by Hölderlin describing "those aspects of elemental nature that escape or at least resist the human organization of them." David Farrell Krell in Hölderlin, *The Death of Empedocles*, 257.

14 In the hymn *Brot und Wein*, for example.

15 In "Remarks on 'Antigone.'"

16 In a letter to Böhlendorff on December 4, 1801.

17 In "Remarks on 'Oedipus.'"

corresponding depiction. There are countless forms of native reversal: political, religious, and moral.

Furthermore, the movement inscribes itself within a larger, more encompassing law, which is the driving force of the world: The law of biological life is the law of the spirit, is the law of "Bildungstrieb" (of the "drive for education/formation" that gives birth to civilizations and art) and is the law of the universe; it is an expansion–contraction movement, in our lungs as in the universe. Is that it? So, it isn't simple, but rather simplistic and incomprehensible, right? Certainly, as long as the paradigms of Hölderlin's time (linear model with the hegemony of rational thought and hierarchical organization starting from the summits of the living and coexistence) are still in place and active, which is unfortunately the case.

Let's now connect the above-stated keywords of the native reversal and translate them into our 21st century. Let's think about how for Hölderlin, the native reversal may be the only thing for humans that enable that which saves to grow and have an effect proportional to the danger. In *The Threepenny Opera*, Brecht paraphrases, "When distress is greatest, salvation is nearest." There is nothing automatic about this since it could also NOT happen! And then what Hölderlin states as the greatest danger does happen, namely that memories of the Divine Ones fade and there is a gap in the course of the world.[18] This is more understandable in our present time than it was for Hölderlin's contemporaries: God is dead, as Nietzsche put it, meaning we have banished from our lives any entity transcendent to humans.

18 See "Remarks on 'Oedipus,'" in *Friedrich Hölderlin: Essays and Letters on Theory*, 108.

WHAT DOES HÖLDERLIN SAY?

a) The basis in which everything else is inscribed is the "reversal of all modes of representation and forms." Sometimes Hölderlin also calls this, "the revolution of convictions and modes of representation." What does this mean? Using the example of the French Revolution, the danger is that good, beauty, and hope will veer into their opposites. If it was not a historical accident, but a law of nature, then this must be recognized. And therefore "modes of representation" are also not primarily a matter of particular political modes, but it must be read as a revolution *of all* convictions and modes of representation. This means, as a principle! *No* mode of conviction or representation, whatever it comprises, should continue forever and in that way become ever more absolute over time, separate from everything else. It then goes mad and becomes wild, veering into its opposite. This is the "schize," the dislocation, the separation of that which should be—under the banner of any kind of ideology or religion whatsoever—from that which actually is. (We are thinking of the first diagram of more–less.) The claim of an absolute truth always leads to war and death and, in Hölderlin's terminology, to dissolution in the aorgic. Before jihadists, there was the reign of terror and the St. Bartholomew's Day massacre and the Crusades.

The revolution of all modes of representation being demanded is a kind of "relativization," but one that is not arbitrary since it belongs to a law and has a place—Hölderlin does not only have an organic idea of biological creatures, but of cultures as well. A culture also develops from a center that contains its full potential (myths, fairy tales, and holy books recount this potential) into its most evolved state, to then find in its reversal the path to a new reality. Expansion and contraction take place simultaneously and in the expansion phase, the potential for contraction increases. They say Heraclitus called this "enantiodromia": running contrary, meaning forces continually working in opposition as a fundamental law of life, inseparable from each other, and mutually connected at the same time like high and low tide. If this dynamic system loses its balance, if one power begins to dominate, then it will automatically veer into its opposite because they are no longer connected.

b) Hölderlin labels this mechanism with the Latin concept of "fas – nefas," which means, that which is allowed and that which is no longer allowed. This should not, however, be understood morally. A car driver who misses his turn drives directly into the void. It is also a matter of physical laws. That which is no longer allowed is that which is too much according to relations—it is the change from "full–abundance" to "overflowing–emptiness." In the "Remarks on 'Antigone,'" using the example of the sun and its effects, Hölderlin illustrates the change from fruitfulness into barrenness, a garden into a desert. These are facts that are relevant to us.

c) In the theoretical texts and in the letters, Hölderlin often talks about the Greeks. He means the world and culture of Ancient Greece. It takes the place of the "other" and "that which is foreign," which he compares to that which is his "own," meaning our culture, which he labels the Hesperian (Greek: hesperos: evening). In his time, this was the intellectual standard for comparisons and the superiority of the Greek model went unquestioned as far as was possible. The logical consequence is that one wants to imitate the model, or at least tries—like Hölderlin with Empedocles—to adopt and assimilate the patterns to one's own time. One's own culture is understood as the continuation of the preceding one. And yet, Hölderlin began to doubt the validity of this assessment, arriving at the radical insight that with one exception, we have nothing in common with them. The exception is "the highest," and this is precisely the fact that we have a destiny and stand under this destiny. To have a destiny means to have arisen out of, and now to stand in a tense relationship of contrary energies and forces. This is, in general, the fundamental law of the living. And yet, this tense relationship shows we are different from the Greeks and, in our situation, the task we must fulfill is different. Task? How does one understand history? As a random flow of a series of events? As a proto-teleological process? As the gradual uncovering of predetermined meaning? As solely the result of human actions? How do we understand ourselves now?

d) The task that we must fulfill within the framework of our native reversal is "to hit a mark."[19] Let us remember the "black sin" and its etymological derivation. Sin is "to aim to the side" and "to hit a mark" is a corrective. Let's think of Hölderlin's diagram and visualize a center and a periphery. We can recall the Hermocrates of "The Basis of Empedocles" who reasserts his "own" again through that which he experienced in confrontations with the "other" and "what is foreign." In this movement of the "reversal of all modes of representation and forms," he meets that which is his own again and again, and in this way learns it anew. "What is one's own must be learned as well as what is foreign," says Hölderlin.

The biblical story of the prodigal son and his return home, the countless sagas about an area that must be run around

19 In "Remarks on 'Antigone,'" Hölderlin names the task of his/our own Hesperian time, which is fundamentally different from that which the earlier Greek culture had to fulfill: "the Greek representations change insofar as it is their chief tendency to comprehend themselves, [...] on the other hand, it is the main tendency in the mode of representation of our time to hit a mark." ("Remarks on 'Antigone,'" 110–114, translation modified.)

in one day, the sea stories of departing and returning home. All the myths of the world trace the same path of life from which the other, linear one differentiates itself as a path of death. Only, how have we come to forget this? The question is all the more interesting since in the natural sciences, the same cyclical, spiral model is shown; nothing is linear in nature! What abstruse linearity of culture did we want to invent? What did we want to escape or to prove? To which law did we not want to bow?

e) The quality of the meditation on precisely this question likely depends upon whether or not there will be a gap in the course of the world. Linearity is an invention of Western culture. It neither exists in nature nor in any spirituality, but thanks to the unbelievable driving force of our ideas, we have imposed it on the entire world since industrialization. Hölderlin saw it coming and gave a warning about the consequences.

Since then, linear, centrifugal forces have massively altered the relationship between nature and culture and torn apart the previous dynamic balance (the memory of the Divine Ones!). From fas to nefas—that which is "too much" becomes "wild." Culture and nature have become "wild," one in the hubris of technology, the other in tsunamis, typhoons, and pandemics. These are exterior reflections of interior conditions. Over the past 500 years, the rational components of our consciousness have established themselves with increasing strength, to the disadvantage of that which is not rational, leading to the liberation of the latter in dysfunctional behavior, violence with and between people, areas in which we have made few advances in spite of our constantly increasing knowledge and our convictions—as shown by the 20th century, among other things.

To hit a mark: nature and culture—equivalent bipolarity—represent danger and that which saves as two directions of a contrary movement and are in a certain way the same insofar as they are the field in which "hitting a mark" must unfold. Wherever we find ourselves, on whatever point of disequilibrium, it is a matter of inventing, living, and trying the largest possible number of variations of "hitting a mark," individually and collectively, in the psychological, philosophical, artistic, scientific, ecological, and economic realm.

The movement of the organic against the aorgic is the coincidence of what is one's own with what is still foreign, which should then return to the organic in an integration of the foreign in one's own self, which has consequently been altered and requires a new name for a coming totality. In the native reversal and "the revolution of all modes of representation and forms," time and space, as we have become accustomed to perceiving them, only play a subordinate role. It is rather a simultaneity of all dimensions. The foreign is one's own inner nature, which comes from faraway, but which also remains inherently germinal in its essence. From a post-quantum perspective, the historically forgotten, and that which still needs to evolve in the future are the same—are present. Let's restore the dynamic relationship as the fundamental law of the living.

f) This is Hölderlin's legacy. This is what he prophesized. And as an answer to the question repeated seventeen times in *Hommage à Vernon*, "Have you not told me everything?" we could respond with seventeen variations of "hitting a mark," attesting our perception of the danger and rendering true that which saves. This is not the place for that.

But let's nevertheless add that the line attributed to Péguy and recalled again and again by Straub and Huillet,"To make the revolution also means to put back into place things that are ancient but forgotten," resounds like an echo of Hölderlin. And likewise, that filmic work is itself an exercise in "hitting a mark" in that, in a singular and unheard-of manner, it demands and itself represents precisely the back and forth between two equivalent poles.

Translated from French and German by Ted Fendt.

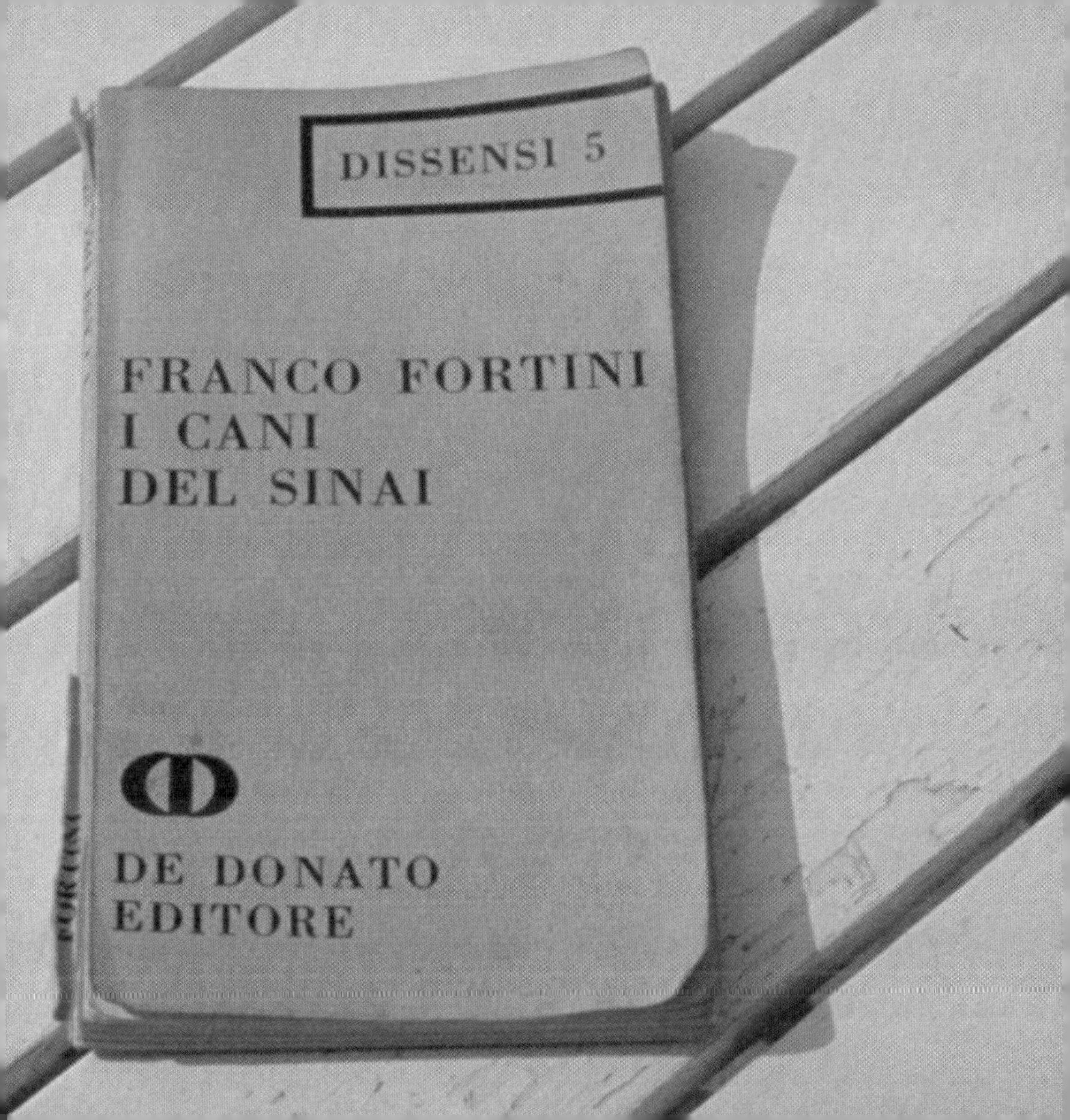
DISSENSI 5
FRANCO FORTINI
I CANI
DEL SINAI
DE DONATO
EDITORE

Paolo Caffoni

A REVOLUTIONARY COPYWRITER

FRANCO FORTINI AND HIS RELATIONS TO FILM

The opening shot shows the book cover of no. 5 in the "Dissensi" (dissents) series by De Donato: *I cani del Sinai* by Franco Fortini. The design of the cover replaces the title of the film, and we might wonder what is actually the subject: the book or its author? The film title, *Fortini/Cani*, which does not appear in the credits, juxtaposes the name of the author and the title of his pamphlet through a typographic sign of punctuation (slash), emphasizing the alternation and the disjunction of the two terms, followed by the names of the two directors, "Danièle Huillet, Jean-Marie Straub," and the interpreters, "Franco Lattes, Luciana Nissim, Adriano Aprà." Here we might notice that the main interpreter of the film does not coincide with the author of the book. "Lattes" is the name of Franco Fortini's father—a Jewish lawyer originally from Livorno—while "Fortini" is the name of his mother—a non-practicing Catholic—and also the name that he adopted as a writer.

The juxtaposition established by the typographic sign in the film title calls into question the writer's own biographical position—he is no longer the person who wrote the text, nine years have passed by—while at the same time it reveals the point of view on the text taken by the two film directors. The "angle" which the film takes on the book is defined by the directors' work of reading and rewriting, an endeavor that produces an openness and a possibility to look from a distance, that is, in the words of Straub, "To give the possibility to see a movie with a character that might also be different from the one who wrote the book."[1] In 1967 Franco Fortini had impetuously denounced, with a written pamphlet, the manipulation of Italian public opinion following the outbreak of the Arab-Israeli conflict in the Six-Day War. With *I cani del Sinai*, he criticized the propaganda of media power and its coercive action. He wrote, "There is no perspective, no order of priorities. You must partake in this fictional passion now just like you did with other passions. You must not have the time to pause. You must ready yourself to forget everything, and soon. You must prepare not to be or to want anything."[2]

Nine years later, in 1976, directors Danièle Huillet and Jean Marie Straub made a film dedicated to that same book.

1 "I cani del Sinai: conversazione," *Film/Straub-Huillet. Quaderni di Filmcritica 18*, ed. Ricardo Rossetti (Roma: Bulzoni, 1984): 186.

2 Franco Fortini, *The Dogs of the Sinai*, trans. Alberto Toscano (Calcutta: Seagull Books, 2013), 11.

Fortini/Cani makes use of the distance in time between the book release and the film shooting—as well as the difference of specific instruments between the two media—in order to establish a discourse on the means of production that is also a "history lesson" capable of transforming Fortini's text into a pedagogical tool: "Vitality, passion, immediacy—in their absence, nothing is done. At the same time, if these do not die, if they are not distanced, stifled, looked at as goods that have been forever lost and are not meant for us, they cannot become 'food for the many.'"[3]

The semiotic analyses of W.J.T. Mitchell on the typographic conventions of "image/text" composite can help us to further articulate the media relation between the book and the film, going beyond simplifications of a comparative approach, such as the idea of "adaptation." They rather point to an unresolved field of tensions, where the cleavage is equally a relation and a nonrelation.[4] Mitchell's semiotic approach nevertheless doesn't seem sufficient for tackling the question of the historicity of the object of filmic representation, its "gestus," to use the Brechtian terminology—which directly invests the pair Fortini/Lattes with the writer transposition to the reader—and its connection with the historical period in which he changed the name following the promulgation of Italian racial laws in 1938.[5]

Recalling the instructions that were given to Fortini on the film set, Straub says, "Read them as foreign texts, as if they were written by someone else. [...] And then always in contradiction with the idea of reading them as the texts of another, we told Franco to read them how he would read a letter to a friend who had been absent, someone who wasn't there as spectator."[6]

In the postface to the French edition of *I cani del Sinai*, Fortini returns to his experience of working with the directors:

> In a note from the time I find this: 'I'm ill, fatigue, trigeminal neuralgia, dizziness. That's what happens, if one tries to re-enter one's biography. But in these few days the two living-dead friends have taught me an extraordinary lesson in meter.'

The lesson taught by the "living-dead" Danièle Huillet and Jean-Marie Straub is the rule of estrangement: "In the in-

3 Fortini, "A Note for Jean-Marie Straub," *The Dogs of the Sinai*, 79.

4 W. J. T. Mitchell, "Beyond Comparison: Picture, Text, and Method," in *Picture Theory. Essays on Verbal and Visual Representation* (Chicago: University of Chicago Press, 1994), 83–107.

5 "Had I at least known the history of the forced conversions, or conversion of opportunity, of the past centuries." Fortini, *The Dogs of the Sinai*, 43.

6 Straub, "I cani del Sinai: conversazione," 188.

structions that I received from Danièle and Jean-Marie, the text estranged itself under my gaze."[7]

The film directors do not alter the text except for the punctuation, combining words that were originally divided, or breaking the fluidity of the discourse by inserting pauses. The film contains about two-thirds of the 1967 text, with sequences corresponding to chapters of the book—except for the long sequence of panning shots of the Apuan Alps that breaks one chapter into two. The selection of the text parts spoken in the film follows a method of montage mirroring the composition of the title (Franco Fortini, *I cani del Sinai – Fortini/Cani*), by mostly using the central part of each chapter without any additions. The only direct intervention Huillet and Straub made in Fortini's text was to change "thirty years ago" to "thirty years before," acknowledging that some time has passed between the writing of the text and the shooting of the film, thus blending a reflection on the year of the Six-Day War into the present. Huillet-Straub's approach, "the most communist possible," according to Fortini, to the book establishes a relationship with the film that is problematized and articulated to the point where it becomes a "figure" in itself, that which embodies the tension between the biographical and the historical. They intended the film to be seen as a movement between two poles: the "romanzo," as an autobiographical (fictional) reflection on the Italian past, and the "documentary," as a general reflection on imperialism. Overcoming the mystical interpretation of the Nazi massacres, Fortini re-inscribes them into the context of neocolonialism and class struggle. "But from Fortini's reflection on imperialism we would not have made a film—Straub says—if the source had not been the personal, concrete reflection on his own biography."[8]

7 "A Note for Jean-Marie Straub," 80–81.

8 "I cani del Sinai: conversazione," 185.

Toward the end of the film, the camera captures a red, handwritten text by Fortini, which contrasts the mechanical typeface of the newspapers (see the vertical panning shot on the pages of *L'Unità*, the newspaper of the Italian Communist Party). The camera's "attention" further emphasizes a tension between the biographical and the documentary through staging their signifiers. Yet there cannot be a simple dualism resulting from the correspondence of meanings and images: the biographical/handwritten and the historical/typewritten. The risk would be that of consuming the truth simply as a "product" and to reinforce "the identity attained by envelope and content"[9] in the same fashion as the Arab-Israeli conflict was covered by the journalistic discourse.

The discrepancy between signified and signifier—which unveils the "regime of truth" of media propaganda and lets the biographical and historical oscillate—is already declared within the epigraph that opens the book and closes the first sequence of the film:

> It seems that 'making the dog of the Sinai' was an Arab expression [...] its meaning oscillates between 'running to the aid of the victor,' 'being on the side of the masters' and 'making a show of noble sentiments.'
>
> —"There are no dogs on the Sinai," the expression is an invention of its author.

TEXT

The "lesson" Huillet-Straub are giving us with *Fortini/Cani* opens up various directions for further investigations, and I propose not to look here into their filmography, in which the film partakes in their so called "trilogy on the Jewish question,"[10] but to rather follow Fortini and his relation to other films he was actively involved in. The voices of Fortini are many, sometimes hidden and often in contradiction with each other, as resonances of a complex personality and a restless intellectual spirit rejecting a strict collocation in the Italian literary tradition. The diversity of the genres frequented by Fortini (industrial cinemas, militant documentary, art film), testify not only to the contradictions inherent to his intellectual career but also to the fact that Fortini has never claimed the right to participate in the cinematographic tradition, except as an "ungrateful guest."[11] What is revealed by looking transversally at the relations of Fortini working with film? Verifying Fortini's position with respect to cinema implies to also verify[12] the position of the text with respect to the images: "the relationship between the argumentations (or invectives) of the text and the attention (the word is Simone Weil's) of the camera," as he writes after the experience with *Fortini/Cani*.[13]

9 Fortini, *The Dogs of the Sinai*, 11.

10 "With Fortini, we attempt, after *Moses und Aron* and *Einleitung zu Arnold Schoenbergs Begleitmusik zu einer Lichtspielscene*, a more direct political reflection on the 'Jewish question.'" Jean-Marie Straub, "I cani del Sinai: conversazione," 196.

11 To problematize Fortini's use of this expression, "ungrateful guest"—somehow self-explanatory—it seems to me the association with another, "internal émigré," which is somehow specular and complementary to it could be interesting. See Franco Fortini, "The Writers' Mandate and the End of Anti-Fascism," *A Test of Powers*, trans. Alberto Toscano (Calcutta: Seagull Books, 2016), 241.

12 In his writings, Fortini consistently makes use of the Italian noun *verifica* and the verb *verificare*. The essay "Verifica dei poteri," and the anthology which bears the same title, was translated into English by Alberto Toscano as "A Test of Powers," yet, inside the book, Toscano

Fortini is using the preface to the book *Tre testi per film* (Three texts for films), published by Edizioni Avanti! in 1963,[14] to reflect upon the problems associated with the writing of texts for "montage films." In the early 1960s, Fortini's encounter with the medium of film is driven by the interrogation of the material conditions of his work and by the critique of his own "expressive instruments." This notion of self-critique occurs in an environment that Fortini understands as conditioned by the power of the industry, both in the form of a repressive State apparatus (censorship) and the subsumption of culture under capitalism (commodification).

also uses the verb "to verify." In the epigraph Fortini quotes, I believe the source of this wording therefore clarifies its political connotation: "'The commissioners of the Nobility... voiced the fear that the test of powers in common implied deliberation in common.' Alessandro Manzoni, *La Rivoluzione Francese del 1979, III.*"

13 "A Note for Jean-Marie Straub," 78.

14 Franco Fortini, *Tre testi per film* (Milan: Edizioni Avanti!, 1963) comprises the commentaries written by Fortini for the movies *All'armi siam fascisti!* (To arms we are fascists!, 1961) by Cecilia Mangini, Lino Del Fra and Lino Miccichè, *Scioperi a Torino* (Strikes in Turin, 1962) by Carla and Paolo Gobetti, *La Statua di Stalin* (Stalin's Statue, 1963) again with with Mangini and Del Fra.

15 Fortini, "Premessa," *Tre testi per film*, 5.

16 Fortini, 5.

On the one hand, Fortini underlines how the task of writing a commentary for a documentary implies certain technical and prosodic (metric) problems that are tightened with the specificity of the medium. The challenges of such a task are first set by the principles of information theory according to which, most importantly, "if information density is increased beyond a certain threshold, the degree of its reception decreases."[15]

On the other hand, the conditions of the contemporary cinematographic production are understood on a more ideological level:

> The 'documentary' genre intended for the current commercial circuit has all the hybrid characteristics of the essay and all the vices of the oratory. It is demonstrative-persuasive but relies mostly on the succession of images, word and the musical score, therefore the editing.[16]

Writing a text for a documentary cannot therefore disregard/ignore the analysis of those limitations that are implicit in its material conditions of existence. On the contrary, it requires a study of the function to which it has been called upon, the selection of a specific public to which it intends to speak, and the definition of a congruent linguistic register. The parallel that unravels between the technical and the ideological understanding of film technique, allows Fortini to question his own position as an intellectual. The Italian economic boom of the 1950s and 1960s created those specific parameters of subsumption of culture under capitalism that rendered regressive the very notion of the "social mandate" of the intellectual, inherited by the anti-fascist tradition.

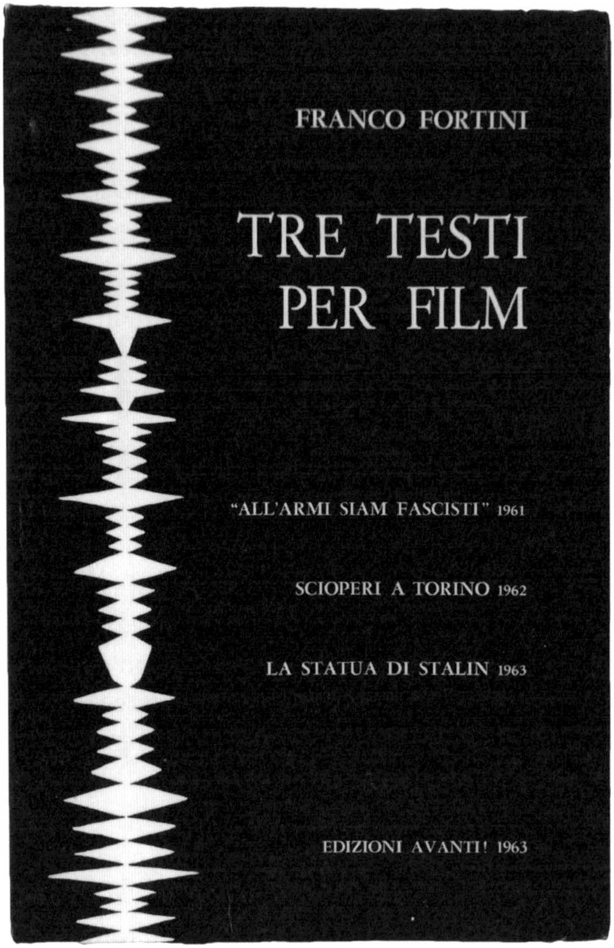

The historical reference made by Fortini with "the writer's mandate," is Bertolt Brecht's intervention at the First International Congress of Writers for the Defense of Culture, held in Paris in 1935. It was on that occasion that Brecht addressed the *necessity* to think about the "roots of evil" (die Wurzel der Übel), and to talk about those prevailing conditions of property ownership (Eigentumsverhältnisse) that made the "barbarism" of fascism *necessary* for their defense.[17]

Fortini questions at length the crisis of the anti-fascist perspective and the relationship of intellectuals to the Communist Party. He seeks to elaborate a historical distance with respect to the present time that, while recognizing its cultural heritage, would prove the possibility to elaborate instruments suitable for today: "I wonder if we should not try to preserve the residual revolutionary capacities of language in a new estrangement, different from the

17 "Many of us writers who have experienced the atrocities of Fascism and are horrified by them have not yet understood this doctrine, have not yet discovered the roots of the brutality which so horrifies them. For them the danger persists that they will regard the cruelties of Fascism as unnecessary cruelties. They cling to the conditions of property ownership because they believe that the cruelties of Fascism are not necessary for their defence. But if the prevailing conditions of property ownership are to be upheld, then these cruelties are indeed necessary. In this particular the Fascists are not lying, they are telling the truth." Bertolt Brecht, "A Necessary Observation on the Struggle Against Barbarism," in *Brecht on Art and Politics*, ed. T. Kuhn et al. (London: Methuen, 2003), 161. Fortini translated Brecht's speech and published it in appendix to the text "The Writer's Mandate and the End of Anti-Fascism," 214–269.

18 Fortini, "Cunning as Doves," in *A Test of Powers*, 146.

19 Fortini, "Premessa," 8.

20 In neorealist rhetoric, fascism becomes an episode suffered and not participated in by the majority of the population, racial persecution, something that did not involve Italians and the massacres of colonial wars are never represented. In *Quaderni*

Brechtian kind but oriented by it."[18] This desire, to look into the "roots of evil," still resonates in the way Fortini structures his commentary in the film *All'armi siam fascisti!*. The text was written directly at the Moviola, right after the first editing, and therefore has a controlling function with respect to the images; it declares a point of view in order to leave no doubts about the ideological-political positioning of the film. At the same time the commentary is also an autobiography, a subjective narrative, which deconstructs the alleged objectivity of the documentary.

The premise of *All'armi* is the definition of fascism as an "armed organization of capitalist violence" that has seen only the workers movement opposing it. The film has a precise thesis:

> That the origins of fascism were above all the interests of agrarian and industrial capitalism [...] a series of choices made by the Italian bourgeoisie, high, middle and small [...] to fight with the maximum energy the class interests of the salaried worker and, in short, the socialist prospects.[19]

The film therefore accepted neither the exaltation of the spirit of anti-fascist unity in Italy (as was instead put forward by neorealism),[20] nor the moralistic condemnation of the "Duce." Among the most significant sequences of the film is the one that records Mussolini and Senator Agnelli at Lingotto in Turin, the FIAT factory, celebrating the alliance that put an end to the "red strikes."[21] *All'armi* was realized ten months after the "Events of June 30th, 1960," when wide-spread protests in reaction to the congress in Genoa of the fascist organization MSI (Italian Social Movement) were brutally suppressed by the police.[22]

The on-screen text concluding the film directly addresses the spectator, providing Fortini with yet another occasion to reflect on the implications of a politics of memory in the present time. He recognizes a latent continuity, invisible but still perceptible, between the fascist age—which only apparently came to an end—and the *unripe* republican age:

> But is fascism still present? / It is. It has rediscovered its face of fifty years ago, / before the Blackshirts. / The face of conservatism / which still offers at a good price on the political market / its little bands

Piacentini of July 1962, Fortini clarifies that he didn't conceive the commentary for *All'armi* as a reply to the fascist time, but to that "hypocrisy, historiography and politics, which sought to attenuate the memory of the revolutionary and anti-bourgeois dimension of most of the anti-fascist struggle to make it a reason for national-popular patriotism or an advance of the 'peace movement.'"

21
The same thesis about the alliance of fascism and capitalist in an anti-socialist perspective, is extended also to the neocolonial enterprise: "Fifteen years later / to half of Europe they will say: better Hitler than the reds. / Thirty years later, that is yesterday, they will say: / better Franco, better Chiang Kai-shek, better Syngman Rhee, better Batista, better Trujillo, better Salazar than the reds. / Better the massacres of Algeria, the prisons of Greece, the massacres of South Africa / than the Socialists. Better the atomic death /—the death of others, of course—then Socialism." Franco Fortini, "All'armi siam fascisti," *Tre testi per film*, 24–25.

22
On July 7th of the same year, the police killed five workers during a trade union demonstration and four people in Palermo during the clashes that followed the general strike of July 8th.

> of provocateurs, / so that the little amount of visible fascism / may better disguise the large amount of invisible fascism.[23]

In the commentary for the film *La statua di Stalin*, Fortini returns to some of the themes that already emerged in *All'armi*.[24] The questions which open the film, "Why did Soviet Russia create Stalin? Why did it destroy him?" highlight the intention to carry out, without compromises, a "verification" of a historical period that was, at least in Italy, still the subject of many hypocritical considerations. Fortini's text was intended to disorient the cinema audience by consciously avoiding the deceptive desire for a conclusion (who is right?). It forced the viewer to "an unavoidable tension between the judgment of the refusal of Stalinism as tyranny and bloody violence and a judgment of understanding Stalin's time as a consequence of certain historical-economic premises."[25] For this purpose, the text had "to be a kind of continuous counterpoint" with respect to the images—of which, for the most part, only a repertoire of official ceremonies was available—and to challenge the spectator's emotional reactions: "To dampen the exaltation that caught each of us when Russian soldiers hurl the Nazi flags at Stalin's feet, recalling, precisely in that moment, Lenin's internationalism."[26]

The final edit of the film was not to be recognized by the three authors. The directors Cecilia Mangini, Lino Del Fra and Lino Micciché, together with Fortini, withdrew their signatures following censorship and cuts made by the production company.[27] In an interview, Cecilia Mangini later recalled that for Italian public opinion, "Stalin had to remain that bloodthirsty monster"—according to the definition given by Alberto Moravia—and not "the diligent and active official, without pity or warmth, that Fortini described in his text."[28]

The film's original length of three-and-a-half hours was shortened to approximately two hours in order to comply with commercial needs. The constraints of the cultural market were interlinked with the ostracism of the Italian Left, who didn't want the images of the anti-colonial revolutions being associated with the banner of the socialist class struggle.[29]

23 Fortini, "All'armi siam fascisti," *Tre testi per film*, 53.

24 In his commentary, Fortini quotes the striking words of Nikolai Bucharin of whom—among the few in Italy—he had read the 1938 Moscow trial reports during his exile in Switzerland: "The roots of evil lies in the complete fusion of the Party and State." Franco Fortini, "La statua di Stalin," *Tre testi per film*, 103.

25 Fortini, "Premessa," 12.

26 Fortini, 10.

27 The film will be released with the title *Processo a Stalin* (Trial on Stalin) and signed by producer Fulvio Lucisano and editor Renato May.

28 Pasquale Iaccio, *Cinema e storia. Percorsi immagini testimonianze* (Napoli: Liguori, 2000). It should also be noted that Fortini's commentary on Stalin was based—in large part—on the writings and the interpretations provided by Isaac Deutscher.

29 Following the sequence of Stalin's death, to represent the end of the darkest time, the film's original cut would have ended with images of struggles in Asia, Africa and Latin America.

This tells of Fortini's problematic relations with those institutions that still pretended to embody the mandate of anti-fascism (namely the Italian Communist Party and its mediating agent with the working class, the trade union). As Alberto Toscano pointed out, "for Fortini, as for other heretics, the foremost task was to wrest communism from its monopolization by state and party," and he never "ceased exploring the question of the relationship between the intellectual and communism understood as a non-state state."[30] In the film *Scioperi a Torino* by Carla and Paolo Gobetti about the strikes of 1962 in the factories of Lancia, Michelin and Fiat, the reference to the fascist past is entrusted to the words of the old worker Cervi, who—unlike the younger generation—is not surprised by the violent police repression, neither then nor today.

30 Alberto Toscano, "The non-State Intellectual: Franco Fortini and Communist Criticism," *The Dogs of the Sinai*, 97–98.

The first line of Fortini's comment reads, "The Turin of today is no longer the Turin of Gramsci," remarking on a historical distance and a discontinuity in the organization of the struggle, and it concludes with: "Saying class unity is not the same thing as saying trade unionism. / Trade unionism is useful, / class unity is necessary."[31] On the one hand, the film interprets the revolutionary potential of the working class; on the other, it underlines "the dangers of collaboration implicit to any union struggle of our time," reminding us that "the power and not the contract is the goal of the struggle; that state company doesn't mean socialist company."

31 Franco Fortini, "Scioperi a Torino," in *Tre testi per film*, 74.

VOICE

In the essay, "Verifica dei poteri" (A Test of Powers) from 1960, Fortini sharply analyzes the writer's role in the growing mass cultural industry, and asks for a verification of the social and historical mandate in the name of which intellectuals claim the right to testify the following:

> Until yesterday, many militant critics thought they were still running around wearing the uniform of Marxism and Catholic spiritualism, ignoring that on their backs was already printed the name of a company producing cultural tyres or literary toothpaste.[32]

32 Franco Fortini, "A Test of Powers," in *A Test of Powers*, 94.

Fortini's criticism turns here to the industrial-corporate sphere of influence which, with the advent of neo-capitalism, seems to have replaced the representative function of the political parties. If once there was the Party—as representative of the collectivity—to organize the ideological life of the population, defining the relationship of the intellectual with the State through appointments and subsidies, now the industry is ahead in the "production of subjectivity."[33]

In this context, Fortini begins a polemical discussion with many of his colleagues from the magazine *Menabò*—Vittorini for example—who saw in the object-user's and the object-producer's alienated relations, a symptom of the crisis of capitalist optimism. Fortini responds that "industry produces not just objects but also human relationships and 'ideas.'"[34]

He is influenced by the Operaist discourse recently started by a group around the magazine *Quaderni Rossi*, a context that will mark Fortini's renewed political commitment with a "bottom-up" perspective:

> I think that today [...] to wish to write about industry, factories, workers, trade union and political struggles is to be fellow-traveller of conservation. To understand the world around us is also to be concerned with industry, factories and workers, with trade union and political struggles. It is to act within them. This I believe must be done.[35]

Therefore, the writer's elective theme cannot be the world of industry—whether in its productive or consumption stage. It has to be, if anything, "the very general historical theme of the 'fundamental conflict' of which the world of industry is both a manifestation and a component."[36] Fortini criticizes a misconception of progress according to which industrial reality should find "literary expression" because it is considered "important." One should instead recognize its historical-ideological reality, that is to say, "industry is not *a* theme, it is a manifestation of *the* theme called capitalism."[37]

Fortini's collaboration with Olivetti as a copywriter began in 1947.[38] The significance of that experience is not merely a side note when trying to understand the shot/counter-

33 I borrow the term from Félix Guattari. In the early 1990s, the notion of "production of subjectivity" was fundamental to the development of the Post-Operaist discourse (Negri, Lazzarato, et al.).

34 Fortini, "Cunning as Doves," 126.

35 Fortini, 146.

36 Fortini, 127.

37 Fortini, 133.

38 And it continued on and off between the 1950s and 1960s. "A first breach with the company took place in 1948, following a political conflict with Adriano Olivetti. Fortini left the firm's staff for five years, but remained a contributor to the 'Comunità' magazine, where he edited a literary column. In 1953 he was hired again in the advertising office [...]. In 1963 he was out again, definitively, partly by personal decision, partly under the pressure of internal downsizing. Only two years later, in 1965, he was renewed a contract as an external collaborator of the same office." See Davide Lamas, "Il significato dei nomi e le macchinazioni delle macchine: Franco Fortini e l'industria," *Levia Gravia*, no. 14 (2012).

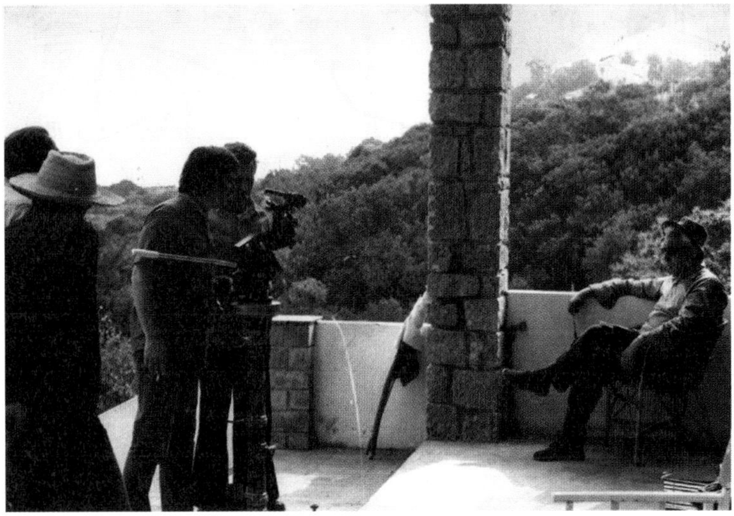

shot of industry film productions and those of militant cinema, which very often looked at the same subjects from opposing angles.[39] It also helps to grasp Fortini's capacity to critically engage with new forms of production and to reframe the possibility of one's own political action.

39
Such as, *Scioperi a Torino* and *Divisione controllo numerico* (Numerical Control Division, Aristide Bosio, 1968) and *Le regole del gioco* (The Rules of the Game, Massimo Magrì, 1968), two of the shorts realized for Olivetti, in which the relation of technology-labor is opposed to that of politics-labor.

The short film *Le regole del gioco* was produced by Olivetti in 1968. The film doesn't advertise a specific product, but summarizes, by illustrating those operations that allow technicians to issue orders to an electronic calculator, the company's ideological vision of the relationship between technology and development.
In the incipit of the voice-over for the film, Fortini writes,

> They say that we will drown in scrap paper, in empty or full tin cans. / They say that the scent of fuel condemned the smell of any grass. / For twenty, thirty years they have been explaining to us that reality is very complicated, that the race for consumption consumes every kind of race. / They say that at the end of the supermarket corridors there is a Minotaur with prizes, that from the jet disembark with us over and underdevelopment, past and future. / We've just read today's newspapers and we must already try to forget them. / But to evils of the present we can only respond with a little more of the present. Machines will win over the other machines. That's all.

Against the backdrop of the technological transformation of the working process, Fortini saw the metamorphosis of intellectual work into abstract mental labor. The implementation of new electronic machines which rationalize production via automation, does not only invert the count of the produced units and that of the employed workers, but also incorporates intellectual labor directly into industrial production.[40] As Sergio Bologna—also working at Olivetti at that time—noted, the integration of the intellectual workforce (writers, philosophers, designers, engineers, etc.) in the electronic department, was achieved through a series of ethical and economical negotiations, and represented a true political matter. Olivetti resorted to the myth of progress in order to make intellectuals fully accept the new social investiture of capital.[41]

In this historical framework, we could look at Fortini's work for Olivetti as a struggle against the ideological mystification that intended to hide, behind the veil of progress, the real transformation of a social group, the intellectuals, who were holding the public monopoly for symbolic legitimation, into a simple waged workforce: technicians. Instead of the apologetic description of Olivetti's vision for the future in vogue nowadays, we should think further about the conflictual (and often contradictory) relations that some few intellectuals—Fortini among them—maintained with regard to the company's philosophy and their role in the industry.

During these years, Fortini's thinking doesn't focus solely on the analysis of the mechanisms of the cultural industry, but it rather becomes a "continuous reflection on the positioning within these mechanisms; therefore on the specific task, on the particular skills and on the general function, on the social role of the intellectual."[42] Fortini's argument, rather than defending the obsolescent social mandate of the intellectuals, would, as Alberto Toscano wrote,

> represent a way of maintaining fidelity to a specific incarnation of the intellectual function, one that assumes the responsibility that comes with a certain degree of specialization (as 'language worker'), so to speak, while affirming the social and economic reification of that specialization itself. [...] Having provided his technical services as a copywriter for Olivetti, [Fortini] envisaged and practiced the idea

40 As Daniele Balicco wrote, "a certain reading of the neo-capitalist development (Panzieri, Tronti, Mandel, Baran and Sweezy) is welded together with an interpretation of the cultural industry (Horkheimer, Adorno, Marcuse) as capitalist self-management of hegemony." Daniele Balicco, *Non parlo a tutti: Franco Fortini intellettuale politico* (Roma: manifestolibri, 2006), 159.

41 Sergio Bologna, "Note sulla nuova forza lavoro alla Olivetti elettronica," *Classe Operaia*, no. 1 (year 2, 1965).

42 Sergio Bologna, "Industria e cultura," in *Uomini usciti di pianto in ragione: Saggi su Franco Fortini* (Roma: manifestolibri, 1996), 20.

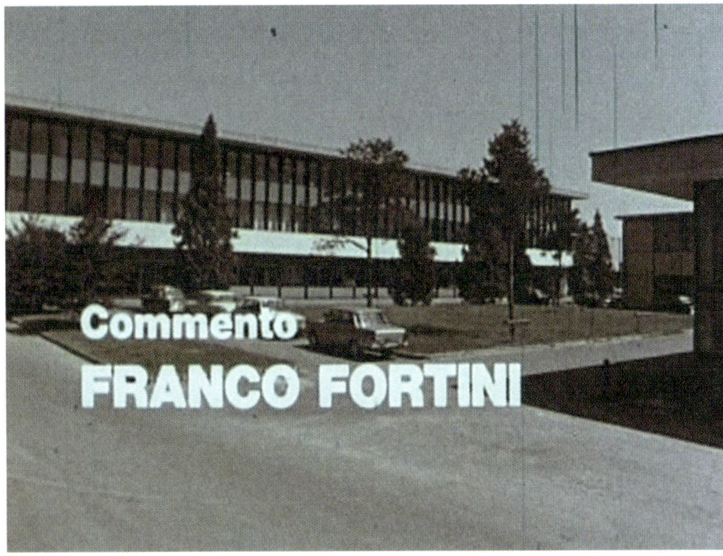
Commento
FRANCO FORTINI

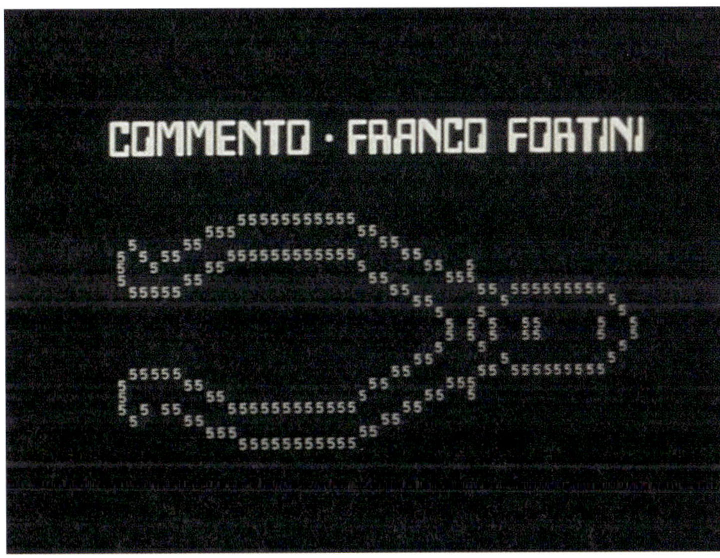
COMMENTO · FRANCO FORTINI

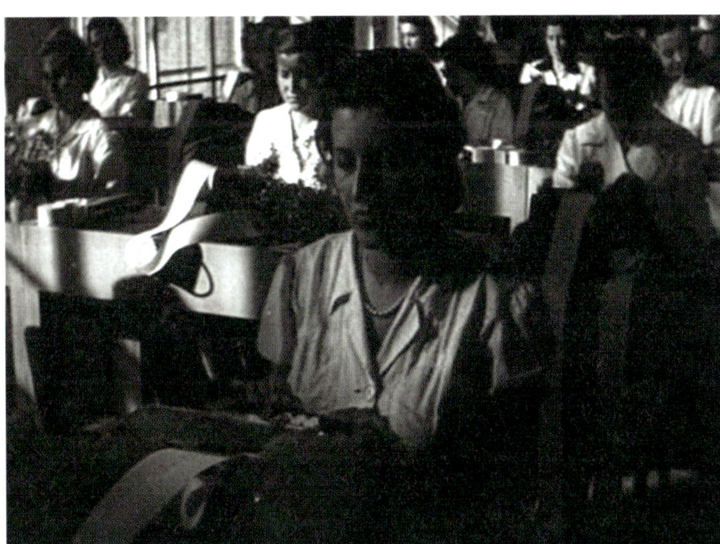

> of 'invisible' service within the movement, provided by writers on the basis of their specific skills.[43]

In this crucial moment of change for Fortini it is necessary to preserve the residual revolutionary capacities of language, to elaborate models of critical writing, of essayistic language, of written information, of organization and investigation of culture, of translation and direction in the field of literary studies. It is in the void left behind by the historical function of the intellectual that he finds the possibility for a collective work capable, in autonomy, of giving shape to one's own activity in terms of what will be named, later on in those years, as "conricerca" (co-research).[44] A "worker's science" that is also a political methodology, that is to say, self-managing the production of knowledge and its practical verification.

In order to make politics within and against the industry, both the *skill* of the assembly line worker and that of the "language worker" are fundamental. Only through a process of collective research would it be possible to overcome the system of specializations imposed by the neo-capitalist division of labor. In "Lettera agli amici di Piacenza" (1961),[45] a sort of manifest of intentions for the political reorganization outside the sphere of influence of the parties, Fortini points to the impossibility of facing these tasks alone, as a sum of separate individualities. He argues for the construction of "groups," micro-organisms of collective thinking able to contrast the cause of the division of workers among themselves and that of each individual in separate parts.

In "Verifica dei poteri" Fortini references once again Bertolt Brecht and the model of a "revolutionary copywriter" in opposition to that of the "engaged intellectual" who provides class struggle with oratory content.[46] In order to grasp the transformation of the intellectual's subjective position that Fortini pursues with the proposal of "revolutionary copywriter," we must consider how he understood his "skills" as the tools of a technician of literary persuasion: "Evaluating which forms and contents are most effective for the intellectual and political mobilization of the masses is specifically intellectual and political work; and even just trying to achieve those ends in exist-

43 Toscano, "The non-State Intellectual," 107–108.

44 See Romano Alquati, *Per fare conricerca* (Milan: Calusca edizioni, 1993).

45 Franco Fortini, "Lettera agli amici di Piacenza," in *L'ospite ingrato primo e secondo* (Casal Monferrato: Marinetti, 1985).

46 Franco Fortini, "The Writers' Mandate and the End of Anti-Fascism," 241. "The point is that after two years in exile, Brecht is issued a political call to arms and gave counsel on how to 'write the truth.' In other words, Brecht advances techniques for the class struggle and tries to fuse his own vocation as an artist with that of the revolutionary copywriter."

ing structures means igniting an uninterrupted series of contradictions. This is a much more difficult road than disguising yourself as a political activist and distributing leaflets at the door of a factory, it is more difficult than writing a book or producing an avant-garde film."[47]

Fortini's proposal for a "politics of syntax" addresses the necessity for a modularity of language that would contrast with the immense wastage of words that characterized the Left's copywriting.

> Instead of carrying out the usual 'political service,' the writer had to focus his strengths mainly on this 'linguistic service.' [...] The stylistic efforts of the drafters [of a political flyer] had to be such as to create, so to speak, a mobile system, by virtue of which [...] one could take advantage of the pedagogical value of repetition. [...] There is in fact something like an ecology of writing, in particular of communicative, political and journalistic writing.[48]

Recalling his public speech in Piazza Strozzi in Florence, during a rally for Vietnam in 1967 (the same year *The Dogs* was published), Fortini reviewed his intentions while drafting a text, written "to be said, not read." His attention focused on the different meanings words can acquire, once the resonance within a context "exalt them and partially verifies them." Responding to this redundancy Fortini conceives his intervention in a modular form, "with variations on a definite and recurrent number of sentences" that could fight against the alleged "immediacy" that would commonly be expected from an oratory. The metric of his text incorporates suggestions for elocution and intonation, "a mechanism of pauses, with Brechtian inflection, which I already used in some texts for films."[49]

Is it possible to draft a parallel between how Fortini designs a political speech and how he writes for film? It would imply an understanding of the "ecology of writing" as a proposal for translating political commitment into literary expression, and to reflect it upon those "limits of communication" imposed by the filmic production. And if it is the voice that performs the relation between text and images, how could we describe its political function?

47 Franco Fortini, "Politica e Sintassi," in *Questioni di Frontiera: Sctitti di politica e letteratura* (Turin: Einaudi, 1977), 138.

48 Toscano, "The non-State Intellectual," 110.

49 Franco Fortini, "Un comizio per il Vietnam (1971)," *Memorie per dopo domani. Tre scritti 1945; 1967; 1980*, ed. C. Fini, (Siena 2014). I would like to thank Luca Lenzini of Centro Studi Franco Fortini for the precious gift of this booklet.

In the documentary films, Fortini's texts "speak" over the images. His commentaries analyze from a privileged position, off screen, the editing and the image sequencing. Positioning the voice outside the frame allows a distance that informs the images in order to leave no doubt about the political-ideological positioning of the film. That "the public would understand immediately and did not stop to recognize that what they saw and heard came from a precise political position, and perhaps only from one part of that position," was fundamentally important for Fortini, but equally essential was that "the public would perceive a significant independence from institutional political parties."[50] Nevertheless, the text materializing in the film inherits a subjectivity through a "hired voice"—Fortini delegates the reading of his text—a representation that we could think of as politically mediated. The voice of the professional speaker is the voice of the expert whose "objectivity" ideologically claims to guide the spectator toward the proper interpretation of the image.

Fortini/Cani also begins with a voice-over: "People don't like to change their minds. When they will have to, it will be in secret." But it articulates its positioning in the discrepancy between the alleged objectivity of the historical and the subjective tension of the biographical. An explicit "acceptance and intention of partiality"—according to Straub—which creates, in the spectator, the necessary conditions for the formation of criticism: "The voice of Fortini is part of this film, it would make no sense to present it with a different one."[51] The film is constructed through the struggle of Fortini's voice with the present time which overwhelms it (the church bells, the traffic jam, the voice of the rabbi, the television speaker). In the initial sequences of the film Fortini's voice challenges that of the journalist Arrigo Levi: "My last name should not count. I'm information, public service, I represent democracy, fair play, civilization, the good." Fortini's voice speaking over that of the journalist reveals that even the latter is reciting a script. But who wrote it? "I'm objective," can only signify that the choice of a part was made earlier, behind the scenes. The manipulative activity of the media aims at co-opting the citizen-spectator, as Luca Lenzi writes,

> into a whole series of fatuous juxtapositions and imposing a discourse or a narrative in which the parts

50 Fortini, *Tre testi per film*, 7.

51 "I cani del Sinai: incontro," *Filmcritica 18*, 208.

had been defined from the outset, and the 'objective' common sense of the unfolding situation had been established (on the one side democracy, progress, the West; on the other their opposite, the 'Arab' enemy, backwardness, a despotic regime, the vassal of the Soviet Empire...).[52]

POSITION

Fortini writes *The Dogs of the Sinai* with the impetus and vehemence of someone who has been directly questioned (despite his intentions?) in a heated debate made of positioning, strong alliances and public accusations. Following the beginning of the Six-Day War he writes,

> If it's not true that I ascribe to the anti-Israeli theses of the PCI, I must declare my solidarity with Israel... I'm familiar with the method. They want to 'file' me? These pages are my file.[53]

To allow his discourse to break with the constraints of those dichotomies within which the conformist thought wants to allocate to the subject a predefined position: "Needless to say, if you wish to avoid ridicule, it is impossible to confuse the notion of 'Jew' with that of 'Israel.'" Fortini must resort to a wholly material, historical and social ontology of the human. After his stay in Israel, at the end of the 1980s, he was capable to sum up in *Extrema ratio* the reinterpretation of oneself and the world, plunging into the unreflected hereditites, the complicities and the ambiguities of class.

> There are causes (of justice and solidarity, of international anti-colonialist and anti-imperialist war, let everyone choose among these the one best suited to them) for which it may prove necessary to break the toughest and dearest bonds, that is, to choose what to put first: loyalty to a country, an ethnicity, a culture, a religious or familial tradition, to one's own dead or instead to something *other*. I who write have put this 'other' first, every time I was faced with a conflict between duties and loyalty.[54]

This "other" to which Fortini makes reference, cannot solely coincide with a solipsistic exercise of the faculty of criticism alone, that would risk to revive the traditional figure of the intellectual as "specialist of negation" in a nine-

52 Luca Lenzini, "Foreword," *The Dogs of the Sinai*, viii.

53 Fortini, *The Dogs of the Sinai*, 17.

54 Fortini, "Un luogo sacro," in *Extrema ratio: note per un buon uso delle rovine* (Milan: Garzanti, 1990), 58. English translation quoted in Luca Lenzini, "Foreword," ix–x.

teenth-century, pre-Gramscian guise.[55] On the contrary, he fought against the idea of the status of the intellectual and of culture as a separate sphere from society, embodying the contradictions between solitary judgment and collective construction. Fortini's political trajectory relies on a form of discourse that operates through continuous disjunctions (Judaism/State of Israel, communism/Stalinism, class union/syndicate, biography/history, image/text, intellectual/worker, we/other) and elaborates further different conjunctions, linking the position of the intellectual to the form of political recomposition that has to be organized around contemporary cultural production. "Other" also refers to a political intention that links the writer to his readership, his audience. But rather than involving readers in an idealized, therefore ahistorical relationship, he seeks an alliance with them that could connect self-criticism and communist pedagogy. In a pronouncement about the addressees of his political writing, Fortini says, "I don't speak to everyone. I speak to those who have a certain idea of the world and of life and a certain work in it and a certain struggle within it and within themselves."[56]

In this regard it is interesting to read across the various moments in which his commentaries for film have explicitly manifested their political intentions via a direct address to the film's audience. The on-screen text preceding the film titles in *All'armi siam fascisti!* reads:

> This film does not intend to persuade anyone. This film just wants to state that we are the offspring of the events summed up by this screen, but we are also those responsible for the present. In any moment, in any choice, in any silence as much as in any word, each of us decides the meaning of one's own life and that of the others.[57]

According to the film's co-director Cecilia Mangini, with this opening statement,

> Fortini had a magnificent and touching idea [...] speaking to 'us,' the spectators felt politically and emotionally involved in history. This 'we' summarizes all that is in the parterre, his feelings, the memories, the actions: the 'we' is a choice, it means taking a side and taking part."[58] The last two lines of the commentary question right away the possible reactions of the spectator: "What does your con-

55
Fortini argued in favor of the possibility to free oneself from the Gramscian notion of "organic intellectual," in order to achieve "each and every one's direct insertion in the national and international political class struggle." Franco Fortini, "Preface to the First Edition," in *A Test of Powers*, 61.

56
Franco Fortini, *Insistenze: cinquanta scritti 1976–1984* (Milan: Garzanti, 1985), 125.

57
This initial address to the spectator wasn't included in the film commentary published in *Tre testi per film*.

58
"Cecilia Mangini interviewed by Federico Rossin," NodoDocFest catalogue (Trieste, 2009): 86.

science have to say? / One must choose, one must decide. Your destiny is yours alone. Now respond.

For the opening sequence of the film *La statua di Stalin*, Fortini had proposed a red writing on the screen: "The film's authors wanted to be useful to those fighting everyday in the world for the capital's power to disappear and to their attention they recommend this work."[59] In this case too, the text situates the film by framing the images within the address to a particular spectator. The relation between the "we" and the "other" is here introduced to further question the internationalist socialist perspective.

> Asia and Africa have taken up arms against the West. [...] these men look towards us and ask: "Does Europe, the home / of the revolution, only think of covering itself / with cars and technology? You cannot help us / unless by helping yourself; unless by freeing yourself / from those who separate us.' [...] But Asia and Africa and Latin America / are wherever there is a struggle / for the power to decide; therefore in Europe, / as well, and among us."[60]

Fortini foresees a certain "positivity" in international solidarity relations only through the achievement of that same "self-criticism" he had already experienced with respect to his status as an intellectual within a certain class.[61] A relentless work of "negation" from which "that courage to one's own history" can emerge, that attitude or hope to "turn into free choices what we still call destiny,"[62] as we can read in the last line of the commentary.

There is only one passage in *The Dogs of the Sinai* where Fortini explicitly addresses the reader. Breaking the self-reflexive accounts of the diaristic form, he writes, "Against biological determinisms, against Enlightenment egalitarianism but also against historicist fatalism and against the more recent attempts to ground an identity of categories on 'systemic' or 'structural' differences ('the savage mind')—my closeness to you, your distance from me are measured by what we do, by how and where we do it, in the context of a confrontation, of an immediate and universal struggle."[63]

In order for the readers/spectators to take charge of their destiny, they must take on a position with regard to the

59 Fortini, *Tre testi per film*, 78.

60 Fortini, 130.

61 In numerous writings Fortini underlines that Third World countries are not our "past"—as a certain ideology of progress would like us to believe—but our revolutionary "present," and that it is in the interest of neo-capitalism to avoid any possible conjunction among the "backward" demands of underdeveloped countries and those "advanced" of the European proletarians. At the core of this reflection is a critique of the white-European ideology of Modernism and it would be interesting to look further at how Fortini intertwines the legacy of a certain internationalist thinking with his often quoted readings of authors such as Franz Fanon and Lu Xun.

62 Fortini, *Tre testi per film*, 131.

63 Fortini, *The Dogs of the Sinai*, 59.

film, an attitude of critical investigation of the sequence and the events exposed. Fortini's reading of Brecht's "separation of the elements" is once again fundamental to understanding his attempt to foreclose the viewer's total identification with the film. Reviewing Brecht's *Dreigroschenroman,* on whose Italian edition he had worked with his wife Ruth Leiser, translator and autogenic therapist, Fortini commented,

> The spectators must be put in the position to turn into translators; from the contemplation of apparent and distant orbits they derive the laws of their own motion, they assert them in order to change them.[64]

When Fortini wrote to Straub in 1976 regarding the latter's proposal to make a film about the *The Dogs of the Sinai,* he already understood that in order to bring "all the relations a step forward," a history lesson, the text and its author will have to be "translated" into objects among other objects. Referring to the film he writes to Straub, "The distance that you introduce between those 'opinions' (text, music, etc.) and the completed object, or your product, is constant."[65] It is the distance among the "objects" which allows them—in Brecht's theater as much as in Straub's cinema—to take a separate and "conscious" position in regard to each other.[66]

In *Fortini/Cani* Huillet and Straub are taking a point of view, which locates Fortini within the space of the scene. Does the frame of the camera "reframe" Fortini and the text in an attempt to "translate" them? Fortini is filmed in such a way that he never has the possibility to look into the camera and encounter the gaze of the viewer. In several sequences he is shown in profile. He himself remembers his surprise—after seeing the film for the first time—about having been shot slightly from above, and appearing as a bent figure, almost humiliated. Or at least an isolated figure, which corresponds to "an intellectual of the 1930s with a Mitteleuropean culture that appears on the screen as an old man who speaks of the past with anguish."[67] Straub's technique of framing highlights "Fortini's limits as an Italian intellectual of a certain generation, born of the petty bourgeoisie [...]. His reflection, even if it goes a long way, remains limited to his condition, that is historically limited."[68] In fact, there are different levels of criticism in the film, each of them corresponding to a different degree of

64 Franco Fortini, "Brecht or the Talking Horse," in *A Test of Powers*, 437.

65 Franco Fortini, "A Letter to Straub: 2 December 1976," in *The Dogs of the Sinai*, 72.

66 I wonder how we could read definitions nowadays in vogue in the field of performance studies, such as "positionality" and "entanglement," in relation to Brecht's attempts to transform the "content" into an autonomous object "towards which text, music and images 'take position.'" See Bertold Brecht, "The Modern Theatre Is the Epic Theatre: Notes to the Opera *Aufstieg und Fall der Stadt Mahagonny*," in *Brecht on Theatre: The Development of an Aesthetic*. ed. and trans. John Willett (London: Methuen, 1964), 33–42.

67 Fortini, "I Cani del Sinai: conversazione con Franco Fortini," in *Film/Straub-Huillet*, 213.

68 "I Cani del Sinai: conversazione," 192.

separation: the first is Fortini's criticism toward himself while he is "forced" to recite a text written nine years before; the second is precisely the point of view of the two directors who stage a particular gaze on the text and on its author; third, the film gives space to the viewers to question in their own way both the framer and the framed, meaning the film and its object, the book.[69]

In the film's last shot—after the overview on the newspapers—Fortini is for the first time seen in the space where he reads. Until then he was almost seen two-dimensionally, while now, he is placed in relation to the house, the hill, in a three-dimensional space. The shot departs from his figure, relatively small, sitting in a corner, and pans over the surrounding landscape, moving to the right toward a conclusion which is at the same time a new opening. Straub said, "This is not a film that turns toward Fortini, but it's a film that turns to the outside."[70]

Thanks to Annett Busch, Tobias Hering and Romy Rüegger for their edits and comments.

69 A short article by Edoardo Bruno appeared as a review of *Fortini/cani* in issue 269/270 of *Filmcritica* in 1976, significantly bore the title *L'uomo che "si" legge e mentre legge si giudica* (The man who "reads" himself and judges while he reads) – recalling Fortini's own words: "The critic judges himself much more than he judges the others." "Verifica dei poteri," 49.

70 "I Cani del Sinai: conversazione," 193.

Manfred Bauschulte

ABSTRACT FURIES: MEMORY AND RESIGNATION

ON THE STORYTELLING OF CESARE PAVESE AND ELIO VITTORINI

I am going to follow a suggestion of Klaus Heinrich's and consider reflection as an act of "consideration." My essay brings texts by the Italian writers Elio Vittorini and Cesare Pavese into conversation and will be an introspective consideration of their dialogical art of storytelling. I am hoping to provide a range of entry points into those of Straub/Huillet's films that were based on works by Pavese and Vittorini. I will rely on passages from the literary texts that are of particular interest in view of the grammar of sounds and images in the films. At the basis of this is a statement by Jean-Marie Straub, "What we try to test are things outside us. We deal with texts that resist us. We try to test them, making audiovisual documents out of them that exist through movements within the frame, movements of light and sound."[1]

"Ritorno all'uomo" (Return to Man) is the headline of an article that Pavese published a few days after the end of the Second World War in the Communist daily *L'Unità* (Turin, May 20, 1945). He writes,

> To speak. Words are our business. One says this without the slightest timidity or irony. Words are gentle things, stubborn and alive, but made for men; men are not made for them. Everyone feels that we are living in a period in which we need to bring words back to the solid and naked neatness of the time when man used to create them in order to use them. And it so happened that because of this, because they are helpful for man, the new words moved and seized us like the pretentious statements of a dying world, like a prayer or a war bulletin.

1 Jean-Marie Straub, "Hölderlin, das ist die Utopie," *CICIM*, no. 30/31/32 (July 1991): 286.

Vittorini founded a magazine shortly after the war had ended, *Il Politecnico*, which did not last long however. In one of its final issues (no. 39 in November 1947), he published a movie review containing questions that are still relevant:

> Last June, I saw *Vredens Dag* [*Day of Wrath*] in Paris, six or seven years after seeing *Vampyr*, I don't remember where, [...] and eleven or twelve years after I saw *Joan of Arc*. [...] *Vredens Dag* gave me [...] the impression that in his films, Dreyer behaves like an "absolute inventor," as Chaplin does, and not just as an organizer [...] In my opinion, his invention is such [...] that it concerns the most advanced bound-

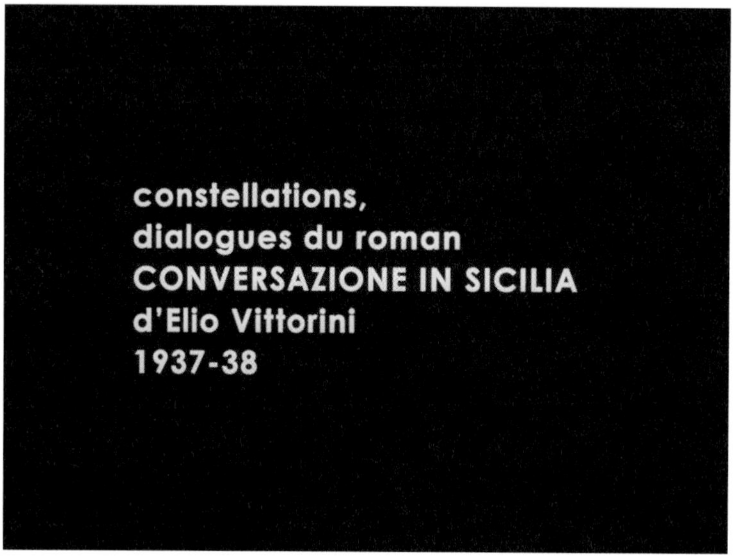

aries of our modernity. I imagine that you too have been struck by *Vredens Dag*, especially the first part, where the tragedy of the old witch takes place with compassion. Singling it out, I can see a legal tragedy that remains relevant today [...]. We have the old witch and we have the men who condemn her... The old woman believes she is guilty: that she is a witch. The "clergymen" are convinced they are looking at a sin that must be punished by upright men for the sake of the world. [...] But the former is not exactly a victim and only a victim because her innocence is abject (like her fat, old-woman nakedness in the torture scene); and the others are not exactly oppressors and just oppressors because they are not conscious of what they are doing. They are not blind, neither the former nor the latter, and the one accepts the others' blindness because she is blind, and the others cover her blindness because she is blind. [...] In fact, what makes it truly tragic is that in order to unveil it, we still need our judgment of men who are historically *less blind* than the old witch or the priests. [...] The horror comes from this ability to look backwards that Dreyer awakens in us. [...] Can we only look behind us, then? Does our judgment ever serve us for ourselves?[2]

In many passages in his diary, *The Business of Living,*[3] Cesare Pavese also acknowledges that for him a realistic perspective is only possible when looking backward. He does

2 Elio Vittorini, "Lettura su Dreyer," *Letteratura, Arte, Società*, vol. 1 (Turin: Einaudi, 2008), 470.

3 Published in English under two different titles: Cesare Pavese, *The Burning Brand: Diaries 1935–1950*, trans. A. E. Murch (New York: Walker and Company, 1961) and Cesare Pavese, *This Business of Living: Diaries 1935–1950*, trans. D. D. Paige (London: Quartet Books, 1980). Quotations hereafter are taken from *The Burning Brand*.

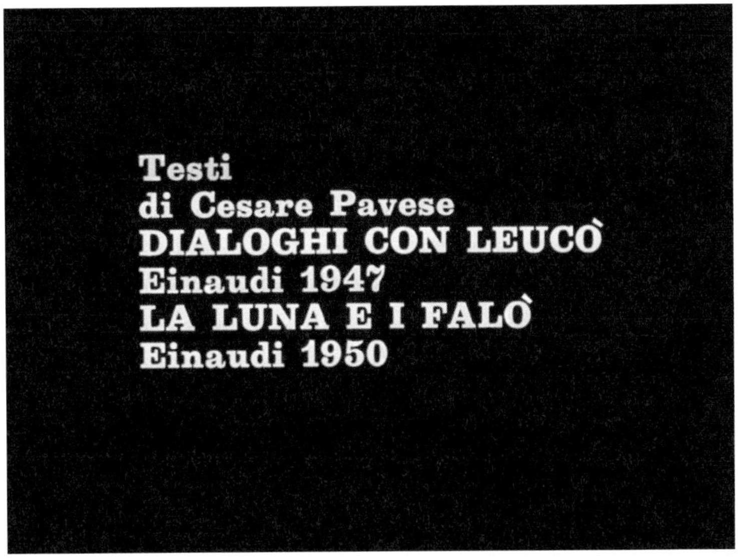

not mean the judgment perspective (like Vittorini), but the storytelling one. German writer Hans-Erich Nossack, who studied Pavese's *Dialogues with Leucò* intensely, describes this backward-oriented "mythological" perspective in a journal entry.

> To write a novel or a short story in which everything is seen from behind. Meaning, by someone who has walked the spiral's circle and is once again coming close to his starting point, but, as said, from behind, and where people from his past turn their backs to him and stand looking in the direction he had gone.[4]

In the early 1930s, Vittorini wrote about an author whose style he really admired.

> [Katherine Mansfield's] figures retain their interior intact. They continually find poetry this way. Their interior is not narrative; it is their expressive medium. They flow along the external reality, they move, they talk, they act perfectly in it, but something from them dives with a voice or a gesture inside, causing refraction. [...] But [...] the story of their "beautiful interiors" is not told. [...] And *Prelude* is instead only a warm reality full of leaves, morning birds, light, chickens, and carts moving along the road to distant cities [...]. Through the same expressive process of representing it, the reality represented is able to continually touch something hidden and mysterious, "differently real" [...] it is adherence to things in the hidden splendor of things.[5]

4
Hans Erich Nossack, *Die Tagebücher 1943–1977* (Frankfurt: Suhrkamp, 1997), 421.

5
Elio Vittorini, "Catarina Mansfield," *Letteratura, Arte, Società*, vol. 1 (Turin: Einaudi, 2008), 531–534.

Pavese characterizes the essential question of linguistic art that occupied his mind following World War II. He firmly defends the dignity of simple and clear man-made words. Using a film by Carl Theodor Dreyer, Vittorini describes the difficult situation of the analyst dealing with images and political memories. He has no other choice; he can merely look into the past. Pavese hopes to be able to use a storytelling technique to resolve the challenge of retrospection. Vittorini uncovers his ideal of writing in Katherine Mansfield's writing style. It aims at sliding over things and appearances in order to grasp reality piece by piece through gestures and voices originating from within.

In 1926, Ernest Hemingway's *The Sun Also Rises* was published in New York by Charles Scribner's Sons. The book had a far greater impact on readers than Martin Heidegger's *Being and Time* (published the same year) and exerted a wide influence. I will quote a passage from the end of the book:

> "Come on. Let's dance," Brett said.
> We danced. It was crowded and close.
> "Oh, darling," Brett said, "I'm so miserable."
> I had that feeling of going through something that has all happened before. "You were happy a minute ago."
> The drummer shouted: "You can't two time—"
> "It's all gone."
> "What's the matter?"
> "I don't know. I just feel terribly."
> "......" the drummer chanted. Then turned to his sticks.
> "Want to go?"
> I had the feeling as in a nightmare of it all being something repeated, something I had been through and that now I must go through again.
> "......" the drummer sang softly.
> "Let's go," said Brett. "You don't mind."
> "......" the drummer shouted and grinned at Brett.
> "All right," I said. We got out from the crowd. Brett went to the dressing-room.
> "Brett wants to go," I said to the count. He nodded. "Does she? That's fine. You take the car. I'm going to stay here for a while, Mr. Barnes."
> We shook hands.[6]

6 Ernest Hemingway, *The Sun Also Rises*, in *The Essential Hemingway* (London: Arrow Books, 2004), 52.

In this scene, one bit of dialogue ties into the next. It is layered over the interior monologue, which is consequently drowned out. The drummer in the background tapping on his instrument maintains an exalted voice. He lends rhythm to the storytelling, moving it toward jazz. At first glance, the scene appears anachronistic to us today, but writers like Vittorini and Pavese (in the late 1920s) immediately recognized themselves in its jolting rhythms, which guide the glances and gestures and separate the situations and feelings. They took the dialogic-rhythmic experiments of *The Sun Also Rises* as a model. As mature authors, they continued to see in Hemingway the "Stendhal of the 20th century" (Pavese). For them, he was not a representative of the "Lost Generation," but an original writer who, along with Gertrude Stein and William Faulkner, was following in the footsteps of Herman Melville, Edgar Allen Poe, and Mark Twain. In his anthology *Americana*, Vittorini characterizes him like this:

> On every one of Hemingway's pages, we find it accepted as an already ancient and accepted fact of mankind that the paths of purity are similar to those of corruption, and that purity is fierce, and that any desire for wildness is a desire for purity, and then we find, implicitly, a stoic ideal.[7]

7 Elio Vittorini, *Americana*, vol. II (Milan: Bompiani, 2002), 744–745.

8 Cesare Pavese, *Selected Letters*, trans. A.E. Murch (London: Peter Own, 1969), 217–218.

Pavese and Vittorini were united in their enthusiasm for American literature. Consequently, both emerged as passionate translators of important works. When the Fascist censors banned *Americana* in 1942, Pavese wrote a letter to the editor in solidarity.

> Dear Vittorini, I owe you this letter, because I think you'll be pleased to hear we are all solidly behind you. [...] I want to applaud your delicate treatment of dramatic contrasts, corruption and purity, ferocity and innocence. It is not by chance, nor by an arbitrary decision, that you begin with *furori astratti* [the abstract furies] [...] of *Conversazione in Sicilia*. In this sense it is something grand. You have brought into it the intensity, the exclamations of delight, so typical of your own views on poetry.[8]

Pavese emphasizes Vittorini's main impulse by mentioning the motif of "furori astratti" from the preface of

Conversazione in Sicilia (*Conversations in Sicily*); the book begins with the following sentences:

> That winter I was in the grip of abstract furies. I won't be more specific, that's not what I've set out to relate. But I have to say that they were abstract, not heroic, not living; in some way they were furies for all doomed humanity.[9]

The lyrical prelude of the Italian original possesses its own melody:

> Io ero, quell' inverno, in preda ad astratti furori. Non dirò quali, non di questo mi son messo a raccontare. Mi bisogna dica ch'erano astratti, non eroici, non vivi; furori, in qualche modo, per il genere umano perduto.

The "abstract furies"—abstract frenzy, undirected and meaningless furor, shapeless rage—no longer have much in common with the late-Renaissance philosopher Giordano Bruno's "furori eroici" or "heroic furies," but they remain part of the tradition of rupture that he initiated.

Italo Calvino, a student and friend, once characterized Vittorini's work in this way: "Every one of Vittorini's novels has as mythical form that of the voyage, as stylistic form that of the dialogue, and as conceptual form that of utopia."[10] I would like to focus on a position at stake with regard to the "furori astratti" in the first paragraph of *Conversazioni*. The resistance novel *Men and Not Men* [*Uomini e no*] helps to clarify Vittorini's position.

> Perhaps that was the crux of it. That one could resist as if one had to resist forever, and as if there could never be anything besides resisting. Resist for as long as men might go down, for as long as they saw themselves going down, always being incapable of saving them, unable to help them, unable to do anything except fight or wish oneself lost and done for. And why fight? In order to resist. As if the doom that lay upon men could never end, and a liberation never come. [...] Resist for the sake of resistance. It was very simple.[11]

Vittorini developed a dialogical art employing experience and imagination in order to face despair and destruction and to resist. Despite resignation and disappointment, he

9
Elio Vittorini, *Conversations in Sicily*, trans. Alane Salierno Mason (New York: New Directions, 2000), 3.

10
Italo Calvino, "Viaggio, dialogo, Utopia," *Il Ponte*, vol. 29 (July-August 1973): 904.

11
Elio Vitorrini, *Men and Not Men*, trans. Sarah Henry (Marlboro, VT: Marlboro Press, 1985), 170–171. Translation slightly modified.

does not give up on humanity. What matters for him is an existential perseverance that is supported by other people and that supports them by bringing them into conversation and including them. Even if reality confronts him with the fact that many positions are futile, abruptly abandoned, or in need of correction, he does not give up on the struggle. It is never in vain to struggle for the cause of the people. Vittorini defends a morality complex enough to provide guidance through the entangled conflicts of corruption and innocence, betrayal and resistance. The constitutive trinity of "travel/dialogue/utopia" in his work is exposed through forms of transition. They provide places and times where solutions and paths can be sought.

Cesare Pavese's intellectual and critical position is fundamentally more ambivalent than Vittorini's. On February 20, 1946, he wrote in the foreword to his *dialoghetti,* as he christened the *Dialogues with Leucò,*

> We have nothing in common with those who flit from one thing to another, experimenting, seeking adventure. We know that the surest, quickest way to find amazement is to fix our minds firmly upon the same object all the time. The moment will come when that object will seem, miraculously, as though we had never seen it before.[12]

Upon first glance, Pavese also seems to be grappling with "abstract furies." But let's read closely what he noted in his diary about his passions only thirty-six hours later:

> 22nd February. You have started spending your evenings alone again, sitting in a corner of the little cinema, smoking, savoring life and the end of the day, watching the film like a child, for the adventure, the brief pleasure of beauty or an awakened memory. And you enjoy it, you enjoy it immensely. It will be the same at seventy, if you live that long.[13]

Although he was endowed with great intellectual alertness and enormous literary expertise, Pavese felt himself on shaky ground. He had a fragile and resigned demeanor. He rejected adventure and travel; he only loves them in his imagination. After the grueling experiences of fascism and the Second World War, exhaustion got the upper hand on him. Outwardly, he espoused the Communist

12 Pavese, *The Burning Brand,* 287.

13 Pavese, 288.

idea, for example in *Dialoghi col compagno* (*Dialogues with a Comrade*), while he also wanted his *dialoghetti* to present a blend of American realism with pre-Homeric mythology. His focus (like Hemingway's and Vittorini's) appears to have been a desire for savagery that should assert itself against all despair. On the other hand, however, the struggle with savagery is a testament to Pavese's deeply ambivalent character. In July 1946, he noted his real view of his fragile position:

> 21st July. Rereading Fraser. What did you find in this book in 1933? That the grape, the corn, the harvest and the sheaf were full of drama and to speak of them in words was to verge upon profound significances that involve our blood, the animal world, the eternal past, the unconscious mind. The beast that strayed into the corn was the spirit. For you it merged ancestry and childhood, your recollections of things that puzzled and alarmed you in the country took on a sense of uniqueness, of something unfathomable.[14]

Pavese's *dialoghetti* are structures charged with awe and tension where he alternately ascribes divine qualities to humans and human qualities to gods. The mythological dialogues implicitly swerve back and forth between these positions, their features sometimes regressive and sometimes destructive. In his diary (April 10, 1949), he has offered insight into his haunted inner life:

> If you had no faith in what you are doing, in your work, the material you are creating, the pages you write, what a horror, what a desert, what a void life would be! The dead escape this fate. They keep themselves intact. Leone, Pintor, even Berto. Fundamentally, you write to be as dead, to speak outside of time, to make yourself remembered by all.[15]

Pavese uses the *dialoghetti* in order to speak with the voices of his mythological protagonists as though from beyond time. The *Dialogues with Leucò* are supposed to appear as if they are written by a person who is glancing back at the suffering and difficulties of the living. Only as a dead man, Pavese said, could he continue to speak with friends like Leone Ginsburg and others who were killed in the struggle against Mussolini. This painful-longing transgression

14 Pavese, 296. Translation slightly modified.

15 Pavese, 388.

constitutes what is fascinating about *Dialogues with Leucò*. These are conversations with the victims of fascism. The *dialoghetti* are cryptic conversations about and with the dead.

Both Elio Vittorini and Cesare Pavese left diaries behind as legacies. Vittorini's *Diario in publico* encompasses three decades from 1929 to 1959. It takes account of what the author saw in the existential and political turmoil of his time, spelling it out and making it readable. The book documents his passionate engagement with his era and the moral conflicts of his partisanship. Integrity and protest are the book's major features. Vittorini rightfully enjoys the reputation of a public intellectual and a person with integrity. Students and friends like Franco Fortini and Italo Calvino felt that their conversation with him continued after his death.

Cesare Pavese's diary bears the title *Il mestiere del vivere.*[16] It is the soliloquy of a writer who has given himself the task of self-analysis, although he denied any connection to psychoanalysis. He has a conversation with himself because he had very little trust in people, friends, and especially women, and felt he was walking on thin ice with them. Prejudice and anxiety sneak in. Readers are embedded in a web of references. His diary is a fascinating document of amazing erudition, extreme self-analysis, and a latent death drive. While Vittorini allows conflicts and problems to come to light and overtly turns them outward, Pavese keeps his encapsulated in an inner universe.

16 The book's German title, *Das Handwerk des Lebens*, means the "craft" rather than the "business" of living.

Both Elio Vittorini and Cesare Pavese were faced with fascism, confronted with crises in a world in which nothing could be relied upon, in which nothing was guaranteed. Despair and denial determined actual relations. In this situation, their dialogue-based storytelling obtains qualities of resistance. Stories surface in which the inner voice is reassured. Voices articulate what the individual fears, where he stands, what he trusts in. Step by step, new strength that can be directed outward grows out of self-discovery and self-discipline. Out of a torturous present emerges a vivid past because perception becomes memory. Crisis remains the basic condition. Grueling and painful conflicts define actual relations. Subtle observations gradually enter into conversations; painful events are touched upon; changes become palpable; people move closer to one another. Sometimes the dialogue serves as reassurance and clarification about an experience of loss. Things and situations that remain unnoticed become dangerous. Something fleeting and impalpable is nevertheless recognized and given a name. Consistent and reliable features emerge during conversations. Witnesses are called forth.

A viewpoint becomes noticeable in Vittorini's works that makes them especially suitable for being transferred to film. He describes the basic condition of his writing:

> The writer commits an error that weighs heavily in relation to the artistic fact when, in the case of emulation, he does not take account of speech (raw or processed), the way people (people in verbal reality) say fifteen, twenty, thirty, or as much as fifty percent with words and everything else with mimicry, gestures, glances, pauses, and the sound and rhythm of their voice (a mimicry and so on that in comparison to raw words are often deeply literate and downright refined). The writer depicts only a part and often only the smallest part of communicable reality if he limits himself only to repeating what is manifested in a turn of phrase or words, even if he chooses or reorganizes. He never fully depicts them and in any case never entirely possesses them if he does not manage to translate into words an individual selection out of everything that exists in communicable reality from mimicry, gestures, glances, pauses, and cadence (and so on) and not from words.[17]

17 Elio Vittorini, *Offenes Tagebuch* (Olten: Walter Verlag, 1959), 447. Editor's Note: Manfred Bauschulte quotes from the German edition in which considerable parts of the text have been rearranged and appear in different order than in the Italian original. The English translation was made from the German text taking into account the Italian phrases wherever they could be unequivocally identified.

Vittorini provides a look into his way of storytelling here. Alongside the theme of dialogue, selection comes to the fore. He implements by means of his own selection what he detected in the storyteller Katherine Mansfield—that she succeeds in retrieving a minimum of a world that is added to external reality, although it had been separated and removed from it. In this way, he became a master of compact story moments.

Pavese is a master of narrative dialogue who gradually clears away models and foreknowledge and subtly brings into play his own retrospection. A diary entry once again demonstrates this particular point of view.

> 13th February. Strange, the moment when (at thirteen or twelve) you left your country home, had your first glimpse of the world, and set out, buoyed up by fancies (adventures, cities, names, strong rhythms, the unknown). You did not know you were starting a long journey that, through those cities, adventures, names, delights and unknown worlds, would lead you to discover how rich in all that future was your moment of departure, the moment when, with more of the country in you than the world, you gave your backward glance. The world, the future, is now within you as your past, as experience, skill in technique, and the rich, everlasting mystery is found to be the childish you that, at the time, you made no effort to possess. Everything is in one's infancy, even the fascination of what the future will be, which only then is felt as a shock of wonderment.[18]

Pavese discloses here what guided him in the writing of *Dialogues with Leucò*, aside from his identification with his dead friends, "the rich, everlasting mystery is found to be the childish you that, at the time, you made no effort to possess." From the very beginning, his dialogue art is in search of his lost childhood.

In the novel *Il sempione strizza l'occhio al frejus* (English title: *The Twilight of the Elephant*), Vittorini finds an explanation as well as a continuation of the *furori astratti* (abstract furies) that have served as a thematic guide throughout this essay. He has his Odyssean protagonist Smut-Face say, "We're always waiting for a stranger to come and tell us something more. And 'something more' means 'the rest of it,' and that's what we need most; we miss it."[19]

This question about the "the rest of it" that we "miss" leads straight into the dialogue in which films by Straub/Huillet are engaging us as listeners and viewers.

Translated from German by Ted Fendt.

18 Pavese, *The Burning Brand*, 334.

19 Elio Vittorini, *A Vittorini Omnibus* (New York: New Directions, 1973), 176.

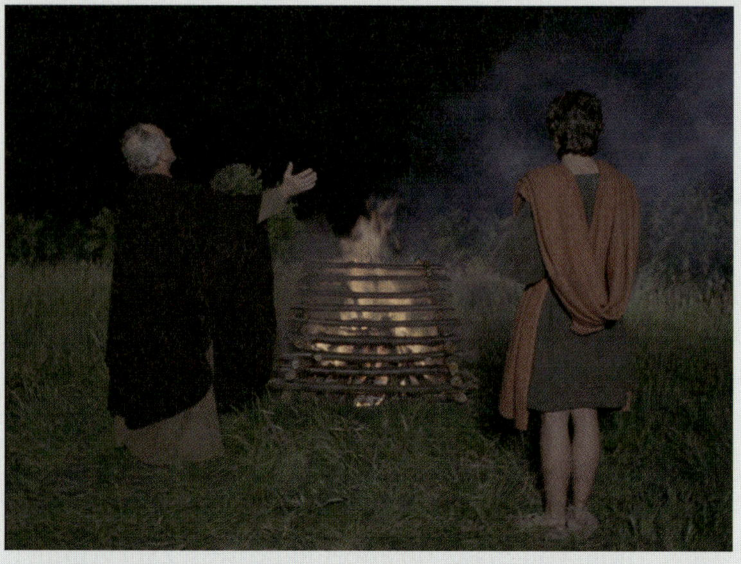

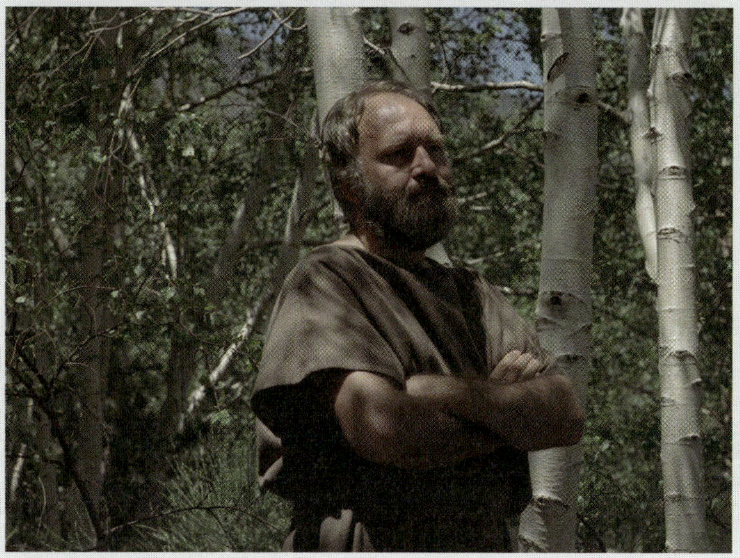

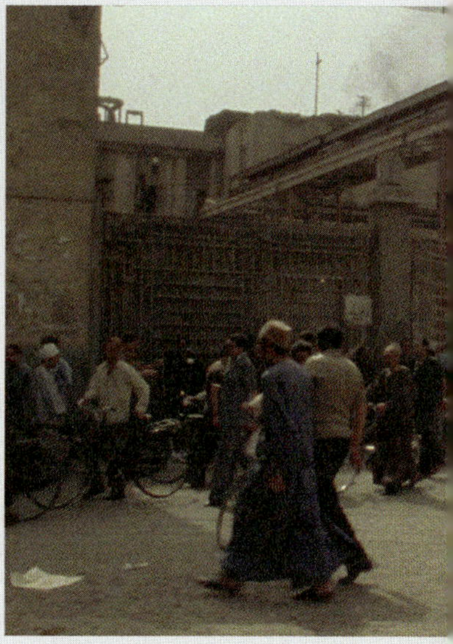

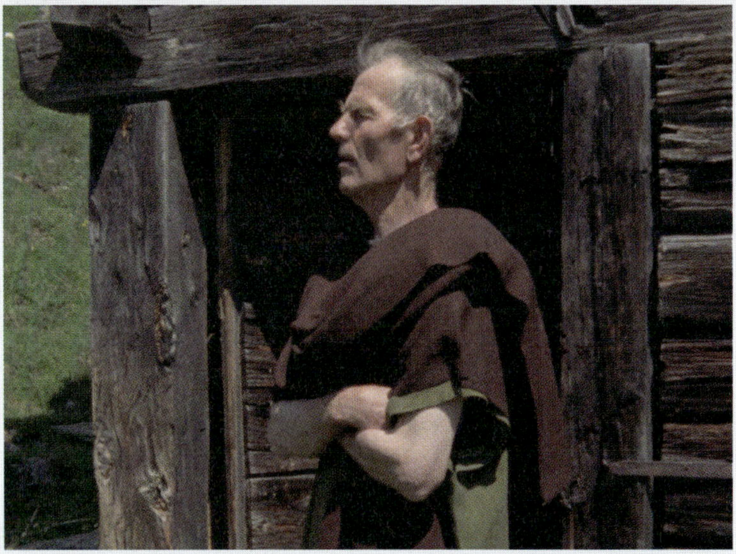
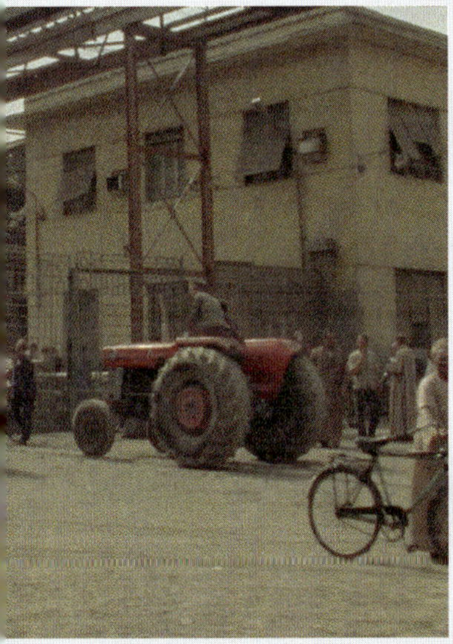
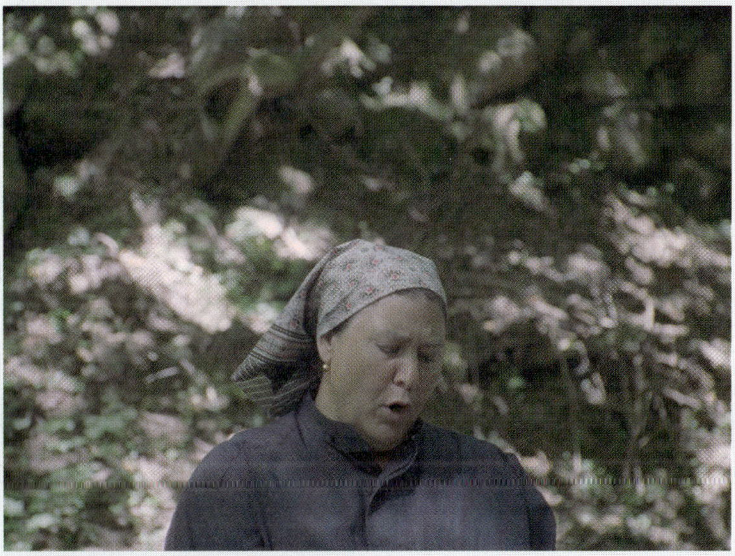
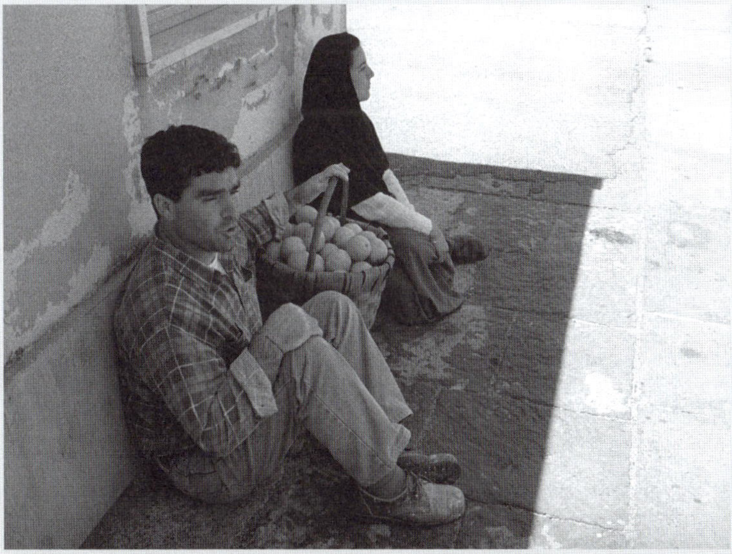

Peter Kammerer, Patrick Primavesi

WORK, PROGRESS

ON THE RESISTANCE OF PEASANTS IN THE WORK OF STRAUB, HUILLET, AND HEINER MÜLLER

[The following text is based on a public conversation that took place on September 16, 2017, at Akademie der Künste, Berlin, in the context of the "Tell it to the Stones" project.]

Annett Busch: There is a statement by Jean-Marie Straub that is quoted again and again, but seems to be readily overheard. Straub says, "I am a peasant from Lorraine." What does this mean? As far as I know, he wasn't born into a peasant family and he never seriously wanted to become a farmer.[1] Is it a metaphor to disassociate himself from "bourgeois filmmakers?" A gesture of solidarity? Appreciation? Provocation?

Peter Kammerer: I would add a second statement to the first. A retrospective dedication of the film *Chronicle of Anna Magdalena Bach* at its premiere in Munich both to peasants in the Bavarian Forest and the Viet Cong, who were in fact leading a typical peasant war. When the Straubs were shooting the Bach film, the Americans were bombing Hanoi daily. In an interview back then, Straub said of the dedication to the peasants, "We meant that the film—if we lived in a democratic society and not in the free market—the film could have interested people who didn't know anything about Straub or Bach and so forth, and who would have discovered something: music and a life, for example."

1 *Translator's note:* the German word *Bauer* means both *farmer* and *peasant* in English. For the French title of their film *Operai, contadini* (and later for the English translation as well), Straub/Huillet chose *paysan* rather than *fermier.* In some contexts in the following pages, I have however opted for *farmer* rather than *peasant* when the context seemed more appropriate

Patrick Primavesi: The combination of these two quotes already makes it clear what questions need to be addressed. And referring to the Bach film, there is a third statement we should keep in mind. More than once Straub emphasized that already in Bach's music, "there are several centuries of peasantry," which contradicts a prevailing interpretation of Bach's work rather from its context of churchly and courtly institutions. What are peasants actually? Out of what perspective do peasants enter Straub's view—as well as in the many different authors with whom Straub/Huillet have been occupied? "Peasants" are not only associated with rural economies, the evolutionary function of sedentariness, and the increasing industrialization and exploitation of

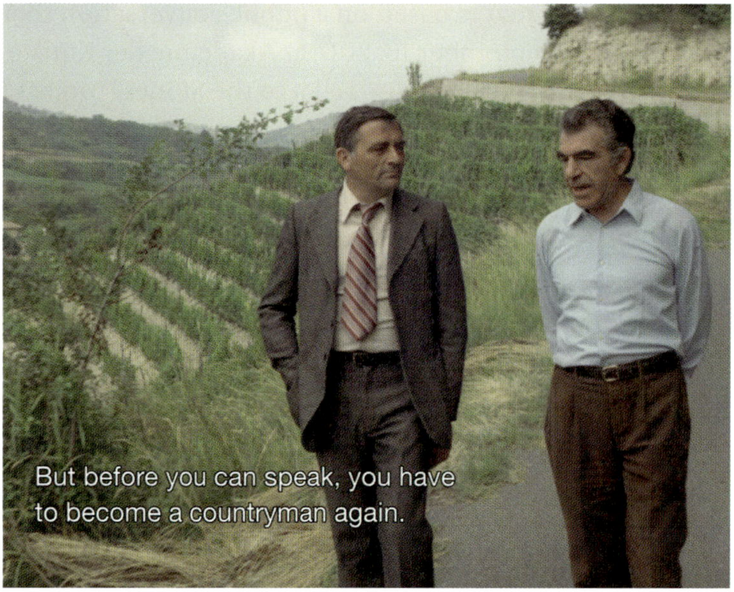

Mauro Monni and Carmelo Lacorte in *From the Cloud to the Resistance.*[2]

nature, or, in the history of ideology, with "blood and soil," but just as much with the East German "worker and farmer state" where much of the Bach film was shot. The word "peasant" has been cast in different ways in texts by Heiner Müller as well, he being someone who lived in the GDR (German Democratic Republic / East Germany) and was always returning from his trips to the West. In 1960, shortly before the construction of the Wall, he finished his play *Die Umsiedlerin oder das Leben auf dem Lande* (*The Resettled Woman or Life in the Countryside*) based on themes from Anna Seghers' short story *Die Umsiedlerin*. It's about the then contentious theme of land reform, which Müller depicts far more critically than the socialist state would have liked. The play appeared in West Germany many years later, somewhat altered, under the title *Die Bauern* (*The Peasants*).

AB: Why was it renamed, and when?

PP: Following the scandal at the premiere, which we can perhaps return to in a moment, Müller was officially banned from publishing and directing. The second version from 1964 was already called *Die Bauern* and could, under this title, be produced in 1976 at the

2
Lino (Carmelo) Lacorte, philosopher, professor at the University of Urbino where in 1968 he starts to reorganize the philosophy department and turns it into a hub for a movement of teachers and students who, inspired by and critically engaging with China's Cultural Revolution, try to grasp and put into practice Marx's dictum: "Philosophy cannot realize itself without the transcendence [*Aufhebung*] of the proletariat, and the proletariat cannot transcend itself without the realization [*Verwirklichung*] of philosophy." (Peter Kammerer)

Volksbühne in East Berlin. However, for Müller too, peasants were not just one theme among others, but also a matter of his political stance toward the state where he lived and some sore points in the history of this state. So between Straub/Huillet and Müller, several correspondences can be developed around the theme of "peasants." But to come back to your question, we should first clarify what Straub and Müller mean with "peasants" and what we associate with the word, now with respect to a potential for resistance that was again and again overlooked in the political history of modernity.

PK: It is an astounding fact that the major revolutions of the 20th century—the October Revolution, China, Cuba, Vietnam—were always sustained by peasants. But in the Italian resistance as well, this is very important for Elio Vittorini and Cesare Pavese, peasants played a very decisive role. Meanwhile industrial labor movements, as we all know, ended up as social democracies that in spite of the invention of "bearers of hope," today seem to have no future.

AB: This also comes up in the film *Too Early/Too Late* from 1981. In that case, Straub was talking about the betrayal of the peasants by president Abdel Nasser: "He betrayed the peasants. He had given them some hopes in the beginning."[3] In comparison to France, there was still a potential in Egypt,

> Despite all [...] Egypt is a country with a future and with a political hope. Thus in the first part one seems to be surveying a dead planet, and in the second one is entering into a future, in some sense.[4]

In a conversation with Helge Heberle and Monika Funke Stern for *Frauen und Film,*[5] Danièle Huillet comes back to the aspect of education, or rather of culture—knowledge that peasants have about their situation, which is a different kind of knowledge than political economy. She comes across fairly upset about the comments of an Egyptian woman during a discussion after a screening at Arsenal cinema (Berlin), "She said that one can expect no revolution from peasants because they are illiterate." Danièle then insists,

3 Huillet and Straub, in "Too Early/Too Late: Interview with Huillet and Straub," *Kino Slang*, (August 22, 2014), http://kinoslang.blogspot.com.

4 Huillet and Straub, "Too Early / Too Late."

5 See "The Fire Inside the Mountain," in the present volume, 250–265.

There's some partial truth to this argument, but nevertheless I can't hear it anymore. The funny thing and the sad thing about it is that the first—not just revolts but also revolutions—came in part precisely from the peasants, for example here in Germany. And they were also illiterate, but the thing was, they had a culture, just not the culture of the clergy.[6]

PK: Peasants are representatives of an "old world" who are making a stand against the bourgeois world, which Straub and his authors Vittorini and Pavese, who have spoken in multiple films, see as essential and do not simply write off as reactionary or anachronistic. I'd like to mention a quote from Marx, who writes about the implementation of the bourgeois revolution in the *Manifesto of the Communist Party.*

All fixed, fast-frozen relations, with their train of ancient and venerable prejudices and opinions, are swept away, all new-formed ones become antiquated before they can ossify. All that is solid melts into air, all that is holy is profaned, and man is at last compelled to face with sober eyes his real conditions of life, and his relations with his kind.[7]

That is a description of the modern situation: nothing can solidify anymore, everything is liquifying, what is newly formed is already antiquated a few days later. Everything evaporates, everything holy is profaned, and according to Marx, this strange reversal must begin: the awful desert that develops here needs to force and enable people to face with sober eyes their mutual relationships, human relationships, and their relationship with nature. And this is precisely what was not achieved, what the labor movement did not achieve. It got addicted to a modern fetishism and technological superstition and in contrast the rural world became a place of retreat. So peasants stand for the protection of the umbilical cord to the earth and also for resistance against the 20th century belief in progress and fetishism of technology. We are still not yet seeing human relationships with sober eyes. But that is the goal. We are no longer peasants, but also not yet sober. If I were to write a book or something for Straub, I would always say *sober eyes*. That is his work: sobering up.

6
"The Fire Inside the Mountain," 259.

7
Karl Marx, "Manifesto of the Communist Party," trans. Samuel Moore in cooperation with Frederick Engels, in Marx/Engels, *Selected Works*, vol. 1 (Moscow: Progress Publishers, 1969), 98–137.

PP: If we ask ourselves where Heiner Müller stands in regard to this point in Marx's work of a necessary sobering up, which he was certainly aware of, then perhaps these early plays—*Die Umsiedlerin* or *Die Bauern* just as much as the plays about industrial production, *Der Lohndrücker*, *Die Korrektur*, or even *Der Bau*—are important because they already deal with this question: what will become of these people who must achieve this system of ideologies through their bodies? How are these ideologies inscribed in bodies?

Now, *Umsiedlerin/Bauern* is a comedy—and we need to look at many of the old questions about the myth of rural work as well as the social conflicts and tensions in the life of peasants from a dual perspective. First, there's a sober and allegorical glance back at missed chances, irreparable mistakes, and omissions. However, there is a comical perspective too that Müller takes on this, which earned him an employment ban for over ten years after the premiere of *Die Umsiedlerin*. He was kicked out of the GDR writers guild (Schriftstellerverband), which was equivalent to a writing ban. Following a party hearing, the director, B.K. Tragelehn, was sentenced to hard labor in an open-pit mine, and the actors in the student theater company in Karlshorst were forced to write a self-criticism of their own roles and thereby disassemble the play and make it impossible. Why was this play so unbearable for the newly forming worker and farmer state? Perhaps it was not only the unfortunate timing of the performance shortly before the construction of the wall, but perhaps as well the insistence on this comical perspective that is linked to the peasants' resistance. In a kind of pictorial broadsheet in fifteen scenes, Müller depicts the phase in which the land of the Junkers, who were being dispossessed in the Soviet occupation zone, was divided among small farmers. The play begins with everyone receiving five hectares, no matter what he did before. Everyone is becoming a small farmer, but also competing with the not yet dispossessed medium and large farmers, the kulaks. In this way, Müller reflects a historical situation from after the end of the war to around

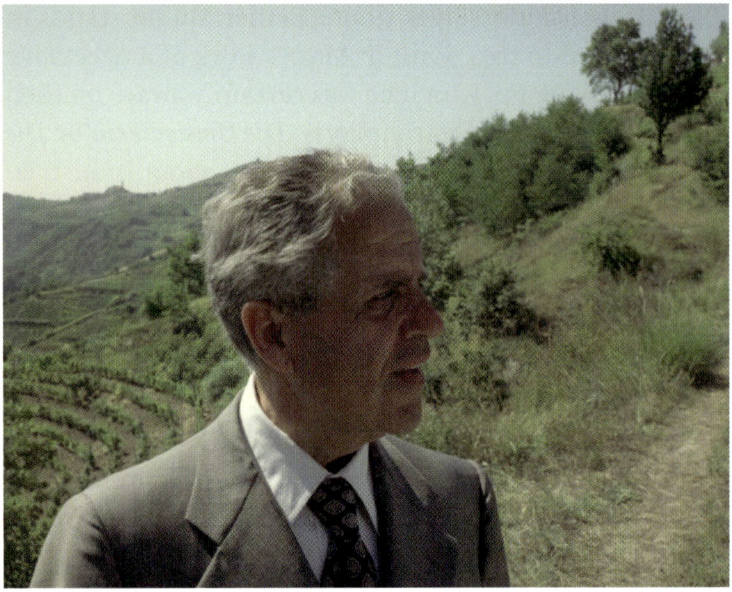

Paolo Cinanni in
From the Cloud to the Resistance.[8]

1950 in which there were not just *the* farmers as a generalized status or class with common interests. For many farmers, land reform was indeed unfair, triggering competitive battles as well as resistance to what the party had already long been planning, namely collectivization, which was then asserted through 1960. In the first phase as depicted by Müller, the small farmers are initially given their five hectares, which however cannot be properly cultivated without horses or machines so they need to begin joining together because they otherwise have no chance. Müller pushes the aggravation of this conflict again and again into comedy, like when the tractor driver tells the farmer that the political goal of collectivization will also be asserted with violence if need be. This is in scene 12 at night on the field:

The farmer measures the furrows with a piece of wood, the tractor driver smokes.

Tractor Driver: What's up? Should I plough you trenches? On your beet bed, too narrow for the cow's piss
It's waste to use the nag. I can be over
The boundary stone in a minute with the tractor.
It'd be easier if you join together.

Farmer: For you.

8
Paolo Cinanni, born 1916 in Calabria on St. Paul's Day which according to peasant myths made him a "friend of snakes" and immunized him against snake bites. Emigrates to Torino as a teenager and loses a leg in a work accident; gets to know Cesare Pavese and the Communist Party, works for the Resistenza in Milano and Cuneo, and is sent by the Party to Calabria in 1948 to organize land occupations and peasant uprisings. In 1967, together with Carlo Levi, he co-founds the Federazione italiana lavoratori emigranti e famiglie, a federation supporting Italian labor emigrants and their families. In the 1970s, he teaches in the philosophy department of the University of Urbino. In *From the Cloud to the Resistance* he plays a landowner. (Peter Kammerer)

Tractor Driver: Am I talking 'bout myself? The tractor, man, needs exercise.[9]

In fact, this includes everything referenced in the concept of "Erziehungsdiktatur" (dictatorship of education)—subsequently established in GDR research. Müller refers in his text to the often violent process of re-educating the rural population, a process marked by lies and force. The play's comical perspective reaches its climax in the diagnosis of the work-shy alcoholic Fondrak commenting on the ongoing (self-)exploitation of the peasants under communism and how the utopia of collective ownership can simply not be achieved with these people. The play was also banned for statements such as these and because the communist utopia in it literally drowns in beer when the peasants refuse their planned re-education into a solidary collective of people. Flint, the party secretary, who from the start tries to improve the mood regarding land reform ("which the people have been waiting for since Müntzer"[10]) finally wants to bribe the peasants with beer, which doesn't help either:

Flint: Beer for all, I said.
Beer for all.
We mistreated it and it mistreated us,
The old earth: ours.
The new technology was not nice to us either
With tanks and bombers, ours now and peaceful.
In one hand, what did not go together
The old earth and the new technology.
No more blood shed, no more sweat, tomorrow.[11]

So much for ideology. The play however shows that this tomorrow is nowhere close to being reached, and perhaps remains unreachable. It has a comic ending with the collectivization (in which no one has really believed), making some progress. Some recognize that they can profit from it in a new manner, by not working and taking sick leave. That is the ending and the play's punch line, which finally demonstrates a kind of domestication of the peasants into slaves of progress. Müller paid a high price for this mixture of sobering up and comical parody of state

9 Heiner Müller, *Die Umsiedlerin oder Das Leben auf dem Lande* (Berlin: Rotbuch/Verlag der Autoren, 1975), 82.

10 Thomas Müntzer (1489–1525) was a protestant priest and one of the revolutionary leaders of the Peasant Wars in German countries.

11 Müller, *Die Umsiedlerin*, 55.

propaganda, perhaps also because he bluntly exposed the deceit of the peasants. Perhaps we can go into correspondences to Straub/Huillet's work here?

PK: What strikes me in the quote from Müller's play is the line: "ours now and peaceful. In one hand, what did not go together, the old earth and the new technology." That's what is at stake here. The most direct parallel between Müller and Straub is probably in the film *Operai, contadini* based on Elio Vittorini's novel *Le donne di Messina*.[12] The war is over and a scattered horde is forming a new community, there are workers and peasants. The workers carry out work that is very much independent from nature. In winter as well, one can continue working at the same pace. But the peasants say, we don't work in winter. Nature has spoken, that's it! In winter we sit in the stable where it's warm and tell each other stories. And the workers say, you're a lazy bunch, and then the conflicts begin. Of course, they come up in Müller's case as well, as does mine clearance in the fields. The fields are all full of mines, which is a terrific metaphor. The question is what we do with a mined field. To put it more sophisticatedly, the earth is wounded. Wars in the last hundred years have also always been wars against peasants. This is continuing today in the Middle East and Iraq where destructive devices produced in Italy, in Brescia for example, or in Germany, are making life impossible for peasants.

But we were talking about the point where it really comes to a conflict between workers and peasants. How does one solve this conflict? In Vittorini's case, the thing blows up. Of course anything else would be a utopia. In the GDR, there were already very concrete, state-organized measures, and I think that in dealing with these problems, Müller had other interests than Straub. However, in the work of both, the question is whether it is industrialization in and of itself that makes us unhappy, alienated, and fearful people? Or is it capitalist industrialization? Is there a different, a truly socialist industrialization, that is not just based in another kind of exploitation? What would that be called, how do such

12 Elio Vittorini, *Le donne di Messina* (1949), new edition 1964, trans. Frances Frenaye and Frances Keene, *Women of Messina* (New York: New Directions Publishing, 1973).

a socialist factory or socialist products look? They must be completely different. But then we are fully in the realm of utopia. The only thing that is in fact obvious to everyone, to all of us in some way, is that the destruction of nature, which has already progressed into the human psyche, into the human constitution, cannot go on this way. And Müller was interested in that. The free space between man and machine—does it exist and where are the possibilities? I think Straub was less interested in that. Straub is in a wonderful way extreme when he says very severely, "industrialization is destroying us." We need to find another way out. This whole discourse about socialism and industrialization, about "How should things go on?" is inappropriate, without the possibility of practice. And where the possibility for political practice is absent, where one only ever chooses the lesser evil and can do nothing else, then of course philosophy also falls apart. After Kant, one either philosophizes up in the heavens or one philosophizes concretely, and today we can apparently do little concretely. And that's the problem for Straub and Müller, I think. It's very simple in Straub's case. He told me, "Peter, you have to step carefully on the earth. That's all you can do." Francis of Assisi says exactly the same thing, by the way. "Brother stone, I'm placing my foot on you now. Are you okay with that?" Francis claims the stones will answer.

PP: The film *Operai, contadini* is definitely a good example of how in this view of Italy after the Second World War—that is, almost contemporaneous with the processes presented by Müller—the conflict between workers and peasants could not be solved. Maybe we can reconsider this from another side as well with the question about the concept of work, which in Straub's case always concerns his own handwork too. What is actually meant by the work or handwork of filmmaking, also in relation to what Brecht called "theater work?" Müller really wrote for theater and always sought that challenge, constantly in dialogue with other artists, especially actors. For him, theater work was a kind of collective situation that should not be confined to the stage but should include the spectators. For Straub, work means first of all, filmmaking as a process that is prepared and performed with extreme care and an awareness of the necessity for artisanal knowledge and skill, often fighting for technologies already seen as obsolete by the mainstream. And he likewise insists that watching films is work too, not just fun and entertainment. In Straub's case, what was actually extreme in the many consciously provoked debates with spectators weren't only substantial political positions, but above all his impulse to rouse spectators out of their comfort seats and to make them realize that watching films is also about work, not least about an examination of what one is blocking out as a spectator or not perceiving and not wanting to realize. Comparable to Müller is an insistence here on discomfort even if the means are different.

PK: But they work in the same direction. Straub says, and ultimately Müller does too, that our task is to see anew and hear anew. And now that is really an eminently political and aesthetic task. For Müller, it was by innovating theater, but Müller always had the misfortune that the established dramaturgical world did not want to accept his actual innovations—similar to the aesthetic revolution in Straub's work, which no one wants, which is then denounced as "actors who drone monotonously," etc. In Müller's work, I've never quite understood the bombardment that he always said one had to increase. He took a completely different path, actually the opposite aesthetically of Straub. Straub becomes quiet, quieter and quieter, longer and slowed down. Whereas Müller concentrates by an extreme reduction. Only then will people understand. I find that very interesting. But both work on the aesthetic education of people so that this aesthetic education can see and shape the future.

PP: This program, which actually goes back to Friedrich Schiller, has however again and again been misunderstood in theater, often discrediting its political aspirations as well, being reduced to an education of the audience about something that would somehow be drummed into them. Therefore we need to be precise here—and Bertolt Brecht always wrestled with this as well: not a top down education about something particular, but the possibility of becoming freer through an aesthetic education in thought as well, and finally self-empowerment instead of indoctrination. That means to put seemingly irrevocable truths and therefore ideologies at risk, throwing light on them from different angles, sometimes reducing them to absurdity. This tendency is consistent in Müller's work, but in Straub/Huillet's as well, especially in their adherence to certain themes, subjects, and locations that they worked on or with, again and again. In this way, the retrospective of the films allows, as does the exhibition at the Akademie der Künste, some elements to return precisely because they cannot only be interpreted one way, but enable many complementary as well as contrasting readings.

The film *Communists*, consisting of five sections, is a great example of how strongly many of the earlier films resonate with each other and that one can really appreciate them as one large nexus now. Similar to how, already in *Introduction to Arnold Schoenberg's "Musical Accompaniment to a Cinematographic Scene,"* extremely different sequences are intertwined or in the *Cézanne* film as well, which likewise already included excerpts from *The Death of Empedocles*. The intertwining of the sections in *Communists*, however, clarifies that for Straub, the themes of work and exploitation or solidarity between people and between humans and nature are closely tied and also connected with the spectator's work of recognizing something only through patient, repeated looking and listening.

But perhaps we can as well talk about the work *in front of* the camera here, which is above all a work of speaking and breathing. In your introduction to *Sicilia!*,[13] you briefly said what speaking meant for you in the case of working on the *Empedocles* film. You play a peasant. In Hölderlin's text, it is the peasant who halfway up the mountain is asked for help by the banished Empedocles and Pausanias, to

13 Referring to Peter Kammerer's introduction to a screening of Huillet and Straub's *Sicilia!* on September 15, 2017, the night before this conversation.

take them in or at least give them water. He rejects them however—out of fear, opportunism, or dread of being punished by the citizens of Agrigento if he helps the banished men. You already said that you were rehearsing for weeks on these ten lines of text. Working through the text via the physical experience is another aspect that we should consider in order to understand what filmmaking as craft and labor actually means. Since in Straub/Huillet's case there is not only a conflict with widespread norms, technical and aesthetic "standards," but also the unusually precise work with those who speak the texts.

PK: That's very hard of course. What is clear is that Straub sees himself as a craftsman and someone resisting the film industry and its dictates. Personally, I experienced how difficult it is to speak ten lines that do not say anything in particular, but only contain a rejection and end with "Away!" We rehearsed for a long time. Straub: "No, say it again." Until I managed my "Away!" and then it still had to be recorded. Weeks and weeks were spent on that. Long before that however is a further decisive activity during the preparations for his films. The search for the location. Each time something decisive occurs. In the case of the Vittorini, for *Sicilia!*, it was oranges that had been thrown into a riverbed and seen by Straub and Huillet in 1971; many years later that becomes the spark while reading Vittorini. That is in fact already the film's entire content. To see the earth where one is filming.

The choice of the actors is another story in itself. We would need to know a lot more about the biographies of each individual actor. If we were to make a list with short biographies of every actress and actor in Straub's films, a whole world would come together. For example, Empedocles. He is the brother of Georg von Rauch, who was murdered here in Berlin. The entire Baratta family (Martina as Panthea, Vladi as Pausanias, Giorgio as a citizen): everyone participating is actually part of a big novel. Paolo Cinanni, from *Dalla nube alla resistenza* based on Pavese, was one of the major peasant leaders during the rural occupation in Calabria in 1945–1949. But in Straub's film, he plays a landowner, a kulak. Lino Lacorte, who plays Nino, was a philosophy professor—I helped with the "casting" of at least two films because those were all my friends and I saw how Straub and Huillet chose people. That is also something quite mysterious, the way they have of looking at people. It's definitely not an industrial way of looking. One should at some point track the development of each working process, for example how they go about the printing. These are processes people are generally not interested in, procedures sort of handled by the apparatus.

PP: In this regard it is not only a matter of casting, inserting suitable human material into clichés, satisfying visual expectations. The extensive series of films partly or entirely shot in Buti that began (after *Dalla nube alla resistenza*) again with *Sicilia!* and *Operai, contadini* and then continued over ten years is also interesting because all of the factors we've just mentioned are condensed in them: people whose histories are partly marked by migration out of Sicily to wealthy northern Italy; texts (above all by Fortini and Pavese) addressing the political history of Italy as well as the connection of myth and the perception of nature; shooting locations where a particular landscape, a wooded valley, has survived and now plays along in the films as living nature; and finally, concerning the work with speech and singing, the re-establishment of a particular performance style with a long tradition in the region of the Pisan Mountains, a kind of epic *Sprechgesang* that is worlds away from the realistic and psychological style of representing people that today has long become the norm, in theater as well. It is not by chance that these films mostly originate in a theatrical production in the old theater in Buti where over the years a very special audience has been able to form. All of these elements show that film work for Straub/Huillet, similar to their theater work, was also a cultural practice developed from their encounters with people and places.

PK: In the last hundred years, Italy attained a very singular balance between urban and rural culture. On one hand, the special characteristic of the cities—each one a big individual. Sienna has a totally urban culture, but also totally rural. Pisa, Lucca, Arezzo, Urbino are all rural cities. One notices that immediately. They are growing out of the ground, out of the landscape. This also belongs to the secret of the Straubian national affiliation, of nationality. They make German films, they make Italian films, French films. Labels that always cause terrible difficulties at film festivals. "Mr. Straub, are you now an Italian filmmaker or a German or French one?"—a question that annoys Straub terribly. But there are enormous differences between the Italian, French, and German films. That's exciting. The Italian films all have something to do with the ground. So, solidarity, nature, togetherness that has sprouted in nature on particular ground, in very particular places. Vittorini and Pavese were both born the same year, 1908. Pasolini was born in 1922. The major Italian writers of the 20th century were born in this timespan. Almost no one before, almost no one after. Whoever was born in this era had a question written on their skin: What is industrialization doing to us and Italy? What do we do with 10,000 years of agrarian history that have shaped this landscape? When a generation has a major question, it also writes major books. Everything else becomes secondary. In this way, Italy's writers were confronted with the question that Mircea Eliade expressed at the time in the text that I wanted to quote as well. In the 1950s and 60s, through his work on mythology and shamanism, Eliade became very influential in the USA and worldwide, for Pasolini and his film *Medea* as well.

The quote comes from the book *The Forge and the Crucible*, first published in 1956, and reads:

As for the crises of the modern world, we must bear in mind that this world inaugurates a completely new type of civilization. It is not possible to foresee its future developments. But it is useful to remember that the only revolution comparable to it in the past history of humanity, that is, the discovery of how to cultivate the land, provoked upheavals and spiritual breakdowns whose magnitude the modern mind finds it well-nigh impossible to conceive. An ancient world, the world of nomadic hunters, with its religions, its myths, its moral conceptions, was ebbing away. Thousands and thousands of years were to elapse before the final lamentations of the old world died away, forever doomed by the advent of agriculture. One must also suppose that the profound spiritual crisis aroused by man's decision *to call a halt and bind himself to the soil*, must have taken many hundreds of years to become completely integrated. It is impossible to imagine the upheavals of all values caused by the changeover from the nomadic to the sedentary life and to appreciate its psychological and spiritual repercussions. The technical discoveries of the modern world, the conquest of Time and Space, represent a revolution of similar proportions, the consequences of which are still very far from having become part of us.[14]

PP: I'd like to address two points here, first the large timespans: "Thousands and thousands of years were to elapse before the final lamentations of the old world died away." That is already noteworthy because we have become used to reckoning with what is now the fourth phase of industrialization. In the digital era, we find ourselves so far from land work that we can no longer imagine that agriculture itself was a revolution. But you're right now in saying, with Eliade, that this revolution has not yet been dealt with. This is why Pavese is so interesting, because he processes this deficit with the help of Greek mythology. When he gives the cloud a voice, it is also a matter of the struggle against a person who has already conquered nature with civilization through agriculture, cattle breeding, and so on. In Straub/Huillet's case, this perspective, partly inherent in the texts, is further intensified when the gaze from the present retrospectively points to the future as well. Namely to catastrophes that are currently happening, when Sicily is being destroyed, when the dock, for example, where the trip in *Sicilia!* begins, is already full of garbage. But to return to Müller again, it should be noted that he integrates 20th century Industrial Revolution themes into a mythological time frame too. In *Zement*, he inserted

14 Mircea Eliade, *The Forge and the Crucible* (1956), trans. Stephen Corn (Chicago: University of Chicago Press, 1978), 177. Translation slightly modified.

the mythological commentaries into Fyodor Gladkov's novel, thereby placing the construction of a cement factory in a larger perspective where the ideology of the "New Man" is also questioned.

PK: We should indeed look into *Dialogues with Leucò* for parallels in Straub with *Zement*. The collision of myth and the future, or the present, the modern present. This same constellation exists in *Zement* as well. But first I want to quote Pavese. On October 15, 1945, he wrote in his diary:

What would you say if, one day, all natural things—springs, woods, vineyards, the countryside—vanish from the earth, absorbed by the cities, remembered only in phrases from bygone times? They will have the same effect as the gods, nymphs, and sacred groves we find in certain Greek poetry. Then the simple phrase: 'There was a spring of water,' will be deeply moving.[15]

That's it, actually. What is added in Müller's case with *Zement* is the intensification of the question about the battle of the sexes. The battle of the sexes is just as hard and actually even bloodier than the class struggle. In the meantime, I've come to think so too. And also: what do we do with the machines? Straub says very practically, we need a moratorium, we need to slow down those processes, make them as slow as possible. Müller already starts from a hybrid between man and machine. That is the major theme, I think. Straub simply just says, "moratorium, step gently on the earth."

15 Cesare Pavese, *This Business of Living. Diaries 1935–1950*, trans. Alma Elizabeth Murch (London: P. Owen Books, 1961).

PP: But there is also another difference in the effect—if we can put it this way. In Müller's work, a very sober perspective is opposed to the quoted emotion that ultimately results from the conjunction of mythology and contemporary conflicts with nature and the earth. We already had this in the *Umsiedlerin* with the openly failed hope of being able to stop and control: "In one hand, what did not go together / The old earth and the new technology." Müller's view of the illusions that are fundamental to the ideology of technological progress also takes on comical traits when, for example, the ideal hero Herakles doesn't notice that he has already transformed into a machine. It is an almost traumatic return of repressed collective experiences that makes each new industrial revolution push up the unprocessed crises and wounds of the earlier ones. Therefore, Müller's writing on man-made disasters not only reflects a work of mourning, but also new wounds and catastrophes—for example the waste-contaminated lake at Strausberg (in *Medeamaterial*) does not only actualize the conflicts of the mythical *Medea* figure, but also makes them forerunners of everything that today more and more strongly imposes on us an irreparable destruction of nature. In this respect, Müller's examination of mythical images in the conflict between man and nature points far beyond that which is sketched in Pavese's work and what also still appears as a mythic past perfect in Straub/Huillet's work. If we can say that there is something like a peasant past of the world, then it is...

PK: ...practically also still our world, it is 10,000 years.

PP: Exactly. This world is still not fully overcome and still has an effect in current conflicts. Accordingly, but from the opposite perspective, Marx (in the third volume of *Capital* and in *Theories of Surplus Value*) states that rural labor is "in no way primordial," but is itself already a product, a kind of precapitalist industrialization, and "exploitation of natural forces." Since then, if we ask ourselves what comes after the third or fourth generation of industrial revolutions, we have to acknowledge that newer and newer forms of the exploitation and destruction of nature have been superimposed and taken on a life of their own. About the moratorium, I am not so sure. In the case of Straub, it is interesting that he is also always reconsidering his interactions with technology. You put it very precisely yesterday that as a filmmaker one cannot naively assume that the improvement of one's tools is simply a given, that one can use them and in the end the quality of the films will automatically improve, as the companies promise. That we need to realize this much more as an experience of loss, that we have no more film labs or that there are almost no more projection-

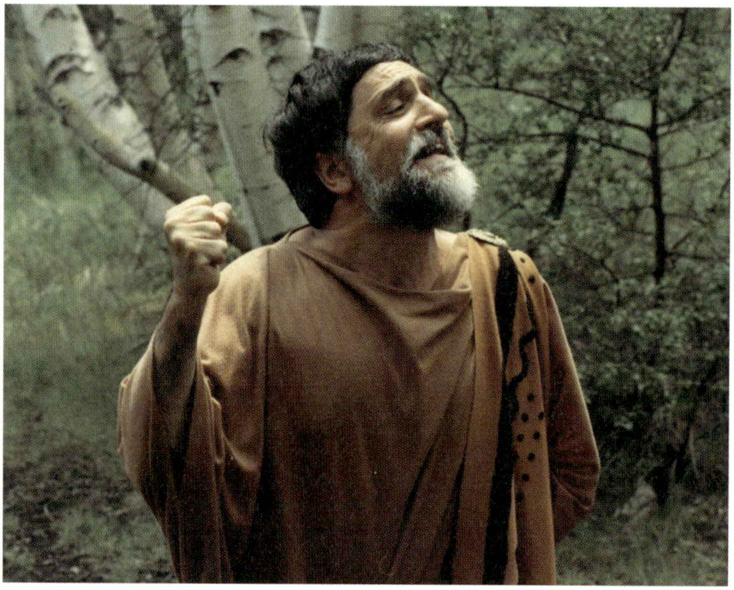

Giorgio Barrata in
The Death of Empedocles.[16]

ists left who can show films as they are meant to be seen, and that the preservation of film is also becoming more and more difficult. The painful experience that an understanding of technology based on physical labor is being lost has also induced a new attitude toward the digital in Straub's case. He shot all of his last films with this technology and still manages to push it beyond its limits, so to speak, which have already ossified into conventions.

PK: As we all know, it took a long time until Straub accepted digital. He is not simply a Luddite who says, I don't want any new technology. But a moratorium means as slow as possible so that we know what we are losing. The joke with progress is that one loses so much, that so much collateral damage is incurred. That's when Straub says, "Stop!" Most Straub films could no longer be shot today. The landscapes have completely changed and people have also changed in the meantime. I mean that very physically. *Moses and Aaron*, shot in Alba Fucens, a wonderful place and at that time deserted, ancient ruins, is today a tourist circus. When they were shooting, the airspace was even temporally closed off so as not to disturb the music being recorded in the open air. Today, the Straubs would no longer find those kinds

16
Giorgio Baratta studied philosophy with Heidegger in Freiburg in the 1950s and built up the research center for migration and people's culture (*cultura popolare*) at the University of Urbino. He devoted a large part of his intellectual life to studies on Antonio Gramsci and worked for the International Gramsci Society. He wrote a book on Edmund Husserl, when the revolution seemed within reach, and others on Gramsci and Leonardo da Vinci, when it was necessary to start over. His children, Martina and Vladimiro, both appear alongside himself in Huillet-Straub's *The Death of Empedocles.* (Peter Kammerer)

of shooting locations and shooting conditions. In regard to all these problems, theater has it easier.

PP: This difference is something I would like to reconsider too. In fact, theater has repeatedly been viewed as strange and anachronistic. During the age of Enlightenment, stage acting had to be justified as an instrument for national education in the German-speaking states and principalities. This resulted in a hollow compromise between morality and entertainment, which was a disaster for authors like Hölderlin, Kleist, and Büchner, some of whose texts could first be performed only 100 years later. In the 1960s, with the after effects of the political compromises of Brechtian theater still in sight, Müller experienced the paradox of being excluded from the theater of the socialist German state for over ten years. We all know how important theater was in the GDR as a kind of surrogate public life and medium for self-understanding not only for intellectuals. However, the further reaching idea of using theater as a social free space or laboratory for non-standardized social behavior was rarely achieved.
In this way, we can also see Brecht as a further reference point connecting Straub/Huillet with Müller. An examination of Brecht traverses all of Straub and Huillet's work, it always returns at the point where a fundamental attitude is addressed. Here, it is a matter of something that could have been directly taken over from Brecht, namely the insistence not only that the world is bad, but also that those who want to change it must change themselves too. With Marx, this moment can also be understood as a principle of the bourgeoisie, its constant drive toward renewal and radical change. However, this contains an anthropological and in another regard political element that has something to do with theater. Müller is very close to what performing in theater is about when he not only extracts comedy from his serious material and acts out the shift from tragedy into farce, but when he also works on a theater that enacts societal conflicts in the concreteness of physical experience. Maybe we can now return to Straub/Huillet's understanding of theater work, which was

not a mere preparation for the film work, but always an autonomous process.

PK: I can only say very little concerning Straub and theater. I experienced three instances: *Antigone* here in Berlin on Cuvrystraße and the others were in Buti, *Operai, contadini* and *Sicilia!* The only thing I can say about it is that Straub was always furious if someone alleged he was using theater to rehearse with the actors what was then simply redeployed in film. It is completely different to perform the same text in theater or, with the same people, to make a film. Where the earth acts too, where quite different co-actors are present. And he insists on this difference, it concerns also the particular manner of speaking. There is a difference if I say something to the spectator or the stones. The stones were those from Segesta and the stones are also different, if I say it to the stones here or the stones in Segesta—the Straubs think in these kinds of differences. And the most important point is the camera position. One can look for it forever. "There are people who just dance around until they find it," says Straub, "but there is the right position." And in film, as in the case of *Antigone*, he built a tower, every shot was calculated to the millimeter. As spectators of the film, we all see the same, we have the same privilege. We all see the same things. In the theater in Buti, I sat like an idiot quite in front, close to the stage. I hadn't thought about a big table that was standing there, meaning I just saw the actors' feet under a big table, nothing more, just the roof. It was an oblique, frog's-eye view. When I told Jean-Marie, he said, "quite an interesting position," and persuaded me finally to consider it a great privilege to have not seen any faces or people, but only the feet, depending on how they moved. He found that enormously important. And that is exactly the difference between film and theater.

PP: In theater, from each point everything appears different and above all fleeting, ephemeral.

PK: Müller says that in theater the actor can die at any moment. It is a life and death struggle.

PP: It goes further: theater is the shared presence not only of the living, actors, and spectators, but also of the potentially dying. In general, as Godard already put it, film watches death at work: everything that we see in a film is changing, is already past in the moment of the take. In Straub/Huillet's work however something else occurs, which may arise from their intense involvement with theater. You talked about your own experience from the *Empedocles* film. In Straub/Huillet's work, this life and death struggle takes place in speech and during production because the actor's speech is not recorded as something happening randomly and later arbitrarily edited and manipulated, but as a physical processing of the text. A very specific form of theater results from this, which is quite different from acting in front of a present audience. Like the green trees in the valley in Buti or the plants ruffled by the wind on Etna, the actors speaking before the camera are also delivered to a sober gaze so that their transitoriness becomes more intensively tangible than all the deaths that illusionistic cinema with its digital effects has to offer.

17 Bertolt Brecht, "Life of Galileo," in: *Collected Plays*, vol. 5, ed. John Willet and Ralph Manheim (London: Methuen, 1980).

PK: Brecht is really a hinge between Straub and Müller, in terms of technological progress as well. If we don't slaughter this cow with all the rituals and everything a ceremonial slaughter requires, then we are lost. I recently looked something up again in *Life of Galileo*, in the final version, where he says,

> I maintain that the only purpose of science is to ease the hardship of human existence. If scientists, intimidated by self-seeking people in power, are content to amass knowledge for the sake of knowledge, then science can become crippled, and your new machines will represent nothing but new means of oppression. With time you may discover all that is to be discovered, and your progress will only be a progression away from mankind. The gulf between you and them can one day become so great that your cry of jubilation over some new achievement may be answered by a universal cry of horror.[17]

That's the point where we stand today.

Translated from German by Ted Fendt.

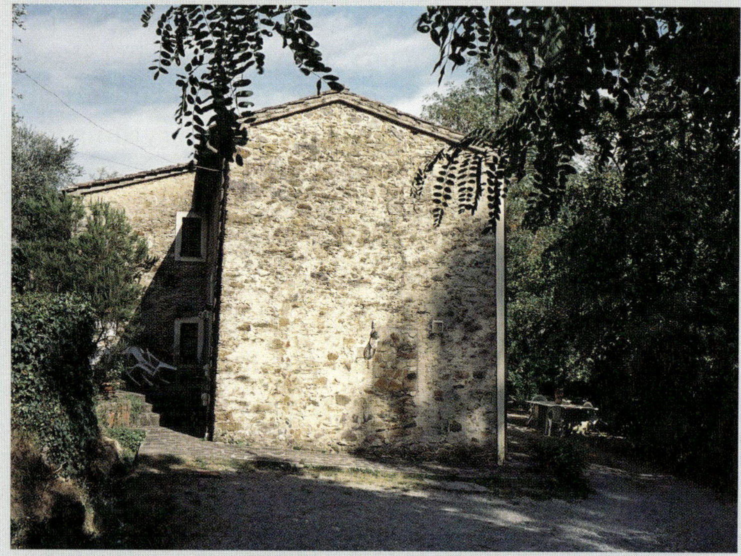

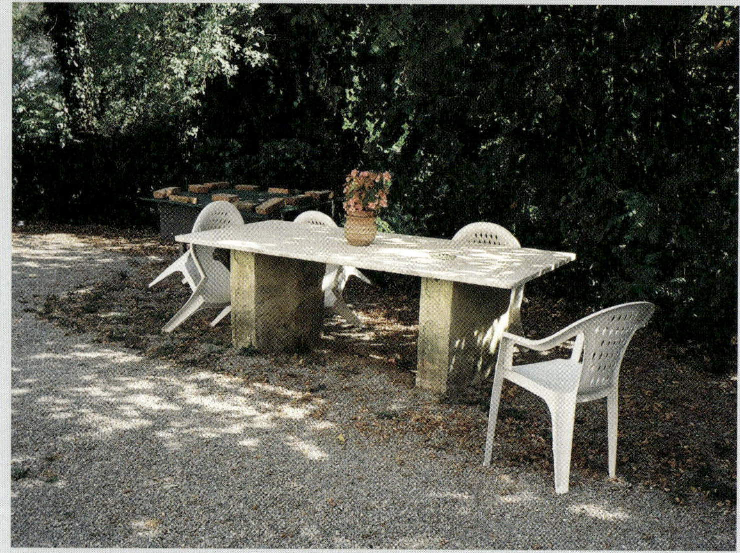

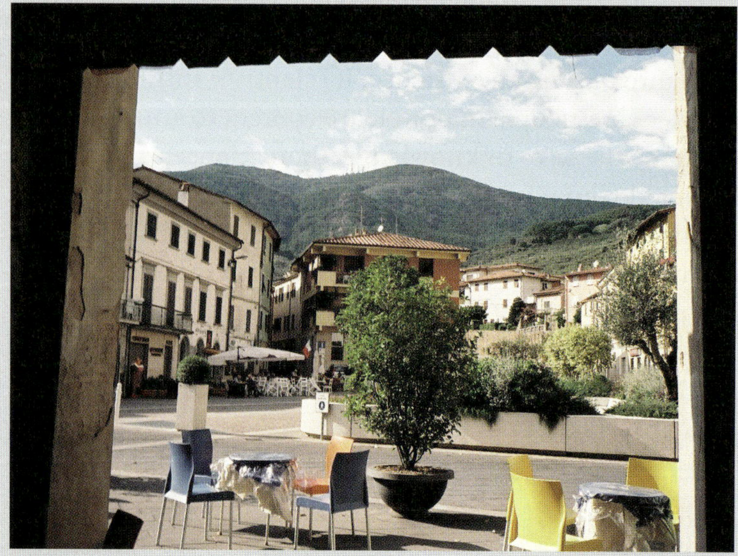

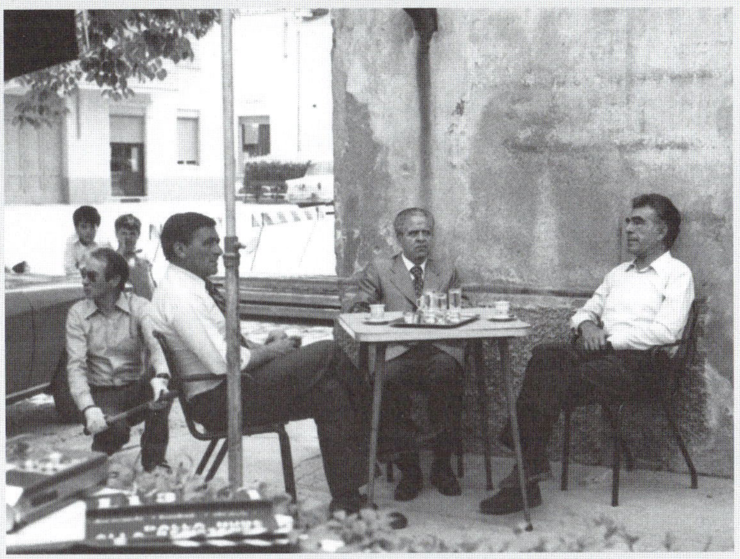

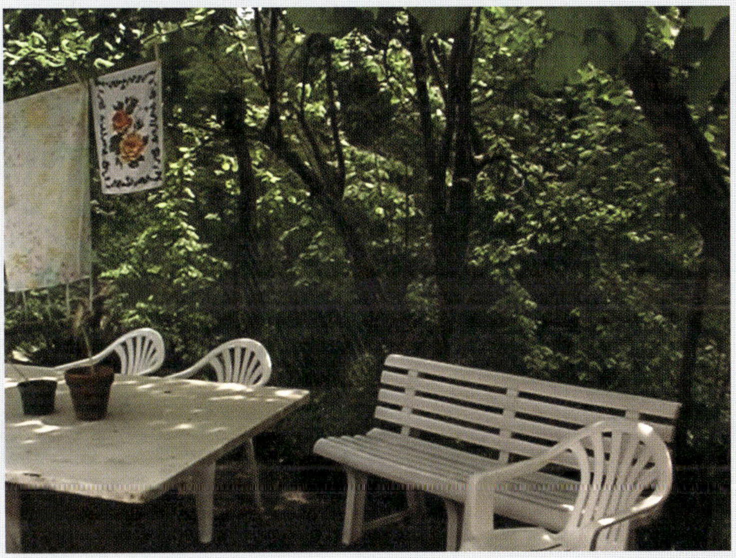

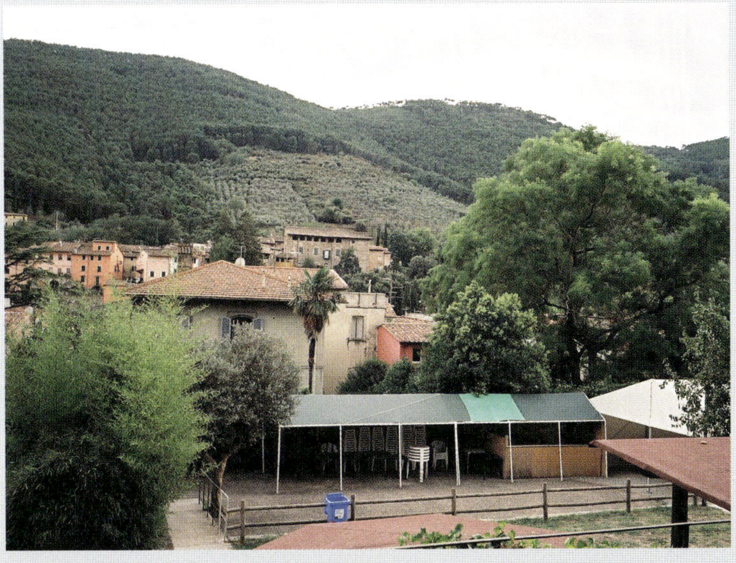

Rinaldo Censi, Giovanna Daddi,
Armin Linke, Dario Marconcini

THE POSITIONS WERE THE SAME, THE SETTING WAS COMPLETELY DIFFERENT.

[The following conversation took place at Teatro Francesco di Bartolo in Buti. Transcribed excerpt from *The green and the stone. Straub-Huillet in Buti*, 2017, 42 min (vimeo.com/236318068), a film by Armin Linke in collaboration with Rinaldo Censi, Giulia Bruno and Giuseppe Ielasi. The other parts of the film were shot at Il Seracino – Cascine di Buti and Monte Serra, with Giovanna Daddi (actress), Dario Marconcini (actor and artistic director of Teatro Francesco di Bartolo), Romano Guelfi (actor and filmmaker), Andrea Bacci (actor and president of Teatro Francesco di Bartolo). Produced on the occasion of the exhibition "Tell it to the Stones: The Work of Danièle Huillet and Jean-Marie Straub," Akademie der Künste, Berlin, 2017. Camera and sound: Armin Linke; editing Giulia Bruno, Giuseppe Ielasi; translation Klaudia Ruschkowski.]

Dario Marconcini: I've been the artistic director of this theater for a long time, and one day I was told that there were two filmmakers here in Buti. They were guests at the home of a man called [Mauro] Monni, who had acted in *Dalla nube alla resistenza* [*From the Cloud to the Resistance,* 1979]. They usually stayed with him whenever they were in the region.

Rinaldo Censi: The mayor?

Giovanna Daddi: No, he wasn't the mayor. He was the mayor's cousin.

DM: He asked me to dinner one evening, where I met Jean-Marie and Danièle. When I met Jean-Marie and Danièle I was struck by their appearance. Especially Danièle, who had this extraordinary rural elegance. She was chic, but at the same time she was so rural French, and very beautiful. He was very cultured with his cigar. Both of them made an impression on me. Straight away, I began thinking of how we could get them into the theater here. So, we tried to find an excuse. I had invited a theater company to do a work on Hölderlin, and as I knew of his film,[1] I proposed that he host a film festival in the front room of the theater, which used to be the meeting room of the Anarchist Workers Society.

1 Probably referring to *The Death of Empedocles* (Danièle Huillet, Jean-Marie Straub, West Germany/France, 1986) or *Antigone*. The theater of Buti produced a version of *Antigone* in 1994. Huillet and Straub came to Buti for *Sicilia!* in 1998, the first time since *Dalla nube alla resistenza*.

So, we set up a small film theater, for fifty or sixty people, and we invited Jean-Marie and Danièle to present their films, including [*Empedocles*]. At that event we talked, and I asked them if they would like to do a performance in the theater here in Buti once a year. We offered to host them and to organize everything.

GD: Something small-scale. He said, "Well see, we'll see..."

DM: Then one day, he called me and said, "All right, I'll come." And for more than ten years, at least twelve years I think, he came to Buti every year, apart from one year. He would arrive in March, set himself up in the small cinema theater, and that's where we would rehearse. March, April, May, June... We would shoot the film in June, and more or less at the same time, sometimes before, sometimes afterwards, the theater performance was staged in here. It wasn't just a replica of the film; it was very similar, with the same dialogue and props, but in a different spatial setting.

GD: The positions were the same.

DM: The positions were the same, the looks were the same, our physical movements were identical, but clearly the setting was completely different. Our costumes were the same in the theater as in the film. The performances took place in here and they were absolutely extraordinary, because of the theatrical language used, the meaning of the language, the meaning of the gaze, the tension of the gaze, the steadiness, the stillness, everything. A lot of us came from what could be called the theater of gestures, from experiences in street theater, avant-garde theater, agitprop theater, call it what you want, and we were now being instructed by Jean-Marie to stay immobile, and having to fix our gaze on these numbers. Seven, eight... and then the only other way you could look was perhaps over there, and hold that position.

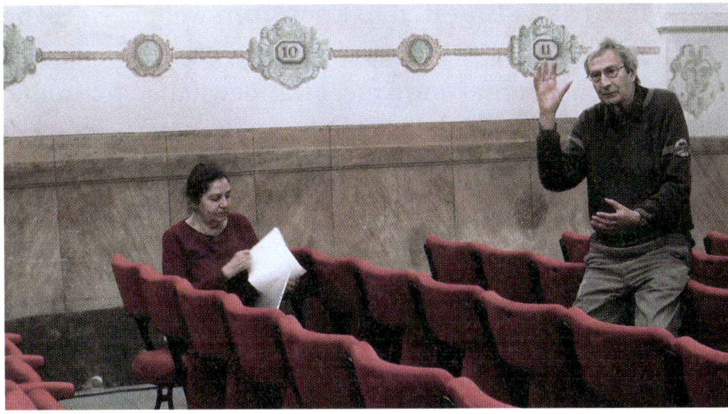

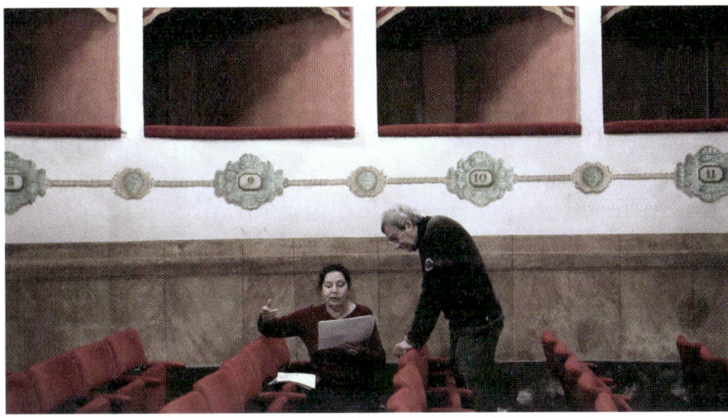

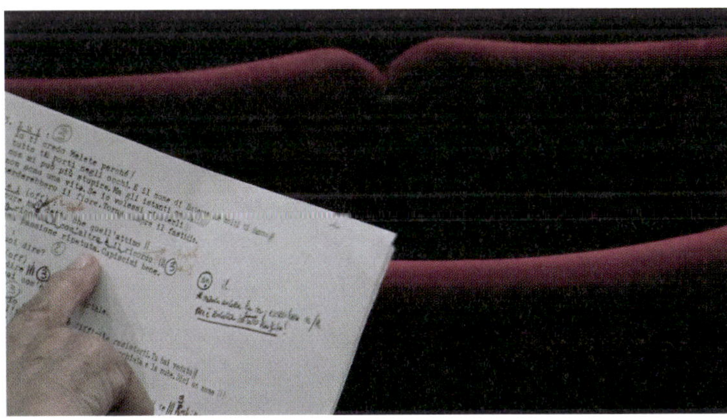

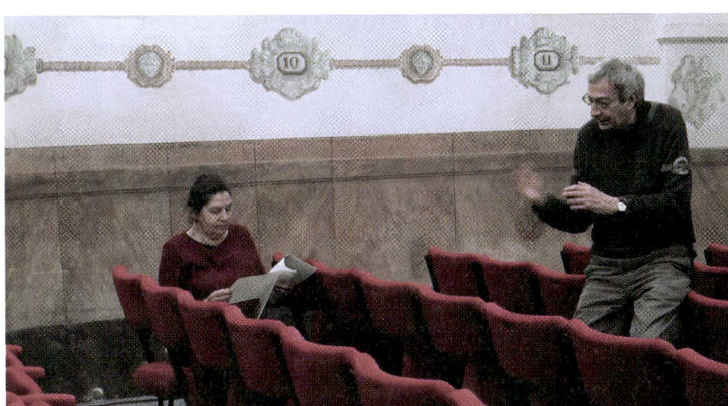

GD: I had already gotten to know him well, because he shot *Sicily!* here before working with us. He worked on it here for a long time. I was bewitched for hours, watching how he directed these people who weren't actors. They had never acted in anything.

RC: So, *Sicily!* was the first film...

GD: The first film he made here—after *From the Cloud to the Resistance*—years later.

DM: He said, "I'll come, but find me some Sicilians that live in Tuscany."

RC: Indeed, these people...

DM: Therefore, we began looking for any Sicilians that lived within twenty-thirty kilometres of here.

GD: He held auditions.

DM: He gathered them together in the room at the front of the theater, he got them to talk, and then he makes his choice. My background was with the theater in Pontedera. The theater in Pontedera was a very important one. It was the first avant-garde theater in Italy. We invited [Jerzy] Grotowski, who was a great intellectual and a great theater artist to move to Pontedera. There was a whole group of artists in Pontedera, such as Eugenio Barba, Living Theater, etc. We invited a lot of different people to come, all kinds of important theatrical artists. Therefore, we were part of a theater that was anti-theater. It represented the search for a renewal of theater.

GD: Yes, but he wants to know about this theater. This is a "bourgeois" theater.

DM: I'm getting there. At a certain point, I left Pontedera, I became the artistic director of the theater here in Buti. Here in Buti, there still exists a very old artistic tradition called "Canto del Maggio." The "Canto del Maggio" are ancient stories, originally written by shepherds, or simply by illiterate people, and therefore completely outside of traditional theater. They were sung during the month of May, when nature is in full bloom, in squares or in clearings in woods. They were sung by so-called commoners, by peasant farmers, who learnt these stories by heart. They were mythical stories of battles and warriors, of heroes who had liberated the area. Normally these were stories about heroes. Secular stories that were sung and were very popular. From the 19th century onward, they began to be considered as something revolutionary compared to "bourgeois" theater, which was staged in places such as this. This theater was constructed by the lords of the area. Each lord gave money toward the construction of this theater, and in turn was given his own box or seat. Operas were performed, as well as modest performances of theatrical works. Theatrical troupes from the area were invited to perform, paid for by the lords. While, the "Canto del Maggio" was completely outside of the theater. It was considered too common to be allowed in the theater.

GD: I don't know if it can be called a technique. When Jean-Marie works he prepares a score. This score is based on breath. That's what he calls it. He inserts pauses based on the actor's breathing. Pause, pause. Pauses of one, two, three, or four—not based on the character, but based on the harmony of the lines. He's extremely strict about this. When we rehearse, he beats a tempo, and if you make a mistake, if you pause for three instead of four, he interrupts, "It was four!" Therefore, his technique is—he gets angry when there is a debate following a screening and he is accused of leaving the actors immobile. "There's no movement in this film." But it's not true. Jean-Marie's movement is all in the voice. Jean-Marie's films are extremely full of life, even if the actors are immobile, because everything is in the voice and in the words. For him, the word is essential. And not just that, one thing that amazed me, was that two French people were so attentive to the Italian language that they would realize if an "a" was pronounced badly. Or if you skipped...

DM: He was fascinated by our "r." He would say, "You have this wonderful 'r,' whereas our 'r' is weak." He used to tell us to use that long "r."

GD: He himself and Danièle had already studied this technique, but they gave it to us in very simple terms. Stop, breathe, look down, look up, breathe.

DM: That's regarding Jean-Marie, however with regards Buti and the "Canto del Maggio," it's very... it has much in common with Brecht. There is this relationship with Brecht, because he talked of estrangement, and the "Canto del Maggio" actor is never a character. Through a gesture or a step the actor takes on stage, with a straight back and a certain look upon his face... First, he might drink a glass of wine and joke, but then he suddenly enters into his role and tells his story, without becoming a character. In my opinion, that could be defined as a Brechtian technique. Brechtian. Very Brechtian. Not being a character, but being the desire to passionately recount what is happening in the scene. Brecht gave us that famous scene on the street corner. And that's how they recount the story of Medea, or any other story. They narrate stories of heroes with immediacy. One moment the body is shown... And we "intellectuals," I say this in inverted commas because we're not intellectuals, have the duty and the responsibility to rediscover this disappearing gestural art, which is being lost. For example, they make these gestures with their arms, which are an expansion...

GD: Like Sicilian puppets!

DM: We have to rediscover it so that it is not simply a game, but something that comes from inside and explodes all at once. It is our duty to rediscover this, because it no longer exists in the youth of today. We have to find it in older people, of course.

RC: Therefore Jean-Marie, who without doubt knew the theater of Brecht, must have found something here in the "Canto del Maggio."

DM: Yes, and what's more he used to say... that they know how to breathe, while the actors of the Schaubühne Theater didn't know how to breathe! "The actors of the Schaubühne don't know how to breathe, but they do!"

GD: And Jean-Marie's instructions... were never, "You are..." But rather, "You have to see what you narrate." If I talk about a garden, then I have to see it. Because only if you see it, can you recount it.

DM: He never spoke of characters.

RC: Never the need for identification.

GD: Never. You have to have visions!

DM: But there are these visions. He once quoted that famous line from Goethe, "Stay a while, you are so beautiful." It's just like a real score, with highs and lows. He used to say, "Let's stamp our feet like we're playing an organ."

2 The Italian sentence she refers to is "ma nei giorni è diverso."

GD: Imagine, for eight minutes of a show. They didn't want to use the word "show." Eight minutes of... How can we define it? Of performance in a short film. We would work on it for two or three months. Eight minutes!

DM: Eight, no! A bit more than that.

GD: Fine, twelve!

DM: Maybe eighteen.

GD: We would work on a single line for an entire afternoon. "Listen." One. "If I think of an event that has happened, of seasons already past, it seems to me that I was happy then. But day by day... " In the original text it's: "But day by day it's different."[2] It's linked to the following words, but he cuts it: "But day by day..." One, two, three. "...it's different. I feel a weariness for things and works that a drunkard feels." One, two. "Then I stop work..." Five. "..and climb up here on the mountain. But when I think back..." High. One, two. "...it seems to me again that I've been happy."

DM: Giovanna, the highs and lows aren't marked here. They're missing.

GD: You didn't mark them?

DM: No, they're not marked.

GD: "But you said that instant was a memory. And what else is a memory..." High. Not: "...is a memory..." "And what else is a memory..." High. "...but an experience repeated in its intensity, do you understand me?" In the original text there is a full stop after "in its intensity," while he unites it and creates a single sentence. Otherwise, it would be: "But you said that instant was a memory. And what else is a memory... but an experience repeated in its intensity. Do you understand me?" It's different. I don't know. Working with them—people would say that they're inflexible and demanding, and it's true. But I loved it. When I was coming here to rehearse, it was as though my heart would burst. I had never felt such joy before. But it wasn't just working with them; it was a profound joy of reading... of reading a text in that way. It was a pleasure doing it.

DM: Our initial job was clearly to perfectly do what they asked of us. The great pleasure came when we managed to do that. But an even greater pleasure came after we did that, when our visions would begin. At a certain stage, the actor would begin to have these visions that were neither prescribed by the score nor explained to us.

GD: They were different for everyone. I had visions right from the start.

DM: While for me the first thing was to repeat the lines precisely, the high and lows, the breathing, the pauses. For example, this line here:

"Listen. If I think of an event that has happened, of seasons already past, it seems to me that I was happy then. But day by day... it's different. I feel a weariness for things and works that a drunkard feels. Then I stop work...and climb up here on the mountain. But when I think back...it seems to me again that I've been happy." I read that in the correct way. Within this precise way of reciting, which the director has established, the breathing, and everything else, you have to begin to see what your "seasons already past" are. Why is it different from one day to another? What is the "weariness for things and works that a drunkard feels?" That's how the actors enrich the lines within themselves, while maintaining the precise score and breathing and everything else. The physical posture must also be precise; you have to look at a specific point, different to where she is looking. This moment here is the part when they meet, and for this meeting Jean-Marie gave me his hat to wear...

GD: Even the positions were already...

DM: There was this photograph of Pavese in a forest wearing a hat; therefore, it was as though I became the personification of Pavese through Jean-Marie's hat. It was very moving to be aware of that.

RC: I remember one rehearsal where he accepted and kept a gesture that one of the actors had unconsciously made.

DM: Yes, that can happen.

GD: Yes, it happens.

DM: It's not expected, but it can happen. "Sold and bought!" [*Venduto, comprato*!] Isn't that what he used to say?

GD: He'd say, "Sold and bought!"

DM: "Sold and bought!"

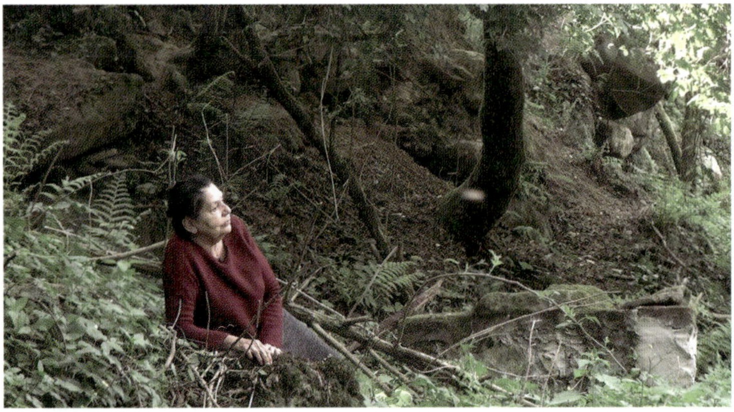

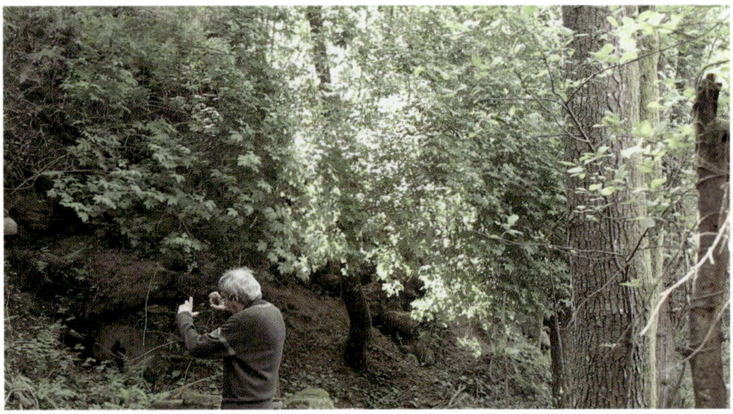

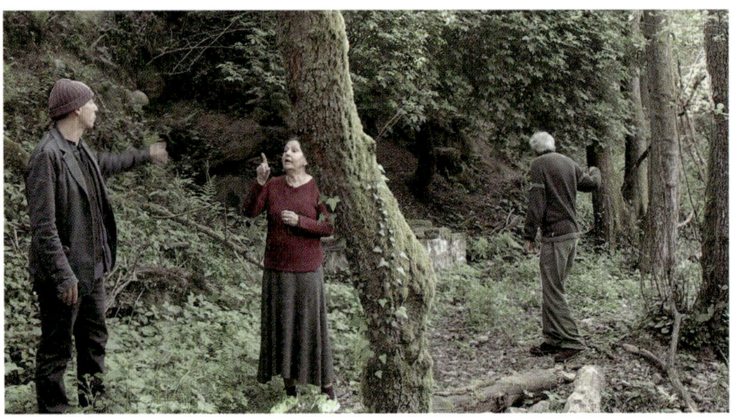

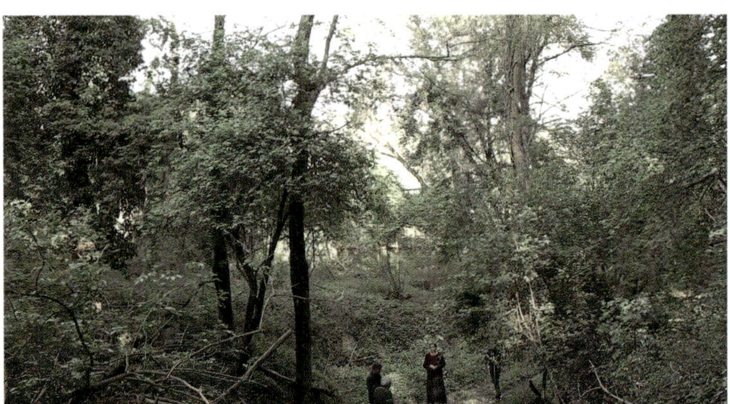

GD: He might say, "Do it a bit differently..."—"Sold and bought!" But only when Danièle wasn't there! All of that came after Danièle had passed away. When Danièle was here, you weren't allowed to make any mistakes. While after Danièle's death, on certain texts, he might say, "Giovanna, try it with a bit more irony." But that never happened with Danièle.

RC: So that's why in *The Witches*...

GD: Yes, it's there in *The Witches*.

RC: You can feel it more because... And Danièle didn't want that?

GD: Danièle didn't want that at all. This is one passage that I always... And he wrote for me: "*The* is still not precise."[3] For example, "The memory," and my pronunciation wasn't perfect. "*The* is not precise." Every day, "*The* is not precise," until you would eventually pronounce "the" in the correct way. It's absolutely wonderful. "Giovanna, you're not breathing."

3 The example he uses is the Italian article "il."

DM: Because often in Italy when we talk, if there are two vowels, one vowel ending and one beginning, we unite them. And he always corrected us and got us to separate them. The pronunciation of the words had to be extremely precise. An "e" at both the end and the beginning of two words are often pronounced as one.

GD: This line here was very difficult for me: I was only allowed a pause or two, not four, in a very long sentence. It goes, "Hesiod, I find you up here every day. Before you I found others... in the mountains to the north, by the barren torrent of Thrace and..." See, I'm already out of breath because it's a very long sentence... and I can't do it anymore. "Hesiod, I find you up here every day. Before you I found others... in the mountains to the north, by the barren torrent of Thrace and Pieria. I like you. More than the others you know... that immortal things are close at hand." It took me a week to get that right.

DM: In fact, Jean-Marie's way of acting is not Baroque at all. We may say that there is a detachment of sorts, a distancing, whereas Baroque acting can confound you as you are inside the role. In Baroque you enter into the character in a certain way. You become part of... Here, you're detached from what you say, there's always a certain distance. And the gaze is... It's an eye that watches—it's something that creates. There's this creative distance that is fantastic. It's difficult to do it because you need extraordinary concentration. You need to have total concentration.

RC: I imagine it takes a lot of commitment.

GD: Yes. This is funny.

DM: Also the gaze, the gaze.

GD: In brackets he wrote: "r" and then "c," "ri," "i"... And then his instructions: "change voice," "loud," "quiet," "everyone together," "change register"...[4]

4 "Cambia voce," "Forte," "Piano," "Tutto insieme," "Cambia registro."

DM: Loud, quiet.

GD: Change register!

DM: They're musical instructions.

GD: Loud, quiet, pause, change register, high, low...

DM: Stamp feet!

GD: That's how it was. ... Danièle would realize... When we were rehearsing the performance she would be behind a curtain, and at a certain point she might say, "Giovanna, you didn't look down." She didn't say it to me because I'm very precise, but she might say, "Romano, you made a mistake." From the sound of your voice she would realize whether your head was facing up or down, or if you were looking to the left or to the right, and without seeing you.

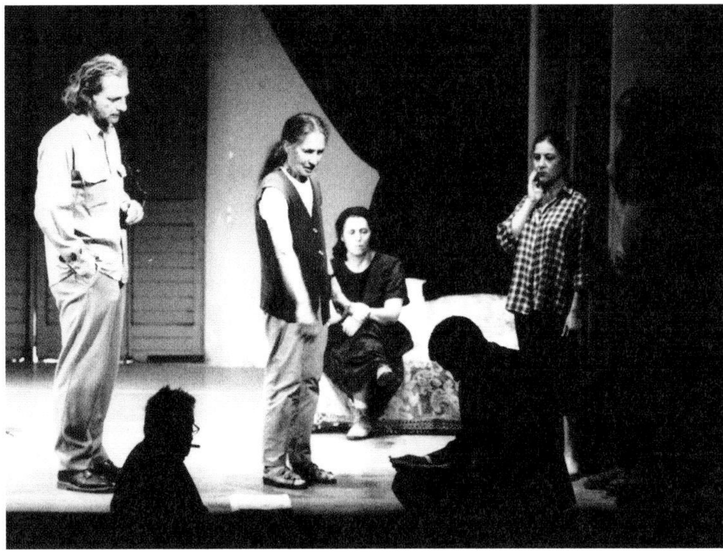

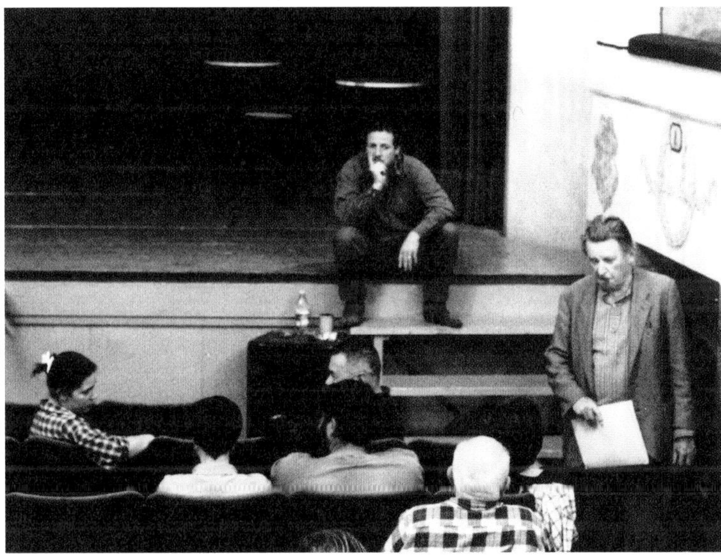

RC: Yes, because she listened a lot...

GD: With headphones. But she didn't have any when she was behind...

RC: But she was very used to...

GD: Yes. When we were shooting films. But when we were working inside the theater...

RC: So, she was able to understand the gestures you made from your voice.

GD: She could understand whether the voice came from

down here or up here. But how did she know where your eyes were?

DM: What was interesting was that you had to look at that number over there, for example. Then, after a precise, set amount of time, you had to look at the ground at another specific point, perhaps marked by a leaf. For example, on set there were these rocks, and if someone happened to move one of these rocks from that point on the ground, it was an absolute tragedy.

GD: One day during rehearsals for *The Witches*, Andrea Bacci... He thought he was helping, and picked up this stick that was on the ground. "No!"

DM: But I wanted to say something else about the way we had to look. There was this sudden jump—what you were saying was linked to this absolutely minimal movement. From up high to down low, like this.

GD: It was very difficult to do this and keep your concentration during a dialogue.

DM: Sometimes at the end.

GD: Yes, but I always had it in the middle.

DM: You'd stay in that position and it was like you had fallen into something, and your gaze had changed. And then you would change your gaze again, perhaps upwards. You might have two or three or four movements in twenty minutes of performance or shooting a film. During all this time you could only move in this very minimal way, and your gaze had to be more than just a gaze. It had to be more like a laser, something that struck where you were going, where your words were directed and where you were looking, and where your visions were. It was extraordinary.

GD: Have you ever seen a hunting dog when it stands still? When it points? And its whole body quivers? And then suddenly... That's a little what it was like.

And it wasn't something studied. It came from this [she points to the text/script].

DM: Yes.

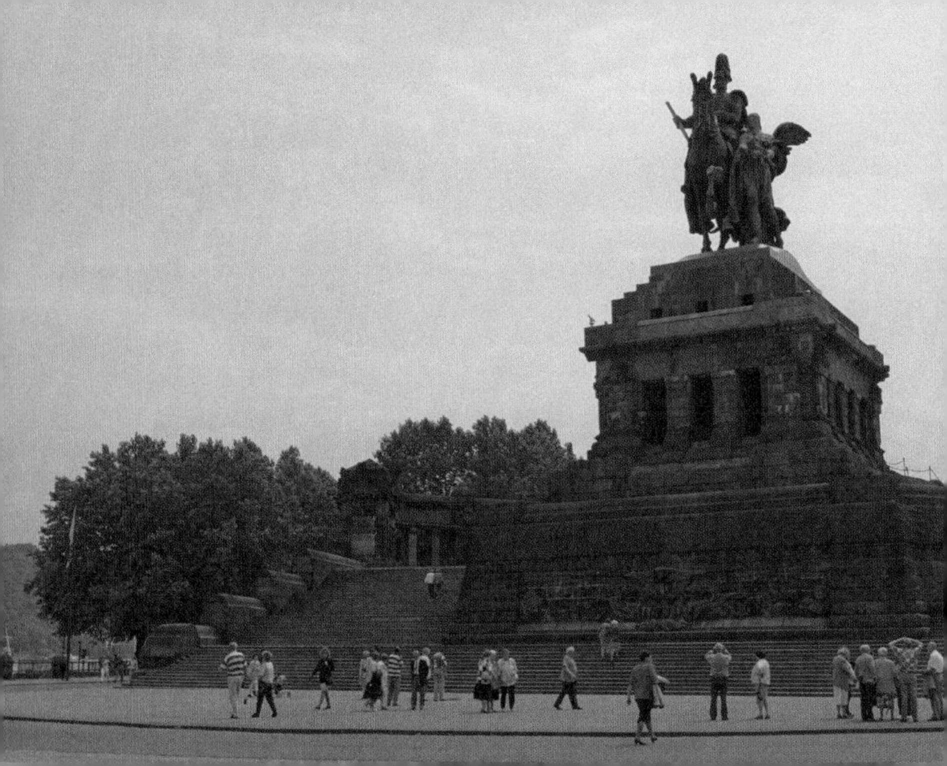

Volko Kamensky

YOU FASCISTS, YOU IGNORAMUSES, YOU HYPOCRITES

[The following text was presented as an introduction to a screening of two films by Danièle Huillet and Jean-Marie Straub, *Lothringen!* and *Sicilia!*, on October 27, 2017, in Zeughauskino in Berlin.]

In 1975, the New York Film Festival wanted to fly in Danièle Huillet and Jean-Marie Straub in order to present their film, *Moses and Aaron*. The festival's director Richard Roud applied for a travel subsidy from the Export-Union der Deutschen Filmindustrie, an organization funded by the department of commerce for the promotion of West German films abroad that today bears the supposedly more casual and international name German Films.

Richard Roud received the following response:

> Dear Mr. Roud,
> Thank you for your letter of June 30, 1975, regarding the German participation at the New York Film Festival. We are sorry to tell you that we are in no position to help you with airfares for Danielle [sic] Huillet and J.M. Straub to come to your festival as both are French nationals and therefore the German authorities will not give any funds for such a trip. The airfare for Werner Herzog will be paid so that there is no problem that he will be present at your festival. With warm personal regards, we remain, sincerely yours,
>
> EXPORT-UNION der Deutschen Filmindustrie e.V.
> Dr. R. F. Goldschmidt

Jean-Marie Straub's written response, published at the time in *Filmkritik*,[1] has also come down to us through the collection *Augenzeugen: 100 Texte neuer deutscher Filmemacher*[2]:

> July 28, 1975
> You fascists, you ignoramuses, you hypocrites.
> Richard Roud sent me a copy of your letter from July 9, 1975 (DR. G/El). I would not think of accepting a single penny from you pimps (Roud wrote without my consent), but: I call your attention to the fact that I am registered in the German Federal Office for commercial activity as a German film

1 *Filmkritik*, no. 225 (September 1975): 432.

2 Hans Helmut Prinzler, Eric Rentschler, eds., *Augenzeugen: 100 Texte neuer deutscher Filmemacher* (Frankfurt am Main: Verlag der Autoren, 1988), 64. Also available in English in *Jean-Marie Straub, Danièle Huillet: Writings*, ed. Sally Shafto (New York: Sequence Press, 2016), 177.

director, and I will seek all possible publicity for you—with your own letter.

With hatred,
Jean-Marie Straub

I do not begin with this correspondence only in order to contribute further to this publicity myself. Instead, in what follows regarding the 1994 film *Lothringen!*, space will be given to a few of the problems mentioned in this letter:

The question of who is supposedly German and who is not;[3]

The fact that one is sometimes forced to be or to become German;

Very generally: nationalism, fascism, exclusion.

But *Lothringen!* is also an exemplary demonstration of how Danièle Huillet and Jean-Marie Straub once again manage with words, images, and sounds to create a free space within a system that uses all of its forces to prevent such free spaces.

That I will leave out *Sicilia!* and limit myself in the following to the shorter film in the program has in no way to do with there being nothing to say about *Sicilia!*. Instead, *Lothringen!* seems to me simply to be the film that in Germany has been too little discussed and too often misunderstood—and that German audiences did not *want* to understand. This is arguably *because* it deals explicitly with Germany ("you fascists, you ignoramuses, you hypocrites").

Colette Baudoche is the title of the literary work behind the film *Lothringen!*. It was composed in 1909 by a conservative French writer named Maurice Barrès, a nationalist and Catholic.

The novel's plot is set in Lorraine around 1905, meaning in a Lorraine annexed by the Prussians that is slowly being Germanized and where all that is French is supposed to

3 Almost immediately after their application for a scriptwriting subsidy for the planned film *Moses and Aaron*, several of the relevant, appointed advisors attempted to use the Federal Republic of Germany's film subsidy law in order to "remove" the project "from the selection process" since the author "in his own words feels he belongs to the French cultural sphere." Quoted in Leo Schönecker, "Warum muß ein 'zu fördernder Film' 'deutsch' sein?," *film-dienst*, vol. 24 (February 9, 1971). See section 7 of the Act on measures to promote the German film industry of December 22, 1967.

disappear. A 25-year-old East Prussian named Fritz Asmus (called "Monsieur Frédéric Asmus" virtually throughout the novel) is dispatched in his capacity as teacher to the city of Metz in Lorraine. There, he is supposed to replace a French teacher or, to be more precise: supplant him. He moves into a room in the home of an old woman, Madame Baudoche, who lives together with her 18-year-old granddaughter Colette Baudoche. Financial difficulties alone force the two women to rent the room to the Prussian, whom they initially only address with extreme reserve.

And yet, little by little the merits of French culture are revealed to the Prussian. The French language arouses a deep interest in him, he learns quickly, questions the "pan-Germanic" feeling of omnipotence of his fellow Prussians, and knows how to win over and, with tiny steps, get closer to the two women. The 25-year-old ends up falling in love with the 18-year-old, asks for her hand, and, after anxiously waiting, is rejected. Colette Baudoche thinks it over carefully, however charming the man may be, she will never marry a German. "Do not be angry with me," this is how she bids farewell to the Prussian suitor.[4]

Throughout the entire novel, what is French is designated as old civilization and, in contrast, what is Prussian as young, primitive, or even pagan. At first glance, then, the book appears solely as an anthology of resentment—the German Wikipedia page for Maurice Barrès describes it as "anti-German."[5] Once written to strengthen the national and conservative disposition of the French public, today only German readers might still find it illuminating. The French view of the German way of life one receives here is, after all, pitiless. Germans, we learn, nourish themselves with all kinds of inferior cold cuts and sausage products, but only until they should encounter the best that Lorraine cooking has to offer: quiche Lorraine. We see and hear the differences constantly and implacably: on one hand the colonizers' disciplined, hammering, Germanic footsteps and on the other "the freer tread of the natives,"[6] as Barrès describes it. The open fireplace—a French invention, it is claimed here—is in every way superior to the oven so adored by the Germans. And lastly: how do the Prussians go to bed? "[P]erspiring for generations under the same big eiderdown quilt,"[7] Barrès de-

4 *Translator's note:* Except where noted, quotes from the book/film were translated by Ted Fendt and Jean-Marie Straub.

5 Jean-Marie Straub reported that before production he proclaimed *Lothringen!* to be an "anti-German film" to the commissioning body of the Saarländischer Rundfunk. See "Straub!," *Le Portique*, no. 33, special edition (May 2014): 113.

6 Maurice Barrès, *Colette Baudoche: The Story of a Young Girl of Metz*, trans. Frances Wilson Huard (New York: George H. Doran Company, 1918), 45.

7 Barrès, 43.

clares in disgust. Finally having arrived in France: a sheet, a blanket—freedom!

And yet *Lothringen!* has little interest in all of this junk. Very much to the contrary, Jean-Marie Straub describes having been unable to read *Colette Baudoche* as a young man because he found the novel's patriotic contents too repulsive. Only later did he manage to do so: "There were thirty pages in it that resisted me," explains Straub, "and because they resisted me, I decided to make a film out of them."[8] And elsewhere: "I'm interested in something foreign to me, that resists me at first, even disgusts me. [...] I don't want to waste my time with something I already know and that comes out of my own head."[9]

At this point it must be stated that Jean-Marie Straub was born in Metz in 1933. As a student, he experienced what he terms the "second German occupation." And even if his German-sounding last name tempts one to suppose Straub might have grown up bilingual and was familiar with the German language from an early age, this is not the case. He first learned German together with Danièle Huillet through the texts and music of Bach, i.e. only after his emigration to Munich as a young man. As a child in Metz, however, under National Socialist rule, the language used in schools was indeed German, but he tried to absorb as little of it as possible. "In the schoolyard," he describes, "we had to speak German—if we spoke French, our parents would be deported to Silesia or who knows where. We simply didn't talk, we were quiet."[10]

During a Q&A following a screening of *Lothringen!* at the Parisian film school La Fémis in 2010, Straub set the record straight about what Alain Badiou had previously claimed in *Libération*, namely that Straub has a "Germanic spirit." "I've made films in German, so what?"[11] says Straub before jumping into a lecture on history before the audience.

The Franco-Prussian War of 1870, to which the novel *Colette Baudoche* constantly refers, was a war started by France in hopes of spurring on its limping economy. This is the usual tactic in capitalist economies, except that once again the situation was deeply misjudged and France was defeated. The Prussian victors demanded indemnities for the slain

8
Le Portique, 90.

9
Le Portique, 100.

10
Quoted in Jean-Lous Raymond, ed., *Rencontres avec Jean-Marie Straub et Danièle Huillet* (Paris: Beaux-arts de Paris / Le Mans: École Supérieure des Beaux-Arts du Mans, 2008), 102.

11
https://vimeo.com/18031783.

troops and destroyed war material. Since the Banque de France had, however, already gone bankrupt prior to the war, the French had no means of meeting the demands, which is why the government immediately resolved to give away part of the country to the victors. This happened to be the country's treasure chest, full of iron ore and coal. Rich in mineral resources but far enough away from Paris so that no one was concerned with what happened to the people living in Alsace-Lorraine. It was simply a territory with a certain economic value whose possessor was changing.

Virtually overnight, the people in Lorraine were confronted with having to make a decision: either stay and "become German" or "remain French" and be forced to leave. Within a very short time and under catastrophic conditions, a mass exodus deeper into France began. Thousands and thousands abandoned Metz alone. The railways were overwhelmed and people set off on the highway with teams of animals or often simply on foot. At the same time as this exodus, a second flow further east was launched: German colonizers set off to take possession of new properties in order finally to climb one rung higher in their administrative career or to grab a better endowed teaching position. 99.9% of Parisians, says Jean-Marie Straub, were in favor of the annexation of Alsace-Lorraine in 1871. Only one person was against it. And this one person was the writer Barrès.

Here comes an objection from the audience: But that can't be, there was the Commune after all. To which Straub answers, "Bismarck helped the Parisians crush the Commune." And the Parisians had even begged him for it, "Please relieve us from the Commune now!"

What of all this is to be seen in *Lothringen!*?

Surprisingly, the film does not begin in Lorraine, but further east. In Koblenz, to be precise, that is to say on the side of the victors, at the so-called Deutsches Eck (German Corner). The film directs its first glance upon the monumental Kaiser-Wilhelm-Denkmal, erected in 1871 in celebration of the victory over France and in celebration of the founding of the German Reich. As always in the films of Danièle Huillet and Jean-Marie Straub, nothing about the choice of the shooting location is by chance. Indeed, this shooting location is once again overloaded with history; we may even be looking at a pile of rubble full of signs and references.

The gigantic Kaiser-Wilhelm-Denkmal at the Deutsches Eck is not the one constructed in 1871. That one was heavily damaged by US bombing in 1945 and its few remains were melted down. Furthermore, initially designated as the so-called Memorial of German Unity from 1953 to 1990, the site became redundant with the implementation of this "German Unity." An initiative quickly formed for the reconstruction of the Kaiser-Wilhelm-Denkmal and in 1988, 80% of the population of Koblenz was reported to speak out in favor of rebuilding. An initially privately funded new equestrian statue was ultimately imposed on Koblenz[12] and placed on the pedestal in 1993. The day of the rededication is revealing: it took place on September 2, the so-called Sedan Day, the day commemorating the capitulation of the French in 1870—a fact "which was merely noted in France," as the German Wikipedia page curtly adds.[13] This "stone fist blow," as Kurt Tucholsky once called it, which we are shown at the beginning of the film is therefore not the one from 1871, but from 1993, erected less than one year before the beginning of the film's production.

The second shot of the film shows a historic map reproducing how Prussian and French troops faced each other in battle in 1870 on the Plateau de Gravelotte near Metz. With bitter losses, the Prussians had to retreat. Jean-Marie Straub claims that Prussia's intelligence, represented by its best young men, was buried here.[14]

In the film, two elements are heard here: on one hand, the piece by Joseph Haydn that became known as the German national anthem; on the other, gunfire. According to Straub, this resulted from training maneuvers of the French armed forces coincidentally recorded during the film shoot in 1994 in the vicinity of Metz.

Only with the third shot in the film do we first find ourselves in Metz. And yet here too there is a double "stone fist blow." The view moves from the main post office to the central train station. Both were built by the German colo-

12
After the art collector and patron Peter Ludwig had announced in 1985 that he wanted to donate his Koblenz cultural prize money to the rebuilding of the equestrian statue, newspaper publisher Werner Theisen and his wife Anneliese stated in 1987 that they wanted to transfer three million German marks to the city of Koblenz for the reconstruction. Although the Prime Minister of Rheinland-Pfalz rejected the couple's donation offer in 1988, in February 1989, the "Bürgeriniative Deutsches Eck" officially commissioned a reproduction from the sculptor Raimund Kittl. In May 1992, the finished bronze casting was transported by cargo ship from Düsseldorf to Koblenz, where it was stored in the port. Despite strong political protests, in August of the same year, an agreement was made between Rheinland-Pfalz, the city of Koblenz, and the Theisens concerning the rebuilding. See Michael Koelges, "Heroisches Kaiserdenkmal oder 'Faustschlag aus Stein'? Das Deutsche Eck in Koblenz," www.rheinische-geschichte.lvr.de.

13
https://de.wikipedia.org/wiki/Deutsches_Eck.

14
Le Portique, 111.

nizers, and every single one of their architectural elements embodies their aspirations to power. Even if we are familiar with so-called Wilhelmine architecture in Germany, we'll find it carried to an extreme in Lorraine. Everything here is supposed to feel well fortified and simultaneously evoke a supposedly ancient or at least medieval-chivalric culture. Labeled "neo-romantic" by experts, Maurice Barrès disparagingly calls this overbearing and inhospitable architecture "style néo-schwob"—neo-Swabian style.

In the story, Grandmother Baudoche explains this very clearly to the young Prussian, "The forms that you create may be pleasant to you—but there is no place for us in them."[15] And the train station in Metz is actually at best only secondarily intended for the transportation of civilians. It is first and foremost a kind of turbine for the armed forces, meaning a giant machine developed with the purpose of literally being able to ship out thousands of German soldiers as quickly as possible. Within twenty-four hours, an entire army could have been brought in and a particular direction for their movement determined as necessary, either West toward France or East, meaning Russia.

15 Barrès, 52–53.

The selection criteria for the shooting locations can in fact be reconstructed for every shot in the film—and even more painstakingly than here. After all, Danièle Huillet and Jean-Marie Straub always objected to the assumption that their films resulted from reduction. Rather, what they were after was concentration—making a very precise choice.

Distinct criteria can also be identified in going through the film's literary template, the novel *Colette Baudoche,* and tracing the lines used in the film. Only those parts were taken, which either directly depict political grievances or conjure possibilities of resistance against such grievances even as a single person. Both Grandmother Baudoche and her granddaughter Colette are depicted as women who in a seemingly powerless situation realize that they can simply say "no."

In and of itself this would not be anything extraordinary since in almost endless variations, cinema has told exactly this tale of powerless individuals who suddenly become aware of their power and use it against evil. We are only too happy as film viewers to identify with such people.

Danièle Huillet and Jean-Marie Straub, however, point us toward another, clearly more uncomfortable place. To me at least, it seems that the filmmakers were making an exception here to their rule of non-identification with the people depicted. Perhaps as viewers we are moving through the film like this Monsieur Frédéric Asmus? Coming from Germany to wander around Lorraine. Discovering landscapes, buildings, and vegetation. In our ignorance, not initially grasping the background and context, although everything is lying open before us.

Only twice in the film do we see a person. Both times it is Colette. The first time from behind as she only briefly and reluctantly turns around toward us in order to make it clear that she can never become a German. The second time frontally: and here, too, only in order to issue the final rejection. The film puts us in the position of the person who, in his novel, Barrès depicts as making an effort but is still too ignorant.

Translated from German by Ted Fendt.

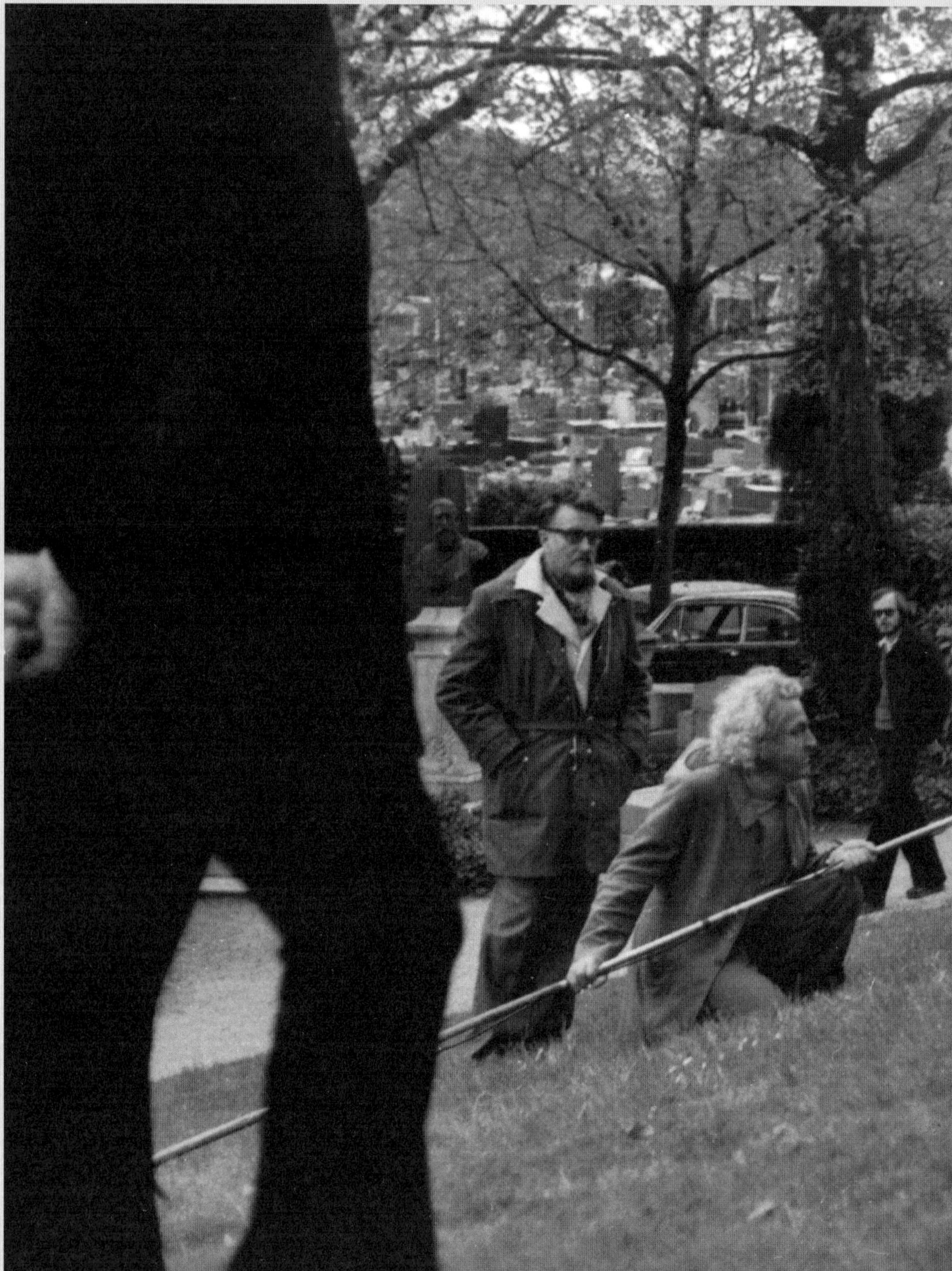

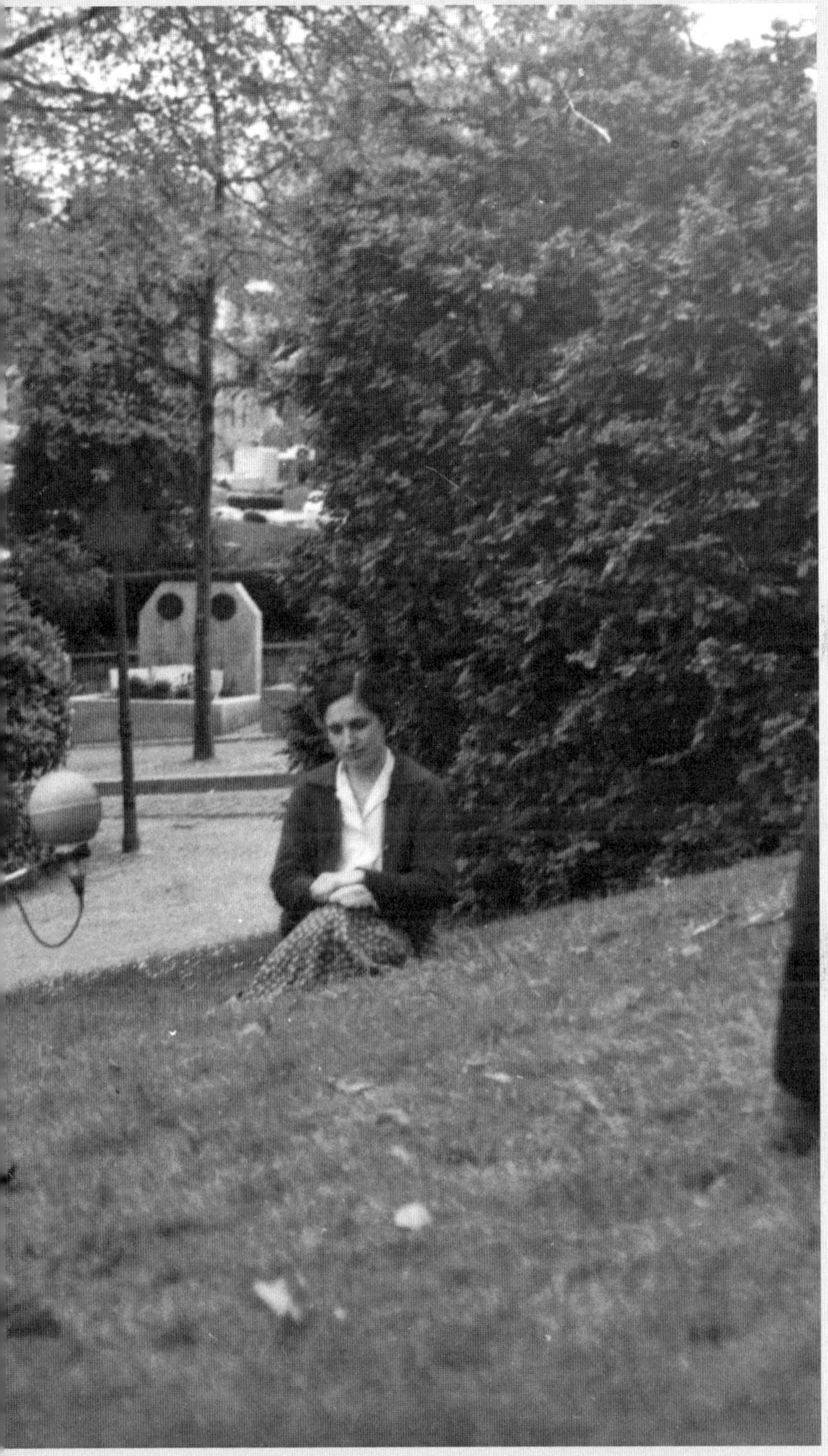

Monika Funke Stern, Helge Heberle, Danièle Huillet

THE FIRE INSIDE THE MOUNTAIN

A CONVERSATION WITH DANIÈLE HUILLET FRAUEN UND FILM 2. 1982

[The conversation with Danièle Huillet took place in Berlin in November 1981 on the occasion of the premiere of *Too Early / Too Late* at the Arsenal cinema and a presentation at the German Film and Television Academy.]

Danièle: I was born in May, 1936. In 1954 I spent a year in a school to prepare for the IDHEC.[1] I saw lots of films, like Buñuel's *Los Olvidados*, which really interested me, and I wanted to try to make documentary films. At the end there was an exam, which I took as well. But after the film they showed us, I just turned in a blank sheet of paper, saying what a shame it was to show us such a film for an examination essay. Then I met Jean-Marie in November. I remember it quite well, because that was when the Algerian Revolution began. He had his idea for a film about Bach, and asked me if I would help him write the thing. In 1958 he had to leave France because of the war in Algeria. He didn't want to shoot at Algerians, and toward the end of 1959 I came to Germany too. So, that's it.

All footnotes are the translator's, unless otherwise noted.

Monika: And since then you've worked together?

1 Institut des hautes études cinématographiques.

D: Yes, we've done everything together. Only back then it wasn't fashionable to mention the women, so no one noticed it. Then it came into fashion, and all of a sudden everyone noticed that I'd been in the opening credits all along. That was amusing.

Helge: The concept of your films, which are quite distinct from each other and which distinguish themselves also from the films of that time, you developed that collaboratively?

D: Yes, but that also came about through our life.

H: The two of you emigrated to Germany. Is that when you first began to learn German?

D: I had learned a little German before, but only with the texts of Bach cantatas, and that was admittedly an odd sort of German. Besides, I didn't learn German very well, because we spoke more French together. There are things that we can only say in

German, but otherwise usually we speak French with each other.

H: What does the time in Germany mean to you, now that you have already left again?

D: The time in Germany, that was the discovery of the class struggle and of a kind of violence that, though it exists in France and Italy too, never appears so openly and clearly. Probably because the hypocrisy is greater.

M: The talk of class struggle often elides the fact that men and women belong to two separate classes. The difference reveals itself also in the way in which your film work is perceived. In the book *Kluge/Herzog/Straub*[2] there's somewhere at the back a mention of Huillet and a short biography, and at least Karsten Witte is polite enough to speak of "the Straubs"—is your name actually Straub, or Huillet?

D: Well, we're not married. I have kept my name. But it's not so easy to pronounce. Straub is much easier. I don't think it's all that important. It has never bothered me. I don't actually enjoy talking about stuff and answering questions. Everyone has their way, and what you don't do well you shouldn't do. There are other things that I do better, and besides, what interests us are the products and not the names.

M: For you, the distribution of your films is important. You travel around with the films and talk about them afterwards. I've understood your silence as a form of refusal vis-à-vis auteur-cinema, vis-à-vis representation.

D: When we're dead, then we won't be able to talk about the films any more. The film material is extremely sensitive, and the negatives won't last forever; but the films will outlive us for a certain amount of time, and I hope they will still speak to people. The fact that we discuss the films is because the distribution system doesn't function at all any more. Straub

2
Editor's note: She refers to *Herzog/Kluge/Straub*, ed. Peter W. Jansen, Wolfram Schütte (Munich: Hanser, 1976).

is better at discussing than I am. I don't know if he likes to do it. I think one destroys part of the work that way.

H: What do you think is destroyed that way?

D: A film is a work one has seen through to the very end. A discussion is always something where one only says half-truths or forces things that one has tried to hold in balance in the film. Also, in a discussion, one can never take the time to really reflect, otherwise one would have to say—It might be eight days before I can give you an answer. Thus *per forza*, as the Italians say, one sometimes answers too quickly or sometimes even falsely. By contrast, when you're making a film, you try to leave all the possibilities open for the person who's going to see and hear it.

M: How do your respective functions look while working?

D: For example, with *Too Early / Too Late*. A certain Straschek—he's a friend of ours—came for a visit as we were recording the orchestral part of *Moses and Aaron* in Vienna in 1974. He brought two heavy suitcases full of books with him—the entire correspondence of Marx and Engels. I thought, I'll never read that, so many books, I don't have the time. I'm only able to read a little bit before bed. Nevertheless, I read the entire thing, and among it the letter from Engels. I read it out loud to Straub and he said—Maybe we can make something about France. Then we were in Egypt for *Moses and Aaron*. We wanted to see how people in Egypt live, what sort of clothes, what gestures, what living conditions and so forth, before we chose the costumes. Once in Egypt, we started asking ourselves other questions than the ones that had to do with the film. In Rome then, Jean-Marie saw a book with the title, *Social Struggles in Egypt*,[3] with statistics and explanations about what was going on there at that time. We always had such a nostalgia to go back to Egypt. I believe I said then—We could make a film out of these

3 Mahmoud Hussein, *La lutte de classe en Égypte de 1945 à 1968*, English title: *Class Struggle in Egypt 1945–1970*.

two things. It was easier with the text by Engels, which held up somehow. We had to check the references, since Engels wrote it to Kautsky by memory from a Russian historian. There were incorrect quotes. We researched it all in the archives in Paris, where the parishes of 1789 had sent the notebooks in the great hope that if everyone would say what doesn't work, then something would change. The notebooks are still lying there and hardly get used. It's somehow moving when they're handed to you. We checked the numbers and names, we drove to the locations and decided together where the camera could be set up, what one can see, and sometimes we quarrel quite fiercely as well.

Things were easier in France. We kept going back to the locations; in Egypt we could only do it once, and it was difficult to find the locations. There are no maps apart from those of the colonial administration. The names are given in Egyptian and underneath in European. We looked for the places using photocopies. Five kilometers from a village, the people don't even know what the village is called. We did our reconnaissance with a friend from Paris, an Egyptian, using his car. Sometimes we needed a whole day just to find a single village. More or less the same work the people did who drew the maps to begin with. Except that we only had 20 days for Egypt. After our return came the organization phase. What one can do with the money one has. What one has to pay for immediately, and what can wait. The discussions one has to have—I do that more than he does. When he says—I can't do it that way, then I look for another way. Then comes the shoot. The people have to be paid, hotels arranged, etc. When we're shooting, I'm usually more involved with the sound and he with the camera. He frames the shots. During editing, I'm operating the editing table, while he does a few things now and then, things that one would normally have an assistant for, spooling and so forth. For the first short film, we had a cutter, and it lasted a week. When Jean-Marie started saying, 'Well, here we need to take away five frames and here three,' the guy had a nervous breakdown. Since then, we've never had a third person involved. The way we do it, we always watch the rushes without sound, because I never want to let the sound out of my hands until it's been transferred. Some good friends of mine have lost parts of their location sound between the location and the lab. Or where the transfer wasn't right when they did the mixing or transferring. I want to be present for that. Jean-Marie is also there, because you continue to discover things listening to the sound recording that you otherwise wouldn't hear. When we edit and begin to make selections, that's the most difficult part: We have three, ten, fifteen takes of the same shot—choosing one is sometimes painful.

M: When you take the source material: the documents from the 18th Century, the reports on the villages and Engels's texts—one could also imagine totally different pictures to go with them. The reports for example say that a certain number of families live in poverty, a certain number can scrape by, a certain number are rich—and in the pictures, one sees no families at all, not even a single person. One sees now and then a truck drive by on the asphalt country road, the village sign. How do you arrive at this visual concept?

D: What interested us was clear from the start, which was to see what traces remained today, and what had completely changed. For example, a city like Rennes, of which it is said that a third of the population lived in constant danger of pauperism, is now much richer. A lot is being built there. But at the beginning you see villages in Bretagne that have perhaps become even poorer. What interested us: to see this today, what traces remain and what has been entirely swept away and has left no traces at all. And moreover, a topographical film: with camera and Nagra with image and location sound as the tools of an investigation.

H: I'm reminded here of the discussion at the DFFB.[4] There you spoke of how during the long drive along the canal in Egypt, you went through as few villages as possible, because it would have seemed intru-

4 Deutsche Film- und Fernsehakademie Berlin (German Film and Television Academy).

sive to you to drive through them. So in the first instance, this investigation has a distanced relation to the people.

D: Yes...

H: And in a different context it was said in the discussion that in this film the human being does not stand at the center. And yet I experienced it quite differently, because through the panning movements and through the intrusion into the space from the edges—whether through a bird or a butterfly or through various noises—one sensed much more emphatically the presence of the filmmaker. That is to say, on the one hand a world is visible that is empty of people, while over against it stands a human presence without a face.

D: But this research applies also to the landscape. The human being is of course there, because these landscapes are processed and altered landscapes. They are historical. This is not Nature. This is a Nature that has been totally transformed by human beings. Of course. But what interested us was also how to understand a landscape. Why a village was built there where it stands. Why the irrigation in Egypt functions this way, with a larger canal and the smaller ones. All of this is from human beings, that's clear. That we didn't want to drive through a village—that wasn't the theme either, because after all, we're told that fighting and revolts took place, and when one sees for example the plains near Luxor: at the beginning the camera is still, then comes a pan to the left toward the mountains, where there is a mountain village, and then you go back to the right—that's where we're told how many people have been massacred. If one had driven through a village during this and had seen the people—that would be false somehow. These places are also fundamentally cemeteries, where human beings are still there, but where many have died. And that again has to do with human beings. But despite this we also wanted to let it be felt that these landscapes are transformed and to some extent threatened not only by human beings, but also by the wind, by the dust, by everything that transforms itself and where the human being is powerless, has no control over it.

M: It's also entirely clear from the text that someone is standing there and observing the landscape from a certain visual perspective and with a certain intention. I find this to be the fascinating thing about your films, that you eschew absolutely and consistently any form of staging this landscape: it is shown here and now and not dressed up in period costume, as repetition of a former time, but rather shown now, how it is now with all the minutiae and historical forces like wind, water and rain that move the country. This point of view saturates itself with history through these elements and also above all through the text that is read to it. But these are texts that proceed from a certain class conflict, the Engels text just as much as the Brecht text in *History Lessons*. For them the class conflict is defined through ownership and not for example through gender identity. To my way of thinking, these images of landscapes, of a city like Rome with its paving stones, charge themselves with history, but this history defrauds the history of women, who also took part, who took large part in the history, and whose sweat, blood and tears were drunk up by the paving stones of Rome just as much as the blood, sweat and tears of the men who are quoted and named. I don't know to what degree it interests you or you're aware of it, of making the case of women present in the historical charge of the images.

D: I can say three things to that. First—I've said this before—there are rules of the game, and one has to hold to them. For example, to put a woman in the middle of a staging of Brecht where he didn't have one would be false for the woman as well. In Egypt, in front of that factory, there you see a woman, clothed entirely in black, walk once through the frame. She's carrying something on her head, probably she's bringing something to eat for her husband or her son. And then you see a second woman, who is dressed like a European, coming out of the factory—probably a secretary. And otherwise, no women, only men walking around. On the country roads you see more women: at one point a woman with a child on a donkey. During the long drive, you see also a woman on a donkey, she's reading a book and is probably going to school or coming home from school. That is one answer. A second answer is, I believe, a film like *The Bridegroom, the Actress and the Pimp*. That is a film in which the oppression of women is quite explicitly present. That is material that comes more from us, the structure did not originate with someone else. Admittedly there is no sentence in it that comes from us, all the texts are from others, but the structure and the story came from us and it began like this: We were in Munich—we lived there at that time—and we once went to the cinema in the suburbs. We came back on foot, because it was very late and there were no more buses. It was pretty far away, and we came upon this street where the women stand on the sidewalk and only men in trucks or automobiles drive past and stop. The rest of the film turned on this. We drove through there twice, and even camouflaged the license plate on the car, because there are also pimps there who observe everything. That is the second answer, and the third answer I have is that I believe women liberate themselves much more easily and quickly—and on this point Marx was somehow right—when there is a total revolution. For example in Vietnam, the women won equality with a single stroke. That doesn't mean that afterwards there isn't a reactionary backlash also in this area. The struggle there is no less necessary once the war is over than it is in other areas. That is totally clear. But I mean, something happens there quite suddenly, precisely because an overall movement takes place and not just that of the women; instead the women are in the middle of it.

M: That's also very clear in your films, the hope for the Third World, for a total revolution, which then also dissolves the secondary contradiction, the women's issue.

D: But more radically than the Egyptian woman at the Arsenal represented it.[5] I was very, very sorry about that, because she came with arguments that originate with political scientists, which she adopted. Certainly, when you hear it from men it's already stupid enough, but from a woman it's still worse. She's not only colonized as an Egyptian, but also as a woman. She said that one can expect no revolution from peasants, because they are illiterate. There's some partial truth to this argument, but nevertheless I can't hear it any more. The funny thing and the sad thing about it is that the first—not just revolts but also revolutions—came in part precisely from the peasants, for example here in Germany. And they were also illiterate, but the thing was, they had a culture, just not the culture of the clergy.

M: The absence of women in the images is also an historical document. But that's not what concerns me here. You decide upon certain texts that interpret history. It is a decision whether to take Engels or Brecht, or whether to critique them in their image of history. This is something the new women's movement does, for example. I am very skeptical whether the situation of women would change with a revolution. Perhaps temporarily during the phase when they are needed and do the legwork. That's always been the case, whenever the women are needed during and after the war and they support the effort but aren't fundamentally representing their own interests. I don't know if you would be interested in thematizing other texts beyond this material, in which the issue of women is dealt with.

5 Huillet is referring here to a public discussion following the film screening which was the occasion for the interview (see introductory note).

D: But that is also an encounter. The love story doesn't only happen when one encounters another person, but it can also be a text in which something appears right. It's always only partly right. I believe the two of us are in agreement, that one can't make a film with general ideas, but rather that one must have something concrete and precise, and the text by Engels is concrete and precise for something very, very small and limited. One could make another film that would be a critique of it, but that wouldn't be the same film, and for that an encounter must somehow take place.

M: One can for example experience something as a deficit and then undergo a development. Speaking for myself, that such a process of becoming conscious takes place. After the discussion at the DFFB, you said, after *History Lessons* something like a deficit is open; at the end stands this fountain sculpture, a woman—albeit a very mythologized one that I didn't even really experience as a woman—and the water is flowing from her mouth. She's puking. She speaks the last word of this film, vomiting over the path of history. In an early film of yours, in the Böll adaptation *Not Reconciled*, the sub-title reads, *Only Violence Helps Where Violence Rules*. For me that's a masculine motto, which also determines our politics, for example the politics of the arms race. The ideology that one must arm oneself, because the enemy is arming himself, thus only violence avails against violence...

D: I interrupt only to say, "violence," that is not only violence with weapons. A strike is a form of violence. If we take a utopia, the greatest utopia there is—that suddenly all intellectuals, women and men, would strike, and this shit-society would collapse, that would also be a form of violence with which to deal with it, which in essence would be much greater than all other forms.

M: But you have shown approaches to alternative figures, the elderly Mrs. Fähmel...[6]

6 A character in *Not Reconciled*, the film mentioned previously.

D: But she stands there for a kind of counter-violence, only she's deranged. And the pressure is too great, so she is destroyed by it. Not only the pressure of the war or the whole period, but rather also what she as woman feels and had to experience.

H: I would very much like to know which films by women you admire. For instance, does Marguérite Duras speak to you?

D: I do admire her. She has a tremendous energy and is quite acerbic. But I admire more a woman who manages everyday life, not just as an intellectual, but a woman who manages things with husband and children, who doesn't kill herself but can live with it. I consider that much more difficult than making films.

M: But you don't want that?

D: I don't have the strength to do both at once.

M: You would rather make films?

D: That would also be a love story. When one chooses, one is still very young, and the experience only comes afterwards. Perhaps there are women who can do both, perhaps Caroline[7] will be able to do it, to have a husband and a daughter or several daughters. Perhaps in the younger generation... It is very difficult to do that without oppressing the others, which wouldn't be a solution either.

7 Caroline Champetier, camera assistant on Huillet-Straub's films *Too Early/Too Late* (1981) and *Class Relations* (1983).

M: What is your opinion of the films of Chantal Akerman, for example, *Jeanne Dielmann*?

D: I can say that some of it was unbearable to me. For example how the actress Delphine Seyrig peels potatoes and one sees immediately that she's never done it before in her life. That's unacceptable. And another thing I don't like in film is obstinately systematic shots, so that whenever for example someone sits upright he cuts off his own head.

M: But I mean, you have pretty explicitly turned away from the cinematic language developed by Hollywood, shot/counter-shot, where the important thing for the moment always appears in the frame, the head, and perhaps that would have to somehow meet you half-way—a certain obstinacy in staging, which then perhaps points more to the dress or a random detail...

D: But I don't believe that one can replace one suppression with another, and I also don't believe that one can contest one system by means of another, because then the whole thing just becomes rigid and that's the end of it.

H: So you have the feeling that in terms of cinematic language a lot happens arbitrarily?

D: At some point it becomes systematic, and then something isn't right for me. That's all.

M: Although I experience your films as explicitly systematic in their rejection, in the reflection on the ways cinematic language is commercialized.

D: But I believe, I hope, that is not so much a system as it is a method for exploring something; it can also be exploded, for example the set-up of a shot. I believe it is the third village one sees in Egypt, where at the beginning you have the sign and then you go left, then come back all the way to the right, and you see the village, and people are walking in the background. And a donkey. In the foreground, on the street, cars, trucks, and wagons and a donkey—that happens very much in the foreground. That was for example not planned. It was also a surprise for us and we wanted to keep it, precisely because we didn't want to clear away the reality for the benefit of the set-up we had planned. Because otherwise, if we were to make the set-up for what happens on the street, we would never have edited that way.

M: Don't you think that, for the comprehension of your films, a great deal of knowledge of film history is prerequisite?

D: Well, in my experience people are very moved who hardly see films, or at least see very few. I believe there are two sides to it: there are people who have a film culture, who have seen lots of films, and with whom the films sometimes go over really well, for whom they are interesting. But the people who are most moved and who, I believe, perhaps experience the films best, are the people who have no film culture.

H: What does that mean, they don't have a film culture? Today there is also television...

D: But in television people watch mostly news, sports, and the people I'm talking about hardly ever see feature films. They watch television just as one used to read the newspaper. Or yes, sports. They're right to do so, since that's about the only thing that is semi-decently filmed. It gets difficult with people who think they know what film is and what it ought to be. They come in and immediately start talking like this Egyptian woman, like, 'That is not a film, it is not filmic.' There's a narrowness. They believe film should be this or that, and they refuse to accept that actually it can be different. And was different, too.

H: In the interview that Karsten Witte conducted with you, there is a passage where you say that you want to make films that cannot be understood through cinema, through film history, but that can just be understood as such.

M: But I do think that there is such a thing as tradition and the tradition of cinematic language, in which people are trained. Somewhere bound up with the cinema, the conventional cinema, are ideas like the dream factory or awakening illusions. And I think it's also a thing that one shouldn't speak of only pejoratively. Because with the possibility of constructing illusions comes the possibility of thinking and proposing and dreaming utopias—also positive ones.

D: But I don't believe that it has much to do with utopias. The dreams one has come only from reality and are only partly distinguished from reality and are an attempt to escape from it. But always from reality, and not from nothing...

M: Okay, fine. One can make it very intellectual. But I think, your images are still somehow a refusal, there's a kind of sparseness and austerity about them.

D: I hope not only that. I hope that one can still experience sensuousness and desire, sense the fragrance of things. Right?

M: What really fascinated me was your reference to Cézanne, who paints the mountain over and over again, the exterior of the mountain, over and over again, and he knows that the mountain has burned. But in spite of that he paints the exterior over and over again. Through the energy that he expends on it, the fire begins to appear.

D: I can tell you something else about Cézanne. When I was fourteen years old, I saw paintings by Cézanne for the first time in the museum. There was the impudent thing with the naked woman, *Les Grandes Baigneuses*. My first impression was, he can't paint, it's painted badly. And nevertheless there was something in it that made me think about it for a long time afterward, and that made me unable to look at the pictures by the other painters, because I had the impression that they paint badly.

Translated from German by John Crutchfield.

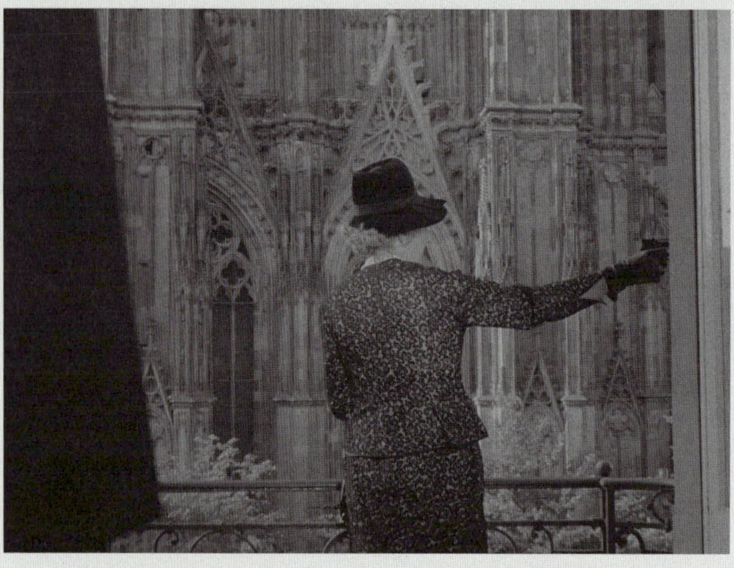

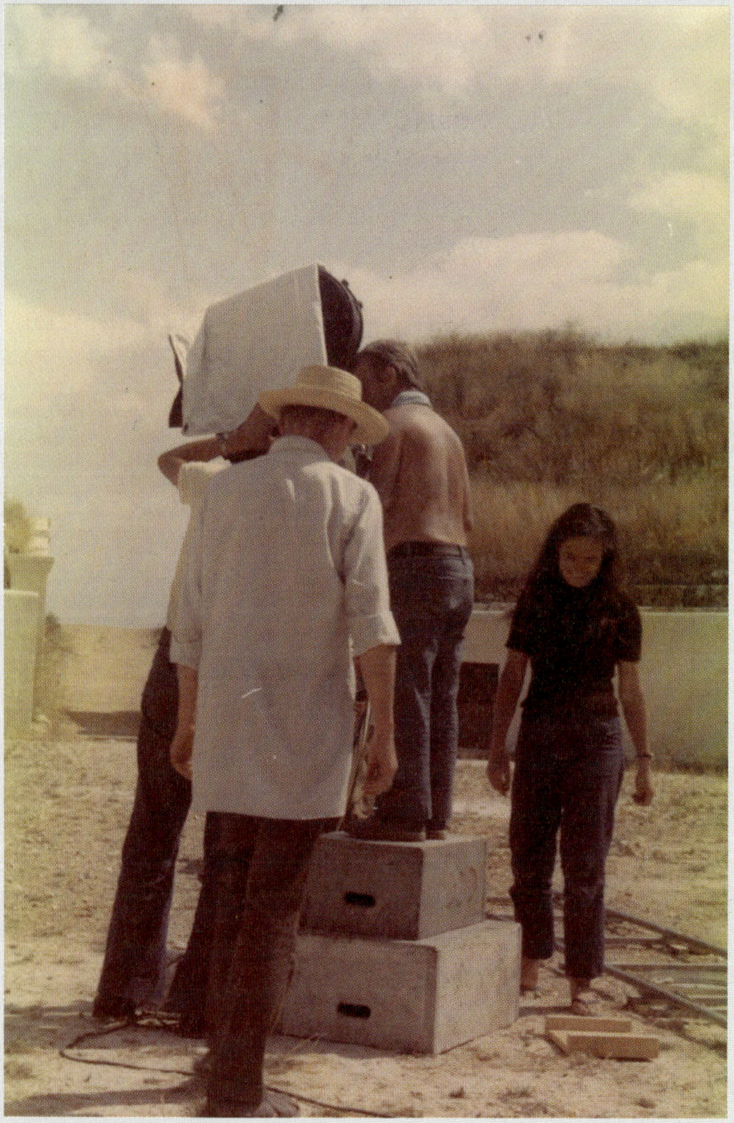

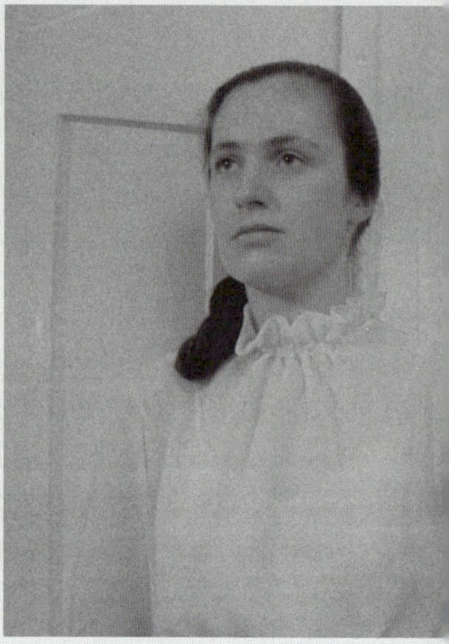

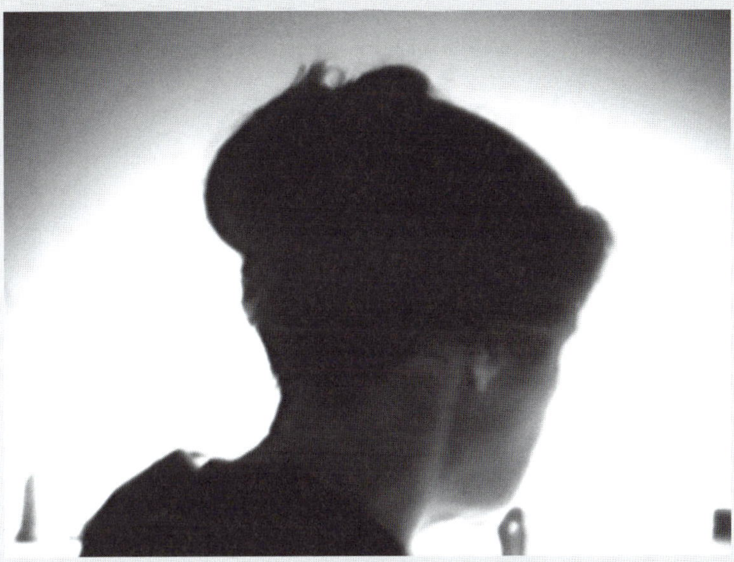

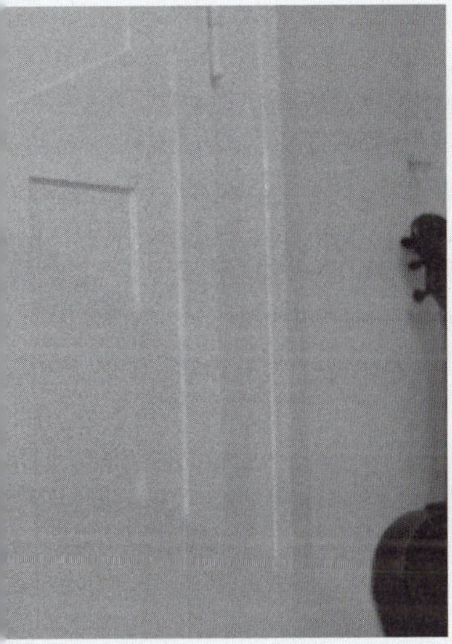

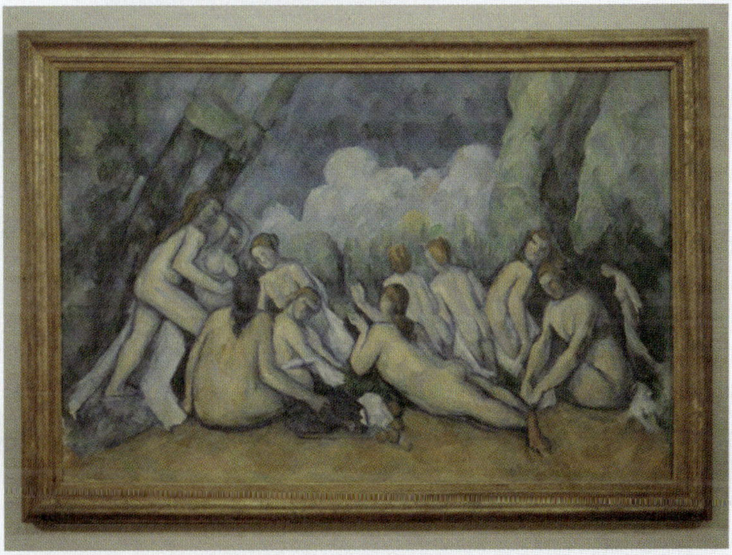

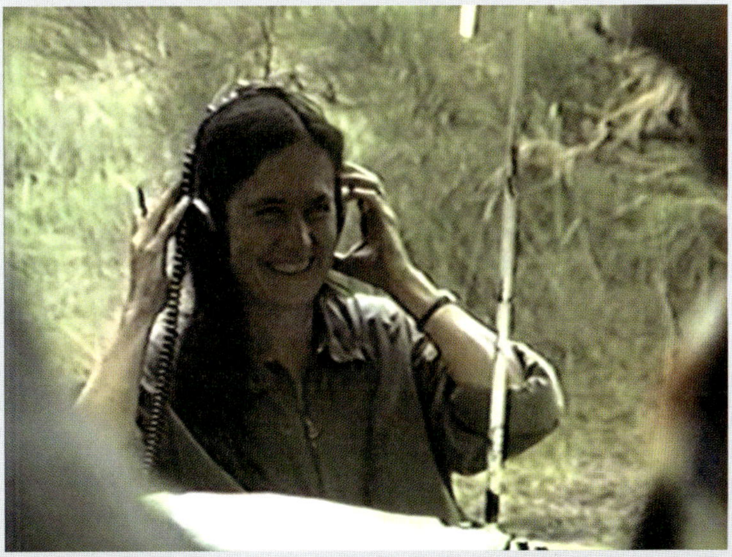

Luisa Greenfield

HISTORY LESSONS BY COMPARISON

The concept of progress must be grounded in the idea of catastrophe. That things are "status quo" is the catastrophe.[1]
—Walter Benjamin

The catastrophe is progress, progress is the catastrophe.[2]
—Bertolt Brecht

The first film I saw by Danièle Huillet and Jean-Marie Straub—*Nicht Versöhnt oder Es hilft nur Gewalt, wo Gewalt herrscht* (*Not Reconciled, or Only Violence Helps Where Violence Rules*)—immediately challenged my preconceived notions of what narrative and filmmaking were and could be. Its fragmented time frames and absence of transitions between them, the long and dense German monologues combined with pared-down subtitles, made it nearly impossible upon a first viewing to grasp a narrative strain in the film. In no particular order, *Not Reconciled* jumps between three different eras: The First World War, 1930s Third Reich, and 1960s post-war Germany. It describes a family of architects who are trying to understand their place in Germany's violent first half of the 20th century and the effect of Nazism on three generations. Collapsing the different time frames gives the sense of a continuous present in the lives of all three protagonists and works as a reminder that violent and oppressive systems of the past can regenerate and operate in new ways in the present.

While preparing for *Not Reconciled*, Huillet and Straub had made multiple visits to the Berliner Ensemble to see Brecht's plays performed by Helene Weigel since they were considering her for the part of Johanna and wanted her to read the script, which was drawn from Heinrich Böll's novel *Billard um halb zehn* (*Billiards at Half-Past Nine*).

> We were set on casting an actress for the part of the old lady so she could "recite" the past [...] She read it and suddenly told us, "Why do you insist on having a professional actress play the part? Actors are always bad in films! Why don't you try a non-professional?" So we said, "Thank you very much." [...] That proves that Weigel had certain meaningful personal experiences and had learned something from living and working with Brecht.[3]

1 Walter Benjamin, "On the Theory of Knowledge, Theory of Progress," in *The Arcades Project*, trans. Howard Eiland, Kevin McLaughlin. (Cambridge, MA: Harvard University Press, 2002), 473.

2 Erdmut Wizisla, *Benjamin and Brecht: The Story of a Friendship* (London: Verso, 2016), 173.

3 Jean-Marie Straub in "Sickle and Hammer, Cannons, Cannons, Dynamite! Danièle Huillet and Jean-Marie Straub in Conversation with François Albera," in *Jean-Marie Straub & Danièle Huillet*, ed. Ted Fendt (Vienna: SYNEMA, 2016), 124–125.

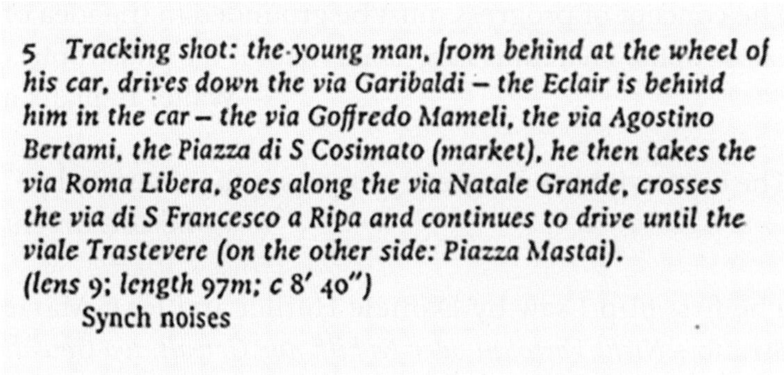

5 Tracking shot: the young man, from behind at the wheel of his car, drives down the via Garibaldi – the Eclair is behind him in the car – the via Goffredo Mameli, the via Agostino Bertami, the Piazza di S Cosimato (market), he then takes the via Roma Libera, goes along the via Natale Grande, crosses the via di S Francesco a Ripa and continues to drive until the viale Trastevere (on the other side: Piazza Mastai). (lens 9; length 97m; c 8′ 40″)

Synch noises

History Lessons script, shot no.5, indications for first drive sequence, 1972. From *Screen* 17 (Spring 1976), see note 4.

What held my interest during that first experience with their work was the unfamiliarity of it all—the stilted manner of speech, the use of direct sound, the unusual camera angles, and indeed also the lack of an easily perceivable narrative. At the same time that a sense of unfamiliarity pushed back against engrained expectations, the persistence and exactitude of the underlying structure of their films, which one can sense even upon a first encounter with their work, offered something rare—it prompted searching.

Transformative events are often remembered retrospectively by the first encounter, and with hindsight, it can be said that the experience lays groundwork and sets one on a certain course. This was absolutely the case for me after experiencing Huillet and Straub's *Geschichtsunterricht* (*History Lessons*) for the first time while living coincidentally in the same neighborhood in Rome where the filmmakers shot the film and had once lived. I saw the film repeatedly, then began to read about it and sought out the script, which had been translated into English by Danièle Huillet and published in a back issue of *Screen* magazine.[4] The *History Lessons* script details not only the exact routes that were filmed, giving indications for direction on precise streets, it also provides specific information about camera position and angles, naming the Éclair Coutant camera they used, the size of lenses, the length of each shot expressed in both meters of film stock and duration of time, and also indications for the use of synch sound. In doing so, Huillet and Straub elevate the importance and specificity of the materials used in the craft of their filmmaking by giving them a place of priority in the scripts.

4 *Screen* 17, no. 1 (Spring 1976): 54–76.

Additionally, their scripts list both the text from which the film was drawn, in this case, Bertolt Brecht's *Die Geschäfte des Herrn Julius Caesar*[5] (*The Business Affairs of Mr. Julius Caesar*) and the film credits, registering the importance of their collaborators by inscribing them in the material of the film script text. As Huillet expressed,

> What makes cinema great is the collective work, something it shares with theater, except that theater is made by an elite. They don't even try to work with people from the street, it's even worse than in film! Collective work is what makes it fascinating. That's where the relationship with politics lies.[6]

All of this set in motion a need to more actively engage with *History Lessons* from the perspective of its making. The idea emerged of retracing the three driving sequences that had so captured my attention, those scenes that had stayed with me and repeatedly returned to the forefront of my mind. Although at the time of the film's premiere, many viewers found the driving sequences "empty, puzzling, uninformative,"[7] and "interminable,"[8] I found the extended tracking shot structure of the drives fascinating, revealing tiny details gleaned from hundreds of fragment stories documenting quotidian life in the labyrinthine streets of Rome in 1972. Each crumbling façade and political poster, the tone of voices, car horns, the changing light and wind moving through trees on the Janiculum—the heterogeneity of daily rhythms that constituted Roman street life at that moment in time are recorded in the approximately ten-minute long unedited scenes. The car runs along the streets like the mechanism of the camera is running through time, for the length of a 16mm film reel. The camera is fixed and unmoving in the back of the car, and although the drives are all unedited, hundreds of visual cuts and sound fades happen by chance when the car passes a building or a person leaves the frame. The drives are slow, meandering and without an end point destination, however, the extended duration of the shots also serves as a respite in the film, as a rare gift of expanded time spent dwelling in a scene much longer than filmgoers are conditioned to expect. The duration of each driving shot in *History Lessons* in order of appearance in the film, and as indicated in the script in minutes and seconds are:

5 Bertolt Brecht, *Die Geschäfte des Herrn Julius Caesar* (Berlin: Gebrüder Weiß, 1949).

6 Huillet, "Sickle and Hammer," 123–124.

7 Maureen Turim, "Jean-Marie Straub and Danièle Huillet: Oblique Angles on Film as Ideological Intervention," in *New German Filmmakers*, ed. Klaus Phillips (New York: Frederick Ungar, 1984), 339.

8 *Variety* review of *Geschichtsunterricht*, which was screened in 1973 at the New York Film Festival, and was found in the Fondo Straub-Huillet at the Cineteca di Bologna. To the side of the clipped-out review Straub wrote: "VARIETY (Organo dei Ruffiani del Cinema Americano ed internationale) J-M.S." Organ of the pimps of American and international cinema.

8'40", 10'20", and 10'39". Landing in the outer limits of "tolerability," in fact the objective of *History Lessons* is to leave the audience feeling irritated and sick at patterns of oppression repeated throughout history, enough so as to incite action and, as Straub repeatedly asserts, "Cinema must set fire to life."[9]

History Lessons is based on playwright and poet Bertolt Brecht's lesser-known, apparently unfinished novel *The Business Affairs of Mr. Julius Caesar*, which was mostly written between 1937 and 1939 during part of his fifteen years in exile. In the novel, Brecht sought to debunk the myth of Caesar as a "great man of history" and thereby contribute to the de-mythologization of the cult of personality around Hitler by indicating how dictatorships are constructed and how empires are built—sometimes haphazardly. The fragmented story begins with a young man, the researcher historian, who is searching for information about the "real" Caesar for a biography he's writing thirty years after Caesar's death. Brecht's aim was not only to dismantle the image of Caesar but also to shed light on the socio-political and economic structures, as well as the aesthetic frameworks, that conspire to create such an image and allow for such figures to take power. The novel offers a fragmented view of Caesar, subverting the linearly structured narrative form that is traditionally used to write history, specifically a cumulative narrative that builds upon itself and follows a seemingly inevitable course through time. Brecht saw this type of historical narrative structure as a support system that helped to promote the "great personality" evidenced in dangerous leaders. He held lifelong interest in the figure of Caesar, dating back to his school days and researched his life as a means to understand why destructive patterns of history persist and repeat.

Brecht intended connections be made between the figure of Caesar and both current and future dictators. In a fragment from his working notes written when he was still planning a dramatic version of the material, in what appears to be a commentator's introductory line, Brecht wrote, "If it is true, ladies and gentlemen, that a new age of Caesars lies before us, then we are in no doubt that you will be profoundly interested by the life and doings of the great Julius Caesar."[10]

9 Jean-Marie Straub in "Rage and Resistance: Jean-Marie Straub and Danièle Huillet Interviewed by Claude-Jean Philippe" (1976), trans. Sally Shafto, *Senses of Cinema*, no. 83 (June 2017).

10 Brecht, *Business Affairs*, 9.

The *Caesar* novel opens with the young researcher, the narrator, seeking authentic historical materials, in particular, a manuscript called “The Diaries of Rarus” penned by one of Caesar’s domestic slaves, his secretary, who took firsthand notes on Caesar’s career. In an attempt to track down these diaries and seeking to confirm his pre-existing view of Caesar as one of the “great men” who ultimately write history, the researcher carries out interviews with four people who had known Caesar personally: a banker, a jurist, a poet, and a peasant who was a former legionnaire in Caesar’s army. Through these accounts, the myth around Caesar is gradually challenged and eventually disintegrates. In the face of mounting contradictions, the researcher—and the reader—is confronted with an alternate view of history to the one that was once learned and originally presumed to be true. The novel challenges the reader with the monuments of imperial progress—the ‘official history’—contrasted against the reality of a dictator’s grasping self-interest. The researcher must face, as Walter Benjamin described in his 1937 essay on the collector and historian Eduard Fuchs,

> [...] that state of unease which marks the beginning of any consideration of history worthy of being called dialectical. Unease over the provocation to the researcher, who must abandon the calm, contemplative attitude toward his object in order to become conscious of the critical constellation in which precisely this fragment of the past finds itself with precisely this present.[11]

Brecht lived in exile in the village of Skovsbostrand near the town of Svendborg, on a small island in southern Denmark from 1933 to 1939, and it was during the latter years in Svendborg that he was writing *The Business Affairs of Mr. Julius Caesar*. He shared early drafts with Benjamin, who visited him there for three extended summer periods: the first in early summer 1934, then again in the summers of 1936 and 1938.[12] This marked a period in their relationship of intense intellectual exchange, from reading and commenting on each other’s work, in which they shared deep political and aesthetic commonalities, to occasional collaboration. Brecht’s summation of the *Caesar* novel can be found in a letter dated Svendborg, September 1938, and

11 Walter Benjamin, *Selected Writings, vol. 3, 1935–1938*, ed. Howard Eiland, Michael W. Jennings, trans. E. Jephcott (Cambridge, MA: Harvard University Press, 2002), 262.

12 Howard Eiland and Michael W. Jennings, *Walter Benjamin: A Critical Life* (Cambridge, MA: Harvard University Press, 2014), 451.

addressed to The American Guild for German Cultural Freedom, an organization founded in 1935 in the US to provide aid for exiled German artists and intellectuals. In it he wrote:

> My main work at present consists in the satirical novel *Die Geschäfte des Herrn Julius Caesar,* which calls for a great deal of historical research. It deals with the founding of an imperium and the establishment of a dictatorship – on a strictly historical basis, I might add. It is not a disguised biography of Hitler or Mussolini. It will provide the modern reader, I hope, not only with valuable information about wars, democracy, etc., but also with a picture of how the persistence of slavery leads to general enslavement, i.e. of all classes of society.[13]

The 1972 film script for *History Lessons* consists entirely of large segments quoted directly from Brecht's *Caesar* novel. Notably, in the script, Huillet and Straub omitted Brecht's 'Rarus Diaries' (Books 2 and 4), which display Caesar's utterly flawed and commonplace side, especially with regard to his personal and self-serving business dealings. Instead, for the film, they retained only passages from the interviews conducted between the researcher and Caesar's contemporaries featured in the novel. As Straub said of their building the script for *History Lessons,* "With Brecht, when we cut we didn't cut the interior, so to speak. We didn't cut into the economic discourses, but only made anecdotal cuts. So there we didn't really put Brecht into question."[14] The diaries create a narrative structure in the novel and removing, as Straub called it, the "anecdotes and psychology"[15] from the text, takes it "beyond the 'Brechtianisms' of the 1970s [...] distanciation, anti-illusionism, deconstruction, the critique of identification processes and the dismantling of 'classical' narrative."[16] In the film the young, male researcher from the early 1970s shares the same temporal space as those contemporaries of Caesar, who appear dressed in costumes that reference antiquity. So the collapsing of eras, as in *Not Reconciled*, sets up a scenario where we see that history could have been, and still could be, made differently. In a journal entry from July 25, 1938, Brecht writes that the conception of Caesar is inhuman, "and i cannot just

13 Bertolt Brecht, *Letters 1913–1956*, ed. John Willet, trans. Ralph Manheim (New York: Routledge, 1981), 292.

14 "*Moses and Aaron* as an object of Marxist reflection," Joel Rogers, *Jump Cut*, no. 12/13 (1976): 61–64.

15 "Andi Engel talks to Jean-Marie Straub, and Danièle Huillet is there too," *Enthusiasm*, no. 1 (December, 1975): 21.

16 Barton Byg, *Landscapes of Resistance*, (Berkeley: University of California Press, 1995), 118.

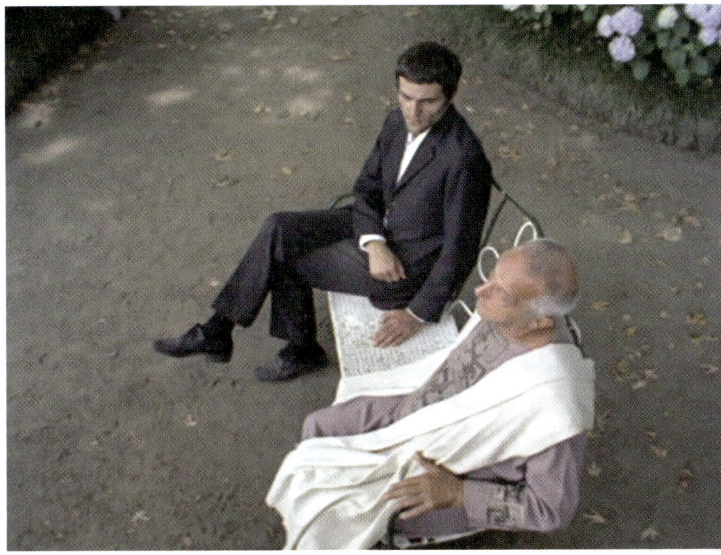

describe things from today's position, i have to make the alternative way seem possible from the perspective of those times too."[17]

When experiencing a film by Huillet and Straub, one is witness to a process of searching that always begins with working through texts and develops into the material act of making films collectively. When asked about their approach to making the films *History Lessons* (1972) and *Moses and Aaron* (1974), Straub replied: "We tried to find a subject that resists us because we have to live with the subject for many years."[18] Their working process involves multiple visits to locations over the course of months and sometimes years of preparation. At times Huillet referred to their practice of returning to potential film locations as "reconnaissance"[19] in the sense of surveying, as in plotting a course, and also a kind of geological, strata-like survey of the land based on the history layered therein. It involves hours spent working out exact camera angles. Caroline Champetier, one of the cinematographers on Huillet and Straub's 1980/81 film *Too Early/Too Late*, and their 1983 film *Klassenverhältnisse* (Class Relations), said their fastidious shot construction was the way to, "most intelligently respect the existing space, to take into account its lines of force."[20] They searched for a geometry in the framing—exactly the correct position from which to orient the camera and frame each shot—based not only on visual considerations, but also to highlight the tension that exists within a given space and between characters. And

17
Bertolt Brecht, *Journals 1934–1955*, ed. John Willett, trans. Hugh Rorrison (London: Methuen, 1993), 10.

18
"Straub/Huillet Talking," Peter Gidal (*Edinburgh Film Festival Catalogue*, 1975): 92.

19
"Das Feuer im Innern des Berges: Ein Gespräch mit Danièle Huillet von Helge Herbele und Monika Funke Stern," *Frauen und Film*, no. 32 (June 1982): 4–12. English translation by John Crutchfield in this volume, 250–264.

20
Daniel Fairfax, "Straub, Jean-Marie & Huillet, Danièle," *Screen* (Sept. 2009).

decision-making was collaborative between Huillet and Straub at every stage, on every level as Straub illuminated,

> And the discussion is often very violent...before, when we are writing the script or afterwards, when we are editing—she is in front of the table, but she is the only one who touches the buttons because I have no right to touch that button. (She's very intolerant.) Never have we made a decision without the other. During the shooting she is working more with the sound people and I am more on the side of the camera people. But even when I am preparing a frame with the cameraman, when I think I'm ready, she says "okay" or "not okay." Brecht said, "Love is to work with the capacities of the other." And so, since we love each other...[21]

Their working process also involves prioritizing the use of direct sound, knowing that sound will determine where a cut in the image is made. As Huillet has said,

> [I]f you have decided to make a film with direct sound, the locations that you choose have to be right not only in terms of the images but also in terms of the sound. [...] You can't edit direct sound as you edit the films you are going to dub: each image has a sound and you're forced to respect it.[22]

This means allowing sound in a scene to run its full course before making a cut, overturning the usual hierarchy of image over sound—of sound functioning merely in support of the image.

Filmic decisions are made based on an inherent respect for the original written material, but that is not incompatible with their desire to test the limits of the text's capabilities. Their practice involves extensive syntactic and gestural work with actors to determine precisely where the emphasis in a sentence or in a word is placed, and to acknowledge the inherent musicality of language. In their films, the voice is a singular instrument of recitation that connects film as a medium directly with oral traditions, as Straub stated, "We're not interested in competing with literature, but in pushing it to the other side [...] when people gathered around the fire to tell stories. Let's call it going from a writer-based civilization to an oral tradition that has been to-

21
"An Aesthetic Inquiry," Phil Mariani, *Wedge*, vol. 2, 1982.

22
Elisabeth Weis, John Belton, eds., *Film Sound: Theory and Practice* (New York: Columbia University Press, 1985), 151–152.

tally repressed."[23] They spent months breaking down a text into a tonal sound structure filled with pauses that were counted out based on natural breathing and the placement of syllabic stress, whose lines in the end more resembled a protracted theatrical monologue or a poem than a film script. Following this initial syntactic work with language, which involved creating blocks of text, more months were concentrated on rehearsing in an apartment or on a stage with actors to create notations for the script, based on the capacities of the actors, their patterns of breath, reciting the texts hundreds of times until it became a part of them, until according to Huillet, the actors "start claiming the text for themselves" and it "enters their nervous system."[24] They are committed to that which is not reproducible, as Straub describes: "In each character in the moment, noise, air and wind, and upon the effort that actors make and the risk they face, like tightrope walkers, throughout long and difficult texts recorded live."[25] In rehearsals Huillet worked as the primary language coach and both she and Straub took daily notes, transcribing them into a complex, color-coded system of annotations creating what they called a score of the text. At the same time they never change the writing in a source text; through the working process with actors who draw on their own life experiences, the words are taken to a limit and transformed into something other, something revitalized, related to musicality, and contemporaneous with the present time.

HUILLET: [...] it's hard with the audience. They are so—partially through their own fault and partially, because of the products that they always see—they are so distant from the notion that music has something to do with cinema. That which they would accept in music, it wouldn't occur to them that that also...
STRAUB: ...has something to do with cinema.[26]

The films are about the re-telling of stories, mostly through non-actors who invoke oral traditions by the recitation of texts learned by heart and sometimes delivered in a language that is not their mother tongue, so that they "will face obstacles which in my opinion, should make the text more alive," as Straub said.[27] This struggle is fundamental to Huillet and Straub's approach to reignite and enliven a text through non-native speakers. In *History Lessons*,

23 Straub, "Sickle and Hammer," 120.

24 Huillet, "Sickle and Hammer," 123.

25 Jean-Marie Straub is referring to their 1969 film, *Les yeux ne veulent pas en tout temps se fermer ou Peut-être qu'un jour Rome se permettra de choisir à son tour* (aka *Othon*) in "Orality and Objectification: Danièle Huillet and Jean-Marie Straub, Filmmakers and Translators," Benoît Turquety, *SubStance*, vol. 44, no. 2, Issue 137 (Johns Hopkins University Press, 2015): 50.

26 "A Conversation with Danièle Huillet and Jean-Marie Straub about *Class Relations*," trans. David Perrin, MUBI, 20 Aug. 2019. mubi.com

27 Straub, "Andi Engel," 15.

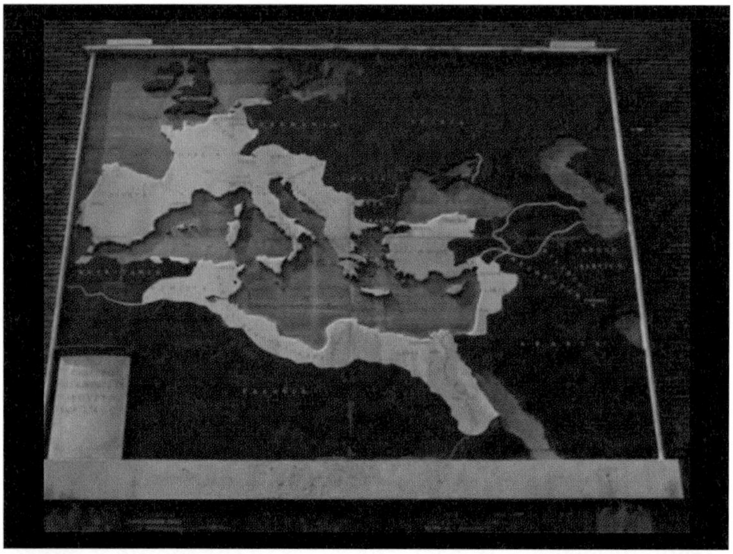

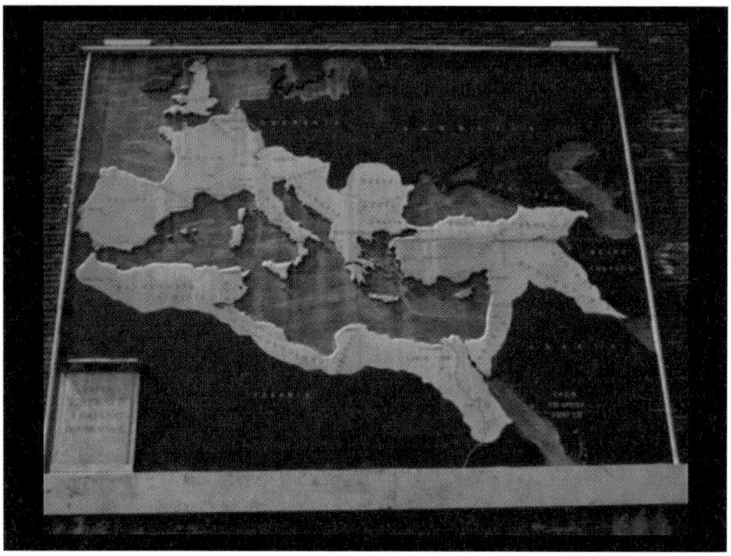

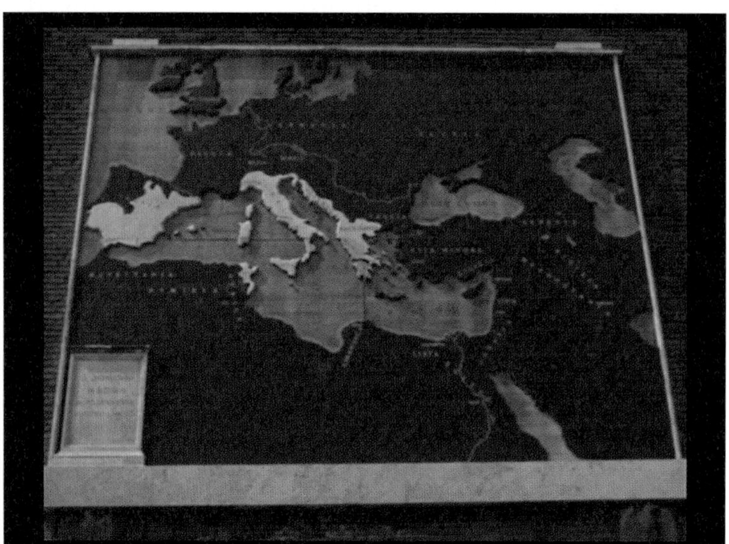

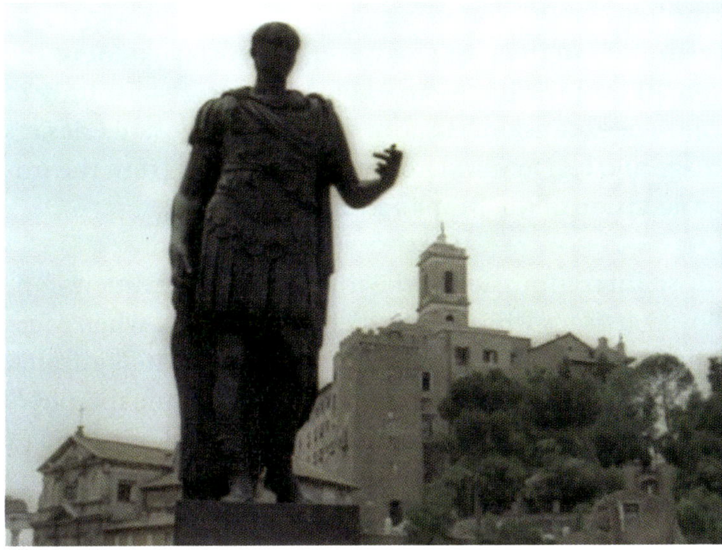

however, the dialectic, that "state of unease" is brought about by native German speakers reciting Brecht's words in German, but as Romans in Rome. Since Brecht had originally intended the *Caesar* project as a play, the oral component remained inherent to the original material that Huillet and Straub drew from to make *History Lessons*.

The film *History Lessons* was shot primarily in Rome in 1972 and it opens with, as the script says, "Noises of the viale dei Fori Imperiali" running over a black screen. While the opening credits roll, underneath the dominant sound of cars and trucks driving on the street, two North American tourists are heard. Their chatting runs over the image of three fixed shots of large-scale stone maps supported at the lower corners by an imperial eagle and mounted on a brick wall. The first shot, holding for five seconds, is a map of the Mediterranean world when the Roman Empire was at its pinnacle of power. The second shot holds for two-thirds of a second on a map of the Roman Empire in AD 14, and the third shot holds for one and one-half seconds on a map of the territory of Rome after the Punic wars. By filming the maps from right to left, in reverse chronology, the Roman Empire no longer expands but contracts—its dominion quickly and drastically reduced in size. The fourth and final shot in this preamble to the first driving sequence is a low angle view of a Roman replica statue of Julius Caesar standing on a plinth by the side of the Roman Forum, which holds for eight seconds.[28] Mussolini had the statue and the maps[29] erected during the mid-1930s with

28 "*History Lessons* – Scenario," *Screen*, vol. 17, no. 1 (Spring 1976): 54–55.

29 Although three maps are recorded in the film, there are four maps mounted on the Basilica Maxentius. Huillet and Straub chose not to film the fourth map, which depicts the beginnings of the Roman Empire in the 8th century BC where the extent of it consists of one small white dot labeled "ROMA."

the intention of promoting fascism, the maps serving as a reminder of the past glory and territorial extent of the Roman Empire and as an exhortation to Fascist Italy to continue expansion. His aim was to reinvigorate Caesar's image and call to mind notions of grandeur from the imperial vision of the Roman Empire.

Mussolini commissioned the maps from government-employed artisans who constructed them in 1934 when Mussolini was preparing to invade Ethiopia. He inaugurated the maps on April 21, (Fascist) Labor Day, while members of the military youth groups, moving from one level of the party to the next and initiating new members in the rites of passage, intended to display the growing strength of the Party marched in goose step down the Via Dell'Impero, past the ancient Forum and in front of the maps. But there was also a fifth map, larger than the rest. The new map was a continuation of Roman conquests and brought the Fascist imperial project up to date, celebrating their campaigns in Eastern Africa and the conquest of Ethiopia as the event that finally established the Italian empire. It depicted current events rather than those of the ancient past but enshrined and commemorated in the same way—set in stone and implicitly pointing to future conquests.[30]

Four of the five maps remain in the same location in Rome, mounted to the outer wall of the Basilica of Maxentius. After Mussolini's downfall the fifth map was defaced with red paint and broken in half, removed and stored away for decades. The exact whereabouts remain unclear but it is now thought to be located somewhere in the EUR complex (Esposizione Universale Roma), the planed architectural example of Mussolini's new Rome set to open at the world's fair in 1942 that never took place.[31] But to understand the maps one must understand the street itself, the sole purpose of which was to enshrine Fascist ideology. The Via dell'Impero was one of Mussolini's most treasured urban projects and it became a major site for ritual display. The plans of the street, drawn by Mussolini, carved a straight line from the Roman Colosseum past the Forum directly to Piazza Venezia where he had his office headquarters. The maps were completed in eleven months at breakneck speed to be ready for the 10th anniversary of Mussolini's semi-fictional "March on Rome," the history of which was

30 Heather Hyde Minor, "Mapping Mussolini: Ritual and Cartography in Public Art during the Second Roman Empire," *Imago Mundi International Journal for the History of Cartography*, vol. 51, ed. Catherine Delano Smith (London: Imago Mundi, Ltd. 1999): 147–162.

31 Minor, "Mapping Mussolini," 155.

carefully choreographed, scripted, and documented by photos, resulting in the founding myth upon which the regime was built.[32]

All three car drives in *History Lessons* were plotted based on Huillet and Straub's walks in the historic Roman districts of Regola (drive 3) and neighboring Trastevere (drives 1 and 2), where they were living at the time.[33] In the early 1970s, when *History Lessons* was made, the maze-like streets that the car winds through were predominantly working class residential neighborhoods where families, artisans, and craftspeople of all kinds lived and worked. Using a shotgun microphone from the back seat of what must have been a borrowed, pine green Austin Mini Countryman, real time sounds in the streets of Rome mixed in with sounds from the workings of the car, are all that is heard in the driving scenes. As the viewer passes through these streets, one is keenly aware of the specificity of the perspective imposed by the fixed camera in the car's back seat. These long, unedited car rides incorporate the element of contingency, enabling an aspect of the film to escape the strictures of authorial intention, at the same time highlighting the filmmaking apparatus through the fixed frame of the front wind shield. The other windows of the car that are visible to us: the front side windows, and the sunroof, expand the view by letting the sounds of the street come in and are reminders of the world that exists outside of the film frame, with the exception of the rear-view mirror, where we only see the eyes of the researcher/driver. The rigorous planning and specificity of structure, only to allow for everything possible to take place during the moment of filming, is emblematic of Huillet and Straub's filmmaking procedure.

32
Minor, 151.

33
Byg, *Landscapes of Resistance*, 127.

The role of passenger in any context is generally a passive one—a passenger is taken somewhere. A sense of containment, isolation, and distance between oneself and the outside world is felt as the frame of the camera/car passes through the streets of Rome. In *History Lessons* Huillet and Straub replace Brecht's "Rarus Diaries" with the three driving sequences, serving as a corrective of Brecht by essentially replacing the everyday life of Caesar with the everyday life of the Roman people. The driving sequences can be understood as moments of filtration, where the researcher allows all the disappointing contradictions that he is learning about Caesar to awaken him to the birth of rage. However, the driver is not the protagonist in these scenes, he is a connecting thread. The protagonist is the street, and during these scenes it is incumbent on the passenger (us) to engage with the world outside the car windows where each fragment story is a marker of a time and place, that will never repeat in exactly the same way again, but is nonetheless materially connected to events of the past. The way to engage comes to us through sound; the sounds of the street spilling into the car and liberating us from its containment, "Everything—the insect suffering in one corner, or the wind coming through the frame or the space itself, or a changing light—everything is as important as the human being you are framing."[34]

Whereas Brecht's *Caesar* novel combined time frames through the use of colloquial language and an overall stylistic structure with its story within a story, aimed at collapsing eras, the film *History Lessons* goes further. It rejects a linear notion of time in favor of a variegated, stratified sense by allowing multiple eras to co-exist in the film through the figure of the contemporary researcher who is in literal dialogue with the contemporaries of Caesar he interviews—filmed in locations, chosen for their historic specificity in relation to the original text. As Danièle Huillet has said in reference to the written materials they are drawn to work with as the basis of their films, "It's a question of epochs—instead of taking away one adds, the things written five hundred years earlier are not removed, they're left. In a film what interests us is the stratification, like in geology."[35] The collapsing of chronological time, where a researcher from the 1970s is in direct conversation with people who had known Caesar first hand, with actors reciting their texts while standing on ground referred to in the script where people have suffered or profited from the suffering of others, is a recognition that all things are in a continual state of change as a result of interactions and conflicts, and many small, sometimes obscure changes add up, until the thing in question has been qualitatively transformed into something different. In this case, it is the consciousness of the researcher—the surrogate for the audience—that has been transformed by the end of the film. In this orientation, the past is no longer viewed as a fixed

34 Susan Dermody, "Jean-Marie Straub and Danièle Huillet, The Politics of Film Practice," *Cinema Papers*, no. 10 (September–October, 1976): 130.

35 "Straub/Huillet Talking," Peter Gidal (*Edinburgh Film Festival Catalogue*, 1975): 93.

point in time but rather, as accumulated experiences that are accessible to the present and can be engaged with, and the point of entry is both literary and filmic.

History Lessons By Comparison is the result of my attempt to inhabit the structure and premise of Huillet and Straub's film. Originally filmed on 16mm, both films were transferred to digital and are screened in a double projection, on a loop with separate speakers for sound. The driving scenes from Huillet and Straub's 1972 film and its accompanying direct sound recording are projected onto the left screen, and my direct sound retracing is projected simultaneously on the right. The slow drives search after predetermined routes that nonetheless, allow for contingencies of everyday life to play out over the course of each uncut reel. Artifacts from the process of filmmaking, the sonic and visual resonance revealed on the same streets that were filmed forty-five years apart, occupy the same temporal space. The two films are in dialogic relation, wherein history is conceived of as an open-ended conversation, one that accepts contradiction and ambiguity.

The idea of retracing the drives, knowing that I would ultimately place those from 1972 in juxtaposition with my contemporary filming of them, also led to curiosity about the streets: the ways in which they had stayed the same, how they had changed over the decades, and what factors determined those changes. I was able to create maps that showed exactly where Huillet and Straub had filmed, and begin to plot out my retracing on a current day street map of Rome. The map of the city is somewhat altered from the 1972 version: what was once a through street is now one-way, some roads are now blocked for pedestrians only, and so on. It was clear that sometimes I would drive on the same streets that they had in 1972, and other times I would have to make my way back to their streets, which became an accepted restriction of the structure for filming. I made a first attempt at drive number one in 2010 as a sketch of the idea, with a digital camera, recording direct sound and driving a borrowed Fiat 500—the most commonly driven car on the road at the time *History Lessons* was made.

From the start it was clear to me that the car I drove should be of the era in which the film was made, as a way for the

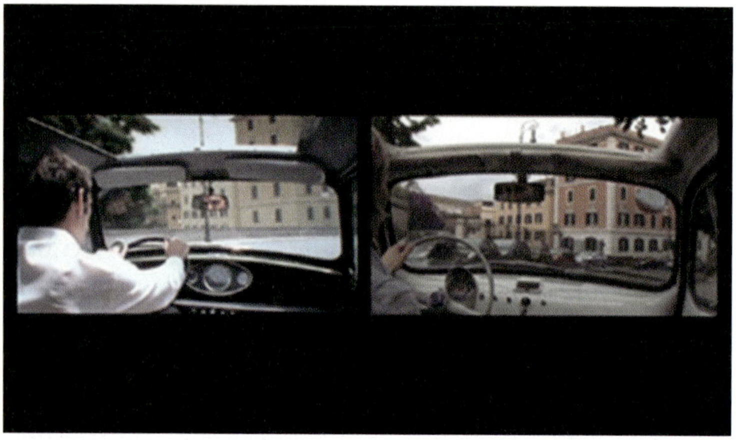

interior frame of my driving sequence to connect to the era of their 1972 film. The task was simply to attempt to drive through the same streets, and only later, during editing, would I be able to compare the drives, to discover convergences, and set up potential visual, sonic, and temporal dialogue between the two films by screening them together.

The project of retracing *History Lessons* was repeated again in 2017, this time filming all three drives with a small crew,[36] using matching film stock,[37] and filming with the same model of camera, the 16mm Éclair, that Straub and Huillet had used, recording direct sound, and again, as in my 2010 attempt, driving the most common make, model and color of car on the streets of Rome at the time. Since the idea was to ultimately juxtapose the two drives, I became interested to see where they would intersect and where they would be forced to separate. In keeping with their practice of developing a well thought out framework for each of their shots that nonetheless allowed for every contingency to come into play as soon as the camera was running, I was curious to see and hear what artifacts of chance this structure would reveal and once the two films were set side by side, how they would differ between the eras.

The relationship of *History Lessons* to the original Brecht text departs radically from conventions of cinematic adaptation, drawing on the broader questions of economic exploitation, power, and resistance that form the basis of the novel. As Barton Byg states in his *Landscapes of Resistance*, it is the form of both the novel and the film that draw connections between fascism and consumer capitalism and "forces a shift of attention away from Caesar and onto the

36
I worked with Gustavo Jahn (camera) and Melissa Dullius (sound) also known as Distruktur, as well as with Terril Scott (production assistant).

37
Huillet and Straub filmed *History Lessons* using Eastman Kodak 7254 film stock, which Kodak no longer produces. We filmed the driving sequences in *History Lessons By Comparison* with Kodak 7203, the most similar film stock available today.

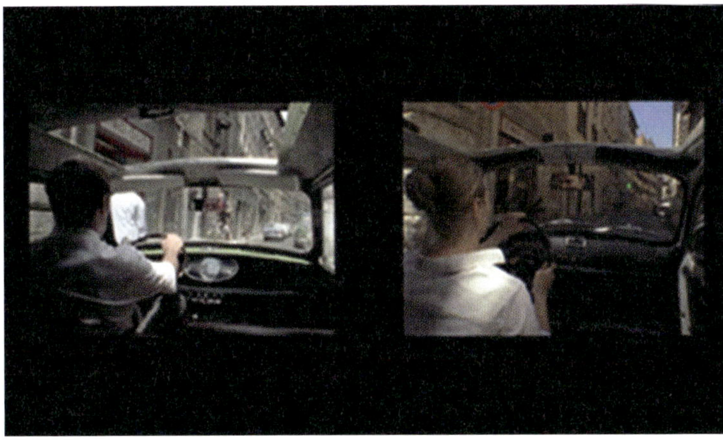

processes of history and the inadequate tools available to understand them."[38]

While Brecht was working on *Caesar* during the time in 1937 when he still envisioned the piece as a play, he indicated, in a letter to his friend and mentor Karl Korsch, that he didn't want to make it a "*pièce à clef*"[39] simply describing real life behind a façade of fiction.

> Nevertheless, Caesar is the great model, and I can throw light on at least two things: 1) the way the dictator swings between the classes and in doing so conducts the business of one single class [...] 2) that wars [...] are undertaken to exploit one's own people, not just the ones under attack. [...] The difficulty: Caesar nevertheless signifies some progress, and the inverted commas round 'progress' are hugely difficult to dramatise.[40]

Benjamin, Brecht, and, decades later, Huillet and Straub were still critical of the Social Democratic notion of progress with its optimistic faith in technology and policy of moderate, incremental political reform, while still working within a capitalist system as opposed to the revolutionary Marxist position. It was in Benjamin's various texts from 1936–1940 that he developed his particular vision of history, dissociating himself more and more radically with the illusion of progress. Benjamin and Brecht shared the view that material progress (mastering nature) coexists with the retrogression of society displaying, as Benjamin wrote in his thesis *On the Concept of History*, "the technocratic features that later emerge in fascism."[41] Likewise, in an interview conducted in 2001 Straub states:

38
Byg, *Landscapes of Resistance*, 137.

39
Brecht, *Letters*, 271.

40
Brecht, *Business Affairs*, 5.

41
Walter Benjamin, *Selected Writings, vol. 4, 1938–1940*, ed. H. Eiland, M. Jennings, G. Smith, trans. E. Jephcott (Cambridge, MA: Harvard University Press, 2003), 393.

> [...] social democracy keeps taking flight into the future; people don't even have the right to experience the present time anymore. They're being told that progress must go on, that there is no alternative but to rush down into the abyss of progress until disaster takes place. [...] Therefore we live in 'the best of all possible worlds' and all that preceded us was necessarily not as good. This is exactly what Walter Benjamin rebelled against when he said that revolution is a 'tiger's leap into the past.' So a political film must remind people that we don't live in the 'best of all possible worlds,' far from it.[42]

Huillet had read all of the correspondence of Marx and Engels aloud to Straub during their work on their film *Moses and Aaron* two years after making *History Lessons*.[43] In that case, she might have subsequently come across a letter written by Engels to economist Walther Borgius from 1894, where he warns that,

> In Germany the greatest hindrance to correct understanding is the irresponsible neglect by literature of economic history. It is so hard, not only to disaccustom oneself of the ideas of history drilled into one at school, but still more to rake up the necessary material for doing so.[44]

In the novel Brecht shows how democratic measures can be exploited financially through land speculation, how war is a business that exploits the people it claims to benefit, and as Brecht wrote in a correspondence drafted from Skovsbostrand on November 19, 1937, regarding the *Caesar* project, "The main political idea is that dictatorships come into being at times of violent class struggle. The dictator as the pointer of the scales. And the dependency of dictatorships on the ruling class."[45] The idea of chance playing a crucial role in the building up of such leaders preceded Brecht by Engels who in the same correspondence points to the contingencies of history:

> This is where the so-called great men come in for treatment. That such and such a man and precisely that man arises at that particular time in that given country is of course pure accident. But cut him out and there will be a demand for a substitute, and this substitute will be found, good or bad, but in the

42 Straub, "Sickle and Hammer," 110–111.

43 Huillet, "The Fire in the Mountain," in this volume, 253.

44 *Marx and Engels Correspondence*, International Publishers (1968), first published *Gestamtausgabe*, trans. Donna Torr, www.marxists.org

45 Brecht, *Letters, 269.*

> long run he will be found. That Napoleon, just that particular Corsican, should have been the military dictator whom the French Republic, exhausted by its own war, had rendered necessary, was an accident; but that, if a Napoleon had been lacking, another would have filled the place, is proved by the fact that the man has always been found as soon as he became necessary: Caesar, Augustus, Cromwell, etc.[46]

Accident and contingency, however, is not the same thing. Accident has the stumbling quality of an unavoidable mistake, and contingency can be invited, like a partner, to participate. Contingency is a very present partner in the films of Huillet and Straub. In *History Lessons*, during a moment in the conversation with the banker, a leaf blows onto the young researcher, first-time actor Benedikt Zulauf's lap just before he is about to start to speak. In a moment of recognition, he grins slightly, glancing presumably in the direction of Straub as he brushes the leaf off, takes a pause, and begins to speak. Letting this intervention of the wind and the tree be included, is in awareness of the place where they are, a living garden, and an acknowledgment that there are other "players" at work in this film. Zulauf knows that Straub won't stop and ask to do a new take when the leaf falls because of the welcome acceptance of other non-human elements operating in the film that are out of their control. Of the falling leaf moment in the film, Straub said, "At the editing table, of course, those kinds of things are kept because they came about by chance during shooting."[47] Having many takes to choose from, Huillet often said, their one luxury is film stock,[48] and since they filmed multiple takes, (for *History Lessons* up to as many as thirty-two of each scene)[49] they must have chosen this take as the best one for precisely that reason.

By 1940 Brecht felt compelled to abandon the *Caesar* novel due to lack of available research materials during his exile[50] and perhaps also the lack of support from peers he admired, although he wrote proudly in his journal about how three "German workers" had read the text and "they grasped everything, even the details."[51] He stopped work on the project a year before fleeing to the US in 1941 where he continued to live in exile in Los Angeles for almost sev-

46 *Marx and Engels Correspondence*, www.marxists.org

47 "A conversation with Danièle Huillet and Jean-Marie Straub," Wilhlem Roth, Günther Pflaum, (Mannheim, 12.10.1972), in a booklet called "Jean-Marie Straub Filme von 1969–1972," 32–39, archived in Fondo Straub-Huillet at the Cineteca di Bologna. Trans. Ted Fendt.

48 "At Work with Straub and Huillet: Thoughts and reflections from their collaborators," in *Jean-Marie Straub & Danièle Huillet*, 140–141.

49 Straub, "A conversation," 32.

50 Brecht, *Letters*, 329.

51 Brecht, *Journals*, 41–42.

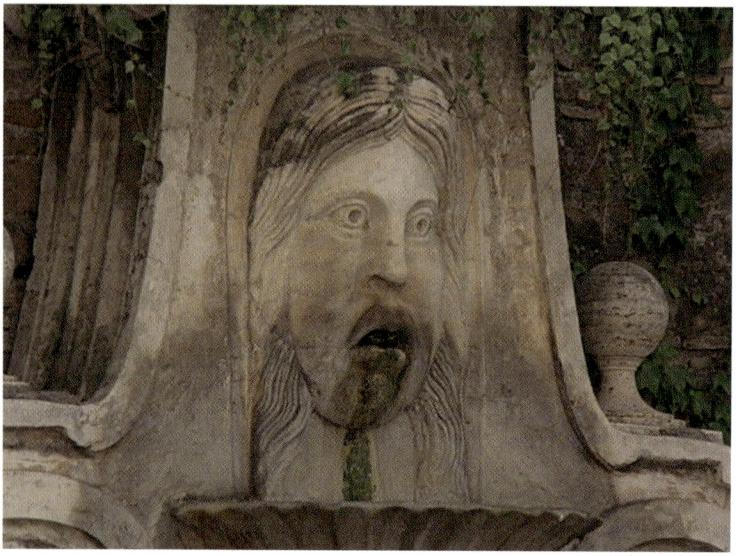

en years, a place he lamented, "almost nowhere has my life ever been harder than here in this mausoleum of *easy going*."[52]

In Brecht's journal from August 9, 1941, days after he learned of Benjamin's death, he noted after having read Benjamin's *On the Concept of History*:

> the little treatise deals with historical research, and could have been written after reading my CAESAR (which b. could not make much of when he read it in svendborg). b. rejects the notion of history as a continuum, the notion of progress as a mighty enterprise undertaken by cool, clear heads, the notion of work as the source of morality, of the workforce as protégés of technology, etc. He makes fun of the common remark about its being astonishing that fascism 'should still be possible in our century' (as if it were not the fruit of every century).[53]

History Lessons, Straub said, is "the story of a crisis of conscience. There's the birth of the political conscience of a young man who is completely unconscious, naïve, in the beginning, who is in compliance with the banker, and who suddenly begins to see. The film tells a story of the birth of anger, which explodes at the end."[54]

The quest that the researcher has undertaken, initially intending to confirm his high estimation of the great leader slowly turns, over the course of his journey, to rage brought

52 Brecht, *Journals*, 157.

53 Brecht, *Journals*, 159.

54 Straub, "Moses and Aaron," *Jump Cut*, 61–64.

on by the measured revelation that history, as it is written and taught, is filled with elision, distortion and lies. Rage is never expressed in the spoken text or gestures of the young man, but a film that opens with fascist monuments, ends irresolutely, in an abrupt camera zoom that lands in extreme close-up on the fountain of the Mascherone, the stone face of a woman with an expression of utter shock, slobbering, vomiting on the via Giulia. Straub remarked, "The reason why I wanted that in *History Lessons* was because it is a woman's face in a film where there are only men."[55] When asked why there were no women in the film, Straub responded, "Because they have nothing to do with power. The film is very contemporary, at least to the extent that it ends up talking about imperialism."[56] In a later interview, Danièle Huillet explained,

> What also interests us in the films we make is to leave the various layers, not eliminating anything. This is contrary to a whole Western artistic tradition, bourgeois of course, which consists of destroying, in effacing the traces and destroying the layers. There are other traditions. Western civilization is only a little drop in the bucket.[57]

At the end of the film, running over the image of the stone mask fountain, Bach's Passion According to Saint Matthew booms out a message for all past, present and would-be imperialist dictators:

> Open your fiery pit, o Hell:
> Wreck, ruin, engulf, shatter
> With sudden force
> The false betrayer, the murderous blood![58]

The film trails off with the sound of angry water gushing from the fountain over black screen, no conciliation, as Huillet has said, "no appeasement."[59]

In *History Lessons By Comparison* I am driving a car that regularly appears in the 1972 film, and the effect is that my car is weaving in and out of the temporal space of the researcher. As opposed to reenactment or recreation, where I might have cast a young man who resembled Benedikt Zulauf to be the driver of the old car, it is instead germane to the overall method of retracing that I assert my own

55 Straub, "Andi Engel," 19.

56 "After 'Othon', before 'History Lessons,' Geoffrey Nowell-Smith talks to Jean-Marie Straub and Danièle Huillet," *Enthusiasm*, no. 1 (December 1975), 26.

57 "Straub/Huillet Talking and Short Notes on Contentious Issues," Peter Gidal, *ARK Magazine, Journal of the Royal College of Art,* vol. 1/52 (Spring 1976): 93.

58 Drawn from Danièle Huillet's English translation of the *History Lessons* script published in *Screen* 17, no. 1 (Spring 1976).

59 Danièle Huillet in "No Appeasement," *Jean-Marie Straub and Danièle Huillet: Writings*, ed. Sally Shafto (New York: Sequence, 2016), 253. "That you want to call 'our' cinema—our films—tragic is a compliment, especially as today's society tries hard to eliminate, to erase the feeling of the tragic, even if the earth, and life, remain tragic. But of course, as in Corneille, the tragic and the comic reinforce each other... Happiness, by flashes, horror, all around. No appeasement."

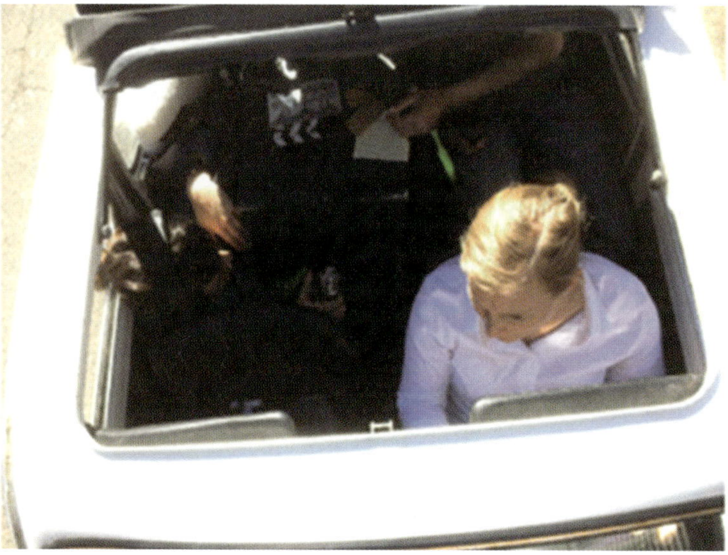

status as researcher, assume the role in the film, and drive the car myself. Present in the car during the making of *History Lesssons* was: Benedikt Zulauf driving, Renato Berta behind the camera in the back seat, to his left sat Jeti Grigioni operating the Nagra sound equipment, and Straub was also squeezed into the back seat to the right of the camera.[60] Huillet was not present in the car which meant that she did not know, until the film reels had been printed and viewed on an editing machine, exactly what elements of the street had been documented in the drives, each one filmed twice,[61] in order of appearance in *History Lessons*: morning, noon and early evening.[62]

60
Straub,
"A conversation," 34.

61
Straub, 33.

62
Albert Cervoni,
"Entretien avec
Jean-Marie Straub,"
Cinéma 75, no. 203
(Nov. 1975): 45–51.

Straub never used the typical blunt directorial commands, "action" and "cut" with their actors, instead he would confirm that all of the technicians were ready and then say the words, "If you please," as an invitation to enter into a scene and simply, "thank you" when the scene was over and as an indication to stop the camera and sound.[63] Taking this level of care in the collaboration and respect for the actors and technicians was moving to read about, but enacting it myself while making *History Lessons By Comparison* directly showed me the humbling power of these words.

63
John Gianvito,
"Tough Love,
Reflections on Some
Ideas and Practices
of Daniéle Huillet and
Jean-Marie Straub,"
in *Jean-Marie Straub &
Daniéle Huillet*, 146.

Huillet and Straub first discovered Brecht's Caesar text six years before making *History Lessons* and at first they thought of making the film only about the diaries of the slave Rarus as "an economic reflection on the historic district, life in the historic district, handworkers and so on. [...]

The Hitler/Ludendorff putsch was on the 8/9th Nov. 1923. Hitler wrote 'Mein Kampf' in Landsberg prison in 1924.

History Lessons: Benedikt Zulauf (the Young Man).
Renato Berta with camera inside car.
Jeti Grigioni and Benedikt Zulauf inside car.

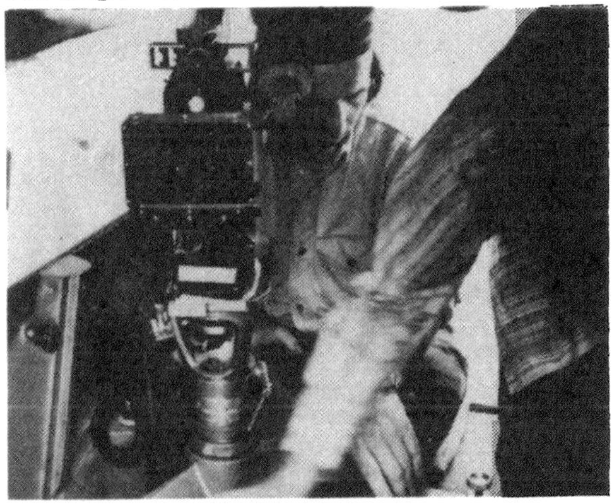

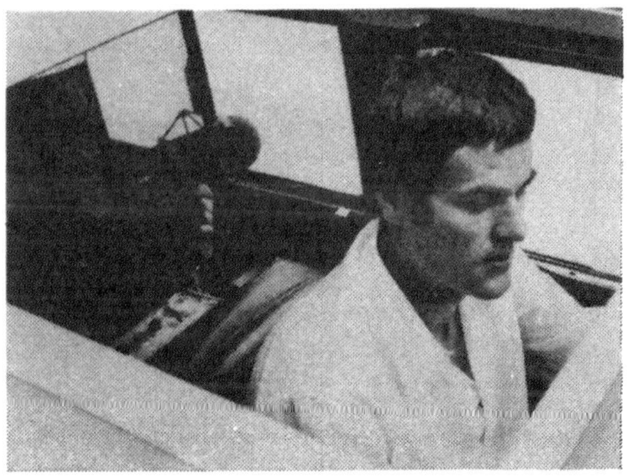

Sebastian Schadhauser (2)

16

Then we noticed that the project was reappearing in these car rides. Rarus' journal and the life of a handworker are in them."[64] What I did not expect in my attempt to learn by doing, by working with others in a collective manner, with the same analogue camera, by using direct sound, and by driving a car of the same era, was how embodied the experience would be. The old car responded to my gestures and movements in a very physical relationship. The frame of the car designated the camera frame and where I pointed the car determined exactly what the camera could see. This relationship between the car, the camera and myself, allowed me to understand the dynamics of the street

64 Straub, "A conversation," 32.

much more clearly—how every cobblestone felt and what it would mean in relation to the camera body, and ultimately to the film image, and to sound. This led me to think about how the streets had been constructed: by whom, using what tools, what stones, under what conditions?

"When people walk on the pavement, do they think of the hands that laid the cobblestones there? Do they think of the hands that buried them there? I do not know. But there is blood there also, and sweat. Sweat is also blood."[65]

65
Straub, quoted in "Tough Love," 152.

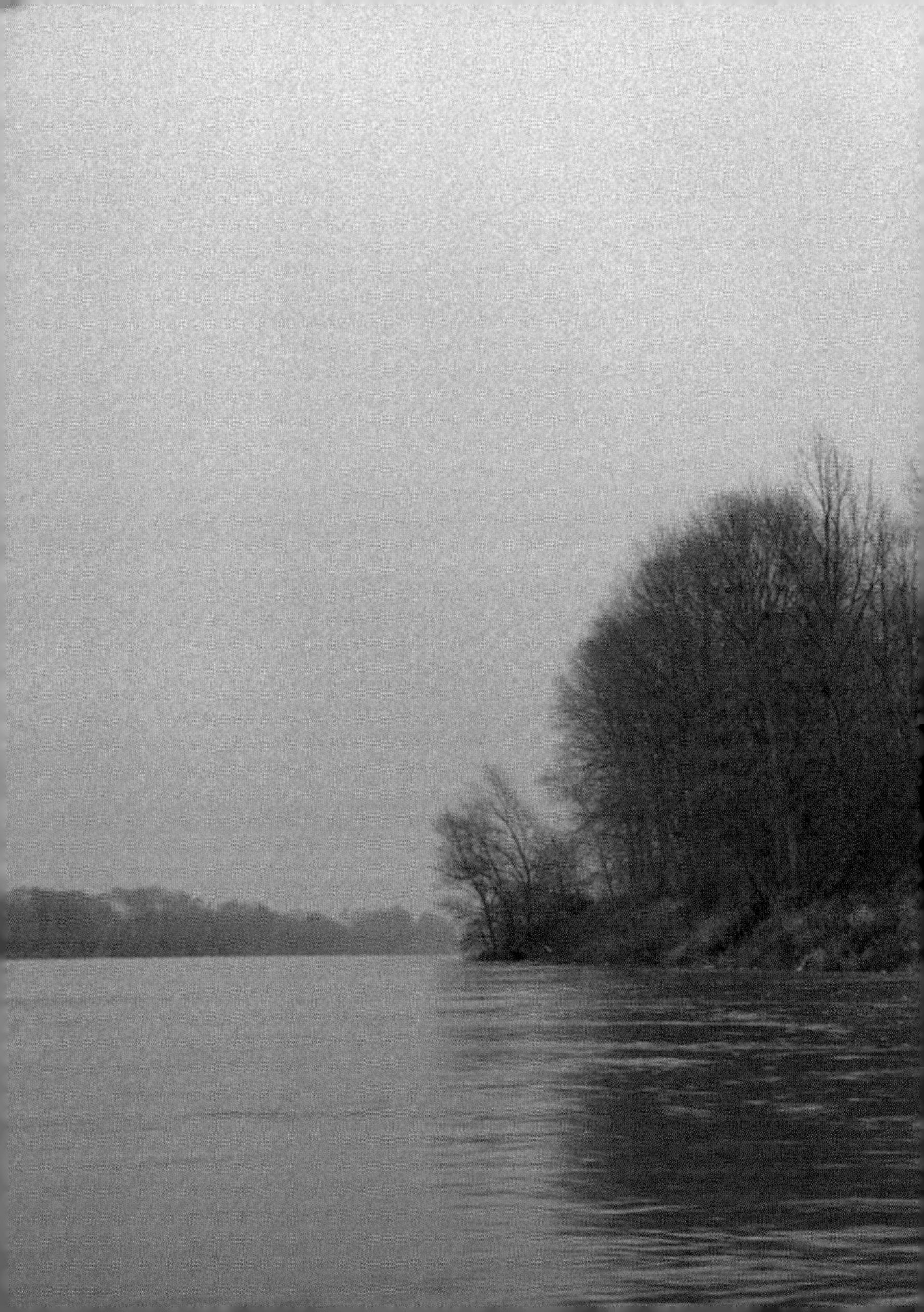

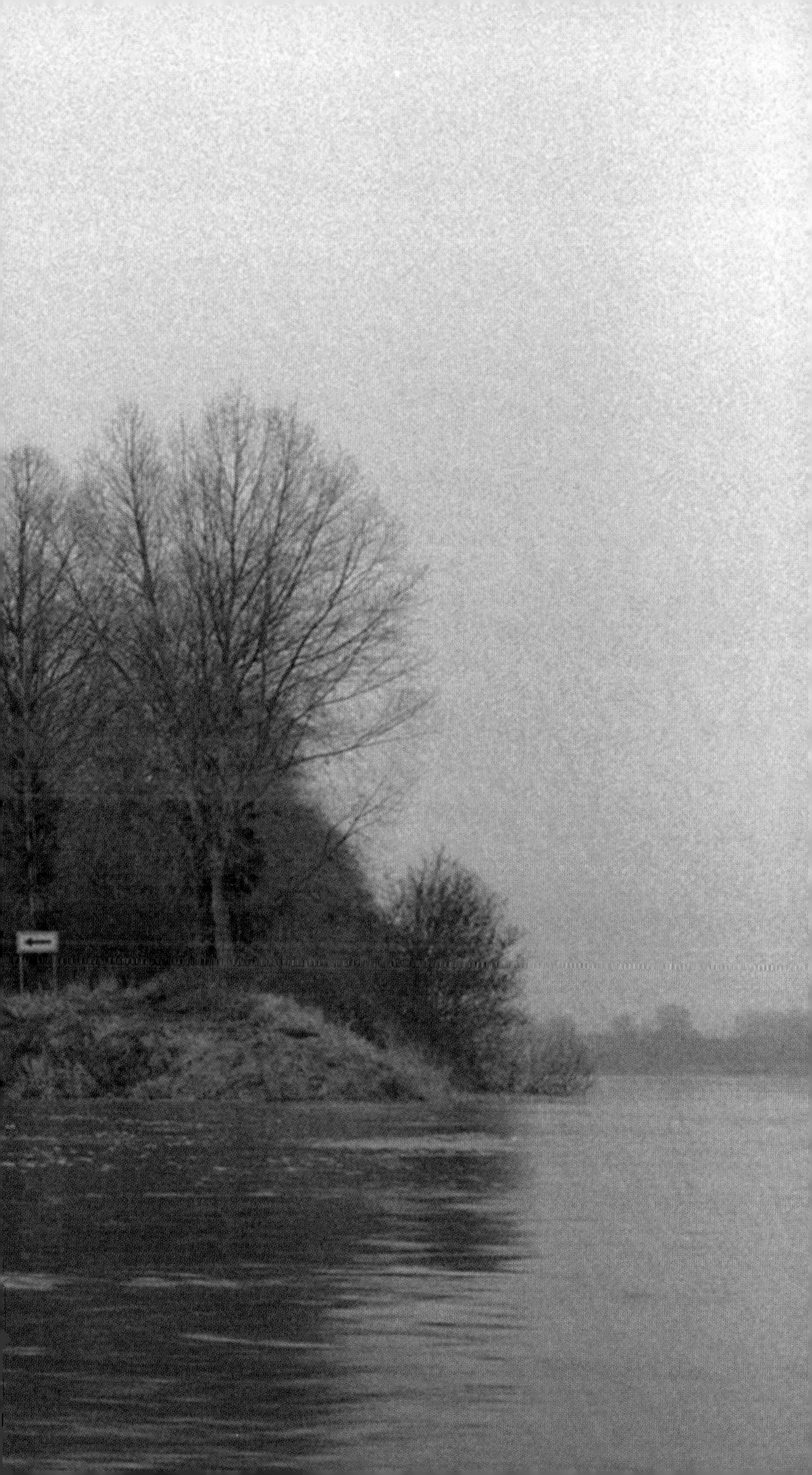

Annett Busch, Louis Henderson

HOW TO FRAME LOSING CONTROL

Dialogue

Let's start with beginnings, the idea of beginnings, with affinities, with Jacques Rivette. In one of our first conversations[1] you mentioned *Out 1: Noli me tangere*[2] as a starting point, a source of inspiration, to think about the play *Monsieur Toussaint* by Édouard Glissant. Which made me curious and triggered a range of associations: How to go from Rivette to Glissant via Straub and Huillet? How and what do you see, read, and hear to make these connections? How did the process of decision making evolve and how do these influences transform into your own approach to filmmaking? Can you recall that idea-giving moment, before the actual working process, that later became *Ouvertures?*[3]

I first saw *Out 1: Noli me tangere* at the BFI during the Rivette retrospective in London in April 2006. There was a small crowd of committed people that came to the cinema over three days and collectively worked through the twelve and a half hours of the film. That experience had a profound impact on me in various ways. I was particularly taken with the way in which Rivette treats acting, improvisation, and direction. At that time I was studying film and video at London College of Communication, and I had started to develop a (continued) problem with the idea of directing action, of directing people in general. What interested me about *Out 1* was how Rivette creates a space for the actors to unfold their characters on their own terms, how he allows for the actors within that space to be active agents in the development of the mise-en-scène, and how this engages a kind of improvised choreography with the camera, the streets they are shooting in and the passersby that happen to be included in scenes. The idea of playing became important for me, especially when thinking about adapting a piece of theater for cinema, and how to play this game of improvisation between us all as a dialogue, as a process. Here I am reminded of an interview with Rivette about *Out 1* that appeared in *La Nouvelle Critique.* The interviewers ask him what the film is about, and he answers:

> To begin with, play in all senses of the word was the only idea: the playing by the actors, the play between the characters, play in the sense that children play, and also play in the sense that there is play between the parties at an assembly.[4]

1
These conversations began during the preparations for the exhibition "Tell it to the Stones" at the Akademie der Künste, Berlin, 2017. Displayed in two vitrines, Louis Henderson exhibited "Overtures: I Build My Language with Rocks," 2017, Mixed Media; assembled as "material for a film on Toussaint Louverture" after shooting in the Jura Mountains, which later became the first part of the film *Ouvertures* (2019). The conversations continued in shared documents between September 2019 and September 2020.

2
Out 1: Noli Me Tangere (1971) dir. Jacques Rivette & Suzanne Schiffman.

3
Ouvertures (2019) dir. The Living and the Dead Ensemble. France-UK-Haiti, Spectre Productions. The film was developed and written by the artist group The Living and the Dead Ensemble, consisting of: Mackenson Bijou, Rossi Jacques Casimir, Dieuvela Cherestal, James Desiris, Louis Henderson, Léonard Jean Baptiste, James Fleurissaint , Cynthia Maignan, Sophonie Maignan, Olivier Marboeuf, Mimétik Nèg.

4
Jacques Rivette in Jonathan Rosenbaum, ed., *Jacques Rivette: Texts and Interviews* (London: British Film Institute, 1977), 46.

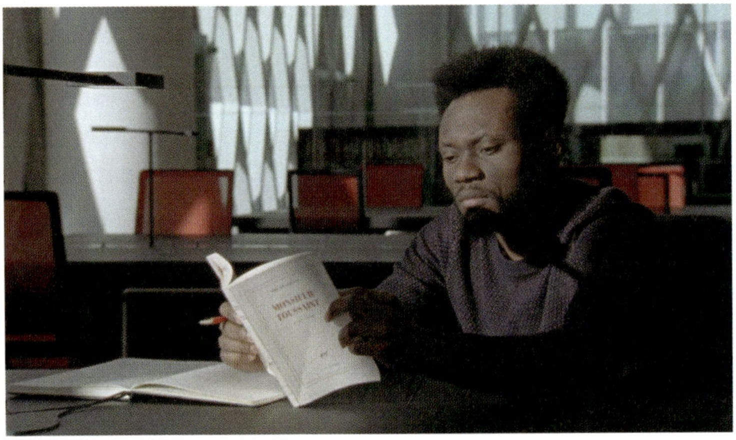

"Improvisation" seems to be an explosive concept to start with, full of traps and misunderstandings. What also resonates with that term is something like an ultimate contradiction to what the filmmaking of Huillet and Straub stands for—which is probably not what you're alluding to. We know from jazz-musicians that the moments of "free play," of improvisation, can only happen within a strictly framed constellation. Jean-Marie repeatedly recalled a similar, dialectical relationship: to set-up a strong and very well prepared frame in order to allow something unpredictable to happen.

> I don't blow it up; I wait until reality does it. Or I work in opposition to the whole. And the air and the light and so on, the sounds and such—the film begins to live in all that isn't foreseen. But only because of the frame-work, otherwise there wouldn't be anything unforeseen.[5]

Or, to put it differently: How to create a set-up that is in itself research, that allows something new to happen in front of the camera, something that exceeds or contradicts what the director is expecting, that goes beyond intentions. "Improvisation" unfolds in response to something, a challenge, a problem, a constellation. What are the given elements, the tools to play with? What is given in *Out 1*, in various ways, are texts. In almost every sequence we see printed matter. We don't experience text as a story to serve as a script to be learned and rehearsed *before* the shooting starts, and then acted out in front of the camera as if the story were real. Written and printed text, books or slips of paper, remain a kind of character leading to an interplay. We see people "dealing" with texts, struggling with its meaning, its authority. Your starting point is the play

5
Mikhail Lylov, Elke Marhöfer, Jean-Marie Straub, "A Thousand Cliffs," in *Der Standpunkt der Aufnahme – Point of View: Perspectives of Political Film and Video Work*, ed. Tobias Hering (Berlin: Archive Books, 2014), 343. Reprinted in this volume, 377.

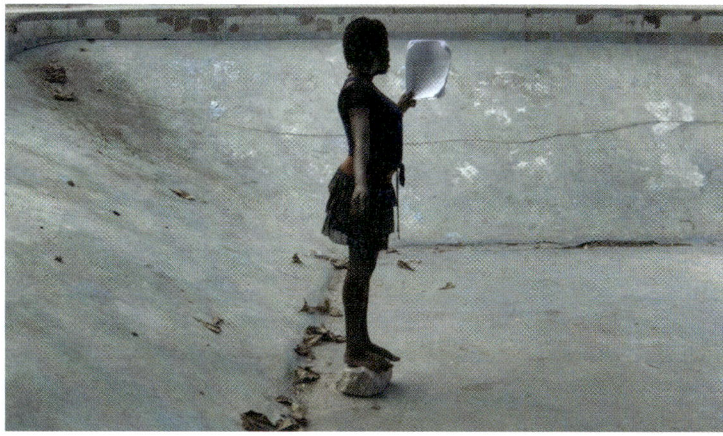

by Glissant that led you to Haiti. Can you describe how you came across the play *Monsieur Toussaint* by Édouard Glissant? Why was it important? What did the play do?

The film *Ouvertures* begins with images of a researcher reading Louverture's handwritten letters in the National Archives in Saint-Denis as we hear how he wrote these letters up until his death, imprisoned by Napoleon in the Château de Joux in the Jura Mountains. Those letters contain evidence of a once enslaved person who had learnt to read and write, battling with the French language mixed with the as yet unofficial language of Haitian Creole, in order to claim his innocence and demand once again his freedom from Napoleon. From the very beginning of the film, written and spoken language become the means through which a struggle with authority is both put into place and made possible.
Then as the narrative proceeds, the premise of the film is in fact a struggle with a text by Glissant, the struggle to find a way to voice and perform Glissant's *Monsieur Toussaint* in Haiti in 2017. The problem arose from the fact that Glissant wrote the play in French, and generally there is an issue with the continued authority that French has in Haiti as the language of an upper class elite that suppresses Haitian Creole. This power dynamic contains within it remnants from the afterlife of slavery in Haiti as French was the language of the ex-colonizers, slavers and plantation owners. However this is very nuanced and complicated in Haiti, as the majority of people do not speak or read French, yet the first constitution of independence, convoked in 1801 by Toussaint Louverture, was written in French, and it was the language of the political rulers during and after the

revolution. So for us with this work it became a struggle with how to appropriate and reconfigure the inherent violence of the French language (within Haiti specifically) through a translation of a work by Glissant into Haitian Creole; the language of a people that organized the only successful slave revolt in history, abolished French slavery and created the first free black state in the Americas.

In addition, the whole project has a trajectory very much related to books. In 2013 I was in Ghana trying to make a film that spoke about Ghana's independence from British colonial rule in relation to certain animist practices. Toward the end of my time in Ghana I went to the George Padmore Research Library in Accra on various occasions. There I found a copy of *The Black Jacobins: Toussaint L'Ouverture and the San Domingo Revolution* by C.L.R. James, and was immediately taken with James' descriptions of the famous night of Vodou ritual in Bois Caïman of August 28th 1791 that started the Haitian Revolution. Later, after reading the book, I found it particularly interesting that James had written *The Black Jacobins* in 1938 as a historical account of the Haitian Revolution so as to imagine a future of independence on the African Continent.

This encounter with C.L.R. James in the George Padmore Library in Accra was the beginning of my interest in the history of Haiti, and the impetus for making a film. In the summer of 2013 I started writing a treatment for a ghost film set in the Jura Mountains where Louverture had died. The film would then travel across the Atlantic, back the other way, with the ghost of Toussaint Louverture returning to his native land after more than 200 years of exile. Finally in Haiti he would discover a group of actors rehearsing C.L.R. James' play: *Toussaint Louverture, The Story of the Only Successful Slave Revolt in History,* which had been performed once in London in 1936, and whose manuscript was found again in 2005 after previously thought to be lost. Then I received Édouard Glissant's *Monsieur Toussaint* as a gift from a friend in the winter of 2013 and started to think that this book could become the source material for the rehearsals in Haiti rather than the play by James for various reasons, notably because Glissant sets his play in a prison cell in the Jura.

Before we continue following the traces of Glissant and C.L.R. James, I would like to stay with the idea of beginnings and influences. Besides Rivette you mentioned Huillet and Straub—when and where did you come across their work and how were their films important for you? You seem to have developed a pretty good strategy to process influences in a way that they shape your movies, and at the same time they are hardly visible.

The films of Straub and Huillet were introduced to me initially through a screening of *Une visite au Louvre* at the Tate Modern in London as part of a Pedro Costa retrospective in 2009. Since then I have been fascinated with the idea of cinema as a form of archaeology, and how this entails a kind of cinematographic stratigraphy, or the writing, imaging and sounding of layers through a vertical montage. Certain of their films excited me very much, such as; *Cézanne, Fortini/Cani, Dalla nube alla resistenza, Toute révolution est un coup de dès, Trop tôt, trop tard, Geschichtsunterricht,* all films that deal with how history can be brought alive in the present, from books and archives into landscape and voice, and then this connection between literature and geology, which is to say that stratigraphy is primarily a literary form; strati-*graphy*, the writing of strata. When thinking about stratigraphy in cinema my questions were always: How can we read what is written in this strata? How can we hear the voices that are silenced in strata?
The idea of burial is important for Straub/Huillet, I think—the burial site as a way to make monument of landscape, a marking of death against forgetting within the land, so that people can be remembered posthumously. Post-*humus*—a Late Latin spelling that added an H to *postumus* so that the idea of earth and burial becomes present within a word that already indicated something existing after death. Yet in the case of my interest with Louverture, the fact remains that he never had a real burial within French soil. His bones were thrown into an unmarked grave for prisoners, which was dug up later when making fortifications for the Chateau de Joux. Over these last few years I learnt that for many Haitians, if someone as important as Louverture does not receive a proper burial he will continue to haunt the earth. When visiting Louverture's ex-prison cell in the Jura for the first time, I was troubled by the lack of a grave and went looking for his presence within the surrounding landscape. The Jura was once a tropical ocean that disappeared and left behind many layers of stratified

limestone. Walking within that landscape you can see how it was created, and the fossilized remains of that tropical ocean exist today. In the tradition of Haitian Vodou, when people die their souls go "beneath the waters" and I started to think that perhaps Louverture's ghost might be fossilized within this ocean-mountain landscape. His bones were ossified into France and thus his soul must still haunt the countryside of the Jura.

Before his death Louverture wrote profusely from his prison cell, so much so that Napoleon banned him from writing, yet in an act of defiance Louverture continued to write and would hide his letters in a scarf wrapped around his head. After death these letters were found and eventually ended up in the French National Archives in Saint-Denis. In 2013 I went to the archives to read Louverture's handwritten memoirs, and then went to find the place in which they were written. Of course when I arrived in the Jura there was really nothing to be found of Toussaint Louverture, all that was left was the landscape in which he wrote his letters. In *Ouvertures* the first act shows these landscapes in a series of sequences in which we see the limestone strata that make up this territory of France, and we hear a voice narrate Louverture's words on the revolutionary ideals of liberty and equality and the importance of "uprooting the tree of slavery" in the French territories overseas.

London 1936. We can imagine the city as a condenser, a catapult, a crossroad—to get an idea of what's "in the air," of what makes it, in the end, possible for you to find a book in 2013 in a library in Accra named after the theorist, adviser, organizer, writer George Padmore, born in Trinidad, like C.L.R. James. At the time Amy Ashwood Garvey had just opened the *International Afro Restaurant* at Oxford Street which became something like a hub for black intellectuals, writers, entrepreneurs, artists, journalists, lawyers and future presidents, where Padmore, James, Kwame Nkrumah, Jomo Kenyatta, Claudia Jones, Una Marson, Ras Makonnen and many others were sitting together, debating, plotting, probably laughing, arguing. James' play, *Toussaint L'Ouverture*, was staged in London's Westminster Theatre—right in the governmental center, not in some off-theater—with Paul Robeson, a star actor and activist, in the role of Toussaint L'Ouverture. From James' biographer Anna Grimshaw we can learn that, "It was planned as an intervention in the debates surrounding the Ethiopian crisis."[6] The invasion of Ethiopia by the Italians had an important mobilising, politicising impact for many, as it was crucial for somebody like James, to see and articulate these connections, between the historic exemplary revolt in Haiti and a future struggle for independence in the African countries. A year later, Padmore and James had co-founded "The International African Service Bureau."

James' thoughts about the connections between historic revolt and future African independence are something that he directly addresses in both the foreword (to the 1980 edition) and the end pages of *The Black Jacobins*. In the 1980 foreword he mentions how his book had been of important political use for "some Pan-African young men from South Africa"[7] that he had met during celebrations for the independence of Ghana in 1957. In the last two pages he makes his intentions with the book very clear: "Finally those black Haitian laborers and the Mulattoes have given us an example to study." And then the penultimate line reads: "The African faces a long and difficult road and he will need guidance."[8]
This method of historical speculation is something that Glissant uses and has written about in relation to his own work. For example, in the preface to the 1961 edition of *Monsieur Toussaint*, Glissant's first sentence mentions *The Black Jacobins* and then a paragraph later he says of his own play, "The work...refers rather to what I would call, by paradox, a prophetic vision of the past."[9] This appeared to me to show some sort of lineage with what James had been trying to do with *The Black Jacobins* and what Glissant then tries to do with his own work on Toussaint Louverture. I became increasingly interested in the working with *Monsieur Toussaint*—initially because Glissant's play is set in Louverture's prison cell in the Jura Mountains—a place I had been visiting and a landscape I was becoming interested in—but also because Haiti is represented through memory and the haunting of ghosts in the present, a particular attitude toward death that had intrigued me for some time and had already formed the basis of nearly all of my earlier films. Then something else became apparent and eventually important: in the *avertissement* to the 1978 edition of *Monsieur Toussaint*, Glissant writes about the (French) language of the play.

6 Anna Grimshaw, *C.L.R. James: A Revolutionary Vision for the 20th Century* (New York: Smyrna Press, 1991), 16.

7 C.L.R. James, *The Black Jacobins: Toussaint Louverture and the San Domingo Revolution* (London: Penguin Books, 2001), xvii.

8 James, *The Black Jacobins*, 303–304.

9 Édouard Glissant, *Monsieur Toussaint: version scénique* (Paris: Gallimard, 1998), 9. "L'ouvrage...il se réfère plutôt à ce que j'appellerai, par paradoxe, une vision prophétique du passé."

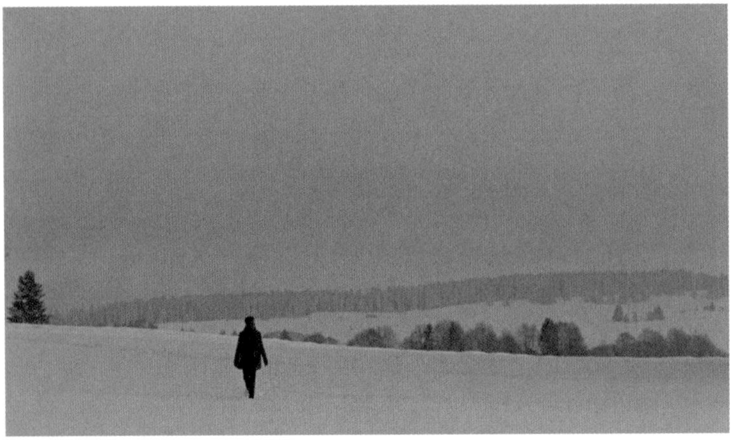

> I tried, however, to resist a simple mechanism of creolisation, the artifice of which was quite obvious. The mise-en-scène of this story can choose its own linguistic environment; and the Creole language is sufficiently free in its written non-fixity for the director and actors to come together and complete, through improvisation, the intentions of the author.[10]

This seemed like a challenge perhaps—indeed, why were certain characters like Mackandal, a maroon from the 18th century, speaking to Louverture in Glissantian French? When in Haiti in 2016 I spoke of this very matter to a friend of mine, the slam poet and actor Rossi Jacques Casimir, he said that if we wanted to work on the play in Haiti we would have to translate it to Haitian Creole as a practical but also political imperative. This was not simply a question of adapting the play from one language to another, but also from 1961 to 2016 as we thought it was important to transform the words of the play with the contemporary slang particular to the actors' lives and situations, essentially creolizing Glissant's play.

10
Glissant, *Monsieur Toussaint*, 12. "J'ai tâché pourtant de résister à un mécanisme simple de 'créolisation' dont l'artifice eût été bien évident. La mise en scène de cette histoire peut décider de son environnement linguistique; et la langue créole est suffisamment disponible dans sa non-fixation écrite pour que le metteur en scène et acteurs rejoignent ici et complètent par l'improvisation les intentions de l'auteur."

That's a series of interesting shifts. With the two very different, both non-Haitian authors, also comes a move from the anglophone to a francophone Caribbean perspective (C.L.R. James, born 1901 in Trinidad; Édouard Glissant, born 1928 in Martinique). James, at the time connected to the Trotskyist movement, sets his piece in the middle of action, crisis and decision making; he is using the stage to play through the role of revolutionary leadership in relation to a people, while Glissant begins and unfolds his play when this action driven battle has been lost for Louverture,

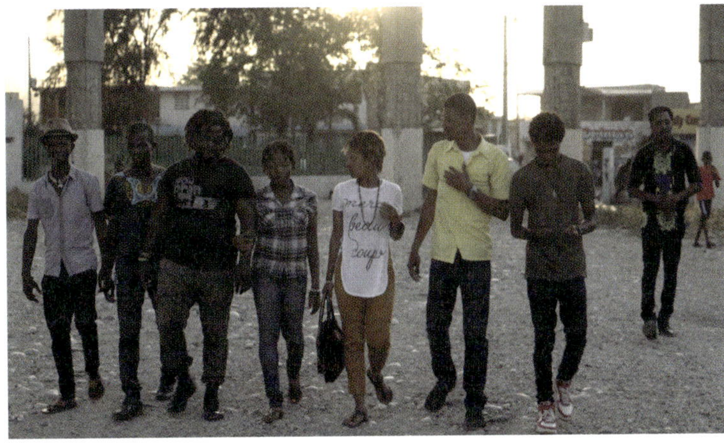

sitting in the prison cell. What he can still do is to write, secretly, while the battle continues for the people in Haiti. You mention the importance of language, of vernacular language, which also means to draw the attention toward the people, how they speak, and how they think and act in very different ways. A shift that is quite fundamental, and raises the question of leadership in a very different way, it's more a distribution of various responsibilities and roles. Translated into the language of performance, theater, and then also film, "improvisation" could mean not to respond unprepared, but to re-act in ways that were not anticipated by the director, to capture a kind of collective, polyvocal momentum.

Since a few years I have been engaged in a conversation with the French writer and producer Olivier Marboeuf about the necessity to dissipate the individual and often narcissistic voice of the artist within an artwork. To find new ways of making films that would fight against the insistence of a certain capitalistic impulse in cinema and art toward the celebration of the singular voice and point of view. In many ways this is connected to a shift away from heroism toward collective action, and this is what both Glissant and James attempted to show with their respective works about Haiti. In the case of *Monsieur Toussaint* we have a hero on his deathbed confronted with various voices from Haiti's past, haunting and taunting him, revealing his individualistic ambitions to become governor. In the introduction to the play, Glissant develops James' and Aimé Césaire's respective theses that Louverture had to allow himself to be taken by Napoleon's forces, that he had to sacrifice his life and his position of power in order for the revolution to achieve its purpose for the collective good. Furthermore, In *Le Discours Antillais* (1981), Glissant has written of the importance of writing "the novel of the We,"[11] by which he means a novel that experiments with a polyvocal narrative as an expression of a collective We. Glissant conceives this as a way toward imagining a postcolonial Caribbean society that is brought together through difference and not fragmented through nationalism. This was and still is an idea that interests us greatly, and so we started working together trying to understand how to make films as collective conversations, as study sessions, as workshops. Films that could be discursive objects opening up an array of activities at the edges of the project itself.[12] Around this time we discussed the possibility of turning the treatment I had written about the ghost of Toussaint Louverture into a collective project that could incorporate the choral voice of a We.[13]

Monsieur Toussaint thus became the starting point from which we tried to bring a chorus together. We translated the play from French to Haitian Creole and then put on the play as a one off performance in the cemetery of Port-au-Prince in December 2017. The play was very important for the project, but as a way to create something that didn't exist yet—and this was the theater group that we formed in 2017, *The Living and the Dead Ensemble*. Our initial impulse to create the group came from the shared desire to find a multivocal and choral method of authoring a work. Furthermore, I was interested in trying to incorporate methods of free improvisation (in the musical sense) into the film, and so we set up the theater group and the event of putting on the play (which eventually took on an existence of its own) and then filmed it as it gradually unfolded, the action becoming increasingly fictionalized as the film progressed. This was the basis of the process; to create a situation that was entirely pre-considered and constructed, based on fiction, and then allow for life to intervene within that space and to bring with it a type of reality that we would never be able to imagine. Much like you describe above, improvisation can only come when there is a clearly defined space to work within. These are the boundaries that are necessary in order for people to move freely. When I speak about mise-en-scène, this is what I mean, it's constituted by the situations that we created through research and work, and this then allows for

11
Édouard Glissant, *Le Discours Antillais* (Paris: Gallimard, 1981), 267. "On me dit que le roman du Nous est impossible à faire, qu'il y faudra toujours l'incarnation des devenirs particuliers. C'est un beau risque à courir." [I am told that it is impossible to write the novel of the We, that it will always be necessary to provide the incarnation of particular destinies. This is a beautiful risk to take.]

12
This process culminated in an exhibition at Olivier Marboeuf's now closed art center in the suburbs of Paris, *Espace Khiasma*. The exhibition was called *Kinesis*, and it encompassed a program of events, talks, screenings, performances, and workshops, all around the idea of collectively remixing and reediting a film I had made in 2015 called *Black Code/Code Noir*.

13
In the essay, "Du boucan chez Glissant," in *Sonic Acts: Hereafter*, ed. Mirna Belina (Amsterdam: Sonic Acts, 2019), Olivier Marboeuf writes of how *Monsieur Toussaint* describes the process through which Louverture's dying body (and heroism) is decomposing in order to create a fertile ground upon which future collective action can recompose, the spiraling together of life, death and rebirth. This is something we tried to translate into the processes of working collectively in Haiti, and is the basis of the work we continue to do.

the film to live in what is unforeseen, as Straub says. It was a question of trying to make a film through dialogue with people from Haiti rather than going to Haiti and imposing a story onto a landscape and people.[14]

14
This approach is not least indebted to Cinéma Vérité, and I love how Rivette describes his own form of Cinéma Vérité as coming from working with Jean Renoir: "The three weeks I spent with Renoir... made quite an impression on me. After a lie, all of a sudden, here was the truth. After a basically artificial cinema, here was the truth of the cinema. I therefore wanted to make a film, not inspired by Renoir, but trying to conform to the idea of a cinema incarnated by Renoir, a cinema which does not impose anything, where one tries to suggest things, to let them happen, where it is mainly a dialogue at every level, with the actors, with the situation, with the people you meet, where the act of filming is part of the film itself."—"Time Overflowing," Jacques Rivette interviewed by Jacques Aumont et al., trans. Amy Gateff, www.dvdbeaver.com/rivette/OK/TXTINT-time.html *Cahiers du cinéma*, no. 204 (1968): 8.

One of the most powerful moments in the third part of *Ouvertures* is the long conversation between Léonard Jean-Baptise (Léo) and Zakh Turin while walking in the outskirts of Port-au-Prince that evolves from the question of belonging, of being "a citizen of the world." There is an unresolved intensity within their dialogue and I keep wondering what happened to make it possible. It sounds and looks like a perfect example for a non-scripted dialogue within a completely scripted frame, an estranged familiarity—and familiarity understood as a feeling that is produced by endless repetition that is put under pressure (estranged) through the presence of the camera.
If I make a link here to Huillet and Straub, what comes to mind is the intense presence of the actors in *Operai, contadini* (*Workers, Peasants*, 2000). The actors hardly move physically, they just stand at a particular place in the woods, reading from a sheet of paper, static in a way that nothing unpredicted can happen, so it seems. Most people would call this utterly boring. Over time you realize that the actors are not professional actors, they are probably peasants and workers and the story they are reading might be familiar to theirs. Their bodies and minds inhabit an experience that becomes present on screen and the way this is happening is unpredictable and not under control of the directors, to achieve anything but representation. It's a result of hard work with text and the act of speaking, to let something appear that exceeds the intention of the directors and of the actors.
What I am trying to emphasize, by putting these two sequences next to each other, are possible similarities rather than a difference—beyond the quite different circumstances and starting points. What also comes into play in relation to creating the frame, of course, are the means and circumstances of production.

In shooting with a small digital camera and only one or two people doing sound means that we have a very small technical presence in the space we are shooting in. Our crew was always much smaller than the situations we were trying to film, what was around our frame was always much larger than what we were trying to contain in the frame. Such as the Rara sequence at the end of the film, when we had an entire Rara band, a huge amount of extras, a storm and the night approaching, the ocean, the full moon, the sunset and also eight actors. Because of the unfathomable nature of what is outside our frame we can only allow for the unforeseen to start to take place within the frame. In these instances we can allow the camera to run for hours, but we always need a well-organized rhythm section to keep us in order.

In respect to the conversation about being a "citizen of the world," this was a topic that had come up in various conversations with the group, it was often presented by Léo as he thinks of himself as a citizen of the world rather than simply a Haitian citizen determined by pre-existing sociocultural constructs. We often felt that Léo represented a kind of Glissantian figure in this regard, the later Glissant from after *Poétique de la Rélation* in which he has abandoned the national specificity of Martiniquan politics and argues his totalizing concepts of rélation and Tout-monde. And Zakh, as an avid reader of both Frantz Fanon and Aimé Césaire, seemed to represent a position more in line with the Négritude and Caribbean autonomy of the earlier Glissant. Neither of them had had this conversation beforehand, however, nor had we really discussed this scene at all. All we had decided on was to shoot a scene where the character of Toussaint is finally walking with the group in an area of Port-au-Prince called Pont Rouge, the place where Jean-Jacques Dessalines was assassinated in October 1806. The first part of the scene was based on a loose script where Léo expresses his interest in the notion of being a "citizen of the world" to Toussaint, whom we often discuss in the group as being the first diasporic Haitian. After we shot this scene I had the idea that Léo, while ambling around, could run into Zakh who would take issue with him on what he had just said to Toussaint about world citizenship. Even if this may seem like an ad hoc decision taken within the moment, it was in fact based on the knowledge we all had of each other from spending considerable time together and conversing on a wide array of subjects. Léo was completely unprepared for what Zakh would say to him, and so the conversation in this scene unfolded as we filmed everything in one take that lasted about twenty minutes. In this instance, as with many others in the film, the frame is organized according to the location, the time of day, the amount of light we have left to shoot with, the choice of people talking and the subject loosely decided beforehand. Then within that frame the actors are free to decide upon which part of their narrative they will convey, and that is perhaps where the element of free improvisation comes in.

You mentioned before your interest in strata, how history and time materializes in the landscape and how to make these layers "speak." For the first part of *Ouvertures* you were filming with a 16mm camera in the Jura, in a wintry, unpopulated landscape; you bring a researcher whom we have seen sitting in the library in Paris before, working through a huge pile of archival papers; we watch him walking and running—away and toward the camera. From a bird's eye view we see him looking around in the cave, touching, almost caressing the surface of the sediments; his bodily movements seem cautious and curious, maybe frightened. We watch him looking for history. We hear a whispering voice and the music of Purcell and Monteverdi. There is something slightly obsessive and abundant within these camera movements, a crescendo unfolds, as if there are doubts if the methodology will actually work. And once we arrive in the second chapter and know what happens next, it looks almost like an escape—to leave the lonely position of a researcher, to leave the false end of history, to leave deserted France.[15] Between the first and the second chapter we fall through the earth, taken away by something blue, following an underwater travel—and arrive at the other side of the world, in Haiti. And within a second we, the spectators, enter a very different zone; the soundscape has changed completely with street noise and rap music, the frame is populated with people, debating, arguing, laughing. The silence of the library, of books, the lonely reading—all gone. The camera is now following the theater group and it seems that step by step, they are taking over and start to direct you instead of you directing them.

You are right in identifying a movement from the lonely archive researcher toward something in which I am directed by the situation rather than directing it myself. Indeed,

15 "In June 1980, the Straubs spent two weeks filming in the French countryside. They were seen in places as improbable as Treogan, Mottreff, Marbeuf and Harville. They were seen prowling close to big cities: Lyon, Rennes. Their idea, which presides over the execution of this opus 12 in their oeuvre (already twenty years of filmmaking!) was to film, as they are today, a certain number of places mentioned in a letter sent by Engels to the future renegade Kautsky. In this letter (read off-screen by Danièle Huillet), Engels, bolstered with figures, describes the misery of the countryside on the eve of the French Revolution. One suspects that these places have changed. For one thing, they are deserted. The French countryside, Straub says, has a 'science fiction, deserted-planet aspect.' Maybe people live there, but they don't inhabit the locale. The fields, roadways, fences and rows of trees are traces of human activity, but the actors are birds, a few vehicles, a faint murmur, the wind." See "Cinemeteorology [Serge Daney on *Too Early/Too Late*]" originally published in *Libération*, February 20–21, 1982. Translated by Jonathan Rosenbaum, jonathanrosenbaum.net.

we move from something quite formal, about landscape, text and archives toward improvisation, the gradual loss of authorial control and a focus on people, stories and play. This is in fact quite a personal movement of mine, toward trying to do things differently while remaining very close to the work of Straub and Huillet. I think this is how I have engaged with the methodologies of Straub and Huillet since I first started making films. Not as a way to identify a problem with their work, but as a way to think critically through it as I try to work with it.

My short film *Black Code/Code Noir* (2015) opens with a shot that quotes the opening of *Too Early/Too Late*. We have a camera mounted inside a car circling the roundabout at Place de la Bastille in Paris. The principal gesture remains the same, but I try to create a détournement within their own revolving shot through a series of small changes. Their shot is in the bright daytime, whereas mine is at night (which is also a reference to *Les Mains Negatives* by Marguerite Duras, a further complication in the reading of this image). Danièle Huillet reads a letter from Friedrich Engels about the failings of the French Revolution, whereas Ana Vaz reads from *The Black Jacobins* about the beginnings of the Haitian Revolution. In creating a cinematic quotation that détours from the original I wanted to ally myself with their working methods but create an image that could be the other side of the original, the reverse or underneath, a quotation-image in negative.

With *Ouvertures* however, comes a clear shift from one method to another within the film; so rather than a way of making changes to a quotation, this was actually an attempt at speaking in a new way, yet the questions—of how to work with actors and language remain. The formal shift in the film was a way to mark a departure for me into a new kind of cinema informed through experiments with collaboration and improvisation that I had never done before to this extent. Furthermore Glissant's play is slowly discarded and forgotten altogether and what constitutes the narrative of the film is a blending together of scenes written with the Haitian members of the Ensemble and translated to Haitian Creole, and scenes that are entirely improvised—both in terms of what is said and the movements that the scenes create for the camera. In this sense, the mise-en-scène unfolds as the film develops, as the shot rolls out into the space of the situation we were filming in.

Hence why we have many shots of people walking as they talk about their experiences and ideas—the landscape that constitutes the image is determined through the duration of what is being said.
My role in this instance as a filmmaker was one of stepping back from talking about something, and rather listening to what was being spoken of. It is a kind of cinema that follows an ethical principle of images imbued with sound, a cinema that *listens to* rather than *taking from* a community. This comes down to a question of knowledge also, and the difference in French between the words *entendre* and *comprendre*, the first is a form of understanding that learns through being attentive, the latter through grasping something. Yet the film is of course very much constructed and follows a form of "critical fabulation" in order to tell the stories it needs to tell, but this was done through a long process of learning how to write and speak, both with the camera and the people on screen, as a choral voice, as an Ensemble that allows the space for a series of different solos or duets within a piece that follows and eventually discards its score.

The notion of listening is interesting. Or to put it more provocatively, "Listening" has become the ultimate good, nothing can be wrong with listening. As if we could escape power structures through listening sessions, while an expression like, "I hear you" doesn't do much more than affirming exactly the same existing structures. I mean, to listen is certainly an absolutely crucial point of departure, but then, to do what with what we heard? In the context of our conversation, when you talk about listening, it makes me think of a series of pictures of Danièle Huillet sitting next to a Nagra with headphones on—many of which are in the documentary *J'écoute!* (2006), realized by Giulio Bursi, but also in other film set documentaries such as Jean-Paul Toraille's *Les Avatars de la Mort d'Empédocle*. Danièle was the one who stayed close to the sound engineers (often Louis Hochet), she listened with full attention, which made her interact and object when she heard disturbances or intonations that seemed wrong to her. The act of listening is here connected to a technology, it's dependent on microphones, recording devices and so on, amplifiers, which allow and enable a very different approach to the environment. And it certainly affects the way of engagement with it, maybe in a more immediate way, less mediated. What is maybe interesting is that through the absence of the "heavy" recording devices, like schlepping around a Nagra, you have to re-appropriate, re-introduce certain mechanisms of listening in different ways, to remember what it means. The act of listening, to which you refer, triggers a process *before* the actual recording—and when you say "scenes written together with the Ensemble" on what were they based and how did these develop?

I appreciate your provocation about listening very much, and I agree that it has become a means through which people attempt to justify a position from an apparently unquestionable ethical high ground, both within art and academia. There is a particular problem with this gesture of "hearing people" and then enabling them to have a place to speak. Often this is bound up with the problematic notion of using one's privileged position (as a white, European artist for example) to give voice to other people from less privileged places. In this scenario the people "giving voice," maintain their positions of power as gatekeepers of what or who should be listened to while exuding a false sense of passivity, as if the ears cannot do the harm that eyes have done in the past. I don't think this is what we are doing in Haiti with the Ensemble. What I am trying to express is that it took some time to learn to listen to people and to learn the language they are speaking in, and to try and translate that within an artistic collaboration. What interested us from the very beginning was how we could make cinema as and through conversation. In terms of writing together, the process was rather varied and depended on what stage we were at socially as a group. As we got to know each other better through spending more time together in different periods we worked out various ways of writing.[16] Initially our work together was focused on translating Glissant, and the production of the play. In our first two weeks in Haiti, Olivier and I didn't really understand Haitian Creole very well, and so we were partially deaf as to what was happening exactly with the translation. We had many discussions around how to best translate the play based upon what meaning we could gather from discussing Glissant's text together, yet often meanings would escape us and the interpretation would take on a life of its own. It was only much later, in editing

16
We first went to Port-au-Prince for two weeks in June 2017 for the translation workshop of Glissant's *Monsieur Toussaint* and then I returned for two months in November 2017 to work with the group on rehearsing the play. Olivier arrived in December and we put on the play at the Ghetto Biennale 2017. We returned to Haiti to shoot the last third of the film over one month in August 2018. Then in July 2019 we all spent a month together in Clichy-Montfermeil on a residency at Les Ateliers Medicis working on a new project called *The Wake,* which eventuated two weeks of shooting in Haiti in January 2020 and one month of rehearsals in France in March 2020.

the film, that I started to realize how misunderstandings had led to misinterpretations and that in certain scenes we had in fact moved quite far away from Glissant's original intentions with the play. Much of the translation was based upon Haitian idioms, contemporary slang, jokes and double meanings, and as such we had created a version that was quite alien to the original. For all of us it was a mutual process of learning through the act of translating the play and we listened closely to suggestions from the actors in terms of how to construct the mise-en-scène of the play, how to build it together rhythmically with elements of song and slam. So the actors and writers in the Ensemble; Mackenson Bijou, Cynthia Maignan, Dieuvela Cherestal, James Desiris, Léonard Jean Baptiste, Rikiki, Rossi Jacques Casimir and Zakh Turin (Mimétik Nèg) worked at speaking for themselves through the words of Glissant placed into relation with their own experiences. The Ensemble in this instance acted as an echo chamber for history, politics, and poetry, and again I believe this complicates the idea of direction and authorship both within the play and the film. We came back to Haiti in 2018 and worked together on shooting the third act of the film. Initially the general structure was decided by me and Olivier; how the story would be plotted and what locations we would film in, yet in terms of what words would constitute what was being said, we approached collective methods of writing in various ways. For example, one of the methods was based again on close listening. During conversations certain things would come up that people would want to elaborate upon in a scene the next day, so that person would set out to draft a small statement about this idea and we would film it the next day—usually in three or four takes, improvised in relation to someone else who would act as a respondent. This is how the theme of the spiral came into the film, from a conversation one evening in a bus driving back to the hotel from the Grotte Marie-Jeanne in Port-à-Piment. James Desiris was discussing the importance of the spiral within Vodou iconography with me, Léo and Olivier, and Léo responded by adding that it was also an important form for Haitian literature and not just within the Vodou religion.[17] Over the following days this eventuated two scenes in the film improvised as discussions on exactly these topics. It was in this manner that I personally was working toward losing authorial control,

17 Olivier and I had both been attracted to the spiral via the work of Édouard Glissant. In the introduction to *Poetics of Relation*, Glissant describes his work as being "a reconstituted echo or a spiral retelling" of his earlier book, *Caribbean Discourse*.

and allowing for the film to unravel while making it. Life intervened so much that it naturally shaped the film's process into something unruly and perhaps, at times, chaotic. When we first went to Haiti neither Olivier nor I had read any of the works of Frankétienne, yet all of the Haitian members of the Ensemble knew his work intimately and his poetry would come up from time to time. However it wasn't until we filmed the scene with Léo describing *Spiralisme* and the work of Frankétienne that it became solidified within the narrative itself. Thanks to these discussions in Haiti I started to develop a keen interest in his work and began reading his novels and plays, and also theoretical writing around his work. Then I started to realize that in fact the ideas we were trying to explore in relation to questions around authorship and voice, the blending of personal stories with fictional narratives, the oscillating between author and character, were precisely the foundations of the Spiralist mode of writing. Frankétienne had been there all along, accompanying our work and thinking from the beginning and in many ways this makes perfect sense considering how important Frankétienne is in the literary and artistic landscape of Haiti. In the autumn of 2018 I read an essay by Kaiama L. Glover, a professor and translator of Frankétienne, in which she describes the characters in his novels as follows:

> These beings are ultimately more relational than individual: that is, their value to a given text is primarily a function of their manner of insertion into the narrative collective. Like musical passages in textual symphonies, his characters literally and figuratively bounce off, echo, double, and reflect one another.[18]

I feel that this reads as a perfect description of what we were trying to do with the film, especially with the third act in which we started to fictionalize a set of characters based upon the lives of the actors and also the historical figures they were playing in *Monsieur Toussaint*. In the third act, part of the narrative is based around two people who are haunted by the characters they act in the play and so the division between life and fiction becomes completely blurred. They improvise at being themselves in front of the camera, themselves rehearsing the characters in the play, and also act as people speaking with the voices of the ghosts of their characters from two hun-

18 Kaiama L. Glover, "Showing vs. Telling: 'Spiralisme' in the Light of 'Antillanité,'" in *Journal of Haitian Studies*, vol. 14, no. 1, Special Issue on Frankétienne (Spring 2008): 95.

dred years ago, precisely in a spiraling movement that constantly doubles itself through echo and reflection.

Let me abstract the figure of the spiral as form and practice and think in connection with the cinema of Huillet and Straub. The spiral as a line that tries to make a circle but loses it's direction, so the ending lands slightly displaced and becomes a new beginning, which starts with a circling curve and so on. A movement that describes slow progress and the idea that every repetition leads to a difference, while at the same time, to create a difference, to advance one has to turn around, rethink, rehearse, revise, to get just one step ahead. Which almost describes Huillet's and Straub's general approach, but is also something I can see in their pleasure and insistence to make takes, variations, and then different versions. Or maybe we could think of *Itinéraire de Jean Bricard* (2007) as a spiral movement—shot on 35mm in black and white by Irina and William Lubtchansky. When at the beginning an island in the Loire is circled by a boat, whose engine we hear but we only see the flowing water and changing parts of the island, mostly trees, which creates a double, inverse movement of a passing landscape through the fixed frame while moving onward. And when the boat starts moving again toward the end of the film, we have heard in between about the life, work, and resistance that happened on that island in the 1940s—and the same passing trees begin to look differently, once we know.

But to end with, I found a beautiful quote by Benoît Turquety from his comprehensive book *Danièle Huillet, Jean-Marie Straub: "Objectivists" in Cinema*,[19] recently published in English in a translation by Ted Fendt:

> The first scene in *Moses and Aaron* is entitled 'The Calling of Moses.' It is filmed in one, nine minute and 35 seconds shot [...] It is a panning shot shaped like a spiral, if not a slight spinode: it begins looking down at Moses in a close-up three-quarters from behind, pans diagonally upward to the left, then horizontally, before finally stopping—covering a horizontal angle of about 300°. It traces a shape from interior to exterior, below to above, beginning close to its centre (Moses, next to the camera) and ending at the point in the distance marking it's edge: a double mountain (Monte Velino). But the

19 Originally published in French: Benoît Turquety, *Danièle Huillet, Jean-Marie Straub, objectivistes en cinéma* (Lausanne: Editions l'Age d'Homme, 2009).

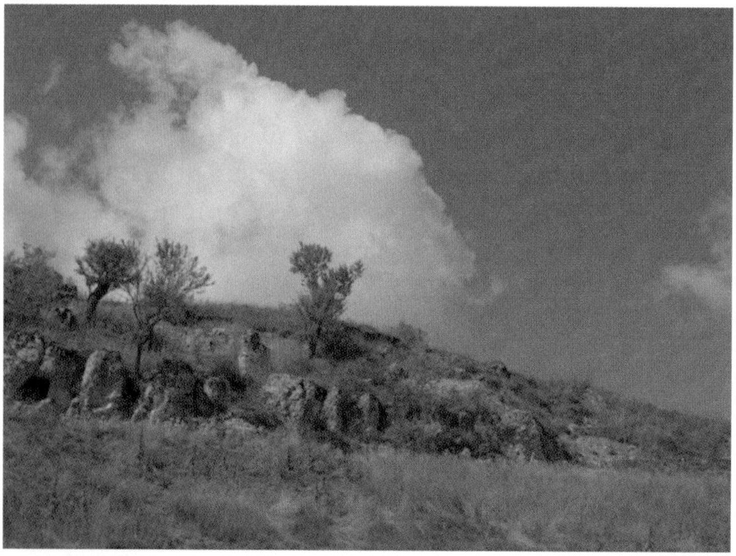

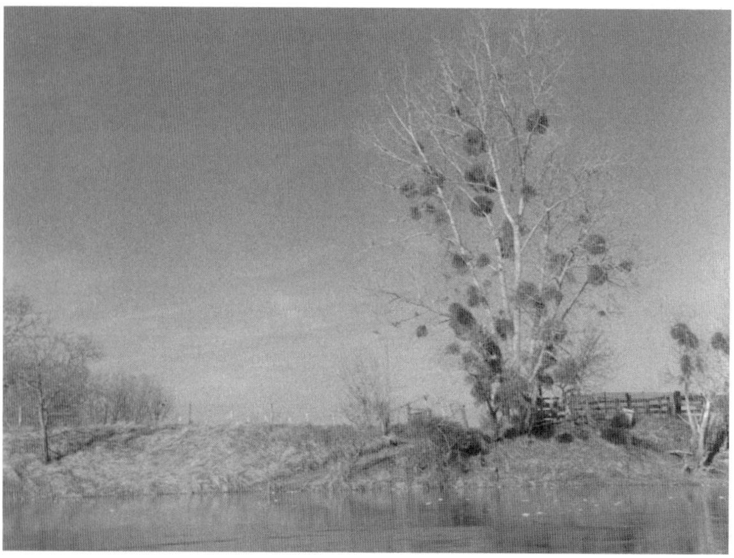

spinode, the non-rounded angle the camera traces as it moves from the diagonal to the horizontal pan, throws doubt on the spiral. Perhaps it is instead a portion of a circle attached to a diagonal.[20]

To throw doubt on the spiral could mean to throw doubt on the spiral metaphor as a seemingly unstoppable movement, either upwards or downwards. But if we understand the spiral as a relational figure, as you just described it with Kaiama Glover, the panning shot in *Moses and Aaron* actually describes correlations between the decision making of the directors, a camera movement and the request of the landscape in its own right—that which constitutes the image.

20 Benoît Turquety, *Danièle Huillet, Jean-Marie Straub: "Objectivists" in Cinema,* trans. Ted Fendt (Amsterdam: Amsterdam University Press, 2020), 77.

Ala Younis

THIS LAND FIRST SPEAKS TO YOU IN SIGNS

Cairo, February 11, 2011
Mubarak steps down. The eighteen days of sit-ins are referred to as a revolution.

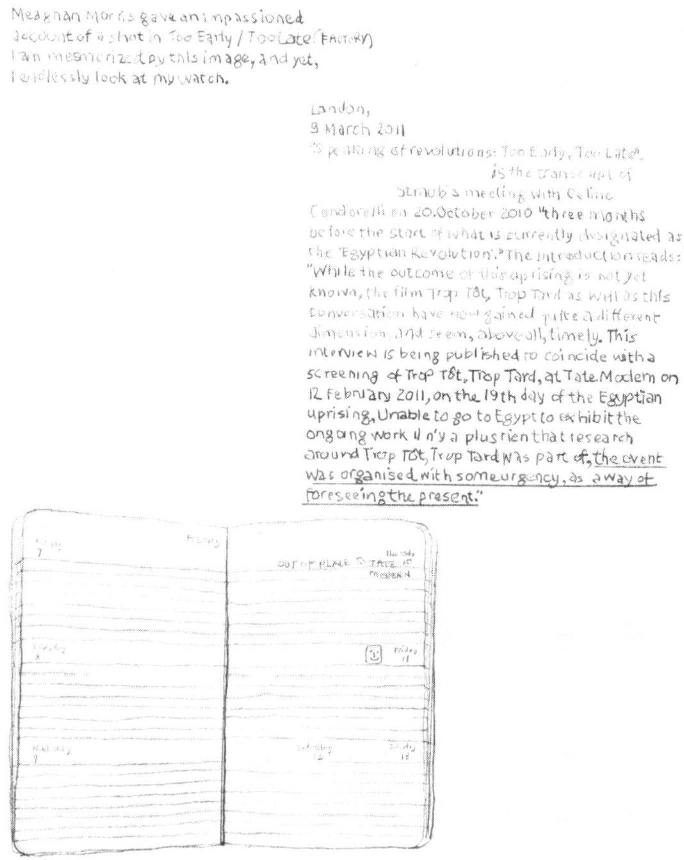

London, February 12, 2011
It is the morning after the opening night of the "Out of Place" exhibition I co-curated at Tate Modern. I am sitting with one of the artists as I receive an SMS: "Resigned."

London, February 12, 2011

Tate Modern shows Straub and Huillet's *Too Early/Too Late*, 1981. Announcement text:

> Momentous events have been unfolding in the Middle East, pressing for meaningful ways to engage with what is happening in Egypt. As instantaneous newsfeeds pull us in different directions, there is a need to counter the speed of media coverage overwhelming our present. This event features a screening of the rarely seen film as a means to open up and reflect on the current moment.

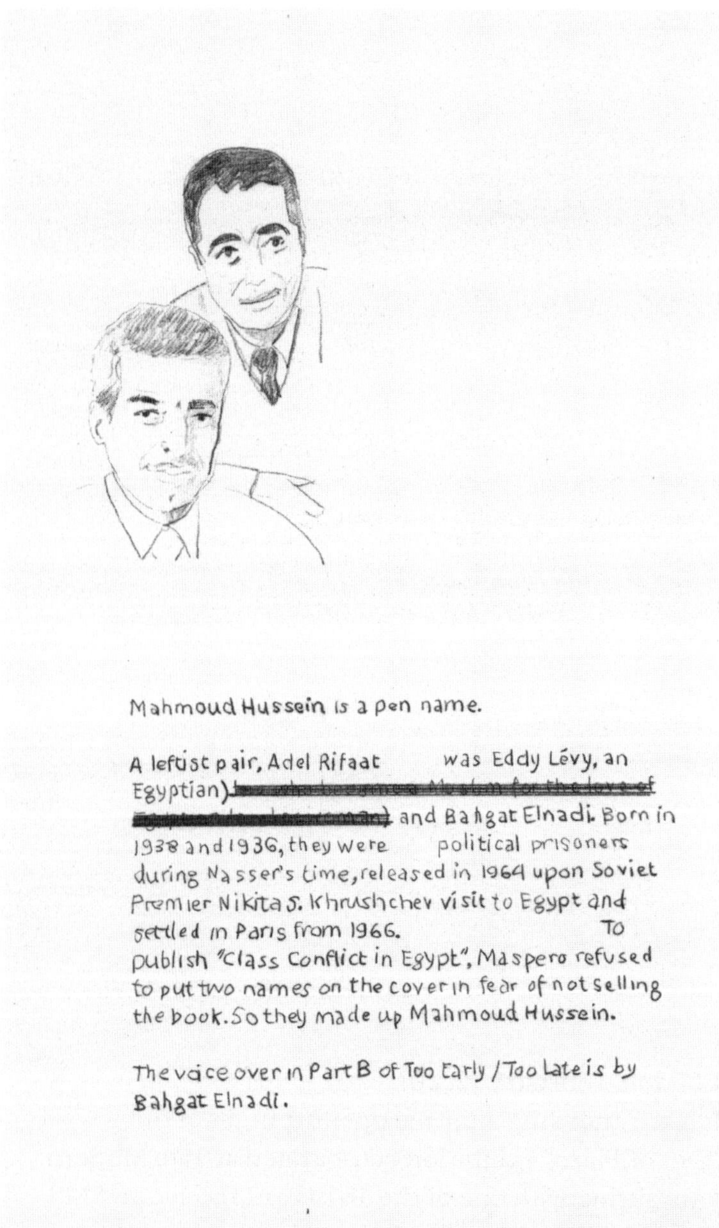

In their two-part film, *Too Early/Too Late*, Jean-Marie Straub and Danièle Huillet return to sites of revolutionary movements in France and Egypt. They attempt to capture the contemporary condition of these sites, mainly through recording rural landscapes. In the film's first and shorter part, shot in France in June

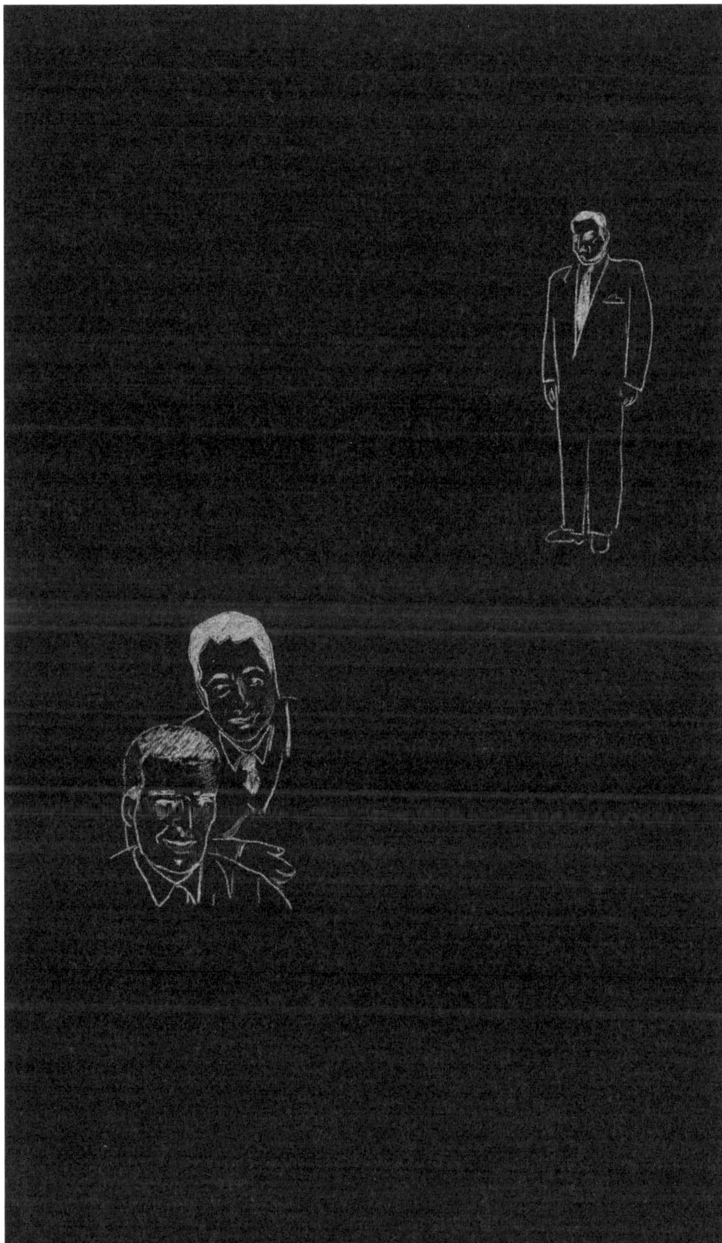

1980, Huillet reads excerpts from a letter by Friedrich Engels to Karl Kautsky on the miserable state of the French peasantry on the eve of the French Revolution. In the second and longer part, shot in Egypt in May 1981,

Bahgat Elnadi[1] delivers a timeline of local rural and urban revolts from the book *La Lutte de classes en Egypte de 1945 à 1968* (published in English as: *Class Conflict in Egypt, 1945–1970*), which he co-authored with Adel Rifaat under the pseudonym of Mahmoud Hussein.[2]

The film was proposed for a screening at the Tate Modern on February 12, 2011, as a means to reflect on the "momentous events" that broke out in Cairo on January 25, 2011. The screening date fell (accidentally) on the day after president Mubarak resigned. Then, for several months, the film circulated in contemporary art and film contexts, in attempts to foster a discussion of the new revolution. The present essay aims to analyze this proposition, and the elements that constitute the value assigned to the film before and after its relaunch. Text excerpts from the contexts of planning, producing, speaking about, screening and re-screening *Too Early/Too Late* (1981) guide this analysis.

Engels to Kautsky:

> London, February 20, 1889
> I would say much less about the new mode of production. An enormous gulf always separates it from the facts you speak of, and presented in this direct form it appears as a pure abstraction which does not make the thing clearer but rather more obscure.

A 16mm print of *Zu Früh, Zu Spät* (the German version of *Too Early/Too Late*) is kept in the archive of the Arsenal – Institute for Film and Video Art in Berlin, probably from its premiere at Kino Arsenal on November 8, 1981, or from its later screening in February 1982 at the Internationale Forum des Jungen Films of the Berlin Film Festival. I watched *Zu Früh, Zu Spät* for the first time on an editing table at Arsenal in April 2012, while researching films that accidentally predicted the end of states or regimes. Between the contexts they were produced in and the new readings they might give rise to, I was hoping that movies as protagonists would lead this research into the sorts of utopian impulses that appear latent in film. I was especially interested in part B of *Too Early/Too Late*.

Part B starts with the names of its crew members, followed by an urban pan from Cairo's citadel. The voice-over of

1 Bahgat Elnadi is heard in the French and the English versions. The Straubs also made a German version and an Italian version of the film.

2 Mahmoud Hussein is an Egyptian leftist pair. Adel Rifaat (born Eddy Lévy in 1938, converted to Islam in 1956) and Bahgat Elnadi (born in 1936) were political prisoners during Nasser's time. They were released in 1964 upon Soviet Premier Nikita S. Khrushchev's visit to Egypt, and settled in Paris from 1966. When they wanted to publish their work, *Class Conflict in Egypt*, Maspero, the leftist French publisher, refused to put their names on the cover for fear of not selling the book because of their young age and unknown names. They picked the familiar combination of Mahmoud Hussein, which they have kept ever since. They are based in Paris, where they have long worked with UNESCO, and authored several other books.

Bahgat Elnadi makes a statement on the working and rural classes leading or uniting in local revolts during Napoleon Bonaparte's time in Egypt. This time mark is shared with the film's first part that refers to sites of pre-revolutionary unrest in 18th century France. The events Engels quotes are

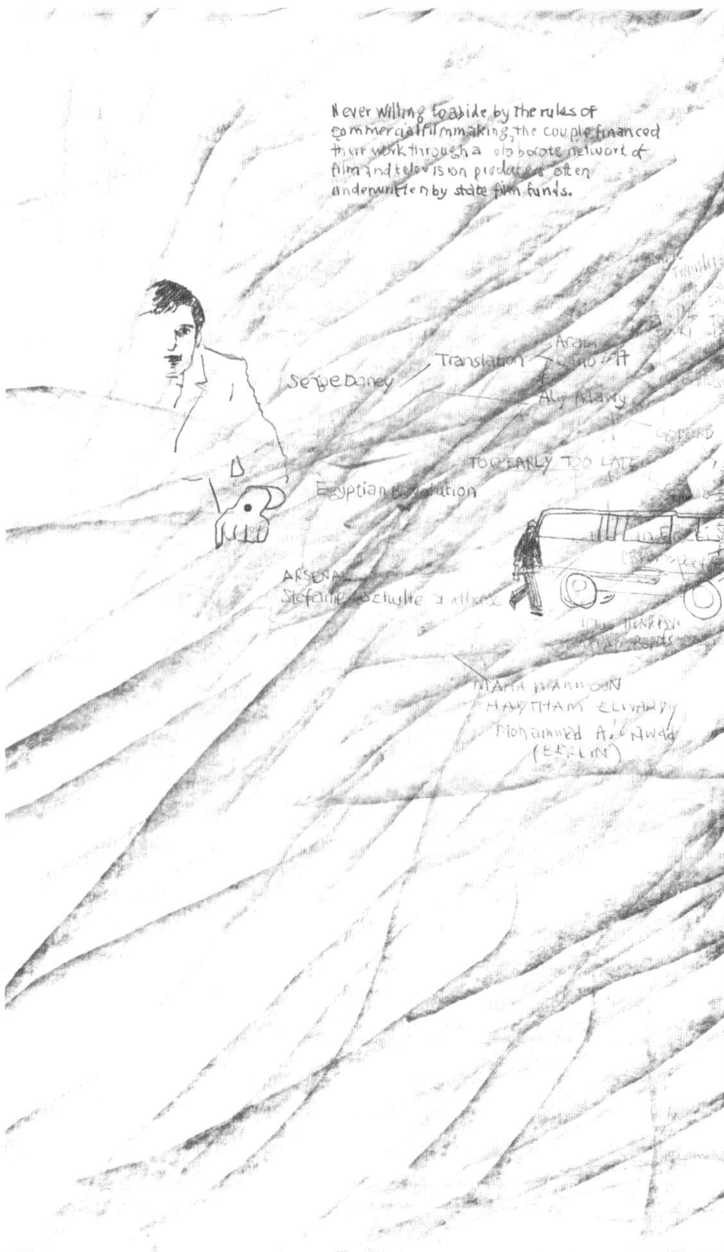

from the years closely preceding the 1789 revolution. In the second part of the film, the camera moves from one Egyptian location to another referring to the locations that carry the history of revolutionary movements that protested Muhammad Ali's centralized regime, or created their own

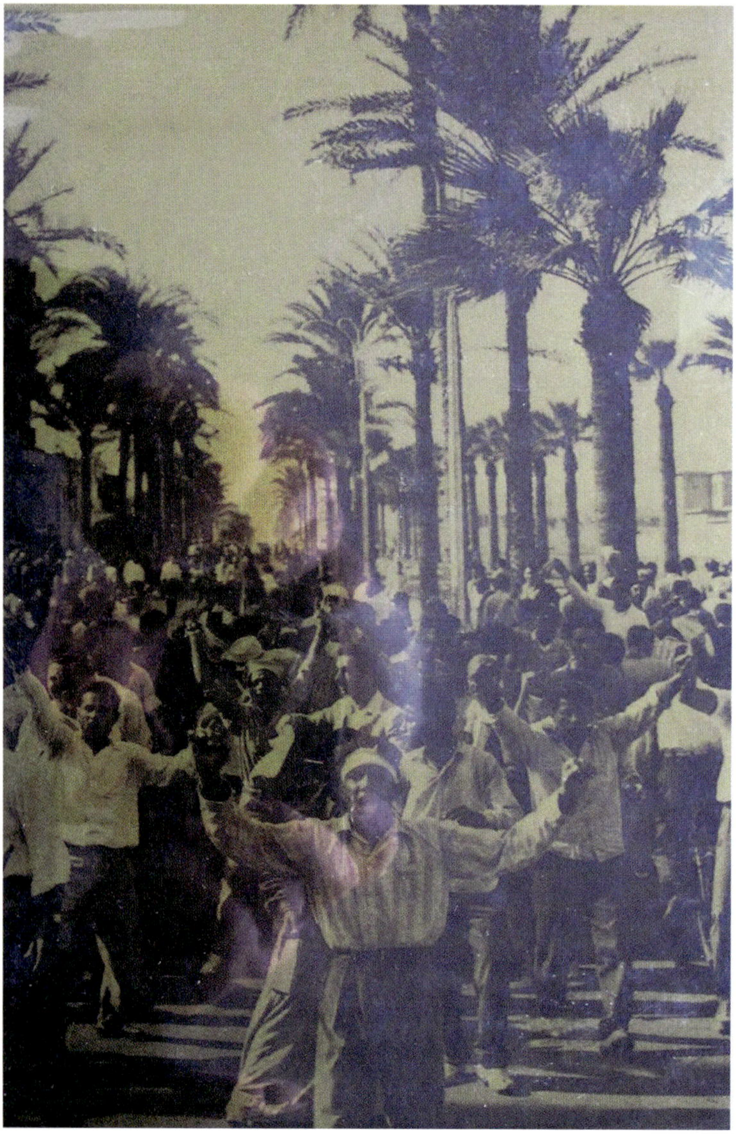

3
Too Early/Too Late (1981), directed by Danièle Huillet and Jean-Marie Straub, [1:37:00].

popular governments, were crushed at times, or ended up under occupation at others. There is no dialogue. No sounds interrupt the narration other than sounds of nature, rattling vehicles, and people's random, distant chatter. However, the film's finale is a compilation of archival footage that shows British soldiers' brutalities against Egyptian peasants, images of local resistance, King Farouk and the speech that was delivered on the day he was overthrown, "the reformed forces of the petit bourgeois that emerged from the army"[3] in 1952, Muhammad Naguib, who became president after he delivered his speech ill in his bed and his successor President Gamal Abdel Nasser heading a cabinet in which the future President Sadat is seen. Before the film closes on the Nile, the voice-over delivers the closing line: "And from 1955 to 1967, the mass movement could be dismantled and co-opted by a new ruling class inheriting all the vices of the old and betraying the national dignity which has served its ascension."[4]

This being a German version, I had to watch it again with an English translation of Engels' letter at hand. The parts read by Elnadi are taken from his book that Straub and Huillet found in "the Lusitania bookshop in Rome, on a shelf all covered in dust, and I bought it. [...] It was the Italian version, we obtained the French original later."[5] The book was able to fulfil the filmmakers' curiosity upon their return from an exploratory visit to Egypt in 1971. In Cairo, I spotted the English edition of Mahmoud Hussein's book by chance in the library of a friend's place. It was 2014, and I was too busy to browse or borrow the book at the time. In 2016, I ordered an ex-library copy online that was lost in the mail, and finally, I bought an affordable copy from Amazon, and was happy to receive it and see it was still in mint condition.

The first chapter of the book presents Egypt's cotton culture as a means to politically control the population and reduce it to poverty. It also tackles Gamal Abdel Nasser's project of fighting the feudal system through what Hussein describes as a capitalist transition. The second chapter centers on Nasser's rise to power, while the third deals with Nasser's post-1967 state structure, worn out by new, violent forms of mass mobilization.[6] Mahmoud Hussein (Adel Rifaat and Bahgat Elnadi) wrote the book in the wake of the Arab defeat in the 1967 Arab-Israeli War.[7]

> In forming a response to the questions this defeat so brutally thrust at us, we were attempting to define the politico-social contradictions of the Nasser experience, beginning with its genesis.[8]

The writers warn that,

> absent from this work is an intrinsic understanding of the forces making for revolutionary social change and consequently, of the specific laws governing the revolution of the Egyptian people. In short, this survey lacks what is most essential. This is because this essential knowledge does not exist today in anyone's head.[9]

4
Too Early/Too Late

5
Danièle Huillet and Jean-Marie Straub in conversation with Hans Hurch, Berlin, November 10, 1981. Originally published in German, *Falter – Wiener Programm-zeitschrift*, no. 1 (January–February 11, 1982): 15–28. Translated by Ben Brewster, posted as "Too Early / Too Late: Interview with Huillet and Straub," kinoslang.blogspot.com, August 22, 2014.

6
Fuad Faris, "Class Conflict in Egypt: 1945–1970," *MERIP Reports*, no. 29 (June 1974): 24–26.

7
In 1976, Straub and Huillet also made a film based on a text written at the time of Mahmoud Hussein's *Class Conflict in Egypt*. The film was titled *Fortini/Cani*, and the book is *The Dogs of the Sinai* by Franco Fortini.

8
Mahmoud Hussein, *Class Conflict in Egypt: 1945–1970* (New York: Monthly Review Press Books, 1974), ix.

9
Hussein, 12.

The two Marxists, born in Egypt, were imprisoned for their political activism during Nasser's time, and left for Europe upon their release in 1964. Their book was first published by Maspero in Paris in 1969. Huillet and Straub chose to center some of their film's discourse around Nasser, though he was already dead when they visited Egypt in 1971, and when they returned around 1973, Sadat was very close to his victory in the second Arab-Israeli War. When they later came back to shoot in 1981, Sadat's *infitah* (open, or neoliberal) policy had prevailed over Egypt's social classes and economy. Unlike Nasser, Sadat was now a

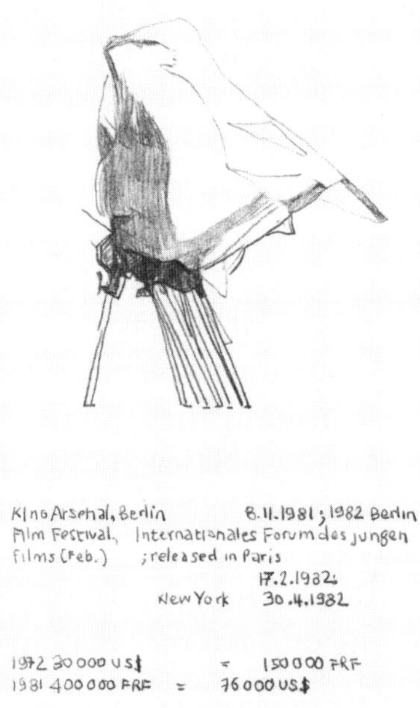

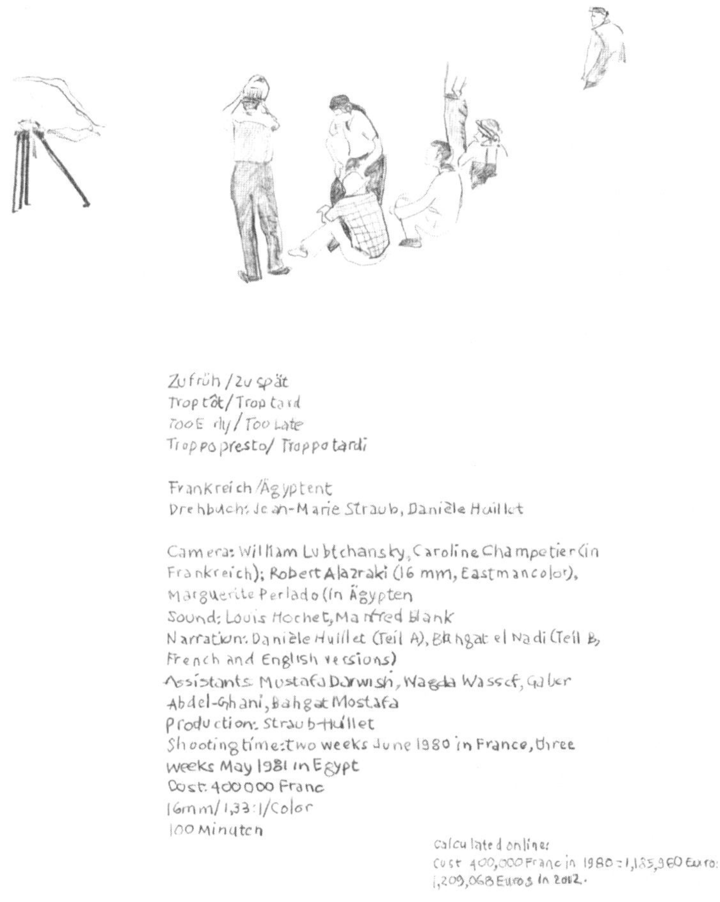

friend of Israel, antagonizing almost all Arabs. Bread and anti-peace-treaty riots loomed over his reign. Sadat would be killed during a televised celebration of his own victories a few months after the Straubs left with their footage from Egypt. It is perhaps Nasser's promises to the peasants, promises of sovereignty that the Straubs attempted to unfold. In the interview from 1981, when Straub used the phrase "Nasser's betrayal," Huillet corrected, "with Nasser it wasn't even a betrayal, he acted as a member of his class." Straub then explained, "He betrayed the peasants.

He had given them some hopes in the beginning."[10] Still, when comparing Egypt to France, he saw that, "[d]espite all [...] Egypt is a country with a future and with a political hope."[11]

The film is a survey of the Egyptian landscape transformed by all the forces that have held power over it. Here is a chance to look at the land alone, as the filmmakers use no actors and let their camera capture the daily happenings in villages, on agricultural roads, and at the gate of a factory. Huillet acknowledged,

> And the landscape itself, I mean, when I saw the film, after it was finished, it suddenly struck me: this is something new. That is, no one has ever shot landscapes in a film and then held and, as it were, caressed them. As if they were precisely characters.[12]

The film appears peaceful, as if minding its own business. Save for the archival footage and the few buildings, or compounds, reminiscent of a city sprawl, nothing illustrated any brewing anger nor a shift in the rural landscape or the industrial zone embedded within it. Factories were used by Nasser to counter the work of the "agricultural trap" enforced by the past ruling classes and colonial powers, as mentioned in Mahmoud Hussein's book. They were also hubs of mass movements in his time, and were positioned in or near rural areas as evidenced by the film.

10
Huillet and Straub, "Too Early/Too Late: Interview with Huillet and Straub."

11
Straub, "Too Early/Too Late: Interview."

12
Straub, "Too Early/Too Late: Interview."

One scene from *Too Early/Too Late* is included in Harun Farocki's *Workers Leaving the Factory in Eleven Decades* (2006), and I first encountered it on February 7, 2010, the closing day of Farocki's retrospective show at Raven Row in London.

Farocki's survey of film fragments is not only a collection of scenes that carry a resemblance to cinema's first ever moving images, but also of what they tell us about different modes of production. In the factory scene in *Too Early/Too Late,* a siren sets the workers free after their day's work. They leave only to find a camera awaiting them at some distance across the gate. Some acknowledge the presence of the camera by looking at or speaking about it, or slowing down distracted by it. Others continue to leave or pull back their distracted colleagues away from the gate of the factory and the camera. About this unidentified relationship with the camera in this factory scene, Straub said, “That’s the little aspect of the film which I’m very proud of.”[13] The scene is ten minutes long, and critics such as Meaghan Morris noted, “I am mesmerized by this image, and yet, I endlessly look at my watch.”[14] Huillet responds,

> That’s also the reward of patience, [...] it’s a risk as well, because at the beginning the text almost carries the shot. Then the text stops and for a time

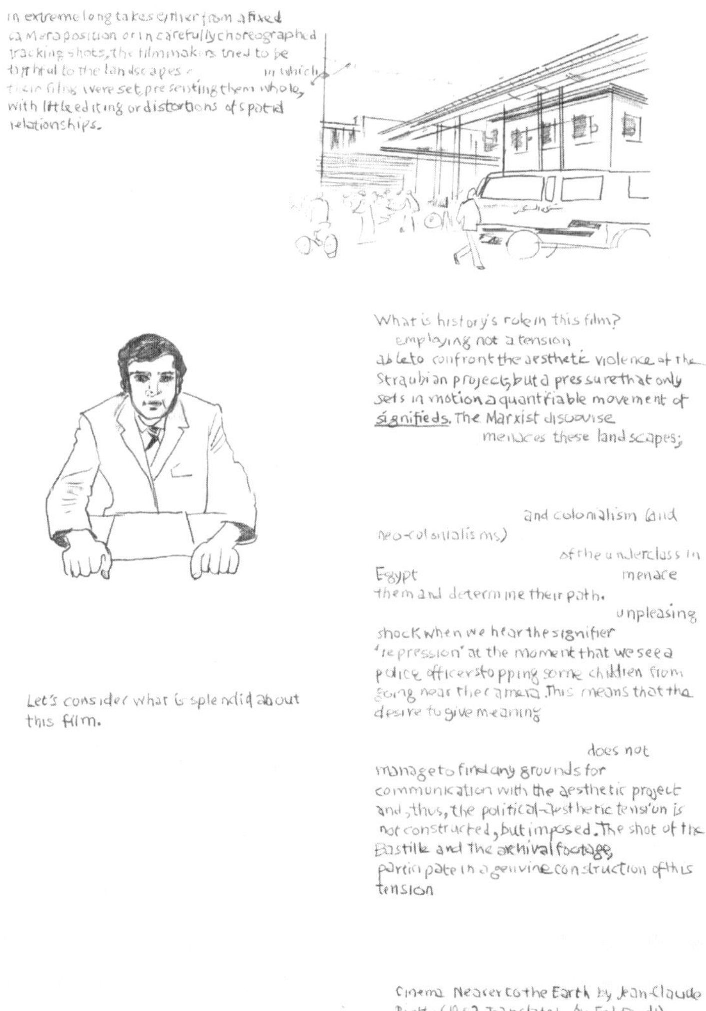

13
Straub,
“Too Early/Too Late:
Interview.”

14
Meaghan Morris,
Too Soon Too Late: History in Popular Culture (Bloomington: Indiana University Press, 1998), xxiii.

> it's not clear whether the shot can carry itself. And suddenly one realizes that it's getting stronger and stronger.[15]

Similar interactions happen in the following scene where, in the distance, policemen appear to be keeping kids away from the business of the camera people. None of the Arabic chatter is translated, although it is clearly audible on the soundtrack of the film.

In the script submitted to secure permissions to shoot in Egypt, the Straubs included plans to shoot three factories and their surroundings: a sugar factory in Hawamdieh, and two cement factories in Tura and Helwan. In the factory scene, a bus passes by; on it the name of the Egyptian Sugar Company can be read. In 1981, Huillet said, "It is our first documentary film, really."[16]

Libération, February 20–21, 1982
Serge Daney writes,

> One therefore has to see the second part of *Too Early/Too Late* as an odd performance, made up of approaches and retreats, where the filmmakers, less meteorologists than acupuncturists, search for the spot—the only spot, the right spot—where their camera can catch people without bothering them. Two dangers immediately present themselves: exotic tourism and the invisible camera. Too close, too far. In a lengthy 'scene', the camera is planted in front of a factory gate and allows one to see the Egyptian workers who pass, enter and leave. Too close for them not to see the camera, too far away for them to be tempted to go towards it. To find this point, this moral point, is at this moment the entire art of the Straubs.[17]

For Serge Daney, the camera was at the right distance from what it was filming—not in the way nor totally out of it. In February 2013, Jean-Marie Straub told Elke Marhöfer and Mikhail Lylov that he was bothered by the phrase, "the viewpoint of the take."[18] He considers a take the result of a process, that of searching for the viewpoint. "One discovers that in a village the search often ends where the water tower stands [... The camera] is placed

15 Huillet, "Too Early / Too Late: Interview."

16 Huillet, "Too Early / Too Late: Interview."

17 Serge Daney, "Cinemeteorology," *Libération* (February 20–21, 1982). Translated by Jonathan Rosenbaum for the catalogue of a twelve-day Straub/Huillet retrospective at the Public Theater in New York, November 2, 1982. jonathanrosenbaum.net

18 Jean-Marie Straub in conversation with Elke Marhöfer and Mikhail Lylov, February 2013. Published as "A Thousand Cliffs," in *Point of View – Perspectives of Political Film and Video Work*, ed. Tobias Hering (Berlin: Archive Books, 2014), 355. Translated by John Barrett. Republished in the present volume, 368.

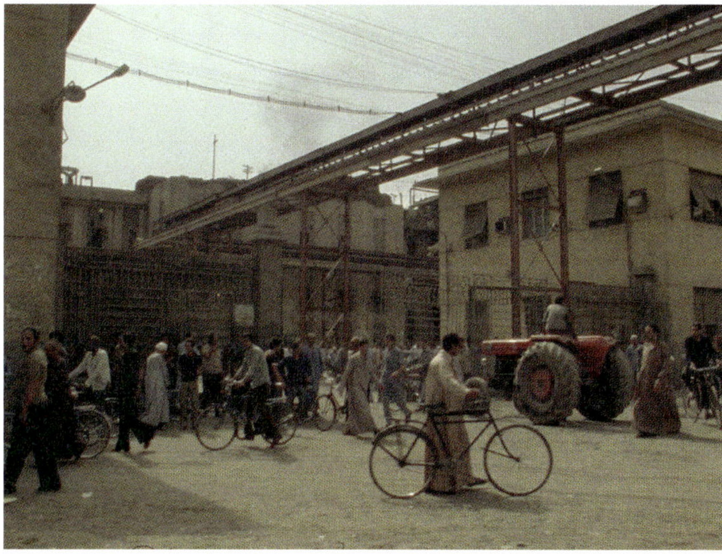

exactly on that spot where water can be fed to the entire locality."[19] To film from that spot, for Straub, is to "show an entirety." To think of Straub, Farocki, and Mahmoud Hussein together is to understand how the exit from the gate of a factory can sum up the entirety of a community of people and the laws that govern their relationship to that factory socially, economically and politically. To make a film on Nasser is to make a film on Egypt's masses, those anonymous presences in the form of distant chatter, claiming agency over their land's historical shifts.

Daney was fascinated by the way the film was emptied of actors ("especially not extras") except for the landscape ("This actor has a text to recite: History"[20]) and the wind that sculpts the film's silence. Daney argues that,

> (1) the Straubs are stout-hearted, and (2) voyages into the impossible are very instructive. With *Too Early/Too Late*, an experience is attempted, with us and in spite of us: at moments, one begins to see (the grass bent by the wind) before hearing (the wind responsible for this bending). At other moments, one hears first (the wind), then one sees (the grass).[21]

In their interview on November 10, 1981, in Berlin, Danièle Huillet told Hans Hurch, "I think that the fact that there aren't characters that we have selected in the film isn't really so important. There are landscapes and they are handled just as if they were characters."[22] The wind animates the limbs and lips of these usually and seemingly silent (or silenced) characters.

19
"A Thousand Cliffs," 368.

20
Daney,
"Cinemeteorology."

21
Daney,
"Cinemeteorology."

22
Huillet,
"Too Early / Too Late:
Interview."

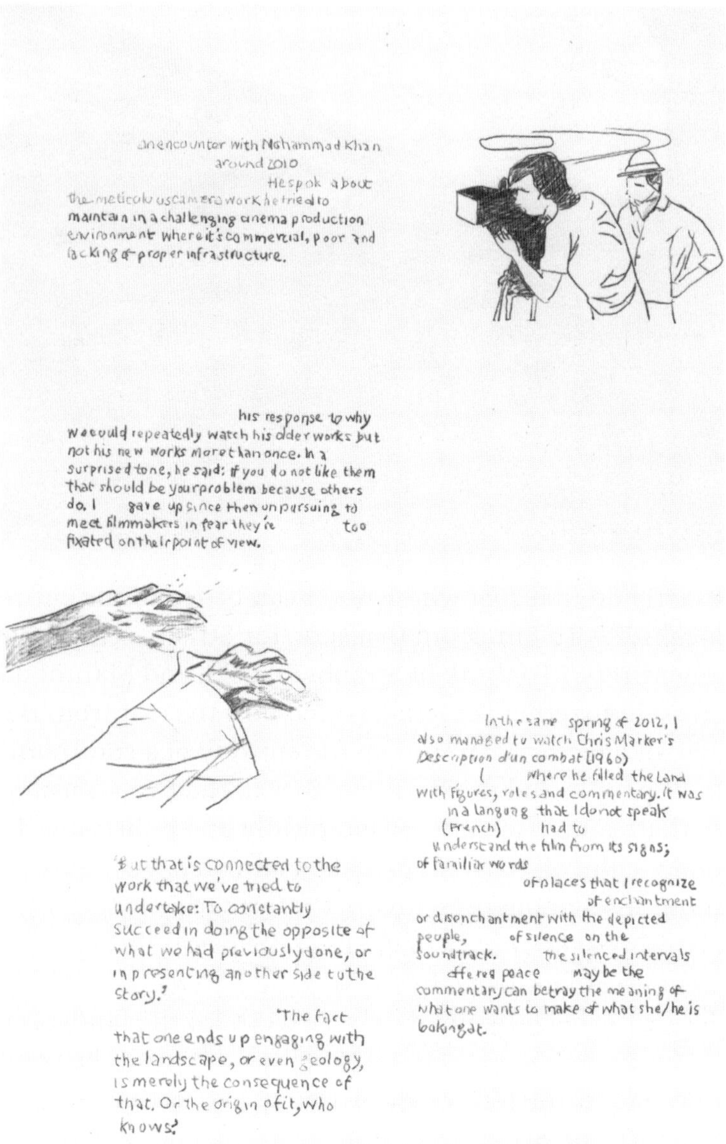

The wind is one of the most difficult sounds to record because it is normally considered a disturbing noise that needs to be filtered out. This makes the Straub's decision to sculpt the space of their film with it an element to take interest in. One way to visualize Daney's point of employing the wind as an actor, is to look at the film's production stills of Maggie Perlado in Egypt. She was one of the assistants during the shooting, and her photos show some of the crew sitting under the sun, or standing next to a 16mm camera on a tripod, while the wind shapes the camera's white cover into interesting formations. Another photo shows the sound engineer (Louis Hochet) listening from his equipment close to an abandoned gas station and an empty green lot. The wind blows the attire of the young peasants who come to speak with the crew; they stand in front of the camera looking like the angry men in the photo that was used for Mahmoud Hussein's English cover. One can also look at the way Robert Alazraki is bending his knees and closing one eye to look through the camera lens onto Cairo's urban fabric with a green roundabout in the background. To understand the silence, one need only look at his bare feet. At times, he puts a foot on Danièle Huillet's back at her request, in order to minimize all the extra sounds that would come from operating the camera and stain the sound experience of the film.

From Rome, on August 19, 1980, Danièle Huillet sent a letter to William Lubtchansky and Caroline Champetier, the cinematographers of the French part of *Too Early/Too Late*.

> Willy, take care of your eyes, particularly in Egypt, where the sun is not at all like in Brittany! Twice, there was a blue velatura (stain) in the middle of a take that comes from the eye moving away from the viewfinder. That didn't bother us, but more care should be taken! And finally, Willy again: pay attention to the noises during the shoot; there are quite a few noises from jackets, some small cell noises ... and some noises from the shoes. In *Fortini[/Cani]*, Ciccio [Renato Berta] moved around barefoot so as not to make any noise; as a result, it was less noisy. This is not to persuade you to go to Egypt barefoot—but just that you'll need to think about that, too, when you're preparing a camera movement; 'for expediency,' JM would say. Absolute Ruhe (silence).[23]

23 *Jean-Marie Straub and Danièle Huillet: Writings*, ed. Sally Shafto, Katherine Pickard (New York: Sequence Press, 2016), 347–349. In the margin of the letter, Danièle's handwritten notes indicate that the couple had shot over 12,000 meters of 35mm and 40,000 meters of 16mm film, and they were mostly exposed, developed and titled in Germany and Italy.

The film's pans look familiar, from the numerous Egyptian films that millions watch every day. The pace of events is non-existent, except for the narrated timeline. The filmmakers made subtitle-free editions in four languages, none of which is Arabic, and, upon the request of Mahmoud Hussein, never showed *Too Early/Too Late* in Egypt. What does this make of the Arabic chatter with the camera? Does this reduce the viewership of the film squarely to the West?

Digital copies of the film were hard to find. That a personal encounter with the work is so improbable perhaps contributes to its appreciation. In 2015, for its inaugural program, Cairo's Cimatheque–Alternative Film Centre wrote to BFI [British Film Institute] inquiring about the film's English 16mm print. BFI's response was that a print exists but is not in good enough condition to be screened. Cimatheque had to screen the English version from a DVD, and produced Arabic subtitles. It was the centre's testing phase so its DCP burnt, software crashed, and electricity sometimes went off. The film's new subtitles similarly did not run for the planned screening so an English-only version was shown.

The film was announced a few days before the screening. The description that was circulated read:

> Shot in the summer of 1980, this film from long-time directorial partners Straub and Huillet investigates the changing relationship between people, the land, and society in France and Egypt. Based on texts written by Friedrich Engels and exiled writer (or writers?) operating under the pseudonym Mahmoud Hussein, the film's history is just as enigmatic as the fragmented images of Egypt's landscapes and peasantry it presents.[24]

People on social media expressed their excitement. Some wrote that finally a cinema space in Cairo is programming Straub and Huillet. The seventy-seat screening room was packed. By mid-screening, people started to walk out.

The factory scene lasts around ten minutes.[25] Long takes can feel like a luxury of raw film at a time when local filmmakers struggle to secure production funds. Egyptian filmmakers shot similar scenes but included them within larger stories of how factories and their owners and workers are challenged when the Egyptian pound is continuously devalued and foreign currency channeled through the black market. Film critics underlined the ways in which local productions were held captive to their leading actors and actresses, which allowed for less expenditure on the other elements of the movies.[26]
In some of his films, Egyptian director Youssef Chahine edited out transitions, cut scenes at the end of dialogues, and experimented with the work of Egyptian writers and

24 Screening of *Too Early/Too Late*, Cimatheque, Cairo, June 10, 2015.

25 The duration of the shot reflects the length of a 16mm reel on which it was filmed.

26 Viola Shafik, *Arab Cinema: History and Cultural Identity* (Cairo: American University in Cairo Press, 2007), 27. Shafik writes, "Many Egyptian producers take up production loans offered by distributors from the Gulf states–mainly those who can fix the selling price and thus the budget of a film according to the popularity of the cast. For this reason, actors' fees are enormous in comparison to the total budget. The average budget of an Egyptian feature film at present is approximately LE750,000 (LE = Egyptian pounds), i.e., about US$230,000. Up to LE300,000 may have to be spent on fees for the stars, which means that little remains for props, set, costumes, transport, and wages."

with political upheavals. *Al Ard* (*The Land*, 1969) was his attempt to depict a land that was brewing a revolt. It centered on peasants, and was released in the wake of the 1967 Arab defeat. It also focused on the villagers' precarity as they depend on the only educated man among them, whose cowardice makes him an accomplice of the feudal neighbor: he tricks them into signing a paper that gives away their land for the benefit of the road the neighbor wants to build. The film's finale—the revolt leader, and elder peasant, clinging to the land as he's pulled out of his cotton field—brings some spectators to tears. *Too Early/Too Late* looks for the rural surge on this land while *Al Ard* animates it. Based on a novel from 1954 with the same title, this film was, like Hussein's book, made in the wake of the defeat in 1967, yet as an attempt to defend the 1952 revolution and its resulting ruling system. It attempted so by illustrating the peasants' close relationship with the land they cultivated, and their resistance to the alien forces that were trying to remove them from their land could be a metaphor of the land lost in the war and its displaced people. It is difficult to watch the images of agricultural land in *Too Early/Too Late* without thinking of *Al Ard*; both show the same fields, feature the same palm trees, and show us a cow making its way out of water, yet the films present opinions that are opposite each other.

Al-Asfour (*The Sparrow*, 1972) is Chahine's second attempt to reflect on the defeat, and to separate Nasser's ideals from the corruption that surrounded his figure. The film's finale is a sort of mass movement that spontaneously formed on the day Nasser admitted defeat and resigned on television. Just like the ending of *Al Ard*, the last moment in the film becomes an intense popular expression of how to fight for the land you love. In his autobiographical film *Hadduta Masriyya* (*An Egyptian Story*, 1982), Chahine included a re-enactment of shooting *The Sparrow's* re-enacted demonstrations, along with the anger and anxiety that drove this process. His point in the 1982 iteration was to exploit the old fellows who had shifted their views in the post-Nasser era, and refused to fund or give permission to make *The Sparrow*. Following Nasser's death in 1970, politics were shifting, and Chahine failed to secure funds for a film that would be somehow still on Nasser's side. What does not appear in the autobiographical film is how Chahine managed to make *The Sparrow* eventually; he received a one-word

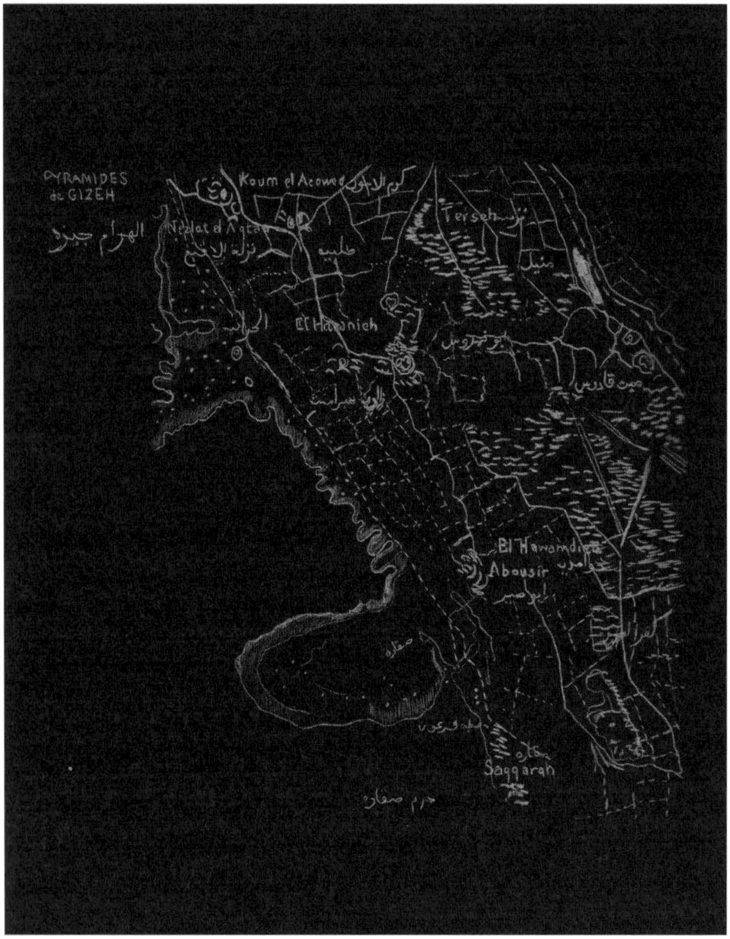

telegram from Algeria; it reads "Viens!" [Come!].[27] Algerian film historian Ahmed Bedjaoui told me that Lotfy al-Khouly who wrote *The Sparrow* was a classmate of the (second) Algerian president Houari Boumédiène who also admired Nasser. When Boumédiène heard of Chahine's troubled production, he instructed L'Office National pour le Commerce et l'Industrie Cinématographique (ONCIC) to write to the filmmaker. Algerian filmmaker Ahmed Rachedi told me he wrote the one-word telegram. The Algerians could give US$ 30,000, half of the budget Chahine had planned to work with.[28] The film was eventually made for E£ 42,000 (US$ 75,000[29]) and not released in Egyptian cinemas until 1974, following the 1973 war. It made E£ 4,815 (US$ 8,675) in five weeks of projection.[30] Chahine's films in general were not seeing great turn out at cinemas, and also made people leave in middle of their projection.

In 1981, the Straubs hired no actors to pretend history for us; they spent their budget of 400,000 French Francs (US$

27
Personal interview with director Ahmed Rachedi, Oran, September 2013.

28
Salim Aggar, *Youssef Chahine and Algeria*, 10th International Arab Film Festival, Oran, 2017.

29
US Treasury Reporting Rates of Exchange as of March 31, 1972.

30
Al Asfour (*The Sparrow*) on El Cinema database.

80,000).[31] The filmed landscape, captured sounds, and the materials and cameras involved, needed export permits of the film issued by the Egyptian Ministry of Culture. These permits indicate that the film's working title was *Egypt from 1798 to 1951*, that it was to be sent to France, and that by end of May 1981 the filmmakers were allowed to take out the undeveloped 16mm film reels and sound recordings.[32] The film script in French was sent for approval by the Egyptian authorities on October 23, 1980, along with a list of locations to be filmed. It was presented as a short film and with the subtitle *Places of revolt against Franco-British colonization*. A note at the bottom of the first of nine pages of the submitted dossier confirms that the landscapes and the villages will be filmed as they are—without historical reconstruction.

The film's copy in the archive at Arsenal in Berlin is in two 16mm reels; total duration is 104 minutes, weight is 5.2 kilos, length is 1140 meters, with an optical sound track.

Straub says his guide to filming the landscape was a set of maps.

> [W]e went to Egypt one year before the shoot to do location scouting in the villages. We had the maps drawn by the expedition of Napoleon. The geographers who accompanied him made precise maps, with the wheat fields. When we showed the maps to the film crew, they didn't know how to read them, so Danièle had to write out very explicit itineraries.[33]

Huillet said that the Egyptians invented the land register in order to organize "where the water should run."[34] She said, "It's an incredible piece of work. [...] The evil is what is done with it."[35] In *Adieu Bonaparte* (1985), Youssef Chahine also makes use of knowledge produced by Napoleon's expedition, but his treatment of it is different. In particular, he includes three local characters: one joins the Egyptian resistance against the French, another collaborates and learns the language of the French, while the third one seeks their knowledge in order to employ it for the local resistance movement. By putting these parallel film efforts next to each other, it is interesting to see what is made of the materials the filmmakers resorted to, or experiences produced by the historical events themselves. There might also be a link or influence if we think of the possibility that

31 US Treasury Reporting Rates of Exchange as of March 31, 1981. Philip Widmann provided a scan of an interview with the French magazine *Révolution* from 1982 in which the Straubs mention that their budget in actual money was $10,000 from Hubert Bals of the Rotterdam IFF, and the rest were debts that they tried to repay through sales of the film.

32 The permits show that the Straubs took out 11 and 43 reels of undeveloped 16mm film weighting 6.5 and 24.58 kilos, and 8 and 34 of sound recordings weighting 1.8 and 8.5 (34 x 0.25) kilos.

33 *Writings*, 340.

34 Huillet, "Too Early / Too Late: Interview."

35 Huillet, "Too Early / Too Late: Interview."

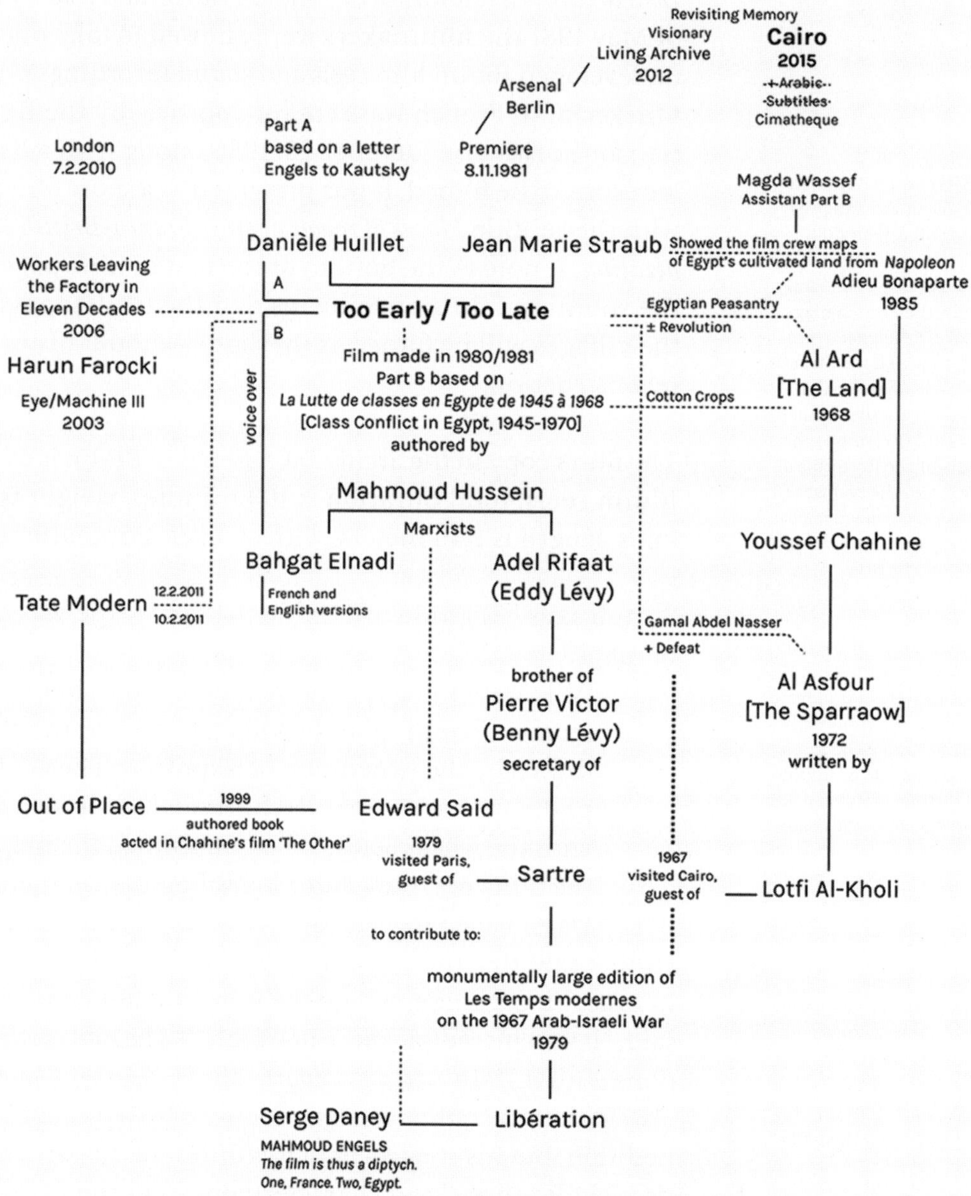

Revisiting Memory
Visionary
Living Archive
2012
Cairo
2015
+ Arabic
Subtitles
Cimatheque
Arsenal
Berlin
Premiere
8.11.1981
Part A
based on a letter
Engels to Kautsky
London
7.2.2010
Magda Wassef
Assistant Part B
Danièle Huillet
Jean Marie Straub
Showed the film crew maps
of Egypt's cultivated land from Napoleon
Adieu Bonaparte
1985
Workers Leaving
the Factory in
Eleven Decades
2006
A
Too Early / Too Late
Egyptian Peasantry
± Revolution
B
Harun Farocki
Film made in 1980/1981
Part B based on
La Lutte de classes en Egypte de 1945 à 1968
[Class Conflict in Egypt, 1945-1970]
authored by
Al Ard
[The Land]
1968
Eye/Machine III
2003
voice over
Cotton Crops
Mahmoud Hussein
Marxists
Youssef Chahine
Bahgat Elnadi
Adel Rifaat
(Eddy Lévy)
Tate Modern
12.2.2011
10.2.2011
French and
English versions
Gamal Abdel Nasser
+ Defeat
brother of
Pierre Victor
(Benny Lévy)
secretary of
Al Asfour
[The Sparraow]
1972
written by
Out of Place
1999
authored book
acted in Chahine's film 'The Other'
Edward Said
1979
visited Paris,
guest of
Sartre
1967
visited Cairo,
guest of
Lotfi Al-Kholi
to contribute to:
monumentally large edition of
Les Temps modernes
on the 1967 Arab-Israeli War
1979
Serge Daney
Libération
MAHMOUD ENGELS
The film is thus a diptych.
One, France. Two, Egypt.

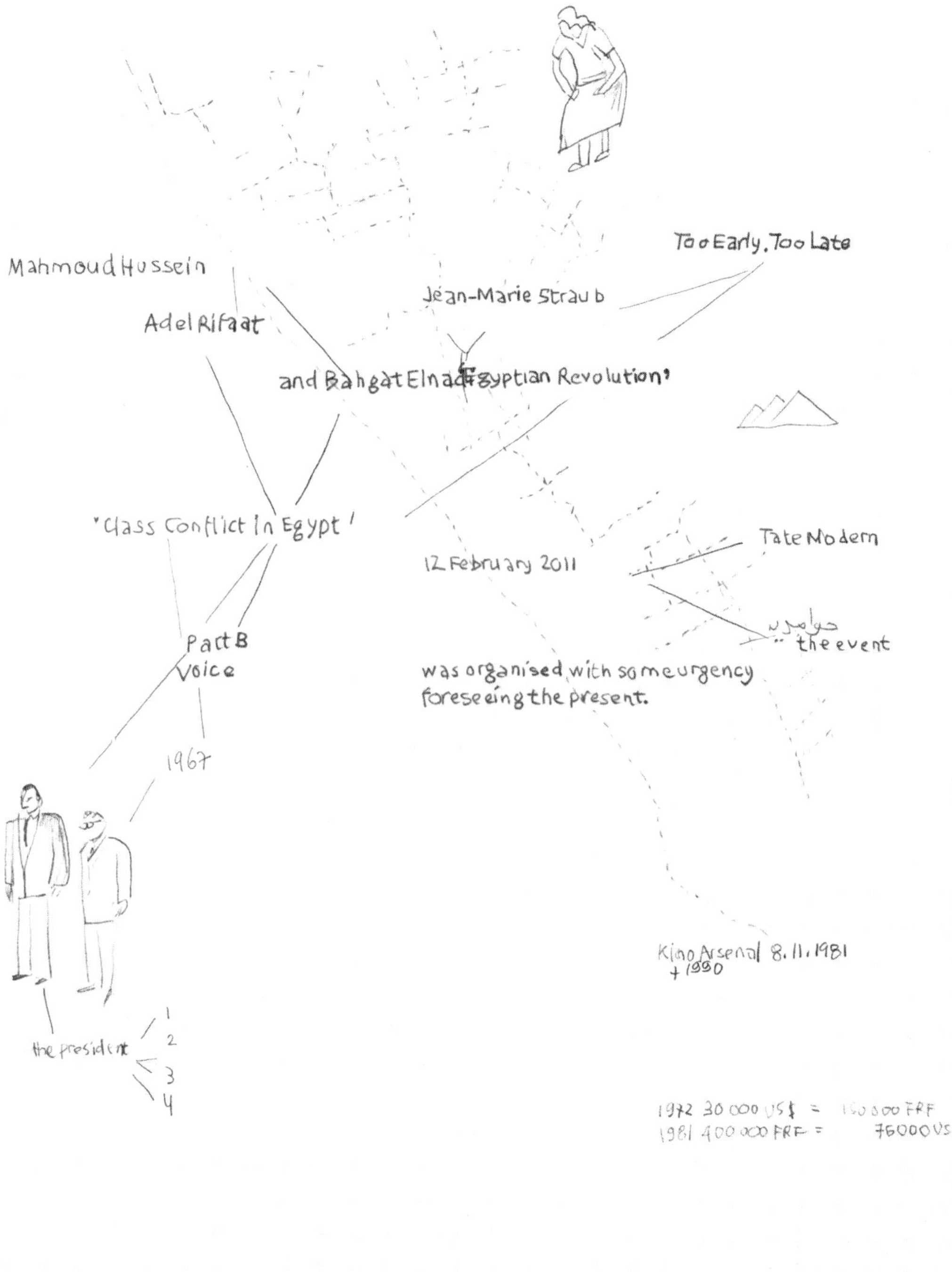
Mahmoud Hussein
Adel Rifaat
and Bahgat Elnadi
Jean-Marie Straub
Too Early, Too Late
'Egyptian Revolution'
'Class Conflict in Egypt'
12 February 2011
Tate Modern
the event
Part B
Voice
was organised with some urgency
foreseeing the present.
1967
the president
1
2
3
4
Kino Arsenal 8.11.1981
+1990
1972 30 000 US$ = 150 000 FRF
1981 400 000 FRF = 76000 US

Chahine might have seen any of the Straub/Huillet's films on his trips to Europe.

As I watched *Too Early/Too Late*, I was constantly thinking about its embedded critique of a ruling system. A film not made or presented to those who are on the land, but to those who are elsewhere. In other words, it was talking about Egypt, or on its behalf, but not to it. Straub said once that he would be happy if the film eventually goes to Cairo, but the film has locked its images out of Egypt, and its commentary out of its language. In the same spring of 2012, I also watched Chris Marker's *Description d'un combat* (*Description of a Struggle*, 1960) where the land is filled with figures, roles and commentary. It too was in a language that I do not speak, this time French, and I had to make an effort to understand the film from its signs; signs of familiar words that appear in a foreign language, signs of places that I recognize from other images, signs of enchantment or disenchantment with the people depicted, signs of silence on the film's soundtrack. It was the silent intervals that offered peace, for the commentary sometimes betrays the signs the land itself communicates. It was the 'gaze' that the films presented, despite how Straub resented the ideological stakes in a 'point of view.'

Gilles Deleuze was fascinated by the stratigraphy in the Straubs' film. He wrote,

> But they are again essentially the empty and lacunary stratigraphic landscapes of Straub, where the camera movements (when there are any, notably pan shots) trace the abstract curve of what has happened, and where the earth stands for what is buried in it: the cave in *Othon* where the resistance fighters had their weapons, the marble quarries and the Italian countryside where civil populations were massacred in *Fortini/Cani*, the cornfield in *Dalla Nube alla Resistenza* fertilized by the blood of the sacrificial victims (or the shot of the grass and acacias), the French countryside and the Egyptian countryside in *Trop Tôt, trop tard*. To the question: what is a Straubian shot? one can reply, as in a manual of stratigraphy, that it is a section comprising the stippled [pointillées] lines of vanished features and the complete lines of those that

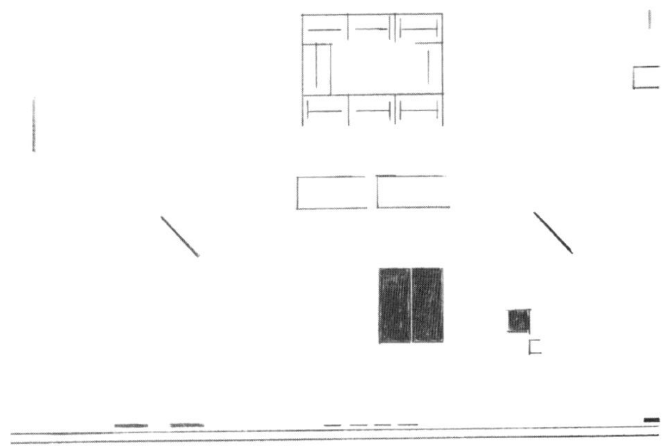

36
Gilles Deleuze, *Cinema 2: The Time-Image*, trans. Hugh Tomlinson. (Minneapolis: University of Minnesota Press, 1997), 244.

37
Céline Condorelli, "Speaking of revolutions: Too Early / Too Late," *LUX*, March 9, 2011, lux.org.uk

38
Condorelli, "Speaking of revolutions."

> are still touched. The visual image, in Straub, is the rock.[36]

"I am really wondering how to address a country like Egypt,"[37] Celine Condorelli asked Jean-Marie Straub in 2010, three months before the events of January 2011, "of the situation following the Egyptian revolution [of 1952]. What is the appropriate position? The film *Trop Tôt, trop tard* is very clear in these terms, explicitly locating where it looks and speaks from, or reads from. My three questions are all about this, about positioning. ...Why Egypt, why the Egyptian revolutions?"[38] He answered that it was an informative encounter related to unanswered questions that they took back with them from their visits to Egypt in the 1970s, "and we found a book, in which we found information, which is the one from these two gentlemen [Mahmoud Hussein]."[39] Straub argued that the film "does not have anything to do" with the writing of Mahmoud Hussein or the things and facts they mention, because, in his view, "they had not seen what they talked about." Straub wanted an engagement with the geography of places, and "to check those informations' topography, the geography of the thing." The introduction to this interview reads,

> While the outcome of this uprising is not yet known, the film *Trop tôt, trop tard* as well as this conversation have now gained quite a different dimension, and seem, above all, timely. This interview is being published to coincide with a screening of *Trop tôt, trop tard*, at Tate Modern on February 12, 2011, on the 19th day of the Egyptian uprising. Unable to go to Egypt to exhibit the ongoing work *Il n'y a plus rien* [There is Nothing Left] that research around *Trop tôt, trop tard* was part of, the event was organised at Tate with some urgency, as a way of foreseeing the present.[40]

In Jens Maier-Rothe's review of a 2015 show in Bologna that approached the Middle East through contemporary art and took the title of *Too Early / Too Late*, he argues that, "Following the events in Egypt in 2011, the film's title would come up quite frequently during debates on the untimeliness of artistic practice vis-à-vis major political transformation."[41] Condorelli hosted the screening at Tate Modern, and took her project *Il n'y a plus rien*—whose third movement, on revolutions, was inspired by *Too Early / Too Late*—to Alexandria Contemporary Arts Forum (ACAF) in December 2011.[42] Maier-Rothe screened the film in April 2012 at Beirut, the Cairo-based initiative that he co-founded. With Tobias Hering, I screened the film at Arsenal in July 2012 "to take a critical perspective on [...] how the film can be positioned in relation to its production process, temporality, circulation, and appreciation."[43] In the same year, Louis Henderson went to Cairo to film his *Logical Revolts* (2012) at Tahrir Square to "see what was left of the struggle."[44]

39 Straub, "Speaking of revolutions."

40 Straub, "Speaking of revolutions."

41 Jens Maier-Rothe, "Tout va bien? 'Too Early / Too Late: Middle East and Modernity' at the Pinacoteca Nazionale di Bologna," *Ibraaz*, March 31, 2015.

42 In a conversation published as an advertisement on *Art Agenda*, titled, "Céline Condorelli + Uriel Orlow's 'There is nothing left' at Alexandria Contemporary Arts Forum," December 9, 2011–January 12, 2012. Condorelli said that the last movement of her piece was "that of revolution, taking its cue from the 1981 film *Trop Tôt, trop tard* by Straub-Huillet that now appears to be almost prophetic."

43 "Special Screening on July 1: 'Trop Tôt, trop tard' ('Too Early / Too Late')," Arsenal –Institute for Film and Video Art, June 2012.

44 Amira Gad, "On Logical Revolts: Louis Henderson in conversation with Amira Gad," *Ibraaz* 10, June 6, 2016.

> This idea of doing a topographic study of an archival text actually came from reading an interview that Celine Condorelli conducted in 2011 with Jean-Marie Straub about the film, *Trop tôt, trop tard,*

Henderson continues,

> This film inspired *Logical Revolts* in many ways: in terms of its method of research of archival topography, the symbols and images used to evoke the idea of revolution, the space, time and distancing created through camera placement and movement.[45]

When Henderson is in Egypt, his camera is not welcome at Tahrir square and his journey takes a turn through history, by what he articulates as means of unearthing the stratigraphic image: "layering of image and text (and sound) can construct a rereading of history in the present by proposing it as a living and transmutable thing." Tahrir resistance against his camera pushes the filmmaker to feel that his collection of images "contradicts what is being told [by the images of Tahrir calling for solidarity for the revolution] and shows how Henderson is never actually close to understanding or really commenting on what surrounds him." This negative reception at Tahrir did not happen in the other locations where Henderson filmed, nor did it happen in Tahrir only to him; many have reported that after a heavy image-documentation as well as development of political events, people pointing their cameras to events in Tahrir were not tolerated by people in the square itself. Henderson concludes that he is more "inclined to believe that revolts are not necessarily logical or reasoned events and are impossible to rationalize."[46]

45
Henderson,
"On Logical Revolts."

46
Henderson,
"On Logical Revolts"
See also Ala Younis,
"Violent Relatedness,
Embeddings, Hindsight,"
Ibraaz 10, July 22, 2016.

In the light of the huge Straub/Huillet oeuvre that was for many years hard to see in its entirety, the process of encountering *Too Early/Too Late* is the foundation of this text. Among the materials that unfolded in the process was a text found by Tobias Hering in the Straubs' archive in Bologna in 2016. Hering was unable to read it in Arabic, and wrote to seek help from those who might understand it. It was a scanned article, written in Arabic, signed by Magda Wassef. Throughout the article I wasn't sure if it was originally written in Arabic: the language is good hence it doesn't sound like it's a translation. However, toward the very end of the article I noticed the mistranslation of a title of a film by Mustafa Abu Ali—if Magda wrote this in Arabic, I thought she would have had the correct name. Magda was the director of the Cairo Film Festival in 2016, was educated at the Sorbonne and headed the cinema department at the Institut du Monde Arabe for some time, so I suspected her text was originally written in French. The first part of the text is on Godard's *Ici et Ailleurs* (*Here and Elsewhere*), and his choices of scenes, mostly in relation to a line in the film on "how we did it like others, arranged the images and raised the sound/voice very high." The second part of the text was on *Fortini/Cani* and the Straubs, and she weaved their films together with Fortini's views on the Palestinian cause and anti-Semitic claims, etc. She mentioned Fortini's book *The Dogs of the Sinai* as an important mark. The title of the article was "هنا/هناك" و"هناك/هنا"، "نحن" و"جودار وستروب" ("'*Here/Elsewhere*' and '*Elsewhere/Her*e'. 'Us' and 'Godard/Straub'"),[47] and the text was split into two parts, each with three sub parts. The first subsection titles were: "Godard and subjects," "Godard and sounds and images," "Godard and the viewer," and the second: "Straub and subjects," "Straub and sounds and images," "Straub and the viewer." The last bit was on why both works are important for us and for the scenes in which they emerged, to resist the dominant norms and voices in their contexts. Now, to me, the most interesting thing in this is that Magda is credited in *Too Early/Too Late* as segment B assistant director. And that among the authors in this issue is Ahmed El Maanouni, director of *Alyam Alyam* (*Oh the days!*, 1978) which I screened at Arsenal in Berlin to compare to *Too Early/Too Late* back in May 2012.

47
Magda Wassef, "GODARD/STRAUB et la Palestine," *Cinemarabe*, no. 6 (1977).

"What is history's role in this film?" argued Jean-Claude Biette about *Too Early/Too Late* in 1982,

> It consists in employing not a tension that would be able to confront the aesthetic violence of the Straubian project, but a pressure that only sets in motion a quantifiable movement of signifieds. [...] It menaces [the people we see] and determines their path. It even goes so far as producing a sort of very unpleasing shock when we hear the signifier 'repression' at the moment that we see a police officer stopping some children from going near the camera. This means that the desire to give meaning (here, during the length of a second, and in a more constant man-

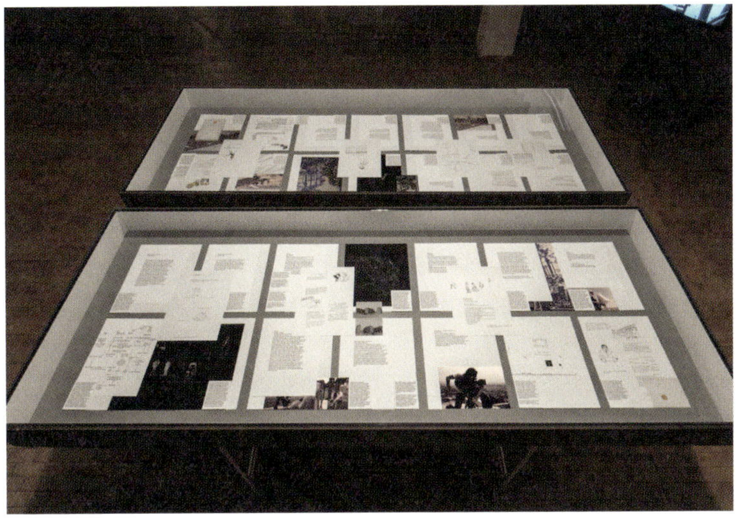

> ner by the commentary) does not manage to find any grounds for communication with the aesthetic project and, thus, the political-aesthetic tension is not constructed, but imposed.[48]

The final line in this quote brings closer the issues addressed in this text on the uneasiness of imposition that this film might communicate to some viewers. Children not permitted by a policeman to approach the camera is only one scene in a film where the majority of its scenes do not show 'oppressive' figures standing in the way of the people's interaction with the camera. The only oppressive device that might be imagined in the filming process could perhaps be the camera apparatus that the people saw filming, feared to interrupt its business, or were curious but too reluctant to interfere in. Uninformed as to what the camera was filming, their images, reactions and reluctance traveled unsolicited onto Straubs' celluloid.

As I watched *Too Early/Too Late* in Cairo, I enjoyed its scenes and the tension it created with the impatient viewers. How I wished it was in Arabic, or perhaps that the land depicted is not a place (that I think) I know.

48 Jean-Claude Biette, "Cinema Nearer to the Earth," *Cahiers du cinéma*, 1982. Translated by Ted Fendt, posted on kinoslang.blogspot.com, November 17, 2010.

Manfred Blank

Chance and the Cinematograph

[This text is a slightly modified version of a lecture given by the author on September 16, 2017, at the Akademie der Künste in Berlin as an introduction to the films *Every Revolution is a Throw of the Dice* and *Too Early/Too Late.*]

What follows is a reprise of a talk I first gave to introduce both of these films at the same location in early 1987. On my initiative, the Straubs had made the premiere of *Too Early/Too Late* a gift to *Filmkritik* on its 25th birthday and since then *Filmkritik* had in this potlatch system remained committed to the Straubs. Before we ever published anything about the film, however, we had to abandon the magazine's publication. Shortly thereafter, I dragged *Too Early/Too Late* into the program of an event at the Akademie der Künste about essay films initiated by Harun Farocki and largely sustained by former *Filmkritik* colleagues. I was driven to establish a program proposal as an apparatus of discovery: If I combined *Too Early/Too* Late with *Every Revolution is a Throw of the Dice*, edited both of these films together so to speak, they would mutually illuminate each other.

1.

If the apparatus worked, it would be unnecessary to precede the Mallarmé film with an interpretation. Decades before, both Susan Sontag and Jean-Marie Straub had made declarations against interpretation. With an interpretation, one would need, moreover, if I may use the language of the secret service, to break the poem's code, and minds more refined than mine have already failed at that. I would merely claim—and this is not only a mere hunch—that both films have more to do with one another than one might expect from two films by the same filmmaker. I take the Mallarmé film for a heuristic model.

But I would like to begin with an anecdote. The Straubs have told a lot about the story behind *Too Early/Too Late*, most elaborately and most illuminatingly in an interview with Hans Hurch for the Viennese magazine *Falter*. Remarks about the Mallarmé film are sparser and more cryptic. In 1955, Jacques Rivette shot his first short film, the approximately thirty-minute long *Le coup du berger* (*Fool's Mate*). During the first half of the opening titles, we see two

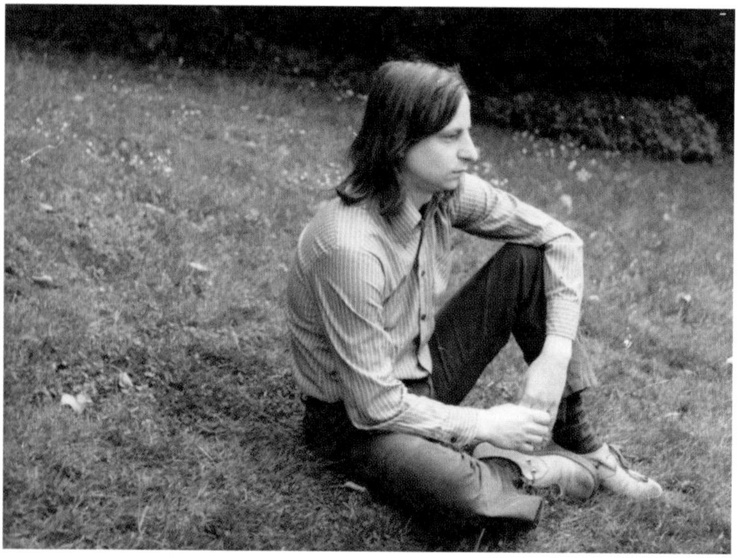

hands and a chessboard playing out the so-called "Scholar's Mate" or "Shepherd's Mate," which would be the correct translation of the title. This very short series of moves comes out of the playbook for absolute beginners—only very inexperienced players allow themselves to be duped by it. The film follows the intrigue of a young wife and her lover, who as cheaters are absolute beginners. The cheated husband checkmates them with a surprising, well-planned move. The title sequence is therefore *cum grano salis* a metaphor for the entire film. At the same time, the metaphorical image is also reminiscent of a statement Jean-Marie has often made: In a certain way, filmmaking is like playing chess. And the film's title refers to that famous saying by the one, who Rivette calls "the master" in his film portrait, Jean Renoir, that all of his adepts took to heart: filmmaking is about pulling a job with friends. He used the word "*coup*."

The only time in his life Jean-Marie worked as assistant director was on *Le coup du berger* when he was twenty-two years old. The same year, he probably also watched Bresson in Lyon during the making of *Un condamné à mort s'est échappé* and Renoir in Paris on *French Cancan*, but those were merely brief, friendly visits. During production, the then-twenty-seven-year-old Jacques Rivette—Jean-Marie told me—constantly recited Mallarmé's poem, which he knew by heart. With a certain degree of certainty, we can therefore conclude that this is where the nucleus of the Straubs' Mallarmé film lies, possibly even the nucleus of the Straubs' and Rivette's filmmaking. And, more boldly, that for all three of them, the poem is a metaphor for filmmaking itself.

For many, *Le coup du berger* is the first film of the Nouvelle Vague because it is so entirely an inside job, a *coup* following Renoir's dictum. The film's mastermind, the cuckolded husband who dupes the young cheating pair and presents them in turn his mistress wearing the *corpus delicti*, the young cheater's fur coat, is played by then-editor-in-chief and co-founder of *Cahiers du cinéma*, Jacques Doniol-Valcroze. Chabrol was the film's production manager and Truffaut, Godard, and Rivette himself appear in the final sequence as party guests. We have here nearly all of the pupil's of the charismatic, leftist Catholic André Bazin, those whom he named "young Turks" and esteemed as experts—of American films above all. The Straubs thus appear—not only through their lifelong friendship with Rivette, with whom they exchanged film tips, directors of photography, producers, and crew—from their youth onward as filmmakers marked by the ideas, preferences, and strategies of the Nouvelle Vague—contrary to the popular perception of them as German filmmakers whose native language is French.

2.

Too Early/Too Late has been designated the Straubs' first documentary film. They have begrudgingly accepted this. There are no characters in the film that are actors, but they said the landscapes are like characters. This is also true of the *Cinematographic Scene* film, where Günter Peter Straschek reads a letter by Schoenberg and of *Fortini/Cani*, in which Franco Fortini reads from his own book. But this genre classification does not bring us any further with the Straubs' films. Furthermore, Jean-Marie has correctly pointed out that every so-called fiction film is a documentary about its actors. And I wonder, is not every film a documentation even when it is staged and is not every document a staging? When I first gave this lecture, for contemporary examples I referred to Bernd Eichinger's productions as documentations of desperate attempts to spend lots of money and Klaus Wildenhahn's participatory observations as the staging of undeserved trust. Today everyone can look for corresponding examples.

What is to be seen in *Too Early/Too Late*? What is to be heard?

The film's individual elements as well as what the images and the sounds concern are disparate. Almost at random, I will list a few that are noticeable on first glance, on a first listen. A film in two parts. The first is based on a segment of a letter from Engels to Kautsky, which in turn has two or perhaps even three different parts—an initial, abstract exposition of the French Revolution followed by the enumeration of places, whose social conditions are supported with figures and, at the end, another short theoretical chapter. The second part is based on excerpts from the book *Class Conflict in Egypt 1945–1970* by two Egyptian authors working under the pseudonym Mahmoud Hussein.

Very different kinds of shots: made with a telephoto lens, with a wide-angle lens; tracking shots, static shots, occasional pans back and forth. Black leader. Excerpts from an old newsreel. Two entirely different texts: one historical and one (at the time the film was made) contemporary. A female and a male narrator. Shots in which we can hear the sound of the moving air and ones that are full of human and animal voices. Again and again, there is a kind of extension at the beginning and end of the shots and then camera movements cut very short. There is the postcard-like view from the Sacré-Coeur and shots that—off-centered, Johan van der Keuken would say—only show a small patch of vegetation and lots of sky. (This is only good for a first viewing because the visual system in the work of the Straub-enthusiast van der Keuken is entirely different from the work of the Straubs themselves). The first part comes with an austere text, where in some passages, only figures that are not representative are listed and whose meaning is hard to grasp. The second part has a text written like journalism, with something curiously unclear in the construction of the sentences and whose transitions remain vague, a vocabulary like something out of the program of a political party.

A few critics as well as viewers and friends with whom one speaks grumble that the texts in this film and many

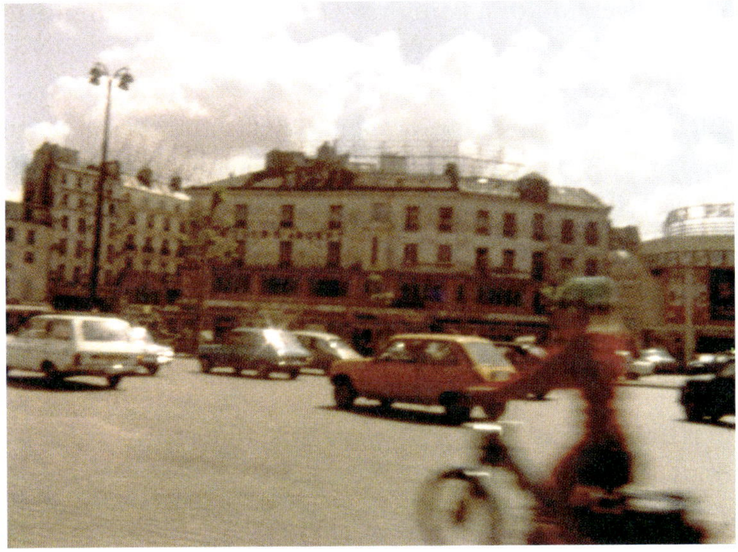

others by the Straubs are ugly. To my taste, this is a little bit true of the Egyptian part. But anyone who knows the Straubs a little understands that there is no error in taste here. Jean-Marie works with texts because he claims he himself is unable to write. He takes what he likes from the texts. More precisely, he uses them for his own purposes. His attitude toward them is not that of a servant of noble literature, but, as he once said with a wink, that of a censor. That may be an exaggeration but it hits the nail on the head. And it shows that, even if both occasionally take hold of the incunabula of world literature, the quality of the texts is not of primary importance.

We find shots in *Too Early/Too Late* whose entire duration is filled by the text and ones in which only one or even no words come.

4.

A shot.

It is the first one in the film after the titles. Therefore the first in the French part of this two-part film. The second part shows cities and landscapes in Egypt. In the script, the shot is called, "La Place de la Bastille en carrousel." This describes the effect better than the German word *Kreisfahrt* ("arc shot"). It is a relatively fast tracking shot, filmed out of the right, passenger side door of a car. The French term refers to dizziness, colors flying by, and the impression of a kaleidoscopic effect—to something strange. Vehicles that drive onto the roundabout seem to be pulled in—an impression emerging from the non-parallel movements of camera and objects and through the short focal length with which this is recorded—and then in the end seemingly blown away. Vertical lines, corners of buildings, and the road are distorted, including a building that houses a Banque de France.

Constant returning, *all for nothing,* is not what the shot says—not futility, but grotesquery. This is surprising at first sight because it in no way corresponds to preconceptions about Straubian images.

The shot of the historical site—in the sense that the one who frames is taking a position on what he shoots—is blasphemous. The view is not of the Place de la Bastille monument, the spirit of liberty on the column. It is behind the camera's back. The monument is, moreover, only indirectly related to the *Grande Révolution* of 1789. It was built in memory of the 1830 July Revolution and later dedicated to the Revolution of 1848. Although a "Spirit of Liberty" stands on top of the column, the monument has less to do with liberty, equality, and brotherhood as with the "*enrichissez-vous*" ("enrich yourselves") of the *Juste milieu.*

That the Place de la Bastille is actually the subject here does not appear essential. One does not even need to know it.

5.

Another shot.

The first shot without voice-over comes in the final third of the film, in the Egyptian part. Four more follow.

This looks like a break from the principle of the film, which one could concisely characterize as: two texts as a guidebook for two different countries. The silence in the voice-over can however easily be explained on an abstract level: there are sites to see that the text does not name, but that it sweepingly implicates. The travelers who are following their guide have made a discovery without it.

But the first shot without voice-over is striking for an entirely different reason. It is the longest one in the entire film, 10 ½ minutes, the length of an entire 120 meter roll—if there had only been longer 16mm rolls, the shot would likely have been even longer.

Upon first glance—when I say *glance*, I am including the ears—the shot might look like the counterpart to the one just described: no circle, no carousel, a forward tracking shot. However, just as little as the shot at the Place de la Bastille deals with circularity in the sense of futility, is it here a matter of *moving forward:* the future, optimism. The shot's gesture—and by that I mean a combination of framing, movement, camera position, and duration—does not permit it. The shot makes a gesture toward seizing the land, and I do not mean the driving of a tank or a low-flying helicopter—camera positions are never so clear. Seizing the land in the sense of an expedition—the Straubs have pointed out that cartographers came to Egypt with Bonaparte's military expedition—which is also a bracket holding both parts together. The French military cartographers drew up the still reliable maps of the Egyptian provinces. The Straubian expedition is therefore an echo of this earlier one. They actually used the old French maps while location scouting. Seizing the land in the sense of conquering it. Even the disempowerment of the British, foreigners, and aristocrats did not free this land.

Also relevant is that later in the shot, before the voice-over ends, we can hear in the distance, but loudly, a donkey braying; that during the entire forward tracking shot we hear the motor of the small bus through the front windshield of which the shot was made; and that every time a tree or group of trees is passed, an excited concert of birds can be heard. I think that the Straubs did not seek these out but found them. That they were gifted them. This brings us to the concept of the cinematograph.

The fourth shot in the film shows the sign for the town of Tréogan. We are then back in the first part, the French part. We are in Brittany. The shot is connected with the previous one: a pan ending on a street, by a meaningful correct/false sound edit. A car drives out of the shot; we can still hear the sound of the vehicle as it moves away.

After the cut, we hear a car coming closer that drives past the sign and into the distance of the image. Like two opening shots in a fiction film—even if the cars are of course not identical. A shack with advertisements and a bush in front of it can be seen behind the sign. Half of the image is made up of the street and its vanishing line. During the previous shot, we hear: "Tréogan: ten well-off families, ten impoverished, ten beggarly." Bearing in mind the false introductory sound edit, with this shot—and this is the first town that is shown—the film misleads us. It acts as if it wants to represent continuity, "two hundred years ago, this town was already poor and it still is, nothing has changed," as if the film wanted to confirm a historical fact in a text with an image. This shot is what Godard in his film *Week-end* calls *faux*tography, *faux* as in false.

If the film permits a doubling in this shot (the text talks about poverty and we see an image that upon first glance seems to mean "poverty"), it permits, especially in the first part, a contrast and stays true to a dialectical gesture so important to the Straubs: to allow the counterpart to appear within what is shown and what is said. This contrast entails that given the amount of towns listed whose inhabitants were once beggars, paupers, and people living on the edge of poverty, the series of pans over green fields and pastures imposes a consideration of how fruitful this land nevertheless is, and yet in which the majority of people suffer from hunger.

Images in films may only exist to put flesh on the bones of the text. The language gives the idea and the image brings the accompanying music. In the Straubs' films, the state of affairs is, at least occasionally, exactly the opposite.

7.

Two shots from the second part.

Twice while the Egyptian central government in the 19th century is being discussed, we see a shot of the citadel in Cairo, the same static shot twice. From an extreme, wide, low-angle—I'm avoiding the word "fish-eye" perspective, because it would make this all too cute—we see a piece of wall at the very bottom of the frame and small towers on the left and right, distorted by the perspective; overhead, filling up most of the image, the white of the sky.

There is an analogy between image and text here. The text's often loudly enunciated diction, especially in the Egyptian part—significantly not so distinct here—finds its equivalent in the idea of an image. It is the idea of an image gravitating toward a pictogram. Straub was fully aware how *un-Straubian* this perspective and this frame are. He showed it to me, grinning, when he had set up the camera. "Looks a little like something out of Eisenstein," I said. "Sometimes he has to do the opposite of what he likes," said Danièle. This is a kind of shot that does not allow an *impression*, Godard would have said, but an *expression*. This image is an expression, the expression of an attitude of the person who made it. The shots showing the Cairo Citadel are an expression of disdain. Not disdainful images, but images for disdain.

8.

After all of these preliminaries, now to the shot I have been driving at. It can be seen upstairs in the exhibition, in the middle of the room, as if it were its focal point, its centerpiece.[1] *Un coup de dés jamais n'abolira le hasard.* A throw of the dice will never abolish chance.

1
Editors' note: Manfred Blank refers here to the exhibition "Tell it to the Stones" at the Akademie der Künste, on display when he was delivering this talk in the auditorium of the same building.

A factory gate, the text is speaking about a revolution in the year 1919, the word "worker" is heard for the first time. We might recognize such a connection and such an image. The filmmakers, who were not authorized to go into the factory because capitalism hides work and wants to make it invisible, wanted to meet the workers at a spot where they were still workers and only just beginning to become private individuals again, in front of the factory gate, in order to see a little bit of the work, the *production relations*, perhaps in the workers' faces or their gestures. And here is the site at which visible altercations occur during factory occupations and where statements are delivered during strikes.

Also in *Too Early/Too Late*, this shot, *sortie d'usine*, is not free of some of that hypothetical revolutionary pathos even if it was filmed in 1981 at a time when nobody was filming this kind of thing any longer, even if through the distance from which the people are filmed and the length of the shot something distinctive and unique is obtained.

Faire la revolution, reads one of the maxims in the script of the film *Chronicle of Anna Magdalena Bach, c'est aussi remettre en place des choses très anciennes mais oubliées*. This is a quote by Charles Péguy: Making a revolution is also putting very ancient, but forgotten things back in place.

Straub/Huillet are traditionalists, so much so that they—accepting how unfashionable this connotation has become—mean something far older: the invention of cinematography, of the cinematograph. The Lumières' factory gate in Lyon, filmed at the end of the working day with the newly screwed together cinematograph belongs, along with *Arrival of a Train at La Ciotat* and *Déjeuner du bébé*, to the archetypes of cinema. It is not merely being quoted here. The Straubs are positioning themselves in the frequently forgotten tradition of the Lumières' cinematographic images. While these were at first home movies of the employer's family, soon camera operators were sent out into the world with the new device in order to make panoramas and moving views for fair stands and diverse programs in newly opened movie theaters. The Lumières themselves were thinking of widespread uses for the new recording and playback device for scientific purposes. In the final years of the 19th century, a massive amount of first cinematographic pieces emerged almost everywhere in the known world.

When I was commissioned in 1993 on the occasion of Jean-Marie's 60th birthday to make two short documentaries for a Straub/Huillet evening on ARTE, the French interviewees were unanimous in saying that: *the Straubs are going back to the cinematograph*. In my little film, Helmut Färber stated this in detail in German, but we were unable to reach the ordinary German arts and leisure bureaucrat. When I was invited on local Berlin radio in 2003 for a short interview for Jean-Marie's 70th birthday and explained this as an essential characteristic of the Straubs' work, the moderator looked at me pitifully, thinking I had nothing more to say than the tautology *cinema is cinema* and was therefore using the quaint term "cinematograph."

She could not grasp that I was talking about something very specific.

For the Straubs, it goes without question that it is meaningful to travel around with a camera and sound recorder and sometimes to record events with fervor and wrath; that by watching these moving images it may be possible to find out something that we could not otherwise find out. How a horse gallops, for instance. That the heart of filmmaking lies in the cinematograph, an instrument for studying the world. This approach is programmatic for an essential aspect of *Too Early/Too Late* and for the Straubs' cinema in general.

9.

But what does any of this have to do with the Mallarmé film and to what degree does the Mallarmé film provide a key to *Too Early/Too Late*?

During my lecture in 1987, I made myself into a reciter, reading a number of lines from the poem aloud without commentary, complete with the German translation that Danièle, Jean-Marie, Andrea Spingler, Helmut Färber, and I had prepared during the shooting in Paris. (This translation can be seen upstairs in the exhibition as a subtitle list.) Mallarmé's poem, in which, on the one hand, a logical system is constructed through the elaborate typography and in which pure musical language reigns on the other, did not become easier to understand through my recitation. Therefore I would now like to attempt a short paraphrase of the play's in fact hardly important *plot*: in a precarious and hopeless situation (*du fond d'un naufrage*—from a shipwreck's deck) characterized hermetically and with numerous nautical metaphors, a man—called *maître* and *vieillard* (old man), formerly ship's captain, among other things—attempts, in a titanic effort, to throw a particular number that would allow him to free himself and others from this situation and for them to escape. The endeavor cannot guarantee success however. He remains ultimately surrendered to chance.

The final line of the poem, *Toute pensée émet un Coup de Dés* (*Every Thought emits a Throw of Dice*)—a straightforward line, so to speak—makes it clear that each and every mental activity is meant, in other words: the mastery of life itself, which includes the composition of poetry and the shooting of films, as Rivette probably once meant by his recitation. It is relatively easy and obviously appropriate to relate this titanic struggle around "l'unique nombre qui ne peut pas être un autre—the one number that cannot be another" to Mallarmé's thirty year wrestling with this, his final poem. The Straubs do not simply record Rivette's recitation again. They place it in a very Straubian context. Their Mallarmé film is called *Toute révolution est un coup de dés*—Every Revolution is a Throw of the Dice. There is therefore a further connection to *Too Early/Too Late*. The theoretical passages of the Engels letter (at the beginning and end of the first part) are about how a revolution is by no means to be taken for granted, but depends on concrete historical facts and ultimately on chance.

The title of the Mallarmé film is a quotation; a line that the historian Michelet wrote decades before the Commune and decades before the development of the Mallarmé poem, which was published for the first time in 1897 shortly before Mallarmé's death. The Straubs sat us, the reciters, in a semicircle on the burial mound in Père Lachaise cemetery that covers the remains of the 147 fighters of the 1871 Commune who were shot here and rises before the so-called *Mur des fédérés*, the monument for the 30,000 who died during the Commune and over which the film's opening pan sweeps.

The quotation-title is an answer to or a variation on the poem's final line, Every Thought emits a Throw of Dice. It is the third element of the montage that makes up the film: the quotation-title, the site of the events, and the text of the poem. Mallarmé was not exactly a political man, but it is doubtless that he witnessed, not in Père Lachaise, but in his apartment near Gare St. Lazare, the Commune and the struggles. And it is irrelevant whether he meant the Commune as well with this poem. Nothing is meant in poetry, metaphors and the music of language reign.

Jean-Marie often said that with every film he and Danièle tried to go one step further. That sounds very abstract and could easily be written off as a vague, conceited comment. And yet it is probably true. In the 1977 Mallarmé short film, there is a new concept for them that grew in importance over time. On the slant of the burial mound in Père Lachaise, all of the reciters were filmed from almost the same camera position, which their arrangement of course made possible. We find this again in a few of the "crowd scenes" in *From the Cloud to the Resistance*, filmed one year later, it nearly becomes a rule in the multi-person spectacle *Class Relations*, and is more or less an iron law from the "theater film," meaning from *Empedocles*, onward. For this to work, one must calculate the positions of the actors exactly. One must play chess, says Jean-Marie, meaning to anticipate the consequences of a decision far ahead. Such rigorous pre-planning, determination, and commitment exists in other areas than the camera position, and this is how the Straubs gained a reputation as workaholics, control freaks, and fanatics for precision. Even in 1974, Rainer Gansera joked in *Filmkritik*, "no false move, Moses and Aaron."

As I was the Straubs' assistant for the first time in 1978 and, among other things, brought the exposed film stock to the lab in Rome every two or three nights and picked up the work print that we watched the following evening in a cinema near the shooting location, I noticed that the production was simultaneously poor and rich. The catering and hotels were rather poor, all of the assistants were working for free, the department heads had accepted very low wages because they liked the Straubs, and the lead actors were non-professionals and worked on an expense basis. But the quantity of exposed and printed footage was a pure luxury. The Straubs shot a minimum of at least twenty, usually thirty, and often more than forty takes per shot. And when we saw the dailies, it became clear that this was not because something had gone wrong technically or the actors had made a lot of mistakes. That was taken care of during the technical tests and rehearsals.

When we made a short trip around France in 1980 for the first part of *Too Early/Too Late*, Danièle decided on June as the production period because at that time in northern France, where we were mainly moving around, there was little rain but lots of wind and therefore changing clouds to deal with, meaning both textured skies and frequent changes of light. Only so-called landscape shots were planned, lots of static shots and a few pans, which for an artful camera operator like Willy Lubtchansky did not present any technical problems. But we shot two to three shots a day over a time period of nearly an entire month. A crew working on a TV production might have received ten days for this task. We would wait and wait and we would shoot and shoot, although we lost no shooting days due to the weather or technical problems.

For both films, more or less all of the dailies were good technically and aesthetically speaking. Since this luxurious use of film stock and time—which as you know is also money—was not about the perfection of the results, the Straubs must have had something else in mind with the many slates and the waiting. Looking at our heuristic model, the Mallarmé film, it becomes clear what this is. They were waiting for an unexpected, unique moment. They wanted to provoke something unplanned, they wanted to let something happen, which might happen entirely independent from their intentions and that had nothing to do with prefabricated meanings. They made a calculation. But not in order to control something. They wanted the appearance of "the one number that cannot be another." They pursued the calculation of chance. They wanted to go back to conditions in which the film images become documents again, like in 1895 at the factory gate in Lyon; not propaganda, not language, not a concept, but a document.

This is not about workaholics being redeemed because they strive with all their might. This is about the mercy of "kairos–καιρό"ς, of the right moment, neither too early nor too late. This is about receiving "a gift" in humility. That is a word that Jean-Marie always used in this context, "gift."

11.

It has been said that the text in *Too Early/Too Late* is a pretext—a pretext to travel to the locations it speaks about. To travel to them and to record what is happening there.

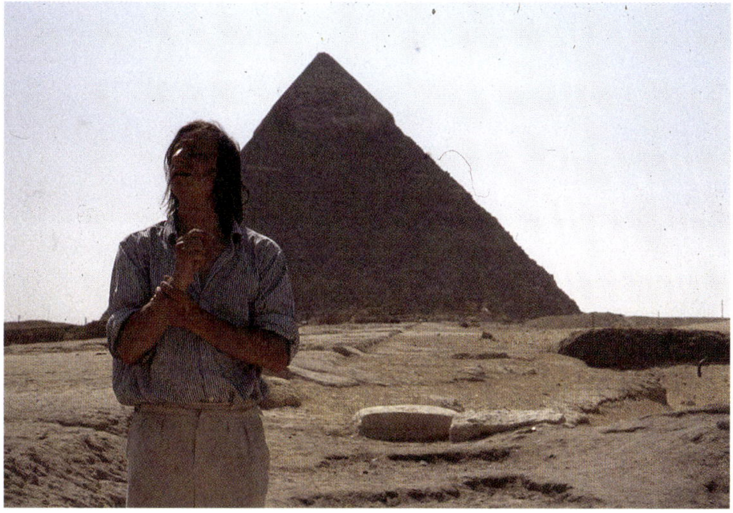

Or with the help of recordings, to measure the facts in these locations. Actually, a little what a cartographer who surveys does and who from the sum of his measurements creates an image of a landscape, a map.

Now, a sound recorder and a camera do not measure meters, height, etc. Maybe one could say that both instruments are carried to these areas in order to consider what is alive there. Alive in the people, the plants, and the animals, and this series has no hierarchy. In dramatic moments, interviews, discussions, and press conferences, Straub often refered in this context to Rosa Luxemburg: "For Rosa Luxemburg, the fate of an insect fighting in some corner for its life without mankind noticing was just as important as the fate and the future of the revolution in which she believed."

A suggestion as to how he would like the film to be watched and listened to; and it is a principle that one should perhaps follow in life.

Translated from German by Ted Fendt.

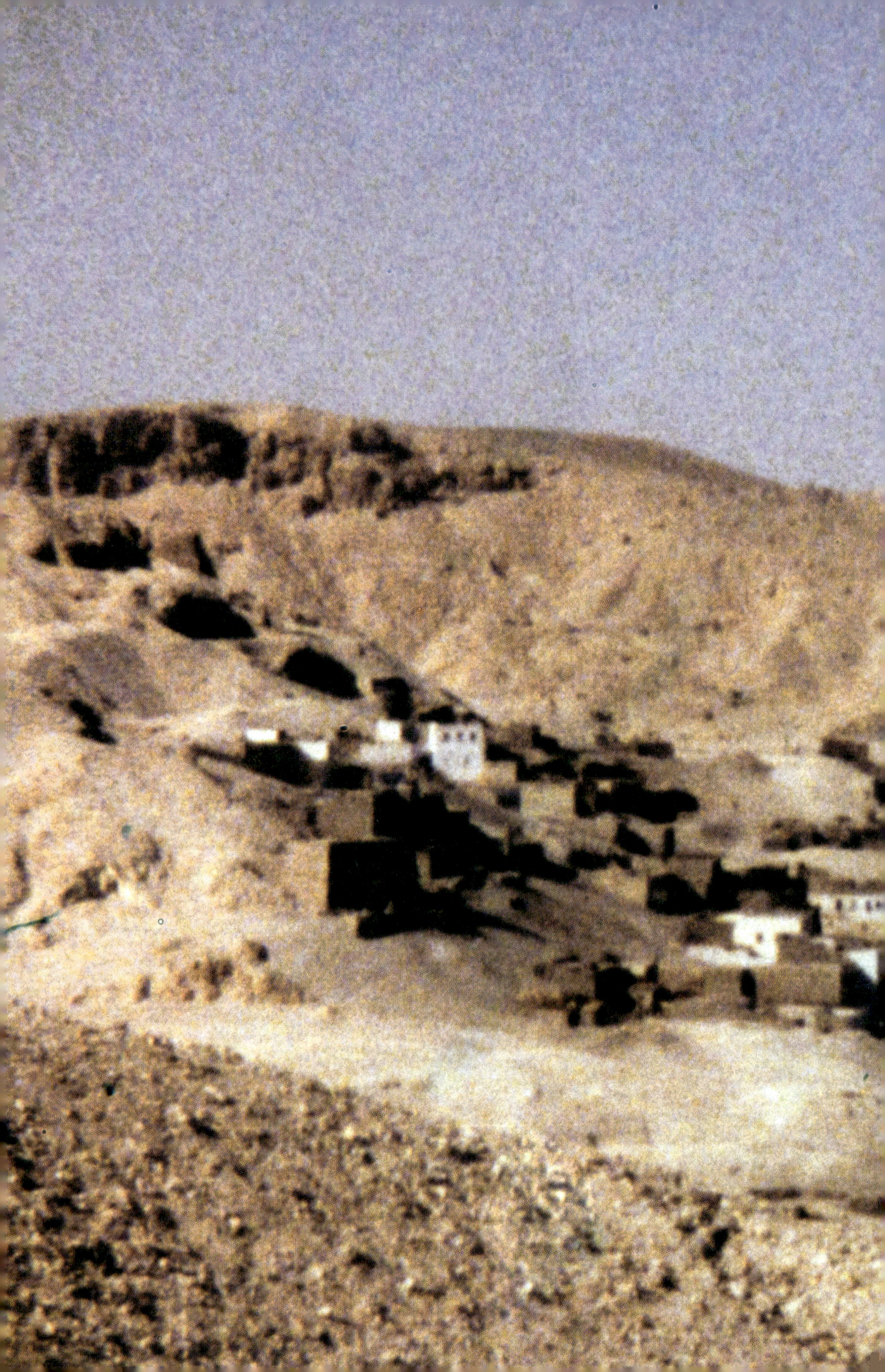

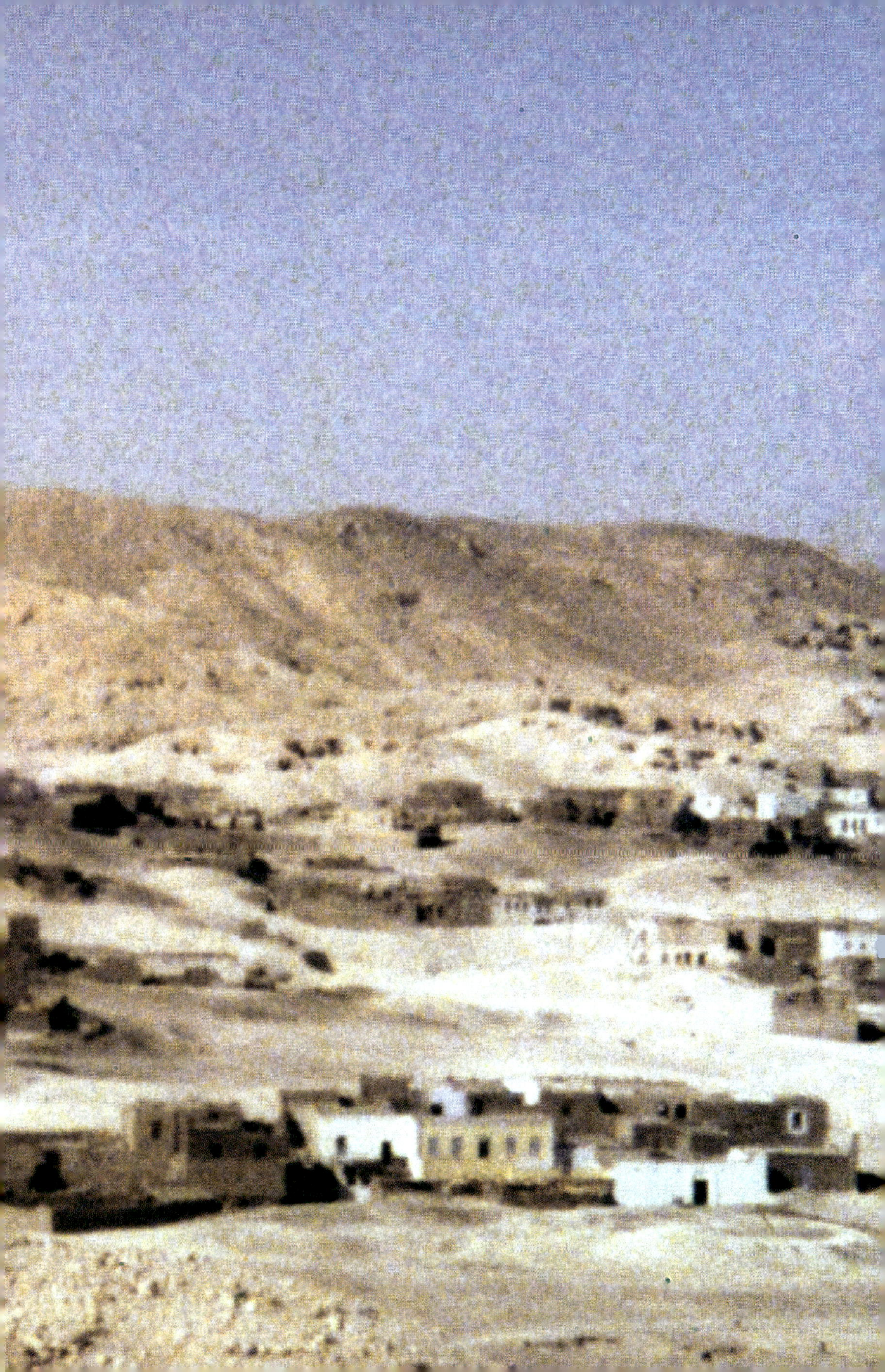

Mikhail Lylov, Elke Marhöfer, Jean-Marie Straub

A THOUSAND CLIFFS

[The following text is an edited transcription of a conversation that Elke Marhöfer and Mikhail Lylov had with Jean-Marie Straub on three consecutive days in February 2013. It was originally published in German and English in: Tobias Hering, ed. *Der Standpunkt der Aufnahme – Point of View* (Berlin: Archive Books, 2014). It is printed here slightly revised.]

Elke Marhöfer: This question deals with a model that Jacques Rancière outlined in relation to your films, namely the shift from a dialectical *dispositif* toward a lyrical *dispositif* after *Dalla nube alla resistenza,* the film you made in 1978.[1] In Rancière's view, the earlier, dialectical *dispositif* presents a form of "workers' communism" that centers on a model of disagreement and disassociation. On the other hand, the lyrical *dispositif* is a type of "peasant communism" based upon agreement and affirmation. How would you describe your and Danièle's films in relation to this concept of peasant communism? I'm referring here to *Trop tôt, trop tard, Dalla nube alla resistenza*, and *Operai, contadini.*[2]

Jean-Marie Straub: But that's not me at all. Rancière is Rancière. I can't comment on Rancière. I don't even quite understand what he means. What am I to say about it? That Rancière got it right? About something, which for me is quite abstract. Perhaps that is concrete for him, though I ought to read his book, or read it again. I can't make out what all that is supposed to mean. I don't make a film to illustrate or to represent "peasant communism." Besides, *Operai, contadini* is not only about peasant communism. It is also a love story between Ventura and the woman. A love story based upon mutual respect. These are people that built a community after the war. They tried to live their lives out together, and then afterwards this community is destroyed from without, for that's when McCarthy[3] comes along, and after McCarthy comes the Italian Christian Democratic party and it colludes with the Americans to such an extent that they even plan assassinations in cahoots with the CIA for the sole purpose of preventing them

1 EM refers to a line of thought elaborated by Jacques Rancière during a public interview with Philippe Lafosse following a screening of *Dalla nube alla resistenza* and *Operai, contadini* at Cinéma Jean Vigo in Nice. A transcription of the discussion translated by Ted Fendt has been published on mubi.com/notebook

2 *Too Early / Too Late*, 1980/81, *From the Cloud to the Resistance*, 1978, and *Workers, Peasants*, 2000. In this conversation, films are henceforth refered to by their original titles.

3 Joseph McCarthy (1908–1957), American politician from whom the "McCarthy era" took its name, instigated an anti-communist campaign in the U.S.A. in the early 1950s that stretched several years, developing into a nationwide phase of repression, character assassination and occupational bans.

from working together with the Italian Communist party.

EM: I agree with you insofar as Rancière's model is too abstract in its binarism, but I find it helpful to clarify the point when you began focusing on "peasant lifestyles." And when one examines the film *Trop tôt, trop tard,* the historical text, and also the images from present-day France, one senses nonetheless a palpable interest in this way of life.

JMS: Those numbers in the film didn't come from me but are taken from the *Cahiers de Doléances,*[4] drawn up before the French Revolution. Engels makes use of them, and I go there and drive around in search of sites, places. I search for what you refer to as the "point of view of the take,"[5] in light of this information, these figures. That's the French section of the film. In the Egyptian section, it's no longer about figures but again about specific locations where rebellions broke out. I don't know what I should comment about that. Were I able to pass comment on that, I wouldn't have made the film. I made that film precisely because I was unable to talk about "peasant communism." In *Operai, contadini* the word communism is never once uttered.

EM: I find it interesting, however, to describe Danièle's and your approach by using the word "communism." Your films are characterized by an affirmation of equivalence among the elements, be it text, the wind, birds, crickets, the people who recite the text. Everything exists as though in an equally significant form. Everything exists: snow, ice, stars, trucks, petrol, cheese making. What significance does this community you've just described have for you? Why did it interest you and Danièle?

JMS: I could answer cynically, like Buñuel who said he interested himself in insects too. That sounds a little disparaging, but a film is no model. A film is woven from feelings, stories, and experiences. That which is transmitted by texts, not written by Danièle and me, but by others, doesn't in any way impede; if

4
The *Cahiers de Doléanaces* (List of Grievances), a directive of the Ancien Régime in France, were lists of grievances, criticisms, and pleas from all classes in society recorded in a register that deputies regularly had to present to the king.

5
Jean-Marie Straub refers here to the title of the book (then in-progress) for which the interview was conducted, *Der Standpunkt der Aufnahme,* literally: the standpoint of the take, or the point where one places the camera.

anything, quite the opposite, what emerges is yet another layer for the fiction. The second section of *Operai, contadini* is the story of what could almost be described as a lynching. The storyteller is almost lynched. And then there's the other side of the story, that is the love story with Ventura and that is then linked to the community. It's a love story that could only happen in a community, and for that reason is at once concrete and beautiful. But that has nothing to do with peasantry as such.

EM: For me, *Trop tôt, trop tard* is a particularly important film, more so than *Operai, contadini,* in that it engages with the landscape and brings it to the fore as a protagonist.

JMS: Someone once referred to that as "closeness and distance." Hence it's interesting that you've focused on these two films. The Egyptian part particularly, and also the French part, really deals with distance—the distance of numbers. Let's call that landscape, or for all I care, geology—a geological theater of figures. By way of contrast, in the film set in Italy [*Operai, contadini*] we are no longer dealing with the distant but with the near. But that is connected to the work that we've tried to undertake—to constantly succeed in doing the opposite of what we had previously done, or in presenting an other side to the story. So as to contradict, or so as to do the opposite. But who is to say that one or the other is more important? I wouldn't know on what grounds. One could also say, somewhat cynically: the theater of that which you're talking about, the theatrical space. The fact that one ends up engaging with the landscape, or even geology, is merely the consequence of that. Or the origin of it, who knows.

EM: How would you then describe the space in *Trop tôt, trop tard*?

JMS: I don't know if I can describe it; only those who have nothing to do with it can do that. Someone on the outside makes a description, and I am on the inside. A film is something that works with space, and if a film really exists, the space should be toiled in such a way that one reaches time with it. That is all, there's nothing more I can add. It would be a lot more interesting were you to write what you have felt and experienced. Whatever I have to say on the subject is irrelevant. What I have to say is embedded in the subject matter, not in words that one later finds to chatter about it. It becomes interesting when an outsider does it. It would then be based upon experiences and observations he had had with the films, that come from the films but are yet mixed with his personal experiences. That's when it becomes interesting.

EM: What first strikes me as important in the film is the equivalence of that which you refer to as theatrical space and I call landscape, of the soundscape and the unfolding accounts. Every single instant is treated equally and therein I see an equal status for the narrative in relation to, for example, the physical space itself and all that exists.

JMS: One must search and search until one finds what you refer to as the "point of view," and then the subject matter comes into being. In the same way as when one wants to film a village, one needs to know the spot from where to do that. This phrase, "the viewpoint of the take," bothered me. The take is the result, and the viewpoint is what one searches for in order to achieve that result. And that involves driving around the village a lot, going up and then going down until one finds that spot from where one can simply see something. Where one sees something. It's important to repeat that. And then one discovers that in a village the search often ends where the water tower stands, for needless to say the water tower's location isn't arbitrary. It is placed exactly on that spot where water can be fed to the entire locality. And the standpoint from where the locality can be supplied with water just also happens to be the filmmaker's standpoint, who is likewise attempting to show an entirety. Hence the take of a village then operates like an irrigation system. And Brecht would say, "What one films then belongs to the irrigators." What one reveals belongs to the irrigators; the world belongs to the irrigators. But that is humbug.

EM: You not only show a village, you also show everything that surrounds the village, its setting.

JMS: One doesn't just irrigate a locality, one irrigates the earth.

EM: And the earth is one of these elements in your films. Is there a form of "film ecology"?

JMS: I don't know what ecology means. I know what *logia* means; that's the word *logos* and *oikos* is the word for household. Ha! *Oikos* is the economy, hence the man, the manager, the house management. That comes from the Greek and there's no getting around that. I would prefer to say, "Oh earth, my cradle."

EM: That lyrical response opens up another space than the word "ecology." Well then, what does "the earth as cradle" mean?

JMS: Now we're coming to the crux of the matter. It means nothing more than what it says, "Oh earth, my cradle." Just as it is with a film—it is in and of itself enough. I don't see why one should improve upon that by means of a description or an explanation.

EM: In *Trop tôt, trop tard* the French countryside comes across as singularly strange, because it has been so completely emptied.

JMS: That was obvious to us because we just didn't simply drive there and start shooting immediately but rather we traveled back and forth repeatedly so that we could draw closer to that which we wanted to film. We were well aware that in France, from the standpoint that we required, there wouldn't be a lot of human activity to be seen or to be heard. Firstly, because the standpoint is at a distance, and secondly, because of the fact that France has just become what it has become. Nonetheless one senses that the countryside was once worked and that it was worked intensively, even though it seems so deserted now. Whether that was the case in Egypt? One could say that it is the opposite. But that is just being rhetorical. Opposite, in the sense that every single patch of land close to the Nile has been cultivated. But once the fertile Nile valley ends and the desert begins, all life ceases and it is even more drastic. And there is a point that could almost be a common denominator for both films, although they initially might appear as quite contradictory. In *Operai, contadini* we are right in the middle, in the middle of what's happening and the people are in the foreground.

EM: *Trop tôt, trop tard* and *Operai, contadini* are almost ethnographical.

JMS: Yes, I hope so. That is also what I attempted to sneak in before, when I mentioned Buñuel and the insects. He once said, "I'm simply filming these people in the way I would film insects." As long as we can assume it has nothing to do with scorn or with indifference, then it is a worthwhile undertaking.

EM: Ousmane Sembène said something along those lines to Jean Rouch, "You film us as though we were insects." I didn't know that Buñuel quotation, but he put it in identical terms.

JMS: Ousmane said that in reference to Jean Rouch's films?

EM: Yes.

JMS: And did he regret or complain about that?

EM: Sembène meant it as a reproach.

JMS: Oh yes, he meant it as a reproach. But if they hadn't been filmed like insects, then how would they have been filmed...? Like clowns? Like a Punch and Judy show?

EM: But Buñuel's film *Las Hurdes* [*Land Without Bread*] is precisely a critique of ethnological films and the spectators' expectations. I don't for one second believe he wants to film the village and its inhabitants like insects.

JMS: He didn't say that in reference to *Las Hurdes*. He made that statement much later about the films he shot in Mexico and in France. And he made that comment in relation to the bourgeoisie that he filmed, and not about the people in *Las Hurdes*.

EM: Why do you want to ascribe this quotation to your films? Why even do you want to be cynical and aloof?

JMS: That which comes to pass between the workers and the peasants, for example, is very tough. There is a chasm. And the first third of the film deals with this chasm. And one really can't blame either side, they are equally torn asunder—Neguib! (*He calls his cat.*) He makes an appearance in *Trop tôt, trop tard*, toward the end.

EM: Who, the cat?

JMS: Yes, yes, he sits on the bed and telephones. He is sick and will soon die. And his name is Neguib.[6]

6 Mohammed Neguib (1901–1984), prominent figure in the Egyptian "23 July Revolution" (1952) as well as the nation's first president after the proclamation of the republic on 18 June 1953.

EM: There is also an ambiguity in *Dalla nube alla resistenza*, an intermediate state between the mystical and the historical, between the human and the animal, between man and woman. There is a wolf that was a human, and a man who was a woman. What lies behind the interest to tone down these fundamental distinctions? In other words, to be able to shift back and forth between these powerful distinctions, and also to modify them.

JMS: That has to do with mythology, as it is called.

EM: Yes, what is nonetheless important is that in mythology these divisions, which are of such importance to us nowadays, are not so common. And I would like to know what it was that sparked your and Danièle's interest in the fact that these divisions are not so common.

JMS: You mean that the wolf was of no less interest to us than the couple who prattle on so much about his death? That's substantial for the film.

EM: And that a man can be a woman. Exactly, that is substantial. And what is the reason to bring these occurrences to the fore?

JMS: I'm not versed in mythology. While Danièle was familiar with the subject, I was completely ignorant. I was attracted to these stories just because they were comical, and nothing else. And mostly comical stories by the peasants.

EM: What is significant about these comical stories?

JMS: That they simply seem comical and quite outlandish and that they be told as if it didn't exist, this outlandishness, and then always and again the opposite. So we're back to Brecht, there's no way around him.

EM: I found these comical stories noteworthy because they question our present day life and times with its regulative divisions.

JMS: They not only question our present. As Tiresias sits on his cart, speaking of the Gods, he suddenly utters, "First they deprive of your strength and then become indignant as you become less than a human being." That has partly to do with mythology, but not entirely. The whole film is like that, whether it's directly mythological or just implicitly so.

EM: Yes, we can give up using that word; I also don't have much use for it.

JMS: It came from me, unfortunately.

EM: There's something about this "neither man nor

woman, neither beast nor human" that defies the separation of the living into specific types or genders, and I find that very liberating.

JMS: Yes, my goodness, aren't they ... If a woman betrays, then she betrays as a woman, she rebels as a woman. Because she finds the man-world so loathsome, and not because of man and woman and so on. It's quite the opposite. She doesn't betray herself or the world around her or nature. She betrays the betrayer, and that is something entirely different because they are just that, betrayers.

EM: The texts you employ are invariably lyrical texts and their content is but *one* part among other elements. Everything is directly palpable and doesn't allude to something off-screen. One could then perhaps say that your films operate by affect.

JMS: Affect ... I would prefer to say feelings. Because to be specific the word affect doesn't derive from Greek but from Latin.

EM: If your films are based upon feelings, is it due to the fact that you abandon abstract images of representation and thereby produce something akin to an immediate awareness? Is it a question of breaking loose from representation?

JMS: Yes, I would say it's about showing things and the feelings, so that the person watching the film gets the impression that: What kind of a planet is this on which we are living? Or, what kind of a world is this that such things are possible? Or such feelings, or where such things can occur. And here again we find ourselves in the mire with Brecht, in the positive sense. What kind of world is this then where such feelings, such things, such incidents, such stories can happen? Is that right or not right? Could it be otherwise? One day, however, we will have to change that. Yes. That's it.

EM: The manner in which you and Danièle film, namely based more on feelings, is somewhat different to when someone simply attempts to make the depiction of a problem into a film. You don't present a problem through film but instead you film more directly.

JMS: Yes. Without that, which some carelessly call "distance." And yet in such a way, that whoever watches the film has the possibility to ask how that came about; whether it *must* be or whether it ought to be. Brecht never spoke of *Distanzierung* [distantiation]; the Americans and the English misinterpreted it. He spoke of *Verfremdung* [estrangement], to show things in such a light that they become strange.

EM: You've just said that you would like to show things without this sense of distance, and yet the observer should have the possibility to reflect and ask, "Why must the world be like this?" This shift from direct, non-distant sensation toward this very question: Why must it be like this—how does it operate?

JMS: Ha! But you know better than I do how that operates. I'm just the cook. I don't know how that operates. I just hope that it operates somehow, what more can I say.

EM: Gilles Deleuze remarked that your image is a "rock" and your take is a "tomb." The earth is abandoned and yet, as it were, it is filled with generations of corpses. When, for example, toward the end of *Operai, contadini*, you make a long sweeping pan across the hillside, the physical space comes across as being strangely humanized in the light of what was said beforehand. The hillside seems to be populated by people. Hence history becomes the humanization of nature. What is "human" in this panning shot and what is "nature"?

JMS: "Nature" in itself doesn't intrinsically exist and whether human beings ever actually existed or still exist, that is the other question. For me, this landscape incorporates something feminine, and what are called human beings, if one wants to push the point, incorporate something manly.

EM: While you search out very specific shooting locations, historic sites, you don't produce any illusory cinematic construction of these locations. Sometimes you shoot a wide-angled or a panning shot but they don't explain the physical space in this illusionary understanding of film. Why do you resist employing film conventions, whereby a series of takes render the physical space tangible?

JMS: It must remain a secret. If by filming one destroys a secret, one films absolutely nothing. It's about the opposite of a violation. I don't know... we should, we must, we may only film that which we don't violate. For heaven's sake, what we love, or—and I dislike the word, but, respect. To analyze literally means, "to unravel." Aaron says in *Moses and Aaron*, "Let me unravel it." He's referring to an idea by Moses and then he continues, "To unravel, that means to become opportunistic."

EM: And the filmed space, which you and Danièle produced in your films, would it be okay for you to say that this space is fragmented? A space composed of parts in contrast to a continuous space?

JMS: Yes, but on the other hand it mustn't be blatantly fragmented, for then it wouldn't make sense any longer. A filmmaker is by no means a surgeon. "To unravel" implies something else. When Aaron says, "Use appropriate force to make yourself understood by the people. Your Commandments shall be strict, but obeyable." Here, he's giving voice to pure opportunism. The filmmaker has got to banish and avoid all temptation for opportunism.

EM: You have always stressed that there's no such thing as "film language." You have sought to fight against any psychoanalytical or semiotic presentation of film.

JMS: Film language is advertisement.

EM: What then constitutes your basis for clarity in film?

JMS: That one avoids anything metaphorical.

MIKHAIL LYLOV: Yesterday we discussed how you produce in *Dalla nube alla resistenza*, *Trop tôt, trop tard* and *Operai, contadini* a very specific "plane" relationship between bodies, text, sound, lighting and locations. If these elements form the film space, which forces arrange them?

JMS: That involves contemplation, contemplation, and more contemplation, and the forces are the elements of a construction. When the construction is right and solid enough, the forces within it are free like the stars in the sky. For a film to exist requires that it be constructed beforehand. And that is exactly the relationships between these so-called forces and then everything within this frame must function freely. Without a rigid structure, there will be no film. And there must be diversity there. What interests us is the diversity of the different small stories that are told and then become part of a web. It is a web. It's not enough just to set up camera and start rolling. An abstract frame and construction must be developed beforehand that later will be concretized in situ and that then will operate freely. One needs a rhythm even before one starts shooting the film, or works at the cutting table. One needs to know why one chooses particular angles from which to film, how long the individual shots will last, and then choose another standpoint or an identical one, but nearer, or the same, only a little more distant. One needs to have all that in mind already or written down. If one has nothing thought out, there'll be nothing on screen, and if one has no feelings, or nothing in one's heart, there won't be anything either.

EM: You say that one needs to construct and set up a framework and the elements must operate freely within it. That means there's a casing that also needs to be put in place, and the freedom within this casing. My question is what kind of relationship exists between the casing and the freedom. In terms of control, how do they impact on each other? How do you work with them?

JMS: If the idea behind the film is powerful enough at the outset, then everything operates of its own accord. But such freedom only evolves out of something that in the beginning is the opposite of freedom. There's nothing more I can add. It is a configuration and also a *dispositif*. But all that needs to be torn asunder, it must be blown to pieces. The film only really gets rolling once all that has been blown up.

EM: And how do you blow it up?

JMS: I don't blow it up; I wait until reality does it. Or I work in opposition to the whole. And the air and the light and so on, the sounds and such—the film begins to live in all that isn't foreseen. But only because of the framework, otherwise there wouldn't be anything unforeseen. The old man in *Nicht versöhnt* [Not reconciled] says, "The unforeseen struck me hard." In this case it is the woman that embodies the unforeseen. One might add that in this sense the film is a woman who suddenly blows everything to pieces. The unforeseen is an integral part of the subject matter. If the film exists, then the unforeseen is never an external factor but arises from within.

EM: When the film has been shot—then yes. Can the "unforeseen" crop up after shooting has finished. Is the editing process also part of the "unforeseen"?

JMS: No, that is always the unforeseen. But it's purely skilled manual labor. Editing is nothing other than handcraft, handcraft, handcraft. If one has two blocks, one only needs to know what occurs in-between. One learns the strength of editing. And yes, it becomes a strength if the editing cut works, and if the cut is right in relation to the lot and to the story itself, to the relationships, to the physiques and the rest—then it's precisely a strength, otherwise there's nothing there.

EM: Halfway through the second part of *Trop tôt, trop tard*, the voice-over lapses into silence, but the landscapes continue.

JMS: That's what's referred to as a *développement*. Film works with space and only exists if one works it to such an extent that it becomes time, until something suddenly is freed. We made a film titled *Fortini/Cani*. Have you seen it? It is a story of a Jew from Florence who recounts what happened there during the war. And he suddenly says, "The town council of the Apuan Alps announces that it will adapt a comparable stance to the commune of Marzabotto."[7] And then one sees Marzabotto. What happened there is ten times the scale of Oradour,[8] and in northern Italy. That was the so-called Gothic Line that stretched from coast to coast. As the resistance erupted, the Wehrmacht attempted to destroy the villages and to massacre the women because they provided food for the men.
What I just wanted to say is that here is a much more drastic development that goes way beyond that which happens toward the end of *Trop tôt, trop tard*. With three sentences we get a ceremonious, historical explanation, and what follows is a series of panning shots in, I think, ten villages in the vicinity of the Gothic Line. For close to twenty minutes one sees nothing but landscape, silent, without commentary. That's a development in the film. That's what's called a development. A sort of geophysical, geographical, geological sequence that at the same time is a spectacle, a site of resistance.

7
The complete sentence from *Fortini/Cani* to which Jean-Marie Straub refers is: "The Apuan Alps Commune Council, where 23 years previously Reder and his people had slaughtered citizens in their hundreds, declare that they will take an identical stance to the Community of Marzabotto and reject the appeal for pardon."

8
On 10 June, 1944, soldiers of a German SS Division perpetrated a massacre on the inhabitants of Oradour-sur-Glane, a village in the Limousin region.

EM: You mentioned that in the second half of *Trop tôt, trop tard*, after the historical references, something is freed; and I find that one sees that. I have the impression that it has got something to do with the situation on site, with Egypt, that suddenly the countryside is populated again, in contrast to France. That's when suddenly the construction collapses. In other words, does a development happen only in the script, or does it also occur while filming is underway?

JMS: No, that is exactly what I call the construction. We read that phrase and thought to ourselves: "Good grief, what is this all about?" And so we drove there and went in circles for three-weeks on end searching for these villages, for documents that finally indicated to us the whereabouts of these villages. And some people didn't know anything whatsoever and so we had to go there on several occasions and discover. You see a village toward the end of the film, in which the SS locked up the entire remaining population in a school on a hill, the women and children. They then sat the school ablaze and started to shoot into it. The pan shot ends on this school, a village school, somewhat small albeit with many windows; and that we discovered on-the-spot. In order to do so, we had to ask around a lot and drive around a lot. We traveled to Egypt twice, once with the maps drawn up by cartographers who accompanied Napoleon on his campaign there. These are the only topographical maps of the villages and the fields that exist. There were no modern-day maps of Egypt. We then had to ask all the truck-drivers: Where is such-and-such a village? And at times we were smack in the middle of it and nobody knew its location, not even the truck-drivers. Shall we watch *Fortini/Cani*?

EM: Yes, we'd be glad to.

*

JMS: There is a French word: *dilatation,* expansion. The term is also used in music, as when suddenly something expands and then it suddenly contracts. That is the task at hand. And nothing more. And that hinges upon what one encounters before filming begins and not during the shoot. But surprises also come about. In *Fortini/Cani* the synagogue in Florence was one such. One Saturday we entered there and experienced the religious service in full. And then we filmed it, too. It can be seen in the film, although it hadn't been envisaged. One can only film what one has seen, and one can only have seen something when one has gazed long enough. Cézanne remarked, "Look at that mountain; once it was fire." Mont Sainte Victoire—that is the mountain he painted or drew some fifty times, but that approach ought to pertain to every single frame in every film.

EM: I also believe in the inherent power of the situation, in that moment in which something happens. Not only in the course of a thorough pre-production phase but also in the actual situation when one sees something afresh, or for the first time. If this moment can be captured on film, something will come across.

JMS: But one needs to be very careful about that. I don't believe in "spontaneity." It might happen on occasion within a context that had been thoroughly worked out in advance. In contrast, at times one needs the courage to do without a particular shot and to push the button so that filming is *stopped*. Take, for example, Jean Rouch's *La chasse au lion à l'arc* [The Lion Hunters]. Rouch was filming and filming and then at the very moment they shot arrows at the lion he stopped the camera. His comment was, "That shouldn't be shown." That is a moral question. Aesthetics has to do with morals.

EM: The hunt was part of a ritual that is holy in some way.

JMS: That, too, but it wasn't only that. There are moments in which we must intervene and not stand by with our hands in our pockets and film.

ML: *Operai, contadini* introduces texts taken from Elio Vittorini's *Women of Messina*. The narrative focuses on how a group of people creates a community and how they sought to come to terms with life's hardships in post-war Italy, to overcome hunger and survive the lengthy winter. The story is centered on their daily activities and the relationships that emerge from these interactions. Everyday activities constitute the material life of the commune, their daily chores. The film *Operai, contadini* is enacted in the woods. Here, the protagonists are surrounded by uncultivated countryside. Hence an asymmetry exists between the life of the commune as told in the story and the life of the commune as depicted in the film. Is this asymmetry necessary?

JMS: Of course it is better than had we filmed right in the middle of the fields. That is where they actually live; it is not just anywhere. Besides, had we shown them in cultivated fields it would have been flat and illustrative. Here they are in a physical space, in a place where they are undergoing a trial, a trial in the sense of being before a court. They stand in court and are asked to testify about the entire circumstances and how it all came about. That's why at times they read, as though reading a statement aloud at court.

ML: Yet the people in the film also represent a community.

JMS: But one doesn't see the community as such, even though it exists. One sees all that is told. It is a series of stories, a good many tiny little stories. Just as someone recounts a tiny detail in court, something precise and exact.

ML: If one accepts that every film is in a certain sense a documentation of itself, then there is a distinction to be made between Vittorini's novel, that is to say between a book that describes in a straightforward manner the setting, and your film, *Operai, contadini*. My concern here is the different representational politics employed with respect to the work. In the filmed version, one sees a group of people who speak about the commune, but is the presence of the commune established in the film? Wherein lies the connection between the commune about which they speak and the speakers themselves?

JMS: One doesn't get to see the commune while it exists and functions as such. We don't enter the dining area, we don't go to the fields. One experiences the commune by means of a fiction that is a tale for the court. It's the commune according to how people say they experienced it. It consists only of stories about petty quarrels between peasants and workers. They tell stories about what happened when the commune existed.

ML: In view of my own experience nowadays, that stems from several attempts to set up a collective in the artistic sphere for instance, it doesn't suffice just to speak of the commune to get it launched. Making an official declaration won't produce a collective. In Vittorini's novel, which describes life within a commune, there's also the materiality of everyday life that is independent of the debates about the commune. It seems that in *Operai, contadini* the commune is meant to be established by talking about it.

JMS: You can't establish something that no longer exists. Reconstruction is often difficult and fails because one cannot materialize it. But talking about something one has lived through, that's something concrete. One can do that, or at least it was possible to do so during the era of Soviet films, for instance. The circumstances in this case are not comparable, it is impossible to do so, and there was no other solution. And besides, the aim was not to present or to film a commune. Our intention was to *allude* to a commune. The word.

ML: That film dates from 2001. Why this necessity to reintroduce this word commune, where did this need arise?

JMS: Who knows? Because that was all suppressed and because current official policy strives to suppress it even further.

ML: In *Dalla nube alla resistenza* Tiresias says to Oedipus that *before* the Gods existed objects had governed themselves. The Gods began to give names to the objects, thereby determining their destiny. Old Bellerophon cannot kill himself, because death is a matter of destiny. In the bar scene in the second section of the film, one sees the philistine's contempt for communists enacted. They say, "Those who are called communists are always such-and-such..." Is the struggle against destiny a communist struggle?

And if "communism" were a label, what would it then entail to be a self-regulating communist or a commune?

JMS: There's a character in the film who returns. He had been the joiner and he says to the other, "What are you then? Communist?" To which the communist replies, "Italian." These are all concrete and moral precisions, it's not about pie in the sky communism. He says, "We are too ignorant in this country. A communist is not he who wants to be one. We would need people who are not ignorant, who won't tarnish the name." That is all. They discuss something that doesn't exist. Let me remind you that the word "commune" is never once uttered by anyone in the film. At the end Ventura once refers to "this *riunione* of people." That is to say, "this togetherness of people, this meeting of people"; he never once uses the word "commune."

ML: In the opening scene of *Trop tôt, trop tard*, the camera is positioned in a car that repeatedly drives around a roundabout.

JMS: Seven times.

ML: The camera movements blur the coordinates in physical space. By means of this movement, the space is continuously transformed. Hierarchies in space are obliterated. The left-right, north-south axes that guide the observer don't exist. Even though this sequence has a starting and finishing point, the camera movement doesn't follow a particular direction. Why did you create this dis-figurative space? Is it a non-human or an anti-human space?

JMS: It is no longer human; it is only full of traffic, or engulfed in traffic and hence no longer human. But once upon a time it was a human space, for it was a public square and above it, on top of the column is the statue of the "Spirit of Liberty," which you don't see, because you're circling around it recounting how the bourgeoisie were always betrayers. The human figures are locked into their vehicles, as though imprisoned. One also says, to go around in circles. That is quite concrete. And this very ferocious shot right at the beginning of the film, which contains all that you've pointed out, was for us, however, a game to show something spectral. After all, one shouldn't feel abashed about playing!

THIRD DAY

EM: We would like to discuss *Trop tôt, trop tard* in a little more detail. In the Egyptian segment there is a panoramic shot of Cairo as observed from the perspective of a fortress.

JMS: That is the citadel.

EM: You mentioned how if you want to film a village, you need to search out a standpoint, and that this standpoint is often located where the water reservoir irrigates the area. If one shoots from a fortress, or in a village, let's say, from the point where it is irrigated, do you consider these as two different standpoints?

JMS: In an ideological sense, yes. Some villages don't have water reservoirs and depend on another village for their water supply, and so on. But one needs to find such a standpoint. It could also be the church, if it looks down over the locality. But that has the consequence that one can't film the church itself, for one is either inside or on the rooftop.

EM: But is there really a need to make this ideological distinction?

JMS: The water reservoir isn't shown anyway. But this particular fortress, if that is your standpoint, you show it, because it was really a point of departure for the Egyptian resistance movement.

ML: So then the camera position is strategic?

JMS: I don't like strategy because strategy comes from *strategos*, the Greek for "the general." The term applies to conquerors or to armies, but it does not apply to the film. A film has nothing whatsoever to do with war. One doesn't want to conquer the earth, one wants to caress it. A film has to do with eroticism and not with strategy. It has more to do with geology, with geology and geography. That is related to *geo,* Greek for the earth. Geology is the study of that which is not visible, or barely so; that which is underneath. Geography deals with that which is on the surface, a description of the earth.

EM: You say you dislike strategy because of its military connotations. But couldn't it also be pointed out that construction and editing are components of a particular strategy?

JMS: During preparation, yes. But what emerges afterwards is the opposite of strategy.

EM: And what might that be?

JMS: Eroticism, or observation, or ... it has a mystical aspect. It has nothing whatsoever to do with mysticism but with the mystic. What do they call it in the Bible, the "Song of Songs"? In Bach this is also the basis for a duet: "When will You come, my Saviour? I wait with burning oil." We once took the liberty of making a music film so to speak and that is the closing chorale from the Ascension Oratorio with these lyrics expressing impatience. In *Der Bräutigam, die Komödiantin und der Zuhälter* [*The Bridegroom, the Actress and the Pimp*] one sees the people there, the women on the sidewalk with this closing chorale as a soundtrack. Then one hears the words "when will we greet the Saviour, when will we kiss the Saviour?" Now! If that isn't erotic.

EM: I find that your and Danièle's films also work very much on an archeological level; searching out ruins, localities, towns and streets, that which remains, the historical and spatial vestiges. Yet at the same time these films are also very anthropological because they are principally concerned with human life. But human bodies aren't filmed as in ethnological films, as Rouch filmed them, for instance. When filming a landscape, you follow more the lines created by the landscape, the contours drawn by the mountains, for instance, or the route a street takes, but not the people that are going about their business within the frame.

JMS: That would be another film. One can't undertake two things at once. From this distance people are in the distance, or they're not there at all. Our intention and aim is not to show the people.

ML: The question concerning strategy and tactic arose so as to comprehend how the various elements involved in making a film relate to the whole.

JMS: Why should they? They needn't be in any way. One can show blocks that interact like geological blocks. But that is a question of millennia! Millennia. In *Der Bräutigam, die Komödiantin und der Zuhälter* the question goes: "O day, o day, when will you be?" That is impatience personified. "When will we greet the Savior, when will we kiss the Savior? Come, present yourself now! O day, o day, when will you be?" That is a block in itself with the music.

EM: Some blocks of a film could fit in with each other in the way that tectonic plates do geologically. They don't need to be strategically linked, yet they have a bearing on one another—is that what you're getting at?

JMS: At times yes, then that is what's called a sequence. But with landscape that need not be the case, that one element has bearing on another for they can also be separate. Blocks like granite boulders that collide with each other.

ML: A geologist or an archeologist can just *know how* the granite blocks, the geology of a locale is pieced together. That is the point—if we undertake geological surveys or archeological digs, our investigations are exclusively limited to how landscape is formed. We can't construct the geology. And then when it comes to the process of creating a film, in which blocks are interconnected.

JMS: It's not a concept; it's a working method. We are not there so as to present ourselves and declare: "Now we'll become geologists." No, it's not like that; it's a method. It is connected with geology but it involves filming. It doesn't reveal anything about geology as such, but yet it works partly like geology.

ML: Is this method based upon mimesis?

JMS: No. The opposite of mimesis: Coincidence. That has more to do with coincidence than with mimesis. In film anything tainted with mimesis is fatal, as is anything metaphorical. Kafka writes in his diary, "Metaphors are one of the many things that make me despair when writing." Film must avoid metaphors, and it must also, as a film, avoid a painterly approach. If one starts and says, "We will now reveal this in a light that has to do with Rubens or with Goya," then the film is already destroyed before it even came to life. The camera is no paintbrush—it's a camera. And just in the same way the camera was never a weapon as many claimed in May 1968. It is not a weapon—it's a camera. Brecht already pointed out, "It's no eye, it's no eye!"

EM: If not, what is it then for you?

JMS: It's contemplation. And then we're back to Meister Eckhart, or what?

EM: Is the camera a work-tool for you?

JMS: Yes.

ML: To link your films with strategy was not meant as a statement on our behalf but rather an attempt to understand. Just as one follows a thread and sees where it leads. A fortress isn't built just anywhere; it doesn't suddenly pop up out of nowhere. It is invariably linked to the surrounding landscape and its geology.

JMS: Are you referring to *Trop tôt, trop tard*?

ML: That's a case in point. And then we followed this thread by regarding the camera as an extension of a geological feature, as a fortress, it uses granite to designate its standpoint, or it uses that water-reservoir that we discussed yesterday.

JMS: Not bad. That's true. Why are you sitting here? It would be better if you'd write something about it.

EM: It's important to have your take on the subject.

JMS: No, it's a pity. For with such ramblings one partly destroys what the films are all about. The films are what they are thanks to the effort that goes into making them. What I am rambling on about is in itself of no interest. For that is already embedded in the material we've filmed and you are better placed to describe what is embedded there. For that is then concrete, an experience or something that you have lived through. And what I'm rambling on about is the opposite, it's theory, poor theory, or shallow theory, thus in a nutshell: clichés. And the greater part of the work during pre-production and when shooting is namely that—to avoid the clichés, and to blow them up, to dynamite them. There's a word that has frayed with usage, that has turned into something of a cliché. It is linked to *dialectic*. Damn! One should never say or show something in which one cannot sense the possibility of its opposite as an intrinsic resistance.

EM: *(laughs)* I am naturally full of such "shallow theories." When considering what we would like to discuss with you here, it also struck us that we could merely touch lightly upon "shallow constructions."

JMS: It's nevertheless all a lot of retroactive crap. What I have to say is all embedded in the films but when it is articulated, it is somehow watered-down. What we're discussing here, even if it is partly right, ends up as caricature or generalities. Brecht said "To unearth the truth under the debris of the everyday, to combine the individual with the general in the greater process." Filming concerns itself with the individual and not with the general. And the whole must remain a mystery. That is subject matter for a film, that's not a sermon.

ML: And film isn't a reconciliation of this dialectic?

JMS: No, never.

ML: When I watch a film, how does the dialectic affect me? What should be the dialectical effect? It seems that for Brecht it's about a calculated provocation aimed at manipulating the outcome. The "Brechtian effect" is the production of an unreconciled subject. That is the power inherent in dialectical approach; one becomes part of this irreconcilable logic in which there's no solution. Hence it is a form in which the dialectical approach affects us. Is this understanding of things close to your approach?

JMS: Our first feature film was called *Not Reconciled.* How could one reconcile oneself to such a world? I tried to express that earlier on when I alluded to the subject: One needs to be all that one shows. We have something concrete beneath our feet, the earth, and we must have the ability to enjoy the earth, so as to be in a position to protect it. That's all we have.

EM: Would you describe your films as "in defense of the earth"?

JMS: Yes, of course. There's a scene in a film by Dovzhenko in which a peasant in a sudden fit of impatience begins yanking hard on his horse's reins. He's all on edge as a result of what happened to him earlier on and then he suddenly is confronted with the horse, and then one hears a very cautious commentary: "Ivan, Ivan you've mistaken the enemy." Cynicism has never been so prevalent as it is nowadays. We have reached such a level of cynicism that everything which existed previously... and what's the source of that? Money, capitalism, one has to put it so puerilely.

EM: That's why I was somewhat surprised on the first day when you quoted Buñuel: "One could say it cynically: that I filmed them like insects."

JMS: To be more precise he was then referring to...

EM: ...the bourgeoisie.

JMS: Yes. The idea was along the lines of, "How curious that such creatures exist." One doesn't do that because one finds it good or beautiful, but rather so that people will say, "But how can that be possible? By no means ought it have been like that, it shouldn't have been like that, and it can't be like that and it shouldn't be like that." This feeling is embedded in our films, and were we to be pretentious, it is embedded in every single take we shot. Unless we worked all for nothing, Danièle and I. And it is thanks to this whole thing that I'm here like a maniac. Yet the films, despite all that I've said are anything but manic. To wit, it is coercion, a caricature that is then carried out... while always with caution and utmost patience, patience, patience... despite all we attempted to work... That is why I... you are both dear to me but I should have said in the beginning: No, I don't want that. I've already gone on too long with too much claptrap; I don't want to continue because you are both dear to me. Yes. That was a trap.

EM: Misha, he thinks that we've laid him a trap.

JMS: A trap, exactly, a trap.

Translated from German by John Barrett.

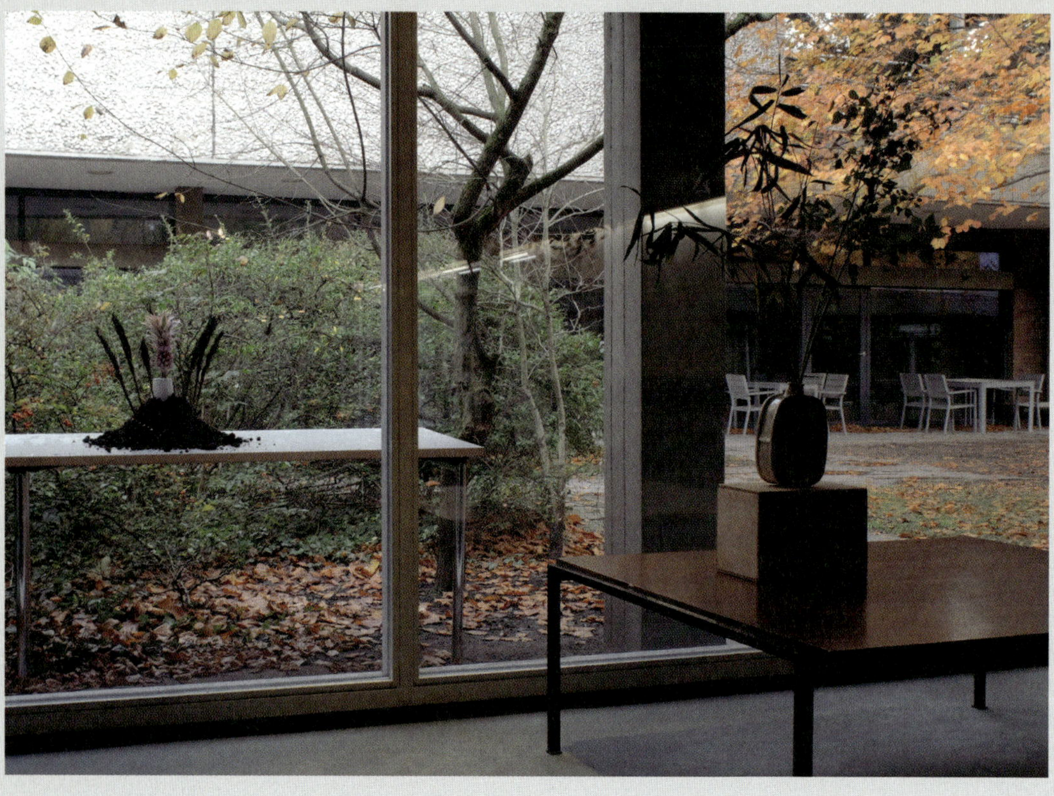

Mikhail Lylov, Elke Marhöfer

SOILS_HABIT_PLANTS
A PUBLIC CONVERSATION

[The conversation took place on November 11, 2017, in the foyer of Akademie der Künste, Hanseatenweg in Berlin, following the premiere of Elke Marhöfer and Mikhail Lylov's film *Soils_Habit_Plants*, which was screened from a 16mm projector installed in the same room. Prior to the event, Marhöfer and Lylov had prepared two flower arrangements on a table to the left side of the screen.]

Mikhail Lylov: Like some of the films we have seen today and yesterday, our film *Soils_Habit_Plants* also has to do with the notion of landscape, even though we prefer not to use the term. One can speak about landscape as a material entity that bears readable marks and through these marks enters into history. A film can be an exercise of reading these marks. The landscape can also become an intensive character corresponding with the mood of the film's protagonists. But I think that in our work we understand landscape in a different way.

Elke Marhöfer: The idea of landscape is problematic, because it messes all the different protagonists into one kind of perception. And maybe this relates a little bit to what we are trying to do, which is not to mess everybody up, and still being out in something that is called "landscape."

ML: *Soils_Habit_Plants:* The first and the last element of the title are very present in the film. So maybe the middle element, the interstice, should be highlighted. Our informal proposition may be: instead of a notion of landscape, to consider the place in terms of 'habit,' or 'habitat.' This is important for us, because we try to work with protagonists that are not always inscribed into the human history: plants and animals. They are always commented upon, represented. But they have a certain autonomy, a certain resistance toward this inclusion into the commented space, into the filmic space which puts them in relation to human concerns. On the one hand, it is very important politically to bring things into our human concern, but on the other hand, this concern also bears the risk to initiate a form of violence. We believe that we can speak

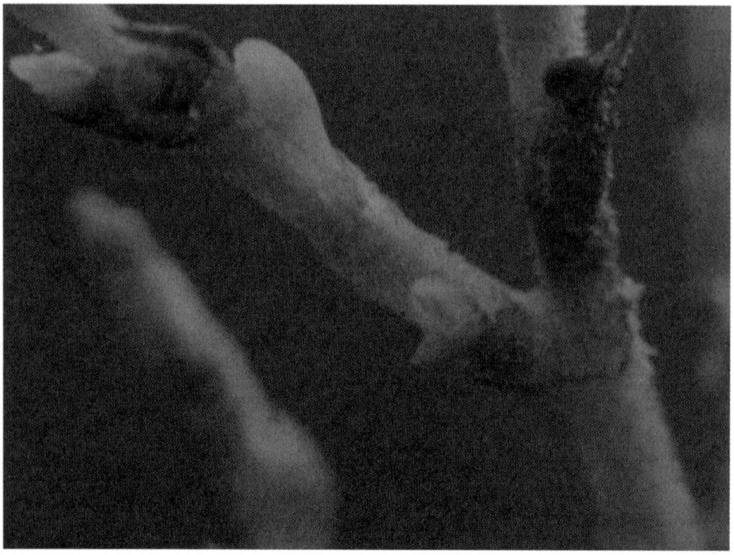

about the non-human perspective through the notion of the habitat or habit, and by not putting these protagonists into a 'landscape.'

EM: We are in Japan and we are doing some research on disturbances there, ecological disturbances. And we understand 'disturbance' in a way that it isn't necessarily destructive but it can also be productive. Human and non-human disturbance can cause, for example, bio-diversity, higher bio-diversities. So this is what we are learning, let's say. Actually, I would like to replace the term 'learning' with 'experiencing,' and then put it into relation with other experiences that we previously had through reading or being out somewhere else. Learning, experiencing, to read—about plants for example, soil for example, habitat for example. We could tell you a couple of things about the plants that we saw in this film, but we wanted to share this with you not by way of a voice-over, that would kind of bring it into a place already.

ML: It's a complicated question how you can actually learn something from the soil or from the plant. For the conventional idea of learning, communication is the central point; but the soil and plants they don't communicate very well in a direct way. If we were trying to use the voice, this would mean to bring these things into our concern and to express our concern about them, but at the same time it would mean to already include the representation, which we would not like to include in the film.

[Audience: Kajsa Dahlberg] I have a question, which might be related to what you just said about reading, text, and the film. Can you please say something about the [unstable] use of focus in your film, which is also of course a matter of allowing one to see or not to see, and how that came into the film.

EM: Thanks for this question. Certainly it has to do with a form of resistance, in a sense of unlearning the seeing, to kind of resist the expectations toward the image. At the same time we don't want to close the door to anybody, to the viewer. There's always a [negotiation] how much you can disclose of some singularity by exposing it to the camera. How much can you actually film some of these? If it is soil, it seems to be less problematic, because soil does not appear as a singularity. But if you have a flower, it's quite an exposure and kind of violent what you do to this plant, while trying to learn from it in alternative ways, or to learn its language. These are some of the thoughts that sometimes made us go in and out of focus.

[Audience: Philip Widmann] Is this also a way to show respect? I remember that in the conversation you had with Straub there was a part about the secret and keeping a secret and also respecting the secret.

ML: You just don't want to pretend that you know everything and it is always good to have a mistake or imperfection on your side. Rather than pretending that we have a perfection, we are trying to keep imperfection on our side. On the one hand, this can lead to a learning experience when it comes to the imperfections of the production of the film itself and the failures that we experience sometimes. And on the other hand, it is a way to keep a useful distance between us and between what we try to work with, because I think the distance between you and what you film is an extremely important notion. So this unsharpness is definitely a way to keep the distance.

EM: We wanted to give the camera an acting position in this as well. But in terms of the secret, it's also important not to *make* a secret. It is important to be as open and... bland, I think is the term, as possible. But there is nothing as such, not even a secret. So in a way the secret is part of a construction, it comes with the process of production, but it's not something planned. Of course, one could strategically use a secret, which could be interesting as a method, but I think this is not how we work. If there are secrets to us, I guess we keep them in a way, in the sense that it is not necessary to unveil them.

[Audience: Luisa Greenfield] I think it's interesting that you break down this term landscape and question its use. Of course we think about cultivation when you show the close-up of the soil. If it's healthy soil, we see life in it, and we can see life in that soil in the close-ups in your film. But it also makes me think about the history of the soil in Japan and the history of cultivation and farming in Japan. As I understand it, the US brought industrial agriculture and chemical agriculture to Japan, sold it to the government and basically devastated the soil there. But then I also think about the history of rice-paddy farming and how flooding the paddies is also an extreme intervention and cultivation into the land. Then came this movement in the 1970s toward Natural Farming where you basically create an environment that allows for the land to do what it wants to do naturally.

I appreciate that the text material is over here, separate from the film, because the first thing that came into my mind when watching it were actually books that I'd read about the soil in Japan. I just wonder how much of that is 'revealed' in your film, in terms of what you just said about the secret. I mean you end it with a shot of the cars and the highway and the garden underneath it. How much of that comes into play for you?

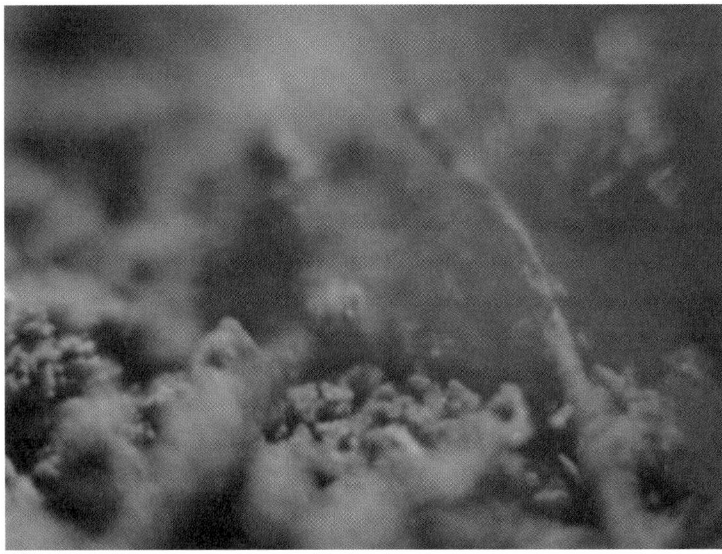

ML: Okay, thanks, that's an extremely informed comment, everything you mention matters for us very much. Let's switch the mode of discussion to "communication," since we have matters of fact to talk about. The second plant that we see in the film is a wild relative of millet. Millet is a very interesting *personage*. It was part of the staple diet in Japan before the events you mention, before the '70s. Some parts of Japan never actually cultivated rice, be it because they were too high in the mountains, or because it was too cold. This fact of course totally contradicts the image, created by the Japanese agricultural lobby, of Japan as an essentially rice-eating culture. The wild millet somehow interacts with this version of reality: it fully mimics rice, pretends that it does not exist, up until a certain stage of its life cycle. It is indistinguishable from rice until it produces seeds. To counteract the repeated attempts by people to kill it off in their fields, this plant created a camouflage technique and an incredible resistance to agrochemicals. Wild millet is a great example of guerilla resistance to industrial farming. One can see this plant as an agent of biodiversity in a monoculture of a rice paddy. Also it draws attention to other edible types of millet, who because of their robustness require much less labor and much less industrial efforts to cultivate them. But since the change of the agrosystem, plants like millet are treated as good as weeds. I think this gives quite an interesting example of the history of interaction between plants and people. But of course, when I speak of "history," I only speak of plants as food, which means I speak of *my* concern, which is not necessarily the concern of the plant—to be my food, right? So that's also in parenthesis answering why this is all in the printed texts and not in the film.

In relation to this, I would like to read a quote, which leads us back to the aesthetic questions. Elke and I argue so much about this quotation, it is extremely important for us. It comes from Gilles Deleuze and Felix Guattari and their book *What Is Philosophy?* They write,

> A plant contemplates by contracting the elements from which it originates—light, carbon, and the salts—and it fills itself with colors and odors that in each case qualify its variety, its composition. It is sensation in itself.[1]

I think this understanding of a plant as sensation in itself, is something which for us was a very important entry point for our efforts to make this film.

1 Gilles Deleuze, Felix Guattari, *What Is Philosophy?*, trans. Hugh Tomlinson, Graham Burchill (London: Verso, 1994), 212.

EM: And other films.

ML: It is extremely interesting how they bring together the production of an image and biological processes.They don't explain the molecular processes or they don't use the scientific parlance or jargon to explain this, but they conceptualize the plant as having the capacity to contract the outside, contract an image, contract itself as an image. The plant produces itself from the soil and we try to produce the film as a kind of documentary of plant production, which passes through political notions that we have just discussed.

EM: The plant contracts an image not only from the soil but also from the sunlight and the all critters and insects that roam around. In a way, Deleuze and Guattari gave us a tool: 'contraction,' the idea of production to explain the sensibilities of plants, their brain, their knowledge, their beauty. Producing whatever senses, images, the luring and these mimicking capacities that we see in the wild millet;

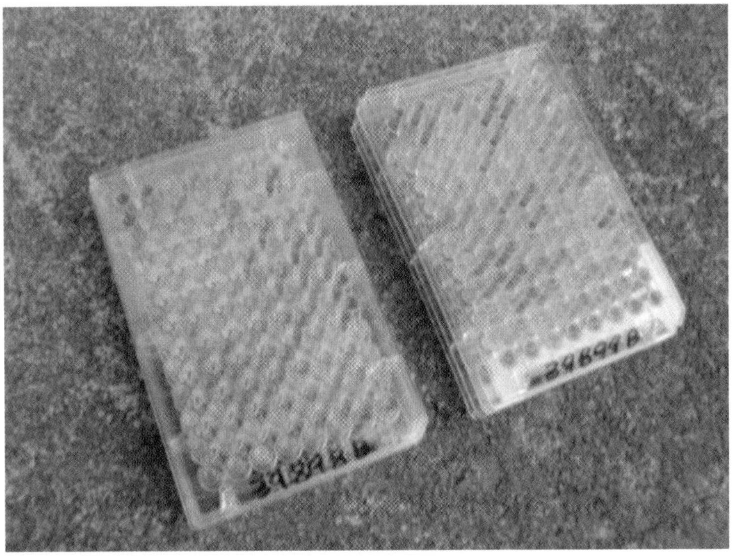

like being the joker in the rice field, pretending that they are rice just to have a habitat for their endurance. Deleuze and Guattari gave us this concept of contraction to understand these great capacities. The going in and out of focus of the camera is a mode of contracting an image. And that's how we used it, as a concept and as a way to communicate with you about this.

[Audience: Annett Busch] You have used the term personage. I have been wondering if it is ironic. And also the term communication; you want to communicate, but how does it work, how do you communicate?

ML: 'Personage' refers to the fact that they are singular for us. 'Persona,' the singular persona. They are unique, just like Florian was pointing out today that the moment of learning has to propose a singularity, so that's why learning is not really about communication, but it's an encounter. What happens is you encounter these protagonists, plants, and then you exercise your capacities of being *aufmerksam* [attentive]. And this is the obligation of the viewer, because as a filmmaker there is a part where you create an image but there is also a big part where you just see it and passively contract it.

This is very similar to what the two philosophers write, that contraction is not really an action. There

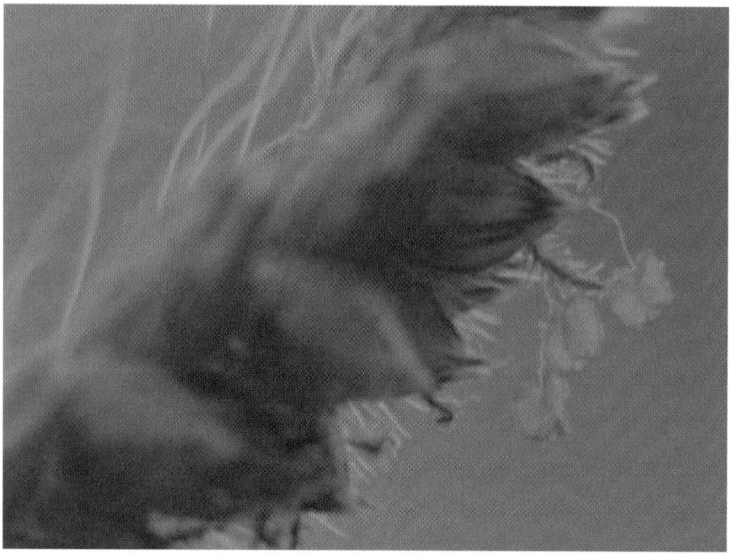

is a moment of contemplation in this, a contraction of an image. So I think, this film is about arranging encounters with things in a way that you can become more engaged, more interested. This is maybe the process of learning as we understand it.

[Audience: Makoto Mochida] I want to ask you a question. While I was watching your film, I remembered the word 'eroticism,' which Jean-Marie used in the interview that you made with him. Now you were talking about 'capacities." Does the word 'capacities' have a connection with eroticism?

EM: It's a very nice comment, thank you, very interesting. 'Eroticism' came from Jean-Marie. It's a bit difficult. The idea is a bit masculine for me. But concerning capacities and eroticism I can just refer back to what I already said: the capacities of a plant to be erotic I guess. To lure or seduce for example and to mimic.

ML: To lure a bee to enter it. An insect comes inside to pollinate; it's an erotic capacity of a plant that's directed toward, not a plant, but toward other species, animals. So it's interspecies eroticism. When the plant contracts all these elements from the soil or from the earth, I think this is an erotic process. It's not masturbation, it's a narcissistic notion. Narcissism includes eroticism and it is simply because there is a certain affirmation of pleasure in this process. When the plant contracts itself, it affirms its own pleasure and it further expects that it will continue and this is the kind of duration of this eroticism. And yes, definitely, there are these blurry images and then something comes into focus... I never thought about this as being erotic. It's a great question. Thank you very much.

Makoto Mochida

I IS AN OTHER

EROTICISM IN *SOILS_HABIT_PLANTS*

The embers in the 'irori' fireplace were redder than nuclear fire —Masanobu Fukuoka[1]

1

In the essay "A Tomb for the Eye" (1975)[2] Serge Daney uses the term eroticism in his discussion of the short film *Introduction to Arnold Schoenberg's "Accompaniment to a Cinematographic Scene"* (1972) by Danièle Huillet and Jean-Marie Straub. The eroticism Daney detects in this film is represented by an ankle of Straub or a knee of Huillet that protrude into the screen. When Daney evokes eroticism in the Huillet and Straub film, he thinks of "the most neutral parts of the body, the less spectacularly consumable." According to Daney, eroticism in the film has nothing to do with the naked body as a commodity that has exchange value on the market.

1
Masanobu Fukuoka, *Wara ippon no kakumei* (*The One-Straw Revolution*) (Tokyo: Shunjusha, 1983), 171.

2
Serge Daney, "A Tomb for the Eye (Straubian pedagogy)," sergedaney.blogspot.com, September 15, 2014.

3
Mikhail Lylov, Elke Marhöfer, Jean-Marie Straub, "A Thousand Cliffs," in *Der Standpunkt der Aufnahme – Point of View: Perspectives of Political Film and Video Work,* ed. Tobias Hering (Berlin: Archive Books, 2014), Republished in the present volume, 384.

2

More than thirty-eight years after the publication of Daney's "A Tomb for the Eye," Jean-Marie Straub is interviewed by Elke Marhöfer and Mikhail Lylov and talks about eroticism in the following way:

ML: So then the camera position is strategic?

JMS: I don't like strategy because strategy comes from *strategos*, the Greek for "the general." The term applies to conquerors or to armies, but it does not apply to the film. A film has nothing whatsoever to do with war. One doesn't want to conquer the earth, one wants to caress it. A film has to do with eroticism and not with strategy. It has more to do with geology, with geology and geography. That is related to *geo*, Greek for the earth.[3]

For Huillet and Straub, filmmaking is intimately connected to the desire to caress the earth. Perhaps Jean-Marie Straub intuitively understood that the three of them shared this desire. In fact, four years after the interview with Straub, Marhöfer and Lylov created a film in Japan that looks like the crystallization of that desire of caressing the earth. In *Soils_Habit_Plants* (2017), Japanese plants, namely wild mil-

let, Japanese knotweed, Sugi (Japanese cedar) and Hinoki (Japanese cypress), along with the soil from which they absorb nutrients, are the main protagonists.
The most characteristic quality of the film are close-up images which are hardly ever entirely in focus, and even if they are, it only happens for a brief moment. Close to two thirds of the less than twelve-minute-long film are spent on out of focus close-up movements.

In 2016, Elke Marhöfer was interviewed by Martin Grennberger for the online journal of contemporary art *Kunstkritikk*. When asked about the short film *Shape Shifting* (2015), which she had created together with Lylov in Japan, she explained the camera work in the following way: "If it (the camera) wants to get closer, it doesn't zoom in, it really gets closer."[4]

Marhöfer explains the refusal to use a zoom lens and wish to approach a subject as a shared desire that dwells inside the actual camera as much as in the person holding it. While speaking of the camera in such a way, Marhöfer refers to *living cameras*, a term used by the visual anthropologist Jean Rouch.

4
Martin Grennberger, "Ten Questions: Elke Marhöfer," *Kunstkritikk*, August 31, 2016, kunstkritikk.com.

5
Jean Rouch, "The Camera and Man," 1973, der.org.

3

Rouch discusses the term *living camera* in his text "The Camera and Man," (1973).[5] He explains that *living cameras* differ from cameras that are fixed on a tripod and approach the subject with the aid of a zoom lens which, in Rouch's words, leads to a kind of "involuntary arrogance." A "living camera" instead can only be in the hands of a filmmaker for whom the only way to film is "to walk with the camera, taking it where it is most effective and improvising another type of ballet with it, trying to make it as alive as the people it is filming." A filmmaker holding a camera is, in Rouch's words, not a human being but a "mechanical eye" accompanied by an "electronic ear." Rouch calls "this strange state of transformation" *cine-trance*.

In the *Kunstkritikk* interview, Marhöfer further explains that the term *cine-trance* not only means that the filmmaker and the camera are in trance, but that the "other-than-human" or the "more-than-human" environment must be included. She defines her understanding of the term "more-than-human" as "not human-centered." "I think this trance is not only the trance of the filmmaker, but also that of the camera together with the environment." When Grennberger asks Marhöfer, "Could one even talk about the becoming animal of the camera?" she replies, "One can say the camera can become animal, but also plant, or microbe... "

The camera can become an animal, a plant, a microbe, or soil because the camera, the person, and the environment in which they are entangled overlap each other on the same plane. They become "companions," and thereby "heterogeneities."[6]

"Free indirect discourse" refers to the fact that the subordinate clause that forms the indirect discourse is constructed independently from the subject and verb of the main clause. As an example, Gilles Deleuze mentions a passage of "Canticle to St. Eulalie" that is quoted by Mikhail Bakhtin in *Marxism and the Philosophy of Language* (1929): "She gathers her strength: better that she undergo tortures than lose her virginity."[7]

The following passage from *Marxism and the Philosophy of Language* helps to understand the concept of "free indirect discourse" as used by Deleuze:

> The narrator's speech is just as individualized, colorful, and nonauthoritative as is the speech of the characters. The narrator's position is fluid, and in the majority of cases he uses the language of the personages depicted in the work. He cannot bring to bear against their subjective position a more authoritative and objective world.[8]

If we use Deleuze's words instead of Bakhtin's, the phrase, "the narrator's position is fluid" translates into "the Ego=Ego form of identity ceases to be valid," and "the narrator uses the language of the personages depicted in the work" translates into "the filmmaker declares that I is another."

When Deleuze speaks of "free indirect discourse," he probably has Rimbaud's words "I is another," or "I is an-other" in mind. In *Moi un Noir* (1959), one of Rouch's most repre-

6
In "A Tomb for the Eye," the word "heterogeneity" is used by Daney in order to describe Huillet and Straub's way of making films: "taking seriously the cinematic heterogeneity."

7
V. N. Vološinov, *Marxism and the Philosophy of Language*, trans. Ladislav Matejka and I. R. Titunik (New York: Seminar Press, 1973), 150.

8
Vološinov, *Marxism*, 121.

sentative works, Deleuze observes that the main characters, who come from Niger, have adopted white people's names such as Dorothy Lamour and Lemmy Caution. Their Egos as black people are making their own "free indirect discourse" by becoming "an-other" as white people. According to Deleuze, however, not only the depicted characters are making a "free indirect discourse." When the filmmaker Rouch shoots a film with black characters, his Ego as a white man makes his own "free indirect discourse"[9] by becoming "an/-other."

Like other contemporary filmmakers, Marhöfer and Lylov have been influenced by Rouch. And like Rouch, they construct their own "free indirect discourse" by becoming "an-other" when they film their characters. However, Marhöfer and Lylov are not visual anthropologists. They rather understand their work as "not human-centered." Therefore, when they make their own "free indirect discourse," their Egos as human beings become not someone but something, that is, "an-other" as the "other-than-human" and the "more-than-human."

5

As if to justify André Bazin's statement in *What Is Cinema?* "The human being is all-important in the theater. The drama on the screen can exist without actors,"[10] the main characters in Marhöfer and Lylov's *Soils_Habit_Plants* are not human beings but wild millet, Japanese knotweed, Sugi and Hinoki trees, and their soils.
The human body does not appear at all, not even partially. The most artificial thing that is shown, is a photograph of a forest, placed on the Sugi cedar forest floor. As Marhöfer and Lylov explain in an accompanying text[11] the photograph shows a forest in Sarawak, Malaysia, and was taken when the area was still a British Colony. The shooting of the photograph calls to mind the historical fact that the Sugi cedars and Hinoki cypresses appearing in the film are not completely "natural," but actually they are trees of the monoculture forest plantation promotion that was uniformly carried out in the past to meet the demand for timber as construction material in Japan. Later, when cheaper wood became available for import from Malaysia and South East Asia, the value of these plantations decreased

9
See Gilles Deleuze, *Cinema 2, The Time-Image*, trans. Hugh Tomlinson and Robert Galeta (London: Athlone Press, 1989), 183.

10
André Bazin, *What Is Cinema?*, trans. Hugh Gray (Berkeley and Los Angeles: University of California Press, 1967), 102.

11
Elke Marhöfer and Mikhail Lylov, "Soil_Habit_Plants," mikhaillylov.com.

rapidly. As a result, the plantations lost their commercial interest, and today, many of these forests are neglected.
Another artificial thing drawing special attention is a container that looks like a scientific test instrument. From the above-mentioned text we learn that the container is a micro test plate used to examine soil microbial diversity. The conducted soil tests show that soil in which a diverse range of vegetables, weeds and wild millet grow contains the highest microbial diversity.
Like the forest plantations, the wild millet and the Japanese knotweed, that are part of the film, are not simply "natural." Wild millet is considered a "pest" in rice monoculture fields and the endless target of weeding, while Japanese knotweed is an "invasive species" and a target of extermination in the UK. Generally speaking, they are both considered to be harmful plants. However, as the soil tests indicate, these plants are not at all harmful but rather helpful from the point of the view of soil microbial diversity.

6

In "A Tomb for the Eye," Daney describes Huillet and Straub's way of making films as "the stubborn refusal of all the forces of *homogenization*." Following this idea, we could describe Marhöfer and Lylov's way of making films as the stubborn refusal of all the forces of *monoculture*. However, that refusal is also affirmative. The filmmakers' NO is a NO that is actually at the same time a YES. When Huillet and Straub stubbornly refuse all forces of *homogenization*, and when Marhöfer and Lylov stubbornly refuse all forces of *monoculture*, at the same time they fully affirm the desire to caress the earth.

> A film has nothing whatsoever to do with war. One doesn't want to conquer the earth, one wants to caress it. A film has to do with eroticism and not with strategy.[12]

If Marhöfer and Lylov's *Soils_Habit_Plants* is filled with eroticism, then that is why: *I am a wild millet, a Japanese knotweed, a Sugi cedar, a Hinoki cypress, soil...*

12 Jean-Marie Straub, Elke Marhöfer and Mikhail Lylov, "A Thousand Cliffs," 405.

Rinaldo Censi

Site Inspections

Something that has always fascinated me in the work of Jean-Marie Straub and Danièle Huillet is the cartographic exploration of the places they will shoot. Before making a film, the locations are studied by them, crossed, walked, traversed. They are measured. It is well known that the inspections made for *Moses und Aron* lasted many months.[1] Jean-Marie and Danièle toured Italy in Danièle's mother's car, looking for the right site. They finally landed in Sicily, in Segesta, past the Abruzzi, in Alba Fucens (where they shot the film). We can imagine them on the road equipped with maps. Taking photos, choosing lenses, making notes. Jean-Marie Straub once recalled,

> For the Egyptian portion of *Too Early/Too Late*, we went to Egypt one year before the shoot to do location scouting in the villages. We had the maps drawn by the expedition of Napoleon. The geographers who accompanied him made precise maps, with the wheat fields. When we showed these maps to the film crew, they didn't know how to read them, so Danièle had to write out very explicit itineraries. It was the same for the French segment. No one had ever gone to these Breton villages. That said, we made these itineraries primarily for ourselves. Danièle used to send them also to members of the film crew just in case they got lost on the way.[2]

The idea of site inspection and moving around using a map, has always reminded me of the gesture of Land art artists, Robert Smithson in particular. I doubt that Jean-Marie and Danièle have ever heard of Smithson. I have never asked them. Domenico Carosso, a scholar who, together with Danièle, translated the movie dialogues taken from Hölderlin and Kafka from German to Italian, wrote a book about Huillet and Straub entitled *Straub e la resistenza del cinema (con Pavese, Kafka, Hölderlin, Cézanne).*[3] In the appendix, one can find a passage dedicated to *Schwarze Sünde*, "The whole dispositif operates as an artefact, an 'artificial' object, also, close to those of Land art." What could be associated with Straub is when Smithson says,

> I very often travel to a particular area; that's the primary phase. I began in a very primitive way by going from one point to another. I started taking trips to specific sites in 1965: (...) when you take a

1 Regarding the process of the shooting, see the wonderful "Journal" written by Gregory Woods and annotated by Danièle Huillet. G. Woods, "A Work Journal for *Moses and Aaron*" and D. Huillet, "Notes on Gregory's Work Journal" in *Jean-Marie Straub and Danièle Huillet: Writings*, ed. Sally Shafto (New York: Sequence Press, 2016), 276–331.

2 Jean-Marie Straub, "Itinerary for *Too Early, Too Late*," *Writings*, 340.

3 Domenico Carosso, "Peccato Nero" in *Straub e la resistenza del cinema (con Pavese, Kafka, Hölderlin, Cézanne)*, (Turin: Mille, 1990), 45.

trip you need a lot of precise data, so often I would use quadrangle maps; the mapping followed the traveling."[4]

Maps are often linked to a stratigraphic conception, a geological space, this is an aspect that has always been of interest for Danièle Huillet and Jean-Marie Straub.[5] We find the same idea of the stratigraphic in Lucy Lippard's book *Overlay*,

> The map, and the map-derived art, is in itself fundamentally but an overlay—simultaneously a place, a journey and a mental concept; abstract and figurative; remote and intimate. Maps are like 'stills' of voyages, stasis laid on motion.[6]

SITES, NON-SITES

For Huillet and Straub, the sphere of the map also relates to the space of history and memory. Smithson expresses something similar, but in a rather provocative way. Like a geologist he argues, "I think we all see the landscape as coextensive with the gallery. I don't think we're dealing with matter in terms of a back to nature movement. For me the world is a museum. Photography makes nature obsolete." In short, what is important is the study of specific sites. Dominique Païni, in his book *Le Temps Exposé*, even if not citing Land art, describes the work of Huillet and Straub as a "mise en site" of the places that they project to film.

> The Straubs' mise en scène does not only involve familiarizing themselves with a specific space, sometimes a highly organized site," (as at Segesta), "it also relates to a veritable 'mise-en-site' [settling-into-site], the occupation of a space determined by invisible yet imposing contours, in other words, a sacred era.[7]

Dialectics are at work between the *site* (a natural space), and what will become the *non-site* (the material gathered on site, shown in a gallery, a museum, or a movie theater in case of a film). In "Fragments of a Conversation" (1969), a text that deals with Cézanne, Robert Smithson talks about the way he frames a site,

> I'm interested in making a point in a designated area. That's the focal point. You then have a dialec-

4
"Discussion with Heizer, Oppenheim, Smithson," in *Robert Smithson: The Collected Writings*, ed. Jack Flam (Berkley: University of California Press, 1996), 244.

5
See essays by Serge Daney and Gilles Deleuze, for example: "To the question: what is a Straubian shot?, one can reply, as in a manual of stratigraphy, that it is a section comprising the stippled [*pointillées*] lines of vanished *features* and the complete lines of those that are still touched." Gilles Deleuze, *The Time-Image*, trans. Hugh Tomlinson and Robert Galeta (London: Athlone Press, 1989), 244.

6
Lucy Lippard, *Overlay: Contemporary Art and the Prehistory* (New York: Pantheon Books, 1983), 122.

7
Dominique Païni, *Le temps exposé. Le cinéma de la salle au musée* (Paris: *Cahiers du cinéma*, 2002), 115.

tic between the point and the edge: within a single focus, a kind of Pascalian calculus between the edge and the middle or the fringe and the center operating within a designated area. And usually when you focus on it with a camera, it becomes a

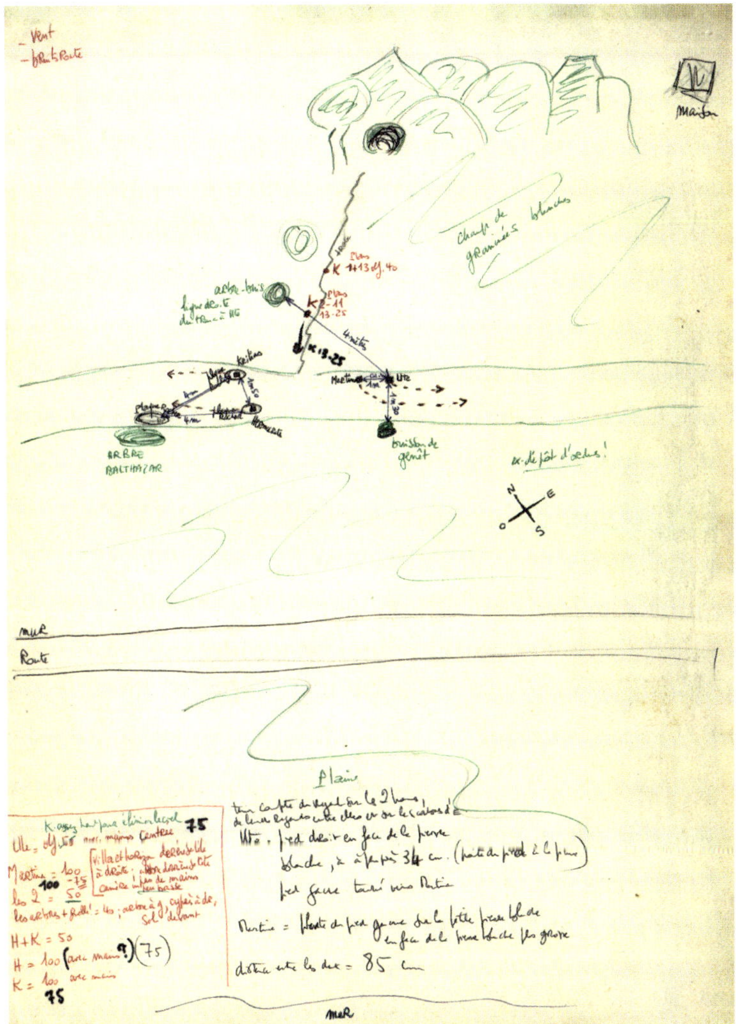

Diagram for the shooting of *The Death of Empedocles*.

rectangle. The randomness to me is always very precise, a kind of zeroing in. But there is a random element: the choice is never abolished. I would say the designation is what I call an open limit as opposed to a closed limit, which is a non-site usually in an interior space. The open limit is a designation that I walk through in a kind of network looking for a site. And then I select the site. There's no criteria; just how the material hits my psyche

> when I'm scanning it. But it's a kind of low level scanning, almost unconscious. When you select, it's fixed so that randomness is then determined. It's determined in uncertainty. At the same time, the fringes or boundaries of the designation are always open. They're only closed on the map, and the map serves as the designation. The map is like a key to where the site is and then you can operate within that sector.[8]

Jean-Marie and Danièle close those fringes as a frame—although the filmed frame is never entirely closed (the Bazinian difference between *cadre* and *cache* comes into play here). A lot of information arrives from outside: sounds, atmospheric conditions, natural objects, flying insects.
To survey *sites*. Often with a map. To travel, measure and observe and make a site inspection. *Too Early/Too Late* opens with the framing of a site par excellence, Place de la Bastille. A camera-car circles the roundabout and the monument located in the center. Here, in this single frame, there's a whole lesson about the historical-geological "layers" that their panning movement or their framing can produce. The rotating movement on Place de la Bastille circumscribes a revolutionary reference as well as the here and now, what that place has become: the emblem of an impossible revolution. The square at the time of François Mitterrand.
Think of the panoramic movements on the Apuan Alps in *Fortini/Cani*, or the movements that open *Othon* and *Toute révolution est un coup de dés*, or the panoramic movement on the "Pont du Carrousel" in *Une visite au Louvre*. Think of *Antigone* (the ancient Greek theater of Segesta) and *Der Tod des Empedokles*, or the labyrinthine movements in the camera-car along the streets of Rome (a city that is a concentrate of geological-historical layers) in *History Lessons*. In *Too Early/Too Late* the whole film is a long treatise in dialectical form on the measurement, the capture of places charged with history: empty, abandoned Breton places, and vital places such as the Egyptian countryside.

Each of Huillet and Straub's films, each one of their shots is the visible result of an invisible labor of surveying. Again, regarding *Too Early/Too Late*—just to give a better

8 William C. Lipke, "Fragments of a Conversation," in *Robert Smithson: The Collected Writings*, 188–89.

idea of the meticulous effort associated with their inspections and shooting—it is worth quoting excerpts from a letter by Danièle Huillet, dated Rome, August 19, 1980, addressed to Willy Lubtchansky, director of photography of the French part of the film, and camera assistant Caroline Champetier (the Egyptian part of the film would be filmed by Robert Alazraki). After compliments, what follows is a precise account, a sort of technical history related to problems in development and printing: positive defects, "red spots," and "white dust," hair on the frames and traces of "anti-halo" spread all over the negative. Considering the shoot in Egypt, Huillet writes to Lubtchansky,

> Willy, take care of your eyes, particularly in Egypt, where the sun is not at all like in Brittany! Twice, there was a blue *velatura* (stain) in the middle of a take that comes from the eye moving away from the viewfinder... That didn't bother us, but more care should be taken! And finally, Willy again: pay attention to the noises during the shoot; there are quite a few noises from jackets, some small cell noises... and some noises from shoes. In *Fortini[/Cani]*, Ciccio [Renato Berta] moved around barefoot so as not to make any noise.[9]

9 Huillet, *Writings*, 348.

The "holiness of accuracy"—that's what "communism" deals with, says the protagonist of George Steiner's novel *Proofs and Three Parables*. An Italian professor, portrayed in the figure of the famous philologist Sebastiano Timpanaro, states that if "the holiness of accuracy" exists, it is precisely this; and we find it in the continuous work of axis setting, measurement, preparation: in meteorological, stratigraphic and optical study. This incessant attention to every detail is intended to vanish at the moment of the shoot. The much-quoted "severity" of Straub and Huillet's work is basically the obstinate attention to things, so that everything looks like it is under control.
But this precision is just insurance, a pledge that has to be paid in view of the "gifts" that will be fixed on the film. For Straub and Huillet, each shot is a *coup des dés*: a fight between the precision of the inspection and the framing, the diction of the recited text and the meteorological whims. It seems paradoxical, but all the effort, the

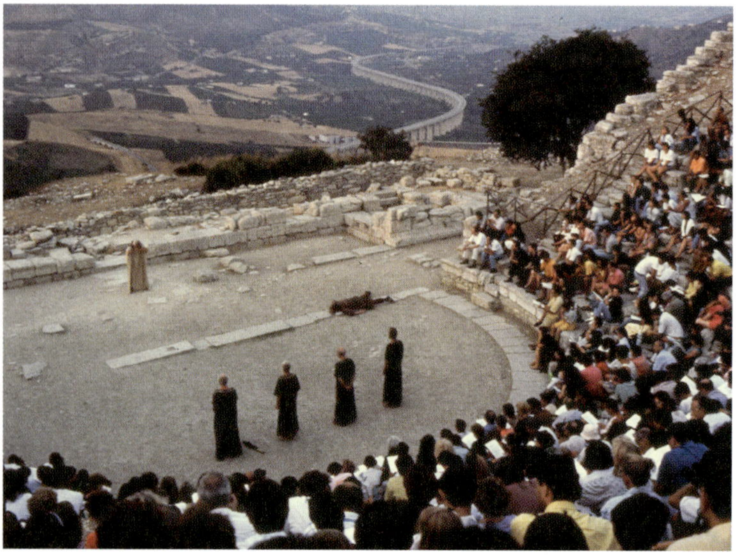

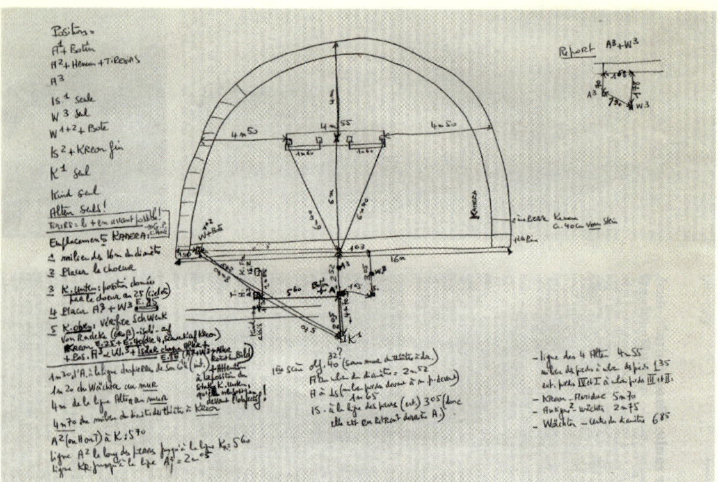

Arbeitsskizze des Teatro di Segesta von Danièle Huillet. Darin eingetragen die Positionen und Wege der Darsteller, die Entfernungen zwischen den Figuren, ihr Verhältnis zur Architektur des Theaters und der fixe Standpunkt der Kamera.

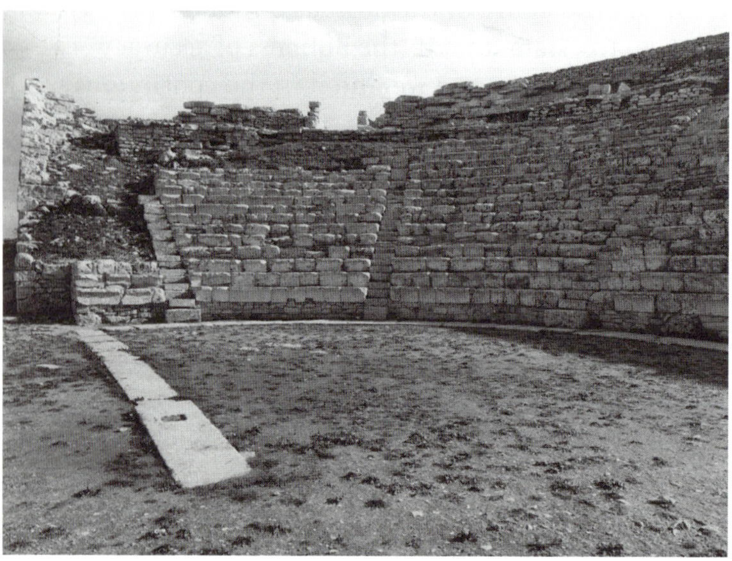

preparation, converge on the idea of letting things happen—nothing is fixed, ready to welcome the unexpected, letting some events take place.

An equally informative example for their approach to a site is the series of drawings related to the shooting of *Der Tod des Empedokles*. As Jean-Marie Straub recalls,

> Danièle did these drawings for Renato Berta [the cameraman] but also for us. I think that they were even more useful to me, to refresh my memory during the shoot, than to the cameraman.
> We visited the filming location several times, the year before. We imagined the actors, what they said to each other, their position in relation to each other, and their movements. This location work is essential; otherwise you do any old thing during the shoot. If it is not mastered by patience and time, it's worth nothing. It must penetrate and it must take root.
> This work was done together with Danièle. We would look and I would choose the lenses; very quickly we saw that there was only one lens possible for what we had in mind. You can't let the cameraman choose the lens half an hour before shooting; that only results in confusion.[10]

10 Jean-Marie Straub, "Diagrams for *The Death of Empedocles*," in *Writings*, 352.

The idea of taking root and penetration indicated by Straub was the result of a prolonged study and location survey and deals with the quest for a regime of intensity and concentration. Can we draw an analogy from Straub's "only one lens possible" to Smithson's "point"? When he says, as cited above, "I'm interested in making a point in a designated area. That's the focal point."
There is only one point from which things must be filmed. To take root and penetration, precision of framing, concentration and intensity, are the necessary elements for the quest of the exact point, what Paul Cézanne called *motif.* All the site inspections, Danièle Huillet's drawings, Jean-Marie Straub's attempts with lenses, all the postures played, all these procedures converge, serve to stabilize, harmonize, fix the boundaries of the frame. As Cézanne said, "Il faut se faire un optique." But how should we read this phrase? The term "optique" could be considered as the goal toward a "logic" or a "logistics" of sensation.

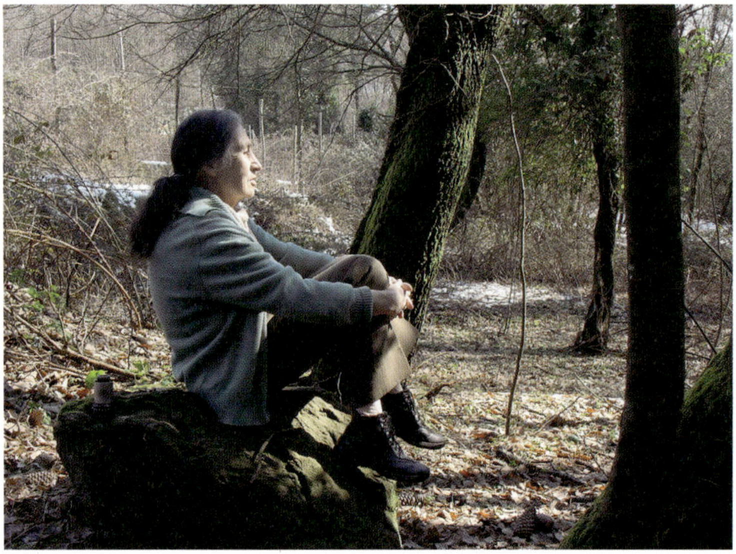

GEOLOGICAL IMPLICATIONS

In the above-mentioned text, Robert Smithson talks about Cézanne as a starting point to talk about his own work on sites:

> Cézanne and his contemporaries were forced out of their studio by the photograph. They were in actual competition with photography, so they went to sites, because photography does make Nature an impossible concept. It somehow mitigates the whole concept of Nature in that the earth after photography becomes more of a museum. Geologists always talk of the earth as 'a museum'; of the 'abyss of time' and treat it in terms of artifacts. The recovery of fragments of lost civilizations and the recovery of rocks makes the earth become a kind of artifice.
>
> I do think an interesting thing would be to check the behaviour of Cézanne and the motivation to the site. Instead of thinking in formalist terms—we've gotten to such a high degree of abstraction out of that—where the Cubists claimed Cézanne and made his work into a kind of empty formalism, we now have to reintroduce a kind of physicality; *the actual place* rather than the tendency to decoration which is a studio thing, because the Cubists brought Cézanne back into the studio.

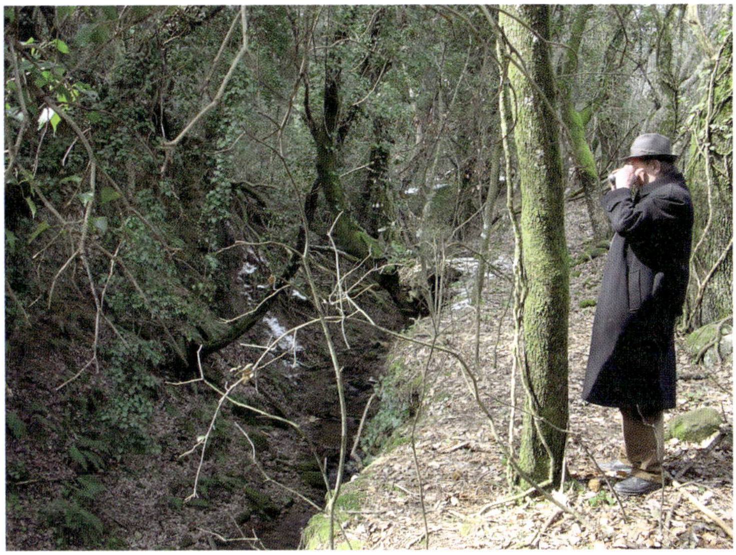

> It would be interesting to deal with the ecology of the psychological behaviour of the artist in the various sites from that period. Because in looking at the work today, you just can't say its all just shapes, colors and lines. There is a physical reference, and that choice of subject matter is not simply a representational thing to be avoided. It has important physical implications. And then there is Cézanne's perception: being on the ground, thrown back on to a kind of soil. I'm reversing the perspective to get another viewpoint, because we've seen it so long now from the decorative design point of view and not from the point of view of the physicality of the terrain. That perception is needed more now than the abstract because we're now into such a kind of soupy, effete thing. It's so one sided and groundless.[11]

11 Lipke, "Fragments of a Conversation," 188.

12 Eric Michaud, "Les sensations de Cézanne,"*Critique,* no. 390 (November 1979), 953–963. Later in E. Michaud, *La fin du salut par l'image* (Nîmes: Jacqueline Chambon, 1992), 51–60.

This point of view of ecology, physical reference, of physicality of the terrain is close to how Danièle and Jean-Marie prepared their films. The subject matter has important physical, geological implications, depicted with images and sounds. In an essay dedicated to Paul Cézanne, Eric Michaud has clearly outlined some aspects related to the achievement and to the process of painting conversions conceived of as possible by Cézanne's method. Cézanne was not interested in theoretical disputes, since he was engaged in reasoning and understanding some movements, on *site*, through nature.[12] Cézanne tries to explain this process to Joachim Gasquet as he describes a scene in which Cézanne takes from the shelf a book by Balzac, *La peau de chagrin* (The Magic Skin) and reads, "a tablecloth as white as new fallen snow and on which the place settings rise symmetrically, each one crowned by little blonde rolls." Whereupon Cézanne declares,

> Throughout my youth, I wanted to paint that, this tablecloth of fresh snow. I know now that I must paint only 'place settings rise symmetrically' and 'little blonde rolls.' If I paint 'crowned' I'm ruined. Do you understand? And if I truly balance and nuance my place settings and my rolls as from nature, you can be sure that the crowns, the snow, and all the flickering will be there too.[13]

The interpretation of this extract, proposed by Eric Michaud, appears to be very illuminating, "Cézanne does not paint any effect: he paints the *conditions* of the *production of the effect*. In other words: prepares the conditions for its possible emersion for other gazes."[14] Cézanne avoids painting "crowned," he avoids painting the *metaphor*, the literary, Michaud insists, in order to avoid the fixation of the *sense*, and reduce reality.

To shoot the *conditions of the production of the effect*, the conditions of the possible emersion of other gazes, isn't that also the goal that Danièle Huillet and Jean-Marie Straub have tried to achieve with their furious preparatory work? We witness the study of a delimited place, a landscape, a *motif*, and we witness the emersion of a series of "effects," their resonance in other gazes. These conditions include a physical, geographic, geological dimension linked to an idea of *sensation* that is charged with memory: a place of historical memory (panning the Apuan Alps, or Place de la Bastille), but also a place where a personal memory is at work (*Lothringen!*, *Itinéraire de Jean Bricard*).

Like Cézanne in his last years, a motif painter addressed to the present, we could say that Danièle Huillet and Jean-Marie Straub have always filmed memory areas. For both, the painter and the filmmakers, this temporality must be understood *geologically*. In his wonderful work on Cézanne, art historian Jean-Claude Lebensztejn elaborates that in Cézanne's work the present is only a way to "conceal the layers, superficial or buried, of memory"[15]—historical

13 Michael Doran, ed., *Conversations with Cézanne*, trans. Julie Lawrence Cochran (Berkeley: University of California Press, 2001), 158.

14 Michaud, *La fin du salut par l'image*, 51–60. Translation: R. Censi.

15 Jean-Claude Lebensztejn, *Études cézanniennes* (Paris: Flammarion, 2006), 30.

or personal. In other words, we can paint (or film), "here anticipating, there recalling, in the future, in the past, *under the false appearance of a present*."[16]

Commenting on the "diagrams" for *Der Tod des Empedokles*, Jean-Marie Straub remembers that during the surveys Danièle drew the space, sketched the landscape that would be filmed near the Etna volcano—their *motif*. In the lower left corner of the paper is written: "Balthazar tree." What does that mean?

> 'Balthazar Tree,' that's where we left the dog on a leash all day while filming. He was used to it. When we'd come, we would unleash him, and would let him go free and he would go lie down under his tree. But we tied him out of precaution, so that he wouldn't come out of curiosity. Balthazar was fine there, in the shade, under this tree; he chose it himself.[17]

On September 2, 1906, before going to the river to paint *Les Baigneuses*, Cézanne wrote to his son, "There are tall trees, they form a vault over the water."[18] But as Lebensztejn points out, "[Theodore] Reff noted [...] that the vault of *Les Baigneuses* evokes not so much the trees that Cézanne saw on the Arch River in 1906, the year of the painting, but rather the lanes of chestnut trees at Jas de Bouffan that he had seen since his adolescence and painted in the 1880s."[19] Like Cézanne, Straub and Huillet's work deals with these huge dimensions of memory—historical, first of all. Still, something intimate seems to be hidden in their films, a personal memory.

Consider the following hypothesis: the directors of "severity," who never grant anything to the viewer, are not only the ones who have tried to give the spectator more freedom, but, in addition, in contrast to the refrain that calls them hermetic, incomprehensible, they are also the ones—thanks to Cézanne's lesson—that have attempted a similar enterprise: to blend into their filmic process "with the same intensity, and at the same time, observation, memory, imagination, and mental construction."[20] Past, Future, Present. There is a sort of temporal instability that puts Cézanne's canvases and the films of Straub and Huillet in contact. They remain slippery, because they are

16 Lebensztejn, *Études cézanniennes*, 35. Lebensztejn is quoting Stephane Mallarmé's, "Mimique" (1886). See *Divagations* (Paris: Fasquelle, 1897), 189. Translation: Barbara Johnson in Jacques Derrida, *Dissemination* (London: Athlone Press, 1981), xxii.

17 Straub, *Writings*, 352.

18 Alex Danchev, ed. *The letters of Paul Cézanne*, trans. Alex Danchev (London: Thames & Hudson, 2013), 266.

19 Lebensztejn, *Études cézanniennes*, 34. Translation: Ted Fendt.

20 Lebensztejn, 35.

seized in a false appearance of the present. Or rather, inside image and sound a subterranean, thinner, completely mental dimension that complicates this present is embedded. Making it complex indeed.

Strokes on a canvas. Single units of sensations. Sudden shifts of light during the shoot, or a sound, a sudden shadow projected over an actor while reciting, and set on that exact word—everything looks so concentrated, intense, sensual. Perception, memory, imagination, intellect, affectivity, in short, sensation and temperament. Could all this emerge and be triggered by a meticulous study of a space, a landscape to be filmed? "Sensation, the encounter between temperament and the world," Lebensztejn writes, "is that to which Cézanne's touch is trying to provide an equivalent in painting: that touch that strikes us as the *vibrato* of his emotion. In its quantum of energy, it releases the maximum information, dissolving the conventions dissociating the mind from the heart, perception and illusion, the present and what is not present—absent, past, phantom."[21]

21
Lebensztejn, 43.
Translation: Ted Fendt.

By reviewing *Il ginocchio di Artemide* [*Artemide's Knee*], while the camera pans over the woods and the clearing near Buti, a memorial monument comes into the picture / frame, for the victims of a Wehrmacht execution on July 23, 1944, when eighteen men were killed, mostly farmers, one realizes that all layers are there, sensation and history. Andrea Bacci, the "actor" that Danièle probably respected most, told me, that location scouting, site inspections were made years before, when Danièle was still alive. You can get to Mount Piavola only with a camion. It's difficult to get there. And if you look at the end of *Artemide's Knee* you can perceive in those pans also the physical, intellectual and durational efforts to capture the present, past and the intimate at once—hidden in plain sight.

Renato Berta, Rinaldo Censi

WHEN THE IMAGE DOESN'T EXIST YET

[This text is the transcript of a public conversation that took place at Akademie der Künste, Berlin, on September 16, 2017, in the framework of "Tell it to the Stones: The Work of Danièle Huillet and Jean-Marie Straub."]

Rinaldo Censi: Renato is surely one of the most important directors of photography in the field. He has made more films with Jean-Marie and Danièle than anybody else and knows them extremely well. I want to begin with Buti, this Tuscan village, I want to start out from there, from the last place where they worked together. The first film they made in that place was *Sicilia!*. It is an area outside the village, in an agritourism called Il Seracino, where there's a sort of small wood and a clearing... that time, Willy Lubtchansky was the cinematographer...

Renato Berta: ...and in Buti they were only interiors.

RC: Yes, they filmed between Sicily and Buti, and in Buti only the interiors. The next film, *Operai, contadini*, [*Workers, Peasants*] was the first film to be made entirely in this area. Can you tell us something about Buti, about this space that returns in all the films they made up until... well yes, even after the death of Danièle.

RB: I would like to start, if I may, by making a small comment about everything you said before, above all about the relationship to the work that I do, in the sense that all the comments you have made always begin with finished works...

RC: Yes, of course...

RB: The fundamental difference between you and me is actually, I begin with the works that don't yet exist. This is the absolute, fundamental difference. I will reply to your question, but from another angle, another point of view. It might be interesting to know, how we get to certain outcomes and what are the elements that come into play. Creating the shots, for example, on the basis of what we shoot, of what kind of observation is there already from the point of view—you might say direction to agree—that is, from the point of view of the work of Jean-Marie in particular... I say Jean-Marie in particular because it was Jean-Marie who above all was interested in photography and the shots while the one on the ground was rather Danièle. Danièle took care of the sound. In a mise-en-scène, you can't separate the two things.

Before going to Buti, I was sent a screenplay, for that first film I made in Buti, *Operai, contadini* [*Workers, Peasants*]. So when he hands you a script, Straub has already experimented the shots with a viewfinder, with a visor, in other words, with a small device for more or less seeing the shots, a device that is not at all precise. In the preparation phase we try to check if shots work or not. How we get to this result of the shots is the most interesting part. First, from Jean-Marie's point of view and later, *hop* with my intervention. Voilà. Here we already have a first observation of theoretical nature: How is a shot created? The most important thing, I believe, is not so much what you put in each shot but what you leave out.

In other words, what you don't film. And above all, in the case of Jean-Marie, all this kind of reflection has already been made, on his part, to an extent that, together with the team, decisions have already been made. In Buti, we would often film at about fifty meters from the house we were living in. I always stayed with them, in Seracino, not the whole team, but I lived with them there, because I preferred to, it was better... yes, together with the dogs, the cats. What I find to be really interesting, what I often discussed with Jean-Marie, and precisely in the preparation phase, is why some things were not filmed. And there were often very interesting discussions around this, but it's really hard to understand why a director doesn't film some things and does film others. I'm referring here, in particular, to fixed shots.

So, the problem presents itself in diametrically opposed terms at the moment the camera starts rolling. At the moment when there are panoramas, at the moment when you can't control the framing. When there are fixed shots, Jean-Marie and I spent hours creating the shots, "No, a bit further up, further down, no, more to the left, but there, that branch there, mmm, but you're limiting the shot there, yes why don't we put it a little bit more to the left..." Discussions with Jean-Marie could last for hours. Danièle, a bit off, says, "But are you still at it? You haven't finished yet? But Jean-Marie, didn't you say you were more interested in the sound than in the images?" [Imitating Straub]: "But, no, no, I..., very important, yes but, very important..." So, some very colorful conversations arose.

What is interesting in the fixed frames with Jean-Marie is that once you've established a frame taking into account all these kinds of elements, the frame has become an almost autonomous moment of life, in the sense that everything that happens within the shot are elements that you don't control, voilà. And this equilibrium between the extremely rigid control of a shot and then allowing everything that happens within that shot... Yesterday evening, watching *Empedocles* I found that this point of view is very interesting: everything that happens within the shot are elements that we can't control and we're in the hands of God. This is the great fundamental difference that exists between painting, between Cézanne, if you like, and Jean-Marie Straub.

At the moment when we organize the panoramas, other discussions start. Generally, we fix points in the landscape, that is, the panorama starts from here, goes through here, this way, let's see here. And in a given moment you need to pace this panorama. So I say, "Jean-Marie, how are we going to do this?" It's blind trust. In the sense that he says, "No, you do them, it must be you who has to work within the vista." Time is practically in my hands, at this moment. And this is when it becomes really interesting. And, in fact, if we look closely at all the films I've made—I'm generalizing a bit here—in lots of films I've made, there isn't one shot that looks like another, there is no time that looks like another. The different takes are different, but simply because all the elements that are controlled in the fixed shot, that happen: the wind, the leaves, etc., inevitably condition you and your vision. So you find times that are truly different. The caricature of this fact is in the last shot of *Il ginocchio di Artemide* [*Artemide's Knee*]: there are these shots that go to the right, and then return, just the time to stop and then return, *hop*. For all these kinds of timings, Jean-Marie says, "You do it." Voilà.

RC: But the starting point...

RB: ...and end point, yes, those we agree on together, but, even then, they can change a bit, in the sense that you're never sure, especially when you're filming in nature, the plants move, you're never sure if you're going to get there. In other words, it's simpler in urban environments. In nature it becomes a bit more difficult. But also, Jean-Marie isn't ever going to say to you, "Ah, no, this is a mistake" in an instance when you go a bit further on. But it depends on what is guiding you, you see?

From this point of view, I find the double panorama that we created in *Fortini/Cani* interesting. I'll tell you, how this thing happened. Jean-Marie and I discussed the shot at the start and the shot at the end and they were supposed to be the same. I said, "But, sorry, Jean-Marie, if we start from here, we do the whole panorama here—wouldn't you like to have the possibility, when you edit, to cut in the movement, without the stoppage?" In other words, so that there is only the panorama, which would mean starting a bit earlier... There was a long discussion... starting a bit earlier, then going a bit further in the second [take], so that he can cut the end or the start of the shots. Do you see? I said, "let's start with this shot here and do two panoramas so that you choose the panorama that works best when you're editing."

RC: And he kept them.

RB: Right. To put it bluntly, he screwed me over and kept them both.

RC: Nonetheless, he had thought about this movement, it was something he'd already done...

RB: Yes, but just once...

RC: Once...

RB: Just one panorama, not the two.

RC: This is also a bit linked to some fixed shots where there are continuous repeats and continuity... I can't explain it well, but it's as if there's a moment in which...

RB: It starts again...

RC: Yes, we do another one...

RB: Yes, we do another one. But he always... I don't remember ever having experienced a second take without the "clap." There is always the clapperboard. The shot begins: ah, and clap, "action," it's never "action" but "...Bitte!" or how do you say, "please!" It depends on the actors—"please," and finally, at the end, "merci." The rest and the timings that exist, often there are times that I find interesting, at the end of the shot on Andrea Bacci, where in one take he leaves, in another not; it depends very much on the sound. It depends on how the actor is—and the actor, I thought, was genius. I mean, Bacci, wow! Undaunted, there aren't many actors with whom you can do those kinds of things.

RC: Something interesting that is also linked to the idea of the picture, of the shot, here in this space, in this area of the Seracino, where these films are made: the difference between one film and another may be only twenty centimeters from one point to another. The shot changes, the space changes... For example: *Il ginocchio di Artemide, La Madre* [*The Mother*], or *L'inconsolabile* [*The Inconsolable*] are more or less...

RB: Yes, more or less...

RC: Shot at the same spot, probably from a different angle.

RB: Yes, in fact we often laughed because we'd say, "Oh, Jean-Marie, you're a real idler—you don't want to hear about meters being too long... no, no, no..."

RC: But this is interesting, it means understanding how space is...

RB: Yes, well, how it's interpreted...

RC: How it's treated also because space is what it is, it's always what it is.

RB: So there are various things to be said there. First of all, you have to understand that films are always made one shot after another. In other words, we don't film everything on the run, we film a shot then *hop*, the next shot, if it's a reverse shot and then we go back to the same shot. We already have to find, that is, gradually—this is a first comment—we gradually carry on with the film. If I'm talking about *Fortini/Cani*, the positions, even the positions in the story, and the positions of the machine, were rather rich from this point of view. We gradually advanced, going toward a unique point of view, within certain sequences. In *Artemide*, it's really incredible, we were effectively within a field of two. Marconcini was always with his back to us because we didn't want to have him... we wanted to be on Andrea's side. You have to assume that Marconcini is always with his back to us, in the shots of the two of them, in the shots of him and in the shots of Andrea. That means changing lenses. Then, in *Empedocles* we only had fixed lenses, that is, we gradually proceeded, we began to introduce zooms in the sense that we looked for the frame with the zoom in the same way. In this way, the point of view that came in was absolutely essential taking into account that we were in a system that we could call more rigid in *Empedocles* than in *Artemide*. Do you see? It's clear, isn't it?

From this perspective in the development, I would say I've collaborated on a lot of films that we made together from '69 onward and, you know, I saw Jean-Marie go toward... slowly toward, I'd say, toward a minimalism of the point of view while increasing a bit the [choice of] lenses. Voilà. This would be my comment.

In other words, the essential thing, anyway the most important, is that—how can I say this—within a system that you could call very rigid, even too rigid, there are lots of people who say: it's always the same. As the audience you're already forced to see some things that you're not used to, I'm thinking, in particular, about *Empedocles*. Reviewing yesterday evening a film from a long time ago, a beautiful copy, very good projection, very good sound—congratulations, well done—having this richness of reading images, nonetheless, as an audience, you need to give yourself the means. Of course, there's the text and you can see how this text works within the shots and how you can *fruire* from this text. What's "*fruire*" in French? In English? I don't know, but I believe it's an expression that only exists in Italian. How can it be said, *fruire*—that's the idea of pleasure, isn't it?

So, I heard Danièle say, many times—when we were talking about financing the films, about means at our disposal, her favorite expression was, "Look, our luxury is the amount of film stock." In the sense that we shot loads of takes; in *Othon*, I remember we arrived at... good God, every shot we took had six, seven minutes behind it, we did more than fifty, and yes, in effect, there were those that had even more, yes more, but ultimately they laid claim to the fact that their real luxury was the film stock. A small anecdote: I had a discussion with Danièle and Jean-Marie during the last film we made on Monte Serra, *Quei loro incontri* [*These Encounters of Theirs*, 2005]. While we ate, a discussion ended in tragedy, because with them, the tension went up when there were different positions, psychodramas, and a discussion on the digital. Both, Danièle and Jean-Marie said, "We will never use digital! You're *Kleinbürger* [petty bourgeoisie] because you present this kind of problem." In other words, we were treated like dogs because we brought up the problem of the digital. The conclusion of all this stuff here is, nobody is... In other words, let's say contradictions are part of being human.

At the time, my first reaction was: Jean-Marie, it won't be you who decides, but there are interests that go beyond our decisions and one of the reasons why the effective disappearance of analog film is such a real drama, is that you can't choose. There are certain films that you can film on celluloid, but well... The problem is not so much the disappearance of celluloid but the way of working, the whole system of work that generated a form of reflection. Today, I believe, the digital is a clear democratization on this level, but when we see today what we do with our democracies, it confronts me with some very profound questions.

Translated from Italian by Nicola Iannelli-Popham.

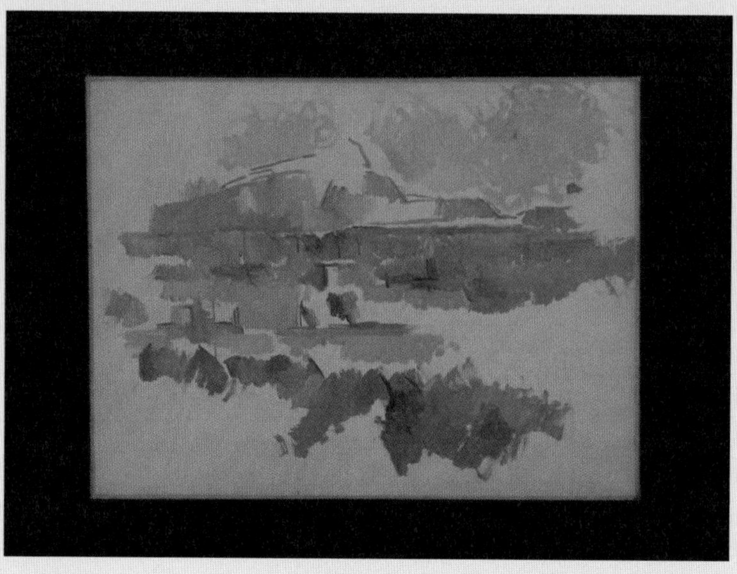

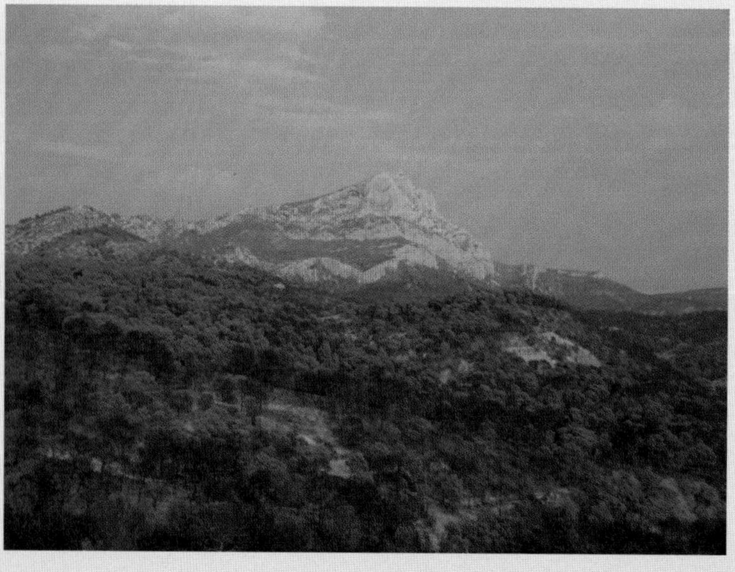

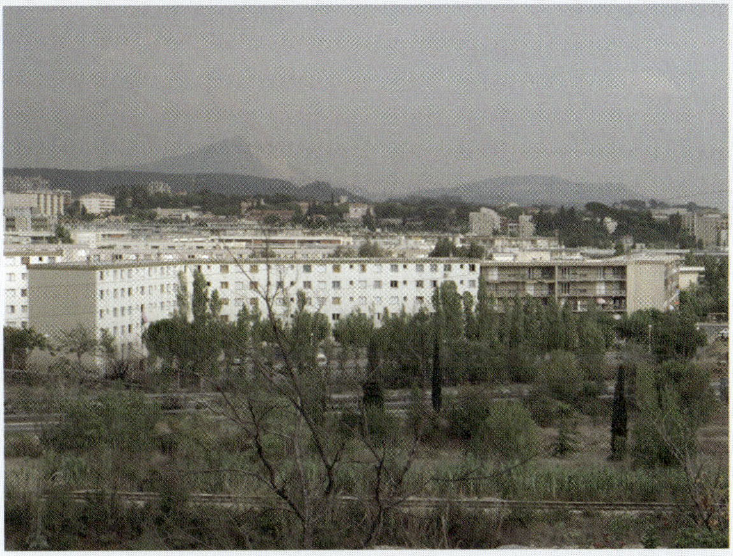
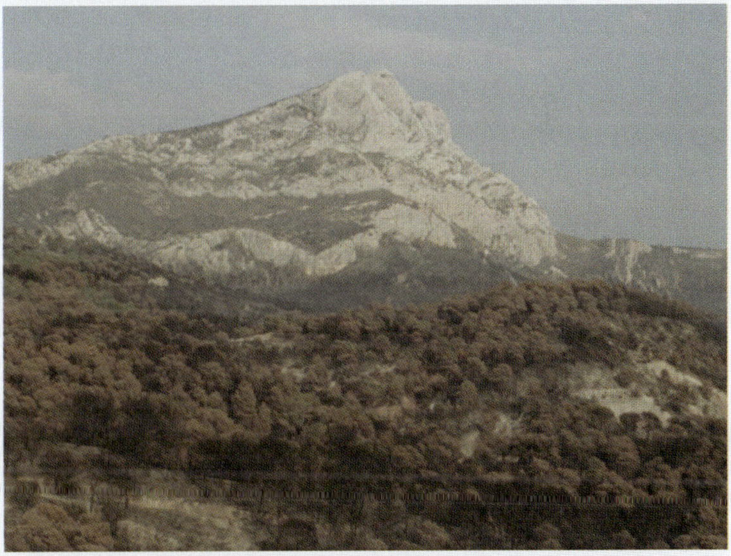
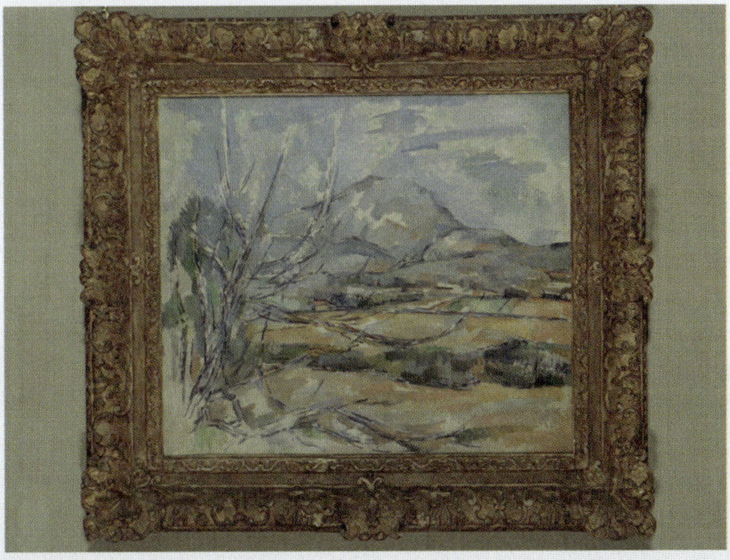

Barton Byg

Paul Cézanne Directs a Film

As I initially told friends that I was working on Cézanne and Straub/Huillet, the most common response would be: "Now that means you can go to France!" Instead, it seemed more consistent with all three artists' practices and the film to walk to the Smith College Museum as often as possible to stand in front of its only Cézanne: *Route tournante à la Roche-Guyon* (1885). Now, since the coronavirus pandemic has made even that impossible, the concentration on everyday, repeated contemplation of what is close at hand resonates more strongly than ever.

The study of Cézanne would be helpful for seeing films by Straub and Huillet even if the artist had never been their subject for two films, *Cézanne, dialogue avec Joachim Gasquet* (*Les éditions Bernheim-Jeune*) (1989), my focus here, and the more recent *Une visite au Louvre* (2003). The painter's work has accompanied theirs for decades. Huillet had first seen Cézanne's *Bathers* (1898) when she was sixteen.[1] And they hitchhiked to the Barnes collection to see the Cézannes outside Philadelphia in 1975.[2] A print of *Apples, Bottle and Chairback* (ca. 1904–1906) had a prominent place in their apartment soon after they moved to Rome in 1969.[3] Postcards of two other still lifes—including *Apples and Oranges* (ca. 1899) which like *Apples, Bottle and Chairback* appears in *Cézanne, dialogue*—were placed above the fireplace of a house in Buti as they filmed interior shots from *Sicilia!* around it. Jacques Rivette noted the aura of Cézanne in the long landscape pans of *Fortini/Cani* (1976),[4] and I cannot look at the close-ups of the pine branches beside Empedocles or the Autostrada behind Creon in *Antigone* without thinking of Cézanne's *Montagne Sainte-Victoire with Large Pine* (1887) and similar renditions of the motif.

I also insist on seeing *Cézanne, dialogue* as more Huillet's film than Straub's and a culmination of her contribution to their collaborative filmmaking over the decades. As a counterpart to Straub's introducing Schoenberg in their short film of 1973,[5] Huillet here takes the role of Cézanne, with the "dialogue" of the title consisting only of a few questions interjected by Straub as the voice of Gasquet. I'm convinced that Huillet speaks more in the interviews about this film than in any other of the filmmakers' recorded conversations, and Cézanne is the focus of one of her very few publications as sole author: "Quite a Lot of Pent-Up

1 Sally Shafto, "Artistic Encounters: Jean-Marie Straub, Danièle Huillet and Paul Cézanne," *Senses of Cinema*, no. 52 (September, 2009) [cited from here on as "Encounters"]. Extended reference at the end of the essay.

2 Danièle Huillet, "Quite a lot of Pent-Up Anger...," in *Jean-Marie Straub and Danièle Huillet: Writings*, ed. and trans. Sally Shafto, with Katherine Pickard (New York: Sequence Press, 2016), 229 [cited from now on as *Writings*].

3 Visible between Straub and Huillet during interviews in Michael Klier's 1970 WDR television piece, *Nicht Versöhnt. Jean-Marie Straub in Italien.*

4 Cited in Shafto, "Encounters."

5 *Einführung zu Arnold Schoenbergs 'Begleitmusik zu einer Lichtspielscene.'*

Anger..."[6] And in her description of the greater possibility of "singing" the text in German rather than in French, thus providing a distance to the Old Masters but retaining a "brotherly" tone, it becomes clear that for this film she was directing herself.[7] To round out the connection between *Cézanne dialogue* and Hölderlin, Huillet appears in the final scene of the companion film, *Black Sin* (*Schwarze Sünde*, 1988), their second film based on the *Empedocles* fragments.

The elements that make up this film, like those in a Cézanne painting, are deceptively simple and few. They include three photographs of Cézanne himself, ten Cézanne works, an excerpt from Jean Renoir's film *Madame Bovary* (1934), two excerpts from Straub/Huillet's *Death of Empedocles* (1986), paired with contemporary shots of Mont Sainte-Victoire, and a final shot outside the painter's studio in Paris.[8]

Although far from a biography or filmography, this film at least points toward key facts in the lives and work of Straub, Huillet, Cézanne and even of the cinematographer Henri Alekan. What follows here will explore some of the formal terms of the film's engagement with Cézanne's life and work, but always with a connection to the most elemental aspects of film art—such as time and editing, fragment and structure, framing and composition, color and space.

Cézanne, dialogue presents a filmed documentation in situ of ten Cézanne works. All but *The Old Woman with a Rosary* (1885–1886) are in the film's second half, culminating with a full-screen image of Cézanne's *Bathers* (1894–1905), the only art work accompanied by the ambient sound with which these filmmakers are often identified. But unlike the live sound in all their other films, and the Empedocles excerpts and other exteriors here, the sound accompanying the *Bathers* is only of the wind blowing in an unknown location. In this shot, they thus have employed their most "documentary" tool almost as a special effect, calling attention perhaps to Cézanne's wish to take classical, studio painting outdoors. This wind, and the ambient sound at the film's start and outside Cézanne's studio in Paris at its conclusion, also invoke the saying from D.W. Griffith Straub has often quoted: "What the modern film lacks is beauty, the beauty of the wind moving in the trees."[9]

6
Writings, 229–231.

7
Paul Cézanne im Gespräch mit Joachim Gasquet. Film von Danièle Huillet und Jean-Marie Straub, Kinomagazin, WDR, 1990.

8
In addition to multiple viewings of the film(s), appreciation of its multiple connections to art history can be gained through Sally Shafto's "Encounters," which also details the ten Cézanne works that appear.

9
Cited in Richard Roud, *Jean-Marie Straub* (London: Secker and Warburg/British Film Institute, 1971), 72.

The rest of the film seems to arise from the first reference to Cézanne I heard Huillet make, and often repeat, including through his voice in this film: "Look at this mountain; once it was fire."

Perhaps more than any other film in the Straub/Huillet oeuvre, which constantly seeks to rediscover and build on the powerful simplicity of silent cinema, this work is a breathtaking exploration of what film can be if it remains open to its own potential and does not seek to obey the rules of narration and film "language." I thus attempt to take seriously Straub's description of the film as a "detective novel."[10] My conclusion is that it is more like a picture puzzle than a mystery, a puzzle that produces beauty no matter how the pieces are assembled, and all the more because so many pieces are missing.

10
Jean-Marie Straub on the occasion of the pre-premiere of *Une visite au Louvre* on March 15, 2004, at the Cinémathèque Francaise in Paris. See newfilmkritik.de, blog entry of July 8, 2004 (in German).

11
Writings, 229.

12
Producer: Jakob Hausmann; Director: Jochen Richter; Glashaus Film Production / RM Arts.

CÉZANNE AS POLEMIC

Given the restraint and simplicity of *Cézanne, dialogue,* it is difficult to perceive its origins in a polemic against contemporary art-world and museum practice, which is more obvious in their interviews and in Huillet's essay "Quite a Lot of Pent-Up Anger..."

Here and elsewhere, Huillet expresses her exasperation at the lack of respect museums show for the works in their charge and for visitors who wish to actually see them. Instead, they endanger paintings by installing them behind (inappropriate) glass, only for insurance purposes. For the *Cézanne* film, leading museums even suggested using existing slides of the works instead of actually filming them as objects in the world. By contrast, Huillet recalls the difficulty of reaching the Barnes collection in the 1970s, then far outside Philadelphia, where "we were happy to have finally found a museum where it was considered normal for people to come to the paintings [...] and not the paintings to the people."[11]

In one interview Huillet also makes it clear that this film was provoked by the video *Cézanne: The Man and the Mountain* (1985),[12] sold widely at museum gift shops. That film is a glaring example of the use of paintings merely as illustration for a re-enacted, kitschy biopic of the artist in period costume and setting. Segments of Cézanne's works are cut out and cursorily panned over, usually on screen for only three to six seconds and never longer than fifteen seconds. The romanticized nineteenth-century setting excludes any intrusions of actual modernity, even those Cézanne had painted, such as the railroads. Instead we are given a horse-drawn cart and bucolic fields—where the painter finally is discovered having collapsed and near death. As Huillet remarked, "... and at that point we just wanted to vomit—enough of Cézanne, enough of the pictures, of the mountain and everything! And so it was clear that the film [their *Cézanne, dialogue*] is also directed against that."[13] According to Huillet, this is the "fraud" emanating from the reliance on reproductions: "... to make people think they have 'seen' (and thus taken possession of) a painting, when without the matter, they have only a shadow, a piece of information."[14]

FRAGMENT AND STRUCTURE

The simplicity and fragmentary nature of many of the elements of this film stand out, and refer strongly to Cézanne's own principles. Only the photographs of Cézanne and each work of art on paper or canvas are presented as integral and complete, with space around them on the screen. Thus, as Cézanne urges in the voice-over text, there is "air" between the elements. Everything else is a fragment, and the number of these in the film's fifty-one minutes (or sixty-three in the German version) is very few. But the separateness of these fragments allows us to connect them in any number of ways: The five separate shots in two excerpts from *The Death of Empedocles* (1986) and its mythologizing, spiritual drama could echo Cézanne's artistic strivings.[15] But these could just as aptly contrast with the drama of bourgeois domesticity found in *Madame Bovary* (1856), or echo the intergenerational dialogue in Gasquet's book itself. Conceptually, visually, and dramatically, these blocks of text are set against Gasquet and Flaubert, as poetry in contrast to prose, as German vs. French, as portraits, landscapes, and portraits in a landscape as opposed to the confinement of the "portraits" of Madame Bovary, her contemporaries, and the *Old Woman with a Rosary* (1895–96).

13 In *Paul Cézanne im Gespräch mit Joachim Gasquet. Film von Danièle Huillet und Jean-Marie Straub*: "... und da war es uns zum kotzen, also da hatte man genug von Cézanne, von den Bildern, vom Berg von allem und da war es klar, dass der Film auch dagegen ist."

14 *Writings*, 229.

15 Nenad Jovanović discusses the function of the excerpts from the Hölderlin drama at length in: "Jean-Marie Straub and Danièle Huillet: The Caveman's Avant-Garde," in *Brechtian Cinemas: Montage and Theatricality in Jean-Marie Straub and Danièle Huillet, Peter Watkins, and Lars von Trier* (Albany: State University of New York Press, 2017), 63–112.

A sense of place is one of the most powerful aspects of Straub/Huillet films, but a sense of location is elusive in *Cézanne, dialogue*. Where does this film take place? It almost seems as if the "dialogue" between the older Cézanne and the much younger Gasquet is "staged" at Les Lauves where the photographs were taken, also by much younger visitors. This mountainside setting echoes the similar Etna dialogue between the older Empedocles and the young Pausanias, for which the long pans over Aix that open the film could serve as establishing shots.

Aside from the distant views of mountains, the film is striking in its visual lack of depth. This seems fitting since the confinement to two dimensions within a frame is a condition of painting. Aside from the *Madame Bovary* scenes, almost all of the visual, spatial drama of the film consists of movement of the eye and the mind within two-dimensional confines. The camera never moves forward or back, and objects within the frame, if they move at all, move laterally and not into and out of the depth of field.

Even the still photographs of Cézanne at work do not reveal either the canvas he is working on or the motif he is painting—both are at a ninety-degree angle to the photograph and the cinema screen, and thus only revealed elsewhere in the logic of the film—as works by Cézanne or in the contemporary views of the mountain itself. As the canvases are seen only from the side in the photographs and Cézanne's palette appears in black and white, only later do these elements reach fulfillment in the paintings. Thus the strong presence of the easel and its geometry also remain a motif throughout the film, as does the changing pattern of shadows in the film's compositions. Between the two-dimensional photos of the painter and the final few paintings in the film, most works are photographed in such a way that their frames cast dramatic, yet varying, shadows. The latest works however are not visibly framed or hanging on a wall, so the easels on which they are placed cast even more striking shadows. The progression in the film is thus: full frame with landscape and sky, with shadows (Aix and Sicily); work within the cinema frame almost as silent film narration (with easels or frames, with shadows); the easels but the cinema screen as frame; then easels with shadows; and finally, full screen cinema again (Paris with live sound).

In distilled form, then, the process of representation from drawing to painting, from line to color, is visible here. On one black and white photo and on the stylized opening title of the *Madame Bovary* excerpt we see the only examples of handwriting in the work, the only two references to a time and place in the entire film. The photos' only indexicality consists in recording what the painter looked like, and we do see the gestures of both Cézanne looking and his hand applying the brush to the canvas, and his placing of a completed canvas on the ground. The empty easel then points to the second half of the film, where pictures will be presented.

Like so many "planes" of space, time and history included in this film—and "plane" is a key term for Cézanne—these photos gesture provocatively to the oblique geometry of memory. The progression of the angles of the easels, from tools to frames to structures in space to sources of shadow, are analogous to the progression from drawing and line in black and white to the paintings with their "taches" of color. They are also a subtle record of the biography of the great cinematographer Henri Alekan at work here. Even the quotation of the Renoir film could point to him, since he was starting out as a camera assistant at the Billancourt studio when *Madame Bovary* was shot there. In the context of painting, he is mainly known as the author of the work *Des lumières et des ombres* (Of Lights and Shadows),[16] which explores deeply his connection of lighting to the paintings of European masters. Straub has underscored how important it was to have Alekan's skills applied to the filming of Cézanne's works, claiming that only this film represents photographs of the art that have been carefully calibrated to the color temperatures of the originals.[17] As a provocative distillation of Alekan's career, the film concludes with breathtaking contrasts in the final four shots: The *Bathers* and the outside of Cézanne's studio are given ample time, with all possible fullness of color and ambient sound. Between them, Cézanne's final statement of exasperation accompanies his unfinished last portrait of the gardener, leaning on an easel toward the left of the frame in front

16
Henri Alekan, *Des lumières et des ombres* (Paris: Librairie du Collectionneur, 1991). Excerpts from Alekan's book appear in German translation in *Die Metaphysik des Lichts: der Kameramann Henri Alekan*, ed. Heidi Wiese (Marburg: Schüren, 1996).

17
Julien Goetz and Catherine Simon, *J.M.S. de A à Z* [*J.M.S. à Metz*], 2011, youtube.com

of a white painted brick wall—a restful image beneath an agitated narration. Then for just a few seconds appears the image of the nude drawing of a woman, with subtle color, to the right of the frame with the most striking shadow of the easel on which it rests, beside it to the left.[18]

TIME

> "...the idiotic and arrogant idea that you can act as if time has not passed!"
>
> — Danièle Huillet[19]

The intersection of art and cinema crystallized in this film is deeply connected with time in a wide range of its meanings. We can see the discussion of the easels above as a simple example of film narration: from empty easel to full canvas to empty easel to full film screen again; and the sequence is loose enough, as in early cinema, that one can easily imagine it running from back to front, or in some other order. For Jean-Louis Raymond,

> The Straubs' frame conveys time; it is inscribed within the duration of the image. Its precision, so propitious for the grasping of the cinematographic movement, opens up a space which gives rise to an experience that is unique, new every time, an experience inscribed within a place whose primary analogy is the frame of painting.[20]

The simplicity of the film's structure foregrounds the passage of time as duration: how long it takes Huillet to deliver each text and how long she pauses (There is much more silence in the German version), how long each "quoted work" is on the screen, how long it takes a truck to enter and leave the frame in the initial pans over Aix, etc. But moments in historical time are equally striking in their presence and juxtaposition. The "vibrations" among them are simply limitless; as several critics have noted, time flows both forward and backward in the film.[21] It is a liberating element.

For instance, only two precise dates are present in the film: one seen handwritten on the edge of the second photo of Cézanne at Les Lauves (by Gertrude Osthaus) from 1904, and one, in stylized handwriting, as part of the title introducing the Comices Agricoles sequence of *Madame Bovary*

18
Granting objecthood to the easel and its shadow as well as the painting finds a parallel in other post-1960s encounters with modernism, such as the work of Robert Irwin, about whom Lawrence Weschler has written, "From the early 1960s onward, Mr. Irwin had been engaged in a successive phenomenological reduction of the art object, insisting that he was pushing cubism's most famous achievement, the collapse of figure and ground, yet further forward: for how, he demanded to know, could that achievement be limited to the action within the frame of the painting—what about the shadows on the wall? Why should they be considered less figure than the object they grounded?" *New York Times*, February 17, 2020: C2. On Cézanne and the objecthood of the landscape, the comments of contemporary Land artist Robert Smithson are equally resonant. Cf. Guillermo Solana, "Ruins of the Landscape," in *CÉZANNE Site / Non-Site* (Madrid, Museo Thyssen-Bornemisza, 2014), 17–27.

19
Writings, 231.

20
Miguel Abreu Gallery, *Jean-Marie Straub & Danièle Huillet: Films and Their Sites*, July 2006; miguelabreugallery.com.

21
Cf., for example, Gilles Deleuze, *Cinema II: The Time-Image* (London: Bloomsbury, 1989 [2013]), 260–262.

(including the date of Juillet 1841). Yet the quoted fictions in the film extend from the fourth century BCE (Empedocles and Greek culture) to Hölderlin around 1800, when as Dominque Païni notes, the origin of a "modern" concept of nature originated.[22]

While the linear presentation of Cézanne's biography would be anathema to Straub/Huillet, placing him and his work in a striking relation to time is one of the film's most radical aspects. The Bovary references are, for instance, related to his contemporaries: the author Flaubert and the painter Renoir, replacing here Cézanne's fraught friendship with Emile Zola. The Flaubert settings and the architecture in the contemporary Paris shots come from the mid-19th century. The class and provincial milieu of Cézanne's origins are similar to those depicted in the film of *Madame Bovary*. That film, however, "repeatedly described as one of Renoir's darkest, [...] reflects the somber mood of the early 1930s when it was made."[23]

There are no images of living human beings from the present day in *Cézanne, dialogue*; the only "present-day" aspects are the varied shots of Mont Sainte-Victoire (two across contemporary Aix-en-Provence and two from the artist's favorite vantage point at Les Lauves), and the final shot of Paris. In the contemporary images in the film we see the mid-century modern architecture evident in Aix and the "present" of Europe in the 1980s—Sicily and France—perhaps echoing Straub's reminder that Cézanne had Italian origins.[24] Other parts of Europe are "present" but only as the locations of the paintings: Scotland, Switzerland, England. Germany is there only in the language we hear, in *Empedocles* and in the translation of the voice-over in the second version of the film. This provides another kind of balance between the two versions: *Empedocles* has French subtitles in the first while Cézanne/Gasquet are translated into German but *Bovary* is not subtitled in the second.

Beyond this, many of Cézanne's statements to Gasquet orient him in time, from the origins of the world ("two atoms...") and the geological past of the mountain to references to Antiquity (Apuleius—providing a parallel to Empedocles) and his own place in art history (as distinct from Impressionism). What eludes him (Nature resisting

22 Cited in Shafto, "Encounters."

23 Mary Donaldson-Evans, *Madame Bovary at the Movies : Adaptation, Ideology, Context* (Amsterdam: Rodopi, 2009), 65.

24 Jean-Marie Straub, "Cézanne/Empedocles/Hölderlin/von Armin," *Writings*, 208.

the artist) is the ability to capture the perceptions—colors, temperatures, smells—of any given moment. The fact that only one image in the entire film is presented twice also makes us conscious of "film time" and the construction of narrative: It is the first photo of Cézanne looking off into the landscape as he reaches toward the canvas to apply paint. After one of Alekan's contemporary shots of Mont Sainte-Victoire, we again see the same image of Cézanne reaching forward with his brush, as if the film's investigation, too, must begin again and again.

CÉZANNE DIRECTS

From the first words of the film, "Greife ich zu hoch... / si je passe trop haut..." (If I reach too high...) the presence of each image in the film can be either immediately or indirectly related to Cézanne's quest to see, understand, and record Nature, what is before his eyes. We are directed at particular points in the film to consider why each image is before us, and at what time.

The painting of the *Old Woman with a Rosary,* the only Cézanne work in the first half of the film, is also the first example of the artist's "illustration" of a point he is making about color, and then about avoiding the "literary" in art. It is most striking that the cut to the Comices Agricoles scene of *Madame Bovary* is one of the few examples in all Straub/Huillet films where the image obediently shows what the sound track is indicating. Here, the words Comice Agricoles are the cue to the cut, which then repeats the phrase in text on the screen. So the words Flaubert, Madame Bovary, Old Woman, and Comices Agricoles are all promptings in the Cézanne text for the Renoir film excerpt.[25]

But the resonances also run in the other direction: Not only is the agricultural fair scene in *Madame Bovary* an example of the "literary" or perhaps auto-biographical environment out of which Cézanne's art emerges, and which he abjures, it is also noteworthy as an anticipation of cinematic style—commented upon by Eisenstein among many others.[26] Yet the "cinematic" in Flaubert is overlaid with the "painterly" emphasized by scholars writing on the Renoir film,[27] a black and white contrast with the rest of the Straub/Huillet film and all of the works by Cézanne in color.

25 The segment representing the Comices Agricoles is accompanied merely by the tinny band and dancehall music to fit the setting and not the much more atmospheric, and in passages strikingly modernist, "Album de Madame Bovary" by the film's composer, Darius Milhaud.

26 Sergei Eisenstein, "Through Theater to Cinema," in *Film Form: Essays in Film Theory* (New York: Harcourt, 1949), 12–13.

27 Robert Stam, "The Proto-Cinematic Novel: Metamorphoses of Madame Bovary," in *Literature Through Film: Realism, Magic, and the Art of Adaptation* (Malden, MA: Blackwell, 2004), 156–157, 163; Mary Donaldson-Evans, *Madame Bovary at the Movies*, 55–56.

As noted earlier, the dynamics introduced by *Old Woman with a Rosary* and its juxtaposition with Jean Renoir's film of *Madame Bovary* hint at biographical resonances such as Cézanne's relationships with others, whether younger men like Gasquet or peers like Zola, Renoir, or Flaubert. The provincial, bourgeois family setting does not narrate Cézanne's biography, but could allude to aspects such as his dependence on his father (echoed here with the painter Auguste Renoir's sons Jean as director and the actor Pierre Renoir as Charles Bovary), his relationships with women, his friendships with Renoir or Zola, etc. Madame Bovary's rebellion against the constraints of society, her wish to go outdoors—while the Renoir film frustrates all these—echoes the artist's similar desires. Not only is Madame Bovary a decidedly "painterly" film, but the interiors in this scene seem to refer to the painter Auguste Renoir's ornate domestic settings. On the other hand, the costume and body language of the film character of an old peasant woman receiving a medal at the fair seem to explicitly quote Cézanne's painting: Renoir positions her obliquely to the other very rigidly symmetrical arrangements in the scene just as Cézanne's painting positions its subject low and to the left of the frame, with an inward-turning mien and an oblique gaze.[28]

The portrait itself was actually owned by Gasquet—apparently a gift from close to the time these dialogues supposedly took place. This detail in turn recalls Cézanne's distrust of the art market. Gasquet later sold his Cézanne painting of Mont Sainte-Victoire,[29] but in the film the only hint of this transaction is the name of the gallery, the same as the original publisher of the Gasquet dialogues. But nothing could be more prominent than Straub/Huillet's adding it to the title of the French version of the film: Bernheim-Jeune.

And finally, in the claustrophobic confinement of Madame Bovary within frames of windows, doors and draperies, it is easy to overlook perhaps the key homage to Cézanne: there seems to be a framed image of Mont Sainte-Victoire on the wall behind her as well.

The static camera of Straub/Huillet does not emphasize confinement in the frame as the moving camera of Renoir

28 In Shafto's discussion of this in "Encounters," she also provides side-by-side images.

29 John Rewald, *Cézanne, Geffroy et Gasquet. Suivi de souvenirs sur Cézanne de Louis Aurenche et de lettres inédites* (Paris: Quatre Chemins-Editart, 1959), 50.

manages to do. Instead, it allows the multitude of detail of light, motion and color within the frame to echo the boundlessness of nature and the freedom it offers—in both texts, that of Hölderlin and that of Cézanne/Gasquet.

But when Empedocles speaks to the light and to the benevolent gods, from where is he speaking? The presumption is that his point of view is ours and that he is present; but he is also already dead. The same is true of Cézanne in Huillet's voice looking at Mont Sainte-Victoire. Unlike the confined and physical Emma Bovary, the voices in the mountains take on the totemic quality Jean Rouch once described.[30] Rouch has likened the long speeches of Empedocles to what ethnography calls the entrance of the hero into a totemic realm—and this is particularly true of speeches from off-screen. They are there and not there; as Huillet put it in regard to the actors, "We showed them how they could extinguish themselves."[31]

30
Jean Rouch, "Kassiber aus der idealen Stadt," newfilmkritik.de, blog entry from July 8, 2004: comments by Jean Rouch on films by Huillet & Straub made in a radio feature in the series "Le Bon Plaisir," broadcast on France Culture on April 24th, 1993 (accessible via franceculture.fr).

31
Writings, 206

It is hard to imagine, then, a greater departure from Staub/Huillet's usual approach to narration than the moments in the film where Cézanne tells us to "look at this." As Huillet has so often quoted, he urges Gasquet to "look at this mountain," which we are also doing—but at both Etna and Sainte-Victoire. He speaks of "my still lifes" just as, or shortly after, the still life *Apples, Bottle and Chair-back* appears on the screen. He speaks of the geometry of representing fruit when *Apples and Oranges* appears. But at one decisive moment he says "over there to the right" and indeed, the camera pans to the right (but not at the precise moment, and at different moments in the French and German versions). Cézanne says to "look at the Pilon du Roi" to the right—where the light of the sea is visible.

This blunt consonance of verbal instruction and cinematic pan forces us to reconsider the two other pans in the film (aside from the busy camera work of Renoir): the two opening shots. If the film is largely made up of paintings, the shots composed by Straub/Huillet that do not show Cézanne or his work should also be seen in this context: as landscapes and portraits. The three pans of the film invite a motion that is conceptual and abstract and not visual—motion from the valley to the mountains, or from the mountains to the sea. The two at the opening both end at Mont Sainte-Victoire, but as in a Cézanne painting, the planes of space are separate and there is no avenue that would lead from the spectator to the mountain. The lush park with trees and shadows framing the first shot, a pan from right to left, keeps the attention in the foreground, not at the arid Mont Sainte-Victoire barely distinguishable in the hazy distance. I suspect some viewers don't even notice it.

The foreground of the second pan has a good deal of lateral motion echoing the camera movement: traffic moves in both directions on the highway (A51) along its light-colored concrete, which echoes the horizontal lines of the modern architecture in the foreground. Despite the vehicles entering and exiting the frame, there is no sense of motion outside but only a confirmation of the flatness of this plane, underscored by the section of railway in the immediate foreground that also leads nowhere. By contrast, the progression of the eye from the trees shading the restful green park in the foreground to the arid first view of the mountain they frame is all the more dramatic.

Recalling these pans to Mont Sainte-Victoire is important later in the film when Cézanne speaks of the difficulty of seeing the geometry of the mountain and its shadows, of representing the psychology of the stone. The later images of Mont Sainte-Victoire, either photographed by Alekan for Straub/Huillet in the first half of the film or as painted by Cézanne in the second, connect as well to the shots from *The Death of Empedocles*, especially the cloud obscuring Mount Etna above a shadowy meadow and stark birch trees as Empedocles invokes Nature and the Gods.[32]

A concrete illustration of this conceptual merging of presence and absence is the third pan of the film, left to right like the second. It is the one "narrated" by Cézanne's text: "look to the right over the Pilon du Roi." He says this is a view of the sea, but visually this is only represented by the light; neither the Pilon du Roi nor the sea is visible. As Cézanne says elsewhere, one cannot depict the sun, only what it does to color. As is often the case in Straub/Huillet films,[33] we spectators do not see what is pointed to, any more than we see the sea over the Pilon du Roi, as

32 In the history of photography, this contrast between mystery and "information" is discussed by Rosalind Krauss in her "Photography's Discursive Spaces," regarding two versions of Timothy O'Sullivan's *Tufa Domes, Pyramid Lake, Nevada* of 1868 and 1875, in *Visual Culture: The Reader*, ed. Jessica Evans and Stuart Hall (London: SAGE, 1999), 193–209.

33 In Straub/Huillet films indirect light and other gestures underscore the significance of a vision outside what the viewer can see: The light of the window as Bach's death is narrated at the end of *Chronicle of Anna Magdalena Bach*, and at the end of *The Bridegroom, the Actress, and the Pimp*. The Rhine, which Straub has called the "pagan river" is the unseen view out the window at the end of *Not Reconciled* and the last image from the veranda in *Machorka-Muff*. Women at windows narrate their unseen memories (the mother in *SICILIA!*, Therese in *Class Relations*) or Laura Betti as Brunelda urges Karl Rossmann to "look" from the balcony in the Kafka film as well, to which he simply replies, "I see enough."

Cézanne instructs. In addition to reminding us of what art and film cannot show, we are also made aware here of the resistance that both art and Nature offer.

OBJECTHOOD AND RESISTANCE: NO RENUNCIATION [KEIN VERZICHT]!

It has been observed that *Chronicle of Anna Magdalena Bach*, Straub/Huillet's first project together, is a film about resistance against death, "the most unnatural thing in the world."[34] And as Laura Mulvey,[35] André Bazin,[36] and many others have stressed—and as Max Raphael argued in the context of Cézanne's Mont Sainte-Victoire[37]—this aesthetic resistance against death is related to political resistance against oppression of any kind. It is a drive toward liberation. Here, let Deleuze speak for the rest:

> What resists death?
>
> Take the case, for example of the Straubs when they perform this disjunction between auditory voice and visual image, which goes as follows: the voice rises, it rises, it rises, and what it speaks about passes under the naked, deserted ground that the visual image was showing us, a visual image that had no direct relation to the auditory image. But what is this speech act that rises in the air while its object passes underground? Resistance
>
> This act of resistance has two sides. It is human, and it is also the act of art. Only the act of resistance resists death, whether the act is in the form of a work of art or in the form of human struggle.[38]

The "objecthood" of art as presented in this film connects to the "objecthood" of Nature, and is given material force by the attention drawn to it by the variation in modes from painting to photography to film. As Bazin writes,

> ...the photograph allows us on the one hand to admire in reproduction something that our eyes alone could not have taught us to love, and on the other, to admire the painting as a thing in itself whose relation to something in nature has ceased to be the justification for its existence."[39]

34 Jean-Marie Straub, "Gespräch mit Danièle Huillet und Jean-Marie Straub," *Filmkritik*, no. 10 (1968), cited in Barton Byg, *Landscapes of Resistance: The German Films of Danièle Huillet and Jean-Marie Straub* (Berkeley: University of California Press, 1995), 69.

35 Laura Mulvey, *Death 24x a Second: Stillness and the Moving Image* (Chicago: University of Chicago Press, 2006), 22.

36 André Bazin and Hugh Gray, "The Ontology of the Photographic Image," *Film Quarterly*, vol. 13, no. 4 (1960): 4–9.

37 Max Raphael, *The Demands of Art* (Princeton: Princeton University Press, 1968), 27–29. It is striking that both the motif of Mont Sainte-Victoire and the Old Woman with Rosary figure so prominently in Raphael's work. However, there is no evidence that Raphael was known to Straub and Huillet. Cf. also John Berger, "Revolutionary Undoing: On Max Raphael's *The Demands of Art*," in *Landscapes: John Berger on Art* (London: Verso, 2016), 44–53.

38 Gilles Deleuze, "Having an Idea in Cinema" in *Deleuze and Guattari: New Mappings in Politics, Philosophy, and Culture*, ed. Eleanor Kaufman and Kevin Jon Heller; trans. Eleanor Kaufman (Minneapolis: University of Minnesota Press, 1998), 19.

And both Max Raphael and Gilles Deleuze connect this view toward art with the possibility of human freedom as well—and for them Cézanne is also the best example. The response in the present, however, on the part of the viewer, is political. All the imagery in Straub/Huillet films presents the world as it is and as complete and sufficient as it is: not as beautiful but as "other." Straub/Huillet's insistence on the "otherness" of both Nature and art, a refusal to commodify either as "information," explains perhaps the visceral dislike some people initially feel for Straub/Huillet films. But as with the reproductions Huillet so vehemently despised, if the adequacy of the dominant film apparatus is its main message, the viewer has nothing to add, nothing to look forward to, nothing to hope for. By radical contrast, the incompleteness of these fragmentary works by Straub/Huillet and Cézanne's impassioned description of his own inadequacy to his task are our source of hope. Here is the hopefulness of Straub/Huillet films, and the deadly despair of the culture they reject. As Jean-Charles Fitoussi puts it: "One can never sufficiently stress how much the famous Straubian 'resistance' is based on an affirmation. [...] The 'no' is meant for those who negate the real."[40]
There is more at stake here than a biopic of a French painter or an exercise in film form or cinema history. What is at stake is the survival of the planet in the face of human "time." Is there time enough, we wonder. The movement of time in all directions in this film is one answer. The dignity of nature as "object," of artworks as objects, or Cézanne's search for the psychology of the stones could be another. Giving Nature its due is to see it as having the right to exist, not to be consumed, used up or even "depicted" by humans.

The accomplishment of this film—which it shares with Cézanne's art—is that it does both: it points to a world of nature that is unattainably and inexhaustibly perfect while presenting an artistic engagement with the world that is as incomplete as it is finite and concrete.

39
André Bazin and Hugh Gray, "The Ontology of the Photographic Image," *Film Quarterly*, vol. 13, no. 4 (1960): 9.

40
Jean-Charles Fitoussi, "Der Marmor hat geblutet. Über *Une visite au Louvre* von Jean-Marie Straub & Danièle Huillet," newfilmkritik.de, July 8, 2004. Translation from *La Lettre du Cinéma*, no. 26 (May 2004).

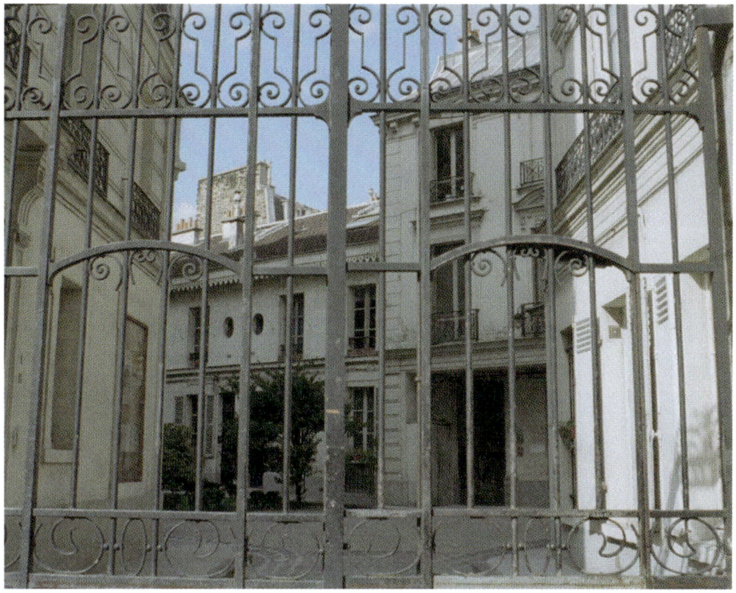

ACKNOWLEDGMENT

In addition to the editors of this volume, it is to Sally Shafto that I owe the greatest debt for inspiring and supporting my work on this topic over many years. I rely on her *Senses of Cinema* article as the landmark analysis of Straub/Huillet's relationship with Cézanne, with details on the exact works contained in *Cézanne, dialogue*. That essay, as well as Shafto's translation and introduction to the *Senses of Cinema* publication on *Une visite au Louvre* (2003)—as well as Dominique Païni's text—are essential. Sally Shafto, "Artistic Encounters: Jean-Marie Straub, Danièle Huillet and Paul Cézanne," *Senses of Cinema*, no. 52 (September, 2009) [www.sensesofcinema.com]; Dominique Païni, "Straub, Hölderlin, Cézanne," *Senses of Cinema*, no. 39 (May, 2006), translation and introduction by Sally Shafto; and Sally Shafto, "On Straub-Huillet's *Une visite au Louvre*," *Senses of Cinema*, no. 53 (December, 2009), followed by her "Transcription of *Une visite au Louvre*." My thanks also to Michael Esser, John Gianvito, Copper Giloth, Catherine Portuges, Andy Rector, Barbara Ulrich, and Klaus Volkmer for their help.

Florian Schneider

REFRAMING WHAT IS ALREADY FRAMED, OR: WHAT IS WRONG WITH PRIMITIVISM?

"I don't like the Primitives." The sentence that opens Danièle Huillet and Jean-Marie Straub's *Une visite au Louvre* alludes to the paintings of late Gothic and early Renaissance masters, most prominently Giotto, or his teacher Cimabue, and Uccello. Paul Cézanne's words continue in the voice-over: "I don't know Giotto well. I would have liked to see him."[1] But what is wrong with the Primitives? Why doesn't Cézanne appreciate these works, yet complains that he didn't have enough chances to encounter their art?

Disentangling the layers of virtual understanding and possible misunderstandings sparked by a sentence or two put deliberately at the beginning of a 47 or 48-minute film—though they appeared very much in the middle of Cézanne's conversation with his friend Joachim Gasquet—might seem like an esoteric challenge suited to ivory-tower academics. On the contrary: the questions that flow from contemplating these lines present a sharp insight into some of the most fundamental aspects of the peculiar ethics of a cinema that can reframe otherwise mutually exclusive alternatives like fiction or nonfiction, expression or abstraction. Furthermore, since it is mainly concerned with the difficulties and conditions of the passage from old to new, questioning the problem of Primitivism can also be seen in the wider framework of an aesthetics of subsistence rather than resistance.

The notion of the 'primitive' is two-fold, at least. The word alone sparks confusion involving, on the one hand, its Latin meaning as 'the first of its kind,' and, on the other, more current and vernacular uses, which derogatorily suggest a value judgment.

In art-historical studies, the term Primitives was coined to distinguish artists of the Early Renaissance period, such as Giotto, from those of the High Renaissance. More specifically, it points to what is nowadays widely considered Northern Renaissance or Early Netherlandish Painting. "Primitifs flamands"[2] denotes several generations of artists who worked in present-day Flanders in the 15th and 16th centuries, ranging from Jan van Eyck to, as some authors like Max Friedländer claimed,[3] Peter Brueghel the Elder. Across the various connotations of Primitivism and

1
Joachim Gasquet, *Joachim Gasquet's Cézanne: A Memoir with Conversations*, trans. Christopher Pemberton (London: Thames and Hudson, 1991), 175.

2
The enthusiasm for Flemish primitivism culminated in the highly influential exhibition "Les Primitifs flamands à Bruges" in the Provinciaal Hof in Bruges from June 15 until October 5, 1902.

3
See Max Jacob Friedländer, "The Flemish Primitives. An Anthology of Max J. Friedländer," *Art News Annual*, no. 26 (1957).

its Italian, Flemish or French flavors, it is supposed to mark the cornerstones of the passage from medieval to early modern art.

Erwin Panofsky prefers the term "ars nova" or new art, as it is used in music where it distinguishes a radically new form of music that appeared in the 14th century, in a break from the preceding "ars antiqua."[4] He insists that a "nouvelle pratique" in painting emerged from a "fusion of sophistication and candor, worldliness and piety, brilliance and truthfulness."[5] What is widely described as 'primitive' must be considered as an "undeniable revolution" that took place in painting in the years between 1406 and the 1420s.[6]

This revolution was international, and it had three main aspects. It introduced, perfected and spread new techniques of painting, such as the blending and mixing of pigments or superimposing layers of paint with different degrees of opacity, usually referred to as the "new oil technique."[7] Furthermore, the science of optical perspective resulting from "the encounter between painting and Euclidean optical geometry"[8] renders the artwork constructible as a "view through a window."[9] Panofsky concludes, "Pictorial space is subject to the rules that govern empirical space."[10] On the basis of these technical and technological innovations, large-scale projects could be carried out in parallel which both required and enabled the implementation of new divisions of artistic labor within a new setting: the workshop. Last but not least it prepared the ground for the exploration of new distribution channels: painting, formerly immobile, gained mobility as a profane object no longer tied to the architecture of a sacred premise but, instead, beginning its transformation into a secularized commodity form.

It is not by chance that Karl Marx described a similar unease with the term 'primitive' when, in his response to Adam Smith's "previous accumulation"[11] in Part VII of *Das Kapital*, he elaborates on "so-called primitive accumulation."[12] Here, the 'primitive,' rather than deriving from an earlier process, points to its metaphysical function as a "legend of theological original sin"[13] and exposes its tautology: How can the new come into being while it is still governed by the very conditions it is about to overcome?

4 Erwin Panofsky, *Early Netherlandish Painting, Its Origins and Character*, vol. 1 (Cambridge: Harvard University Press, 1953), 150.

5 Panofsky, *Early Netherlandish Painting*, 150.

6 Otto Pächt, *Van Eyck: And the Founders of Early Netherlandish Painting*, trans. David Britt (London: Harvey Miller, 1994), 20.

7 Panofsky, 151.

8 Jim Hillier et al., *Cahiers du cinéma: Volume Four, 1973–1978 : History, Ideology, Cultural Struggle: An Anthology from Cahiers du cinéma, Nos 248–292, September 1973–September 1978* (London: Routledge, 2000), 197.

9 Panofsky, 4.

10 Panofsky, 141.

11 Adam Smith, *An Inquiry into the Nature and Causes of the Wealth of Nations* (Nashville: Thomas Nelson, 1843), 111.

12 Karl Marx, *Capital: A Critical Analysis of Capitalist Production*, trans. Samuel Moore and Edward B. Averling (London: Swan Sonnenschein, 1889), 736.

13 Marx, *Capital*, 736.

Smith had argued that capital evolved naturally from increasing specialization, due to division of labor, which allowed for hoarding and stockpiling, but Marx rejects his attempt to explain capitalism's starting point. Instead, he conceived of it as "the historical process of divorcing the producer from the means of production"[14]—or, in the words of Ivan Illich, it becomes "a war against subsistence."[15] But privatizing the means of production, which enabled the idea of capital and surplus value, was preceded by the exploitation of natural resources in the colonies and a system of slavery that "signaled the rosy dawn of the era of capitalist production."[16]

The subtlety or even complexity of Marx's relies on (and reveals) a use of the term 'primitive' that is technical, not judgmental. If there were something like a critique of the political economy of creative practices, Primitivism would indeed function as a "so-called primitive accumulation" within modernity. As a metaphorical device it links the origins of a process of emancipation of artistic work from earlier regimes to its instrumentalization under a new command; and it reframes the urgencies of the Old as outdated, compared to the sophisticated character of what is considered as New.

14
Marx, 738.

15
Ivan Illich, "Vernacular Values," *Philosophica* 26 (1980), 47.

16
Marx, 775.

Rather than a distinct moment in history or a peculiar style, Primitivism refers to a process that insinuates the revolving patterns of consumption of Otherness and the subsumption of difference under a regime of supremacy. Inasmuch as it involves the appropriation of first and foremost exocitized practices ranging from the Spanish Netherlands to French Polynesia, it is the founding myth of modern art as we know it—or as we may take it for granted. But we should take nothing for granted.

Une visite au Louvre starts with a 270-degree panning shot across the southern facade of the Louvre, filmed from the bridge across the Seine. Just as the camera passes the museum building, it suddenly turns back, without the slightest hesitation. The noise of the street, with all its contemporary sounds, accompanies the image as it re-centers the museum in a proper frontal perspective. Then, just as suddenly, a black screen, and the voice-over by Julie Koltaï begins.

Jean Marie Straub met Koltaï on the streets of Paris. He knew her from a neighborhood bar where she "used to make speeches all the time."[17] Until their random encounter, Straub had considered asking the prolific French actor Michel Piccoli to read Cézanne's commentaries, but he was persuaded by Koltaï because, "she spoke with a vocabulary not at all up to date." Straub called her "a pearl, a ruby."[18]

As in many other films by Danièle Huillet and Jean-Marie Straub, the division between professional and nonprofessional actors is at stake; and questioning it was a key part of a systematic revaluation of the purpose and meaning of enactment. Rather than optimizing the illusion of authenticity to encourage empathy and immersion, Huillet and Straub adopted a counter-intuitive method: recognizing ordinary people as experts while treating professionals as if they were lay people.[19]

"I don't like the primitives." The screen remains black while Julie Koltaï recounts Cézanne's reservations about what is not even seen, "It's not my kind of painting," before concluding with the verdict that, "there's no flesh on those ideas."[20]

At first glance, it might seem to be nothing more than a bit of sarcasm. Cézanne repeatedly referred to his technical failings, labeling himself more or less ironically as a Primitive. In a conversation with his student Bernard, he described himself as, "no more than the primitive of the way he had discovered."[21] Also, Cézanne's young friend and admirer Joachim Gasquet was a young Provençal poet who recorded his conversations with the painter from his memories. He happened to be involved in a literary group that operated under the slogan: "We are without doubt the Primitives of a future race."[22]

In this spirit, *Une visite au Louvre* could easily be understood as the kindred meeting of artists who seem equally modest, unrecognized by their contemporaries. Despite the shades of bitterness and self-doubt, they nevertheless believe—strongly—in their art and their ways of working with and in it, no matter what others might think. But even this understanding of the artist being fully immersed into and absorbed by his or her artistic practice,[23] falls short

17 *Jean-Marie Straub and Danièle Huillet: Writings*, ed. Sally Shafto (New York: Sequence Press, 2016), 489.

18 *Writings*, 489.

19 See also Harun Farocki's film, *Jean-Marie Straub und Danièle Huillet bei der Arbeit an einem Film nach Franz Kafkas Romanfragment "Amerika"* (1983).

20 Gasquet, *Cézanne*, 176.

21 Michael Doran et al., *Conversations with Cézanne*, trans. Julie Lawrence Cochran (Berkeley: University of California Press, 2001), XXV.

22 Doran et al., *Conversations*, XXV.

23 See the announcement of the television broadcast by 3sat in 2013: "Ihre Beziehung zu Paul Cézanne ist eine geistige Verwandtschaft. So wie Cézanne sich restlos in seiner Malerei realisierte, so gehen Straub/Huillet in ihrer filmkünstlerischen Arbeit auf." 3sat, "Ein Besuch Im Louvre," programm.ard.de.

of grasping what is really at stake. Right before Cézanne expressed his reluctance to sympathize with the early Renaissance Primitives, he told Gasquet, "But look, see how complicated everything is, life and realism are far greater in the 15th and in the 16th centuries than the elongations of the primitives."[24]

So what is it that could account for, as Cézanne himself saw it, such a surplus of life and realism in the High Renaissance? One possibility would be to attribute it to what Sally Shafto called the "reflection of an age-old debate in the history of art between the followers of Poussin and the followers of Rubens, between the painters of Florence and those of Venice."[25] But that might be misleading, again. Danièle Huillet and Jean-Marie Straub show no interest in reducing *Une visite au Louvre* to just another round of illustrating the artificial dichotomies of art history's desire for binary periodization. They withdraw from the epic battle of style: Renaissance versus Baroque or Classicism versus Romanticism—oppositions according to the criteria that Heinrich Wölfflin identified as the means of art criticism: linear or painterly, closed or open form, multiplicity or unity, and absolute or relative clarity. [26]

By emphasizing color and light, Cézanne argues for a different way of seeing that is more synthetic than idiosyncratic. His "penetrative gaze" is supposed to help us "to see anew, to see better, to really see canvases that we do not know well." "Il nous faudra revoir, voir mieux, voir vraiment, des toiles que nous connaissons mal," as Huillet wrote in a letter proposing the film project to possible supporters under the working title "I am Cézanne."[27]

"People who expect cinema to make them feel do not interest us; I do not consider myself Cézanne, but in front of a Cézanne painting, the sensations are not provoked in you, but you see them there, materialized."[28] Although Danièle Huillet and Jean-Marie Straub do not dare to seduce the spectators to empathize with Gasquet and Cézanne, their film creates an urge to constantly reframe what one assumes as self-evident and might have taken for granted. In 1548, Francisco de Hollanda retells a conversation by Michelangelo and Vittoria Colonna about the main difference between Italian and Flemish Renaissance:

24 Gasquet, *Cézanne*, 130.

25 Sally Shafto, "On Straub-Huillet's *Une visite au Louvre*," *Senses of Cinema*, no. 53 (2009).

26 See Heinrich Wölfflin, Evonne Levy, and Tristan Weddigen, *Principles of Art History: The Problem of the Development of Style in Early Modern Art: One Hundredth Anniversary Edition*, trans. Jonathan Blower, Texts & Documents (Los Angeles: Getty Publications, 2015).

27 "We have to see anew, see better, really see canvases that we do not know..." Translated from a French typescript at Fondo Straub-Huillet, Fondazione Cineteca di Bologna.

28 Serge Daney and Jean Narboni, "De La Nuée À La Résistance: Entretien Avec Jean-Marie Straub Et Danièle Huillet," *Cahiers du cinéma*, no. 305 (1979): 19.

> The painting of Flanders, Madam, will generally satisfy any devout person more than the painting of Italy, which will never cause him to drop a single tear, but that of Flanders will cause him to shed many; this is not owing to the vigour and goodness of that painting, but to the goodness of such devout person.[29]

Empathy and immersion in a work of art—or maybe with or within it—relies on a process of identification. The viewer identifies with what is depicted, in large part by suspending disbelief based on a tacit, mutual agreement that is informed by the experienced degree of proficiency, acquaintance, or relative familiarity. Rather than regarding the artwork in terms of its supposed quality, rather than endowing "things with substantiality,"[30] it pleases the narcissism of the viewer to project a sufficiently developed self onto a commodified image as an object diverse from and yet not its own. This proliferation of the pleasures of representation is, according to Guy Debord, the secularized, "specious form of the sacred."[31] Endlessly played out across society, the spectacle becomes "the normative form of visual experience in modern life."[32]

In contrast, Maurice Merleau-Ponty considers Cézanne's people as "strange, as if viewed by a creature of another species. Nature itself is stripped of the attributes, which make it ready for animistic communions... It is an unfamiliar world in which it is uncomfortable and which forbids all human effusiveness."[33] Almost a century before Debord finished *The Society of the Spectacle*, Cézanne seems to have struggled with the question of how creativity and artistic innovation could subsist in an environment that was increasingly defined by the reification of visual experience—a disruptive experience and profound transition whose beginning he and his contemporaries were witnessing. Cézanne, by making the familiar unfamiliar, anticipated the concept of aesthetic estrangement. More than that, he applied it to nature in ways that emphasize subsistence in the Stoics' notion of a "derivative mode of reality"[34] and gives sensory account to immaterial entities: "Look at the mountain. Once it was fire."

29 Charles Holroyd, *Michael Angelo Buonarroti* (Project Gutenberg, 2006), 280.

30 Paul Smith, "Cézanne's 'Primitive' Perspective, or the 'View from Everywhere,'" *Art Bulletin* 1, no. 95 (2013): 116.

31 Guy Debord, *The Society of the Spectacle*, trans. Donald Nicholson-Smith (New York: Zone Books, 1994), 20.

32 Smith, "Cézanne's 'Primitive' Perspective," 116.

33 Maurice Merleau-Ponty and Galen A. Johnson, *The Merleau-Ponty Aesthetics Reader: Philosophy and Painting*, trans. Michael B. Smith (Evanston, IL: Northwestern University Press, 1993), 66.

34 Vanessa de Harven, "The Coherence of Stoic Ontology" (PhD diss., University of California, Berkeley, 2012), 1.

Une visite au Louvre begins, after a half-minute of black screen, with two complementary views of a masterpiece of Hellenistic sculpture, the *Winged Victory of Samothrace.* There is no doubt about the extraordinary status of this artwork, but at an earlier point in his conversation with Gasquet, Cézanne had already concluded, "I would like to be classical, but that bores me."[35] And, in a brief, almost cryptic remark, he said enviously of the Primitives that they were "looking at the present without being bothered by a past."

For Cézanne, painting is a "means of expressing sensation," as he wrote in a letter to Émile Zola in 1878.[36] It results from a "personal way of seeing," and, as Paul Smith pointed out, "it shows him what this was like."[37] Cézanne reframes immediate visual experience with a self-critical reflection on (or perhaps of) the means of visual production: "The re-forming process which a painter carries out as a result of his own personal way of seeing things gives a new interest to the depiction of nature. As a painter, he is revealing something which no one has ever seen before and translating it into absolute concepts of painting. That is, into something other than reality."[38]

Although the *Winged Victory of Samothrace* has been partly reconstructed, it still lacks its head. But, for Cézanne, it was the absence of the head, its invisibility, that rendered it perfectly present: "I don't need the head to imagine the expression, because all the blood that pulses, circulates, sings in the legs, the thighs, the whole body, has poured into the brain and risen to the heart. It is in motion, the motion of the whole woman, of the whole statue, of Greece. When the head came off, the marble must have bled."[39] In comparison, if the martyrs of the Primitives were decapitated, "A little vermilion, some drops of blood. They fly straight off bloodlessly to heaven. You don't paint souls."[40]

Nearly two minutes into *Une visite au Louvre*, one begins to get a sharper idea of what Cézanne might have intended when he spoke of a surplus of life and realism: it reverberates with what the art patron and theorist Konrad Fiedler has identified as "seeing in the sense of the artist." Unlike scientific evidence, this surplus only begins where "any possibility of language to name and to describe has come

35 Doran et al., *Conversations*, 130.

36 Paul Cézanne, *Letters*, ed. John Rewald, trans. Marguerite Kay (Oxford: B. Cassirer, 1946), 129.

37 Smith, "Cézanne's 'Primitive' Perspective," 102.

38 Ulrike Becks-Malorny, *Paul Cézanne, 1839–1906: Pioneer of Modernism* (Cologne: Taschen, 2001), 47–48.

39 Gasquet, *Cézanne*, 176.

40 Gasquet, 176.

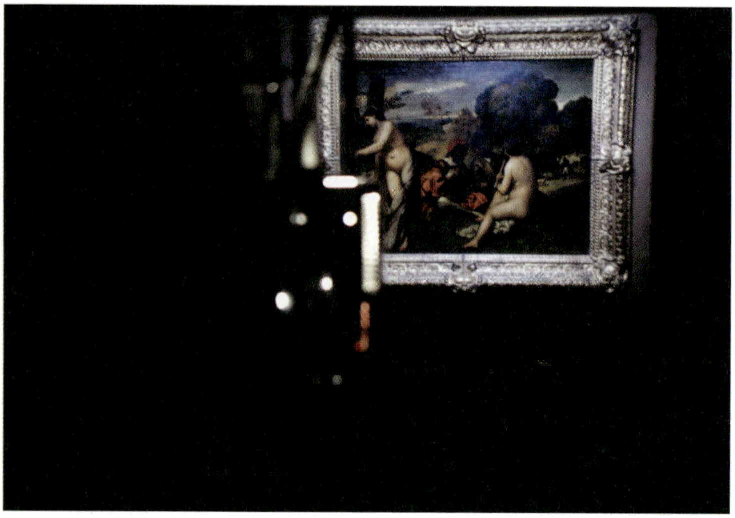

to an end."[41] More than merely translating and transposing sensations from one register to another, the artists' way of seeing—original, unconventional, and even radically different—appropriates and creates abstract concepts rather than representing or augmenting reality.

Cézanne's new way of seeing, as much as it consciously brings together and contains multiple projection systems within the same image, also refers back to what is widely recognized as the pre-Renaissance Primitives' inability to fully conform to the rules of perspective. Paul Smith acclaims Cézanne for reinventing "primitive perspective" and connects it to what he, with Merleau-Ponty, calls a "view from everywhere."[42] It rejects the scopic regime of individualized, linear perspective by combining spatially and chronologically disconnected aspects of sensation juxtaposed within one frame. In doing so, Cézanne counters impressionism, which privileges a subjective point of view and, as it were, outsources the production of sensation to the mind of the beholder. This quasi-objective "view from everywhere," in contrast, paves the way for what later came to be called Cubism. Ultimately, Picasso and Matisse declared Cézanne "the father of us all."

However, despite the best efforts of generations of art historians to persuade themselves otherwise, the histories of art do not follow linear genealogies according to logical, dialectical progressions based on hoarding and stockpiling formal assets and features of style. Instead, they seem to go in circles, sometimes vicious, sometimes virtuous,

41 Konrad Fiedler, *Der Ursprung Der Künstlerischen Thätigkeit* (Leipzig: S. Hirzel, 1887), 95. "Das Kunstwerk wird unwillkürlich mit demselben wissenschaftlichen Interesse betrachtet, wie das Naturding; man meint ihm gerecht werden zu können, wenn man das in ihm wieder zu finden sucht, was man als sichtbar in der Natur vorhanden benennen und konstatieren kann, und begreift nicht, dass das Sehen im Sinne des Künstlers erst da anfängt, wo alle Möglichkeit des Benennens und Konstatierens im wissenschaftlichen Sinne aufhört."

42 Smith, "Cézanne's 'Primitive' Perspective," 112.

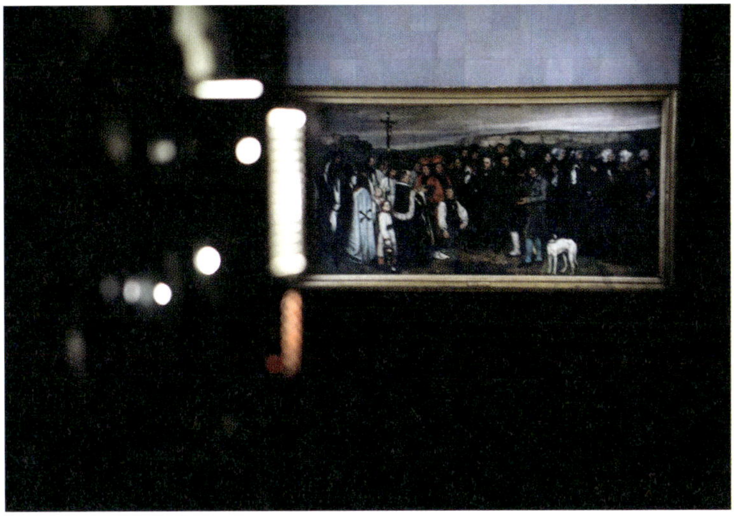

but always reframing what had already been framed. This is what is at stake with Primitivism: whether it is understood as a primal scene or, conversely, as the indicator of a certain "degeneration"—as it was during the Fascists' attempt to purify German culture. In promoting purportedly classical ideals, they sought to exterminate what they claimed to disdain and ridicule as 'primitive'—"a category that included, along with the mentally and physically deformed, avant-garde modernism, Bolshevism, and Jewish culture."[43] Such hatred and contempt for Primitivism does not come out of the blue.

43
Holland Cotter, "First, They Came for the Art," *The New York Times*, March 13, 2014.

44
Wilhelm Worringer, *Abstraction and Empathy: A Contribution to the Psychology of Style*, trans. Michael Bullock (Chicago: Ivan R. Dee, 1997), 5.

45
Worringer, *Abstraction and Empathy*, 15.

Two years after Cézanne's death in 1906, Wilhelm Worringer summarized the psychology of art by Theodor Lipps: "Aesthetic enjoyment is objectified self-enjoyment. To enjoy aesthetically means to enjoy myself in a sensuous object diverse from myself, to empathize myself into it."[44] In "Abstraction and Empathy," his doctoral thesis from 1908, Worringer argued that empathy and abstraction respond to opposing relationships between human beings and the external world. He claims, "Whereas the precondition of the urge to empathy is a happy, pantheistic relationship of confidence between man and the external world, the urge to abstraction is the outcome of great unrest inspired in man by the phenomena of the outside world."[45]

Remarkably, Worringer suggests that we understand the urge for abstraction as a feature of 'primitive' cultures in contrast to the sophisticated technologies of empathy, mimesis and identification (*Einfühlung*), which he assigns to the ancient Greek and Renaissance periods: "Just as the urge to empathy as a pre-assumption for aesthetic experience finds its gratification in the beauty of the organic, so the urge to abstraction finds its beauty in the life-denying inorganic, in the crystalline, in general terms, in all abstract law and necessity."[46] His notion of empathy stems from the idea of the domination of nature through science. The mastering of otherwise-hostile spatiality, he argues, produces a "relationship of confidence between man and the external world."[47] Consequently, Worringer frames the urge toward abstraction as a "spiritual dread of space"[48] among 'primitive' cultures that, he claims, lack control over nature and things.

While Worringer's views had had immense influence on a large number of contemporary artists he later branded as "Expressionists," such as Kandinsky, Marc, or Klee, he also met fierce opposition. The writer and art theorist Carl Einstein argues in his seminal study "Negro Sculpture" from 1915 against the predominant conception of Primitivism among his contemporaries. He sets out to expose the sentiments regarding what is rendered 'primitive'—whether inspiring or derogatory—as ignorance that rests on prejudice: "In all of his judgments the European proceeds from one assumption, namely that of his own absolute, indeed fantastic, superiority."[49] In opposition to Worringer's claims, the abstract conception of space where the artist's work stands "at an immeasurable distance" proves to be "the strongest realism."[50] It allows for a simultaneity of different views, or in Merleau-Ponty's terms, "a view from everywhere."

46 Worringer, 4.

47 Worringer, 45.

48 Worringer, 16.

49 Carl Einstein, Charles W. Haxthausen, and Sebastian Zeidler, "Negro Sculpture," *October* 107 (2004): 124.

50 Einstein, Haxthausen, Zeidler, "Negro Sculpture," 129.

When Danièle Huillet and Jean-Marie Straub visit the Louvre, they re-enact a guided tour by a painter, whose statements and judgments are already framed by the words of his young friend and admirer who recounts the conversations they had in front of the paintings, years before. But the act of reframing what is already framed gains yet another meaning, this time in the most literal sense.

Rather than representing a collection of artworks and their systematic order in terms of form or content, Huillet and Straub risk a collision of frames—the result of two different image-making processes that are genuinely incompatible, the pictorial frame of the canvas, and the cinematic frame of the camera. Conventionally, a reframing of irreconcilable frames runs the risk of a recursive paradox, an image within an image, a state within a state, so to speak. Because of this, most filmmakers try to de-frame the frame of the painting by zooming in on details and more or less imitating the movement of the eyes in order to direct the attention toward selected, partial views. When they do so, the artwork as a whole exists only as a relation, outside of the frame of the film.

It should come as no surprise that Huillet and Straub refuse this temptation as well. In their film, paintings are shot from fixed camera angles, which—despite its apparent simplicity—gives rise to both an immediate as well as abstracted conception of space: in their physical frames, contexts, backgrounds and natural light. The intense colors of the walls reflect the daylight with different intensities, which further reveals material structures and patterns. According to the frame ratio of the artworks, the filmmakers technically and conceptually reframe the paintings—as transpositions of images that are re-synchronised with Cézanne's unconventional, subjective evaluation of their relevance and qualities, notably from an *hors-champ* that is absolute and not relative.[51]

51
See Gilles Deleuze, *Cinema 1: The Movement Image* (London: Continuum, 2001), 19.

52
Doran et al., *Conversations*, 130.

Rather than representing the artworks by the means of filmmaking, the fourteen paintings that follow the *Victory of Samothrace* actualize sensations which subsist in both their materiality and totality. More than the sum of their parts, they exceed their subjects and ingredients far beyond what could be measured and reduced to information. They become too strange to be merely legible or simply visible. In this context it is remarkable, that Huillet and Straub shot two takes of each artwork, resulting in two different versions of *Une visite au Louvre* which are supposed to be projected back-to-back. While hardly distinguishable, the two versions nevertheless, differ in the time that has passed between the takes which mainly becomes manifest in the changing lighting conditions.

"And yet, it seems to me that there is everything in the Louvre,that one can learn and love everything in the Louvre,"[52] Cézanne says. Rather than seeing an exhibition of artworks as the outcome of a learning process, it should be seen as the very environment in which learning takes place.

While Cézanne is often credited with the reconciliation of classicism and romanticism that is supposed to have prepared the ground for modernism, the learning experience of *Une visite au Louvre* makes clear that this tension was not, indeed cannot be resolved, neatly summed up, or reduced. More than that, the continuous framing of what is assumed and consequently consumed as 'primitive' is, ultimately, what constitutes modern art, and, more specifically, the complications of modernism in the 20th century or maybe even beyond it.

But the lesson to be learned—especially for a "society *after* the spectacle"—is about confidence and trust in the power of abstraction to create a community[53] out of field or *hors champ*. That community does not exist on the basis of shared preferences in terms of style, or identification with one's contemporaries, let alone through mediation by technologies of empathy or immersion. Instead, such a community subsists on—and must insist on—its ability to reframe what is already framed.

Burial at Ornans by Gustave Courbet, the painter of the Paris Commune, is the last artwork that Cézanne presents: "We've got a masterpiece like this in France and we hide it. Let them set fire to the Louvre right away. If they're afraid of something beautiful."[54] *Une visite au Louvre* ends with a long, slow panning shot across ferns and trees in a wooded area near Buti, a small town in Tuscany. Birds are singing, a babbling brook—maybe it is the same place where Danièle Huillet and Jean-Marie Straub shot *Operai, contadini* three years before, in summer 2000. When the camera takes a turn in the wood, the greens of the leaves alternate in a harsh, nearly artificial polarity of shadows and bright daylight that seems to exceed the contrast range the film stock is able to handle. Together with the film credits Bach's cantata starts, *Ein unbegreiflich Licht erfüllt den ganzen Kreis der Erden*—an incomprehensible light fills the entire circle of the earth.

53
See Antonio Negri, *Art and Multitude*, trans. Ed Emery (London: Wiley Blackwell, 2011), 11. "The abstract is our nature. The abstract is the quality of our labour. The abstract is the sole community in which we exist."

54
Gasquet, *Cézanne*, 204.

Oraib Toukan

PALACE OF THE SLAVE

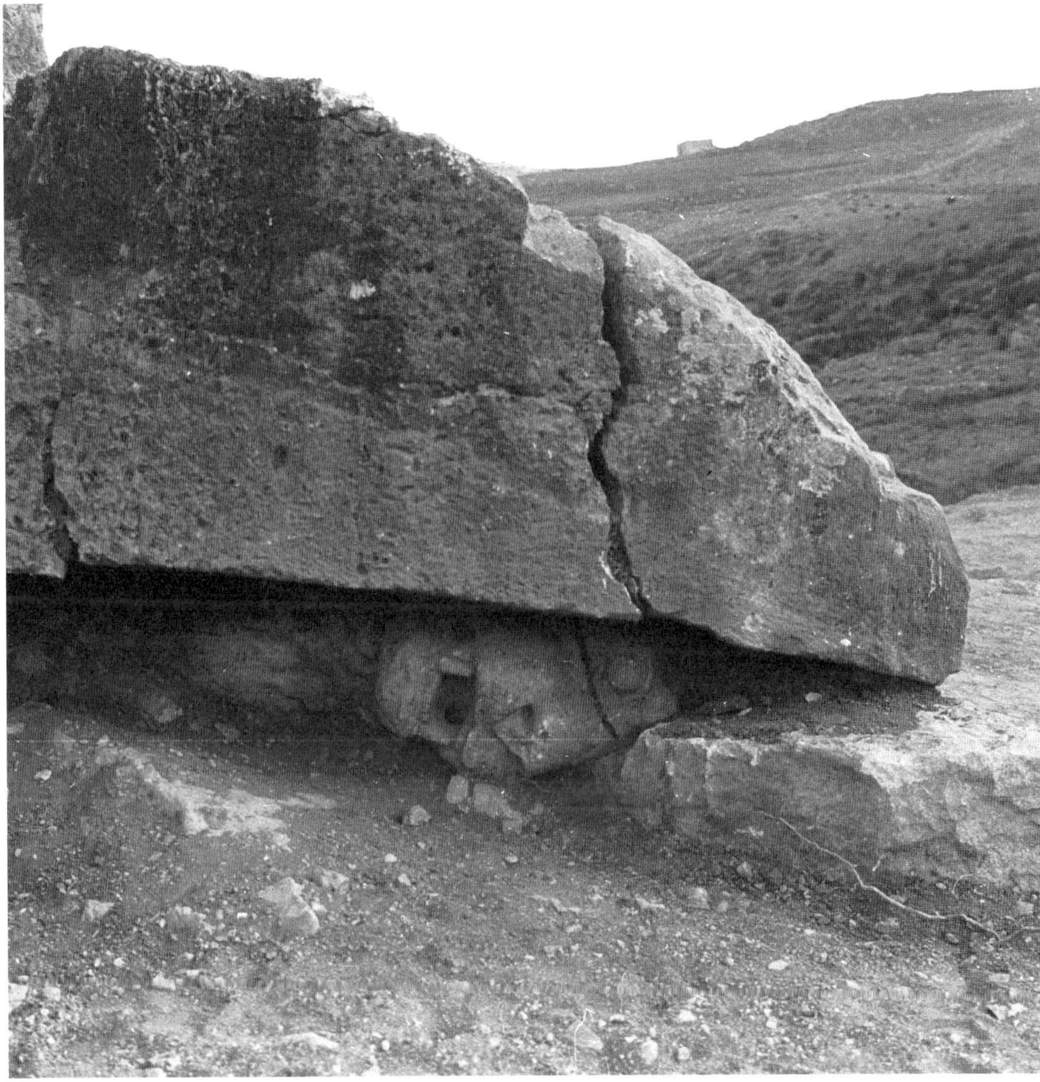

1

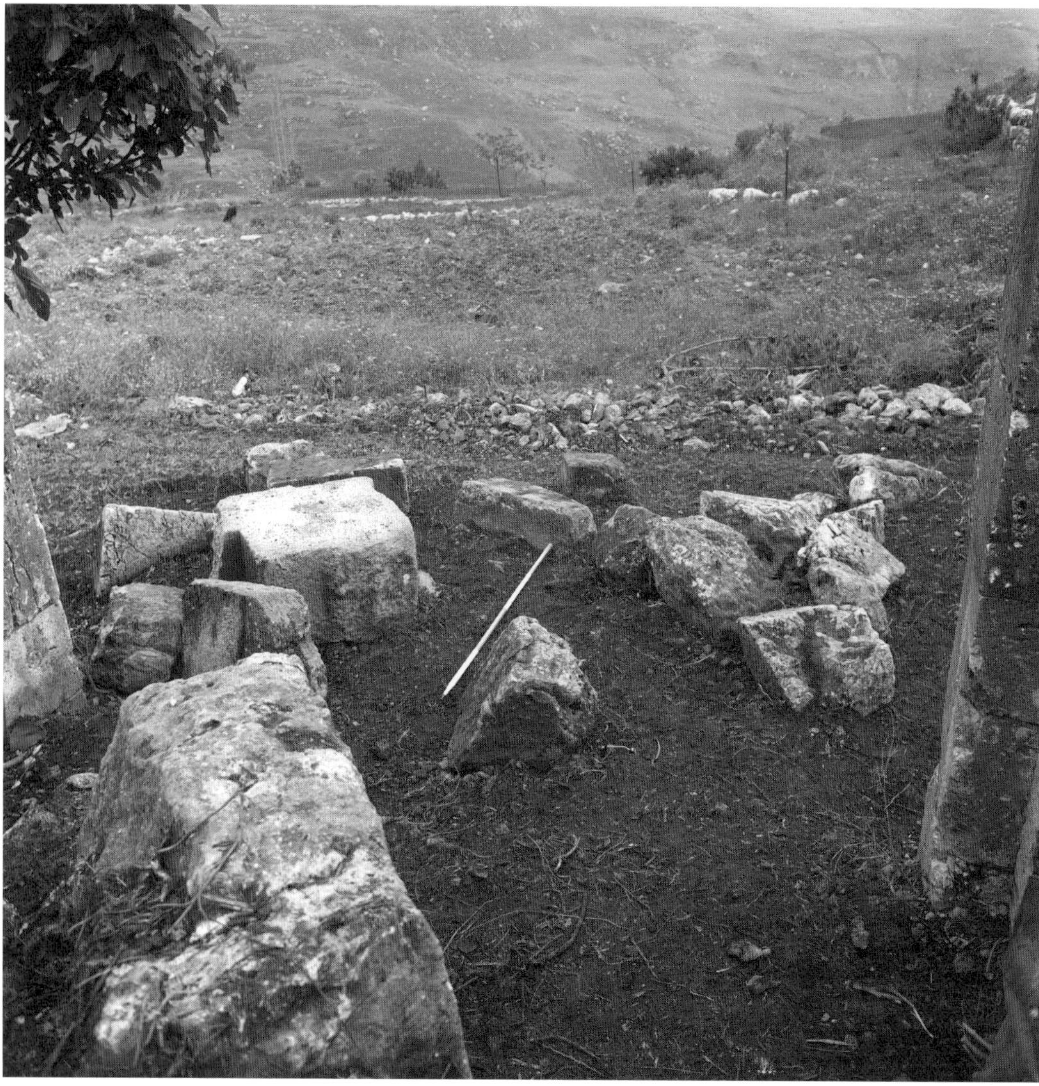

2

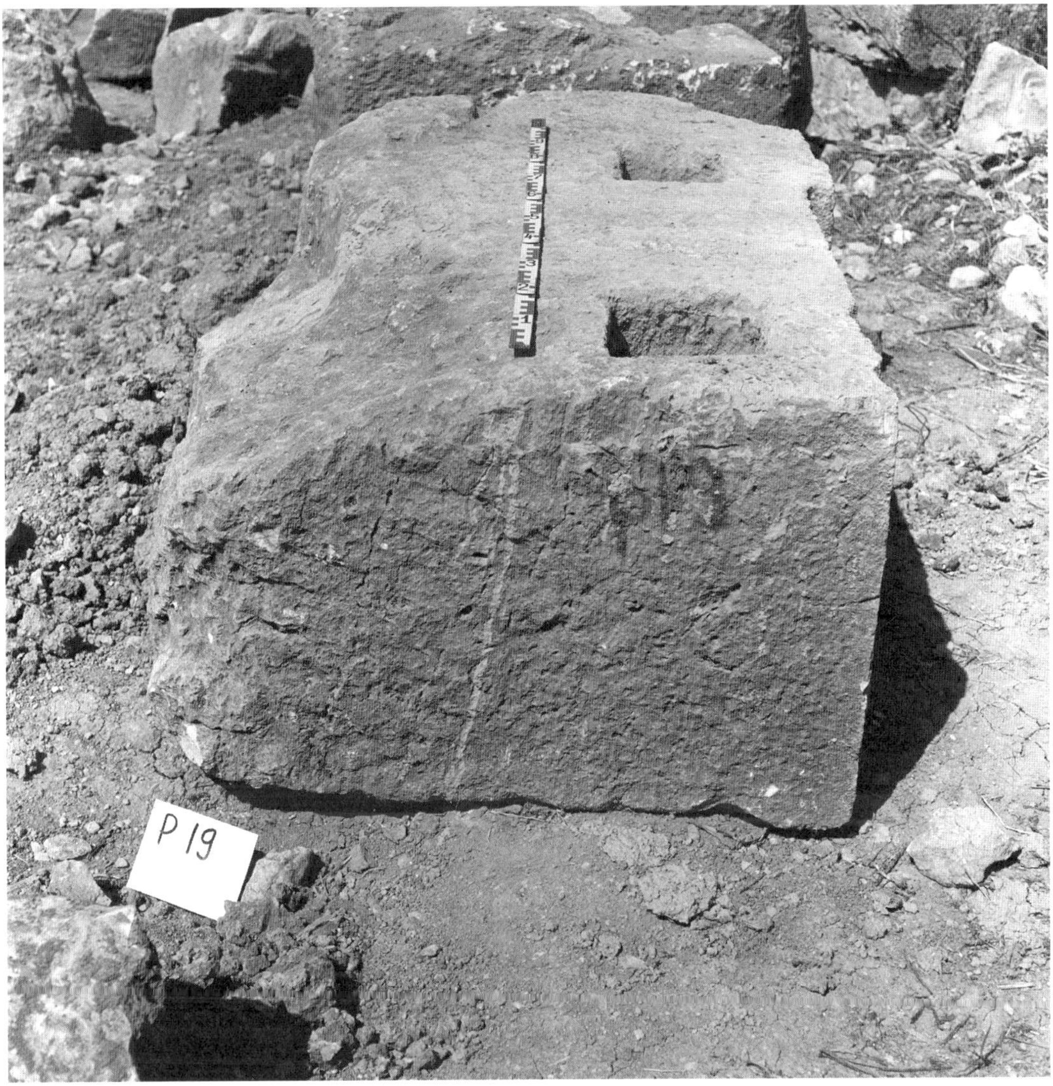

3

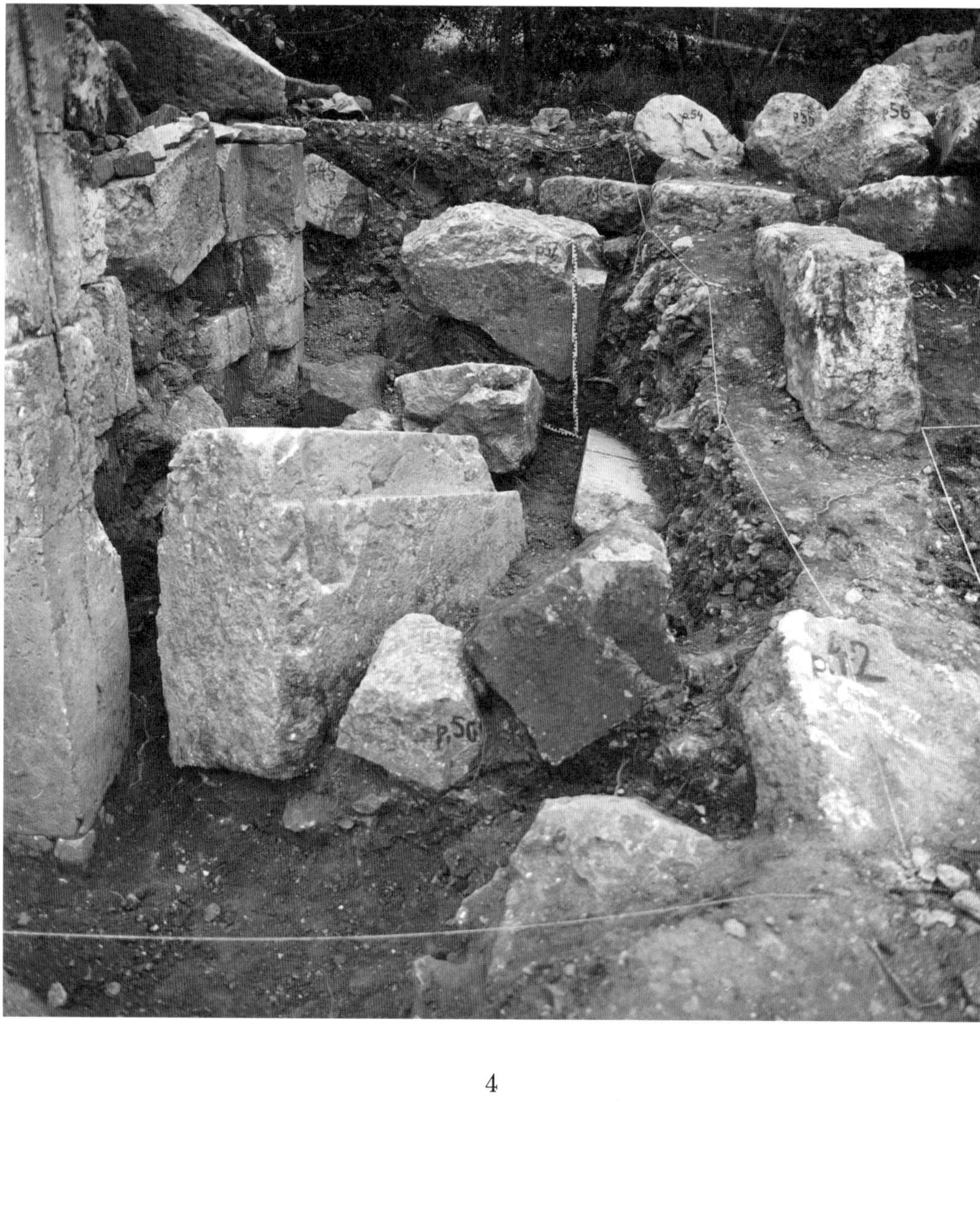

4

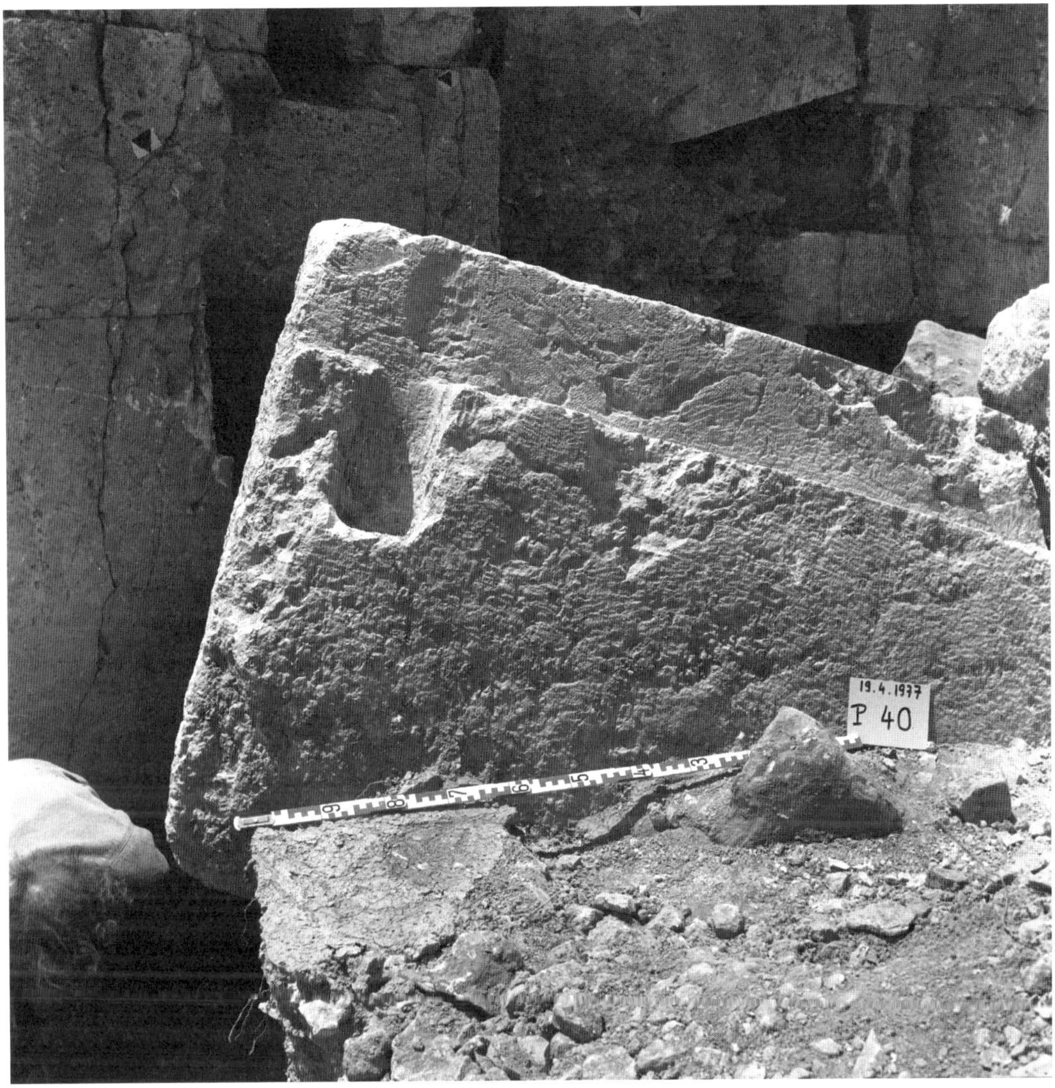

5

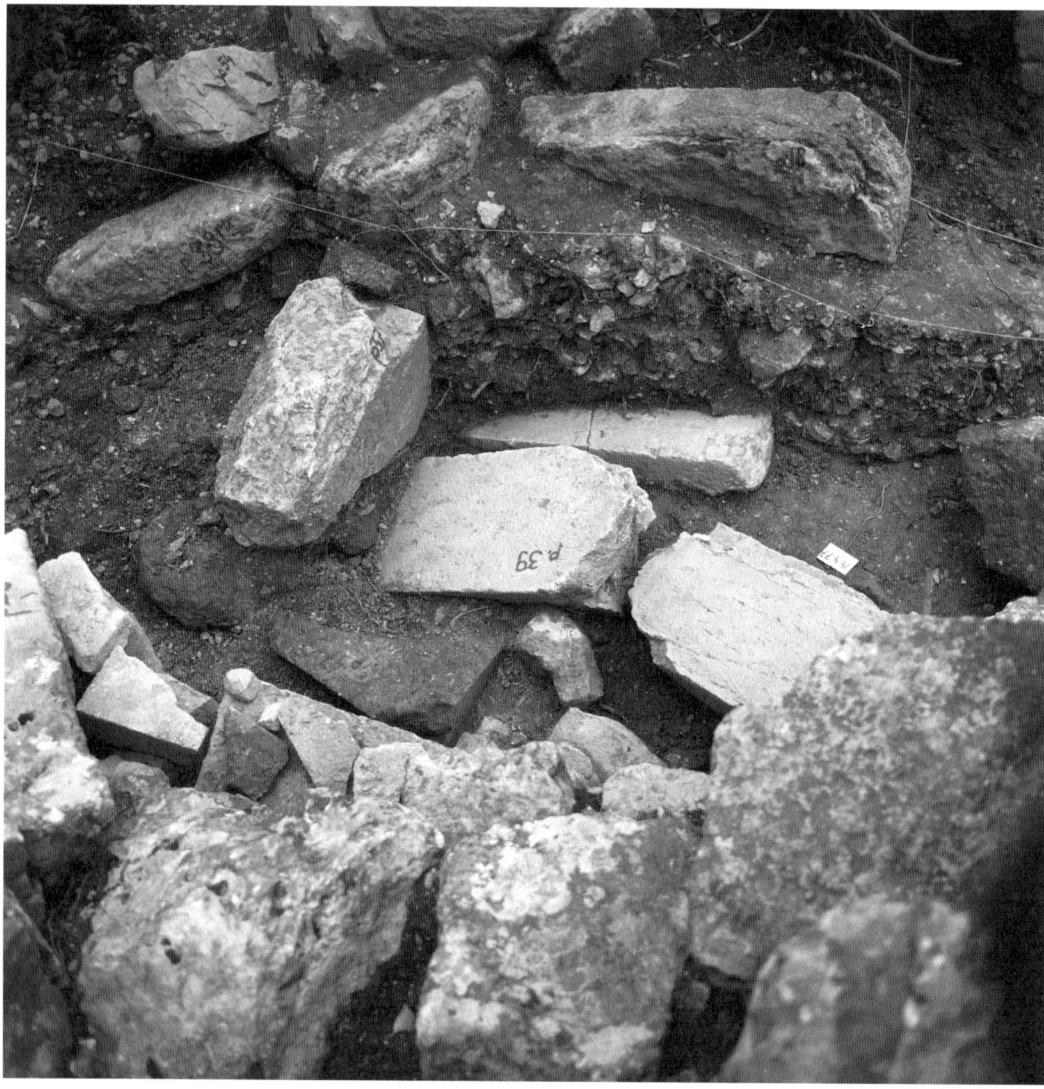

6

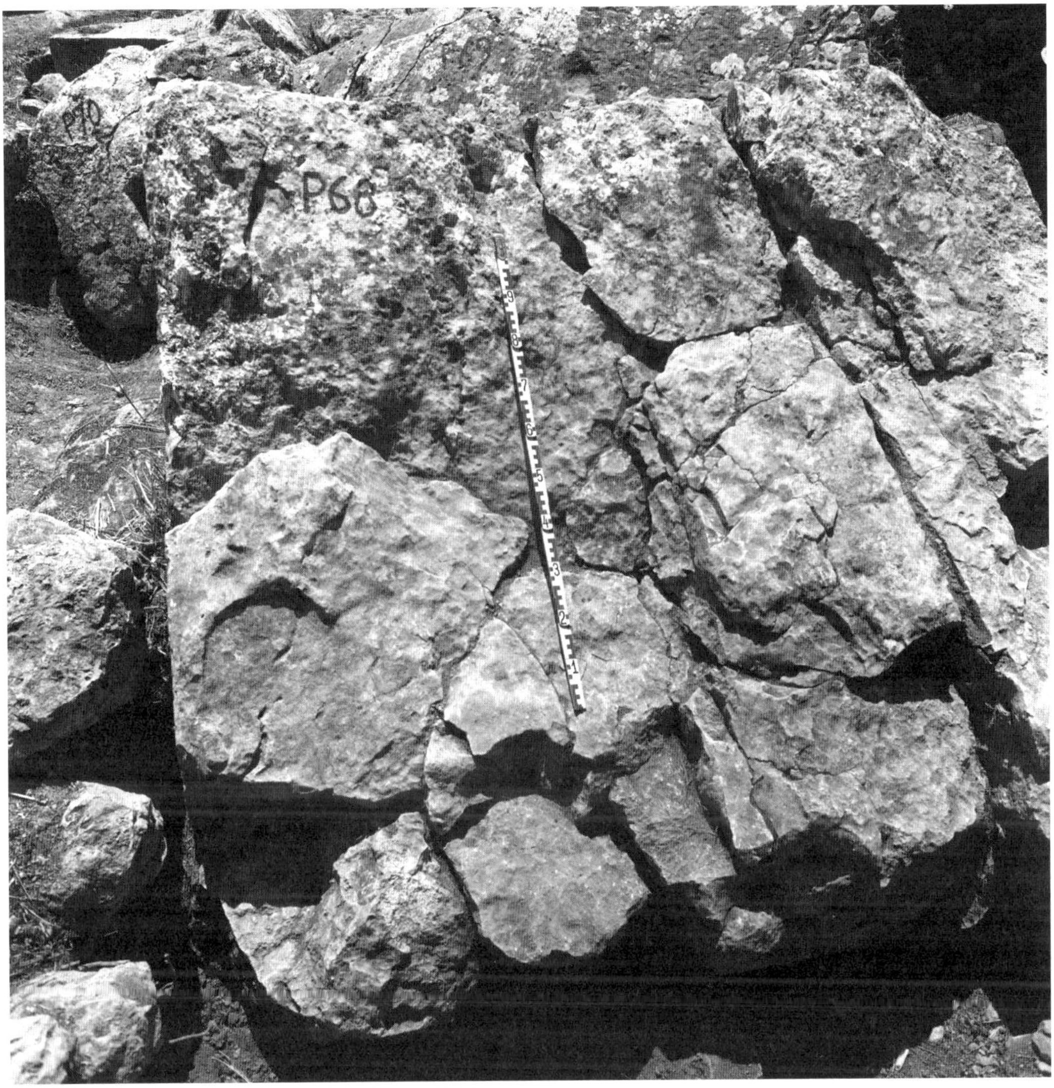

7

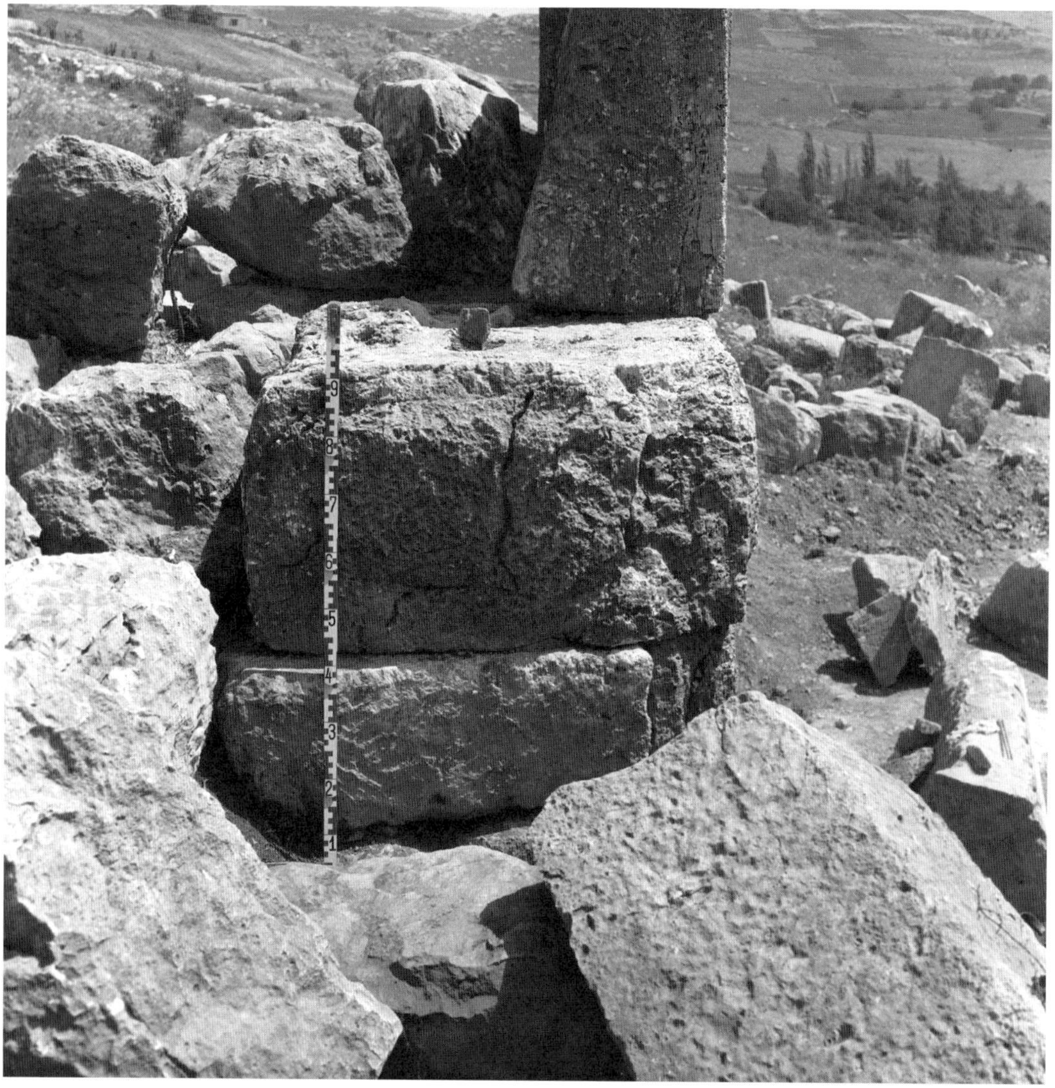

8

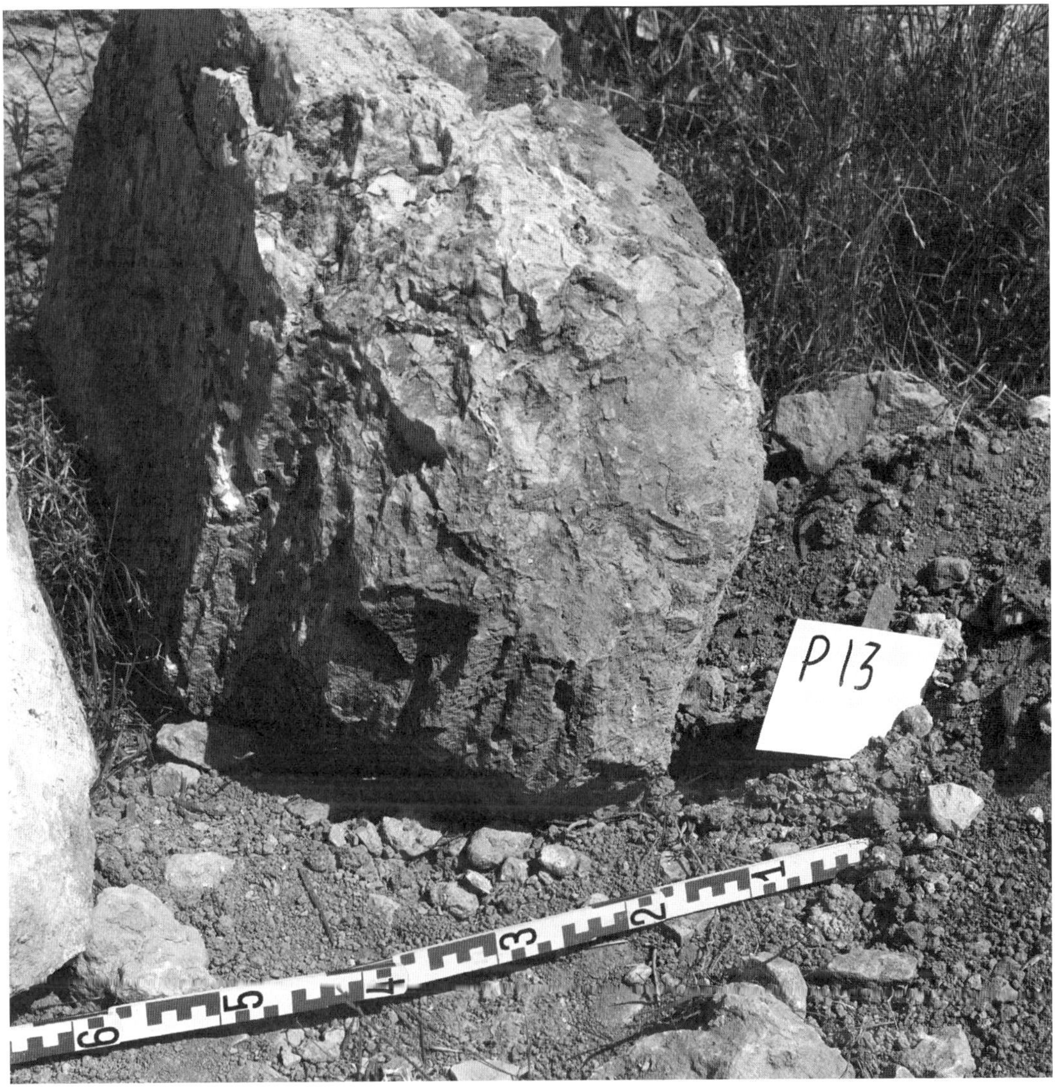

9

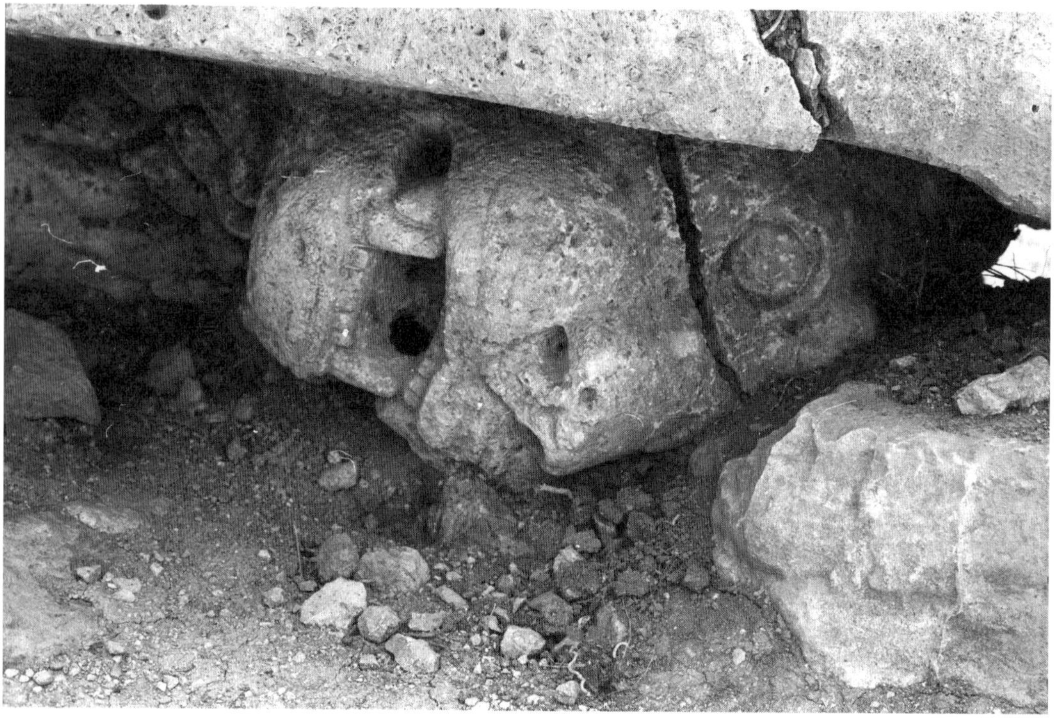

10

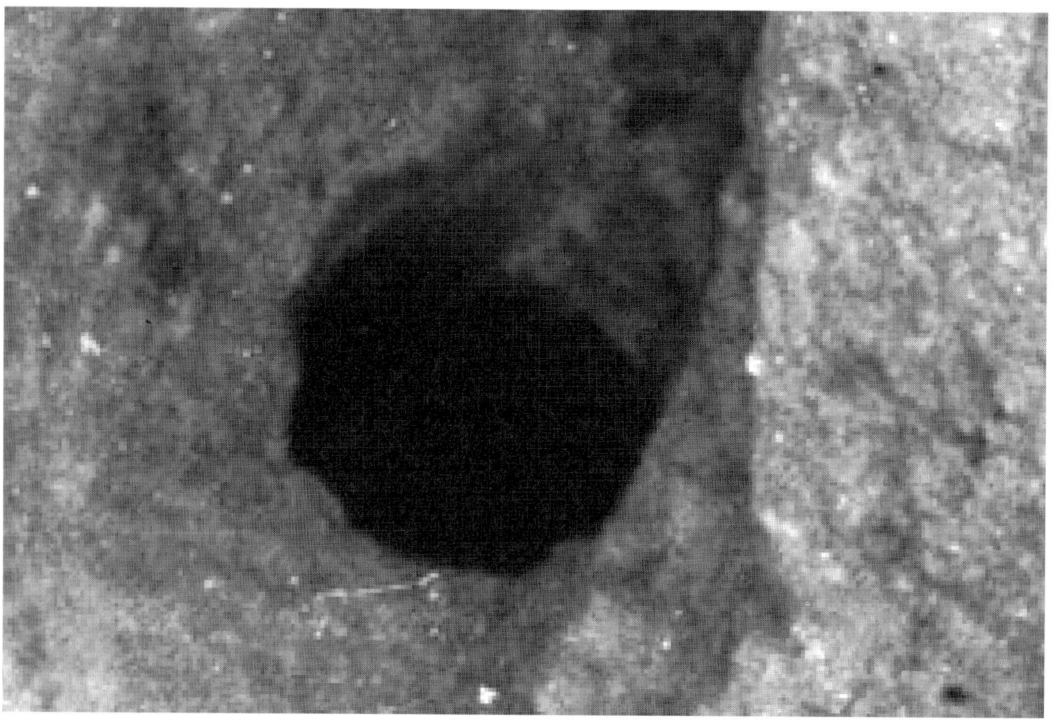

11

Holes are engulfing, because they are not about shapes, or scapes, or objects, but about dispossession.[1] The writer Reza Negarestani notes, holes are about the possibility of another world, or, the idea of possible worlds. "You cannot diagram a hole," he says. Because cavities represent continuums. And continuums cannot be measured.

So how do we write an image that for all its fierceness comes to represent nothing? Unutterable, undecipherable, unfathomable. No matter how much you measure, classify, typologize, analyze it, its cruelty comes to represent nothing.

The Russian poet Daniil Kharms writes:

> There was a redheaded man who had no eyes or ears. He didn't have hair either, so he was called a redhead- arbitrarily. He couldn't talk because he had no mouth. He didn't have a nose either. He didn't even have arms or legs. He had no stomach, he had no back, no spine, and he didn't have any insides at all. There was nothing! So, we don't even know who we're talking about. We'd better not talk about him any more.[2]

Images 1 to 9:
Courtesy Francois Larchè.
Archaeologist's personal slide collection of
Palace of the Slave, Iraq Al Amir, Jordan.

Images 10 and 11:
Stills from Oraib Toukan,
Palace of the Slave, 2017.
Two-channel video (color), 9'47"

1 Jean-Luc Moulène in conversation with Alain Badiou and Reza Negarestani on *Torture Concrete: Jean-Luc Moulene and the Protocol of Abstraction* (New York: Sequence Press, 2014). University Settlement, October 29, 2017, New York

2 Danill Kharms, *Today I Wrote Nothing: The Selected Writings of Daniil Kharms*, trans. Matvei Yankelevich (London: Overlook Duckworth, 2007).

Patrick Primavesi

Violence and the Stones

Danièle Huillet's and Jean-Marie Straub's film *Antigone* confronts its audience with a complex notion of violence. A violence that somehow reproduces itself, as in the famous quote of *Saint Joan of the Stockyards* by Bertolt Brecht in the title of their earlier film *Not Reconciled, or Only Violence Helps Where Violence Rules* (*Nicht versöhnt oder es hilft nur Gewalt wo Gewalt herrscht*, 1965), after Heinrich Böll's novel *Billiards at Half-Past Nine* about the continuity of fascism and the need for resistance in the Federal Republic of Germany. Straub/Huillet's entire work reflects the topic of a political counter-violence by enacting various kinds of violence, including on a rather structural level. There have been recurring complaints about their all too violent and uncompromising attitude toward an established norm of perception, which is part of the political, cultural, and economic conditions they constantly address. This also applies to the film *Antigone*. The issue of violence, as emphasized by the plot of the tragedy, accompanied the history of the text and its translations as well as the project of staging the play and producing the film. A first impulse was the acquaintance with the ancient theater at Segesta in Sicily. Then, much later, the work on Brecht's version of Hölderlin's translation of Sophocles' *Antigone* led to rehearsals and performances at the Berlin Schaubühne in spring 1991, to the shooting in Segesta, and finally to the editing of the film and its premiere in 1992. Based on this whole process, the film reflects different kinds of violence in a unique form, resulting from unconventional decisions against any comfortable consumption. Instead, spectators may feel challenged to decide, to take a stand, on their own.

VIOLENCE IN SOPHOCLES' ANTIGONE AND IN HÖLDERLIN'S TRANSLATION

In a long sequence of translations and transformations between Sophocles' tragedy and the film by Huillet/Straub, the term violence plays its own part—a part that is already split and redoubled, starting from the original. Whereas the Greek word *bia* refers to physical violence, the term *kratos* designates power or governance. Accordingly, modern concepts of violence presume a strict, yet questionable distinction between *violence* and *power*, separating both terms by an ethical judgment: physical violence is damned, whereas institutionalized violence as a medium of power

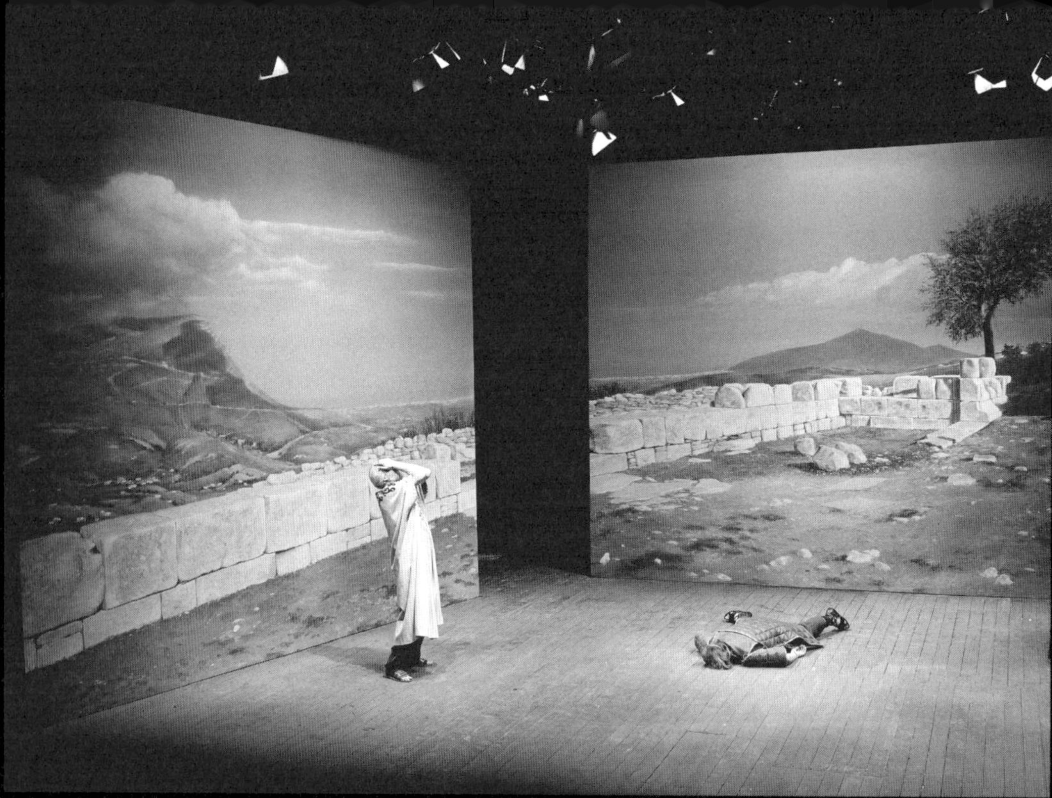

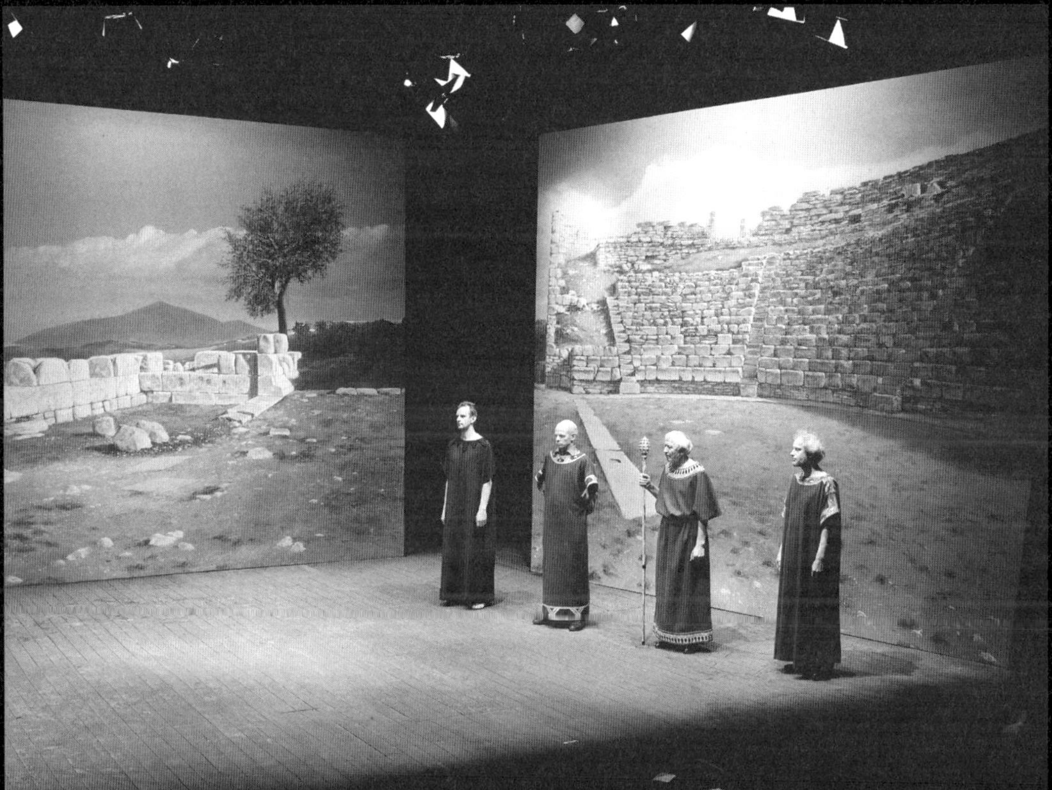

and command is justified. Greek tragedy negotiates the transition from mythical to rational and juridical interpretations of violence with a remarkable interrelation of *bia* and *kratos*, violence and power. One of the most famous examples is in fact the violent clash in Sophocles' *Antigone*, between the political law of the state, represented by Kreon, and the religious law of the family, the "unwritten laws" of the dead, that oblige Antigone to bury her brother Polyneikes although he was banished from the city of Thebes as aggressor and traitor.

The case of Antigone is often interpreted as the struggle of an individual against the power of the state. However, the decisive question is, if Antigone's resistance runs *against* the laws of the city, or if it rather manifests a more democratic understanding of law and order, *in favor* of the city. The first scene already establishes a certain tension between violence and power when Ismene warns her sister Antigone about the consequences of her action. "If against the law we break with violence (*bia*) the decision of the ruler or the power (*kratos*)," translated by Hölderlin as, "wenn/ Gewaltsam wir des Herrn Befehl und Kraft/Verfehlten" (if/ violently we would miss the ruler's command and force).[1] Only a few lines later, this apparently obvious distinction between violence and power is blurred, when Ismene once more rejects Antigone's endeavor to bury the dead brother: "This civil act of violence (bia) is nothing for me." Hölderlin again translates quite clearly, "Zum Schritt allein, den Bürger/Im Aufstand thun, bin linkisch ich geboren" (for this act that citizens in an uprising would undertake, I am not fitting). The question, in whose name violent action would be legitimated, is the problem of every translation of the Greek text that remains ambiguous here. The term in question is *bia politōn*, meaning either violence against the citizens (and the state), or violence performed in the manner—and interest—of citizens, as Hölderlin translates, which is clearly amplified in Brecht's version: "Nur/ Mich aufzuwerfen bin ich nicht gut genug,"[2] (but/to act rebellious I am not good enough). Hölderlin focuses on the political dimension in Antigone's behavior again in translating *bia politōn*, when used by herself, as *uprise*: "hätt' ich mit Gewalt,/Als wollt' ich einen Aufstand, diß errungen." (had I achieved this with violence, as if I would have aimed for an uprising).[3]

1
Friedrich Hölderlin, "Antigonä," in *Sämtliche Werke*, vol. 16: *Sophocles*, ed. Dietrich E. Sattler (Frankfurt am Main: Roter Stern, 1975–2008), 270–271. This volume includes the Greek text from the old Juntina edition (1555) used by Hölderlin with a new interlinear German translation by Michael Franz as well as Hölderlin's translation from its first printed edition 1804. Here and in the following, the English translations (based on this edition) are my own.

2
Bertolt Brecht, "Antigonemodell 1948," in *Brechts Antigone des Sophokles*, ed. Werner Hecht (Frankfurt am Main: Suhrkamp, 1988), 74.

3
Hölderlin, "Antigonä," 358–359.

Although the other interpretation of *bia politōn* as "violence *against* the citizens" has been established nowadays, in the course of the play it becomes obvious that violence is needed to resist Kreon's violent and autocratic regime in order to save the city, as his own son Haimon argues as well. Here in particular we may get an idea of the *deinos*, the monstrosity of man, whose actions may prove to be in favor of, or against, the city (the community of the *polis*) only in retrospect, when it is already too late, as is the case with Antigone and Kreon. Hölderlin's translation is unique in reflecting this problem of violence and power, both on the level of the translation itself, by which he explicitly tried to *improve* the Greek original, and on the level of tragic dramaturgy. In his famous comments, he prefers an anti-classicist and revolutionary manner, once more comparing Antigone's action to an uprising of citizens, in a patriotic and republican reversal of all conventional ideas and forms ("Umkehr aller Vorstellungsarten und Formen").[4] This interpretation leaves space beyond human reason for something unforeseeable or even unthinkable: a gap in the logic of the law, a caesura in the dramaturgy of the play, and a potential of the *political*, beyond the economy of means and ends, beyond the politics of power and strategies.

4 Hölderlin, "Anmerkungen zur Antigonä," in *Sämtliche Werke*, 16, 419–421.

STONES AND EMPTY THEATERS

The complete title of the film *die Antigone des Sophokles in der Hölderlinschen Übertragung für die Bühne bearbeitet von Brecht 1948 (Suhrkamp Verlag)*—the Antigone of Sophocles after Hölderlin's translation adapted for the stage by Brecht 1948 (Suhrkamp publishers)—already manifests the particular complexity of the text, its versions and layers. Brecht explained his interest in Hölderlin's translation by a familiar Swabian tone in his language, but it was obviously his interest in a political interpretation of the tragedy as well, that made him choose this version. Together with his stage designer Caspar Neher, he reworked the translation and added another ending: now Kreon, engaged in a war about raw materials and overestimating his power, causes the decay of his state. He had killed Polyneikes himself, and the war campaign has just started. Brecht also wrote a prelude, situated in Berlin in the last days of World War II, when the Nazi police seizes two sisters because they tried to help their brother who had just returned as a deserter. However, Brecht himself was rather skeptical about this prelude and he acknowledged that his attempt to rationalize the whole tragedy had failed. The new version does not take sides as clearly as one might expect—neither Antigone herself nor the chorus of the elder citizens may stand in for a sufficient civil resistance, and both seem somehow corrupted.

Huillet and Straub had already reflected the issue of violence in the transition between the space of theater and film. The ancient theater of Segesta in Sicily marked an interspace, presented on the painted backdrops in the rehearsal stage of the Schaubühne, where the theater performance took place. The constant presence of the theater ruins echoed Brecht's recommendation, in case the prelude was skipped, to show at least "a plate depicting a modern city in ruins."[5] The performance of *Antigone* in Berlin in 1991 was related to a contemporary crisis—concerning not only the new 'world order' already threatened by the war in Iraq and the decay of the former Soviet Union, but the theater venue itself, situated on Cuvrystrasse in the Kreuzberg neighborhood, quite close to the former wall of a collapsed system of dictatorship. By its spatial arrangement, the playing area framed by the backdrops was reminiscent of the first premiere in 1948, when Caspar Neher's stage had artificial backdrops too. Huillet and Straub used the scenery in an anti-illusionist way too, letting the actors enter or leave between the painted canvases. From the space of the ancient theater of Segesta, these backdrops showed the intersection between the remains of the Roman skene, and on the other side, the comparably well-preserved cavea with stone tiers from an early Hellenistic period. Thus the actual theater space in Berlin relied on the previously developed concept of the filmic space that itself referred to the site of the ancient theater in Segesta. The spectator's perspective of the painted backdrops on stage anticipated the film's final point of view, showing the landscape and the sky above the ruins. In both situations, the stone tiers of the ancient theater are featured as stones in bright daylight and as witnesses to the absence of the people[6]—a recurring manifestation of the violence or the force of the political in the cinematographic œuvre of Huillet and Straub, as Gilles Deleuze has pointed out,

5 Brecht, "Vorwort zum Antigonemodell 1948," in *Brechts Antigone des Sophokles*, 52.

6 In his detailed chapter on *Antigone*, Barton Byg somehow ignores these scenes in order to separate the filmic space from a conventionally theatrical point of view. However, during the first song of the chorus and later on in all its encounters with Kreon, the empty seating rows of the theater are clearly visible and not just left to the spectator's imagination, as Byg suggests. See Barton Byg, *Landscapes of Resistance. The German Films of Danièle Huillet and Jean-Marie Straub* (Berkeley: University of California Press, 1995), 228–229.

"the people are what is missing."[7] This absence reaches its utmost visibility, as in *Moses and Aaron* (and in the later Schoenberg film *Von heute auf morgen/From Today Until Tomorrow*), in an empty theater—in particular when a ruin of ancient stones recalls a time when open-air theaters were often places of political convention and decision-making. In shooting the *Antigone* film there were two positions of the camera, differing only in their height, on a scaffold placed almost in the middle of the theater ruins. From this perspective could the choir in the orchestra, as well as the actors, appear in front of the old stones. The camera was placed just above a stone plate on the floor, perhaps the former position of a sacrificial altar. The film refrains from showing a panoramic view from the perspective of the audience. Therefore, the distinct choice of a position (standpoint and viewpoint) and of the particular shots, mark an important difference between the film and the theater performance. As Deleuze (inspired by film reviews by Jean Narboni and Serge Daney) pointed out, Huillet and Straub have constructed "astonishing amorphous shots, deserted, ambiguous or deepened geological spaces, theaters emptied of the operations which took place there."[8] Moreover, there is a material resistance, manifested by *stone* as the ground of any experience in these films, "The visual image, in Straub, is the rock."[9] Deleuze hereby also addresses the particularly violent act of speaking in these films, distanced from any representative humanist understanding of literature, tradition, and conventions of embodiment. The effort is to free the political violence already inherent to the texts, like rocks in the desert.

> [P]eople talk in an empty space, and, whilst speech rises, the space is sunk into the ground, and does not let us see it, but makes its archaeological buryings, its stratigraphic thicknesses readable; it testifies to the work that had to be done and the victims slaughtered in order to fertilize a field, the struggles that took place and the corpses thrown out. (*Dalla nube alla resistenza*, *Fortini/Cani*). History is inseparable from the earth [terre], struggle is underground [sous terre], and, if we want to grasp an event, we must not show it, we must not pass along the event, but plunge into it, go through all the geological layers that are its internal history (and not simply a more or less distant past).[10]

7 Gilles Deleuze, *The Time-Image. Cinema 2*, trans. H. Tomlinson, R. Galeta (Minneapolis: University of Minnesota Press, 1989), 217.

8 Gilles Deleuze, *The Movement Image. Cinema 1*, trans. H. Tomlinson, B. Habberjam (Minneapolis: University of Minnesota Press, 1986), 121 and 233 (note 22), cf. Jean Narboni, "Là," in *Cahiers du cinéma*, No. 275 (April 1977), Serge Daney, "Le plan straubien," in *Cahiers du cinéma*, no. 305, 1070.

9 Deleuze, *The Time Image*, 244.

10 Deleuze, 254–255.

These observations on and under the ground, of the always violent and ambiguous work of human 'culture' in its relation to a physical ground, reflect various traits in the work of Huillet and Straub that have culminated in their *Antigone* film. In order to set free the political energies of Sophocles' tragedy, Hölderlin's subversion of German classicism, and Brecht's failed attempt to rationalize a barbaric ground of the play, a double scene was needed. The spatial dispositif of that film connected the ancient site and the contemporary theater venue in Berlin, where the "other" scene became visible already. Thus, Huillet and Straub took up Brecht's *Antigone-model* (including the controversial reflections on violence and its legitimation by the dead) on the theater stage, but with the film space in their minds.

"TELL IT TO THE STONES!"

For the theater performance, Huillet and Straub completely trusted in a polyphony of voices and contrasting manners of speaking and playing. Particularly the chorus combined different voice pitches and melodies into a complex rhythmic structure. The rehearsals (which I had the chance to attend personally) were quite unusual regarding a commitment to each single word, phrase, and breath, affixed in the script with all details. After a first phase of studying the text in the Berlin film academy, the rehearsal work focused on accentuation and pauses, postures and gestures, with the aim to "free the pure act of speaking" that needs to be *torn away* from the text, as Deleuze described it,

> This tearing-away does not take place in a fit of rage or passion; it presupposes a certain resistance of the text, and all the more respect for the text, but on each occasion a special effort to draw the speech-act out of it.[11]

For the work on *Antigone*, this particular process also required a certain violence with regard to some conventions of professional acting.

At Schaubühne Berlin, one of the most renowned German theater institutions, Huillet and Straub had conflicts about the question of how the different competences and potentials from lay actors and professional actors should be treated and perhaps combined. Playing Kreon, the ex-

11 Deleuze, 253.

perienced Werner Rehm from the Schaubühne ensemble was confronted with Astrid Ofner's Antigone, who had studied philosophy and film directing, and with her sister Ursula Ofner, who had only started an acting education in Berlin, in the role of Ismene. Haimon and the guard were performed by the young actors Stephan Wolf-Schönburg and Lars Studer, while the messenger was Libgart Schwarz, who, like Werner Rehm and Michael König (the other messenger), was a star at the Schaubühne and had problems to focus on the act of speaking without the habituated "fit of rage or passion." The blind prophet Tiresias was played by Albert Hetterle, who for decades had been actor, director, and manager of the East Berlin Maxim Gorki Theater. Not by chance, the cast and the chorus too were divided into various German accents and into actors from East and West Germany. Kurt Radeke came from the Gorki Theater too, whereas the younger actors Rainer Philippi, Michael Maassen and Hans Diehl belonged to the West German Schaubühne.[12] Theater rehearsals in spring 1991 were full of quarrels about the professional self-image of the actors, challenged by the way Huillet and Straub worked. In particular the verism Werner Rehm tried to use for his Kreon was not accepted. For his first entrance, when he lies to the chorus by claiming that Argos was destroyed, Huillet and Straub suggested he should look down to the floor while speaking, whereas Rehm wanted to perform the strategist with an open gaze toward his men. This conflict about the direction of the gaze was a hard one, and it demonstrated paradigmatically the problem of credibility, with regard to the dubious and contradictory representation of a triumphant ruler.

12
For detailed credits see the filmography in *Jean-Marie Straub and Danièle Huillet*, ed. Ted Fendt (Vienna: SYNEMA, 2016).

13
Bertolt Brecht, "Zur Gestik des Kreon," in *Brechts Antigone des Sophokles*, 26.

Brecht had previously summarized Kreon's gestures with an ironic remark, "gestures of public man and bloody clown."[13] Likewise, Huillet and Straub were interested in the tension between extreme ways of acting, not at all to *denounce* the professional actor, but rather to prevent him from flattening down the dimensions of his character. In the struggle with Werner Rehm about where to look and whom to address, Danièle Huillet finally had another proposal for the actor: "Sagen Sie's den Steinen!" (Tell it to the Stones!). This profound formula concerns not only the difficult search for more or less credible gestures, but also more generally, the violence of a speech act, the performance of which should release the various layers of violence inscribed in the text itself. Therefore, addressing the stones—in particular regarding the case of Antigone who refers to the laws of the dead and therefore will be condemned by Kreon to a cruel death in isolation, buried alive among stones—is not just a rehearsal trick in order to avoid the trappings of psychologically motivated professional acting. It precisely marks the border, the threshold between life and death, to which this tragic play and its production in theater and film refers.

By their meticulous staging of speech and physical action, Huillet and Straub consciously renounced the conventional ways to depict violence by rather pornographic conventions. Instead, they came closer to the way Brecht reflected his Antigone-model of 1948:

> Thriftiness in the moving back and forth of groups and individuals safeguarded the meaning of this movement. The specific constellations, even the distances have their dramaturgical function, and sometimes a single movement of an actor's hand may change the whole situation.[14]

However, as a film, the *Antigone* production reinforces the experience of the multilayered text with a different, shock-like intensity. Space is no longer confined to the narrow stage of a black box, but extends to a visible distance. The scene fills with the light of a Sicilian landscape. Wind, clouds, a rare Arolla pine tree, grass, and the bright stone of ruins, then suddenly the sight of a motorway that cuts the entire valley. Instead of merely reproducing the ancient tragedy in an 'historical' environment (as it has been attempted time and again), the *Antigone* film is a completely new work, structured by the editing of sharply calculated shots and the tension between voice-off scenes and speaking on the screen.

14
Brecht, "Vorwort zum Antigonemodell 1948," in *Brechts Antigone des Sophokles*, 48.

In the first caesura of the chorus song about violence and the inadequacy of man, the camera pans toward the stone threshold between the skene and the orchestra of the former theater, and remains focused there during the words of the chorus that follow. While the text depicts the destructive violence of man, both civil and uncivil, the threshold allows our imagination to project various stages of political violence until today. At the end of the tragedy, when the chorus can only sing about its own decline, a last pan leads our gaze from the ruins to the mountains in the back. A stony landscape comes in sight that will somehow outlast the wars of humans against each other. However, the very last take shows a text by Brecht, a warning of coming catastrophes by appealing both to our memory and to our imagination:

> Das Gedächtnis der Menschheit für erduldete Leiden ist erstaunlich kurz. Ihre Vorstellungsgabe für kommende Leiden ist fast noch geringer. Diese Abgestumpftheit ist es, die wir zu bekämpfen haben. Denn der Menschheit drohen Kriege, gegen welche die vergangenen wie armselige Versuche sind, und sie werden kommen ohne jeden Zweifel, wenn denen, die sie in aller Öffentlichkeit vorbereiten, nicht die Hände zerschlagen werden.[15]

The film shows this extract from Brecht's message for the People's Congress for Peace in 1952, while we hear the noise of a helicopter circling above the theater of Segesta. This open and not reconciled ending relates to the context of the wars to come forty years later. At the theater première Straub pronounced an ex post dedication "to Georg von Rauch killed by the police and to 100,000 Iraqis, victims of the international community under their new leader George Bush." The professional spectators and critics were upset, and the audience was split—not too bad for a theater performance. The idea that theater should enable dissent, instead of producing an unanimous community, was already part of Brecht's experimental learning plays (Lehrstücke), including the *Maßnahme* (Measures Taken), which during the rehearsals for *Antigone*, Straub repeatedly mentioned as another Brechtian play he would still like to produce. The quotation itself, readable in cold print at the end of the film, is another reference to Brecht's stance on a particular and sometimes justified kind of violence, related to warfare, in a pacifist and yet resolute call for an uprise against the preparation of future wars, coming close to Walter Benjamin's idea of the general strike as a manifestation of what he called "reine Gewalt" (pure violence), in his essay *Zur Kritik der Gewalt*.[16]

However, the political interest of the *Antigone* film relies on its material quality, without reducing the play to a trial

15 Bertolt Brecht, "Zum Kongress der Völker für den Frieden (1952)," in *Werke. Große kommentierte Berliner und Frankfurter Ausgabe*, ed. Werner Hecht et al, vol. 23 (Frankfurt am Main: Suhrkamp, 1993), 215. "The memory of humanity for sufferings borne is astonishingly short. Its gift of imagination for coming sufferings is almost even less. It is this callousness that we must combat. For humanity is threatened by wars compared to which those past are like poor attempts and they will come, without any doubt, if the hands of those who prepare them in all openness are not broken." Translation quoted from: www.straub-huillet.com

16 Walter Benjamin, "Zur Kritik der Gewalt" (1920), in *Gesammelte Schriften*, Vol. II.1, ed. Rolf Tiedemann, Hermann Schweppenhäuser (Frankfurt am Main: Suhrkamp, 1980), 179–203. "Critique of Violence," in: *Selected Writings* Vol. 1 1913–1926, ed. Marcus Bullock, Michael W. Jennings (Cambridge: Belknap Press of Harvard University Press, 1969).

of individual persons, positions, or forces. Therefore, the film also transgresses the theater as venue, space, practice, and institution, in many ways. The colors of the sky, plants, costumes, and stones, are not just decoration, but a hard and luminous reality that surrounds the play and the monstrous violence of the words spoken by the actors. Thus, the film charges the visible scene, the stones, the ruins of a public, sacred, and political space, with the energies of a text as a musical and rhythmic medium of collective memory. Beyond all ideological messages and arguments, a political quality of this work derives from its particular and violent incompatibility, connecting the visible stone and the audible cry, the breathing bodies and the ancient ruins, through an extremely sharpened sensual experience.

And there is always something more to see which adds to the ecology of the films by Huillet and Straub. The *animals* in their films highlight the close relation between film, life, and death. In addition, they manifest a certain dialectics in the representation of violence including a violence of representation, to be activated in the imagination of the spectator. There are these sudden moments, when little animals appear and disappear, unexpected, without a particular part in the scene, crossing and subverting the efforts of representation. Toward the end of *Antigone*, the failed tyrant Kreon returns from the dead bodies of Antigone and her fiancé Haimon, the tyrant's son. Unable to rescue him from the consequence of his own orders, Kreon bears in hand his bloody cloth. A butterfly enters, a bright spot that flutters around Kreon's head. Once more an accidental and ephemeral moment that does not impose on the viewer's perception, but can be quite irritating. The butterfly, for an instant, may even turn the whole pathos of the reckless tyrant into something comical, encircling the red cloth like a flower.

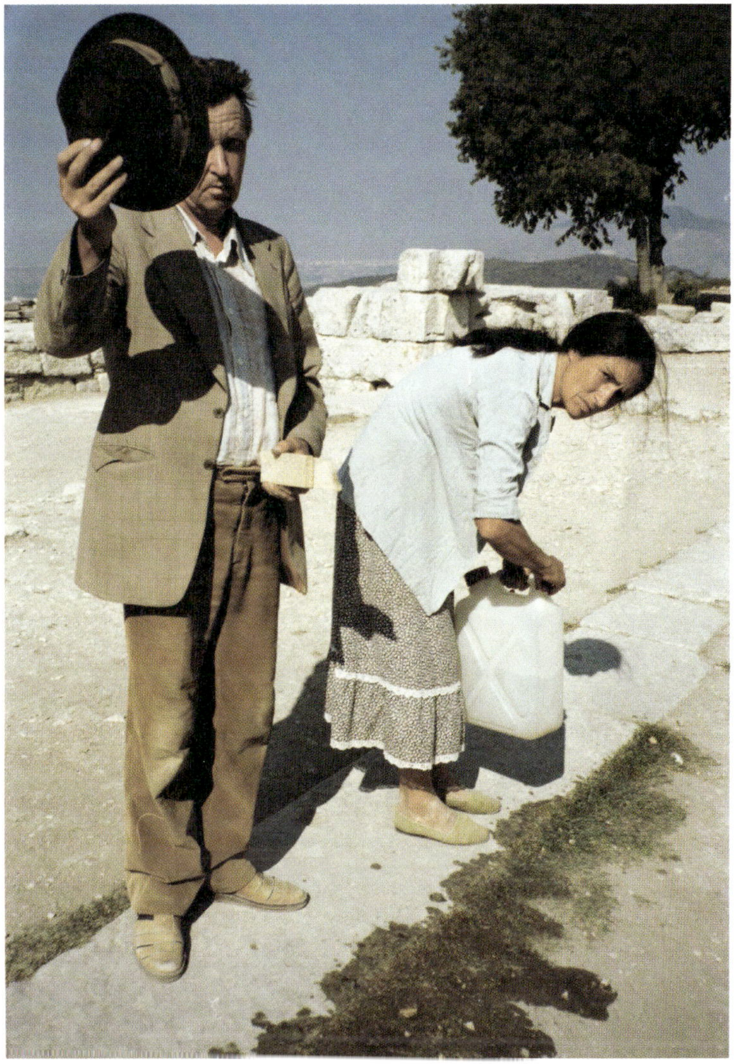

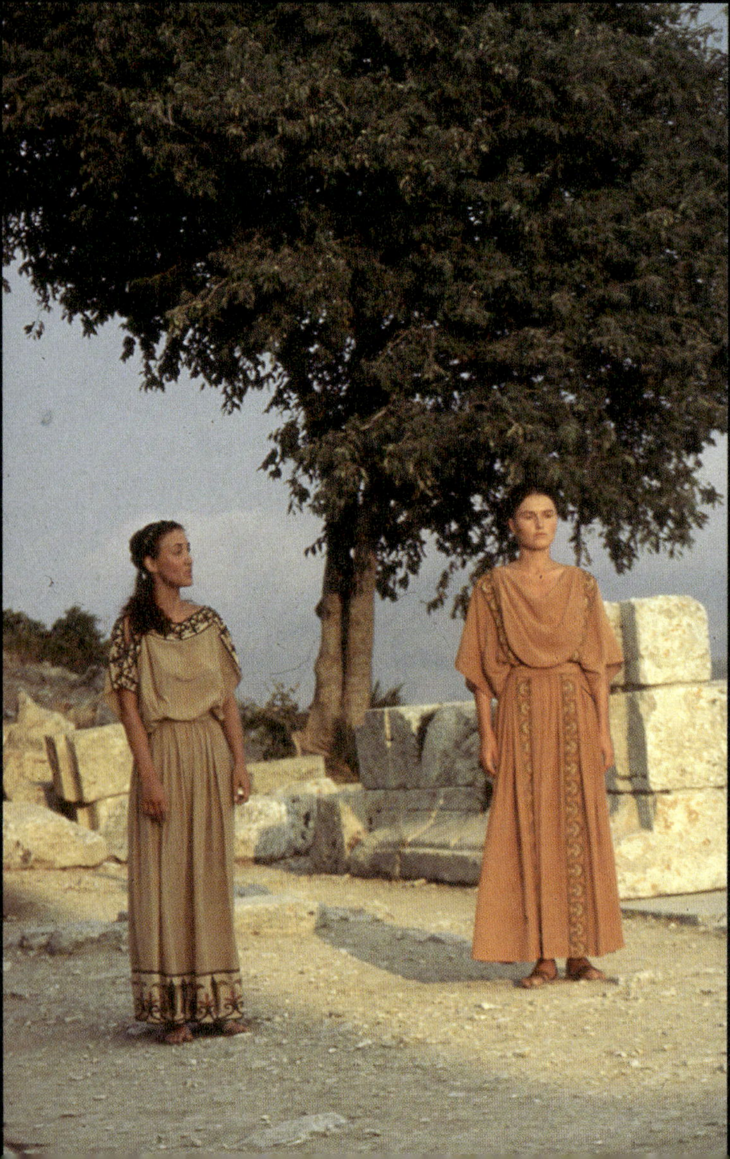

The film was not initiated by the text but by the place; by this landscape which we had seen for the first time in 1971. Everything else just added up. If we hadn't been given the permission to shoot in Segesta, we wouldn't have made the film. And I would even go further: if this tree, this singular tree on this hill, this Arolla pine—in Southern France they are abundant, the wood is used for making wind instruments—if this tree had died... Because we saw it in winter and its condition was so-so; then we saw it again and it was in a very bad condition, and we thought: if this tree dies, we cannot make the film, because this tree was also Antigone. We kept calling in Segesta to ask the old man down there how the tree was doing, and they thought we were nuts. Thank God, the tree recovered. It has very little soil, everything there is rock and the tree is a miracle.

Danièle Huillet, during a seminar at the Freie Universität Berlin, hosted by Peter Kammerer, Ekkehart Krippendorff and Wolf-Dieter Narr in February 1993.

ACKNOWLEDGMENTS

This publication was made possible through generous support from the Mozhai Foundation.

The lead-up to this book began in 2017 with a cycle of events and an exhibition, "Tell it to the Stones: The Work of Danièle Huillet and Jean-Marie Straub," an Akademie der Künste, Berlin, project, funded by the Hauptstadtkulturfonds.

It is thanks to the efforts of many that a book like this becomes possible. Without the staff of Akademie der Künste, and in particular the efforts and expertise of Cornelia Klauß and Mechthild Cramer von Laue, this beginning would not have been possible.

The series of talks, conversations, encounters and artistic contributions taking place between September and November 2017 formed the source material for the conception of this book. It gradually took shape with the authors and artists who had participated in this endeavor by reconsidering their contributions, expanding, focusing and revising their chapters time and again. Our thanks also go to the translators as well as to those who generously provided and licensed the photographs, film stills, and documents reproduced in the book; to Seb Holl-Trieu, Piotr Zapasnik and Marco Cucuiu at Workout Services, who gave the book its unique look, and for their endless patience; and to Luisa Greenfield who not only contributed her own chapter, but has been a great and attentive companion as a copy editor.

Over the three years that the book has been in the making, we have experienced countless gestures of friendship and generosity by many who shared their knowledge, gave insight and access to documents and private archives, worked extra hours, and supported our work through encouragement and criticism. Lists are certainly incomplete by default, but special thanks go to Christophe Clavert, Misha Donat, Helmut Färber, Ted Fendt, Anna Fiaccarini, Jörg Frieß, Alexander Horwath, *Danièle Huillet, Claus Löser, Johannes Odenthal, Volker Pantenburg, Katherine Pickard, Ulrike Roesen, Sally Shafto, Andrea Spingler, Jean-Marie Straub, Elena Testa, Ming Tsao, Barbara Ulrich, Klaus Volkmer, and Antonia Weiße.

CONTRIBUTORS

Manfred Bauschulte, born in 1956 in Ibbenbüren (Westphalia), is a writer, translator and a scholar in religious studies. He lives and works in Cologne. His most recent book is *Henri Michaux: Autor und Artist* (Vienna: Klever, 2020).

Renato Berta was born in 1945 in Bellinzona (Switzerland). Apprenticed as a locksmith and studied at the Technical College in Biel (1961–65). He had an early enthusiasm for cinema and trained as chief cameraman at the Centro Sperimentale di Cinematografia in Rome (1965–67). In the 1970s he was a central figure of the New Swiss Film by collaborating with directors Alain Tanner, Claude Goretta, Daniel Schmid and Thomas Koerfer. Since the 1980s he has been an internationally acclaimed cameraman and has collaborated with all of the important directors of the Nouvelle Vague generation: Godard, Rivette, Malle, Resnais, Rohmer, Chabrol. To this day he prefers to work with directors who are committed to the concept of auteur films: Amos Gitai, Philippe Garrel, Elise Girard. He made eleven films with Danièle Huillet/Jean-Marie Straub, and another nine films under the sole direction of Straub.

Manfred Blank, born in 1949, is a graduate of the Munich Academy for Television and Film (HFF). For many years he was co-publisher, editor and author of the magazine *Filmkritik*. For a decade he was assistant to Danièle Huillet and Jean-Marie Straub and for several years a lecturer at the West Berlin Film and Television Academy (dffb). He has worked and still works as a sound engineer, author, filmmaker and producer on countless films for cinema and television.

Annett Busch works as a curator, editor, writer, and translator, affiliated with the Trondheim Academy of Fine Art/NTNU. Her interest in radical forms of filmmaking and film criticism has led to her thinking of and in juxtapositions. She co-curated "Tell it to the Stones: The Work of J. M. Straub and D. Huillet" (2017, with Tobias Hering) and co-edited *Ousmane Sembène: Interviews* (2008, with Max Annas) and *Frieda Grafe: 30 Filme* (2013, with Max Annas and Henriette Gunkel). Her focus is on creating frameworks of attention for what otherwise goes unnoticed, as co-curating "After Year Zero" (2012–15, with Anselm Franke), "Women on Aeroplanes" (since 2017, with MH Gutberlet and Magda Lipska) and co-editing the accompanying *Inflight Magazine*.

Barton Byg is Professor Emeritus and Founding Director of the DEFA Film Library at the University of Massachusetts Amherst. He has been affiliated with the UMass programs in German and Scandinavian Studies, Comparative Literature, and Communication, and is a founding faculty member of the Interdepartmental Program in Film Studies. Principal areas of research and teaching in addition to the work of Huillet and Straub are GDR cinema and culture, Brecht and cinema, documentary, culture of the Cold War, memory culture, landscape and film, color and film.

Paolo Caffoni is an editor at Archive Books, a Berlin-based publishing house. He is a faculty member of NABA – New Academy of Fine Arts Milan, and was part of the curatorial team of the Second Yinchuan Biennial in 2018. His doctoral project at the Hochschule für Gestaltung Karlsruhe focuses on the methodologies of Naoki Sakai and Antonio Gramsci, investigating the practice of translation among different media (or semiotic systems) as a process of encounter between political subjectivities.

Rinaldo Censi (PhD in Film Studies, University of Bologna) is a writer, translator and film curator. He is interested in the borders of disciplinary areas. He wrote a book on Italian silent Diva-films (*Formule di Pathos*, Ancona: Cattedrale, 2008), and one on Yervant Gianikian and Angela Ricci Lucchi (Milan: Doppiozero, 2013). In 2014 he published a book called *Copie Originali. Iperrealismi tra pittura e cinema* (Monza: Johan & Levi editore). He has curated several film programs on filmmakers as diverse as Straub-Huillet, Jacques Tourneur, Charley Bowers, Pedro Costa, Philippe Garrel, Peter Tscherkassky, Karl Kels, Jean Eustache, and Peter Kubelka.

Giovanna Daddi is an actress whose work in theater, mostly in Italy, spans almost five decades. Throughout the 1970s and 1980s she was part of several independent companies, acting in classical as well as contemporary roles. At the end of the 1980s she joined the Teatro Francesco di Bartolo in Buti and took on leading roles in plays by Bertolt Brecht, Samuel Beckett, Jean-Marie Koltès, Harold Pinter and Heiner Müller, including three different impersonations of Mephistopheles in Goethe's *Faust*. She met Jean-Marie Straub and Danièle Huillet when they visited Buti in 1996 and collaborated on four of their films based on the *Dialogues with Leucò* by Cesare Pavese: *These Encounters of Theirs* (2005), *The Witches, Women among themselves* (2008), *The Inconsolable One* (2010) and *The Mother* (2011). Together with Dario Marconcini, Giovanna Daddi was a nominee for the Italian Ubu Theater Award for lifetime achievement.

In the 1980s Diedrich Diederichsen was editor and publisher of music magazines (*Sounds, Spex*); in the 1990s he was Guest Professor or lecturer in Frankfurt, Stuttgart, Pasadena, Offenbach, Munich, Weimar, Bremen, Gießen, Vienna, Gainesville, Florida, St. Louis, Cologne, Salzburg, Los Angeles, among others. Professor for Aesthetic Theory/Cultural Studies at Merz Academy, Stuttgart (1998–2007), and since 2006 he is Professor for Theory, Practice and Communication of Contemporary Art at the Institute for Art Theory and Cultural Studies of the Academy of Fine Arts, Vienna.

Monika Funke Stern is a media artist, filmmaker, and writer. Assistant Professor for Visual Communication at the University of Fine Arts Berlin (1997–2008); Professor for film and video at the University of Applied Sciences Düsseldorf; independent TV-film- and video productions. Executive film producer in Brazil, Ivory Coast, Nigeria, Gambia, Philippines; lectures and workshops in France and Italy; works are in collections of the Centre Pompidou, Hamburger Bahnhof, Berlin, Deutsche Kinemathek, Neuer Berliner Kunstverein (n.b.k.), Vera Chaves Barcellos Foundation, private collections. Lives and works in Berlin/Falkensee and Crimea.

Luisa Greenfield is a Berlin-based visual artist working predominantly with film and essay writing. She is a PhD candidate in Art and Media at the University of Plymouth, UK, where her practice-based research considers film a form of thought that is capable of offering resistance against an accelerated, future-oriented perception of history. Her current work comes out of a close study of Danièle Huillet and Jean-Marie Straub's 1972 film *Geschichtsunterricht*. Luisa is an active member of the LaborBerlin analogue film collective, and is one of the editors of the book *Film in the Present Tense* (Berlin: Archive Books, 2020).

Louis Henderson is a filmmaker and writer who experiments with different documentary practices to address and question our current global condition, defined by racial capitalism and ever-present histories of the European colonial project. Since 2017, Henderson has been working within the artist group *The Living and the Dead Ensemble*. Coming from Haiti, France, and the UK, they focus on theater, song, slam poetry, and cinema. Their first feature film, *Ouvertures*, was awarded a FIPRESCI special mention at the 70th Berlin International Film Festival 2020.

Tobias Hering is an independent film curator, researcher and writer. Together with Annett Busch he co-curated the program cycle "Tell it to the Stones: The Work of Danièle Huillet and Jean-Marie Straub" for Akademie der Künste, Berlin, in 2017. He is editor of the anthology *Der Standpunkt der Aufnahme – Point of View: Perspectives of Political Film and Video Work* (Berlin: Archive Books, 2014), co-editor of *Luta ca caba inda: time place matter voice* (Berlin: Archive Books, 2017) and *Danièle Huillet, Jean-Marie Straub: Schriften* (Berlin: Vorwerk 8, 2020).

Ute Holl is Professor for Media Aesthetics at Basel University. Her research focuses on audiovisual media in terms of their epistemology, aesthetics and ecology. Her contributions to film history examine anthropological, experimental and Middle Eastern cinemas. Recent research projects are concerned with radio and electro acoustics. She has published the book *The Moses Complex. Freud, Schoenberg, Straub/Huillet* (Zurich: Diaphanes/Chicago University Press, 2017).

Rembert Hüser is Professor of Media Studies at Goethe University Frankfurt. He wrote about Harun Farocki studying Huillet/Straub, Huillet/Straub filming ghosts in *Cézanne*, the typewritten credit sequence of *Class Relations*, and the making of *The Death of Empedocles, or When the Green of the Earth Will Glisten for You Anew*.

Volko Kamensky (*1972) is a filmmaker, author and translator. His film productions include the experimental documentaries *Divina Obsesión* (1999), *Alles was wir haben* (2004), and *Oral History* (2009). He teaches and researches film theory and practice and is co-editor of the text collections *Ton. Texte zur Akustik im Dokumentarfilm* (Berlin: Vorwerk 8, 2013), and *Danièle Huillet, Jean-Marie Straub: Schriften* (Berlin: Vorwerk 8, 2020).

Peter Kammerer was born 1938 in Offenburg (Germany). Studied economics. Diploma (1961), dissertation with Prof. Erich Preiser at Ludwig-Maximilians-University, Munich with a thesis on problems of development in Southern Italy (1965). Since 1962 he has been living in Rome and Urbino. He taught general sociology at the University of Urbino from 1970–2009. Fields of work and research: labor migration, economic development, socialism/communism. Publications on Heiner Müller, Straub and Huillet, Francis of Assisi, Pier Paolo Pasolini, Marx and Engels.

Jan Lemitz is a photographer and visual artist based in Duisburg and Berlin. He graduated from the University of Brighton in 2003 with a BA in Photography, and received an MA in Research Architecture from Goldsmiths College in 2011. His practice relates to landscape, architecture and infrastructure and draws from media archeological finds. His contribution to "Tell It to the Stones," *Blockbuster*, is part of an extensive body of work following traces of NATO supply infrastructure across the Lower Rhine region.

Armin Linke is a photographer and filmmaker combining a range of contemporary image processing technologies to blur the border between fiction and reality. Through working with his own archive and with other media archives, he challenges the conventions of photographic practice and representation. In a collective approach with other artists, curators, designers, architects, historians, philosophers and scientists, the narratives of his works expand the level of multiple discourses.

Born 1989 in Voronezh, Russia, Mikhail Lylov is an artist and researcher, and lives in Sicily and Berlin. His current artistic work adapts the genealogical approach to the investigation of forces forming assemblages of relations, affects and perceptions, proposing various practical, theoretical and artistic interpretations of ecology. Working with moving, photographic and archival images, he investigates histories of the interaction between human and non-human protagonists responsible for the emergence of various environments.

In 1974 Dario Marconcini was a co-founder of the "Centro per la sperimentazione e la ricerca teatrale" (Center for theatrical experimentation and research) at Pontedera (Tuscanny), which subsequently became an internationally acclaimed hub for independent theater groups, including Odin Teatret, the Living Theater, and the Teatr Laboratorium of Jerzy Grotovsky. In the mid 1980s, Dario Marconcini moved to Buti to study local forms of folk and popular theater. He became the artistic director of Teatro Francesco di Bartolo and directed a large number of its productions. In 1996 he met Danièle Huillet and Jean-Marie Straub in the house of a friend when the filmmakers visited Buti. From this visit the idea to present their Hölderlin films in Buti was born, an event, which occasioned Huillet and Straub's ongoing commitment to Buti. "Year after year they would move to Buti for a few months, to shoot their films, but also to have a life in the theater. Thus it continued until 2010. And the lessons learned from these masters will be forever remembered in this little village." (D.M.) Marconcini was an actor in three of Huillet and Straub's Buti projects: *These Encounters of Theirs* (2005), *Artemide's Knee* (2007) and *The Mother* (2011).

Elke Marhöfer is an artist and a farmer based in Berlin and Sicily. She investigates ecological practices that support human and nonhuman communities and works with notions of self-admitted foreignness and radical othering. Linking, for example, the nonhuman with the postcolonial, she discusses how nature evokes situated testimonies of past and current events while simultaneously surpassing historical formatting, with its unique and machinic mode of constantly mutating into something new.

Makoto Mochida is a theater director who lives in Tokyo. He studied German Philosophy at Kyoto University until 1997. He worked as a theater director in Tokyo, and in 2015 formed the theater group PuP (Panthea und Pausanias), whose name derives from Hölderlin's *The Death of Empedocles*. His recent works are *Ko, re, an!* (2015), and *In the shade of the bushes of this metropolis* (2017), both of which originated from Japanese texts written in the period when Japan was heading toward World War II.

Peter Nestler was born in Freiburg (Baden) in 1937 and raised in Bavaria, went to sea in 1955, so avoiding military service. In 1959 he studied painting, then soon started filmmaking (from 1961 to 1966 in West Germany), married Zsóka in Hungary and moved to Sweden. He worked first as a freelance filmmaker, and then was employed for thirty years by Swedish TV, he continued filmmaking (often together with Zsóka), also purchasing and editing children's films from all over the world. From 2002 he was freelance again. In 2020 a film was made in France, *Picasso in Vallauris*, one is in preparation, *Widerstand* (Resistance).

Maggie Perlado graduated in 1978 from IDHEC (Institute for Advanced Cinematographic Studies) with a diploma in directing and cinematography. She worked as a first assistant camerawoman (focus puller) on fiction films and documentaries. Impassioned by image-making, she takes photographs during every film shoot. In 1981, she assisted Robert Alazraki, director of photography for the Egyptian part of *Too Early/Too Late* by Jean-Marie Straub and Danièle Huillet. Maggie Perlado also directs documentaries and worked as a scriptwriter on numerous feature films with Patrice Leconte (*Le mari de la coiffeuse*, *Ridicule*), Anne Fontaine (*Entre ses mains*) Pierre Jolivet (*Je crois que je l'aime*) Gérard Krawczyk (*Taxi 2*) and Michael Haneke (*Happy End*), among others.

Patrick Primavesi is Professor and Head of Department at the Institute of Theater Studies at Leipzig University. He wrote his PhD on Walter Benjamin's theories about commentary, translation and theater and has published widely on Brecht and Heiner Müller, contemporary theater, dance and performance. Current research projects focus on body politics, movement in urban space and archives in digital environments. He has also been writing on the work of Straub/Huillet, in particular on their films *Antigone*, *The*

Death of Empedocles, Black Sin, From Today Until Tomorrow, Sicilia!, Operai, contadini.

Florian Schneider is a filmmaker, writer, and curator. In his work he investigates "imaginary property" relations and new divisions of labor within the cultural and creative industries. Educated as a documentary filmmaker, he has been engaged in a wide range of processes to rethink the impact and value of documentary practices across disciplines. In 2009, he co-curated the exhibition and ciné-club "Of a people who are missing: On films by Danièle Huillet and Jean-Marie Straub" in Extra City, Antwerp. Since 2013 he is Professor for Art theory and documentary practices, and since 2014 Head of the Trondheim Academy of Fine Art at the Norwegian University of Science and Technology (NTNU). Since 2019 he is the Chair of the COST action CA 18136 "European Forum for Advanced Practices" (EFAP).

Oraib Toukan's practice is concerned with the after-life of "cruel images," and how to treat them as object and subject through the making of art. Her method lies in handling and re-editing found archival materials, whereby knowledge is produced through an extreme proximity to the materiality of an image and the dialectics of montage. She holds a PhD in Fine Arts from Oxford University, Ruskin School of Art, and is an artist and scholar based in Berlin.

Ming Tsao writes music with a sensuality that arises out of a focus on the inherent qualities of sound—what the composer calls its "materiality." Many of his works are the result of a critical and deep-thinking examination of the Western classical tradition as well as his serious engagement with Chinese traditional music. Increasingly, opera is the forum where Ming Tsao brings these interests together. In recent seasons his major projects included two works for large ensemble: *Refuse Collection* (2017), a response to the oeuvre of Danièle Huillet und Jean-Marie Straub; and *Plus Minus* (2012–13), the first full realization of Stockhausen's open composition of the same name.

Barbara Ulrich, born 1960 in Baar, Switzerland. Lived in Munich, Paris, in the Vendée, in Paris and now again in Switzerland, in Rolle. Still trying, despite long studies of philosophy, to understand "what holds the world together at its core"—or maybe not (anymore). Friends with Straub/Huillet since the time of *The Death of Empedocles*. Living and working with JMS since the death of Danièle. Founder of BELVA Film GmbH.

Nikolaus Wegmann, a Germanist with a strong interest in media culture, he received his intellectual training at Bielefeld, Cornell University, and Cologne. He has taught literature and media studies at Bielefeld, Cologne, and Potsdam. His research is focused on basic philological and cultural techniques such as (re)reading, collective note-taking, scaling, or searching and finding. Co-editor of *Historisches Wörterbuch des Mediengebrauchs* (Köln: Böhlau, Vol. 1 2015, Vol. 2 2017). Since 2006, he is Professor of German at Princeton University.

Antonia Weiße is a photographer at the Institute for Archaeology at Humboldt University of Berlin. In 1991 she attended the rehearsals for *Antigone*, since then she has followed the work of Huillet and Straub from within the perspective of their friendship and has repeatedly worked on the German subtitles of their films. She is co-editor of *Danièle Huillet, Jean-Marie Straub: Schriften* (Berlin: Vorwerk 8, 2020).

Ala Younis is an artist with research, curatorial, film, and publishing projects. Younis's projects are expanded experiences, relating to materials from distant times and places; working against the archive's play on predilections and how its lacunae and mishaps manipulate imagination. She is a member of the Advisory Board of Berlinale's Forum Expanded, and of Akademie der Künste der Welt in Cologne. Younis co-founded Kayfa ta, a non-profit publishing initiative that uses the popular form of how-to manuals (how=kayfa, to=ta) to respond to some of today's perceived needs.

IMAGE CREDITS

Photographs are reprinted with the permission of those who took them, unless otherwise noted. Stills from films by Danièle Huillet and Jean-Marie Straub were digitally reproduced by Olivier Boischot, unless otherwise noted, and are reprinted with permission from BELVA-Film.

Cover
Film set during the shooting of *Too Early/Too Late*, Egypt, 1981. Photo Maggie Perlado.

Frontispiece
Stills from films by Huillet/Straub whose title fonts were used in the design of this book.

8/9, 12, 28/29
Exhibition views, "Tell it to the Stones: The Work of Danièle Huillet and Jean-Marie Straub," Akademie der Künste, Berlin, 2017. Photos Antonia Weiße.

13
Film stills from *From the Cloud to the Resistance*, *Moses and Aaron*, *Sicilia!* and *Every Revolution is a Throw of Dice*.

20
Film still from *En rachâchant*.

21
Film still from *From the Cloud to the Resistance*.

22
Film still from *Too Early/Too Late*.

24
Graphic representation of the position of the performer-reciters in *Every Revolution is a Throw of Dice*. From: *Apparatus. Cinematographic Apparatus. Selected Writings*. Edited by Theresa Hak Kyung Cha (New York: Tanam Press, 1980).

27
Stage view of the music performance of Huillet and Straub's *Antigone* script by Astrid Ofner and the New Composers Collective (Andi Toma, Jan St. Werner, Michael Rauter, Matti Gajek), Akademie der Künste, Berlin, 11th November, 2017. Photo Antonia Weiße.

43–53
"... on the way from Munich to Pesaro, 25th July, 1966." Photos Peter Nestler.

55–63
Blockbuster, Goch (2016-2017). Photos Jan Lemitz.

64, 65
Film stills from *Machorka-Muff*.

66/67
Film still from *From Today Until Tomorrow*.

78/79
Film set during the shooting of *Moses and Aaron*, amphitheater in Alba Fucens, Italy, 1974. Photographer unknown. Source: Fondo Straub-Huillet, Fondazione Cineteca di Bologna. Reprinted with permission from BELVA-Film.

83, 90, 97, 100
Film stills from *Moses and Aaron*.

103
Arnold Schoenberg, "Begleitmusik zu einer Lichtspielscene," op. 34, measures 1–6 (Wilhelmshaven: Heinrichshofen's Verlag, 1930).

105
Film still from *Introduction to Arnold Schoenberg's "Accompaniment to a Cinematographic Scene."*

119, 120
Ming Tsao, *Refuse Collection,* measures 1–4 (Leipzig: Edition Peters, 2017). Excerpts from sketch and final score. Reprinted by permission.

124
Film stills from *Every Revolution is a Throw of Dice* and *Cézanne. Conversation with Joachim Gasquet.*

125
Film stills from *Fortini/Cani, Introduction to Arnold Schoenberg's "Accompaniment to a Cinematographic Scene," Sicilia!*

138/139
Exhibition view, "Tell it to the Stones: The Work of Danièle Huillet and Jean-Marie Straub," Akademie der Künste, Berlin, 2017. Photo Antonia Weiße.

141
Detail from manuscript, Friedrich Hölderlin, "Wenn der Dichter einmal des Geistes mächtig," Stuttgarter Foliobuch, in *Sämtliche Werke,* Vol. 14, edited by D.E. Sattler, 263 (Frankfurt: Stroemfeld/Roter Stern, 1985).

143
Film still from *Hommage à Vernon.*

158/159
Film still from *Fortini/Cani.*

166
Book cover, Franco Fortini, *Tre testi per film* (Milan: Edizioni Avanti!, 1963).

171
Shooting of *Fortini/Cani.* Courtesy Renato Berta.

173
Film stills from *Divisione controllo numerico, Le regole del gioco* and *Incontro con la Olivetti.* Courtesy of Archivio Nazionale Cinema Impresa, Associazione Archivio Storico Olivetti.

184
Film still from *Sicilia!.*

185
Film still from *From the Cloud to the Resistance.*

194/195
Film stills from *From the Cloud to the Resistance* (top left), *The Death of Empedocles* (center left, Peter Kammerer playing the peasant), *Too Early/Too Late* (centerfold), *History Lessons* (top right), *Workers, Peasants* (center right), *Sicilia!* (bottom right).

198, 202
Film stills from *From the Cloud to the Resistance.*

214
Film still from *The Death of Empedocles.*

218
Buti, 2016. Photos Antonia Weiße.

219
From top to bottom: during the shooting of *From the Cloud to the Resistance,* courtesy of Manfred Blank; film still from *Six Bagatelas,* dir. Pedro Costa, 2001, courtesy Pedro Costa; Buti, 2016, photo Antonia Weiße.

223, 230
Video stills from *The green and the stone. Straub-Huillet in Buti,* a film by Armin Linke in collaboration with Rinaldo Censi, Giulia Bruno and Giuseppe Ielasi, 2017. Teatro Francesco di Bartolo, Il Seracino - Cascine di Buti with Giovanna Daddi, Dario Marconcini and Romano Guelfi.

233
Stage rehearsals for *Umiliati* at Teatro Francesco di Bartolo, Buti, 2002. Source: Fondo Straub-Huillet, Fondazione Cineteca di Bologna. Reprinted with permission from BELVA-Film.

236, 237
Film stills from *Lothringen!.*

248/249
On the set of *Every Revolution is a Throw of Dice,* Père Lachaise cemetery, Paris, 1977. Photo Andrea Spingler. Courtesy Manfred Blank.

266/267
Top left and centerfold: Film stills from *Not Reconciled, or Only Violence Helps Where Violence Rules.* Bottom left: on the set of *Moses and Aaron.* Source: Fondo Straub-Huillet,

Fondazione Cineteca di Bologna. Reprinted with permission from BELVA-Film. Top right: video still from *Schaut euch diesen Berg an, einstmals war er Feuer*, dir. Harald Bergmann, 1991, reprinted by permission. Center right: film still from *Cézanne. Conversation with Joachim Gasquet*. Bottom right: video still from *Les Avatars de la Mort d'Empédocle*, dir. Jean-Paul Toraille, 2010. Courtesy J.-P. Toraille.

275, 278, 279
Film stills from *History Lessons*.

284
Video still from 2010 sketch for *History Lessons By Comparison*, dir. Luisa Greenfield, 2017.

285
Film still from *History Lessons By Comparison*, dir. Luisa Greenfield, 2017.

288
Film still from *History Lesssons By Comparison*, final scene of the Mascherone fountain on the Via Giulia in Rome, 2017.

290
The camera and sound set up inside the car during the making of *History Lessons By Comparison*. Photo Terril Scott.

291
The camera and sound set up inside the car during the making of *History Lessons*. Clipping from "Andi Engel talks to Jean-Marie Straub, and Danièle Huillet is there too," *Enthusiasm*, no. 1 (December, 1975): 15. Original images by Sebastian Schadhauser.

294/295
Film still from *Itinerary of Jean Bricard*.

298, 299, 304, 305
Video stills from *Ouvertures*, dir. The Living and the Dead Ensemble, 2019.

316
Film stills from *Moses and Aaron* and *Itinerary of Jean Bricard*.

318–345
All drawings in this chapter are original artworks by Ala Younis, produced for the installation *This Land First Speaks to You in Signs* on the occasion of the exhibition "Tell it to the Stones," Akademie der Künste, Berlin, 2017.

324
Rendering of image used on the front cover of Mahmoud Hussein: *Class Conflict In Egypt, 1945–1970* (New York, London: Monthly Review Press, 1973).

331
Film still from *Too Early / Too Late*.

345
Exhibition view "This Land First Speaks to You in Signs" within "Tell it to the Stones: The Work of Danièle Huillet and Jean-Marie Straub," Akademie der Künste, Berlin, 2017. Photo Antonia Weiße.

348
Manfred Blank in *Every Revolution is a Throw of Dice*. Courtesy of Manfred Blank.

351
Film still from *Too Early / Too Late*.

361
Manfred Blank during the shooting of *Too Early / Too Late*, Egypt, 1981. Photo Maggie Perlado.

362/363
Film still from *Too Early / Too Late*, photographed by Marian Stefanowski from a 16mm archive print at Arsenal – Institute for Film and Video Art.

392
Akademie der Künste, Berlin, 11th November, 2017. Courtesy Mikhail Lylov, Elke Marhöfer.

396, 399, 401, 402
Film stills from *Soils_Habit_Plants*, dir. Mikhail Lylov, Elke Marhöfer, 2017.

413
Diagram for the shooting of *The Death of Empedocles*. First published in *Danièle Huillet, Jean-Marie Straub: Writings*. Edited by Sally Shafto and Katherine Pickard. (New York: Sequence Press, 2016), 355. Reprinted with permission from BELVA-Film.

416
Top: public performance of *Antigone* in Segesta, Sicily. Print from color slide, photographer unknown. Courtesy Antonia Weiße. Center: diagram for the shooting of *Antigone*. First published in "Stadtkino Programm" no. 238 (1993), the program brochure for the cinema release of *Antigone* in Austria, published by Stadtkino Wien. The caption reads: "Working sketch of the Teatro di Segesta by Danièle Huillet. Marked therein: the positions and movements of the actors, the distance between the characters, their relation to the architecture of the theater and the fixed position of the camera." Bottom: Teatro di Segesta. Source: Fondo Straub-Huillet, Fondazione Cineteca di Bologna. Reprinted by permission from BELVA-Film.

418, 419
Danièle Huillet and Jean-Marie Straub on the set of *These Encounters of Theirs*. Photos Renato Berta.

434, 435, 451
Film stills from *Cézanne. Conversation with Joachim Gasquet.*

460, 461
Screening of *Une visite au Louvre*, November 27, 2009, at Extra Citiy, Antwerp, as part of the exhibition and ciné-club, "Of a people who are missing." Photos Florian Schneider.

467–475
Images from the archaeological site Palace of the Slave, Iraq Al Amir, Jordan. Courtesy Francois Larchè.

476
Video stills from *Palace of the Slave,* dir. Oraib Toukan, 2017.

480, 481
Stage performance of *Antigone* at Schaubühne Berlin (rehearsal stage Cuvrystraße), May 1991. Photos Antonia Weiße.

491
Jean-Marie Straub and Danièle Huillet on the set of *Antigone*, Teatro di Segesta, Sicily. Photo Astrid Johanna Ofner. The photo was taken shortly after the final take for the film.

492
Ursula and Astrid Ofner during rehearsals for *Antigone,* Teatro di Segesta, Sicily.

INDEX

Tell It to the Stones
Encounters with the Work of
Danièle Huillet and Jean-Marie Straub

Published by Sternberg Press

This book was initiated and supported by the Akademie der Künste, Berlin, project, "Tell it to the Stones: The Work of Danièle Huillet and Jean-Marie Straub," curated by Annett Busch and Tobias Hering.

Editors: Annett Busch, Tobias Hering
Copyediting: Luisa Greenfield
Proofreading: Misha Donat, Ted Fendt,
Lili Hering, Antonia Weiße
Graphic Design: Workout Services
(Seb Holl-Trieu, Piotr Zapasnik)
Printing & Binding: Tallinna Raamatutrükikoda
(Tallinn Book Printers)

ISBN 978-3-95679-532-9

Distributed by The MIT Press, Art Data, and
Les presses du réel

Sternberg Press
71–75 Shelton Street
UK–London WC2H 9JQ
www.sternberg-press.com